G. W. Spohn

THE WAY OF A TRANSGRESSOR

The Way
of a Transgressor

BY NEGLEY FARSON

*"It's like a book, I think, this blooming world
Which one can read and care for just so long."*

HARCOURT, BRACE AND COMPANY

NEW YORK

COPYRIGHT, 1936, BY

NEGLEY FARSON

first American edition

PRINTED IN THE UNITED STATES OF AMERICA

BY QUINN & BODEN COMPANY, INC., RAHWAY, N. J.

Designed by Robert Josephy

To Eve and Dan

CONTENTS

viii CONTENTS

Chapter 1

POLITICAL HATE

MY GRANDFATHER kept his three Negro servants by the simple expedient of not paying them. They did not seem to mind. They lived on the place, they ate about the same food that we did; and when good luck came to us, why, good luck came to them. They got paid.

My grandfather and Abner could get more solid contentment out of a pot of wax and a pruning-knife than any two men I ever knew.

They would make plums grow on a peach-tree and (I'm not so sure of this), peaches on plums—half the trees were bandaged on our place—and my grandfather would discourse learnedly to Abner upon how the bees crossed the pollen on the grapes, which explained that cross we had between the Wild Fox and the Concord whose vine trailed along from the stables to the garden gate. A miraculous grape, with all the sweetness of the little Wild Fox in Concord size. The vine that Henderson, the big New York seed man, was always after my grandfather to sell him outright. And of course during all these rambles, in an old black alpaca coat with trailers of alfalfa dangling from its pockets, my grandfather and Abner would talk politics. For my grandfather, who had served four terms in Congress, had just been broken in Pennsylvania politics and was now a ruined man—to everyone but Abner. People used to say:

"General Negley can swing only two votes now—his and his nigger's!"

It was a happy relationship in which money did not count.

But it was vastly different with the tradespeople. My young life was detonated by periodic visits from the butcher, the baker and the Chinese laundryman demanding their bills. The Chinaman was welcomed by my grandfather, who liked anything foreign. He was led to the garden forthwith. There they stood, the old General and the Chinaman, absorbed in our radish beds.

Among the freaks that my grandfather was experimenting with at that time was a foot-long, white Chinese radish, which was finding itself quite at home in our New Jersey soil. The China-man clopped off with armfuls of these, and after that, scented packages of *lichi* nuts began to arrive at our house. In contrast to such celestial understanding was a scene which showed my grandfather at his worst, or best, as it now appears to me.

He had been away for two years in England, trying to recoup his wasted fortunes by representing the Mexican government after the Baring Bros. failed. In order to put up a decent front in London he had taken with him every available red cent he could scrape up. They were two bad years for us. My grandmother, by being ingratiating to people she would have preferred to mur-der, had managed to hold most of the tradesmen at bay. But there was one of them more or less camped on our doorstep when the General returned.

"General," said Simms, our young Negro butler, who spent his time in the butler's pantry reading for the Law instead of cleaning our silver—"There's a man wants to see you."

The General knew that tone. He got up from the dining-table.

Our porch ran around two sides of the old wooden house, and flanking the front door was the "monkey cage," a section of the porch enclosed by fine screens where we used to sit on summer nights when the New Jersey mosquitoes were at play. It was cov-ered with honeysuckle. And in this dark nook my grandfather stood at bay. It was a quiet street, where at nights, except for the occasional clop-clop of a horse, the only sound was the shrilling of the crickets in the graveyard across the way. Our creditor be-gan to shout so loud that we could hear him in the dining-room even through the closed doors. Then there was a loud yelp of protest, a thud, and my grandfather, a little more florid than usual, came inside. The ensuing summons explained that General Negley had kicked Mr. So-and-So off the Negley front steps.

One can hardly blame the old man for being truculent, for he felt that Life—in particular his Country—had treated him abom-inably.

He and his people had helped make this land. The first cabin west of the Alleghenies was built by a Negley. At the age of seventeen he had run off to the Mexican War and enlisted as a private in the Duquesne Grays. His family had him brought back, but he immediately ran off again, taking with him this time his cousin who was killed by his side at Vera Cruz. At the outbreak of the Civil War, which caught him living as a country gentleman, experimenting, as always, with unheard-of plants, he had raised and outfitted a brigade and given it to the Northern Government. He had been breveted a major-general for distinguished services and gallantry on the field of the battle of Stone River. The cavalry charge that he led himself to take the Rebel batteries was the inspiration of the war song, "Who Saved the Left?" He had been given a gold sword, by its grateful citizens, for saving Nashville. He was one of the four generals who plotted and rode with Sherman when they burned Georgia from Atlanta to the sea. He had served his country as a Congressman for a period covering eighteen years, until he was broken by an all-powerful railroad whose Bill he refused to lobby. And here he was expected to stand still and hear some nincompoop call him names—just because people would not allow him breathing space to pay his bills!

Well, he'd be God-damned if he would put up with it.

I could not understand any of it. He put me on the table and sank my hands into his curly head. I grabbed handfuls of grey hair. He roared with laughter when I pulled his goatee. He let me crack hickory nuts for him. I knew all about the sword from Nashville, and I knew that it was fine. It hung over our library mantelpiece and on its hilt was an outstretched eagle with green emerald eyes. When I was last in the States I tried to buy it back from the bankers who are holding it as security against a safety vault that my family has not been able to unlock for thirty-two years. I grew up with his escutcheon citing Stone River facing me over his shoulder at the breakfast-table. I played with the Bowie knife he carried in the Mexican War, and I knew he was in the party that captured Santa Ana, and found his wooden leg full of gold doubloons. I knew he had been shot through the hip at Vera Cruz. I watched him drive off in the carriage in the morning to catch the early train; and then, for some reason, we had no horses; and I watched for him around six o'clock, when I knew that in a little while I would see him come limping around those pine-trees by the graveyard where he had just left the trolley. I could not understand any of it.

All I knew was that he made other men around him look like mongrel dogs.

I did not know how brazenly he had offended the proprieties of his time. For my grandmother was his second wife, and when he married her she was about the same age as his eldest son. This outraged all the hell-fire-and-damnation Protestantism of the Negleys and the Mellons, who at that time were dotting the State of Pennsylvania with churches wherever they could find a convenient site. Thomas Mellon, father of Andrew Mellon, had married my grandfather's sister and thus welded the two clans. They stood together against this pretty woman with her hour-glass little figure and large, blue, unsophisticated eyes. But it was not only the young wife that so scandalised proper Pittsburghers —there was a horse named Billy.

Billy was war loot. I believe he is standing somewhere, stuffed, in a Pittsburgh museum now. He was a snow-white horse without one black spot. He had belonged to a Confederate colonel whom my grandfather had captured; and believing strictly in the spoils of war, when the wretched Rebel was sent to one of those rabbit-warren underground prisons that so disgraced the Civil War, my grandfather sent Billy back to Pittsburgh. When the war ended, the Confederate colonel came North himself to ask for his horse back again, and my grandfather kept it, which was neither nice nor characteristic of him. The reason was that Billy was now my grandmother's pet riding horse. In a riding habit made of regulation army blue, with a white plume in her black regulation cavalry hat, "that flighty young Mrs. Negley" rode around East Liberty Valley.

That was bad enough. But what Billy caused the General to do to his eldest son was one of the reasons why my grandfather left Pittsburgh.

The General had given strictest orders that under no condition was Billy ever to be put into harness. One day when the General came home to his flowered place, which was now called "Negley's Folly," he found Clifford Negley sitting in a trap with Billy between the shafts. Clifford Negley, his eldest son, the same age as his pretty stepmother. My grandfather seized the whip from its socket and lashed him across the face.

Clifford Negley got down from the trap and walked into the house. He packed his bags and never returned. My grandfather saw him only once after that, when he was running to catch a train in the Pennsylvania railroad station in New York. He waved to Clifford to jump aboard. He thought Clifford had heard him; maybe he did. But when the train had started, and my grandfather limped along the cars, Clifford was not there.

Two years later a newspaper notice mentioned his name among the passengers of a ship that had gone down off Buenos Aires.

Pittsburgh never forgave the General for that.

It was years before I found out things like that. That was why, I knew now, my grandfather had adopted me when I was born and made me have his own full name, James Scott Negley, as well as my father's; because his other son had died and he wanted someone with the name of Negley to carry on. When I got old enough to decide he hoped I would drop the name of Farson.

I came to know these things, just as I learned that my grandfather had faced a court martial after Chattanooga, and that it had ruined his life. I did not know what the true story of Chattanooga was. For that matter, no one does to this day. The case was taken to Washington, and there it became a battle between my grandfather and his superior general, Rosecrans. Rosecrans had ordered him to retire and my grandfather had not obeyed. Instead he attacked and re-captured 50 guns which Rosecrans had abandoned. He had held on and found himself unsupported and lost most of his men before he could draw back; and, so the talk sometimes went, he had shot some of his own men when they tried to break. I don't know. That part of it is all in the history books, and it had all seemed so long ago that I hardly paid any attention to it when we came to that part of the Civil War in school. All I knew was that my grandfather had been exonerated with full honours, but, for some strange reason, he had never again held a big command. The history books did not say why. He demanded the court martial himself.

It was only years later that I knew I must have played with the truth of Chattanooga in our stables. For there were stacks of my grandfather's old dispatch books up in the loft interspersed with letters from Grant and Lincoln, and packets of old love letters between the General and his first wife. We used his franked mileage books for tickets in our railway games. It was a historian who told me I had probably held the true story of that mysterious battle in my hands.

"I am writing a book," he said. "It's called *The True Chattanooga*. The court martial was really a rank case of army politics. That wasn't appreciated at the time. It is now, and if I could only get the copies of your grandfather's dispatches I think I have enough now to piece the story together."

I told him he would never see them. My grandfather had been dead for years. And when he died, God preserve us! we had burned all that "rubbish" in the stables. The historian gasped, as well he might. I groan whenever I think of it to this day.

The point was that none of these dusty glories were any good. My grandfather had been too pressed and harassed by financial worries to bother about hanging on to things that were gone. America was not like other countries, where men who had served their country were loaded with honours and for ever afterward invited to big State affairs "with decorations." Glory had to have a bank account to back it up. If a man became poor he just dropped out of sight.

That was the real trouble. We were poor. In fact, we were worse than that; sometimes we were poor—and then suddenly we were not. My grandfather had hit it again. There was something mysterious about that family among the pine-trees on the corner.

The small town could not make it out. To be poor was to be *déclassé* in the United States of those days; and it seemed that my grandfather should have let it rest at that. But we knew that he was always off somewhere abroad. Strange people were brought to our house. Dark dirty Mexicans, who smoked cigars in bed and burned holes in my grandmother's sheets. We would have to eat violent paprika soups. A great big man named J. P. MacDonald came there and frightened everybody with the way he roared at his own jokes. He was called the "Haytian King," I was told; and he and my grandfather were going to build a railroad up into a jungle where they were going to plant some banana-trees. And then there were Hunt and Roberts, and Mr. Hunt had lived so long in Mexico that he had begun to look black and greasy like the real ones. And he and Roberts had a joke; I can still see him telling it. He was originally from Alabama, and he drawled:

"Ye-as, I reckon Roberts and I must have put our money on the wrong horse. I didn't know anything was wrong until I went out for a stroll after breakfast. Just as I came to the porch steps—someone shot. Roberts, I guess I beat you to the boat by two jumps?"

They had backed the losing side in a Central American revolution.

I grew up listening to the talk of men like that. And then there were other kinds. The general who commanded the Spanish forces in Cuba came and stayed at our house. He brought his two daughters, and I could not take my eyes from their black glistening hair; for both of my aunts had hair like the sun and I knew that my mother's was red. My aunts still have the gold Alfonso buckles that the general gave them from his belts.

And always I was detailed to take these people around the place before dinner-time. I walked hurriedly past the little blue gum-tree, for I had just received a thrashing from Abner for tearing off its green shoots. Instead, I led them down into the garden and along to the melon patch, where I would gaze thoughtfully at the one I knew I was going to eat as soon as it became ripe. In time I became quite an accomplished guide.

"This," I would say, "is a Catawba grape."

But I was always wondering why it was, when my grandfather knew so many big people outside, that we were not so important locally as his position entitled us to be.

He was not a popular man. A Colonel von Boskirk lived on the diagonal corner from us; a Colonel Tyler lived two places down on our right—with two very pretty daughters who used to play tennis with my aunts—and an old General Schwenck was dragging out an embittered existence two blocks down on our left. One would have thought that these four old officers, at least, would have had something to say to each other. But as far as I can remember they never spoke.

There was something wrong. Some summers the tennis net would be out and there would be big parties on the lawn with iced tea and cakes. Then the racquets would lie in that cupboard under the stairs until they began to curl and snap.

My grandfather had archaic ideas as far as women were concerned. He would not accommodate himself to changing times, nor would he let his family do it. He still believed that "women should not work." With the result he stopped my Aunt Edith from pursuing her studies to become a doctor. He refused to permit my Aunt Mabel to study singing for the stage. Singing in a church choir was as far as he would let her go. He wanted them to go to Miss Something-or-Other's Private Seminary for Young Ladies in our town. But he would not let them go to college after that. Not that he would have had money enough to send them there properly. And when my father turned up with a yacht and banjo, to court my mother, my grandfather raised the roof, saying he wasn't going to have a damned organ-grinder in his house.

My father was an ass to bring that banjo along. He couldn't play it anyway; he only knew six chords. And it earned him my grandfather's contempt for life. My grandfather was rude to the young tennis parties he found on the lawn in the long summer afternoons. He hated young men.

I did not know that my grandfather had outlived his epoch. Every year, on the 4th of July, a big American flag was hung over our drive, and my grandfather walked down to the sidewalk to take a salute as the Grand Army of the Republic, the Civil War veterans, marched past. Every year more and more of them marched on, never to return; and with them went many of the fine things that had made the United States.

The cash registers marched in.

Chapter 2

NEGRO SANCTUARY

THE EARLY atmosphere—namely the fact that we seemed to owe everybody money—gave me an inferiority complex that would have been worse had it not been for the three happy Negro servants on our place. They were my insulation against the realities of life. I adored them.

Raking up the autumn leaves with Abner and roasting chestnuts in the embers; or, as he showed me, putting the chestnuts in a rain-spout to keep them soft, these were affairs of first-rate importance. Watching Abner make a box-trap for rabbits out of old planks was such a serious business that it made me hold my breath.

"You baits it wid an apple," explained Abner. "Cause rabbits likes vegetables."

The rabbit skins were worthless when we tanned them. For good muskrat pelts, however, we got 25 cents each. Abner showed me how to set the trap at the beginning of their runs—under-water—and tie it to an under-water stake with a light wire so that they could not pull it up on the bank.

"Cause if dey gets dat far de'll bite dey own legs offen themselves!"

Which of course muskrats did.

And he showed me how, instead of trying to chew the skins soft as I had read in a book the Indian squaws did, we should dry them on stretcher boards and then rub the fat off them with a rough stone.

He was pure Uncle Remus, although he probably did not know one of those Negro cabin tales. It was just that animals were not something foreign to him; he seemed to know what they were thinking about things. They had characters. He had a running vendetta against a Buff Cochin cock we had because he thought it was always "sassing" him.

"Watch dat possum!" he said of one of those smelly creatures we kept alive for some time in a barrel, and to whom he had just given a slice of water-melon and a plate of water—"You watch 'em—jes watch how he washes everything he eats, *befo* he eats it, first!"

Which of course opossums do.

Once every year Abner was given me and $5—which was a lot of money in those days—to take me to the Trenton State Fair.

With my hand squeezed to a pulp in his paw we took the train down-State. There in a riot of freshly-painted agricultural machinery, shining galvanised iron windmills, pens of important looking prize pigs, cattle and poultry and rams, Abner would forgather with the other Negroes in the State. Their rendezvous nearly every year was the same place, an old circus tent by the merry-go-round. They would meet there by instinct, just as surely as salmon will gather at the mouth of a river when they feel the spawning urge coming on. I would be one white spot in a sea of black, stuffed with hot-dogs and lemonade by Abner to keep me quiet. There Abner would "confabulate" with his dusky friends. And when he had shaken the hand and inquired about the health of every Negro he knew (and he seemed to me to know every Negro in the State) he would head for the race track.

Because Abner was a racing man! He would lean over the rail. . . .

"COME ON! little red horse!—COME ON! little red horse . . . !"

Then, sadly, as our fancy would come trailing the field into the home stretch:

"Little red horse—*what* am detaining you?"

He had a bad case of stage fright when he once took me all the way up to New York, to Madison Square Garden, to see Buffalo Bill. And I was nearly worried out of my mind, trying to find some place in New York where a Negro could sit down and eat with a white man (without letting Abner know I was looking for one) until we walked boldly into Sherry's and a sophisticated head waiter, seeing this huge black man with me in tow, realised the situation and gave us a table behind a convenient screen.

That waiter was of course a Frenchman!

Then there was Rhodie, the cook. She ruined my digestion by letting me eat all the insides of the doughnuts she punched out. Crisp, brown little balls.

"Bless mah soul, boy—youse *all* stomach!"

Rhodie was Abner's wife.

They had both been born slaves.

I can see as I write that this was a life in the United States that has gone—gone. . . . Young Simms, Abner's nephew, heralded the new era. Simms, as I said, was our young butler. He had gone quite a long way in school. He had pitched on its baseball team. And he taught me a wicked out-curve behind the stables, when he should have been cleaning the silver on summer afternoons.

"Listen, boy—make 'em break fast—like *this!* Not one of those lazy ones a man can see coming for miles! And one of the first things you ought to do, when you steps in the box—is throw the ball straight at 'em! Try and hit 'em, if you can. It marks one ball up against you. But there's a lot of scarey people that will strike 'emselves out after that."

When the day came that I was to pitch for my school I remembered Simms' advice; and, I must say, it did work like a charm.

At other times, he was sitting in the butler's pantry reading Blackstone. The last time I heard of Simms, he was a successful lawyer at the Bar in New York.

But Abner was distinctly of the old school—and treated me accordingly. There was no doubt in that honest head as to what our proper relationship should be.

"Go on, boy—don't you dare call me *nigger*. A nigger's a mean white man, and dat's what you is when you calls me a nigger!"

Smack! A cuff on the ear would send me sprawling on the lawn. He taught me my manners all right!

At the age of eleven I achieved a momentary notoriety by getting shot. My allowance at that time was still my usual 25 cents a week. But by being very prudent and cadging for tips I had collected $3.50 in a cigar box, whose lid I had nailed down. With this I bought a second-hand Flobert .22. A perfectly good rifle as long as one held it straight. And with this I went off in the woods to shoot everything within sight. Red-headed woodpeckers in the apple orchards were profitless game; we could not eat them, and our people made such a row about them when we brought them home! Our real big game at that age was the frisky grey squirrel.

It was a game of wits, played in the stillness of the coloured autumn woods. We would sit there deathly silent, and then a squirrel would venture out. We would hear him rustling across the leaves, or that *tscik, tscik* of his sharp little incisor teeth as they rasped against a hard hickory nut; or we would see him trying to get away from us, unnoticed, by climbing up along the far side of a tree or branch. The marvellous beauty of a squirrel travelling through the tree tops, swinging from branch to swaying branch. And we, with no eyes for the artistry of it all, trying to pot him before he could get to his hole. We got to know the way squirrels would often give themselves away on sunshiny days by lying in a crotch, thinking themselves concealed up there; but we could see the sunlight glinting through the fuzz of their bushy tails.

And often, when the squirrel dropped, we knew the feeling (hastily stifled) that we wished we hadn't shot him.

But on this dramatic occasion a friend and I were stalking a covey of partridges. Not that our chances of getting one with a .22 rifle were any too good. But I was in the act of carefully drawing a bead on one, standing on tiptoe to see over a bush, when a rifle went off. I fell on my face.

"I've murdered him!"

The right side of my head was burning and I felt it with my hands. Through a mist I saw my friend running back and forth and holding out his arms to me.

"Oh, don't tell!" he was crying. "Oh, please, please, please don't tell. I'll give you anything. . . . I'll give you my gun. . . . Oh, please, please, please don't tell!"

Then he ran off and left me. Cries of "I've murdered him!" came back to me across the fields. And then I was alone.

As my eyes cleared I felt around. Apparently I was not shot in the head at all; it was my leg. There was the blood coming out through my boot.

I tried to jump up. I wanted to run—run anywhere to get away from this awful scene. But my leg would not work. My left heel was pulled up and it would not go down. And through the hole in my boot trickled this oozy red stream.

I was done for.

I pictured myself dying in loneliness, like the boy heroes of G. A. Henty, I was reading at that time. But then came the comforting thought that they never did actually die. On the contrary, they were always saved in the nick of time and rose rapidly to become generals or admirals as the case might be. At the last minute, when all hope was lost, some grateful Hindu, or an unexpected Dutchman or Spaniard always turned up. In my case it was two farmers.

I saw them running, zigzagging across the fields, with, I suppose, the cries of "I've murdered him!" still ringing in their ears. Then they saw me crawling along at a record pace on my hands and knees.

"I think I'm dying," I told them. "Can you staunch this flow of blood?"

They laughed. They ran me piggy-back about half a mile across the fields, where we reached a house whose owner was on the point of driving into town. Feeling every inch the hero, I was raced to hospital. But it was discovered I could not be attended to for some time. All the doctors were busy in the operating rooms, and I was left in a chair facing an ugly little girl.

"What's the matter?" she asked.

"I've been shot."

I announced that with stoic calm.

She showed no interest.

"It was an accident," I said determined to impress her. "My best friend shot me."

"Do you shoot bunnies?"

"Sure!" I said.

"Then I'm glad you're shot. It serves you right. I hope you'll die."

Then I fainted.

Chapter 3

COUNTRY-BRED

THESE were some of the delights of being country-bred in the United States.

For some time before I had been shot at the age of eleven, we were building our own canoes. The first creations were made with an old clothes prop for a keel, barrel hoops for ribs and any old canvas or bed ticking for covering. We usually painted them with the carriage enamel. If we sneezed they capsized. Then we organised the Farson Boat Co., and built better craft with moulds up in the stable loft. This company was not really sound financially because it cost about $5 to build a canoe and about all we could ever get for one was 50 cents. Then we were building real sailing canoes, from paper patterns; and going off to places where we could get away from our families in them.

That of course had been our main objective all along.

These were taken down streams or portaged on a handcart over to Newmarket Pond; and to that lonely stretch we rode over on our bicycles, where we used to swim and shoot and fish all through the warm summer days.

Our swimming hole was in a creek at a bend called Fiddler's Elbow. Long before we could swim on the surface the smallest among us would take a long run, dive and "fetch" across its deep pool to the other side where we could stand up and breathe again. Below Fiddler's Elbow lay the swamp.

The smell of that swamp! Suffocating and sickly and heavy; it only added to its mystery. The rubbery resentment of the stretches of spatterdocks as we pushed through them in our canoes was the protest of the swamp against our invasion. We came on turtles there, basking in the sun, rows of evil-looking turtles with dry backs on the branch of an old dead tree sticking out of the water. Turtles that would drop off plop, plop, plop as we came along. There were hideous snapping turtles that we used to call "stinkpots," with corrugated shells. They had a passion for taking our "night" lines; and we had to go through the odious performance of cutting off their heads *if* we wanted to get our hooks back. Usually we just cut the line. We hunted for red-wing blackbird's eggs in the swamp. The nest was always in a tuft of isolated rushes, and the mother would always give it away by clinging on to a reed just above it until the last frightened minute. Then we would collect two or three blue eggs with brown flecks. They weren't very valuable as birds' eggs went, the ivory-like "flicker's," golden woodpecker's eggs were much more rare. These could only be got by shoving one's arm down through a hole in an old dead tree—and one never knew what was down inside that hole! And in the recesses of that swamp of course, there was always an old blue heron, standing on one leg, and then rising—emptying his insides as he did so—to flap off slowly, trailing his long legs across the sky.

I had my first drink of whiskey in that swamp. It was from a disreputable town character known as "Speiler" Welsh, when he and I and another man were fishing for catfish one night. We were baiting with liver. The other man came from a good family, and was more or less our town hero, because he had just come back wounded from the Spanish-American War. He was my first case of hero-worship. And unaware of his "restless foot" and his penchant for going about with such characters as "Speiler" Welsh, my grandmother after a great deal of argument had let me go out with him fishing on this warm, misty spring night. It was adventure for me. We sat on the wooden bridge where the river entered the swamp.

"Don't talk to me!" said the "Speiler," suddenly opening up his favourite topic—"I *knows* that whores make the best wives!"

"But look here—" began Dave Stewart.

"I know, I know what you're going to say—but you got to be broad-minded about these here things! A *whore*, I tell yer, a whore's *been* there! And she *knows* a good man when she sees one. And she knows how to *treat* him. F'ever I marry it's going to be a whore!"

That having been decided, "Speiler" dug his hand in his back pocket and handed me a flask.

"Here, son—have some bait."

I took a gulp and nearly fell off the bridge. I was twenty-four before I could stand whiskey again.

It was Dave Stewart who made me fish-mad for life! The initiation began with a 12 lb. carp that we caught with canned corn in a pond beside Newmarket swamp. I was overcome by his size. I made Dave give him to me and I rode with him ecstatically all the way home tied on the handle-bars.

And then my grandfather told Abner to throw him on the brush pile.

It might have been this lack of appreciation on the part of my Plainfield family, the amazing lack of sympathy with a boy's point of view, that made me so keen to catch fish from the very start.

At any rate, when Dave Stewart took me bass fishing and we caught a 2½ lb. "small-mouth" my fate was sealed for all time.

I can still see it. A big bass patrolling the nest. Dave flicked out a spoon and drew it gently along. I saw it spinning, glittering in the sun with its beautiful tuft of red feathers concealing its three deadly hooks. Then the bass saw it! There was a rush, swirl, and a shining fish flashed out of water in the sunlight. He fell back into the water and made a sharp run. The reel screamed. . . .

When he lay on the bank I knew that I wanted to fish and fish and fish.

Inch for inch and pound for pound the American fresh-water small-mouth bass is probably as good a fighter as any fish that swims. I began trolling for them with spoons, then bait casting with artificial minnows; and finally progressed to the delicate art of fishing for them with live frogs.

We baited the tiny frogs through the lips. It made me sick at first to see the way the frogs grasped the shank of the hook with their hands. They looked so human. But this was all forgotten when we cast the frog, carefully under the willows where the bass would be lying in the hot middle day. The art of casting frogs is: first, not to kill your frog by casting him too roughly— he must hit the water just as if he had jumped in—next, to restrain yourself and not strike when the bass makes his first run. They always run with the frog for some distance before they stop and blow out the frog to swallow it finally head-on. Then, when you see the line slowly moving out through the guides, is the time to strike and sink the hook. Something like an explosion occurs under water at that time. . . .

Surf-casting along the great Atlantic rollers that rush up the New Jersey sands was a more grandiose, if not so subtle sport. We fished for bay trout and flounders and king-fish that way. We would wade out into the oncoming waves until the sucking salt wash swept around our waists, and then with a two-handed Lancewood rod we would hurl a four-ounce sinker hundreds of feet out to beyond where the waves began. In the clear sand channels that lay out there were also the great striped bass.

Some of these bass ran to 40 lbs. We baited with live clams, and, more often than not after a night's fishing it was we who ate the bait. We would build a fire of driftwood and bake the clams on the beach. We were about to do this one moonlit night when a German I was fishing with got into a 25 lb. channel bass. In his excitement he jammed his complicated reel. To play the fish he had to run backwards and forwards along the waves. The big fish gave him a merry dance. The New Jersey coast has a shallow, sandy foreshore and the huge rollers thunder in in sets of threes. When there is an off-shore wind as there was this night, they race in with the spray trailing off their crests like white veils. The German finally got the big bass into the moil of water where these huge combers curled over and crashed to sweep far up the beach.

This is where I came in. The German yelled that he was beaching the fish and ran backwards into the sand dunes to drag it up with a wave. He couldn't get near it himself. When I saw the fish flapping in the receding wave I rushed down to seize it. Instead, I broke the line.

But it did not get away. I dived on it, clutching it as we were sucked backwards. I stuck my arm up through its gills. It gave me a sharp flap with its massive tail. But I had it, its rough gills cutting my hand; and I did not let go of it until I had carried it up into the dunes.

I have had my heart broken by fish. At Laxo in the Shetland Islands, in a burn about ten feet wide, I played a sea trout two hours and forty minutes before my cast parted. He must have weighed 10 lbs.—and he gets a pound bigger every time I tell this story.

In Loch Baddy, on the extreme north-west tip of Scotland, I played a fresh run salmon for one hour and fifty-five minutes on a Hardy Featherweight rod with a frayed 3X cast. But I got this one. He weighed 12½ lbs.; and he had just come up from the sea —the sea-lice were still on him.

I finally got to the point where I could enjoy walking along a trout stream without a rod. I like to watch them. To see them lying there in the food stream, each behind his own particular rock or patch of reed, opening his little nigger mouth for the things that he lives on. They have a great dignity. At such times I feel a great affinity for them.

There is a lot more in fish than those things lying on a fishmonger's marble slab.

That fascinating winter we spent on the New Jersey coast, when I was twelve, I made friends with the coastguards and the local professional fishermen. I used to walk along with them in the high winds at night, when the guards patrolled the coast with a rocket and spy-glass under their arms, and the spindrift and flying sand cut our faces like sharp glass. Marvellous nights with the ocean roaring and churning itself like a wild beast by our sides. And even more marvellous walks afterward, when the seas lay spent, and there were piles of new wreckage and driftwood beaten up by the waves, and huge dead fish on the beach.

By sitting patiently, watching and admiring him while he was mending his nets with a net-needle, I got round a big horny-toed fisherman to take me off in his skiff. They went off to the "banks," and I knew that bobbing up and down out there, they would let lines baited with shedder crab and clams deep down into the blue sea and pull up all sorts of wondrous things.

"All right," he surrendered finally. "You come 'long here about four o'clock tomorrow morning and we'll take you off. Better ask your people, first."

I did. It was arranged that I was to get up at a few minutes before four, but I was awake and dressed and over at the old life-guard station before three-thirty o'clock.

"Hell!" said the coastguard on duty. "They're gone! Pushed off about twenty minutes ago. Don't know what made 'em go off so early this mawnin'. Tide's about right for four o'clock!"

It broke my heart. After that, for some reason, those fishermen always had an excuse when I tried to make them take me off. Again and again. It was not until it was too late that I was told by my Aunt Edith that she had gone to the fishermen and told them that she would make trouble for them if they ever took me out to sea.

That was another incentive to fish, fish, fish; and the further away from home it was, the better it would be.

During such intervals I went to school.

My family never took my education very seriously. I was constantly whisked out of one school and into another because they wished to spend the winter in some fresh place. To begin with, I was sent to school in Plainfield, convoyed by a nurse as a sort of armed guard. This was kept up until they had more or less broken me of the habit of running away. There, in an uncomfortable Eton collar and ridiculous little bowler hat, I was sent to Sunday-school, where, much against my will, I was forced to follow the footsteps of Our Lord on a plaster of Paris contour map of the Holy Land. Once I got an extra month's vacation because we happened to be horseback riding on a shooting trip through the tan-bark regions of West Virginia.

This sort of thing went on. In all I went to nine different schools.

Then the grand old man died. Died just as luck was beginning to turn for him. He was getting a thousand dollars a day from the State of New York, testifying, I think, against the New York, New Haven and Hartford Railway. He was to testify for ten days; and that ten thousand dollars might have been salvation at that moment. It might have saved a situation where one of his Mexican ventures was showing signs of renewed life. And my grandfather was determined to get it. But he had diabetes. The surgeon who had brought me into this world said to him:

"If you persist in going into New York tomorrow, General, I won't answer for the consequences."

"You won't have to," said my grandfather.

He testified three days. Then he came home, fell into bed and into a stupor from which he never woke.

Abner broke the news to me. I had been packed off to a friend's house in order to be out of the way. Abner came up the drive while we were at breakfast, and I saw that he was weeping aloud.

We lived in a steam-heated slit of an apartment in New York for that first horrible winter. I got my first touch of what I would have to go up against; of the European immigrants, when I had to play Red Rover with their small fry across a cement school-yard instead of good red earth. I got a frightful realisation of how much brighter they were than I was, particularly the young Jewish girls, how infinitely more industrious they were, how much harder they were willing to work to get on—and how they smelt.

We had rented our house in Plainfield to a man who owned a string of race-horses. We had made one stipulation: that he would keep on our Negro servants for that one year, just to give them a try.

"But I don't like nigger servants," he protested.

This was within earshot of Simms.

My grandmother winced: "Abner," she said, "has been with us fourteen years."

So the man said he would try them.

At the end of that year he bought our house. He had also bought a little house for Abner and Rhodie. Nothing less than death itself, he assured my grandmother, would ever make him let those two people go. Abner still had the same toothless rake (he felt immensely important now with such fine horses in the stables); and on Election Day, said the race-horse owner, Abner put on his frock-coat and silk hat (once my grandfather's) and went down to the polls and voted the straight Republican ticket from top to bottom.

Abner carried the traditions.

Eighteen years later when I was back in America after being out of the United States for over half of them, business took me back to Plainfield. I had to visit a big engineering works there on the outskirts of the town. But dare I, I thought, as I rode down in the train from New York—dare I go back to that house?

Charlie, the station-master, was no longer on the platform. A taxi, instead of the old tasselled shay, whizzed me to the address. Instead of cool lawns and shady avenues, canyons of fresh brick and stucco struck my eyes. But our house was the same.

There it was—an oasis—white wood, with a slate mansard roof set in its lawns and tall pine-trees. But how small it was! That was the shock. Somehow, wandering around different parts of the world, and often thinking about Plainfield, I had always pictured that house as having wide, spacious halls. The dark porch at night, with its climbing honeysuckle, I remembered as vast. Here was just an old-fashioned wooden frame house. And—yes—there was Abner.

He was raking the lawn. I walked across it. The rake, as always, was minus several teeth. So was Abner.

"Abner," I said as I came up, "do you remember me?"

His eyes had begun to protrude like an old dog's. They were rheumy and wet.

"Foah Gawd's sake!" said Abner. "What does I see!"

My own eyes weren't any too dry either at that moment, as I handed him the traditional gift. I had stopped at the station to buy it. It was a plug of Battle-Axe chewing tobacco. Abner took it and gouged about with his horny thumb nail to get it off its tin-tag.

"Give it to me," I said. "You know I always saved these."

"Bless my soul!" said Abner. "Youse scarcely changed a hair!"
But I knew better.

A GRATEFUL GOVERNMENT

When my grandmother applied for her pension it was found
that there was a "hitch" in it. She was, said Washington, my
grandfather's second wife. She had only married him at the end
of the Civil War. She had not had the full four years' agony.
Therefore she was not entitled to a full pension. The grateful
Government acknowledged my grandfather's service to his country and offered her an insulting pittance. She refused it.

Then a sense of shame stirred in a New Jersey Congressman.
He took up her case. The pittance was increased by a paltry
sum—

"As a special favour, Mrs. Negley."

And on this I was educated. No wonder that when my time
came up to put in for an appointment to West Point (the Army),
as my grandfather had intended I should, my grandmother refused to ask for it.

Chapter 4

PAST TENSE

MY FATHER, from almost the first days I knew him, always spoke of life in the past tense.

"When I owned the *Juanita* . . . when Charley Rutter and I owned the *Javelin* (a marvellous Chesapeake 'sharpie' schooner) . . . when we had the place at Marcus Hook . . . when I was president of the Farson Manufacturing Co. . . ."

But nearly always the when was connected with some yacht. For my father's life could be told from his boats. Their pictures hung around the walls of his study. I often wondered how he could bear to look at them; for after the time he had reached the age of around forty they were in a sadly descending scale. Their apex was a 50-ft. racing sloop, *Juanita*, whose silver cups always decorated our dining-rooms. They ended with a little catboat, the *G.O.P.*, which meant Grand Old Party, for my father was an un-reasoning Republican; but his friends said that *G.O.P.* meant "Get out and push!" The only memento of little *G.O.P.* was a photo-graph of her lying in a shipyard, with my father underneath, caulking her one Sunday afternoon. I sailed in *Juanita* when I was a baby in arms, for I sailed and was seasick long before I could walk; and I rolled strings of oakum and helped with caulking chisel to fit out little *G.O.P.* for spring.

One of the original members of the famous Quaker City Yacht Club of Philadelphia, and No. 2 in the Corinthian, my father's come-down in life found him with the little *G.O.P.* in the Alpha Boat Club of Chester, Pennsylvania. Not that the members of that little boathouse overhanging the Delaware were any descent as far as sportsmanship went. Far from it. Like the wealthier members of Corinthian, who no matter how wealthy, always sailed their own yachts, the Alpha men were mad watermen. And perhaps, sailing smaller boats, they got closer to the water and knew more about it. At any rate, when I came to live with my father, that little boathouse among the reeds, with its racks of

24

rowing shells and float of fine gunning skiffs, was, for me, the most enchanting and only tolerable spot in his town.

There was a farm behind my father's small house. Our back wire fence was against its open fields. In the summer they were full of waving wheat and corn, and in the autumn I used to shoot rabbits among the corn stacks. But the real estate agent did not see any beauty in that farm; he saw a sub-development; so he bought it and turned it into a suburb of houses and dusty streets. Nothing could be safe from a man like that, except a mountain that he couldn't climb, or a desert he could not cross. Nothing could be preserved. When my father looked out of the windows of his house and saw only that he lived next to a farm like that he was of course a poor business man.

It was a relief to get down to the river in a pair of old ducks, and row across to Chester Island on the Jersey side to shoot rail, reed birds, and ducks. My father's only interest in me was in connection with things like this. And at first, until I was big enough to take my turn doing it, he used to "push" the skiff himself, standing on the stern, with a long pushing pole, shoving us along through the high hot reeds. Then we would row home at sunset, with the river turning gold, and the sight of tramp steamers putting out to sea with foreign flags fluttering from their sterns.

My father was never troubled by those foreign flags; he was worried by the factory smoke-stacks that multiplied daily along the river bank. "In a few years," he said sadly, looking back at the marshes, "they will all be gone."

That for my father was life. The minute he stepped ashore he became a changed man. Fretful, surly. The reason was that on the water he knew he was as good as the next man. On shore, the man who lived next to us happened to be the town's most astute banker; and he had a sort of flair for making my father feel small. For these were the days when the banker, the biggest manufacturer, the richest merchant, were the autocrats of the dinner table in every American town. I could have killed old Daddy Turner when I would hear him silencing my father at a dinner party, just because he happened to have ten times as much money as my old man. When my father died the Philadelphia newspapers gave him space on the news page under the lead:

PROMINENT YACHTSMAN DEAD

When my mother sent me the clippings I was in Amsterdam "covering" the Olympic Games. I did not need to read any further than the lead. I knew it was about all the papers would say about my old man. But I knew how he would have loved to have read it. The one thing he was proudest of in life was that he was known by the professional sailors and oyster fishermen up and down the Delaware and Chesapeake Bays, and that they liked him, and called him "Commodore."

He had a moment of renaissance just before death, when, with a little flush of war prosperity, he bought the *Kirawan*. She was a substantial 40-ft. motor-cruiser. She was not sail. Age had got him by then. And it was agonising to watch the old man fearfully taking the *Kirawan* down the Delaware River on dark nights, a jangle of nerves, what with engines and buoys and up-coming traffic, although he insisted in spite of all arguments that "Kirawan" was the Arab name for "Peace."

His people were farmers on the Delaware, on the same spot where the Farsons first settled in America, when Yardley their cousin was the first Governor of Virginia. They lived a pleasant life there, with their schooners riding at anchor just off the lawns of their houses. The first three Farsons were Scots; three brothers who ran a trading ship of their own to America. Beside the farm on which my brother was born was a shipyard that made wooden sailing ships. On visits to my mother as a child I used to sit there and watch the workmen adze the beams of the big ribs. There was a good smell of tar always about the place and the sound of caulking hammers. My father's father, aside from being the hardest drinker along the Delaware, was one of the best brains of the family. In 1849, more for a whim than anything else, he founded the Farson Manufacturing Company—and made the first refrigerators built in America. The venture grew like the green bay-tree—until the epoch of mass production.

But the Farsons were no match for the business sharks in Grand

Rapids, who would sit up all night just to see if they couldn't punch out an ice-tank in one operation—from tin instead of copper—and who knew that nattily painted pine could be sold just as effectively as good straight grained white oak.

My father couldn't compete. When I came to know the old Farson factory it was trying to meet competition from Grand Rapids where they were turning out refrigerators practically untouched by human hands. My father still employed cabinet makers. He had two reasons for this. First, I suppose, he hated change. But primarily it was because he did not want to lose his old men. He hated Unions with a parochial stubbornness and wouldn't tolerate a union man in the place. But it was his sense of duty towards his employees that practically ruined him.

When he saw that the refrigerator game was getting too much for him, he switched over to expensive hand-made furniture. The river yard of the Farson Manufacturing Company began to fill with mahogany logs from South America. The names Sheraton and Chippendale began to be heard at our own dinner table. The little works had always been a family affair and most of the furniture in our Chester house had been made to order in the factory. They were craftsmen, these old cabinet makers, many of whom had first gone to work there under my father's father, and they put love into it when they knew where it was going. As copies they were not at all bad pieces.

But it was an expensive luxury to hang on to this old style of enterprise in the face of American mass production and mass mentality. And this luxury was fantastically symbolised in the person of Johnny Wonderly.

Johnny had worked on a planing machine—until one day he got absent-minded and sent his fingers along with the board he was planing. His right hand came back without any fingers whatever. Then my father gave him another job. I've forgotten what it was, but it was tending a machine of some sort, a machine with belt power-transmission; and when the twelve o'clock whistle blew one day Johnny tried to kick off the belt instead of reaching up to the lever to shift it over to the idler pulley. Johnny was retrieved minus a right leg.

Then my father hardly knew what to do with him. So he made him a checker in the timber seasoning yard. And here one day a board fell off a stack that Johnny was supervising and put out Johnny's right eye. And here indeed was a dilemma; what could be done with or for Johnny Wonderly now.

One hand, one leg, one eye.

"Well," said my father, "I know what I'll do—I'll make him a day watchman."

"But who ever heard of a day watchman!"

"Watch Wonderly," said my father.

"Sure, Commodore, I know," said that remnant of a man. "That's just the job I've been looking for. I'll keep my eye on things. You can trust me for that."

And all day long Johnny Wonderly would sit by the gate, in the shade of a timber pile, saying:

"Now, if *I* was running this here Goddam factory . . ."

When the Farson Manufacturing Company was caught short in the panic of 1907 my uncle was down in Texas playing tennis, my father was down the Bay shooting ducks; and nobody was running the "Goddam factory."

But I hardly knew my father before I was fifteen. My eighteen-year-old mother had "parked" me with her own father and mother after my birth, while she went off South with her husband in the *Juanita*. And the General and my grandmother never let go. I was to all intents and purposes, the son they had never had themselves. There had been of course periodic visits to my father and mother from Plainfield, but none of any duration. It was not until I was expelled from Andover that I came to live in my father's house.

Chapter 5

EXPELLED FROM ANDOVER

ANDOVER was the one bright spot in my so-called education. The headmaster makes the school, and while Al Stearns was alive I feel sure that Andover was the finest prep. school in the United States. To me, as an institution of culture, it was distinguished for two things: (*a*) I went into long trousers there, (*b*) after two years at Andover I played a leading part in probably the most sensational scandal that splendid school has ever known.

I wept for the long trousers. My grandmother had convoyed me up to Andover, where I was to appear as the youngest and smallest boy in school. As we walked around the campus I saw that all the boys were dressed like real men, and some of them, consciously sophisticated second-year men, smiled at my stockinged legs. When we got back to the Phillips Inn (where Harriet Beecher Stowe wrote *Uncle Tom's Cabin*) I lay flat on the floor and howled. I kept right on howling until a promise was extracted that we would take the first train to Boston the next morning. I wanted to get away before anyone else in Andover woke up. My grandmother, who hated to admit to this obvious break with my gentle childhood, fought a losing battle from the start. After a humiliating breakfast where I knew the part of me that showed above the table was all right, I rushed her from the door into a cab, dashed from cab to train, jumped up and down until she hailed another cab in Boston, and made her stop at the first men's goods store we passed.

In there I demanded a long trouser suit—*and I would not take it off.*

No amount of guile on the part of the salesman, no pleadings or threats from my grandmother, nothing could make me shed that ghastly mustard-coloured suit. I wouldn't try on any other, or consider any alteration. I would not take off those long trousers, and was afraid that if I did I would never get another long pair for years. I tried on a little Norfolk suit by proxy, my grandmother being obliged to accept it on the salesman's assurance that the measurements were identical with the long-trousered affair. I bought a little set of golf clubs. And then I was taken to a restaurant where I was given the one meal I have hankered for throughout life—lobster salad and Tutti Frutti ice-cream. Then, stepping out of the train at Andover I knew I was at last a man.

My grandmother almost destroyed me by hanging on in Andover, which she should not have done, and waiting for me after chapel with an apple in her hand. I cried about that, too, pointing out how my grandmother shamed me before all the other fellows, and she gave up a friendship she had formed with the Latin professor (they used to watch football games together) and left.

The expulsion came two years later. My room-mate, Johnnie Meade, was a wealthy young lad of seventeen whose father owned some of the finest early automobiles in the United States. He took these in succession for long drives through Europe. From these jaunts the fortunate young Johnnie brought back trunk-loads of suits from Poole's in London, and some startling ideas about the accessibility of all women. The suits he sold, without even wearing, the minute we hit Andover—taking for these clothes made in Savile Row $4 or $5 or whatever he could get. That he considered was a legitimate way to get extra spending money. Then his thought turned to women. And Puritan Andover was about the last place in the United States for that kind of attitude. There was an unwritten law at Andover that no boy could speak to a girl "on the hill." The penalty was expulsion forthwith. It was, of course, aimed against our forming unhealthy friendships with the town girls. There had been amusing contretemps where boys had been reported by sneaks and professors and subsequently proved that they had been escorting their sisters. But Johnnie's affair was truly shocking—Johnnie was caught red-handed kissing the prettiest waitress in Phillips Inn.

He was caught, and reported, by an habitué of the inn, who, rumour had it, was "sweet" on that waitress himself. And the Professor to whom Johnnie was reported was not "sweet" on Johnnie . . . or myself. It was the Latin professor. The result was that Johnnie was immediately suspended for ten weeks while his case could be investigated. Ten weeks seemed to be a minimum Andover suspension. Johnnie knew that Al Stearns had written to his father reporting his son's behaviour, but he also knew that his father was in Tunis.

So, not having any more Poole's suits to sell, Johnnie went to the local tailor, ordered six suits on account, then told the tailor not to make them but to give him half the money and keep the rest for himself. The full bill could go to Tunis.

Then Johnnie danced around our rooms and took the next train for Boston.

So far so good; I felt a little lonely and jealous, but nothing else. Then a hero appeared on the scene. He was left-end in the football team—afterwards end at Yale. I stood up as he entered.

"Well," he said. "What are we going to do about Meade?"

"I don't know," I said.

I was only fifteen and still the smallest boy in the school, although sprouting fast.

"Well, I do," he said.

He then unfolded the most startling plan, complete to the last detail. Not only concise, but alluring, breath-taking, enchanting, daring, absolutely unrefusable.

Two nights later the Andover campus was mildly surprised by the appearance of a band which paraded round and round the dormitories playing "Onward, Christian Soldiers." It wasn't Sunday, and there was no Salvation Army about, so people began to wonder what it was. Then they saw a long and fast-growing snake of young Andoverites trailing after it and heard the repeated shout—"ALL OUT! ALL OUT!" which command is obeyed automatically in Andover without one moment's thought. In all that crowd there were only six of us who knew what it was all about. Then the rain came and the procession broke up.

The next day there were questions about it. The campus hummed with uneasy gossip. The professors knew that something was up, but they didn't know what. So, next night, when it repeated itself, they watched the growing procession with mixed feelings of apprehension and pride.

"Boys will be boys, you know, and no one can say that this school is not full of spirit. Look at them now, there must be three hundred of them."

"ALL OUT! ALL OUT! ALL OUT!"

The captain of the football team, the captain of the basketball team, the captain of the baseball team; there they were, always leading as those stout-hearted fellows always do. Always taking the lead in school spirit. Always *there* when things were happening. Yes, yes. . . . I didn't know what Kirkpatrick was thinking, but I knew that I was feeling a little scared at the thought of what these people would think if they knew what we were leading them to. . . .

"*Onward Christ-i-an so-oldiers . . . marching as to warrrr. . . .*"

"ALL OUT . . . ALL OUT! . . . ALL OUT!"

The words struck like hammer blows. Kids jumped out of windows to get in on it. Some of the professors got joyous and tagged along with us. "What is it?" they asked. "I don't know." Nobody knew. It was just something—something exciting was going to happen. And was it not!

When we reached the elms that lead up to the shrubbery that befronts that old inn, Kirkpatrick took the lead. He halted us at the steps. Everybody held their breath. Now, *now* it was going to happen.

"SPEECH!" shouted Kirkpatrick.

"SPEECH!" shouted the crowd.

"Who?" asked everybody.

"I don't know," answered everybody.

"SPEECH!" shouted Kirkpatrick.

"SPEECH!" roared the crowd. "SPEECH! SPEECH! SPEECH!"

Hewart, an habitué of the inn (the man who had squealed upon Meade), came out on its railed front porch. He was dressed in an over-natty grey suit, rose shirt and purple tie. He smiled, and at the roar that welcomed him, he held up a modest hand.

"Gentlemen," he began, "I'm sure I don't know why—"

But he was not long finding out. As he spoke, two of the huskiest boys in school, Kirkpatrick and another footballer, vaulted the railing and seized him by his little grey trousers and they threw him to us as you would throw a rat to a pack of dogs.

It was a shocking demonstration of mob violence. For, as the four of us grabbed him and began to drag him towards the duck pond the blood cry gave full tongue. Like a chip on a wave Hewart was rushed before a hundred odd students down the hill of the golf course. A few thoroughly terrified professors tried to avert the stampede. They were crushed underfoot. One boy, one of the finest fellows in the school, stood there and slugged the lot of us as we came past. "Beasts! Beasts!" he screamed. He hit everyone he could, regardless of size. And no one tried to hit back. We just wanted Hewart. And we got him. When we got to the edge of the mire we threw him well out into the pond.

He hit with a splash and sank.

There he stood up, the water about up to his knees.

"There," said Kirkpatrick. "I guess that'll teach you not to squeal!"

We watched him in silence as he waded out of the mud. Evidently he thought the whole show was over, for he suddenly struck a heroic pose.

"I did it!" he said. "And I'd do it again."

At that instant a figure shot past us, and then it flew through the air. A beautiful flying tackle—so it would have been on any football field—it cut Hewart down as abruptly as wheat with a scythe. And then Hewart did a stage-faint . . . and we all went home with our tails between our legs.

Andover had never, probably never again, will be rocked by a scandal such as that. Horror hung over the hill. Horror, heavy and dark as fog. Through this walked about a hundred of us. The die was cast. There was no turning back and no hope for us now. Our only hope lay in organised strength. To secure that Kirkpatrick and I and the four other "originals" got up a round robin.

This was a bold document, carrying revolt a step further, and an outrageous step. It said that its signatories would not go to classes until Meade had been reinstated. We got eighty signatures.

Then the whole school was closed for four days. This was on

the telegraphed order of Al Stearns, who knew how to handle boys in mass or individually. He was lecturing in Pittsburgh at the time. He finished his engagements. Then he took the first express East. On the fourth day after the Hewart episode he called a meeting of the whole school in the chapel—at eleven o'clock.

That hour, picked with such astuteness, gave the eighty of us some two hours of torture after breakfast. Some had already begun to get cold feet. When we marched into chapel old Al Stearns, our ideal of a man, stood up in the pulpit.

"Boys," he began, "you have stabbed a knife in my heart. . . ."

It might have been acting. I doubt it, as a matter of fact. But at any rate, as we sat there we began to feel ourselves the most abysmal lot of swine ever born. Our strike was not broken, for the simple reason that that wise old Principal did not re-open school. Instead, a sort of drum-head court martial was held forthwith. Thirty of us were dismissed from Andover.

The question that fired us was: "Did you touch Mr. Hewart?"

One boy, a friend of mine not much bigger than myself, replied:

"I didn't. But I wish I had."

He must have given them something to think over. Hewart was very unpopular with all of us.

My grandmother had rushed up from New York in a panic. Under her skillful pleading old Stearns broke down.

"But, Mrs. Negley, I don't know what to make of him. I don't know how much money you give him. But I know he is playing poker all the time!"

"But he is so, so young, Mr. Stearns."

"Oh, very well, I will reduce his sentence of expulsion to one of suspension for ten weeks."

But I never went back. It was impossible to remain with the rest of "us" gone. Strangely enough, the fellow that tried to fight the whole lot of us single-handed, in order to prevent that semilynching, also left school. He would, he said, for ever be known as a teacher's pet if he stayed there.

We all went round and shook hands with him before we left and told him what a hell of a fine fellow we thought he was, and how we all admired his guts.

And that ended the only period of my schooling that I cherish. I loved Andover.

Chapter 6

GROWING PAINS

HURLED into the outer darkness from Andover I resigned myself to life in my father's small river town. I complied with the proprieties by going to the local high school, where for a few autumn months I got a certain amount of kick out of life by playing in the football team. But in every other respect I struggled to get away.

That town frightened me. I never witnessed anything more disheartening than the morning rush of business men to catch the trolley at the end of our street. One morning I watched a boy walk out of it. He was going off to a salmon cannery up in Alaska. I leaned out of my window and cheered as he passed by. I was only sixteen then and did not have the nerve to escape.

My first attempts were futile, but satisfactory while they were on. The first winter I lived with my father I bought a boat. She was a second-hand Bridgeport gunning skiff that I picked up for $25 over on the New Jersey shore. I took her home and put her down the cellar where I worked on her in the evenings. I decked her over and cut a slot in her keel for a drop centre-board. I bought a second-hand sprit-sail rig, and built lockers in her for clothes and supplies. I painted her coal black, with buff decks, and called her *Nimrod*. When spring came I had a first rate chance of escape. The only trouble was—I could not get *Nimrod* out of the cellar. That three-inch combing I had put on just made her jam in the door.

So I cut a hole in the door.

After a storm with my father I got *Nimrod* down to the Delaware. The place that I was heading for was the eastern shore of Maryland, where for a couple of hundred miles there was no railroad, and the people were so remote and lazy they didn't know the Civil War was over yet; and a week later another fellow and I were sailing down the Elk River into the headwaters of the

Chesapeake Bay. About two hundred miles of some of the best cruising water in the world lay ahead of us.

We had no objective. We could stop where we liked, and sail where we liked, and stay away all summer if we could manage to keep alive. Our parents had given us each $15, hoping to tie us by a short string; but coming down through the Chesapeake and Delaware Canal we decided we could easily beat that little game. We would live on the country. That, however, turned out to be one of those things that is easier said than done. We had counted too much on the fishing. In the fourteen mile stretch of head-water, where the Elk, Susquehanna and North Rivers pour in, the steamship folder told us there was one of the best perch grounds in the United States. "The home of the famous Betterton perch," was the caption we read under that fraudulent photograph of the upper bay. But as far as we were concerned all of those Betterton perch are living there yet. We never got a nibble.

We would not face this fact, until we woke up in our tent one morning to realise that we had no breakfast and that all of our money had run out.

Have you ever had crabs for breakfast, lukewarm and soggy? Have you ever had crabs for breakfast, luncheon and dinner on the same day? We did; we had them for two weeks.

By that time we were desperate. It wasn't a question of starving in the midst of plenty. There just wasn't anything. It was too soon for the crops to be ripe, or we would have raided those at will. But, even so, we were too young and healthy to be vegetarians, and we wondered what we could do.

"I'm going to break a Commandment," said my companion. "I'm going to steal."

We sat there on the hot beach, talking of a tin of corn he had seen lying in a tempting position outside a grocery store that morning. While I engaged the shopkeeper's attention he could pick it up and saunter off. This fellow, who afterwards graduated second in his class from the United States Naval Academy, had the proper piratical instincts for such a cruise, but we were saved from that temporarily by a 12 lb. carp.

We caught him up a fresh river where we had gone to try for

wretched sunfish. When I saw his bronze side turn over near the surface I nearly fell in. I have never been more afraid of losing a fish in all my life.

Now, in all the British and German recipes for cooking carp there are aloes and spices and wine; everything, in fact, except carp. We had just a dead carp.

So we cut him in steaks and broiled him over our camp grate. He tasted like river mud. Then we decided to boil him. We wrapped him in a clean towel and put him in a pot. But we fell asleep around our fire. When we woke up in the morning, the carp and towel had become one. So we consigned him to the river whence he came.

That experiment had failed.

Then I wrote my grandmother a letter about how hard times were, and I got ten dollars as a result. We picked up that letter over by the Naval Academy at Annapolis, and then Ned and I went on down the Eastern Shore. In the salt water we got some real fish, and Ned and I wrote a masterly description of our plight to his people. But when that money ran out we knew that we had shot our bolt.

We had now reached the end of our objective, which had been to get as far as we could get, and now we had to face the problem of getting home.

There seemed no answer to it at first, until one morning we persuaded an upcoming lumber schooner to give us a tow. She had anchored for the night in the bay on whose shore we had beached our boat. She was manned by three Negroes, and after we had been with them for a day they said we could go on up into the Delaware with them, if we were willing to help them work their way. This consisted principally of helping a little Negro named Sam to get on sail, for once we had hauled *Nimrod* aboard and lashed her on top of the deck load, the two other Negroes just stopped work altogether.

She was called the *Hattie Jenks* and was one of the dirtiest ships that ever remained afloat. Sam, who apparently had done all the work before we came along, cooked in a galley that had no ports.

"Dese yere cockroaches," said Sam; "dey's de mos' intelligent bugs I'se ever met. Dey sits here an' watches me while I'se cookin', and dey picks up what dey can get. An', bless mah soul, when Ah carries de captain's vittles aft—dey's down dere waiting foah me!"

But how even a cockroach could eat the stuff that Sam cooked was a puzzle to us. It was "sow belly," strips of crusted salt pork, mixed up with potato chunks. There was no time limit to how long it should stay on the stove. It just simmered there all day in water until someone wanted to eat.

Sleeping was a problem, because the muddy-eyed captain insisted on closing the companion-way doors and all the ports. The cabin stank worse than a morgue. On clear nights Ned and I slept on the deck-load, under a tarpaulin we rigged from the foremast boom. When it rained we just had to go down into the cabin and stick it out.

But we became quite friendly with those Negroes before they threw the *Hattie Jenks* up into the wind, so that we could put *Nimrod* back into the Delaware off our home town. The captain was nearly always drunk, and he "had religion," a combination that made him tell some startling tales.

Escape came from an unexpected and entirely different quarter that winter when, to everybody's surprise, my own most of all, I won the interscholastic championships in the shot put.

I had put my name down just for the fun of it. The Middle State interscholastic championships were being held in Philadelphia, in the 2nd Regiment's armoury hall. Perhaps the excitement of the whole thing gave me additional strength. Whatever it was I had the surprise of seeing my shot hit the floor ahead of all the other puts.

From that night I went crazy, and I would travel a hundred miles to win a medal of any kind. I was third in the interscholastics held on Franklin Field, and a week later I won the open interscholastic championship at Princeton University by two inches on my last put.

This was the hey-day of many an American boy, this brief

burst of athletic glory, before he settled down for life to rot in an office of some sort. And I resolved to cash in on it for all I could get. In England, where life is more settled than in the United States, my trophies would have been treasured carefully on the mantelpiece. Here, my family hardly looked at them; and I gave the most attractive gold medals to the various girls I happened to be in love with at the time.

For this girl question was beginning to get bothersome. Spring nights were painful affairs. Leaning out of my father's window, the smell of the moist earth in those dark fields would drive me half-crazy at times. I knew what it all meant. I had had my first sexual adventure while I was still at Andover. It was a girl I had picked up on a merry-go-round. I hired a canoe and paddled her out to an island in the lake. She did not know much more about things than I did. But it wasn't the disappointment I had been told it would be.

The best place for picking up girls in my father's town was in the shadow of the old Catholic church that still held its position in the very heart of the main business street. Although we did not know it, the girls were also hunting for us. They always walked out in couples; one pretty one, and one not quite so nice who had to take what she could get. The delights of conquest were immeasurably increased by the uncertainty of the whole affair. It was a long walk out to the fields on the edge of the town.

But success was exaltation. There was no doubt of that.

We used to walk them out of town. Out there in the fields we made love to them. If the girl was decent or frightened we usually got remorse and ended up by apologising. But it was ecstasy out there in those corn stalks under the moon. Then, temporarily, there was peace.

But one of the great shocks of my life was when a friend of mine brought up his "fiancée," and I knew where I had seen her face last.

One of the results of my athletic madness was that I came under the notice of Mike Murphy, that wizard who coached the

American Olympic teams; and he persuaded me to go to the University of Pennsylvania instead of Yale.

"I'll teach you more than these damned professors ever will," said old Mike.

And so it was. Not that the professors did not have a good try.

Chapter 7

BOAT RACE

THERE is not much to be said about my university career, except that I made an unholy mess of it. My guardian, not my father, came down to help me matriculate.

"Don't work too hard," he told me, over a farewell lunch of lobster salad at the Bellevue Stratford. "Make some good friends and make some good Societies—you'll never be an engineer. When you get out you'll be able to buy them for $100 a month."

I took his advice.

He was a spectacular figure, my guardian. My grandfather passed me on to him in his will as a last shot at my father. An old Yale man himself, he made his millions and lost them in the railroad mergers of his day. At one time he was the president of the Seaboard Air Line. When he took me down to college it was a toss up whether he was going to be a millionaire again or blow up. His *milieu* was a suite of rooms he kept in the Waldorf-Astoria Hotel in New York for business purposes. Often, sitting in its Peacock Alley or one of its restaurants, I acted as a stool pigeon for him, lending an innocent air to the deadly conversation he would be conducting with some other Wall Street gambler across the luncheon table.

Life with my guardian was like living in a roller coaster all the time. When he would be without a dollar, and head over heels in debt, he would suddenly order Pentacost of New York to do thousands of dollars' worth of landscape gardening on his estate. Then he would let this information leak out in Wall Street.

"But you're mad!" I protested the first time I watched him do this, knowing the fix we were in.

"No, I'm not," he said, smiling. "I'm doing it to save myself. I have to unload some securities. If those people in Wall Street knew how broke I was they would simply step in and take them away from me. Now they will pay a good price. I've bluffed them. They're all swine, anyway."

Sometimes this worked. When it did not his life became a shell. People driving past his estate in the Catskills would point it out as the show place on the lake. But inside it we knew that I had been out on the water most of that day, trying to shoot ducks, or even hell-divers, for food. The only thing that made such an existence tolerable was the gusto with which my guardian played the game. Whatever other accusations that might have been made against it, life with him was not dull.

But his advice was hardly the right instruction to give a young man entering the University of Pennsylvania to become a civil engineer. The precision of its famous engineering schools was Prussian to the core. The civil engineering school of that university was no place to play the fool.

"Nine o'clock is nine o'clock," was the opening sentence of the draughting professor to his freshman class; "and five minutes after nine might just as well have been yesterday."

At nine o'clock all the classroom doors in the engineering schools closed with a sharp click. And many a morning I stood outside, trying to get in. But that was not the reason why I made a mess of things. My *débâcle*, bitterly enough, was the result of virtue. The last two years before I went to Penn I went to a crammer's school in Philadelphia, where I worked so hard that I got a certificate and entered the university without examinations. Then I rested on my laurels. I didn't do any work.

I carried on with the shot put, and, in order to win more medals, I joined the 2nd Regiment (Territorials) which was trying to build up an athletic team to win the military championships. As it is a tradition of that proud regiment, one of the oldest in the States, that every officer in the regiment must first serve one year in its ranks—they made me a cook. With a thing that looked like an upturned chamber pot on my sleeve, I shot in my company's rifle team around the State, and wearing the colours of the 2nd Regiment, I alternately got 1st and 2nd in both the shot put and broad jump in the Military Championships for two years running. But the high light of that first year at Penn was the boat races.

We raced the Navy first, and went down for five days to Annapolis, where we lived with the cadets in Bancroft Hall. With apprehension we watched Coach Glendon taking his crack crews up the Severn. And it was just as well that we did, for the Navy beat us by three feet.

We thought we had won and were cheering the other crew, when we suddenly saw the Navy's flag go up. Then several of us collapsed in a faint. I rowed in eight races before I ever watched one from shore. And then I was appalled to see how little a spectator could know of the agony that was being felt on those sliding seats!

The ultimate triumph of rowing in the United States is to win the big Poughkeepsie boat race. Lose the Navy, lose Henley, lose all the dual races of a season; but win the Poughkeepsie race, and everything was all right. That was the only race that counted. It was like the final battle of a war.

In Poughkeepsie each university had its own boat-houses, and its training quarters back on the highlands of the shore. In preparation for the race we lived and rowed there for several weeks. It was a Spartan life, where every pat of butter, every ounce of meat, and practically every lump of sugar was doled out. We were kept like a lot of roaring lions in a cage. When, years later, I went down to stay with the Oxford crew, when it was training at Bourne End, I could not believe the casual life I saw the crew living there. They trained on beer!

But, in passing, I might say that I discovered that the average English oarsman rows for more days in the year, and in more races, than does his American brother of the cedar shell.

I got up to Poughkeepsie one week late. For some reason, in three years' rowing, I could never heal a sore that immediately developed in the palm of my left hand at the beginning of every season. At Annapolis, I had trained with a waxed bandage on my hand, and only took it off when we were lying out at the start, waiting to take our places for the race. When Coach Ward used to pour alum over our hands to harden them, I nearly cried with pain. Shortly after the American Henley, it had to be operated upon, and I was out of the boat for two weeks. I came up to Poughkeepsie a week late, with my hand still in bandages; and I thought I had so little chance of being put back into the boat, that I had smoked several cigars on the railway train up from New York. I took a launch across river and found old side-whiskered Coach Ward sitting in lonely glory on our slip.

"Hello, Farson."

"Good afternoon, Mr. Ward."

"Ready to row?"

I nearly fell back into the river, but a chance like this was not to be missed. Thinking that the best thing I could hope for would be a try-out, I went into the boat-house and hurried into my rowing trunks and socks with their soft leather soles. Lancaster, a good friend of mine, was rowing in my place. When the crews came down and he saw me standing dressed on the slip, tears came into his eyes.

"Don't worry," I said to him, "I'll probably crumple up." And then I told him about the cigars.

Vivian Nickalls, the great English oarsman, afterwards coached my university, but for the score of years he was doing it old Coach Ward had the reputation of being the most man-killing rowing coach in the United States. He whipped his crews along like dogs. He was one of four brothers who had set up a world's record for Fours themselves. He was a man with one idea, and that was maniacal—to beat the crews of Courtney of Cornell; an ambition that nearly killed all of us, for Coach Courtney of Cornell was probably the greatest rowing coach that this world will ever see. A Courtney Eight rowed like one man.

The day I arrived at Poughkeepsie happened to be the day of the infamous "break-down" row, the purpose of which was to smash the fine edge of training by getting the crews in such an exhausted condition that they could be built up again and "fined off" to just the right point for the vital race. By that time our muscles and our insides were so delicately attuned that if we ate something that did not agree with us we would go to bits. It is a matter of fact that a famous crew rowed like a lot of amateurs in a Poughkeepsie race, merely because the night before they had been given some fermented apple-sauce.

"Stroke-hup! Stroke-hup! Stroke-hup . . ."

The long shell went down the Hudson. Down, down, down, until I went through my motions as emotionless as a clock. At first the pain in my hand had been unbearable. But now the pain no longer hurt. It was all part of this trance. And what sharp shoots of it that did penetrate through my daze I bit down on with satisfaction, just as one bites down on the agony of a sore tooth. We were turning, the coaching launch *Franklin* lying off our flanks.

"Give 'em tens," we heard Ward megaphoning to the coxes.

This was just sheer murder.

"I watched you," said Reath afterwards, our famous stroke of the year before. "Believe me, I suffered with you."

"No," I said frankly. "I didn't know, I didn't even know what was going on."

"Are you ready, Cornell? Are you ready, Columbia? Are you ready, Syracuse? Are you ready, Wisconsin? Are—you—ready— *Pennsylvania?*"

There they were; *those dreaded words*. Watermen, leaning from the stake-boats, were holding our delicate rudders. A man with a pistol stood in the prow of the steward's yacht. As he called, each cox raised his right arm in signal that his crew was ready for the start. We were leaning forward, ready to catch.

Crack!

For twenty strokes we gave it everything that we had, our blades moiling the water to get the long shell under way. And then we straightened out.

There was a cannon on the bridge and also a signal arrangement comprised of our university flags. The gun would fire at each mile to denote the crew in the lead; fire one, two, three shots, etc., according to the number of our lane. As we passed under the bridge for the last mile, we heard the gun fire twice— *Columbia was in the lead*.

That last mile at Poughkeepsie!

It is a mile that has broken more hearts than any race-course on water, land or air. Broken not only the hearts of the oarsmen, who are sobbing to themselves—"one more stroke, one more stroke—just one more stroke—and then I die!"—but the thousands and thousands of hearts on the palisades of the Hudson, in the hundreds of yachts that line the course, in the long rumbling observation train that follows the race from along the river-edge.

In that last mile every excursion steamer, yacht, launch and Navy torpedo-boat along the course pulls her whistle down. It is the shrieking of hell. And in this inferno the dying crews fight it out. We passed a crew. We began to overhaul another crew. Suddenly—we left it as if it were standing still. Just a dazed glimpse of something wrong with No. 2—he was rocking in his seat. The cox is giving us tens now, stepping it up—then the last sixty—"*Give her everything you've got left!*"

Roars, whistles, firing of salutes. We are lying, drifting on the tide. Our oars drag lifeless. We lie crumpled up. Big Bill Crawford is sobbing behind me. He leans forward and then slowly falls over my upturned face. I try to push him off. . . . We sit up. A crew fresh as paint is already rowing back up the course. It is followed by an increasing gale of cheers.

"Cornell! Cornell! We yell like hell, Cornell!"

Cornell first, Columbia second, Pennsylvania third . . .

Afterwards we went along to the Wisconsin boat-house. We wanted to know what had happened to No. 2. There he lay, blood all over the place, being attended to by a perplexed doctor. Just before we entered the last sixty strokes he had jumped his seat. He had rowed that sixty with his buttock sliding along the brass runners. The brass strips had cut through his rowing shorts, cut through his flesh, until, it seemed, his entire behind was just one wide open sore.

Otherwise we might have been fourth.

Then I climaxed the day. I thought I would jump aboard the moving observation train to ride back to our boat-house. I took a run beside it, leaped up, and caught hold of its rail. My right hand missed its grip. My dud left hand caught. There I dangled, unable to pull myself up. My feet began to drag along, knocking against the railway ties. I could not pull myself up and I dared not let go for fear I would fall under the wheels.

Some girls above me looked down and began to scream. But there was no way to stop the observation train. No signal cord that one could pull. This was about the twentieth car, and the engine was around the bend. Some men tried to squeeze between the observation train railings and pull me up.

Then I felt the tendons in my left shoulder beginning to go. That broken shoulder from football was taking its count. There was a horrible "clunk" inside my shoulder somewhere—and I dropped.

I hit the rails, bounced outward and rolled down the bank. I was all right. Except my arm was sticking out at a funny angle. And it would not go back.

By this time, the rest of my crew had caught up to me. They wanted to carry me at first; but I persuaded them I could walk all right, if only someone would run for a doctor. There was one, gallant fellow; he, risking his own neck, came running back to us from along the disappearing observation train.

"Thank God," he panted, "you didn't get under the wheels. What's this? Oh, a dislocation—well, I'll soon put that back."

He did. Sitting on my chest he forced my arm back behind my head until I thought every tendon would crack. Then *snap*, it was in again, and I was all right, except for feeling the aftermath of pain and the embarrassing predicament of being the centre of so many staring eyes. Then Ward came along:

"Well, hell's bells!" he growled. "If you ain't the gol darnedest person I've ever seen in my life. No sooner out of bandages before you're in them again.

"Well," he finished, staring moodily at the river on which he had suffered so many triumphs and defeats, "the season's over. It's nothing to me what you do with yourselves now."

Chapter 8

MANHATTAN AFTER DARK

MY FATHER had told me so often that life was cruel that I decided to try and find out if it was. He meant business, of course. So that summer when I came down from Poughkeepsie I stayed over in New York and got a job.

I knew the New York manager of one of the big Standard Oil Company's subsidiaries, and he put me on. He gave me a roving commission to cover New York. When the other salesmen complained that I would be treading on their toes, he probably assured them that I would not sell anything anyway and could do no harm. In which respect he was not far wrong.

As far as work went, that summer did not prove anything as I knew all the time that I was going back to college in the fall. But I liked the Italians and seemed to get on so well with the big contractors that were boring and blasting their way through the rock under the river to build the syphon of the Hudson aqueduct that I was told off to cover that particular job. I never had to sell anything. The Italians' air compressors ate up oil so fast that all I had to do was sit there and take orders from them. Meanwhile I shared the chianti and cheese sandwiches of the rock workers, and occasionally drove back home with a prosperous *padrone* to share his solid luncheon of spaghetti and white wine. I liked the simplicity of their lives, and quite saw their point when they said that the trouble with Americans was they wanted to put every cent they made on their backs.

"Everything show!" said one of these rugged Italian contractors of the Bronx. "Maka little money—buy big house. Maka little more money—buy once more bigger house. Looka me. Gots lots of dough—but *I* no buy bigger house. Not your Uncle Tony."

He had a house that was not much more than a shanty among the tin cans and goats on a hillside in the Bronx. But down in his garage were two new Packard cars, with a full-blooded American attending them. A chauffeur who was always dusting

49

his natty blue suit. Tony pointed him out to me one day by jabbing downwards at him with his knife.

"He tinks I'm a bum—ha-ha!"

On the East Side of New York I saw enough misery to make me wonder why the Russian Jews and others down there did not write back to Europe to warn their people not to come to the United States. In some of those slits of fetid streets, where they hang their bed clothing over the fire escapes and empty their chamber pots out of the windows, the people made me think of maggots in a corpse. At least, they did make me think that way at first; but then I saw that their lives were rich and warm and full of colour compared to those of the clerks in the offices along Broadway. Emptier lives I had never seen than those of the young men I saw sitting in offices waiting for the clock to strike five. Their only preoccupation seemed to be the style of a new straw hat, or a pair of shoes, or a trick belt buckle they had seen in a window down below in the street. They were so vapid that if someone put a device that merely made a ticking noise against a store window, half the street would stop and look. But after I had been in New York for a week or so I couldn't blame them; for, aside from eating ice-cream sodas and going to the movies, there was precious little else to do.

At night I explored New York to the depths.

In company with a red-headed real estate agent, Bob Rainy, whose respectable family had long ago given him up as a bad egg; a charming Latin called Caesar Guillimeti, from the Italian Consulate; and a champion bulldog, called Raleigh, I was on the loose.

We had three rules. Never to eat in the same restaurant twice, never to refuse to do anything at least once, never to let anyone else go about with us—at least, no man.

Such a creed was naturally bound to have some surprising results.

One of these was a Madame who had figured rather too prominently in the murder trial of Harry K. Thaw for shooting Stanford White. She had a place on 57th Street, off Columbus Avenue.

A place of assignation, frankly a genteel brothel, whose name was calculated to make several well-known New York families turn pale. Caesar had met her in some curious way during the Thaw sensation. He had taken a fatuous fancy to her, and assured us that she was a *femme du monde*. He saw nothing out of the way in calling in there late at night to have a chat. We had an idea he picked up a lot about the inside of New York politics this way. At any rate, Bob Rainy and I and the bulldog, Raleigh, were induced to drop in there one night late after theatre time. And this became a habit with us. It was the only place in New York where we did eat twice, a host of times.

Our credit, in fact, was too good with Madame. She would never let us pay for any of the ham-and-eggs and coffee we used to have there at midnight. Bob appealed to Caesar:

"This sort of thing simply can't go on," he assured the young Italian. "We can't do it, Caesar, it simply can't be done. It isn't decent. There is only one form of payment that we can give. You must sleep with Madame."

"Oh, *non*," gasped Caesar. "*Non, non, non, NON!*"

"But you must. It's up to you to do this for us. Remember what we said—do anything at least once?"

"I will not do it!" said upright Caesar, his perfect teeth flashing in defiance. "I refuse."

"Coward."

"*Non! Non, non*—you mus' not say that. This is not fair. I simply do not have that kind of feelings towards the lady in question. Eh, *voilà*—it cannot be done."

"Traitor."

"You are a beast!" said Caesar. "Both you and your dog!"

How we loved that Italian!

Then Bob and the bulldog spoiled the show. We had been circumspect on those premises. Some subterranean vein of Puritanism probably held me back. But it was a more or less tacit understanding between us that our relations should be quite *comme il faut. Très, très, très comme il faut!* as Caesar would put it. We even took Madame and a girl friend of hers down to Coney Island, drank steins of Budweiser on the paddle-wheel boat, took them down the shoot-the-shoots and over the water jumps, and sang sentimental ditties with them all the way home on the steamer in the moonlight.

"Caesar!" laughed Madame, "you've given me the first kick I've had in years! I felt like sweet sixteen and never been kissed tonight."

The trouble was that there was a young girl of just about that description who used to flit in and out of Madame's place. She must have been a relative of some sort. She liked Caesar but made no bones about the fact that she could not stand Bob. Nor did she like his dog. The result was that Bob, in an ugly mood, asked her what the hell did *she* think she was doing in such a place. She slapped his face. The dog sprang at her. She screamed. I grabbed the dog. Bob seized me and threw me against the wall, where my head broke the glass covering an engraving of "Wedded." Then I jumped at Bob.

We had an embarrassing argument, clutching and straining at each other, supported by a wall, where I, with young American naïveté tried to deliver a sermon on the impropriety of fighting in such a place. Then Bob, with a final blast of all the invectives he could think of, seized the one thing in the world he really loved, the precious Raleigh, and left the place.

An hour later, on my way home, I stopped at Pabst's Saloon in Columbus Circle to have a beer and cool off. There was Bob, leaning against the long bar. And there was Raleigh, standing on the bar. Bob, three sheets in the wind, was pointing out the champion's points. Raleigh, be it said, was a well-known dog. I hesitated a moment, then walked over and stood next to Bob and ordered a drink. If he wanted to repair our recently broken friendship, here was his chance. But he would not look at me.

"Jes' take a looka thoshe earsh . . ." said Bob.

I went out. Bob had turned his back. But one hairy red paw was gripping Raleigh's hind leg, and Raleigh, straining to be playful, was wagging his broken tail at me. And that was the last time I saw either of them.

But that summer had taught me one thing. I was not going to work in New York. It is probably the most exhilarating city in the world in which to spend a few weeks or a month, if you have plenty of money in your pocket; but, as far as working there is concerned, Manhattan Island was meant for either Red Indians or millionaires. The Indians have gone long ago. Millionaires go to Palm Beach in the winter and take a steamer to Europe in the summer. Just plain physical comfort costs more in New York than it does on any other spot on earth.

I went back to college determined to become a civil engineer. South America was my destination.

Chapter 9

ENTER WOMEN

WAITING in the gymnasium one day for my turn on the long line of rowing machines I saw a red-headed fellow doing the double cut-off on the flying rings. When he was some forty feet above the hard floor he would throw up his legs, and as they came down on the outside of the rings he would let go and grasp the rings as they were flying away from him. He was doing it without a net. If he missed, I reflected, there would be no use in sending for a doctor, except to hold a post mortem.

This was Jo-Jo. There were only two things in the world that he cared for. A chorus girl named Toots, and an eleven-ton yawl, *Anna*. And he embroiled me with both of them.

I shall not give his name because of some of the things I have to say about ourselves. He was killed as a captain in the American army at Château-Thierry and I want to let him rest in peace. But it was not long before my soberer-minded friends in college were swearing that Jo-Jo was my bad angel. The trouble was that our tastes were too similar. After we had talked to each other for ten minutes we discovered that we had both studied civil engineering so that we should not have to work in an office. We did not care how big the position might be, not even in a president's chair; neither of us wanted to sit in some office for fifty weeks out of every year—which was what was called "making good" in the United States of our epoch. And when I saw that Jo-Jo had an eleven-ton yawl I resolved to cultivate him.

It was the ruination of both of us.

The follies of my freshman year had now to be paid for. I had been one of the two men in my class to win three numerals —in crew, track, and basketball. On the strength of this I had been given my Canteen hat and also made a member of that sinister secret society, Gargoyle (later voluntarily disbanded for the sake of the university). I was even given the coveted Gray

Hat of the Junior Society—that holy of Pennsylvania holies—all on the strength of past performance.

And I failed to deserve any of it.

One day, when I was rowing 7 in the Varsity, the stroke threw a copy of the Philadelphia *Evening Bulletin* across to me. We were in the crew trolley, going out to the river. I read:

A severe blow to the hopes of Pennsylvania oarsmen . . . announcement today that Thomas Cartier, a veteran of last year's Varsity eight, has been declared ineligible. He is behind in his law studies. . . .

My mouth became dry. I read on—

. . . Thomas Reath, who rowed at stroke last year, will not be able to row because of an intense pain in his side . . .

Then—

To cap the climax, Farson, a winning member of last year's freshman crew and regarded as a sure candidate for the Varsity eight, has been pronounced ineligible. He is behind in his studies in the college department . . .

That was the way (and I still have the clipping) I got one of the worst blows of my life. The Faculty Committee on Athletics, angered by what they considered was my indifference to my engineering course, had suddenly decided to crack down on me. Now, at the eleventh hour, I was not allowed to take an exam that I had been promised I could take. The fury of Coach Ward cut no ice whatever with the Professor of Physics. Even the intercession of Mike Murphy was in vain.

"Why the hell did you study civil engineering?" cursed Coach Ward. "Why the hell didn't you study dentistry?"

"You'll make a good engineer," said a meek under-professor of physics, in a sad effort to comfort me—"if you'll only give up athletics. You must think of your career."

What I might have been does not concern me now. At that time, in my despair, I fell between two stools. Ward, to give me the bitterest punishment he could think of, shifted me to 7 in the second Varsity, where he made me row for a week until he saw fit to move a man up from the four. Then I rolled my sweaty togs in a bundle, turned my back on the river—and did not go near it again until the next year.

I turned to Jo-Jo and the night-lights of Philadelphia.

Towards the end of that year it was definitely decided that we would head for the west coast of South America the minute we got our diplomas. Another civil engineer, quarterback on the football team, made the third member of our triumvirate. He was afterwards shot down in France as a pilot in the British Royal Flying Corps. Since I, too, was a pilot in the R.F.C. we spent his last night in London together. But these things lay ahead of us; and in those halcyon days we planned to build railroads together over the Andes.

Jo-Jo and I had frittered away many hours, when we should have been working on the drawing boards, fitting out *Anna* for the summer cruise. And as soon as our Corps had finished a mock railroad survey we had been running in the Allegheny mountains I came down to the Corinthian Yacht Club to join him.

We cast off about midnight and went down the Delaware. *Anna* was a stout little ship, and I sat there in comfortable silence on the wheel box while Jo-Jo went down in the galley to make our invariable black coffee. He was gloomy because just a few hours before I came down to join him he had had a violent quarrel with his father, who had intended to come off with us. Pederson, the Swede who rowed me out to *Anna*, told me about it.

"Mister Yo," he said, "has yust struck his fader. He hid him wid a boat-hook."

Jo-Jo's father, a retired U. S. Navy captain, had such a bad liver that his doctors had forbidden him ever to touch alcohol. Jo-Jo, rowing ashore for something, had come on the poor old captain having a whiskey and soda, and promptly knocked the glass from his hand. Then, when his father tried to come out to the boat, Jo-Jo, who adored him, said that he could not come aboard until he had promised not to drink again. Captain G. had then reverted to naval tactics and tried to board *Anna* by force.

Then Jo-Jo had rapped him on the knuckles with a boat-hook.

The result was that Jo-Jo was not at all good company that night. When he was happy he could be as gay as any Negro. When he was sad he was melancholy incarnate. I was not surprised when we locked in at Delaware City the next day and he asked me to lie in the basin for the night as he wanted to take the train back to Philadelphia.

Delaware City is a quaint town. The night Jack Johnson hammered Jim Jeffries to a pulp the white men of Delaware City threw about half of its Negro population into the river. It was their way of showing that the white man's mission of civilising the darker races had not yet been abandoned. But nothing happened during the two days I lolled around under the willows of the lock, waiting for Jo-Jo. It was only when the Ericson Line steamer locked in that I saw anything exciting—and this was Toots, coming down the gang-plank with Jo-Jo.

I could not blame him. Toots was a beauty. She was half-Jewish, with just about double the vitality of any of the girls we would ordinarily know. But what about me? I thought.

"What about your father?" I asked Jo-Jo bitingly.

Jo-Jo feigned surprise. "My father—did I say I was going back to get my father!"

"You didn't say you were going to fetch Toots either."

Jo-Jo grinned. It was impossible to resist that. He was one of those red-headed men who have white eye-brows and great white horsey teeth. "Go forward," he said, "or Toots and I will put you in irons."

Two days later we were lying above the little town of Betterton in the Chesapeake Bay. I felt about as out of things as any man could be. The geography of *Anna* was embarrassing. There were two cabins. The big main cabin was as large and comfortable as a big steamer's state-room. It had two deep bunks in it, lined with cushions of green corduroy. But the only thing that separated these bunks was the centre-board well, whose flapsides pulled up to make our main dining-table. That cabin was no good to me, now that Toots was here. Ahead of that, on the starboard side, was another smaller cabin. I don't know why, but I simply refused to take that. I think it was because it was too near Toots and Jo-Jo; too uncomfortable to lie there and listen to them.

So I decided I would sleep on deck. I did. But having superstitions about the power of the moon to draw the water out of your face, and people going crazy from sleeping in moonlight, and things like that, I slept on the foredeck with a camp-stool tilted over my face.

For the next two mornings, when I woke up—the sun cooking me—I dutifully made breakfast for Jo-Jo and his sweetheart. I put on the coffee-pot. I put nine eggs to boil in the coffee. I cut up a loaf of bread and made it all into hot buttered toast. I opened and took the seeds out of three cantaloups. Then I told Jo-Jo and Toots that breakfast was ready.

They would emerge, hungry as wolves, naked as Adam and Eve, and dive over the side for a pre-breakfast swim.

I stood this for just exactly forty-eight hours. I was, it seemed to me, either a hero or a damned fool to put up with it even that long—and then I struck.

"Look here," I said to Jo-Jo, "I don't mind your having a bit of fun. But I'll be damned if I am going to carry on playing lady's maid. You can take your choice; either Toots goes or I go."

He was upset about it.

"Oh, you *can't* do that!"

"Can't I," pointing about a mile down below us to where the town of Betterton lay. "Well, you'll be seeing me off on the up-Bay boat tonight. Better think fast."

We compromised. Toots, who was not going to have this summer (or her deeper plans) spoiled for anything, said that she had a friend in the show who was simply dying to get out of town. A friend who had a *part!* The friend came down.

She was terrible. She was what the English call "refaned." And any place where Nature had not given her all that she wanted, or too much, Violette had rearranged. She was a dreadful girl! From the instant she teetered off that Ericson liner I had but one strong feeling about her—I wanted to smack her. And, eventually, smack her I did.

To avoid too much publicity we had returned to our anchorage a mile or so above Betterton. But on this night we had decided we would go ashore. There was a dance that night on the town pier. It was to be a social affair of first magnitude, so Jo-Jo and I got into white flannels and our double-breasted blue coats. And Toots and Violette dressed up as if some butter-and-egg man was taking them out to Kugler's. Anyone who was not infuriated by Violette's doll-like pout, would unquestionably have declared she was a ravishing girl. At any rate the young bloods of Betterton all fell in a heap for her. Did I mind? No, I assured her; dance yourself to death for all I care. I hope you do.

I was shuffling about like that, hugging one of the healthy, rather nifty local beauties, when I chanced to take a look at the sky! There was a low line of white at the foot of it. And, as I looked, little whiffs of cold air shot through the dancing couples.

"Jo-Jo," I said, dancing over to him, "take a look at that sky."

He did, and then he stopped dancing. He had Toots by the hand and was dragging her along.

"Don't argue," he was saying, "when I say it's time to go it's time to go. We aren't driving around in a taxicab. We've got to get out to the *Anna* just as quick as we can."

Violette pouted and said, "Oh, whay, whay leave such a go-od time. I think this is so funny, dancing with the farmers."

"You stow that," I said, "and hop into that boat."

We had them down on the beach. And the minute we took a good look at the bay Jo-Jo began to row as if the devil were after him. If ever we had gone through a blow on the Chesapeake, we were going to go through one now. And like idiots we had anchored *Anna* right in the middle of all the shipping.

We told the girls to get down into the cabin, to close the companionway doors, and stay there. Then we kicked off our shoes and socks, threw our coats down to the girls, and began to get on sail.

We had got on jib and jigger, when the first of the squalls hit us. It came at us with a white streak of waves that it ripped up off the ruffled water. It screamed past us fast as a telegraph flicker, and was gone. . . . Then there was a rumble in the sky and the heavens lit up. In that split second we saw the *Anna* among the black masses of the shipping. And we saw all the ships swing at anchors and slew and jerk. I ran forward and snatched the cable in through the hawse-hole. I felt it coming straight up from underneath, and then I braced myself to break the anchor out. We rode on, straight over it, and I hauled it aboard; then I catted it, made it fast. I came aft, and both Jo-Jo and I gave a loud sigh of relief. At any rate, we weren't going to go ashore at Betterton, or get tangled up with that shipping, not with those two girls aboard.

Now the only thing we need do was make for open water. Get as far out as we could in the bay. And either we must ride it out, out there, or, with some luck, we might work across and reach the lee of towering Turkey Point.

We had completely forgotten the girls.

In any case, we were much too busy now to pay any attention to them. One thundering roar after another split the sky, and with each one the gale increased in size. Each blinding flash of lightning showed heavier seas ahead. We tried to turn and run for Turkey Point. It was hopeless. The instant we did that the *Anna* lay flat on her side and each succeeding wave threatened to roll over us. There was nothing for it but to try and ride it out at anchor where we were.

I groped my way forwards and began to unlash the big right bower that we had never used. It weighed 250 lbs. The lightning helped me, although it terrified me at the same time, for it seemed to be tingling in the chains, and the tip of the mainmast was sparkling with Jacob's Fire. I yelled back for Jo-Jo to throw her up into the wind, staggered to the rail and dropped the right bower in the sea.

It fell with a splash. Then I saw that the chain was jammed in the pipe leading from the chain locker. The big anchor was dangling only some twenty feet underneath. The only thing to do then was to try and joggle the chain tangle out as the *Anna's* bows dropped into each succeeding sea and temporarily eased the strain on it.

I was doing this when the tangle came out with a jerk, the

chain caught my hand, snatched my arm into the hawse-hole, and some forty or fifty fathoms of chain raced over my hand.

When it brought up with a jerk and I retrieved my hand, I found I had two broken fingers.

But we were safely at anchor. A hurricane itself could not have broken that right bower out or made her drag. We got in sail, took a last look around, and went below.

Here was a sight. The terrified girls had lighted every lamp and lantern in the boat. Jo-Jo seized one from them to put up as our riding light. Then he turned his attention to me, gave me a white-toothed grin, and bandaged my two broken fingers together with tar-tape.

"That ought to hold you," he said.

Toots had already recovered her composure. But Violette was being seasick all over the cabin floor. Jo-Jo and I cleaned things up as best we could, then he tried to make some hot coffee in the bouncing galley.

The *Anna*, like a balky horse, would snap viciously against her anchor on the sharp up-waves, hang there, then drop with a sickening squash to meet the next wall of water. Sometimes she would swing, and come up with an alarming jerk. Then Jo-Jo and I would look at each other, waiting for that aimless topsy-turvydom that would let us know that our chain had parted.

I endured Violette for the rest of that night. I stood her, when we were still forced to lie at anchor, throughout all that bucking next morning. But when the sea calmed down and she got her nerve back and began to upbraid all of us, I slapped her face.

But as I slapped her with my broken fingers—which were like cucumbers by that time—it hurt me more than it did her. Toots, feeling that perhaps Jo-Jo and I would be happier by ourselves, also went off with Violette on that evening's up-Bay boat. What an outing it must have been for them!

Chapter 10

END OF TRIUMVIRATE

ONE NIGHT the telephone bell rang in my fraternity house and one of the Negro butlers answered it.

It was Jo-Jo's father.

"Negley," he rasped. "Why didn't you tell me that my son was going to marry a whore?"

"Good God, Captain G.—what on earth are you talking about!"

"You know. That Toots."

"Married?"

"Yes—yesterday."

That summer after we had rid ourselves of Toots and Violette, Jo-Jo and I had gone on down the Bay. After that sordid week at Betterton we had felt ourselves re-born. It was a renaissance quite untroubled by wine, women or song. We had spent most of our time cruising along the sweet shores of tide-water Virginia.

"Gennelmen," asked an old Negro in the moonlight, "does you-all mind if Ah comes and sits near you?" He had been attracted by Jo's guitar. He sat there, as if on probation, a ragged figure above us on the wharf. Then he craned his neck and read the gold letters under our tuck—"ANNA—PHILADELPHIA."

"You-all comes from Philadelphia?"

We told him, yes.

"Dat's funny. Ah used to know a man from up dat way—Philadelphia or Connecticut—up that way."

And, although we were three days late in getting back to college, we had promised each other that from then on we would let nothing stand in the way of our South American project. And now Jo-Jo had gone and got himself married!

"I don't believe it!" I said.

"Don't you!"—even over the telephone I could tell that old Captain G. was weeping—"Well, I'll tell you where they are right now. You just go to—" He gave me an address.

"All right," I answered, furious—"I'll go there. And don't you worry, Captain G.—I'll break this damned thing up."

And that I was determined to do.

After dinner I went into Philadelphia and up to that apartment. There they were. Toots sprawled out at full length on a couch. Jo-Jo, sitting on the floor, his red head against Toot's flanks, playing his guitar:

> *"When I was over in Turkey . . .*
> *I never did a damn bit of worky*
> *I met the Sultan's daughter . . .*
> *I knowed I hadn't oughter . . .*

"Sit down," said Jo-Jo, interrupting his ballad long enough to kick forward a chair. "How's the 'Big Swede'?" (Always my nickname in college.)

"Are you married?" I asked.

"Yep."

"You damned fool!"

"Here!" yelped Toots. "Say you, Negley Farson, you let up on this. Why the hell shouldn't Jo-Jo marry me?"

"You shut up," I said. "I'm talking to Jo."

"No, you're not—you're talking to me—see? You're so narrow-minded your ears meet. And if you come around here trying to make any more trouble I'm going to tell Jo-Jo to kick you out—see?"

"You are, are you!"

"Listen," said Jo-Jo, with the most beguiling of grins. "We're married. Nothing you can say can stop that. It's done. Now listen to me:

> *"I met the Sultan's daughter*
> *I knowed I hadn't oughter . . .*

"Anyway," he said, putting away his guitar. "Give me a cigarette; Toots and I have been too lazy all day to go out and get one."

That almost finished me. I had never felt so jealous of anyone in all my life. Jo-Jo looked so happy there.

I spent the night with them, or most of it. We went out and had a late supper at a cabaret. Toots kissed me good-night, and called me Uncle Negley. I shook Jo-Jo's hand.

But that, in a way, cleared the air for me. I saw very, very little of Jo-Jo now. In fact I only saw him twice again before he died. I was in strict training for various forms of athletics. My fraternity brothers began to comment upon my studious turn of mind. My only diversion was the 2nd Regiment, in which I had been made a 2nd Lieutenant in H Company. I was drilling my company of rough-necks one night when I saw Jo-Jo's red head coming across the Armoury floor. His eyes were also red. Jo-Jo had been weeping!

"Got a couple of minutes to spare?" he asked humbly.

I told the top sergeant, an old Spanish War veteran, to take over and walked Jo-Jo up to our Company rooms. There he broke down.

"It's Toots," he said.

"Of course. Go on."

"Well, Toots's just won a beauty prize."

"Well?"

"She won it standing naked on a banquet table."

"Phew!"

"Yes, and—"

It hurt to have to listen to him. There was no question about the fact that he was hotly in love with her. And I wondered whether she knew it or not! The picture of Toots standing like that on the dinner table made me feel sick.

"I'm off," announced Jo-Jo.

"To South America?"

"Yes—I guess that'll do."

Two weeks later I went over to New York with his mother, and saw Jo-Jo off on the *Panamian* for the Canal Zone.

"Let him get it out of his system," I said to her frightened eyes. Then, with great profundity, "Jo-Jo will soon get enough of this soldier of fortune stuff."

But he didn't; he carried on that way. He was the kind of

person who did do such things, and not merely talk about doing them.

With him to South America, and I suppose lying with some bit of him on the field of Château-Thierry now, went my most prized rowing medal.

Chapter 11

THE LAST GAMBLE

THE SAME lightning was beginning to play about my own head. At a Christmas house party up at my guardian's place I saw a chestnut-haired girl with one blue and one grey eye, and I fell in love with her at once. That was at dinner.

I had seen her skating that afternoon, going off with my guardian's son across the lake. I had noticed that she was wearing straight-bladed hockey skates, and not the rocker affairs that are usually worn by girls. I was surprised therefore when she told me she was an actress.

"At least," she said, "I am on the stage."

The instant my family found out how I felt about her, they were rude to her at once. If anything was needed to make me determined to marry her, that was it. When she went down to New York, I made an excuse and went down with her, followed by the scowls of my guardian's son, who fancied his own chances there. It was he who had brought her up to the lake.

From then on my family did the work for us. They were rude to Ann whenever they chanced to meet her in the street, they wrote long, tiresome letters about her to me. They were so furious with her that they even went to see her next show, although how they found out which it was was a puzzle to me, because Ann never played a lead.

Ann's family was equally helpful. I don't know who her father was—I don't think that she did either—but her mother was very much on the scene. Ann, she was determined, was not going to throw herself away on any young man who was just about to set out to make his way. Ann was pretty enough to marry anybody, if she would only use her head.

What with one thing and another, Ann and I did not get much peace. The only peace we did have was when we could get off alone. I would wait for her after the theatre when I had money enough to get over to New York, and for about forty-eight hours we could let down our nerves.

"But don't you think," said Ann, as I ate my usual after theatre supper, "that Bar-le-Duc jelly, Roquefort cheese and hot chocolate will ruin your stomach?"

I did not drink in those days.

I brought her down to the university for the junior prom. It caused a sensation when it was learned that I had brought an *actress* to that sacred hop. Ethel Barrymore, apparently, was the only woman on the stage with whom one could afford to associate in those days without losing caste. But I did not care; the world of Philadelphia was not mine, and I had a strong hunch that something was going to happen to me and my college career.

I had been getting letters from the lake.

My guardian was again in the whirlpools of his risky railroad deals. These breath-taking mergers were getting a little out of date by then, but my guardian was having a last play at the game. During the last three years he had quietly been gathering options on trans-continental "rights of way," which, when the last link was completed, would give him a railroad paralleling the Harriman lines from the Atlantic to the Pacific coasts.

All that was needed to complete this "big play" was to buy one small railway line near the Pacific. To get this far, my guardian had put himself in pawn. Everything he had in the world, and more too, was at stake in this deal. If he did not find some big backer to buy that last stretch of railroad for him, he was sunk.

I got this put to me bluntly, because the letters explaining his schemes at that moment were also written to explain why my allowance had been so abruptly cut off.

It was an ugly predicament.

"I have the man," smiled my guardian at dinner one night. "He has more money than he knows what to do with. But he's not made a name. He is a king out in Montana. But he feels that he is a mere nobody here in New York. I went out to Montana, and I said to him:

" 'Here it is. Here is the biggest chance of your life. Here is a railway line from coast to coast. I have rights of way; I have complete control of some lines; I have a port on the Pacific. Just buy this little section in here—and you will become the most talked about man in the United States. You will have an international reputation. You will be known wherever you go in the world. You will be bigger than Harriman—because you will have beaten Harriman.' "

It was, my guardian knew, his last bid for glory. He was willing, in his parlous circumstances, to take the cash and let the credit go. He would remain the man behind the door. But what a glory it held out to the other man—in the America of that epoch!

No one in the dining-room of the Waldorf-Astoria that night could have suspected the tenseness at our table. The great man had accepted. He was coming East on his way to Europe. For days now my guardian had been expecting the telegram or telephone call to have his lawyers assemble. And days counted, for some of his options were due to expire. And, of course, the essential strategy of the whole affair had been its secrecy.

Financiers knew, of course, that Dewitt Smith had certain options. But no one in the least suspected what he really intended to do with them. Buck the Harrimans? Why, the very idea of it was unthinkable. No one knew of my guardian's secret trip to the colossus of Montana.

"He is as vain as a peacock," said my guardian hopefully.

I had, with what little cash I had left, made a week-end trip to New York to see Ann. She was in a show then, and I was to pick her up at the theatre. After that we would not be separated until I took the eight o'clock train on Monday morning for Philadelphia.

"I don't like the old Senator So-and-So," she said the next morning at breakfast. She had mentioned the colossus of Montana.

"Why, what on earth do you mean?"

"He's a nasty old man."

I laughed. "They all are—look at So-and-So!" I mentioned America's biggest banker.

She shook her head.

"No," she said. "This one's yellow."

I had, of course, told her everything. And in that peculiar world that has its focus around 42nd Street and Broadway, a side of a man's character is exhibited that he would not be at all anxious for his family or business associates to become acquainted with. It was an ostrich-like egotism which provided a gold mine for the American scandal-sheet of that time, *Town Topics*. And Ann at times used to shock me with some of the casual remarks she made about the heroes of our age, the great business barons.

She was all too right in this case. With my guardian sitting there, waiting for him, desperately trying to postpone his options and weighed down with the strain of feeling a great trans-continental railway almost within his grasp, the great Senator sneaked through New York and sailed incognito for Europe with his lady-friend. He was, my guardian afterwards discovered, upstairs in a suite of rooms in the Waldorf on the very night when we were sitting below in the restaurant talking about him. He sailed the next morning.

Senator So-and-So had lost his nerve. He had been afraid to fight Harriman. Before he sailed for Europe he gave the big railroad king my guardian's scheme. Harriman hastily bought up the section that might have made a competing line. The storm broke. Thunder crashed around my guardian's head. The house at the lake, the horses, the sailboat, the sunny paddock and lake shore were no longer his.

Ann and I got through that winter more or less on our own emotions. My fraternity brothers, without making any talk about it, immediately made me "Secretary," which hastily-invented office gave me a professional status justifying my living at their expense in the fraternity house. About the only allusion they ever made to it was to tell me that I *was* secretary. And, as I could no longer afford week-ends over to New York, Ann frequently took the Saturday night midnight train for Philadelphia.

Then, after the Easter "rowing vacation," when I was stroking the 4 out on the Schuylkill, I got a letter from Ann telling me how my family had all cut her dead in the street.

"*I don't mind for myself so much,*" she wrote, but, it seemed, they had done it before a very important producer, of whom she had high hopes.

I left college that night and I never went back.

In New York, the subsidiary of the Standard Oil Co. gave me a job again. I had a good reputation with them, but it was inevitable that after a month with them I should once more be bored to a point of nearly going out of my mind.

I did not like this kind of life. That was all there was to it— I just didn't like it. It didn't make any difference whether it was wrong or right for me not to like it. I could not stand it. And that was that. On the other hand I could see no alternative to it —not with Ann.

We talked it over. Day after day, night after night; sitting on benches on Riverside Drive, sitting on benches in Central Park; lying on the sands when we had taken an occasional jaunt down to the seashore for a swim; eating Roquefort cheese, Bar-le-Duc jelly and hot chocolate in the same cabaret where I took her that very first night in New York, the night I suddenly realised how adorable I thought it was for a girl to have one blue and one grey eye.

"I have to make a break," I told her. "I don't know what it is yet. But something must be done. We just can't go on this way; it's too slow. Either I make a pile or I don't. If I don't—well, we can always count on this. But I must have that one chance first."

But we could never think what that one chance would be. I had all sorts of wild, unconstructive ideas. When it did come, it came in an envelope bearing a Canal Zone stamp.

"*It's all settled,*" wrote Jo-Jo. "*An ex-Petty Officer of the Zone Police and I have got it all worked out. He's been there, and this is no wild-goose chase. You get down here just as fast as you can and we'll go off to British Guiana on the next boat. . . .*"

I got that in the New York Athletic Club on a day when we were entertaining the visiting British relay team at a luncheon. I never heard a word of the brief speeches that were made. I was seeing myself in a dug-out up some tropic stream. . . . Without leaving the club, I wrote a long letter to Jo-Jo, saying that I would sail for Colon around the last of September.

Then I got hold of Ann.

Ann baulked at the idea of prospecting for gold in British Guiana.

"It's crazy!" she said.

"No more crazy than dying of dry rot here."

I talked her into it. Then she began to get some of the tang of it. And, somewhat miserably, I realised that part of her excitement was that she too saw a chance of relief from our usual daily strain. Neither of our families was making things easy for us. Both were fighting against our marriage, just as bitterly as they could. That was now beginning to make us fretful with each other. And Ann did not have even the safety valve I had of dissipating my boredom by sheer physical fatigue at the New York Athletic Club.

Ann, nevertheless, was the only girl I ever took to an athletic meet, where I was to perform. This was at Travers Island, summer home of the New York Athletic Club, where the big New York Fall Games were being held. It was a sorry day for both of us. For though I won my event, the javelin throw, I lost my chance with Jo-Jo, and it was the last.

They gave me three extra throws to try and break the American record. But the minute I finished the first of these, I knew that something had gone wrong. The next two throws were a good twenty feet short of what I had been doing. I felt suddenly as if all the power had somehow leaked out of me. It was the last time I ever threw a javelin.

I did not realise it that day. I was too happy to bother about analysing that peculiar feeling in my side. I had beaten the American javelin champion on that day. I had the gold medal. There it lay in Ann's bag, lying on the table as we ate our lobster salad on the verandah of the Athletic Club. Life, as far as that day was concerned, could give me nothing more.

A week later a pain hit me as quick as you could slap a wall, and I crumpled up on my way up town from business. A doctor

I knew, also a member of the New York Athletic Club and also a shot-putter, lived near by.

"Go out," he said after examining me, "and make your peace with God. You have a ruptured appendix. I will cut you up to-morrow morning."

He was a paleolithic beast of a man, quite insensible to pain, his own or anyone else's. I once saw him operate on himself. But his brusque brutality was more *gemütlich* to me than the usual undertone of terror in the average surgeon's reception-room. My family did not think so, however; when, instead of making my peace with God, I merely telephoned them my predicament and then went up to have an orgy of sympathy from Ann, they called up a big specialist.

"You're to go down and see him right now," they telephoned me at Ann's. "And none of this nonsense. Thank God, you even told us about it at all."

The specialist asked me several questions, none of which seemed to have anything to do with an appendix. He finally unearthed the story of the javelin throw—how I felt that quick rip in my side, as if something had come loose.

"I will telephone Dr. X," he said, "I do not think he will operate tomorrow. The next day probably, when you have been well prepared." It turned out it was not an appendix. I had torn the main tendon off my thigh bone and a deep-seated infection had started.

Dr. X seemed to take it as a personal grudge that I had dared to see another surgeon. The only thing that saved me was that the other one was so big. Yet I think Dr. X purposely made my operation as Grand Guignol as possible. He tried the new local anaesthetic.

"Now you look out of the window," he said, leaning over me, scalpel in hand. "Did that hurt?"

"Y-yes," I said hesitantly. "I felt a lot of pressure."

"Hah!" he jeered—"I haven't touched you."

"Well," I murmured, still staring at that whitewashed window, "I'm sure I felt pain."

"Well, you just take a look," he said.

I did. And there in my side was a gaping hole over five inches long, as wide open as a mouth, with the blood streaming out.

"That all goes to show you," he went on, clipping away with scissors, "how one's Goddamned imagination plays tricks. Now" —clip, clip, clip—"if I hadn't told you to look . . . er . . . yes, here we are . . . nurse, give me those swabs . . . now, if I hadn't told you to look, you'd never have known that I'd touched you, would you?"

Etc., etc.

I caught my breath. "You—you're getting out of bounds now," I tried to joke, biting the pillow to stop from yelling out loud.

"Ought to be," he announced complacently. "You've got a hole right through you now. This'll drain you all right. Nurse, light a cigarette for me. Give him one, too. Want a highball?"

It was his way. He had me up and walking about in a few days. But it got steadily worse. And, after a few weeks, he had another try.

"Must be pocketing," he explained.

He prowled about in my insides like a terrier nosing for rats. In the meantime the end of September was upon us.

"British Guiana!" Dr. X gave a loud guffaw. "Not a chance. With a hole in you like that! No, my boy, you are going to stay right where you are."

I wrote Jo-Jo a letter. I never got his answer until years after he was dead. It read, one part of it—

Here I've been, shooting off your praises all over the Canal Zone. And there we were (the ex-Petty Officer of the Zone police), sitting on the dock at Colon, hardly able to wait for the sight of your ugly mug—and we get a letter instead. . . .

He had, he declared petulantly in that letter, already thrown up his job; without me he would not go to British Guiana; he was off for the west coast of South America—the one spot where he and I had always intended to go.

A few months later he was serving with the French Ambulance Corps at the Front in France, where he was given the Croix de Guerre at Bar-le-Duc.

Chapter 12

OIL ON TROUBLED WATERS

IT WAS a summer's day. The kind of day that New Yorkers never will admit to strangers exists. Nevertheless, the city was suffocating, old people were dying from heat and lack of air, and young people were desperate—especially this one.

I had had my usual morning battle in the subway to get down to work. And all day long I had been trying to sell people oil. Not merely oil, but my oil; my oil was much better, and I tried to tell them why. Up one stifling street and down another; upstairs and downstairs; into offices, lofts and basements, I pushed my way. I had no interest in my job, because I did not believe half the things I was saying. I had learned them, parrot-fashion, in the sales school of the great XYO Oil Company. Viscosity, flash-point, film-skin, vegetable oils *vs.* mineral oil; I rattled them off like a human gramophone. The people I was talking to didn't know any more about these things than I did. Most of them took what I was saying as a personal affront. I had to be polite to people I would much rather have hit.

There had been one bright spot. Over on the upper East Side I had gone into an ironworks. I found its red-headed Irish proprietor sitting with his feet up on the desk in the exclusive draught of the only electric fan. I started to talk oil to him. He did not answer—not at first. He sat still as a stone, his eyes fixed on his sporting page. His little Jewish typist gave me an imploring look. She was signalling to me plain as words that it would be much better for me if I shut up and got out. I was just about to do this when the great man came to life. He hoisted himself out of his swivel chair.

"Say!" he said, walking up to me dangerously. "Do you want a kick in the pants?"

I told him I did not. And, what was more, he could not give it to me.

"No!"

He swayed from sheer surprise.

"No," I told him, pointing to the sign on his window—O'DOOLEY IRON WORKS. "That," I said, "is an open invitation for me to come in here and talk business, for anyone to talk business. I'm talking business; the XYO OIL Co. makes the—"

"*Yeah!*" He had got his breath by now. "Well, you listen to me, young feller. I know whatcher trying to do—yez trying to get me upset! Then yer gonna yell for a cop! Well, I'm not such a damn fool. Hey—Jake!" He turned and bellowed through an open window into the flaming shop: "Hey, Jake—one of youse guys tell Jake to come in here!"

"See this guy?" he said when a greasy works foreman came in. "He works for the XYO OIL Co.!"

"Sure, I know—we use their stuff."

"Well, we don't no more!—get me? Never no more—not a Goddam drop!"

"Okay, Chief."

"Now take a good look at this guy."

"Okay, Chief."

"If he ever sticks his nose in here again, you sling him out on his . . . ear!—get me?"

"Okay, Chief."

I lingered long enough for honour to be satisfied, then I wished him good day. I would have to turn that call in as "Unsatisfactory." But if ever a sympathetic little Jewish behind could wag a farewell salute that typist's did.

But that had been the one bright spot in the day. The rest had been just the usual humiliating and meaningless round of the salesman's routine. A monotonous performance, based upon professional ingratiation, obsequiousness, and a hide like a crocodile. Nothing but an American fatalism induced people to listen to me. When a sale was made it was more often than not from sheer weariness on the customer's part. One thing it distinctly did not have to do with—and that was anything about oil.

"That God-awful Spratt is right!" sobbed another young

engineer who had been put on with me. "It's the tail-kissing that does it."

"Look at me!" Henry T. Spratt used to say, telling us, not altogether for the first time, the secrets of his amazing success in the XYO Oil Co. "*I* don't try to talk oil to them. What I do, I sell 'em myself—see? That's what you got to do—establish confidence. I don't want to know anything about oil. If you start talking oil to 'em you only start them to arguing about it. They want to show off they know just as much about oil as we do. And believe me, gentlemen—arguments never sold anything! You can't catch flies with vinegar. No, siree! What you got to do, boys—always remember—*is sell 'em yourself!*"

Bartlett's lament was that the people we had to do business with were not real Americans at all. New York, he insisted, was one-third foreign born, a third Jew, and a third Negro. Of these the first were the worst. The immigrants had come to the United States to make money, and they were willing to put up with anything and everything to get on. Well, New York served them right. Nothing, insisted Bartlett, could be more unbearably offensive than the suddenly-successful immigrant in the United States. He had had a bad time in the Old World and he was getting his own back as soon as he got his head above water over here. No human being could be so detestable—unless it were that immigrant's son. He had none of the simplicity of the old man, inherited from Old World conditions; he was just a raw, conceited, arrogant oaf—whose swinishness increased in proportion to the money he made.

"I'm going to do something drastic," sobbed Bartlett. "I'm going to get my old man to buy me a seat on the Stock Exchange."

These immigrants, I pointed out, added spice to our dull lives. They were the "colonies." The Germans, for instance, who lived along Columbus and Amsterdam avenues, and seemed to run all our breweries and delicatessen shops. A solid, warm life there, with bowling alleys and Turnvereins and sauerkraut. The French, who ran the cheap but good little restaurants, where one could be sure of a good dinner and a bottle of *vin ordinaire* for 50 cents, across town along 57th Street. The Italians, on the upper

East Side, the most politically-minded section of which had gained the name "Murder Row"; they were our stone-masons, built the subways, dug the foundations of every skyscraper in New York, polished its shoes, ran nearly every one of its fruit stands—and made its best bombs. The Greeks ran its candy shops and cheap soda fountains. The Polacks and Bohunks from Central Europe shovelled the snow off its streets and followed around after its horses with a dustpan and broom. The little Jews were its haberdashers and ran the cloak and suit business. The big Jews ran its banks and big department stores. The smart progeny of Russian Jews, via Columbia University, ran its theatres, wrote its best book reviews, dramatic and musical criticism, and supplied nearly all of its new authors who had anything new to say. And their daughters were the best typists, secretaries, saleswomen and niftiest chorus girls in the city. The Polish girls made the best prostitutes, because they were prettier and lasted longer. And the Irish manned its trolleys, its elevators, its subways, ran its law courts, its politics, its police—and picked the City's pocket.

It was in fact rather a difficult spot for an "American" to fit in. He found himself more of a foreigner than anyone else.

I had run through a cross-section of nearly all of this Melting Pot on this stifling day.

Up in the Negro district of San Juan Hill I had been approached by a handsome mulatto wench:

"Mister—does you all want to have a good time?"

"I sure do, sister—but not what you mean. I want some air!" I said.

"So does I!" she whined.

And then I stood in Canal Street, the great machinery mart. The traffic rattled past me like a clanking chain. Up on 5th Avenue the buses had been sticking to the asphalt, it was so hot. But down here it was just cobbles and clattering drays. Down here the proprieties did not have to be strictly observed. Some brave fireman had taken the law into his own hands, and had opened the hose hydrants so that the children could bathe. I watched them with envy in my soul. For half a dare I'd strip off my shirt and get in with them. My collar had long since become a rag, my body was soaking, my clothes were sticking to me as if I had already fallen in. I did not have any place I could go for a swim. I was broke. I did not have enough money to get down to the seashore where I could lie on the beach and merely look at the sea. I did not even have enough money to get out into the country and lie under a real tree. And this was Saturday noon!

"Dar she blows! Dar she blows!" said the Negro sitting outside the factory when he heard the 12 o'clock whistle blow. "Dinner time for some folks—but it's just 12 o'clock for me!"

I stood there thinking of this sad joke when my eye fell on a sign across the street. It was the name of one of the biggest steel and pipe companies in America. But it was much more than that to me—the son of the president of that firm had stroked the crew I rowed in at Poughkeepsie. I would, I thought, go in and see him. I might even sell him some oil?

"Well, for heaven's sake! Of all the wild coincidences!" Lester had come out to me himself as soon as I sent in my card. "I was talking about you to my father not ten minutes ago!"

"What about?"

"Well, we have just received a cable from our English connection, asking if we wouldn't select someone to be trained over there. Someone who is both a business man and an engineer."

We both laughed.

"But honest," said Lester, "I thought of you the minute I heard of the job."

"All right, I'll take it," I said.

It was not, said Lester, quite so simple as that.

"Let's go in now and tackle the Old Man. He'll do anything I tell him, as long as we handle him right."

He took me in to a keen, grey-haired old gentleman, sitting behind an enormous glass-topped table. He dismissed his secretary when Lester introduced me.

"So," he said, "you are Negley Farson. And you rowed in the same boat with Lester? Well, all I can tell you about rowing is this: it has ruined Lester's health!"

I told him what Coach Ward had said; that rowing would either take five years off or put five years on a man's life.

"So . . . ?" He smiled. He was a kindly old German, of the stock that gave us Karl Schurz. But something in his manner told me that it wouldn't do to get too friendly with him, or to dwell too long on the subject of athletics.

"Well," he said. "What can I do for you?"

Lester jumped in to explain things and made several outrageous statements about me that I would not have dared make myself. Nevertheless, I was grateful; for the old man then said:

"In England you will learn something. You will see what honesty in manufacturing really can be. And you will see engineers, real engineers, getting much less than yourself. But don't forget the honesty part of it. The word 'British' is like sterling on silver in the engineering world. And this company you are going to is one of the finest in England."

I held my breath through all this.

"There is just one little thing," said that marvellous old gentleman, "that you haven't asked me about."

Good Lord, I thought; what could that be? What blunder had I made? What appropriate question had I failed to ask?

"You haven't yet asked me," he said, "what your salary will be."

"It doesn't matter," I said. Then, seeing the suicidal impetuousness of such a thing. "What I mean is, I'm sure you will take care of that end of it for me."

"Well," he said. "You have not got the position yet. The Manchester company is the one to decide."

Outside in his office Lester and I did a small dance.

"The English are queer," he said; "they think that all an American can do is brag. They're the most complacent, self-satisfied people on the face of this earth. But you'll have a marvellous time over there. They wouldn't believe it when I told them a Harvard second Eight had beat their own pet Leander at Henley. I won fifty dollars off an Englishman for doubting that. I don't think he would have believed it if he had seen it. But there is one fellow I want to warn you about. He's a fellow named Brothers. He looks like a sheep—but so did Disraeli. Brothers has forgotten more about engineering than you and I will ever know!"

The first thing I had to do, said Lester, was go somewhere and write my dossier, and send it to him—with my photograph.

"It's an old-fashioned firm; getting into it is like joining a club," said Lester. "They've left it to us; but they want to know all about you, all the way back to Adam, what you look like and everything you've done. Pile it on about the athletics. That helps you a lot over there. It's not like over here where the ex-college athlete usually turns out to be a bum!"

So, with such thoughts in mind, I went down to the office of the great XYO Oil Co. Saturday afternoon was simple now. I would turn in my reports to the manager and then I would tell him that I was going to resign. Then I would telegraph my brother to have *Seabird* ready, and we would take one last cruise before I left the United States.

"Why, what do you intend to do?" asked Mr. Collard.

"I'm going to England," I said.

"England!—why, I'm an Englishman!"

"I know it," I said, and then I told him what I was going to do.

"Well, I think you're mad! You're reversing the process. Do you know why I left England?"

With great patience he then explained to me why he had come to the United States. England was too crowded, he said. There were too many first-class brains and too few even second-class jobs. That was the chief reason why the Englishman had colonised the world. And now I was going to reverse the process. Deliberately! I would learn the folly of this to my cost. Then, seeing that I was beyond the reach of reason on this point, he suddenly asked me why I did not like my present job.

It was one of the most difficult and awkward questions I have ever had put to me. I could not tell him that I thought the life of a salesman was one of the most meaningless existences on the face of the earth. That there was nothing accumulative about it, nothing that you could get your teeth into, nothing about it that gave you any sense of self-respect. I could not tell him that I would not knuckle down to such an empty life. But the one man who epitomised all this horror was sitting in the outside office at that moment.

"I don't want to be like Spratt," I said. "Hitting the pavements when I'm fifty."

Mr. Collard laughed. "Spratt doesn't hit the pavements," he told me with a sudden frankness that let me know my resignation had already been accepted. "I know what Spratt does, just as well as you do. He hardly moves. When Spratt leaves this office in the mornings he goes to the nearest saloon and picks up the telephone book. Then he calls up all his old customers. He's been giving them cigars and theatre tickets for years, to keep them sweet. And they put him on to other customers. Spratt's a 'good fellow,' he is. But what's the matter with that? That's nothing against him! Spratt sells more oil than any two men in this office put together. So what's the matter with Spratt's life?"

"Sell 'em yourself, boy—sell 'em yourself!"

I could not argue about that.

"Anyway," I said, "I'm off."

I felt sorry I spoke that way about Spratt. He was really a kindly man. All I knew about him was that he lived by himself in a little up-town hotel and he was an insatiable "joiner." He belonged to every lodge or brotherhood or fraternal order that he could discover that did not conflict with the other ones. His huge body was hung with elks' teeth, golden crescents, clasped hands and other glittering insignia. Apparently he always bought the most expensive kind. The ones with diamonds in them. And once a year, I knew, he paraded the Boardwalk at Atlantic City, dressed up like a Turk in bloomers and fez and carrying a wooden scimitar.

He gave me a cigar when I left the United States.

Chapter 13

REACHING ENGLAND

THE *St. Paul* sailed for England that year with a strange passenger list. Austria had just delivered her ultimatum to Serbia, and, fearing war, most of the tourists had cancelled their reservations. Fearing that there would not be a war, or that if they did not hurry home they would not be back in time to get into it, a half-dozen sporting young Englishmen were rushing back to join up. For the rest, there were one or two business men, a professional Southern girl of the type Ruth Draper takes off so well, and her even more Southern mother.

Ann and I had parted a few blocks from the steamer's dock, and we both knew it was for good. She had driven down with me in order that we might have these last moments. We kept up the pretence of talking about writing to each other, and when she would come over to join me; but we both knew that our little affair had run its course. I felt a bit shocked when I got out of the taxi and saw her drive off without looking back, but then I hailed another cab and was soon buried under my family's farewells and warnings at the dock. Then the steamer slowly backed out into the stream and for the first time I experienced that luxury of knowing that for the next ten days I would not have one responsibility in the wide world.

For me that trip will always be memorable for two things. One was my first sight of the Gulf Stream, when I woke up one morning to see those unbelievable blue slopes rising up and down past my porthole (for I was in a very cheap cabin, low down near the water), and, looking out, I saw a little silver nautilus sail down a wave. The other was the scene in the smoking-room the night England declared war on Germany.

We all sang "Rule, Britannia" that night, and when the English in return wanted to sing the "Star Spangled Banner," I discovered to my horror that I did not know the words.

There was an Englishman on board who won most of my

82

money at poker, and gave me my first lesson in British *sang-froid*. He was one of the first men I ever saw reading a book in broad daylight, except on Sundays. He sprawled about with a novel all day, in white flannels, using his old school tie as a belt. He had great success with the Southern girl, and I think she was sorry that she had found him so fascinating before we were half-way across. And he spoke, with a little air of apology for speaking of them so familiarly, of nearly every prominent family in the New York Social Register, always alluding to them by their first names. He seemed to know everybody. And no wonder, for he was one of the handsomest men I had ever seen. He had a head like Hermes.

His father, it seemed, was a retired Indian army colonel: "D.S.O., you know, and all that." His father, it seemed, had been a very stout fellow indeed; and, having been brought up on Kipling, I was delighted when Howard invited me to come down to the seaside resort where his father was living and meet the old chap. "Anybody will tell you where it is," said Howard. "We've got a place called 'Armagh.'"

I liked Howard; he filled the picture of what I thought a typical English "younger son" should be. He was, no doubt, what was called a "remittance man"; but, nevertheless, I thought he was a wonderful fellow.

Well, he was.

A couple of months after I had been in Manchester's choking fogs I felt a yearning for some salty air. I decided I would take up Howard's invitation. I didn't write or wire him, as I wanted most of the week-end to myself. I thought I would just drop in on them on Sunday—about dinner-time.

"No," said the woman who ran the hotel in that neighbourhood. "We don't know of any Colonel Howard who lives around here—do we, Alfred?"

The clerk had been perusing the telephone-book.

"There's no such name here," he said, with an ill-concealed note of triumph in his meek voice. He, obviously, did not like Americans; and even then that type of genteel Englishman (remaining at home himself) was asking us why we didn't get into the war. "Sure you have the right name?"

"Yes," I said, "I'm sure of it—Colonel Rodney Howard, D.S.O., late Skinner's Horse. He must be here—got a place called 'Armagh.' "

Finally they put me on the telephone to the proprietor of a livery stable. He had lived in that one spot for forty years. He would know, if anyone does, said the hotel manageress.

"Howard?" came the rough voice. "Did ye say *Colonel* Howard? No, sir, ain't no one of that name around here. . . . Are you there, sir?—there's a *Drill Sergeant* Howard—but that couldn't be the gentleman you're looking for?"

"No, indeed," I said, "this one's a Colonel. I know he's here, because I came over on the boat with his son."

"Eh!—hold up a minute—'is son's name wasn't Willie, was it— Mister William Howard?"

"It sure was!"

"Well, that's him, that's him—fine upstanding lad—used to be an actor in America."

"Well," I said, "where is he now? I want to see him."

"You can't do that, sir—you can't do that. Willie Howard's off fighting for his King and Country. An officer in the 1st Essex, he is! The old drill sergeant's off at a training camp, 'e is, too!"

The next month, when I was in London, on my way to Russia, I ran into a mutual boat-friend in the Savoy grill.

" 'Member Howard?" he asked. "That English Colonel's son? Yep? Killed last week in France."

"Did you know," I said, "that he had been an actor in America? I bet he was a damned good one!"

But that was all I said about my trip to the seaside in search of the country seat called "Armagh."

But these surprises lay ahead of us.

We woke up one morning in the Mersey. Liverpool was just a mass of blur in a pea-soup fog.

"H'Inglish weather," mocked the ship's doctor. "Well, good luck, you chaps."

Howard, the "cute" Southern girl in tow, was already dancing down the gangway. "Hello, there!" he called to me. "Come and have a spot with us."

We had a good-bye drink in the Railway Hotel, where everything was strange, and a bit musty, to me; and then I went into the station for the Manchester train. The troop trains were moving out. I watched the women and girls running along beside the open windows, with their men looking out and waving their arms. I listened with amazement to the men's farewell jokes. And then I watched the women coming back along the platform with their faces in their hands.

My first delight with England, and it has never ceased, was how unspoilt the country was. It was my first sight of how the Old World had kept itself fresh and green, while we Americans have gone across our country like a plague of locusts. Even between Liverpool and Manchester, England was all and more than I had dared hope it would be. It was to be a long time before I got to know the Hardy country, and Exmoor, and the cottages of the Cotswolds; but my first sunsets walking across the Yorkshire moors were enough to make me fall in love with the English scene.

Then suddenly I remembered that it was August, that people were suffocating, gasping for air, dying of heat in New York, and I blessed "the blasted English climate."

Even the moist air seemed friendly.

I was travelling first class up to Manchester, because I did not know anything about England. In New York, when the company had handed me my steamer ticket, I had noticed that it was second class.

"I won't take it!" I said furiously.

There was a dilemma. Everybody, I was assured, travelled that way. In England most people travelled third class on the railway train.

"I won't do it!" I said, by this time beginning to get quite frantic on the subject. "I don't give a damn about first, second, or third class—it's the principle of the thing. If that firm in England thinks so little of me that they are going to bring me across second class—well, they can damn well keep the job. I won't start my life in England that way!"

I was bull-headed on the point. The head of the New York firm laughed. He crossed the Atlantic at least once every year. He said he would arrange matters. With the same money that he was authorised to spend on second class in a big liner, he bought me a cabin class on the *St. Paul,* and a first-class R.R. ticket to Manchester.

"When you get to Manchester," he smiled at my childishness, "you will see that travelling third class is not so degrading as you think."

With these thoughts in mind I approached Manchester with some trepidation. And the first sight of Manchester did not allay those fears. The fog had lifted shortly after we had left Liverpool but in Manchester it had closed down again. I got a vision of a bleak and black city, of ugly high walls and garish shops, of hustle and bustle and traffic clattering over cobblestones depressingly similar to the manufacturing districts along the two rivers of New York. Big black blocks of office buildings and warehouses in the fog.

The taxi clunked to a stop before the most dismal of them all. And, when he saw me struggling with shillings and six-pences, a man in uniform with a row of war medals on his chest came down the greasy steps and helped me and the taxi driver to get my hand baggage up. I didn't know who this man was, whether to tip him or not; he looked so grand.

"Who do you wish to see, sir?"

"I—I don't know."

Then, seeing that he thought I must be mad, what with my strange accent and all, I explained who I was; that I had just come over from America.

"Right you are, sir."

With military formality he did an about turn and left me sitting in the dingy though spotlessly clean reception-room. On its linoleum-covered table I saw a neat pile of catalogues of the various products that the great company manufactured. I was lost in these when a mousy little man, with baggy grey trousers and an apologetic air walked quietly into the room and shook my hand.

"I'm Hill," he said, "I suppose you are Mr. Farson?"

I nodded. Hill, the great Hill! That man with the grimy Aertex shirt was one of the chief directors of this firm! Hill, the great mathematician—Senior Wrangler at Cambridge!

"Leave your bags here," he said, with rather a girlish grimace at their number and size. "I'm going to put you up until you find digs for yourself."

The next morning at breakfast, when he was cutting the bread, he asked: "Will you have a whole slice or will half a slice do?"

I was still at sea. After a walk through the sombre fog-laden offices during which I learned nothing, except that everyone stood up obsequiously when Mr. Hill came in, I was driven out to Didsbury in an antique motor-car and taken into a typical English suburban house. There it was: chintz chair covers, silver trinkets and what-nots on the tables and mantelpiece, a few insipid water-colours on the wall, yellow smoke from the coal fire in the grate, a tea-table with cakes and crumpets and a receptacle which they vulgarly alluded to as the slop bowl, a wire-haired terrier on the hearthrug, and a "healthy" red-cheeked young woman who exclaimed, "Oh, yes?" to everything that I said—as if she didn't believe one word of it!

During tea I felt distinctly on guard, because it was quite obvious that this young woman thought that Americans were queer people, and she looked as if she would be disappointed if I did not do or say something odd. During dinner I noticed they were watching me: I suppose, to see how I ate. After dinner when we arose, and he closed the door after she went out, I was left with Hill. He passed the port to me, making a queer sweep with his arm across the table with it. I thought at first he was handing it to some invisible person on the other side.

"Sorry," he said, "I'll have to leave you after dinner. Mr. Charles and I have a Browning class tonight. Unless you'd like to come?"

"No, thanks," I said.

I had been warned against these literary and social activities of the great manufacturing company. The Directors both sponsored and conducted them. It was, they considered, one form of Social Uplift. And after refusing that first invitation I managed to keep my independence to the last.

"This war," said Mr. Hill, "has rather upset things. Shouldn't wonder if we had to shut up entirely."

" 'Business as Usual' " I repeated to him. "That seemed to be the motto I saw up everywhere today in Manchester."

I did not want him to go off on this tack, lest he got on the subject of my being no longer needed in Manchester, now that the war was going to upset all their plans. I wanted time at least to find my feet in England, from which I was already determined not to be banished.

He left me with his wife, who, the minute I said that I had seen a nautilus on the crossing, politely told me I had not.

"But you couldn't," she persisted. "Nautili do not go that far north."

"I saw it in the Gulf Stream."

Still that infuriating, exasperating, complacent shake of her head. "You must be mistaken, I'm sure," she said.

Then I felt wild. I demanded an atlas. I took the map of the Atlantic, I plotted the course of the *St. Paul*, showing her how we had gone far south, down to the Azores, to dodge imaginary warships of the combat nations.

"There!" I said, deliberately marking their atlas with my pencil. I put a black cross above the Azores. "I—saw—a—nautilus—there!"

"Oh," she said, as if to a naughty child who had been wrongly accused. "Yes—you *might* have seen a nautilus there. What did it look like?"

"Oh—I don't know—just a nautilus. Ever see one?"

No, she said; she had never seen a nautilus.

That night when I climbed into bed I burnt my foot and almost broke my toes. It was my first contact with a stone hot-water bottle. I was also called at seven and a cup of tea and two biscuits were placed on a chair by my side. Hill then came in in his dressing-gown and told me that the bathroom was free when I wanted to use it. I then had my first English breakfast of eggs with marvellous rashers of curly bacon and grilled tomatoes.

I also, when he asked me, said that I thought I could do with a whole slice of bread, upon which I put the remainder of the modest pot of clear marmalade.

I then asked Mr. Hill if he had ever seen a nautilus. No, he said, he had not.

"Well, I have, I saw one crossing the Atlantic—didn't I, Mrs. Hill?"

With the English, I had made up my mind, the best defence is a continued attack.

The salubrity of that breakfast, the ease of tea and bath before breakfast, and the casualness of conversation at the table itself had been like waking in Paradise after the obscene hustle and bustle of an ordinary morning in New York.

The "streets" inside the great, glass topped works were one-fifth of a mile long. They were whirring with machinery, tended mostly by young girls. There was the smell of steel, of sweet cutting oils, of burnt sand from the foundry, the light clink and heavy thunk of hundreds of punching machines, bells tingling when a piece had finished its strip, the purr of thousands of power-transmission chains. It was wholesome, satisfying, exhilarating beyond all description.

I wanted to take off my coat and get to work at once.

There was a most enlivening research laboratory, with precision instruments for testing tensional and torsional strengths, and Brinnel machines for hardness. Strips of steel were brought in here that looked so precious and were handled so carefully and lovingly by the attendants that they might have been strips of chocolate! I wanted to break off a piece and eat it.

And through the whole great works, from spectacled engineer-inspector, in his long white coat, to clog-footed puddler in the foundry, was a feeling of self-respect and pride in workmanship.

They were making the best chains in the world—and they knew it.

They were British workmen.

Chapter 14

BRITISH MADE

MANCHESTER, from the Englishman's point of view, was hardly the place to expect a salubrious existence. Yet I found it Paradise after New York. I found more dignity in "small" lives in Manchester than I ever found in any city in America.

My first surprise was that a man earning £3 a week should dare to have a hobby. Where was his divine discontent? In New York, if his divine discontent did not make him unhappy to live on that, his sense of envy certainly would, and if that didn't his wife would. Yet here in England I saw hundreds of people living on that, or only a trifle more, who were not only happy but had a tremendous sense of prestige and self-respect. When the closing whistle blew the works simply decanted into the playing fields, and people rushed past me with tennis racquets, cricket bats and golf clubs to play some sort of game until almost nine o'clock. They were undeniably happy. And although the roughest of the workers headed immediately for the pubs, they, too, had a sense of self-respect and dignity. In Manchester I got my first insight into that extraordinary world of the British pubs, where there are a thousand levels, and a man can feel decent, and even an autocrat as long as he behaves himself. In college, studying international labour conditions, the only scale of values was by a comparison of the wages paid, and I was delighted to find in England that there were other things that counted more than that. It was what he got for his wages, and in England he seemed at any rate to be getting an amazing contentment out of life.

With the engineers, with which class I spent most of my time in Manchester, I discovered that they were getting an exhilarating sense of pleasure out of their work. This was largely due to the fact that they were working in plants which were trying to make the best possible goods they could turn out. Quality was the prime essential and quantity came behind, and when I landed in Manchester some of the works were distracted trying to reconcile

the two. In the works that I was in there was one definite aim—
to make the best chain in the world. Nothing, price or anything
else, was allowed to stand in the way of that. As a result there
was not a person in the works, not excepting the hundreds of
girls who sat all day (making three motions) to feed the punching machines, who did not feel a pride in his work. This feeling
was so genuine that it left a feeling of satisfaction when a day's
work was done.

It was a stimulating atmosphere to work in. I liked the way the
British built things to last. I liked the prodigal way they used
solid brass fittings in their ships and railway trains. Great slabs of
pure metal, with plenty to spare for sheer bulldog strength. This
was a thing that I noticed everywhere; lamp brackets, toilet appliances, motor-cars, ash-trays—it was part of a sense of solidity that
permeated the whole British life. In America, some thoughtful
person would have calculated that a hollow casting would do in
place of that solid brass bracket, or that that lamp base of brass
could have been filled with lead, or that plate could have been
punched out instead of turned. So they could, of course, and in
some cases without any risk of harm. I was not naïve enough not
to realise how, with our fine inspection system, the Americans
would turn out accurate and substantial products under the mass
production craze. But I liked the way the British did not shave
everything down to as near the safety factor as was safe.

British shoes may have seemed a bit blunt toed to me at first;
but I liked the feel of the leather in them, that I knew would last
me for years. While I loathe potatoes and Brussels sprouts that
both look and taste as if they had been cooked in the bath tub,
and I was distressed by the lack of imagination with which the
British treated a thing they called a salad, I liked the simple but
sound meals at the Engineers' Club. In fact, before I had been
in foggy, dirty, grimy Manchester one week, I had fallen completely in love with the simplicity and substantiality of British
life.

At first I put all their lack of divine discontent and the ability
to find great happiness out of small lives down to a sense of fatalism. In England very likely the class system was so rigid that the

average Englishman had no hopes of breaking out of it. Therefore he accepted his status as a *fait accompli,* and resolved to make the best of it.

There was something in that. I got a disheartening exhibition of this on almost the first day I was in Manchester. I went to dinner with the works' manager. And all through dinner he alluded to the directors of the firm by their Christian names: such as Mr. Charles or Mr. George or Mr. Henry. Not only that, but he spoke of them and of us as if we were two different species of mankind. And the worst part of it was, so far as he was concerned, this was so obviously true. Their class, the Great English Middle Class, was so vastly different in physique alone from their employees that one wondered how the two breeds could both have been Englishmen springing from the same soil. The works' manager, on the other hand, was a product of English Industrialism with all that that means. Undersized product of generations of mill-workers, male and female, whose physique had been dwarfed several inches by unendurable hours, steam and linty looms; he had worked up from being a messenger boy in the works, via a Manchester Technical School (night course), to be its chief engineer. That, as far as he was concerned, was his ceiling. On the floor above lived the owners of the house, and that was the way he regarded them. He was fettered by traditions.

These were the two sides of the question. The happiness and dignity of these stratified lives. And yet the fact that such stratification was accepted so complacently. It made it very difficult for an American who did not know in which level he belonged or to which one he felt he must sooner or later become reconciled.

In fact this class complex began to frighten me. When, one morning, an order was posted that all under-managers should punch the time-clock as they came in and out I flatly refused. "But I do it," said the works' manager, and when I still shook my head he sent me along to see "Mr. Charles." He, after an attempt to explain things, finally gave up and said, "Oh, very well, you need not punch the clock." But I don't think he really liked me after that. I should have bowed down.

The Directors, by their treatment of me, made this class question all the more difficult. Up to Saturday noon, for instance, I was an executive in the works, bearing the sonorous title of "Manager of the English Speaking Agencies." These included the Manchester end of offices in Canada, U.S.A., Australia, New Zealand and South Africa. The title was much bigger than my salary. But during the week I was an employee and was treated as such. I was vastly inferior to the works' manager, or practically any engineer in the firm. But on Saturdays I was very often invited to spend the week-end up in the Old Man's home on the hill.

It means nothing that I was invited up there. If I had been an English engineer of my status I would never have been asked inside the door. But being a man they were training, and an American and therefore somewhat of a freak—the Old Man did not think it would do any harm to the morale of his great company to have such an underling as his house guest. So as far as that was concerned my being there had no significance, it proved nothing.

But it did give me an amazing chance to see the other side, the inside, of British manufacturing. For sitting up there on the hill with that grand old man I could see from the same stand as he did. And I saw that, gazing down on them, those acres of glass topped machine-rooms were his children. He loved them, and he wanted everything that came out of them to be the best of its kind possible. He was obsessed by that one idea—that his products should be the finest in the world. Let someone else worry how to get the costs down. It was not going to be at the expense of either workmanship or material—not while he was alive.

And it was over this that unwittingly I had my one and only serious difference with him. He had stood it tolerantly when I had been called into Directors' Meetings, and, in standing up for my over-seas clients, had found fault with the local managers and costs. That, he evidently tried to tell himself, was probably efficiency, even if it was officious on my part. But one day a letter came from the Fellow's Gear Shaper Co. in America for a sample of our new silent chain, and I sent an order into the works to have a special sample made up. The Fellow's Co. had asked us for a sample from which they could take measurements for making adequate gear cutters. And then the Old Man came into my office.

"What's *this?*"

He was half out of his mind with rage and he banged a length of chain down on my desk.

"How dare you!" he panted. "How *dare* you!"

I jumped to my feet in alarm. I told him why I had ordered a special sample made up.

"*What!* By God, you listen to me!" He slammed the sample of chain down on the floor. "I want you to understand one thing— every foot of my chain is just as good as any other foot. We don't send out *samples* to get orders by!"

There was almost a maniac shriek as he uttered the detested word "sample." He flung himself out of my office and wouldn't admit my existence for weeks. I think he would have fired me if I had not been on contract.

But that was the Old Man, God bless him! It was an honour to work for him.

Chapter 15

FAREWELL MANCHESTER

In Manchester I tried to make up for some of the mess I had made of my college career, and in the few short months I was there I studied more at nights than I ever had in my University. The great major chord of the city was the roar of cog-wheels, trip-hammers and spinning looms; and I was solidly happy to be a part of it. My "home" life was equally substantial and satisfying.

I had digs with a family named Horsley. The little man had been an exporter on an extremely small scale, buying on a commission of 2 per cent for big firms in the Near East and the Levant. The war had brought his tiny business to a full and ghastly stop. He was on the way to being ruined. And I was the first paying guest they had ever had.

It was an embarrassing situation for both of us.

"I'm sure I don't know," beamed his ample Scotch wife—"What shall we charge you?"

We agreed that £1 10s. od. a week was about proper for my bedroom, study and board. I suggested that perhaps they had better make it a bit more:

"Because," I said, "I like game."

That, they hastened to assure me, was quite all right. And once a week I was given a pheasant, half of which I ate hot the first night and the other half, cold (when it is much better), the following night. They gave me mushrooms for breakfast with huge strips of curly bacon and fried eggs. And eating these with the fogs turning the playing fields of Withington into an aquarium—so that I would not have been at all surprised if a fish had swum past my window—I revelled in such breakfasts. I needed them, for every raw dripping morning I had to walk a mile and a half to the works.

The first dinner was awful. Old Horsley had two daughters; and the eldest of them, a pink-cheeked lass of eighteen, had been delegated to wait upon me. To wait upon a stranger—an American, at that. I sat there, quite aware of some of the agony that was going on in the kitchen outside. Then came a knock:

"Are you ready?"

It was worse than waiting to go on the operating table. You see, I had met these people "socially" on Sunday, had tea with them the day before, when I was arranging to come there. And now the daughter who had been so gay and conversational had to appear as a waitress with my food.

When she came in through the door her face was as red as the tomatoes she was carrying. She trembled as she put down the dishes. Jumped like a startled horse when she chanced to touch me, averted her eyes, dashed out.

This, I thought, simply cannot continue. For the first few nights they gave me the solitude usually accorded to someone with a contagious disease. I did not mind this. But I became aware that my "study" had formerly been their modest drawing-room, and that, with me filling it, there was no place for the family to sit, especially old Horsley, whose whiskey and fog-drenched voice could be heard from the kitchen, and whose carpet slippers I found by my cheery coal fire. So I casually asked him one night if he played cards.

"D'ye know Nap?" he asked. "It's a champion game!"

He taught me Nap, playing with painful deliberation, until he got on my nerves. To relieve the tension one night I accused him of cheating:

"*What!*" he began to arise. "How-how-how . . ." His indignation throttled him.

I have forgotten to mention that he was a hairy bandy-legged little man, with an immaculately tended King Edward VII beard. And he had as peppery a sense of independence as his own aloof Airedale.

When I leaned back and laughed he was so outraged it took me half an hour to get him into a good humour again, but that burst of emotion had broken the ice and made things easier for all of us. So much so, that when I did not take my baths at their ordered times he gave me the devil for not doing so.

Unlike the average Englishman, I still adhered to the American habit of bathing at night time. But as I now often dined down in Manchester at the Engineers' Club, and played snooker pool with the engineers until midnight, I occasionally did not have a bath until morning. The result was that the water they had heated so carefully had become cold.

"It's your own business, mind you!" stormed Horsley. "Have as many baths as you like—or as few as far as I give a damn. But I'll no have my wimmin folk carrying hot water up and down stairs for you when you think so little of it all that you're down drinking whiskey and sodas at the club. I'll no *have* it, I tell you."

His voice rose to a scream.

In Manchester I learned how to drink. Nothing less than an occasional whiskey and soda, I discovered, could proof one against those marrow-drenching yellow fogs. I did some of my drinking on the first walks I took, over week-ends with the moor-loving old Horsley. I did a steady amount in the Manchester Engineers' Club. But the drinking I enjoyed most was in the quiet English country pubs.

I did this with Brothers.

Brothers was the man I had been warned against in New York. "He looks like a sheep," had said Lester. "But so did Disraeli!" Curly-haired Brothers wore bi-focal lenses, had worked out the intricate gyrostatics for Louis Brennan's famous Mono-Rail railway, could produce any calculus formula at a moment's notice from his head, devoted his spare time to designing racing motor-car engines, wore the same shirt from Monday to Saturday, lived in digs in Manchester that it would have been cruel to keep a dog in, owned a six-cylinder Daimler (which he kept down in Wales), could drink any dock-worker under the table, and was an emotional impotent the moment he was left alone with a pretty girl.

He was a genius, an eccentric such as only England can produce—or tolerate.

The directors and chief engineers of the big works disliked him intensely, because he would never take anything seriously. At tense moments, when their respectable heads were all bent over a drawing board, attempting to solve some intricate transmission problem, Brothers would light a cigarette with his stubby, nico-tined fingers, and remark:

"Why not use string?"

Then, while they were glowering at him, those nubbly fingers would make a swift, deft sketch. The amazing brain behind those sheep-like eyes would produce a constellation of mathematical formulae. Then when, feeling somewhat abashed by the sight of such genius, they would begin to praise him, he would set them all off again by remarking:

"And lubricate it with sand."

From Brothers I learned another fundamental lesson in my English education. Never let yourself become serious with an Englishman, unless you are certain you are at least his equal on the subject you are talking about. Don't let yourself be lured to your doom by that false air of apologetic modesty.

We used to take the train down to Chester, where the Daimler had been sent to meet us. Then we would have a long week-end driving and drinking through the vales and glens and over the cloud-drenched brown mountains of Wales. We used to shoot snipe and duck at Barmouth.

The first time we shot there I wiped Brothers' eye as far as the snipe were concerned. This tricky shooting, the zigzag flight, I had done almost from childhood up in the New Jersey marshes. Brothers was so impressed that he almost took off his hat to me. But when the sunset flight came, and we sat behind a sea wall shooting at the incoming duck, Brothers, with his sheepy, near-sighted eyes and huge bi-focal lenses hardly missed a bird, whereas all that I bagged was one cormorant.

That first adventure, as with every other week-end, saw us hours late getting back to work in Manchester. The result was that we both strode firmly into the works and to our respective offices. There, being in a rush to catch up with my work, I put my shotgun case in a corner, and—so that they would not be noticed—shoved some snipe I had intended to give Mr. Hill in the filing drawer of my desk.

And there I forgot them.

" 'Ave you noticed a queer kind of smell about 'ere lately, sir?" asked the commissionaire to me a week later.

"Well, I have," I admitted. "I was wondering what it could be."

"So was us. Night watchman tells me 'e's been lookin' 'igh and low for it."

Engineers passing my office held their noses and looked in at me. They made a pretence of moving off when I joined them at the drawing tables. And even the Old Man heard of it when the snipe were found, and asked me not to "hang" snipe in the future in my filing cabinet.

But this, even this equable, satisfying Manchester existence was also playing at life. I knew that I was not going to stay there any more than I could have remained an oil salesman in New York. Too much was going on "outside." Perhaps the war was the chief reason for my restlessness. So many of the men had gone off, and come back to visit us in khaki. And one day I was almost forced to enlist.

I was taking a girl to the theatre. As we passed Manchester's Town Hall I saw that a monstrous sign had been put up. It was a gigantic thermometer, calibrated to show the scale of Manchester's enlistments. It was called "Manchester's War Heat."

And standing below that sign was a Scot. He was a Gordon, in full Highlander kit, kilt, sporran, hairy legs and everything.

"You look a fine lad!" he said to me, before my girl. "Why don't you walk in there?"

He pointed to the gaping doors behind which sat the enlistment clerks of the Army.

"It's not my war," I said with some embarrassment. "I'm an American."

"Maks no deeference—ye're a mon, aren't ye? Go in yon an' put doon yuir name an' come across to France wi' us. To fight the bloody Hun!"

"No, thanks," I said.

"It'll gie ye a free trip to France!" he protested.

"What about the return ticket?"

The crowd around me began to make comments. There was

something like a low growl, and I heard the words, "bloody Americans . . ."

I flushed—and glared at those who stood nearest to me. It was very embarrassing, particularly so as there was a letter in my pocket at that moment from the Manchester Red Cross, thanking me for a pamphlet I had written to help them raise a permanent source of income for the Withington Hospital. But that in itself was embarrassing, a substitute for the one drastic action I felt that I should take—obey that sergeant of the Gordon Highlanders.

It was not that I hated the Germans, or believed the atrocity stories that Manchester was being flooded with. I never felt strongly one way or another about the war. I couldn't, after knowing Franz Ahrens and some of the Germans in America. But it was merely the fact that every other young man of about my age was enlisting. And it was so humiliating to walk about Manchester, scot-free like this, and have to face their fathers.

That was one reason why I wanted to move on. The other was that, pleasant and satisfying as the life in Manchester was, I saw that it was a dead end. There *was* something fatalistic about the way the English accepted the various given conditions of their lives and in the way they resolved to settle down happily in them. I began to be aware that the heads of the firm expected me to do likewise. I could continue to increase my worth and my salary as an engineer; I could, as I was now doing practically all of it, rise to become the head of their advertising department. I had in fact just been permitted to submit my proposals with suggested advertisements (nearly all of which I had done myself) for the next year's advertising programme. A comparatively easy achievement as my predecessor, with true Lancashire determination to get his money's worth, had filled every square inch of available advertising space with every word he could cram in it. But Advertising Manager would be the ceiling so far as advancement in that firm was concerned.

I was not a relative of the family which owned the works. I had no money to bring into it. It was too old, too well established, too solidly a family affair for me ever to rise to the position of becoming a director.

And I found I did not like the circumspect, dignified and re-spectable lives that these middle-class Englishmen lived. They were dull. Therefore when the chance came, I took it.

Some Americans had come to Manchester. I was told off to take them through the works, assist in our business talks with them, and look after their comfort while they were in Manchester.

It was stirring to come into contact with that thrusting, some-what overwhelming American optimism again. I sat in the French Restaurant of the Midland Hotel, having dinner with them. They wouldn't go into the ordinary restaurant, they declared, as they hated English cooking.

"You seem fairly wide-awake," they said. "What are you doing in this place?"

"Well," they said in chorus when I told them how I had been handling a variegated export trade, "why don't you hitch your wagon to our star?"

"Where's your star going?" I said.

Then they told me that they, with some Englishmen, were opening up an export business in London. London was to be their headquarters for all the world. Just at the moment they were trying to get war contracts from the British, French and Russian Governments.

"Boy!" laughed their young president. "You're coming with us. And we aren't going to take no for an answer."

I put them aboard the London train, then I went out to see Mr. Hill.

"But don't you like this life here?" he asked me.

"Love it," I said. "When I leave Manchester it will be with a lump in my throat."

Then I pointed out to him my feelings about it. The dead end of it all. He admitted it. Even if I became head of the advertising department, he agreed that my salary could never hope to be over some £800 a year. That was as much as the works' manager was getting. And he also was understanding enough to admit that he quite realised that I was perhaps wise in not tying myself down.

"You Americans!" he sighed. "You are the most restless people —you never seem to be able to sit still."

A week later I was in London with a Tasmanian for my boss. And for the sake of those people, many of whom I served with later on, I want to absolve all that island from what I have to say about this representative.

He was atrociously handsome, in a villainous sort of way, with curly dark hair like a movie star. He had a streak of genius in him and could put on a terrific air of business propriety when the occasion demanded. But behind the scenes he was a complete bluff, and one of the most untrustworthy mortals I have ever met. We lived in the motor-car and motor-cycle section of London for the first few weeks, and I discovered that the nest of flats in which I joined him was mostly inhabited by the sort of ladies who accost you late at night on Regent Street.

But that was about the only side of London I saw at that time, because about two days after we had moved into a more decorous flat in Great Portland Street, the steamer *Zara* was sunk by a German mine in the North Sea.

We had been angling, through some Danes, for a contract for motor-cycles with the Russian War Department at that time. The contract had become "sticky," the Tasmanian had been on the point of going out to Petrograd to investigate it, when he picked up the newspaper describing the *Zara* disaster; how several people aboard her had died in the frozen boats before being picked up off the coast of Norway.

"Want to go to Russia?" he asked.

Two nights later, with my first passport in my pocket, bearing Norwegian, Swedish and Russian visas, I was on the train bound for Newcastle.

Half-way up I decided to open my letters of instruction. We had had such a thick farewell lunch, at which had been two King's Messengers, that I had asked my secretary to count my gold sovereigns for me—I wanted to make sure, knowing my boss, that the 150 of them were all there. I would not have been at all surprised to find some ten or a dozen of them missing.

But that was nothing to the shock I got when I opened those sealed letters supposed to contain full details as to what I should do upon reaching Petrograd. There was nothing in them at all!— just a Power of Attorney, and a note:

"Good luck. Everything is left to your discretion."

Chapter 16

RUSSIAN QUEST

When I realised the emptiness of those "letters of instruction" that I was carrying to guide my course of action in Russia I nearly jumped off the train and rushed back to London. In Newcastle I did, for a moment, debate the question. I had literally nothing to go upon; in that short note not a word gave the position of the situation in Petrograd, as my boss had promised it would. If the big war contract was lost it was quite obvious that I had been nominated for the post of full blame. It was an ugly start.

But I went aboard at midnight and woke up the next morning to find myself in the old *Jupiter* in the German Ocean, now the North Sea. In the *Jupiter* I found that I could not, as I had fondly imagined, speak French; and from her rail I heard my first words of pure Norwegian. These were a string of curses when our lines broke a barrel of fish-oil at Stavanger.

My fancied French was exposed to me when I tried to tell two Frenchmen aboard that we need have no fear of submarines, because the old *Jupiter* was valuable to the Germans—she always carried spies. The Frenchmen, it may have been their natural insolence to foreigners, made out that they couldn't understand one word, although Norwegians, Swedes and Russians always managed to make out what I was driving at, and I could understand their French. It was characteristic of my having learned French in America that I never have been able to speak it in France.

The passengers, and our few intimate meals together, were thrilling. Princess Bariatinsky, accompanied by a handsome English dilettante, was returning to her native land to wear an attractive Red Cross uniform. I saw her later on, very nun-like in her white cowl and upturned blue eyes, the soul of patriotism and self-sacrifice, in the best hotel tea-rooms in Petrograd. There was a retired English colonel, the dashing, greyhound type, who was an honorary *atman* of a Cossack *sotnia*. Having been rejected as too old for service with his own army, he was going to fight with his old friends from the Don steppes. The two Frenchmen were munition experts, bound for a powder-works outside Moscow. Taking a fancy to me in our last hours they taught me my first Russian sentence:

"*Ya vass lublu!*" said the fat, bearded chap. "I love you. It's the first sentence you learn in any language—and, my friend, you will get more exquisite returns from that one sentence in Russia than in any other country in the world. Russian women are magnificent!—Oh, la, la—say it again—'*Ya vass lublu!*' "

The immaculate cleanliness and comfort of that Norwegian sleeper rumbling through the snow-clad forests and over the wind-swept mountains between Bergen and Christiania! I was still lying in my delectable pale blue blankets with their three little white Scandinavian crowns when the porter brought me a cable.

"HEINRICH OF COPENHAGEN AWAITS YOU GRAND HOTEL CHRISTIANIA PLEASE MEET."

Hullo, I thought, the plot thickens. No instructions in London —what is going to happen to me here? I threw my things into my bag, waved good-bye to my *Jupiter* comrades, and drove to the Grand Hotel. I had three bags, I was going to Russia to spend three weeks—and I spent three years!

Christiania was in a hysteria of war prosperity. The Norwegians were getting fabulous prices for their shipping. I found them drinking champagne at eleven o'clock in the morning.

This comforted me because my first sight of the bleak streets of Christiania, particularly of the palace, had been depressing. I had never seen a palace (I had not had time to see the King's during the few short weeks I was in London); and, with true American naïveté I had expected a palace to be a ginger-bread or fairy-tale affair, like some of mad Ludwig's crag-castles in Bavaria.

Heinrich was waiting for me. He was, I was shocked to discover, a German. A German trying to sell munitions to Russia. Not only that but his big Berlin firm, through its Danish agents, was quite aware of this. to say the least, unpatriotic affair. An ominous atmosphere.

"There is no need for you to go to Russia," said Heinrich.

That clumsy opening sentence put me on my guard at once. It also put my back up. If the man Hakonson, who accompanied him, had been left to handle me, the chances are they would have talked me out of proceeding to Petrograd. Reluctantly, I would have permitted myself to be persuaded that my presence in this subtle dicker with the great Russian War Department was only not needed, but would ruin such extremely secret negotiations.

Hakonson was a Dane, whom Heinrich introduced as his *advocat*. Hakonson sang his words with a sweetness that seemed calculated to charm birds off trees. He had a bushy beard, which he parted in the middle and brushed back towards his ears, and he parted his curly blonde hair even down the back of his head. Heinrich was a fat *bourgeois* from Essen, who exhibited a missing thumb to explain why he was not at the Front killing Belgians, French, or Englishmen as the case may be; and I think he slept with his fat portfolio, which he even took into the toilet with him.

From these two sinister creatures I learned that there were something like nine different men, representing that many factors in the negotiations, between my London principals and the Russian War Department. I also saw, when I began to insist upon proceeding there, how frantically anxious they were that I should not reach Russia. They predicted all sorts of ugly "accidents" that might happen to me. And the Dane so convinced me of the duplicity and highhandedness of the Russian customs officials that I gave him my case of gold and silver athletic medals to keep. Mementos of an early life that I valued so much in my childish fashion that I would not even leave them with my supposed Tasmanian colleague in London.

When, ultimately, I kicked these Danes out of Russia (by giving them forty-eight hours to clear out or else have their Berlin connections revealed) the Copenhagen Company held on to my medals, which, they said by letter, they would return to me when my company had recompensed them for the great loss they had suffered in Petrograd. Needless to say, the medals are there yet, although Princeton University and the Amateur Athletic Union of America gave me copies of several of the most important.

But this bit of swinishness was unforeseen. Heinrich and Hakonson, despite their chagrin over what they eventually came to speak of as my American pig-headedness, were human. The business trip from Copenhagen to Christiania was a little adventure in their lives. It need not be all business. Not when they realised it was hopeless to try and prevent me from going to Petrograd. So, for luncheon, we also had champagne.

I tried to get them both drunk. To me this seemed very subtle. Drink with them, but hang on to my faculties; soon they would become loose-tongued, and I would discover what it really was they feared I might find out in Petrograd. So, without any demur from them, I ordered a magnum for us.

The atmosphere was congenial. So friendly that when we put the German aboard his train that night, we practically poured him into his bunk. We got out of the cab with our arms around each other's necks. But they had not divulged anything, at least anything that I could remember.

As I had nothing to do until the next evening the Dane and I went out to the ski jump at Holmenkollen. I borrowed the skis of a Norwegian officer and tried the baby jump, a twelve-foot affair arranged for children. I went down to it famously, rose, turned a slow somersault in the air, and came down on my head. The Norwegian lieutenant was the first to reach me—hurriedly removing his precious skis from my feet.

We went up to the great sled run. It goes for miles from the top of those lovely mountains, with swerves and shoots, down through the silent pines, banked turns and sharp cuts under the electric railway bridges, almost all the way back to Christiania.

"Let's get a sled," I suggested to smiling Hakonson.

"But do you know how to guide? It is very difficult."

"Nonsense!" I laughed, memories of bob-sleds down New England hills in my mind. "We steer with our feet on these small sleds. These people do the same thing with a pole. Here, let's ask this kid if we can use his."

The dinky little sled was about the size of a tea tray. I put Hakonson in front. wrapped my legs around him, and the kid gave us a push.

Talk about taking one's breath away! The speed that that sled instantly worked up was terrifying. It had the trajectory of a bullet. The Dane, still in a Nirvana from the night's champagne, was quite likely composing a saga about it. I didn't know what he was doing or thinking. I did not have time. One tiny flick of the pole and we were shooting along the ice wall of the snow run, a counteracting flick and we hurtled along the brim of the other side. We flashed past breaks in the bank and bloodstains in the snow which showed where other sledders had misjudged things, and then I saw the electric railway line ahead. I did not see the bridge. The only way I sensed its approach was by the frightening sight of a mounting train, skis strapped along its sides, its windows full of pink-cheeked, laughing faces, highly interested in us.

Ziiiiip!

There was a sharp turn at the bridge. I jerked the trailing stick —*up we went!*

The sled went on, up, into the cold grey undergrowth beside the sled run. I went on, down, around another curve, riding on the back of Hakonson.

He was stretched out under me like a rug. Arms and legs spraddled out like a flying squirrel. I rode him. I rode him until the snow, shooting up his sleeves, began to shoot out behind his ears. He shot snow out of him like a snow plough in the Rockies. Then he fetched up. I had steered him for a bend in the bank. And I hauled him over it.

That instant another black shape, a racing sled, shot past where we had been.

"Saved your life," I said to him.

His little beard had become unparted, as well it might, being used as a buffer as it was. The shape had gone from his bowler hat. And so had the friendship from his eyes. Hakonson was cold sober now.

That night, eating delectable *hjarpe*, that succulent bird which the Norwegians served with brown cream sauce and red berries,

Hakonson was shockingly outspoken about the folly of my going to Russia.

"You are too impetuous. You will spoil everything," he muttered.

And spoil things I did—for Hakonson, and the thumbless German.

At Karungi, in the Arctic Circle, we had a few short hours of daylight. We walked about without overcoats in the blinding snow. The sun glinted on the deep pine forests, their branches cloaked in white crystals. All the way up through Sweden we had passed through enchantment. At intervals the train halted for a half-hour at stations made of pine logs, and we all rushed inside to gorge on goat's cheese and appetising Swedish *smörgåsbord*. Goat's cheese, the colour of peanut butter, for which I got such a passion that the half-hour stops were never half long enough.

At Upsala, a magnificent figure of a Swedish officer got aboard. He was Count von Eckermann, head of the Swedish machine-gun corps. His headpiece was a white sheepskin with a blue and gold medallion. A gorgeous affair. He was, he told me, proceeding to Boden, the great stone stronghold that the Swedes had built against Russia. A fort whose stone walls were twenty feet thick.

"Up there," he laughed, "we used to drink a bottle of punch for every thousand Russians the Germans captured. But we had to give it up—we got so drunk."

Bridges over the smoking mountain currents, that cleft down through the gorges, and still pines, were all protected with barbed wire and sentry-boxes. At one of these the train was halted for a mysterious length of time. Captain Count von Eckermann was summoned, and spent a long time on our end of the bridge talking to two soldiers.

"Someone," he smiled, when he was back in our carriage again, "some nice fellow thought it would be a charming idea to unbolt the fish-plates of the rails crossing this bridge. They were found that way this morning. I suppose he is sitting somewhere up there now, with binoculars, waiting to see the splash."

Years later I stayed with von Eckermann at Ljusne Woxna, an

ancient iron-works built beside a mountain of pure hematite ore. There was a little Swedish village there on the shores of the Baltic where he was *grand seigneur*, and he even built his own steamships. In wolf-skin robes we drove through the pine forests when it was forty degrees below zero. Bottles of Swedish punch refused to take the ice out of our backbones.

Chapter 17

RUSSIAN WAR ORDERS

RUSSIA was just a sentry-box standing in the middle of the frozen Torneo River.

Russia! Holy Russia! I will never forget my first sight or smell of her, nor, *Bog iznat!* what she did to me during those next three years.

The sentry-box was painted with a herringbone of black and orange stripes, the Imperial colours. A sentry stood outside it, solitary in the Arctic. Sullen, heavy-footed, wrapped in sheep-skins, his bayonet protruding above his sentry-box, he raised a long pole to let us pass.

We lay in sleds pulled by ponies and reindeer. The drivers poked the reindeer in the rump with a stick. Our cavalcade re-sumed its trek across the frozen river. We passed the sentry. The pole dropped.

We were in Russia!

The snows were turning dark blue. Our little hour or so of daylight was already closing down on us, for this was but a few days before the Russian Christmas. And we were in the Arctic Circle. In a Customs House, built of fresh-peeled logs on the ice, I got my first smell of Russian boots and church incense. That smell has haunted me ever after. With fragments of Dostoevsky, Tolstoy, Tchehov, and *The Yellow Ticket* in my mind, I watched the scene during the sullen inspection of my baggage. The swing-ing walk of heavy, brutal soldiery; dapper, unconcerned officers; ponderous generals with hands stuffed in the side-pockets of their great-coats standing about like Colossi; golden epaulets, clanking swords, the *pssing, pssing* of passing spurs; and the scent of pretty women. . . .

For they were there. Watching us, breaking out into bird-like chirps of laughter, were three of the most seductive women I had seen for a long time.

They ought not to have been there. They were, I discovered in the two-day ride across Finland, the generals' lady friends. Actresses from Petrograd. But their presence gave just the right note to touch off the barbarism of that Arctic frontier. The sentry, alone at nightfall on the frozen river; the milk-white skin, jewelled fingers and pouting lips of those full-breasted lovely women in the hot-house atmosphere of the *wagon-lit*. The chatty officers, with their swagger black boots and breasts of glittering decorations, extending to each other over everlasting glasses of tea, tasselled cigarette-cases made from blobs of soft gold. A playful slap or bold pinch of a tempting and always-at-your-service female thigh. Bursts of provocative laughter. And over everything, even in the *wagon-lit*, the smell of incense. . . .

The snowy midnight that saw me clambering out of the train at the *Finlandski Vauxhal*, also saw me unable to get to my hotel in Petrograd. I could not pronounce its name.

"Hôtel Europe, Hôtel Europe!" I kept saying ever louder: "Hôtel Europe?"

I could not say to those porters: "*Ya vass lublu!* I love you!" which was the only Russian sentence I had learned.

"*Ah! Ah-ha! Gasteenitza Evrupaskayia? Da! Da-da-da!*"

In an exhilarating snowstorm we crossed the bridges and trotted down the broad Nevsky, past the Cathedral of the Virgin of Kazan—where three years later I was to stand with my hand on a soldier's back as he was shot dead during the Revolution—swung sharp left and pulled up with a flurry of snow before the Hôtel de l'Europe.

Striped porters and a covey of little red-bloused boys with peacock's feathers in their hats, descended and disappeared with my baggage. The bearded driver bellowed and hurooshed for five times the correct fare. The porter took double the right fare from me, gave half to the driver and kept half for himself. The stallion gave a leap and dashed off. I went into a foyer scintillating with lights, gypsy music, medals and women.

"Here iss Frosch."

A man looked up from boldly reading the labels on my baggage and walked up to take my hand. He bowed and clicked his heels together, showing me the top of his shaven pate.

"You are Mr. Farson—from London?"

I felt the hair on the back of my head begin to twitch. It was so unnecessary for this person to be so positive about me, who I was, and from where I had come. And, as I thought about it—it was unnatural.

"You are from the—"

Before I could get the name of the Danish company out of my mouth he checked me with an upraised palm.

"Please," he advised. "We shall talk in your room."

In the Oriental atmosphere of that deep-carpeted curtained room the bald-pated Dane became excessively friendly. "I haf cable from Heinrich. He likes you very much." Fine, I thought; but what now?

"You must not go near the Russian War Department."

"Why?"

"Things are too complicated. Any day, any day now, we expect to get the order any day. The order will be much bigger than you think."

I asked him what was our competition, what prices he was quoting. Had our machines passed any Government test? What deliveries had he promised; what quantities, and when? I must have been rather trying.

"Please!" He held up both palms. "You do not under*stand!*"

He then gave me a brief but, as I afterwards learned, very realistic description of how one went about getting orders from the great Russian War Department. The first rule was never to go to the War Department at all. One found an intermediary. The intermediary knew the right people, he knew how much each official would take, and which official—if he did not get that much—would see that the order went to somebody else. Or that there would be no order at all. Neither the needs of the Russian soldiers being slaughtered at the front, nor the quality of the goods supplied, mattered in the very least.

"It's merely knowing the man who—" Frosch rubbed the ball

of his thumb and the first two fingers together. "So now, Mr. Farson, you see why you have to lay low."

"I see," I said.

"Petrograd is lofly—they say Russian women are best in the world."

"I know," I said. "*Ya vass lublu.*"

He roared with laughter and slapped his knees.

"Well, then, Mr. Farson, good night. I shall report to you every day of course—yes?"

"Certainly," I said, watching him snap the locks on his portfolio.

The door closed.

I sat there and tried to think for about half an hour. But thinking only made matters worse. It merely muddied my judgment. And that was: if ever I saw a crook—Mr. Frosch was it! I went on intuition and threw everything else aside. Most of that half-hour I had spent waiting for Frosch to get well away from the Hôtel de l'Europe. I had really known what I was going to do the minute the door closed behind him. I did it now.

I typed out a cable to London and went down to the desk. I told the concierge to tell the porter to direct my *droshky* driver to the telegraph office. In a few minutes we had galloped across the Marinsky Ploschad and I had filed my wire. It read:

"CONVINCED DANISH REPRESENTATIVES UNRELIABLE STOP ASK PERMISSION PROCEED INDEPENDENTLY."

It was now nearly two o'clock and I went into the crowded restaurant of the Hôtel de l'Europe; had a meditative feast of toast and fresh caviare, and gave myself over to an orgy of melancholy brought on by the gypsy songs. . . .

It was beginning to dawn on me that I had quite unnecessarily assumed an appalling obligation in this whole affair. Having cut myself off from the Danes, the responsibility for the war order now rested solely upon me. Perhaps funny little Hakonson, with his parted beard, had been right when he said I was too impetuous.

I thought so when the answer to my cable got through the censor two days later. It read:

"EVERYTHING LEFT ENTIRELY YOUR DISCRETION."

By that time I had already moved over to the Hotel Astoria, facing on the great square which contained the towering gold dome of St. Isaac's Cathedral, the Imperial Ballet, and the wrecked red-sandstone German Embassy.

I had gone in there for lunch. And one look at the galaxy of officers, diplomats and courtesans in that glamorous dining-room, immediately convinced me that, in the Hôtel de l'Europe, I was distinctly out of the swim.

"Here," exulted one of my French munition experts from the *Jupiter,* "are all the general staffs of the world and all the beautiful cocottes that the Germans have kindly driven out of Poland. And if there is anything better than a Russian girl, it is a Polish girl!"

They were, they said, in no hurry to get on to Moscow. After all, look at the experience that Napoleon had had there.

That would have been sufficient. But the one thing that really made me go through the bother of shifting all my stuff again was that the Hotel Astoria was the centre of all the War Department intrigue at that time. Nothing of any importance, so far as a foreigner was concerned, was ever concluded with the War Department until after long and secret arrangements had been made with the two big "middlemen" who used the Hotel Astoria as their happy hunting ground.

The bells of the holy Cathedral of St. Isaac's ka-bingled and ka-bongled their Asiatic carillon all day long outside the Hotel Astoria and the cocottes from Poland worked the bedside telephones all night.

It was an erotic spot to live and nearly die in at the end of an exciting year.

One of the things that had made me so suspicious of the Danes was the fact that they had never gone near a certain Russian that we had directed them to get in touch with. My misgivings about my own judgment were immediately put at rest when I discovered he was one of the two biggest middlemen.

"You don't have to do nuddings!" he told me with a wave of his fat hand. "You just leave it to Papa."

Frumkin, as I shall call him, looked and talked and was quite as good an actor as Balaieff of the "Chauve Souris," who was running a little midnight place called "The Flying Mouse" at that time.

"Papa knows," said Frumkin. "Papa knows what's what and Papa knows who's who—and how much they want—and that's all there is to it. For instance, the Minister of War always takes two per cent."

"If you and me," threatened Frumkin, tapping me on the stomach. "If you and me agree—the order is done!"

Once when he came into my room and found a Polish girl he pulled a chair across and sat down on it so that he faced the window.

"Go ahead," he said generously. "Don't pay any attention to me."

But "agreeing" with old Frumkin was not so easy as it seemed. His New York education had added infinite devices to a mind that had already been forced to learn every form of duplicity to protect its owner from the Tsarist treatment of the Jews. Frumkin, in fact, had to pay annual "blood-money" to the police to be allowed to live in Petrograd. Yet, when I first saw his bulldog face, Frumkin was already a millionaire.

With the Danes, in Petrograd, I felt we could play our game on neutral territory. When Frumkin emerged from the cruel tenement quarter where he chose to live—a protective colouring of a sort to mask his riches—I immediately felt like a baby in arms. Frumkin could think twice as quickly and around ten times as many corners as I could. He knew it. I knew it. And, when Frumkin knew that I knew it, we became quite friendly and frank with each other after a time. In time I really got to love the old rascal—until one night I found out what his frankness had really meant.

Then he accused me of trying to have him shot for it. Which he very nearly was!

Chapter 18

A YOUNG MAN AT LARGE

PETROGRAD during the first years of the war provided the perfect life of dissipation. I'm not so sure it did not provide the perfect life all around. I know I could never have dreamed a better one. Englishmen who were born in Russia and lived there declared it was the finest life in all the world. They have proved this since they have been cast out of Paradise by wandering all over the world with the most lugubrious and ruined lives. I know of no people I feel more sorry for—nor whom I envied more at that time.

I made up my mind to end my days in Russia the very instant I saw it. And I very nearly did.

These Englishmen were *barens*, and lived like feudal lords. Many of them were the descendants of ordinary Midland mill workers who came out as foremen when British capital began to develop the textile industry in Russia. A few had come there as adventurers. Several of them owned huge timber estates. But one and all, they lived in baronial fashion, with their *abonnement* at the Ballet, their belligerent private coachmen, their New English Club on the Moyskayia, their golf club, their tennis club, their "English Magazine" (the only place in Russia where one could get good shoes or leather goods), and their hordes of servants, whom they treated kindly, but regarded as clumsy St. Bernards.

Even the war-time foremen in the woollen and cotton mills felt themselves vastly superior as human beings to any Russian Grand Duke. As Keyserling somewhere wrote of the Britisher:

"Whenever I meet one of the representatives of this people I am shocked by the contrast between the dearth of their talents, the limitation of their horizon and the measure of recognition which every one of them exacts from me, as from everybody else."

Well, the Russians gave it to them without asking. An Englishman, any Englishman in Tsarist Russia, was automatically a Milord.

There were, of course, the inevitable class distinctions drawn most rigidly in the English colony itself. Lady Georgina Buchanan, the British Ambassadress, was, of course, the titular head of this colony. She was of the purest purple herself, for, as every Britisher knows, there exist only three families:

"The Holy Family, the Royal Family—and the Bathursts."

But her leadership was challenged by at least one woman whose bright blue Scotch eye enhanced the dinner-table of a flat in Millionaire Street that threatened to split Petrograd's English colony in two. A bitter unscrupulous enemy and an amazing friend, she removed me from the Hotel Astoria to her house when my surgeons told her I was going to die, where she pestered me so much with mischievous remarks about "you Amurricans!" that she kept my blood stream coursing until I could reach an operating table in New York.

The American colony did not count. For that matter, it never does.

The American Embassy had nothing to do with Americans in those days. In fact, to Americans in trouble, there was an unwritten sign above its door, as caricatured afterward by John Reed and Boardman Robinson: No AMERICANS NEED APPLY. They were much too genteel to have anything to do with trade; i.e., help us out in our various troubles with censors and obstructive Russian officials at Archangel. They stuck to the Diplomatic Set, or horned in on the English colony, especially at dinner in the flat in Millionaire Street. But, although we never had a first-class Ambassador there during the war, there were, in the three years that I knew them, one spectacular Attaché Honoraire, two brilliant Counsellors, Butler Wright and Norman Armour, a lovable First Secretary from Kentucky—and the most naïve Third Secretary we have ever sent abroad. More of whom later.

Of the spectacular Attaché Honoraire let this much be said. He was a power in Washington politics. He got his nominee appointed Ambassador to the Court of St. Petersburg. In return he was made Attaché Honoraire so as to give him a fling at court life. The Americans never had a uniform for their Diplomatic Corps. From Madrid to the Court of St. James's they turned up in the middle of the afternoon dressed in full dress evening clothes like a head waiter. The Attaché Honoraire ached with envy for the gold breasts, feathered hats and ceremonial swords of his colleagues. So he invented a uniform for the American Diplomatic Corps, and danced into my room with it before a Court Levee.

"Say, Kid, how do I look—Admiral, bell-hop—or what?"

As a matter of fact, in neat navy blue and gold, with his iron-grey hair and clean-cut Western jaw, he was one of the handsomest figures I had seen.

"You're a knockout!" I said.

"Thanks."

He leapt into his flamingo-coloured motor-car and drove off to the Winter Palace.

This uniform by the way was soon dropped. When the Revolution came along, and the Kerensky Government was holding its first Provisional Parliament in the Duma, the American Ambassador, so the tale went round Petrograd that night, went out to its opening in a tweed suit. If the Russian Republic wanted Democracy—well, here it was!

But he discovered himself in the Diplomatic Gallery sandwiched in between Sir George Buchanan and the French Ambassador, both of whom were in full rig. Just then lizard-eyed Kerensky, the political chameleon, strode in and the diplomats stood up . . . all but Ambassador Francis.

He half rose, his hands still supporting him on his seat, and whispered hoarsely to Sir George:

"I say, it's just occurred to me that my Government has not yet recognised the Provisional Government. What position do you think I should take?"

The British Ambassador adjusted his monocle, and looked down over his gold breast at the crouching Francis:

"I think—er—the position you are holding at present is eminently suitable."

Around each young blood in the English colony was a nimbus of Russian bloods. The only Russian who could stand up to the English bloods in their sporting or night-life activity was a Finn. This was Jack Hoth: the Beau Brummell of Petrograd. No bird, bear, woman or gambling table was safe from Jack Hoth. Neither was I. I met him my first week in Petrograd, and it was a most disastrous introduction; for I held a Full House, with Aces up, against Jack's four Queens at the New English Club. In that awful hour in a Petrograd winter, when it is not yet dawn, but all the same about time for breakfast, I walked out into the Moskayia with not a rouble in this world. I saw in Jack the most accomplished rake I have met outside fiction. No author or dry historian could, in fact, have imagined him. He was the perfect Buck. No one could have invented the nuances of that character. Nor, without being bathetic about it, could they have conceived of the courtesy of his rakish heart.

He supported half a dozen discarded mistresses in the style to which he had accustomed them. He took them out to dinner occasionally just for old times' sake. And when, after a particularly sardonic trick he played his father, the old man publicly disowned him, the Grand Duke Paul took Jack off to Monte Carlo, whence His Highness wrote to Mr. Hoth:

"*You have only one gentleman in your family, and that is Jack —and yet you have disowned him!*"

Mr. Hoth immediately took Jack back.

The life I lived with Jack Hoth has gone, faded into the sands, like the Manchu dynasty. It will never return. For one reason, Jack is dead.

It did not need more than a week's contact with the great Russian War Office to know that Russia was not losing the war at the Front—it was being lost in Petrograd.

That was the most heartbreaking discovery that one could

make. Not only were poor devils being murdered by the hundreds of thousands in the trenches—while they vainly waited for the shells and guns and munitions which their own War Office was holding up because of graft—but I saw battalions marching off, one with rifles and the next without, to pick up the rifles of the others after they were dead! That was now a common sight, gruesome as it was. The corruption was so ghastly that it soon made us oblivious of everything except our own immediate selves. We led harassed lives.

Cables began to arrive for me from London. When was the big war order coming through? New York wanted to know. Was I sure I was right about the Danes being unreliable? They were wiring London that I was obstructing their business. They were asking London to call me back. Did I know that representatives of such-and-such companies had just left London for Petrograd? Did I not?

Day after day I watched the carrion crows flock in. Self-assured, arrogant, high-pressure men from the huge American motor-car, motor-cycle, tyre, steel, explosive and railway car firms. It gave me a certain amount of grim pleasure to listen to their talk in the hotel at nights. "Yes, sure. Expect I'll stay here a few weeks, then Paris. Got another deal warming up there." Ha!—a few weeks—for Russia . . . !

I had, for the fun of it, founded an order in Petrograd called "The Knights of the Double Cross." We had the emblem of an order, a double-cross, made up by a jeweller on the Nevsky. It was really an eating club, where once every fortnight we ate American food. Canned corn and things like that. Its first by-law was that the moment any one of us received a war contract from the Russian Government he would have to leave the Knights of the Double Cross. Sawyer, of the Tacoma Tin & Spelter Co., was our first President. He was President for two years.

Day after day I got up just before lunch-time, put on a formal morning-suit, and, with soft felt hat, paid my routine call at the Technical Department. This was merely going through the motions, however. The details and the formal presentation of my offer to the War Department had already been got through with.

I had given Frumkin my lowest price. He had added on to that ten per cent for this person, five per cent for that official, two per cent, of course, for the Minister of War. Then, with a price nearly double the one I would have been glad to make, I went to the Technical Department and formally presented my bid.

"There's nothing to do now," old Frumkin assured me—"but wait."

We even went through the motions of an artillery test on some machine-guns I had mounted on side-cars. We took them out on the artillery range and our machine-gun expert mowed off a row of picket fence. A very impressive performance, watched by a staff of generals, one of whom (evidently bought by our competitor) noticed the band around the peep-sight:

"Doesn't that," he asked in a beardy voice, "interfere with the firing of the gun?"

"On the contrary," I told the interpreter to assure the general, "it helps it."

Then as our expert, pulling back a lever, dropped a small pin from the Colt-Browning, that general pounced down.

"Ah-ha! Ah-ha! Look at that! Imagine losing that in an engagement. Why, the gun is useless!"

A distressing accident. But when I mentioned it to Frumkin the next day at luncheon in the Astoria, he merely frowned and bit through a chicken leg-bone with his bare teeth:

"*Nitchevo!* It doesn't matter as far as the gun is concerned. But it looks as if Visick (the other big Jewish middleman) will make it hard for us."

These two terrific Jews between them practically divided all the spoils of the War Office contracts. One was backed by one huge New York banking group. The other by another group. Both of these groups had their big export representatives in Petrograd. I suggested to Frumkin:

"Why don't you and Visick get together? If you pooled your interests, nothing in God's green earth could stand out against you. You could just sit at the gate and collect toll from everyone."

He went green.

"My God! Don't say things like that!"

But the idea incubated in his mind. I told him Visick had been playing with me, made me a camouflaged suggestion through another American that I should switch over to his side. I had seen and talked with Visick. He was very clever. I told Frumkin I could be an intermediary for him. I could feel Visick out. If Visick was willing would Frumkin be willing to meet him secretly in my room. I, of course, would not be there. If anyone saw them going in the door the most or worst they could think was that it was just a coincidence that they both happened to have called on me at the same time. Frumkin said all right.

So—for one long hour—I sat down in the tea-room of the Hotel Astoria, knowing that I might be the instrument of the most sensational development that could have taken place in connection with Russian war supplies. If it came off, I was sitting pretty, because either Visick or Frumkin would get my order for me. At any rate Visick would no longer stand in our way. I felt as if I held a time fuse in my hand as I looked round at the competing munition merchants in that scented tea-room, all of them battling against each other, not one of them knowing what was going on upstairs.

But then I saw Frumkin come down. He rushed from the elevator out into the street. A few minutes afterward Visick sauntered in. He sat down at a table directly opposite me and ordered tea and a huge slab of strawberry tart. He looked through me as if I had been the Invisible Man.

"Madness!" Frumkin was sweating when I drove over to his office. "Crazy as hell! That guy was simply laying for me. Thought I was going to sell out!"

Months dragged. The wires from London began to get insolent. Was I, or was I not, going to get that war order?—and please say when. Letters came quarrelling with my expense accounts. My requests for further drafts were not answered for days. Then the £100 drafts ceased altogether. I had taken over another American's bills for him, loaned him part of his train-fare to get back to London. He returned it eventually, but for several weeks I was so broke that I could not tip a waiter and ate meals in my own room. I wired London:

"CABLE SALARY WILL REMAIN PETROGRAD OWN EXPENSE."

And every day, either at luncheon in a dingy little Co-operative restaurant they frequented on the Nevsky, or at some prearranged rendezvous, I met those Danes. Their faces were getting haggard by now. Their worried eyes gave the lie to the tongues that kept assuring me:

"Any day, any day now, we will get the order. It will be much bigger than you expect."

Until one day I said to them:

"I've got it."

Chapter 19

GRAFT

PEKING IS MYSTIFIED BY RUSSIAN BURIALS

Seven bodies, four of them said to be members of the Russian Imperial family, arrived at Peking from Harbin yesterday and were buried in the Russian cemetery, outside the city wall. The whole proceeding was surrounded with the greatest secrecy, even the Russian Legation receiving scant information of the circumstances.

The bodies were declared to be those of the Grand Duke Serge Michaelovitch, the Countess . . . It is alleged that they were killed and their bodies were thrown in a coal-mine near Perm. . . .

THAT is a newspaper clipping. Its date is April 17, 1920. For some reason I have kept it. Not that I should be likely to forget!

It is a long way from Petrograd to the walls of old Peking, and as I look at this yellowed clipping it seems even further back into the opaque past; those white nights in the summer of 1915, when I sat and talked with his Imperial Highness in his little red-plaster palace on the Millionayia (Millionaire Street) in Tsarist Petrograd. He was then head of the Artillery Department.

It was the time when the buying of nearly all war supplies was being done through that infamous body known as the Technical Department, and all Russia was watching the struggles of the other component parts of the great War Office in their fight with this department to do their buying independently.

But two men at the head of the Technical Department, a certain Baron and Colonel, were holding all the rest of Russia at bay. I often used to see them lunching at the Astoria, a flamboyant pair; one very black and bearded, the other bald with a blonde Don Quixote moustache—although there was not much of Don Quixote about that pompous pair. One day, when we happened to have a table near them, Frumkin said he would be willing to pay a couple of hundred thousand roubles to move our chairs where we could hear what they were saying.

"It would be worth it," he said. "Those two guys are the works."

In his effort to get past the blockade established by these two men the Grand Duke Serge had hit upon the brilliant, though simple, solution of sending a secret mission to the United States to place orders without the assistance of the Technical Department. He had placed an Englishman whom I knew at the head of it. This Englishman had been a habitué of Russia since he was at Oxford and was a personal friend of most of the noble families. He came into my room one night and told me that if I wanted to cut out all the Petrograd middlemen, here was my chance. I could, he assured me, do business with the Grand Duke without "palm oil." Frumkin had been infuriating me by persistently refusing to do the numerous things he had promised, so I jumped at the chance.

The Englishman made the interview. Ten o'clock one evening saw us sauntering across the square in front of the Winter Palace, and, as we passed a door guarded by two soldiers on the Millionayia Oulitsa, the Englishman suddenly took my arm and almost pushed me into it.

A pale secretary in civilian black led us up a great staircase beneath the heads of countless antelope, water buffalo and African game.

"His Highness," said the Englishman impressively, "is a shot—a great shot!"

"Yes," I couldn't help chuckling—"but look what he's bagged in the United States."

At the top of that regal stairway, perched on the ultimate banister was a Negro boy. Bare-legged, grinning, his cap cocked over one ear, he gave me a grin such as I hadn't seen since I was sailing in Virginia. He was a cigar-store "nigger-boy"—made of plaster of Paris.

That gave me a jolt to begin with. There must be, I thought, a certain unworldliness about this Grand Duke!

Serge had that Borzoi grace that seems to have blessed all the Grand Dukes. In officer's uniform, he was an exceedingly tall, gaunt, less virile edition of the Grand Duke Nicholas, with a patriarchal courtesy in his manner. He seemed too kindly, too virtuous to triumph against the vice surrounding him.

He resumed his seat behind an enormous flat-topped desk littered with sheaves of official documents and a telephone with a battery of ivory-tipped exchange keys. The whole gave an appearance of business-like energy, which the atmosphere of the room and its royal occupant seemed to dissipate at every turn. It is difficult to convey the feeling of futility in connection with that room. Before I had even broached the subject of my visit I had already acquired the feeling that it was hopeless.

The Englishman was asking: "And ammunition—shells—Your Highness?"

"Oh, we have everything going splendidly now!" His Highness sketched listlessly on a pad of yellow notepaper.

I gasped. Surely, he could not mean that! Only two days before the correspondent of the London *Times*, the American, Major Washburn, had just returned from the Polish front, where he said the wretched Russians had only a few shells per gun. After firing them, they had taken their pieces far into the rear to prevent them from falling too easily into the hands of the Germans on their inevitable advance.

I myself had seen regiments marching off to the front, one with and one without rifles—the latter to pick up the rifles of the dead—swinging along a few days back with their heavy tramp-tramp and deep Russian marching chant directly under the window of this Grand Duke on the Millionayia Oulitsa.

At that moment the Hotel Astoria was full of dismayed and astounded American munition experts who were kicking their heels and ruining their morals in gloomy idleness while the venal Technical Department played about and delayed over the placing of the desperately-needed orders for shells, guns, and rifles. And every foreign observer returning from the front had remarked how wonderful it was to see the Russians holding out with hardly any ammunition at all.

"They'll have to fight with pointed sticks next!" one disgusted Military Attaché had told me—as the Russians did eventually have to do in that disastrous retreat from the Carpaths.

Was it possible that the Grand Duke, head of the Artillery Department, was not aware of all this? Was "the Tsar such a long way off," as the peasants used to lament!

"And Archangel?" persisted the Englishman. "Things are said to be in a terrible mess up there!"

This port was literally sinking under war supplies that were being dumped in. The narrow-gauge railway to Vologda could not possibly carry them away. Bribery was necessary to get railway space. Russia's only other open seaport was Vladivostok on the Pacific.

"Really?" His Highness pursued his sketching.

"I know one man here in Petrograd who kills more Russians than any thousand Germans *can* do—every day!" said the Englishman very quietly.

"Who's that?" The Grand Duke woke up. He stared at the Englishman with an expression of annoyance, then smiled. "Who could that be?"

"He is Captain X, of the *Auftomobilnie Narota.*"

Point blank, to my delight, the Englishman had boldly named a notorious grafting official.

But the Grand Duke did not rise. He seemed, if possible, a little more quiet, more solemn, more preoccupied about things; then he pushed his sketch away from him, and leaned forward:

"Can you prove that?"

"I can," said the Englishman. "I can bring a man in this room, an American—if you can assure him of protection from the Technical Department—who is regularly paying so much a machine to have his cars moved down from Archangel. If he doesn't pay Captain X, he does not get them down. These cars are for the Artillery Department."

Then I spoke up:

"Yes," I said. "I've been paying him. This is how we do it."

I then told him what had happened to a shipment of mine that I had managed to get sent into Archangel on the icebreaker *Canada,* the first ship in that year. It was a terrific leg up for me to get those machines in before anyone else. But they might as well have never left New York. I could not get them down from Archangel. Captain X declared he could not get them down in the name of a private person as every square inch of freight space on the narrow-gauge Archangel-Vologda road was already booked months ahead for Government stuff. He could, however, he suggested, "buy" them from me—then they would be "Government" ostensibly for his department and when they got to Petrograd I could "buy" them back. The difference between these two prices would cover "incidentals and things like that."

His Highness made a gesture of helplessness that was tantamount to indifference.

His apathy was obviously not from lack of interest, or disbelief, or any form of sympathy with the corrupt Russians we were trying to uproot. It was much more fundamental than that —it was just Serge himself. The Grand Duke, like most of the higher Russian nobility, was absolutely honest and sincere in his wish to put down this Frankenstein monster, bribery, and save Russia. But now, at the eleventh hour, they were realising their helplessness and the fact that in a crisis most of them were mere figureheads.

I then went on to explain how the first offers of my company to the Russian Government had been through some Danes, and that between our price to them and their price to the Russians there were *nine* men, most of them Russian officials, all getting their whack. The result was that the price to the Russian Government, which lay over in the Technical Department, was so absolutely ridiculous that I had broken with the Danes and forced them to leave Russia.

Even so, I said—the price had been inflated again. I did not say through whom, but I went on to show him how the Technical Department had again raised my price through Frumkin, and how they were stalling us along now in an effort to make us give more. I explained that there was no such thing as direct business with that abysmal Technical Department, as the way was blocked by Jewish intermediaries who were working hand in glove with the members of the department. I went further and as delicately as I could suggested that even above the Technical Department, in much higher quarters, there was "someone" who took a commission on every order that went through. He must have known I was alluding to Sukhomlinoff, the War Minister, who was afterwards exposed.

I forgot, in my eagerness, that he was a Grand Duke and gave him a picture of the nightly talks in the Hotel Astoria between the American businessmen; how we spent our time guessing who was the right man to bribe and how to go about it. That we no longer hoped for or feared tests on our machines. We knew they were fakes, mere gallery play.

I saw the Englishman making faces at me to stop. But I had gone too far.

"If Russia loses this war, Your Highness—it won't be at the Front. It will be right here in Petrograd."

Serge Michaelovitch listened to my youthful outburst and then sighed:

"I know it, I know it," he said, "and we are trying to put an end to it. That is why I am sending a secret mission to buy things in America"—he nodded toward the young Englishman—"someone whom I know we can trust. We are trying to deal directly with the Americans," and then added as a pessimistic afterthought —"if we can."

"You can with my company," I assured him, and we then arranged, at his request, that I forward my proposals to him direct in quadruplicate. One copy was to be addressed to him. The other three, for some reason, were to be left blank. "I will personally care for them and see that—er—they reach the proper person."

To this day I am still wondering who that proper person could have been.

The Grand Duke made us listen to Prince Obolensky's campaign of graft-exposure and the high hopes all the rest of the nobles had set on his efforts. I thought of these nobles trying in a quixotic fashion to stamp out the basis upon which all business had been conducted in Russia since the Japanese War. And then I thought of the smooth, clever middlemen in the Astoria, of old Frumkin & Co. If the battle were to go to the strong, I decided, the nobles were already beaten.

The Romanoffs were paying with their lifeblood for the fact

that they had wanted only two classes in Russia—the nobility and the peasant—and that business was below them. They had let the Germans and the Jews handle such things in Russia. They had made the Jews "live under the floor" and develop an abnormal brain power merely to keep alive. And now the Jews were running away with things.

I had met Obolensky, a sizable, thick-ankled, thick-wristed young man, who wore his blonde hair *en brosse*, and the insignia of the Russian Hospital Corps on his military tunic. Honest as the day is long—and too obvious. Serious—too serious. "Even virtue needs guile to triumph over evil in this world." Prince Obolensky, like most "reformers," lacked the ordinary savvy that would have made him aware of the tricks of the people he was trying to trap. The thought of these patriotic nobles ousting people like Frumkin made me think of a herd of elephants trying to run down some foxes.

The Englishman evidently thought it was time to get on more pleasant topics and informed the Grand Duke that I had done some flying in Sebastopol with the Russian naval aviators. The Grand Duke immediately became a different man. He became interested, the usual charming Russian conversationalist.

"How delightful! To fly over the Black Sea. Don't you think our aviators are splendid?"

I most certainly did. To anyone who had seen them, the Russian soldiers at the front were as brave and loyal as any in the World War. Perhaps they were even more courageous than most soldiers because of their necessity of having to fight without arms.

Serge, greatly pleased at this eulogy of mine, crossed his slender legs and offered us another cigarette. He wanted to know where I had been in the Crimea, and what places did I like best. Had I been to Balaclava? Yes, I had; I had been in jail there:

"As a spy," I added.

He laughed engagingly. "We always seem to arrest the wrong men."

He made me relate my experience with the Crimean Okhrana, the Tsar's secret Third Arm. When we were going, he walked with us to as far as the grinning "nigger-boy" and shook my hand: "Come again," he said, still smiling, "and tell me more about my beloved Crimea. I love Southern Russia—so warm and beautiful!"

He sighed.

"But about those proposals, Your Highness—shall I send them to you at once?"

"Proposals . . . ? Oh, yes! Of course. You must send them to me. By all means."

He turned back into his room with the manner of a man distinctly annoyed that such an unpleasant topic had been introduced at the last minute.

The pale-faced secretary materialised, yawning, out of the darkness, and officially convoyed us down that magnificent stairway. At the door the Englishman drew him aside and held him in secret conversation for a few minutes. I heard the secretary say to the Englishman:

"But, of course, Your Excellency!"

I saw the Englishman reach in his pocket and heard the crinkle of crisp bank-notes. The secretary, all smiles now, bowed us out and said to the Englishman:

"Good night, Your Excellency!"

"So," I said to the Englishman, when we were out in the street. "So that's the way you put down Russian graft! By bribing the Duke's secretary!"

He grinned. "No, it's not that, but I want an appointment with the Grand Duke at four o'clock tomorrow, and Vassilie, there, is the man who fixes his master's time-table. A ten-rouble note dropped into the hand of Vassilie from time to time would not be a bad way for you to start. You will get your appointments with Serge if you do. Don't be so damned puritanical about things!"

He looked over towards the Summer Gardens, behind whose statued walks lay the buildings that housed the infamous Technical Department.

"As for graft—you'll never do away with it here! It's indigenous to the soil!"

My first fear of the futility of the Grand Duke's was borne out. After a few unfruitful interviews with Serge I was expecting a more or less final one, when a note brought by hand from Vassilie informed me that his master had been ordered to the Front. One day my Russian typist informed me that Serge Michaelovitch had never left Petrograd. He had been there all the time. The little typist seemed to have something bothering him, but he wouldn't say what it was. So I told him to take a note across to Vassilie at once. In it, I asked urgently for an immediate appointment with the Grand Duke.

The typist came back shaking his head:

"It's no use," he said. "His Highness, the Grand Duke Serge Michaelovitch, is no longer head of the Artillery Department. He has been—what you call—bust! It is Lord Kitchener that did it. He tell the Tsar Serge Michaelovitch ought to take a long rest from his work. He leaves for the country tonight!"

"Where is he going?"

"To the Crimea—Sebastopol," said Vassilie. "It is so beautiful there!"

Disaster for the Grand Duke, in this case, was also disaster for me—or was it?

I raced downstairs without even waiting for the lift to come up, jumped into the nearest *droshky* without even attempting to bargain with the *isvostchik*, who thought he had a fresh foreign fool for a fare, and drove at full speed to the Artillery head staff, where General Petroffsky, whom I knew, would now be head in a few days.

He sent for me to come in at once. I gave him my copy of the quadruplicate proposal I had given the Grand Duke. I gave him a *précis* of my talks with Serge Michaelovitch; then I made my final, frantic plea:

"It seems monstrous!" I said. "Here we are, sir, sitting so close to each other across the table that we could touch hands. Here is an offer, God knows, something like thirty or forty per cent lower than the one that lies now over in the Technical Department. I *know* how desperately you need this stuff—Serge Michaelovitch admitted that. Here it is: We have the cars, we have shipping space in boats leaving New York and Canada. Why, *why* can't you act!"

He shrugged his shoulders, pinched the paper tube of his cigarette, shrugged his gold epaulets again:

"Can't!" he snapped shortly. "Impossible!"

"But why not!"

He gave me a ghostly smile: "The Technical Department. . . ."

I stood up. "It's all right," I said. "I understand."

I left him sitting there, staring at his desk—a general painted on canvas.

Chapter 20

THE COSSACK GIRL

DURING our struggles with the venal Technical Department Frumkin and I went to Moscow.

We wanted to see if we couldn't open up a new lead with the Zemska Soujouse, that Union of Landowners which, under the incorruptible leadership of old Prince Lvov, was one of the finest institutions in Russia. We had learned that it also was trying to break the grip of the Technical Department, and was frantically trying to buy war supplies on an honest straightforward basis. It would have saved the lives of hundreds of thousands of Russians if it had been allowed to do so from the first. Getting war contracts on a straight business basis was a new idea for Frumkin. But as a last resort he thought he would try it.

As practically all of my business in Russia now consisted of watching Papa Frumkin—to see that he did not double cross me —I went along with him.

I was fed up with the night life of Petrograd. I would never have believed it if anyone had told me so; but even the sight of a nude girl at the piano was beginning to pall. We had nothing to do in Petrograd but go in for one long round of all-night parties, and we were hardly recovering from one party before we were dashing off to the Islands to have another one. Offsetting all this were the nights we went to the Ballet, and I am glad to think that I saw nearly all of them. It is one of the fine things I got out of Petrograd, perhaps the only one. But I saw the Imperial Ballet in all its glory, with the Grand Dukes sitting in their boxes, and such dancers as Gert, Geltzer and the magnificent Karsavina dancing to them. For the ballerinas danced *to* the Court. That was what made the old Ballet. It was not just the dancers. It was the splendour of the setting. Without the Grand Dukes the Ballet was something else. I saw it after the Kerensky Revolution, and it had already lost its lustre. There were the same dancers. It was of course better, but not so much better, than watching Pavlova in New York. And years later I saw Semenova dancing in both Moscow and Leningrad. Then I knew finally that the old Russian Ballet had died with the Romanoffs.

Also, in Russia, I read and re-read all the Russians. Dostoevsky and Gogol took on an entirely different meaning in their own country. Particularly Dostoevsky, who no longer seemed mad. After watching those green prison trains, with their cross-barred windows, waiting for the human freight to Siberia, I understood "The House of the Dead." I went down into the dungeons of Peter and Paul, and saw the one which once held Vera Figner, and the bare cell where a young girl revolutionary had set her bed on fire, having no other way to kill herself. It was a tremendous delight to re-read Russian history, and go over to the Cathedral of St. Basil in Moscow, and see the same steps that were ascended by Boris Gudonoff.

Spring was coming and I wanted some fresh air. I wanted to see the country towns of Tchkov. I wanted to take off my shoes and eat cucumbers. But Frumkin merely transferred me from the Hotel Astoria in Petrograd to the Hotel Metropole in Moscow.

It was in this mood, having an innocent cup of tea in the new grill they had installed in the Hotel Metropole, that I first saw Shura Alexandra Georgievna Tomachova.

She was a Cossack girl.

Our eyes met behind the Tartar bar attendant's shaven head. They met in the looking glass. We were both perched on stools and I sat there and studied her. About seventeen or eighteen, I thought. She was the perfect type of rather heavy set Russian. A high-cheek-boned face, with the usual pointed chin and firm neck. But on top of this beautiful Junoesque head sat the most awful contraption of a red Gainsborough hat. Where she had got it from I could not imagine. I think it was trying to find that out that first made me smile at her. She answered with a little *gauche* shrug of her head. And then she blushed.

Everything was spoilt at that moment by an American, a General in the Russian medical corps, who came and sat down beside me and began to make eyes at the girl.

"Listen, Farson," he said. "Let me have that. I've got to go down to the Front tonight; you can get plenty more." And he began making what he thought were seductive facial contortions at Shura in the mirror.

After a while she got down from her stool and went out.

"Hell!" said the General. "I never have any luck. That was a nice bit of goods, too."

Next day Shura Alexandra Georgievna Tomachova was sitting on her same stool. And I was sitting on mine. We went through the same performance, our eyes meeting behind the Tartar's head. This time she nodded to me imperiously. And I followed her.

We went outside and walked along the walls of the Chinese city. She was seventeen, she told me, and had just run away from her home at Ekaterinodar in the Caucasus. Compared to the professional cocottes I had been consorting with in Petrograd, she was as fresh as the fifth day of creation. She fascinated me. We entered the Red Square and walked slowly below the red walls of the Kremlin. Its piles of golden cupolas were blazing in the sun. Its black Romanoff eagles were outstretched against the sky. And there was not a cloud in that blue sky. Shura sighed contentedly:

"Good," she said, "good, good!"

Our conversation was limited as far as words were concerned.

Then behind the walls of the Chinese city somewhere we sat down to lunch. She hummed as we ate it and seemed completely happy, which made me feel anxious to keep her so. We wandered around the Kremlin all the afternoon. Bit by bit, I pieced out the gruesome truth that she was just beginning to live the life of a Russian tart. She did not say as much, but her gaucheness said that, and more of it, for her. She was charming. We walked along the frozen river. It was a most innocent excursion. Then we came back to the hotel. What might have happened then I do not know, for I found a very excited Frumkin jumping up and down as he waited for me.

"Hurry! Hurry!" he said, announcing that he himself had actually paid our bill. "We got to go to Petrograd on the eight o'clock train tonight."

Someone, it seemed, had been double-crossing him again.

He was rude to Shura. And to make it up, I stood by our *droshky* and had a few good-bye words with her. She waved as we drove off and then called something after me.

"Huh!" growled Frumkin. "She's just called you *Roidninki*—that's peasant for sweetheart—where you been all the day?"

"Some guy," said Frumkin in the train, "I tink it's that damn Visick—some guy's been making it damn tough for me. I tink you and I got to go to Archangel. I thought I got everything fixed up there, but today I get this."

He handed me a long telegram. It was in Russian.

Translated and decoded by wily Papa Frumkin, it was to inform him that the man he had "fixed" in Archangel had been dismissed from there. This was catastrophe. For, after getting an order from the War Department, the next great task of course was to get shipping space from New York, and finally to get it down on the overworked little single track line from choking Archangel. There was almost as much bribery in that Arctic seaport as there was in Petrograd.

"Me," said Frumkin. "We gotta go to Archangel!"

The day after I got back to Petrograd Louis, the manager of the Astoria, telephoned me to come down to the office for a minute.

"I asked you to come down," he apologised, "because I want you to see for yourself. There is someone to see you."

It was Shura.

There she stood, Shura Alexandra Georgievna Tomachova, in a pile of three-ply wood boxes—and the Gainsborough hat!

"*Roidninki!*"

"Good God!" I said to Louis.

"Yes, Mr. Farson—shall I send up her bags?"

Well—

"Certainly," I said.

Then I walked Shura as fast as I could across the foyer and into the elevator. I felt that if I once got her as far as my room I could handle this affair. I simply couldn't argue with her down in the lobby, not in that hat. But up in my room I would have time enough to convince her that such things simply were not done.

It was hopeless. Perhaps my Russian was too weak. All I know is that Shura took off her hat; and, relieved as I was to see that, by that gesture alone Shura signified that she had come to stay.

Nothing could shift her. I gave it up. Why try, anyway. In seven or eight days Frumkin and I were going up to Archangel. In that frozen seaport on the White Sea I could have my sack-cloth and ashes. I stepped on Shura's outrageous hat by mistake and got her another one. I had to go to the War Department that morning so I took her with me. I left her sitting on a bench in the park outside the Technical Department, her head glinting in the sun. Then we bought a hat and went to Kontant's for lunch.

"Well," said my hostess on Millionaire Street at dinner the next night. "How's your little Cossack girl? I hear she's not bad to look at!"

This was said *sotto voce* so that the rest of the table might not hear. Then the next question:

"Where is she now?"

"God knows," I whispered. "I left her with Jack Hoth."

"*Jack Hoth!*"

My Scotch hostess forgot herself. Everyone heard her. An Englishman, son of a great "timber" family, called down. "What's that Jack Hoth's been doing?"

"But really," she said, after the talk had gone off in another direction. "You must be mad! Jack Hoth of all people—why, I'll bet you she's in bed with him now!"

"Not the faintest chance of it," I said, looking down at my soup. "I was brilliant. First, I did not break my engagement with you. Next, I immediately sent for Jack Hoth and introduced him to Shura. I placed her in his charge. He was wild with me. He knew that after that he would have to leave her alone. He was the one person I was most afraid of—so I disposed of him this way at once."

"You *are* a baby!"

That shook me a bit, but I stuck it out. Jack had sent his car

for her, with his English chauffeur; and when I came back that
night I found our room filled with roses. From Jack Hoth—who
was sitting there.

"We're going out to the Villa Rodé," he said. "The car's waiting downstairs."

We drove out through the snow, we ate crayfish and listened
to the gypsies; Shura sang something about watching her heart
die down as the camp-fire died on the steppe. . . .

"Ah, *Roidninki! Roidninki! Roidninki! . . .*" she sighed as
Jack's wretched English chauffeur drove us back. "How lonely
I am!"

Another afternoon when I came home I found a friend of mine
nursing a sore jaw, which made me wonder if he was such a
friend. He made no bones about it; he said he had got it trying
to kiss Shura.

"Say—she's a Tartar!"

"No, she's not. She's a Cossack from Ekaterinodar. It's a place
down in the Caucasus. But you know what Cossacks are. Ever
read *Taras Bulba?*"

I was relieved when Frumkin told me he had booked our reservations for Archangel. Shura was so upset over this sudden ter-
mination of things that she packed her three-ply wooden boxes
and left the hotel while I was over in Frumkin's office that afternoon. She did not stop to say good-bye to me.

"Forget it," Frumkin said, as we drove to the station; "they're
all like that. Bet you if you went out to the Villa Rodé tonight
you'd see her sitting there with Jack Hoth."

I looked at him. Suddenly his fat, greedy face had become
intensely distasteful to me. He was a coarse man. And Jack Hoth,
now that I reflected upon it, was just a worn-out *roué*. I wondered what Archangel would be like.

There was always something dramatic about the departure of
a railway train in Tsarist Russia. The clank of swords in the station, the comic seriousness of business men and minor officials
impatiently hugging their inevitable portfolios—but all very important to their patient wives, the great galumping bustle of the
porters, the mêlée of *isvostchiks* whooping and yelling, cursing,

trying to drive their stallions into the most favourable place to catch the outcoming traffic. And in a few minutes you knew that this would all be behind you, and your great lumbering train would be moving through deep, dark forests of frozen pines.

Frumkin had a Negro secretary, an American boy named Nelson. He had gone on ahead to meet us at the train. When we found him, a very frightened Nelson explained that he could not get us tickets in the same sleeping car. That annoyed Frumkin, because he knew that when we travelled together in the same compartment, I would take the upper bunk and let him have the lower one. A stranger might not be so accommodating. I was also in a bad mood, hating everybody.

But when the porter pulled back the door of my carriage I was relieved to see that I had the lower bunk. It was a half carriage, with only two bunks in it, and the other man had turned in already. So I pulled up the blind and watched night fall on the passing forest. It was a melancholy sight, the ragged tips of those pines against the raw sky. I leaned up to pull down the flaps over the Pintsch light.

"Shura!"

"*Roidninki!*"

There she was. I yelled with delight. I dashed out to get the *provodnik* to make us tea at once. In the aisle, standing just outside my door, was old Frumkin.

"Vell!" he said. "Which bunk did you get?"

"You old rascal!"

"It wasn't me—it wasn't Papa this time! That guy Jack Hoth did this dirty trick on you. Now ain't you sorry—what you was thinking when I said you'd see him and Shura if you went out to the Villa Rodé tonight? Ain't you *ashamed* of yourself for thinking such things!"

Chapter 21

SHURA AND ARCHANGEL

In the spring of 1915, Archangel lay smothered under layers of lead ingots, steel bars, rusting motor-cars, bales of soggy cotton and broken crates of machinery of every description. Over this scrambled a shrieking but dawdling and incredibly ineffective assortment of Big Russians, Little Russians, White Russians, Poles, Letts, Finns, Esthonians, Ukrainians, Mamalukes, Tartars, Kirjez, Samoyede half-Eskimos—and one silent little Scotchman.

A handful of desperate officials, having given it up, stood around this Tower of Babel on the sinking docks and talked women and politics. No wonder they drank themselves dizzy at nights!

Because of Germany's domination in the Baltic, Archangel, which lies almost within the Arctic Circle, had become Russia's only open mouth to the Atlantic. Into it was pouring this avalanche of war material which was meant to feed the "steam-roller!" of the Tsars, Archangel was choking, its mouth was glutted. The narrow gauge, single-tracked railway to Vologda, where it joins the abnormal super-gauge road to Petrograd, was literally sinking into its own road bed. It could not carry off this deluge of supplies that the ships of the world were dumping into Archangel. As a consequence Russia lay like a starving giant, unable to get enough to feed even a pigmy.

An example of the frantic effort to get things down from Archangel was the case of some vitally needed machinery for the big Tregolnick Rubber Works, which was brought down on reindeer sleds, driven by Samoyede, all the way across the Arctic wastes to Petrograd.

Shura and I, watching for the first signs of spring stirring the *tundra* into life, frequently saw bands of women working on the Vologda line, carrying dirt and ballast in their aprons to the railway workers. I don't think Frumkin looked out of the window once all the way from Petrograd. He sat there for two days, drinking tea continuously, scheming, scheming, scheming; furious at his enforced inability to put all his lovely new ideas into action. The naval officer, from the Admiralty, who made the fourth in our present compartment, lay on his back in the upper bunk and sang French *café chantant* ditties from the time he got up to clean his magnificent teeth until he stirred again to clean them at night. We passed his food up to him between times.

Shura and he would have sung all night long if we had let them. The naval captain had been posted to that desolate port on the White Sea more or less for his sins, and he was very unhappy about it. But we four were, as he said:

"*Sehr gemütlich!*"

Beyond Vologda we had the feeling of climbing up on the roof of the world. Everything was flat up here. There were no deep, dark pine forests here to hold the winter snow. Even the lovely green translucent birch woods had dropped behind. Up here it was just marsh, the great Arctic *tundra*, basking in the warm spring sun. We trundled along all day through a low green swamp growth veined with streams of clear slowly flowing water. At sidings where we waited for the groaning trucks of war supplies to pass, there were a few raw log railway stations and a cluster of huts, where, it seemed, half the Russian army was dancing to the inevitable accordion player. On these patches of civilisation there were bare-legged girls who did a war-profiteer business selling us cooked chickens and hard-boiled eggs. And standing utterly alone on the top of the world was an occasional monastery, its white walls and blue and gold piles of onion domes glinting against a cloudless blue sky. Then the painted domes of the monastery would drop behind us over the flat sky-line.

Petrograd seemed so far behind that I forgot my troubles, and the fact that even before we left I had begun to suspect Papa Frumkin of double-crossing me. In this clear scene I began to see him in the right perspective. This was not his setting. He could, at times, be quite a commanding, even sinister figure in the fetid Hotel Astoria. Scented bedrooms and secret intrigue were his *milieu*. But perched uncomfortably in this hard little train on the open *tundra* he, at times, looked a pitiful object, in spite of his millions.

He was a Russian Jew, born within the pale. He guided his life by only one motto: *"God loves the Rich and the Rich love God!"* His waking hours were spent trying to dig himself well within this coterie of God's elect. And he knew how to do it! Wherever Frumkin went he carried with him the germs of corruption. He was like a rat, a large, white bubonic rat, gnawing his way through the Russian structure of officialdom, infecting everybody. He could place a bribe with a shrewdness that would make the American variety of Washington-lobbyist look like a tyro. Moral decay came in his wake; and it was parasites such as he which eventually brought the official structure crashing down.

Warmed by the spring sun, he too stirred to life and outlined his Archangel "idea." It was a hot one!

A recent ukase from Petrograd had announced that the Russian government intended in the future to commandeer all unauthorised shipments to individuals and pay for them at the bare invoice price. Frumkin had been turning this over in his mind in the train. That was why he had never bothered to look out of the window. Then came the "idea":

"Lookit! What could be easier? Now all I've got to do is send myself large shipments from New York—see? And I bill myself, don't I? You got it!—in the invoice price to myself shall be my profit. What's wrong with that?"

I said I thought the military commanders at the port would get on to such an open game. Even if they wanted to they would not dare "commandeer" goods at such fancy prices.

Frumkin laughed and waved my doubts away.

"Fancy! Fancy prices!—go on! Why should they find my prices fancy—they'll get their bit. So will the guys in Petrograd. First thing I must do in Archangel is have some conversations."

He fascinated Shura with his fat air of arrogance, and won her admiration by the way he ate the cold chickens we bought at the little log railway stations. There was, of course, no *wagon-lit* or dining-car on the Vologda-Archangel line. Frumkin was not hampered by the lack of such things as forks and knives. He would bite right through a chicken leg, bones and all. When he saw that it impressed Shura he tried to swallow the bones.

We got in the Naval tug and went across the Dvina to Archangel. There was one hotel, the "Gasteenitza Bar." It had nine rooms, which was shown by a slate attached to its wall on which the numbers of the rooms and the names of their occupants were written. These rooms, needless to say, were all full. Frumkin, however, was on dry land again. After his first "conversation" two of these rooms suddenly became empty, two names were erased from the slate; the name of Frumkin was written after the best room—Shura and I took the other.

I had never house-kept before. I had nothing to do. So I watched Shura do it. She was a Cossack, and had Cossack, but very effective, ideas of cleanliness such as shaving oneself all over, except the head where girls are concerned, in order to leave no hiding-places for insects. After one look at our room she gave a small yelp like a puppy and dashed down into the hotel to find a maid, or its equivalent. When I removed myself I saw her standing in the middle of the room with every movable object being pulled out from its place. When I came back the room reeked with paraffin. I felt that I smelt like a lampwick. But it did not save me.

"Da!" said Shura. "I told you so!"

It was my first experience of this form of animal life, and it was the proprietor's first experience of anyone who made such an insane fuss about it. With some most violent and descriptive sign-language I made plain my affliction and what I was going to do if he didn't sanitate the toilet in that hotel. As a result we all went about smelling like lampwicks.

When the ice broke, that spring of 1915, the little port of Archangel was one of the most spectacular in the world. Masts, funnels and slanting spars formed a fantastic silhouette against the midnight sunsets. All of these ships had run the gauntlet of the German submarines that hung about the frozen mouth of the

White Sea. At first they could only get into Archangel through a broken path of mush ice cracked by heavy ice-breakers.

The docks were a spatter of shifting colours from the head-dresses of the various nationalities working among the jumbled piles of the cargo. The streets were a galaxy of practically every uniform in the world—except German. But by far the weirdest of these was one worn by the little Scot, Dodd.

He had been commissioned hurriedly in Petrograd by the British and placed in full charge of getting out these vastly important shipments of flax for British and Allied aeroplanes. A man with an amazing grasp of detail and unashamed effrontery, he knew where every barge was in the whole north of Russia. He knew every official of the port of Archangel—and his weakness. Dodd went about promising V.C.'s and other decorations to the vain ones; to others he presented somewhat different things. Threats, occasionally.

The chief difficulty about getting anything either in or out of Archangel, after the ice problem was solved, was to get docking space to load or unload. Ships lay anchored in the Dvina for weeks at a time, ships whose charter was worth £1,000's every day. But ships did not lie at anchor long when Dodd had a cargo for them.

One day he went to the captain of a Russian ship which had just got her lines out and was preparing to unload.

"Sorry, Captain," said Dodd, "but you'll have to move out in the stream."

The Russian captain looked at the little man before him. Dodd was about five feet four or five inches. He had got hold of a pair of regulation Army breeks, a tailor in Petrograd had made him a copy of a British tunic from the British Military Attaché's; but above these Dodd wore an Italian blue military cloak, buttoned at the throat with a silver lion clasp, on his clever little head was a cocky French *beret*, and from his waist trailed a British sabre, obsolete pattern, in an imposing pigskin scabbard. Dodd, with this get-up, might have been a field marshal, for all that Russian naval captain could surmise.

"Who says I have to move!" he began belligerently.

"The Captain of the Port," said Dodd, also belligerently. "Shall I bring him here to say so to ye hisself?"

"Oh, no!" protested the humbled Russian, "I'll move."

And the instant that wharf was clear Dodd had *his* ship in, her lines fast, loading flax as fast as she could swing the bales aboard.

But the captain of the Russian boat was rowing around the harbour, looking for the Port Captain. He found him. He told him his tale. Then they both came steaming across the Dvina straight for the little Scot.

"How dare you!" began the Port Captain. "I *never* gave such an order!"

"Ye-eh?" Dodd made out that he could hardly believe what he was hearing, "Captain, ye mean to stan' there an' . . . Well, I'm no blaming you, perhaps ye forgot . . . remember when we were playing cards last night—remember when I told ye how vastly important it was to have this flax get down to England for our aeroplanes—I'm no blaming you, mind you; perhaps ye'd had a wee bit too much to drink—but—"

"Of course, of course!" said the wretched Russian Port Captain, terrified that Dodd would report him for getting drunk and making a mess of his duties. "The flax for the *aeroplanes*—for our glorious *Allies!*—oh, nothing must take precedence over *that*."

Dodd and I and two Russian colonels used to play bridge throughout most of the white nights. When we had all "had a wee drop" the little Scot would seize his near-by pigskin scabbard, flip out its glittering sabre—and do cavalry exercise. Whush! the thrust over the horse's left ear—whish!—the thrust over the left rump. Thrust, parry, cut—Dodd squatting bow-legged on the floor, astride an imaginary horse—the rest of us crawling under the table, beds or whatever was handiest.

When Dodd left Archangel to present a complaint to the British Embassy, Sir George Buchanan, the Ambassador, used to flee from Petrograd, or at least send out word that he had left. Dodd was a perfect example of what a man can do with just will power alone; we called him the Emperor of North Russia.

Shura, of course, revelled in this life. Her Cossack soul was in

Paradise. Moscow had been a glamorous adventure after Ekaterinodar in the Caucasus, but in Moscow she had been frightened by the life she was just embarking upon. She had had, for her, an even more exotic time of it in our short week in Petrograd. But that, too, had been frightening, because it was so transitory. She was still frightened about the way I seemed ready to leave her behind in Petrograd. But up here she felt safe. She did not have to put on any airs or sit around in cafés trying to make people smile at her. She could be perfectly natural. It was just like being married!

We had nothing to do but let Papa Frumkin get through with his "conversations" and wait for our ship to come in. She was the *Tyr*, and Frumkin and I had posted a man down at the mouth of the Dvina River who was to let us know the minute she was sighted coming in from the White Sea, so that we could get docking space. Until this happened, Shura and I had nothing to do but just live.

After breakfasts of tea, black bread and honey, Shura and I spent our days wandering around the chaos of Archangel, watching the new ships coming in and the pandemonium that followed as the fifty-one races of Russia tried to unload them. A couple of dozen Russians would lay hold of a crate and move it a foot at a time—always to the time of a song that they sang. Our favourite perch was the crate of a Rolls-Royce, which must have been brought in on one of the ice-breakers and never had been moved since. Its inspection port was broken open and through it we could see the magnificent car rusting in spite of its grease from the dead salt spray that had been washed in on the way up into the Arctic Circle to get into Archangel.

As the long white nights drew on Shura would lean with her tiger coloured head against the window and sing me heart-breaking Cossack songs. I can still sing one she made me learn. It is the saddest of songs.

There was not an ounce of evil in Shura Alexandra Georgievna's splendid little body.

And that was just the trouble. She was too decent. Too child-

ish. I could not stand it. My miserable puritanical subconscious-
ness began to mutiny again. It said, "You can't do this. You must
send her home! You must, you must! Make her promise to go
home to the Caucasus. Just that. Don't make her promise anything after that, nothing silly about 'being good' and all the rest
of that nonsense. But just get her back home—once."

I lay awake several mornings, looking at her before I could get
up the nerve to suggest it. Then I did.

Shura wept. I wept. Frumkin wept.

We argued for nearly a week.

It was terrible. I was none too well off at that time, but I
bought her a ticket for Ekaterinodar and gave her what was left
over. Frumkin and I took her across the Dvina in a wretched
launch one windy, grey afternoon. We put her on the train at
Bakraritsa, and I rode down with her a mile to the real railway
station. Then the station bell rang twice, the warning, then three
times.

She hung further and further out of the window, waving until
even the train itself disappeared. And I walked back along the
ties to the waiting launch.

"Fool, fool, fool. . . ." I kept time with the railway sleepers.

I saw Shura just twice after that. The first time I might as well
tell here. I was in bed in my hotel room in Petrograd. It was nip
and tuck whether I would ever leave it alive. They were thinking of amputating my leg to save me. Winter had come round
again. Shura came in. Her furs were cool with snow. She lay
across the bed and wept. "*Roidninki*," she said, "I went home as
you told me to." But, she explained, she could not stick it. Her
mother was always reproaching her. She had gone off again—to
Moscow. Now she was trying Petrograd. She had telephoned
Jack Hoth the instant she had got in. He had told her what had
happened to me.

"*Roidninki!*" she said. "They will let me stay with you now!"

She was having her breakfast beside my bed when my hostess
from the Millionayia came in.

"Oh!" she said. "I'm sorry!"

I told her to come in and I introduced her to Shura.

"You've always asked me about her," I said, "here is my Cossack girl."

But the next time I saw Shura we were neither of us the same person we had been at Archangel. No, not by a million miles.

Chapter 22

ARREST IN THE CRIMEA

DURING all of these months a contract had lain in my desk for one hundred machines. At almost any time during that period I would have been willing to turn over the entire Russian business to Frumkin for that. From time to time I had revised it and had added safeguards that the wily old Jew had unwittingly taught me to see. The result was that by the time Frumkin came into my room late one night to deliver his dramatic ultimatum that it was "now or never" if I wanted to do business with him, that document was a fairly water-tight and sophisticated affair.

We had come down from Archangel when we learned that the ship we had been waiting all those weeks for, the *Tyr*, had been in a British Prize Court at Portsmouth all the time; and in a few days we intended to set off for Sebastopol on the Black Sea where I was to act as a sort of *aide-de-camp* to Frumkin in securing some hydroplane contracts with the Russian navy.

In these few days in Petrograd, Frumkin evidently saw a chance to put the screws on me and make me sell out to him at his own price. Things in the Technical Department had also reached a point where he could be practically certain of getting the war contract from them. He merely wanted the complete authorisation, signed by me with my power of attorney, to represent my company in all dealings with the War Department. And he wanted it for as little as he could give.

As I said, I would have been willing at any time during the first months to have given him this outright for a hundred machines. But of course the more I could make him buy from me to begin with, the heavier he was involved in seeing that our stuff was sold, and the less likely he would be to listen to attractive offers from any of my competitors. Up to date I had kept Frumkin in this position; he had not begun to "play" with anyone else; the Technical Department had not yet placed its order for any of these machines, my type or those of any other company, and the first one of us who landed either Frumkin or Sydney Visick for a big contract was now sure of the big order.

Even the Technical Department could not delay much longer. Too many questions were beginning to be asked around Petrograd.

Frumkin made a dramatic entrance into my room about one in the morning.

"Hurry," he said, "we've got to do it right now." He took out his fountain-pen and laid his portfolio open on the desk. "Give me that contract, I'll sign it right away. In a few minutes I've got a private rendezvous with *the* man. He's waiting for me now at a certain house."

He mentioned the name of a well-known but retired *ballerina*.

"Quick!" he said peremptorily.

I took out the contract and picked up his fountain-pen and altered the number from one hundred to three hundred machines.

"Initial that," I said, "and then sign it—and these three copies."

"Hey—what the hell are you doing!"

"Sign it," I said. "Go on, you know perfectly well that you wouldn't sign it even for a hundred unless you had the war order practically in your pocket. Come on, stop this nonsense and sign."

He slapped together his portfolio and stood up.

"All right," he said, "I go. And if I go out that door me and you is finished for ever." He snorted and snatched out his watch. "Maybe it's too late even now—maybe *he's* gone already."

I felt shocked—and yet I felt a strange exhilaration! If he did go out that door I was practically finished as far as any Russian orders were concerned. I knew he would be able to upset London so much with his cables that they would probably cancel my power of attorney. But thank the stars, I still did have that power in my hands; and even with the best of luck Frumkin couldn't get a wire to London and back through the censors on both sides in anything less than three or four days.

"If you go," I told him, "I know it's the finish. Just as soon as you leave this hotel I'm going upstairs to Visick to give him this contract as it is. I don't give a damn if I have to give it to him for a hundred machines—I'll give it. I will, I warn you. I have the power of attorney—and here it is."

I carried that always in my inside vest pocket and on the railway trains had even put the vest under my pillow at nights. Frumkin knew the value I set upon it and he knew that what I was saying was true. Visick would have snapped at getting our stuff for a hundred machines—especially after all the preliminary work Frumkin and I had done on the war contract. It would be a walkover for Frumkin's greatest enemy. Frumkin could also see, that night, that I was a very desperate young man. I was, too.

"And what are you going to do with the twenty-five machines we've already got in," I said, "and that cargo of other stuff on the *Tyr?* Who are you going to sell those to?"

It was not so much the matter of putting the screws on me as it was a question of personal pride with Frumkin; he was accustomed to getting everything he wanted for its absolute minimum price. He was quite capable of bargaining about the price of a postage stamp. But it was quite obvious now that *the* man was waiting, and that Frumkin had to think fast.

"Right," he said, "gimme that pen. Me and you has always been friends. We ought to do some swell business together. Say, you're pretty tough!"

I wasn't, I was as weak as water inside.

The point was that Frumkin had come to put the screws on me at just the wrong time. A little earlier I would have weakened. But of late I had turned into rather a desperate mood. After all, I did not have so much to lose; my salary was not so colossal as all that. And if I did lose my job—well, it might even be exciting for a time. I was stronger than Frumkin because of that. He lived for nothing but material things.

I did not remind him of it or ask him to read the contract again. I knew with his agile brain he had taken in every safeguard and loophole in the contract. But I read it over fearfully after he had gone out. It seemed safe; twenty-five per cent of the total price for all the machines was to be deposited to our credit in a stipulated New York bank before the contract was confirmed; every machine after that as it went out was to be paid for, cash-against-documents, at United States shipping port or Canada; the contract could be revoked at any time by me until the whole shipment called for in the contract had been paid for; and then there followed a list of other safeguards such as that he agreed that he could not make offers to the War Department on competing machines without our (my) consent, nor could he quote a price on our goods which I had not agreed to in advance. All payments, except the initial twenty-five per cent, were to be at the rate of exchange prevailing in New York on the day of shipment.

Before Frumkin left I telephoned to an American engineer I knew in the hotel and he came down in his dressing-gown to witness the signatures.

"You had the old boy sweating!" he said when Frumkin had stamped out.

"Look at me," I said. "Feel my hand."

I had, I told him in poker slang, just won the jack-pot of the evening on a busted straight! But my feet were beginning to get warm again. They took me on a fast run across St. Isaac's Square to the telegraph office where I sent off a long wire both to London and New York. A few days later wires of congratulations came through. New York said that the twenty-five per cent deposit had been duly made in our New York bank. My first task—"sewing up" the big intermediary, was done—I had landed Papa Frumkin.

The next day I faced the Danes. They had two miserable machines with which they were "demonstrating" in Petrograd. I offered to take over these at their original price. I felt sorry for the Danes, but I already knew enough to know that they were never at any time within speaking distance of anyone who mattered in the Technical Department. They had been deluding themselves as much as they had me. I pointed this out to them and asked them to get out of our way.

They began to abuse me in a frantic chorus. They did, in fact, wire to both London and New York making the most startling charges against me. They also sent for their *advocat*, not Hakonson, to come up from Copenhagen, which he did. And Frosch came into my room one night and broke down.

"It will ruin me!" he said bitterly. "I have a wife and two children. I will lose my job."

He made me wretched, but I went over the whole affair with him all over again; how they had never gone near Frumkin as we had ordered them to, how they had wired London and New York time and again over my head—trying to have me lose my job. I showed him copies of his own cables that London had wired back to me. Signed with his own name.

"It's no use," I said, "you're out."

For three days the *advocat* and the Danes and I argued through the entire afternoons. Then they became threatening. They would go to the Technical Department, they said, and spoil my business.

"If you do," I said, "I will tell them about Heinrich, about the German backing of your concern. You might be able to prove there no longer is such a connection, but with things the way they are now in Petrograd I wouldn't advise you to try. I wouldn't, if I were you."

"He *means* it!" said Frosch.

They threatened suit in New York. I told them to bring it. They did. And lost.

"Now," said Frumkin, his feathers having smoothed out again, "it's you and me for the Black Sea. Wait till you see that place— Frumkin is the whole works down there! I've got a fish of my own in the Hotel Kist."

Rumbling down across Russia I tried to let myself ease down. The face of Frosch haunted me. White, with real terror in his eyes. I could imagine, in a small country like Denmark, the disaster of losing a position to which he had probably worked up from a child in the same company. Where everybody on the street knew of his affairs, where they would all know of his disgrace; and where, in his present position, he had been such a "big man" in all the hotel foyers and midnight cabarets. And Frumkin was such a vindictive slut.

We had left Archangel in a blinding snowstorm. Now we

were going through a country bursting with the spring. Through damp, sweet smelling belts of pine forests and then all day across sunny plains. There was magic in the immeasurability of that great scene, of Russia curving across the world. The Tsars believed in space, in great distances between their cities—different Russian worlds—so that Russians could not co-operate against the Romanoffs. The log huts of the little peasant villages seemed as lost and remote in these vast forests as an animal's lair.

At Rostoff I saw my first Cossack *sotnia* outside of Petrograd. I wondered where Shura was now as I saw these slim-waisted men with their shaggy sheepskin hats and silvered daggers and boots soft as gloves.

"Well, Ivan Petrovitch," they asked their *Atman,* "when do we start to kill?"

Simple creatures. It was a shame to send them against Austrian howitzers! A hero, standing up in his saddle as he rode into battle, had no chance whatever against a pop-eyed professor of ballistics in Berlin. And these brothers of Shura were such decorative creatures!

One morning I woke up to see a rim of white along a milky blue sea. This was the Sea of Azov, the Putrid Sea. On the other side we rolled through oceans of blue wheat, with here and there a horseman riding through its wind-ruffled billows, and great beds of red poppies shone in the warm sun. The sky was an unbelievable blue. That night we ate dinner under the olive trees of Sebastopol.

We had dropped across Russia from the White Sea to the Black, from Arctic bareness to Asiatic voluptuousness; and the soul of Frumkin spoke the measure of its appreciation:

"The food is better here, thank God!"

"Tomorrow," he said, as another little red mullet disappeared as if jumping a waterfall into the cavern of his mouth, "tomorrow we gotta go up to the flying station, I gotit some 'conversations' there!"

Our rooms were on a broad balcony facing the Black Sea. At six on an exhilarating spring morning we had tea and rolls and rose-jam out there, as we looked down on to the great grey warships in the harbour, lying behind their booms of mines. Above us rose the yellow redoubts of the Crimean War. At seven an officer dressed in immaculate white came out on the balcony and saluted Papa Frumkin. He wore a little ceremonial dirk dangling from his slender waist with the St. George's black-and-orange knot, showing he had already won the highest decoration that the Tsar could give. On his breast was another St. George, and St. Vladimir and St. Stanislaus medals. He was a blond Russian, with greenish Slav eyes and high, dangerous-looking cheekbones. His long hair had been bleached salt-white. He was Commander Utgof, Russian "ace," and second-in-command of the Black Sea Flying Corps.

He was a magnificent creature, and I hate to think of what life has done to him and his fellow officers. He was the first man I ever flew with.

The Naval launch took us up to Kilen Bouhta, the hydroplane station up the bay. Other young flying officers in their neat white uniforms came running down the landing stage steps at the last minute to jump aboard. Frumkin and I had a Steinmetz bomb. It was a forlorn contraption, meant to be dragged behind an aeroplane on a long wire, the idea being that its hooks could catch in the fabric of a Zeppelin and blow it up. It looked like an eggplant and Frumkin, telling the officers it was loaded, accidently dropped it and grabbed at its triggers.

All of us tried to jump out of the launch. Such jokes, he fancied, made him popular with these gallant officers—and they did. This fat little Jew *was* "the works" on the hydroplane base.

As we stepped out on the slip of the hydroplane base, I heard an accent I hadn't heard for years, and then I heard a clunk and saw a flying spanner hit a huge Russian sailor directly in the stomach. The sailor had been standing on a hydroplane wing. Looking to see where the spanner had come from, I faced a man whom no other spot in the world could have produced, but Texas.

"Hello, bo," he said to me, his Adam's apple jumping up and down. "What are *you* doing in this man's land?"

This was Death Valley Slim.

"I'm not much on looks," he confided to me when we got to know each other. "But I've travelled some and I know my way about."

He had spent most of his life in the alkali deserts, but then an itinerant aviator had brought his aerial circus to Slim's town. Anything that flew was new then to Texas, and when the miracle broke down and Slim repaired its engine he went off with the aviator as his mechanic. This had led to his being taken on by the Curtis Company, Honolulu, the Philippines, and finally to throwing spanners at the Russian sailors on the Black Sea. A Hawaiian princess had ruined Slim's faith in women for ever.

The Crimean peninsula, dozing in sunny languor, was a land of roses, spreading vineyards and Tartar mosques nestling among their straight poplars. Yalta and Aloupka, two of its sea-ports, are said to be among the most beautiful spots on earth. It was a gorgeous sight to look down on from the air. We flew every morning at seven o'clock, usually to protect the fleet from submarine attacks, either going out or coming into the mine-protected harbour. There was, of course, the usual look-out to watch for the *Goeben* and the *Breslau*, who were in the Black Sea and had fired 208 shots into Sebastopol one night in a fruitless effort to hit the Hydroplane Base. Also, our scouting helped other officers to make domestic change-overs. It was just as well to know when "her husband" was coming back with the fleet.

One officer whom I had dined with one night, thinking that both the charming flat and the pretty woman that inhabited it were his, laughed and pulled up the sleeve of his spotless white tunic to make a muscle.

"Ha!" he grinned, "I shall have to be a very strong man when her husband comes home from the war!"

We both packed his bags for him, and I carried one of them back to his own apartment for him after dinner. We flew out together next dawn to meet the incoming fleet. It steamed in—always a sight to make one's heart beat a little faster, and that afternoon he and I and her husband with another officer played doubles together on the midshipmen's tennis courts.

I saw very little of Frumkin. His time was spent closeted with some higher, non-flying officials of the Naval Aviation Corps, and any inquiries of mine as to what he was doing, were always answered with a fat wink and a rub of his thumb against his forefinger—the Russian sign for giving a bribe.

"I am too fat to fly," he said kittenishly. "Besides, I gotit some business. *This war ain't going to last for ever!*"

I often wondered what such splendid pilots as Utgof, Verrain, Nevitsky and Lieutchanygof must have thought of all this. One couldn't bribe men like them any more than one could have bribed the Tsar. They would more probably have shot Papa Frumkin if he had even breathed such a thing. But there it was; Frumkin was getting next to somebody at a satisfying pace. He used to tell me about it at breakfast time, although even to the last minute he refused to tell me who it was.

If he had, I might have been able to help him later on—that is —if I had wanted to do anything then but get Papa Frumkin shot!

Death Valley Slim I saw occasionally as he slaved, oil-begrimed, over his beloved engines. He was the man who kept the Black Sea flying fleet in the air! The Russian aviators were so fond of him and regarded him as such an oddity that they tried to make a pet of him. But Slim wasn't having any. One night when I asked him if he wouldn't dine with a party of officers and me at the Naval Club, Slim blew up:

"*What!* Me?—go down there and eat at that swell hangout . . . with all them classy Russian dames laughing at me! Say, where do you get that stuff?"

The Naval Club with its white columns and huge ballroom was a brilliant scene. It was one of the most beautiful clubs I have ever been in. Frumkin staggered back from it one night and announced that he was off to Petrograd the next morning:

"I just drankit a good dinner," he explained with a horrible wink, "and it's shameful . . . how few aeroplanes they got here . . . leave Russia unprotected like this! I have just arranged it, they should ask for some more . . . with guns on 'em."

This order, he confided as he pulled off his socks, would put him on Easy Street. Maybe he'd marry and settle down. He had a niece in view.

"You know her," he said. "It's Anna."

With Frumkin went the aeroplane expert who had shared a flat with Slim back of the Naval Club, and not wishing to live in loneliness I left the Hotel Kist and settled down with the Texan. He had a keen sense of values. The junior flying officers, he told me, were a happy-go-lucky lot who seldom came near the hangars and knew next to nothing about the inside of their machines. They spent their time dining and wining with the Crimean beauties and flew for the love of the sport. "But if it comes to any scrapping," drawled Slim, "they give anybody a helluva rough afternoon; one thing they ain't got is a yellow streak!"

For the senior officers, admirals, colonels and such-like, Slim had a savage hatred. "When they get that far," he stated, "they've got married and started in to raise a family. They find their pay ain't no longer good enough for them to live on, so they start grafting, and believe me, they're the crookedest outfit of double-cross merchants I ever laid my eyes on."

The velvet night the *Goeben* and *Breslau* made a flying trip from the Bosphorus and fired some two hundred shells into startled Sebastopol, the damages were slight, but from them on, no lights were allowed to be shown after dark. One night when Slim and I were talking about "home," with an occasional rap at Russian apathy, we felt the touch of the Third Arm. The room was stuffy and without thinking I had flung open the board window shutters. At once came an excited banging at our door, and a booted policeman rushed through the room and banged together the shutters.

"*That guy got here too quick!*" said Slim. "He's been watching us."

A few days later I managed to persuade the Commandant to give Slim a day off from his job at the hydroplane base, and the next morning found us in a ramshackle Tartar barouche rolling along the sandy white road to Balaclava. I broke the news to Slim that we would soon see the valley down which had charged the never-dying "Six Hundred." I guessed he must have recited that poem in Texas in schoolboy orations.

We had taken a few photographs along the road, but when we saw the town lying before us I pushed the camera into the recesses of the folded carriage top as cameras were then strictly taboo in Russia.

A Don Cossack galloped up and demanded our passports and military passes. Balaclava was then a closed military zone and the Cossack made a great showing of examining my papers which would have been more effective if he had not been trying to read my passport upside down. Then he let us pass and Slim and I drove on under the warm spring sun into one of the most beautiful little anchorages on any sea.

Balaclava proper lies on the left side of a small gourd-shaped harbour the colour of a robin's egg. Around this are buff coloured hills with green vineyards and little buff coloured houses with nicely sun-bleached pink roofs. The hills come together at its mouth, the Black Sea lying far below in a deep ravine; and as we looked down into this, Slim and I saw a monster fish. It was about one hundred feet long, just awash, moving slowly into the turquoise anchorage. It was a most startling sight to see its back appearing in the sea. We had forgotten there was a submarine in the Black Sea.

"Christ!" said Slim—"so *this* is where they keep their submarines!"

We watched the submarine come in and then tie up at a wharf. "Damn if they ain't hitching her up just like a pinto pony!" said the enchanted Slim. We ran on down the cliff and through the dozing poplar-shaded street to get a closer view of the sub. At the foot of the hill we found our carriage waiting there. It's Tartar driver was half-asleep in the sun, but beside the barouche stood a very wide-awake and ferocious Russian policeman; knee-whiskers, clanking sword, boots and all—and in his mighty paw was our camera.

"*Vash?*" he said. "Is it yours?" poking it at me.

"*Nyett*" (no), I said, pointing to Slim. "It's his."

"Well—for G-o-d's sake! *My* camera! Say, who the hell's been taking the pictures with this thing!"

"I did, Slim," I said, "but you mustn't forget you own it. You wouldn't want me to *lie* to these people, would you? You *own* the camera, no matter what you let me do with it; and, in the eyes of the law, you are the guilty person. You should not have let me use it. I'm sorry, but you see how things stand."

Slim gaped at me. I saw generations of Texas faith passing out of his face. I saw cynicism and hardness come in, I saw disillusion with this world and all there is in it—especially me.

"You're a hell of a pal," he said sadly. Then he turned on the *gorodovoie*. "Well, mattress face, what's *your* complaint?"

The policeman made bear-like noises and signs and more or less shoved Slim and me in behind the Tartar where he sat down facing us on the tenuous flap-seat with a glare that in any language could be read as a threat that any attempt on our part to escape would be met by a shot from the Luger automatic he now held in his hand.

We were taken to a one-storied building, the district prison, placed on a bench that ran along three of its walls facing a pulpit-like arrangement behind which sat two non-commissioned officers with blue-shaven heads. They also read my passport upside down, sidewise, and held it up to see if the pages were transparent. They did not even laugh at my photograph, although they looked at it several times and then at me with just suspicion. Suddenly, as if part of a ritual, they both jumped down from the pulpit and demanded that both Slim and I be searched. Our pockets were emptied, we were "frisked." Slim went through it all sullenly, keeping his hot eyes stubbornly away from me; but when the non-coms tried to examine each one of his cigarette papers and opened his sack of precious Bull Durham tobacco, Slim leaped upon them and snatched them away.

"Lay off that!" he snapped. "Keep your dirty paws off my smokes."

With lamb-like docility the non-coms let him have them back, and then they turned to me. They caught me at a bad moment, for during the examination of Slim I had noticed that our camera was lying unnoticed on the bench. And in a fatuous moment I thought it might be fun to see what the non-coms would do if I tried to take out its film. I found out all right; the first I knew they had finished with Slim was when I was buried under a football charge of the two non-coms, backed up by the policeman, who held me by the throat. In that position he looked up at the two non-coms like a victorious Christian gladiator in the Coliseum watching Nero's thumb.

"Funny!" said Slim. "You think you're funny, don't you? You big boob!"

Politeness had gone. They may not have known anything about a camera's inside, but they were indubitably convinced I was a suspicious character now! Slim and I were practically frog-marched to two cells. They faced each other, but Slim wouldn't look out of his. I did. I saw the huge policeman looking along into our corridor. When he saw my nose between the bars he gave me a beady glare and significantly unflapped the flap of the regulation wooden holster containing his Luger automatic. As I pulled back my nose I saw an even nastier sight come into the corridor. It stood on tiptoes, and a bald, yellow head and rat-like eyes faced me for a silent few moments. Then it went across and made the same inspection of Slim. Then the ratty eyes disappeared.

"Now," I heard Slim, somewhere in his eight-foot cell. "Now, you big boob—try and laugh this off! That's the Secret Police. Laugh!—we got plenty of time to do it in now!"

The details aren't interesting—although they didn't seem so dull at the time. The policeman clumped back about three hours later with a drawn Luger in his hand. I knew that the Secret Police, the dreaded Third Arm of the Tsar, was notorious for shooting the wrong men, and I had begun to wonder if this wasn't going to be another mistake now, when I noticed who was sitting in the "pulpit" this time.

A typical Petrograd social military dandy. Tight-waisted khaki tunic, leg-o'-mutton black breeches; from his waxed, scented moustache to his smart boots he was the beau ideal of a Tsarist officer.

"I," he announced with a fatigued air, "am the Governor of the district. What have you done?"

I laughed and explained about our picnic to see Balaclava and the incident of the camera film. I was, I lied, taking out the film to give to the police. Then I asked him to read my Naval pass, which the police had placed with the pile of our belongings on his desk.

"If you will telephone the *Midshipmanski Courts* in Sebastopol," I suggested, "you will see that I am supposed to be playing tennis there this afternoon with Lieutenants Verrain and Nevitskie. They will tell you who we are. Slim here"—it suddenly came to me that I had never learned his last name—"Death Valley Slim, Your Excellency, is a most valuable person. He is the Curtis mechanic for the hydroplanes. Without him the hydroplanes do not fly."

Verrain and Nevitskie, aside from being excellent doubles players, were both sons of admirals. (Both of their fathers were murdered afterwards, one on the White Sea and one on the Black, by Red sailors of their ships on the very same day!) And their answer to the Governor's phone call seemed to be that if I was not soon turned loose and on my way to Sebastopol they would have to get another partner to make a four. Would I please tell them whether I could make it or not.

With a bored air the handsome Governor politely shook my hand and gave me a million apologies and our camera.

"Nevertheless," he drawled, "what has happened has to go down on the record. Your—ahem—dossier. . . . If I were you I would call at the Grand Natchalnik of Sebastopol and give him all the details . . . so that he will understand this was all . . . just fun. *Comprenez?*"

I played tennis. But the young naval officers did not seem to think the affair very funny. They took it almost as seriously as Death Valley Slim had done. When I was laughing about it next day at the hydroplane base, Commander Utgof said to me:

"You haven't gone to the Grand Natchalnik!"

"Of course not," I said. "Why should I bother him?"

A few minutes later when I missed Utgof who had told me he

was going to let me fly his plane that day, the station doctor told me Utgof had taken the launch back to Sebastopol to see the Grand Natchalnik and explain all about me.

"You fly with me," said Verrain. "I'm going to try out a new machine—a Russian hydroplane!"

Verrain had served under Admiral Rodjesvinsky as a midshipman in the Russo-Japanese war. He had been shot several times through the chest. It would have killed any ordinary man; but Verrain had a Japanese rising sun tattooed around each bullet scar, so that he looked rather decorative when we stripped naked to swim from the hydroplane over in Round Bay.

As far as I know I think Verrain and I are the only two men who ever flew in a hydroplane stark naked—I know we are as far as that type of plane was concerned; because how it ever got off the water at all is a thing I am still wondering to this day!

This Russian model seaplane had been built with usual Russian brilliance from the Curtis designs. But instead of having a hull, the Russians, for lightness—and in that fine careless fervour that Russians have—had built a tiny *nacelle*, with booms like a British FE 2c going back to its tail float and rudder. The result was there was a big gap of nothing but air between the forward *nacelle*— it was a pusher type of prop—and the tiny tail. A sort of flying tadpole. We had no lateral stability. When I kicked on the rudder she threatened to spin round like a top; when I took it off too quickly she corkscrewed through the air. This was just over Sebastopol, into whose sun-drenched streets I looked down enviously, the water evaporating on my hide, turning me into a cooling flask of a sort, and my hair standing straight up in spite of the wind. Both Verrain and I were fighting to put that plane down on the water before we were killed.

We almost knocked off the roof of the Hotel Kist, flew straight between the masts of the flagship—I swear I felt the heat as we slid right over her hot, gaping stacks—and pancaked her in Sebastopol harbour from about twenty feet up. She hit, shot into the air again—where we frantically opened up the motor—besumped again on the water, and skittered along to the hydroplane base like a stone in ducks and drakes.

I understand now why the Russians had made us put on crash helmets and the life-belts they used in the air in those early days.

"Hi!" yelled Verrain, jumping about (with his tattooed scars) like a painted Indian at a sun dance—"Hi!"—to me—"That's the very first time that I flew that plane—that anybody has *ever* flown it. They tell me I break my neck!"

He went around collecting ten rouble bets he had made on his insane affair.

Poor Verrain; I saw him years later, after the Revolution, in the Hotel Waldorf in London, when I was in the uniform of the British Royal Air Force, with my new wings up. He shook his head:

"Lucky dog! They won't take me. I'm a Russian, you see—we don't count any more."

He was wandering around London like a lost soul, literally unable to get into the war again. Lucky dog to you, Lieutenant Verrain.

It took some doing to win back the confidence of Slim. I don't think it ever would have happened if it had not been for that flying freak of Verrain's.

"Boy," said Slim, "when I saw you cake-walking in over them ships I said to myself, 'Make up your mind to walk slow behind him!'—and I guessed that maybe you weren't such a bad guy after all. You know, we're the only two Americans here."

I told him not to let his sympathies run away from him.

We had one last jaunt together. We took a train and then drove miles back into the dozing Crimean peninsula to *Tchefut Khali*—the Fortress of the Jews. It perched on a high limestone rock, looking down over the poplars and turreted palace of a long dead Tartar Khan. The walls of the fortress were of solid stone, cut from the rock itself. A sect of Jews called Kairines now keep it in shape and once a year used to hold pilgrimages there. They are the Jews who have no Talmud. And they believe that *Tchefut Khali* is the home of the Lost Tribes.

There is a white tomb there upon which roses are placed all during the summer. In it sleeps the body of a Tartar princess. She fell in love with the son of the Jewish chieftain. He stole her one night from the Khan's palace. The Tartars attacked, and the young Jewish warrior was killed on its ramparts, his body was flung over its walls, and when she heard of it his little Tartar princess jumped after him.

"There," said the old Rabbi Ghakam, "she threw herself from that window—into the valley of Jehoshaphat."

In the palace of the Khans was a fountain of tears, made of pearl shells, each one filling and overflowing to drop one drop into the pearl shell below. It had been weeping throughout the centuries, and, as I am sure the Bolshies have not destroyed it, it is weeping there now.

There was an open bath rimmed with cool poplars where the water was warmed by flowing in a thin shell over marble slabs and the Khan could sit on his cushions to watch his harem bathe.

On the day I left Death Valley Slim insisted on carrying my biggest bag for me. "You look too swell," he said, "dressed up like that." He would have hit me if I had asked him to carry my bag. We slid together down the Maklokoff redoubts to the railway station below.

A slip of a young Russian girl had come down to wave me off. She was only fifteen, the daughter of a naval designer, in whose country home I had spent a truly Russian week-end, lying on our backs in the flowered fields and watching the larks sing over our heads, eating jam made from rose leaves, drinking tea all day and night and singing, singing, singing the saddest of songs. . . . I gave her my little V.P.K. camera as a memento of that idyll—and her father, the General Rosenberg, gave me his dog.

"But what shall I do with a dog?"

It was a Llewellyn setter of purest breed.

"He is yours!"

"But I can't take him! I don't know where I shall be." . . . I patted the dog. . . . "He can't live in an hotel in Petrograd," I said. "He would die—wouldn't you, old boy, after a place like this. Won't you keep him for me?"

The General pulled his patriarchal white beard. He frowned. A delicate question of honour was involved.

"Da!" he said. "That's how we shall arrange it—Pompey shall wait here for you."

I carried away a picture of them all standing there. The vivacious old mother, her head wrapped in an orange bandana; "Tania," like a colt, all legs and prancing gestures, looking a little sad now and waving the precious V.P.K. at me; the old General, in spotless white uniform, the black-and-red cross of St. Vladimir (with swords) dangling from his neck—all of them going back to that dozing estate in the country, confidently expecting to end out their days in ease and security.

"But where's 'Tania'?" I asked in New York, in 1920.

"I—I don't know."

They did not know. Something had happened to "Tania" during the Wrangel evacuation.

I thought of asking Wrangel about it, in 1925, when I spent a day with him at his country place on the Danube above Belgrade. Then, I thought, I did not want to know.

On my way back from Sebastopol I found myself in a compartment with the Tsar's Flag Lieutenant with the Black Sea Fleet— the Duke of Leuchtenberg, Prince Romanoffsky. A heavy-set, powerful young man, about thirty-four, whose muscles deemed likely to burst his neat white Naval tunic. He sang opera in a deep, sad bass all the way to Petrograd, lamenting his bad luck not to be on the stage. When we came to a station, which was on his estate, the head peasants from several of the villages were down there to meet him, and he held a council with them on the railway platform.

"They ask me how soon shall we beat the Germans!" he sighed. "What could I tell them!"

Chapter 23

FRUMKIN OVERDOES IT

WHEN I got back to Petrograd, to the Hotel Astoria, I found that everything had gone wrong. Frumkin had taken advantage of my absence to break about every promise he had made to me, verbal or written.

I found it out quite by accident. An American gas-expert I was lunching with happened to mention that he was getting an amazingly good exchange for his English money.

"That's funny," I said.

"Why!" he said, "I changed some today and I got so much." He mentioned a figure quite a lot higher than I had since received. "Where did you go?"

I explained that it had been my custom merely to walk over behind the Cathedral of Kazan to Frumkin's office and tell him I wanted the Russian equivalent of forty or fifty pounds. He always wrote the exchange down on a slip and gave me the roubles.

"But, my God! that fellow must have been swindling you all along!"

I checked up the amount of money I had drawn recently and saw that Frumkin had done me out of about a couple of weeks' free living. Then I went over to speak to him about it.

"Sure," he growled. "I don't know what the bank says. I give you the same rate I make for myself when I draw money from the office. That's all right, ain't it?"

Hardly, I explained to him; when he was both debtor and creditor. I asked him was he really serious in what he was saying.

"It's not the money so much," I said to him. "It's that fact that you would do such a thing to me."

"Well, business is business," said Frumkin.

"All right," I said. "If you feel that way."

I walked back to the Cathedral. A huge procession was choking the great Nevsky, a tremendous river of people, led by priests in jewelled robes and shining crowns, carrying holy ikons and swinging incense before them. Everybody knelt down on the streets and sidewalks and on the grass before the circular pillars of the Virgin of Kazan. The trams stopped, the *droshky* drivers got out, crossed themselves, and held their stallions; the police stood at salute. Like a motion film that had suddenly been stopped, like the two minutes' silence on Armistice Day, all Petrograd was still . . . and then with a great boom of resonance the priests began to chant out their prayer for victory of the Russian arms. . . .

I was alarmed. If Frumkin would cheat me in little things, what would he do to me in big things—what *wasn't* he doing! I took the night train down to Moscow. There, after a couple of days' intrigue, I managed to get hold of a copy of my bid he had submitted to the Zemskie Soujouse for the big contract they were alleged to be ready to place. I also had managed to buy a copy of my strongest competitor's bid. I discovered to my horror that Frumkin was bidding on both of them—and that my price was so fantastic that, in that comparatively honest Zemskie, I was completely out of the running. Frumkin had deliberately put a "fancy" price on my stuff that even the venal Technical Department could not have stomached. I was being "killed," I afterwards discovered, to make way for my competitor, who had offered him ridiculously low prices on their machines.

Frumkin had got back at me. I had bluffed the first big order out of him for the War Department in Petrograd. I had already established a basis of trading there. But down in Moscow Frumkin was playing another game. Whether the New York end of his business had managed to get him the agency for my competitor's machines or not, Frumkin was bidding on them; and he was bidding on them in a manner that would let them get it and let me out of it. The next morning I drove straight from the Nicholas Station to Frumkin's office.

"Since when," I asked, "have you been handling *them?*"

There was a catalogue of my competitor open on his desk!

"I'm not," he grinned. "I was merely reading this."

"You're a liar—you have put a bid on those to the Zemskie Soujouse!"

His fat face wrinkled, then twitched.

"So—you've been down to Moscow, have you?"

"I have."

"Vell—what are you gonna do about it?"

"Just this—"

I knew the drawer of his desk in which he kept our correspondence and the contract. It was a special one kept exclusively for our connection. Above it were some cubbyholes full of our catalogues. I wrenched open the drawer and snatched a handful of papers. I did not know whether the contract was among them or not. I did not have time to look; I just ripped them in half. Then I pulled out all the catalogues and threw them on the floor. Then I kicked them about the room; I kicked until the floor was covered with torn pages.

"Stop! You stop that!" shrieked Frumkin. "Nelson, Nelson, come here—for God's sake, stop him, stop him, stop him . . . !"

Frumkin tried to pull me away from the mess.

"By God!" he hissed in my ear. "We been friends, we been friends—you do this to me, you do this to me—in business I cut you to bits! I cut you to bits!"

"Mr. Farson! Mr. Farson!" Nelson's black face and white eye-balls appeared in the door. "Mr. Farson—you do dat at your own risk! Yo' own risk, Mr. Farson. . . ."

I flung him aside and rushed out of the door. I was simply crazy with rage.

Then I cooled down.

I *was* in a fix!

In order to explain the perfidy of Frumkin let it be said that by putting in such a fantastic bid on my stuff he was not only eliminating me from any chance of getting any more orders, but he was making me a likely scapegoat for any muck-raking that might occur in any of the departments. A price such as mine could have only one explanation—that I must have promised bribes to almost everyone. On the other hand, his bid on my competitor's stuff had no more than the usual padding to satisfy those who required "palm oil" before the order was granted; it was not out of line. If the Zemskie Soujouse was honest, and *nobody* was taking it, then Frumkin was keeping it for himself. And with the bargain-counter price at which he had gobbled up the right to get my competitor's machines old Frumkin had not only removed me from his trail, but added an infinitely more remunerative account to his swollen list.

Anyway, whatever the reason, I was being quietly disposed of.

It took me all of that summer and almost into mid-winter to win back the ground that wily Frumkin had stolen from me. In the meantime things began to happen to Frumkin.

A few days after our argument he had left Petrograd and gone back to Sebastopol. And there the dreaded Third Arm of the Tsar caught him. The first I knew of it, or even that he had left Petrograd, was when an American millionaire, one of Frumkin's New York banking-backers, came into my room in the Astoria and told me with an aggrieved air that the Russian Secret Police had thrown Frumkin into prison the minute he reached the flying station. It was, he growled, a serious affair. Did I know anything about it?

"Why should I?"

"Well, I was only wondering," he muttered. "I know that you and Frumkin had a colossal row."

I laughed. I wasn't, I told him, in league with the Secret Police.

"Well, he's in there."

I laughed again. This was irony!

The millionaire was accompanied by the Third Secretary of the American Embassy, who was obviously highly impressed by the great man's position and wealth.

"Well, what are we going to do about it?" asked the millionaire.

"*We?*"

"Look here, Farson," he exploded. "You know as well as I do that Frumkin is an American citizen—that's why I brought this gentleman along"—he nodded domineeringly towards the young Third Secretary. "We're going to make a complaint about it. I'm going to take it up with Washington."

The whole thing was fantastic, he said. Frumkin had **evidently** been a bit too cute. That must be admitted. At any rate, it did look as if he must have double-crossed someone about bribe money over those aeroplane contracts. Somebody, obviously, had it in for him. Frumkin had been thrown in prison charged with being a German spy—and somebody behind the scenes was trying to move heaven and earth to get him shot.

"He would be—if he were a Russian," said the millionaire with an unctuous sigh. "But, thank God, he's not! Frumkin is an American citizen. And I'm not going to stand by and see any American shot!"

"I just told the Secretary here"—the millionaire now bowed condescendingly in the direction of that worried young diplomat —"that you would vouch for Frumkin being an American . . . we are going to have the Embassy take up the case." He looked expectantly at me.

"I'm sorry," I said. "I can't vouch for that."

"Why the hell can't you!" The millionaire was obviously used to being obeyed. "Why not?"

"Because he isn't an American," I said. "You knew that when you came in here. You know he travels on a Russian passport. I've seen it dozens of times."

"That's—"

"What's more," I said, "he's registered as a Russian in the Sec-ond-Class Guild of Merchants in Petrograd. You can look that up, if you feel like it," I said to the Third Secretary.

"What are you trying to do?" sneered the millionaire. "Do you want him shot!"

"I don't care a damn!" I said.

To do myself justice I never thought for a moment that they would shoot him. The aeroplane order had come through with such pace that it must have taken Frumkin's breath away. It had been too easy, and he had probably felt that the bribe money had not been sufficiently earned. Or else, perhaps, thoughtful Frumkin had not expected any more aeroplane orders, and saw no reason to give it. But as the weeks dragged along I began to feel qualms about it. I might have told a white lie to influence the Third

Secretary—not that it would have done any good. Or, if Frumkin
had only told me who it was he was having "conversations" with,
I might have given the millionaire-backer the name of an officer
in Sebastopol, whom it might have paid him to placate. But now
the Secret Police had their hands on Frumkin, it was clearly a
case of "hands off" as far as any outsider was concerned.

The case of Frumkin began to look desperate.

It was like a scene out of *Karenina*, one rainy night on the
Moscow-Kharkov railway station, when I saw Frumkin's two
nieces mutually supporting each other on the dimly lighted platform. They were in mourning and both weeping their eyes out,
as if fat old Frumkin were already dead. They had been down to
Sebastopol in a vain attempt to see him, to see that fat, bull-dog
face they so adored.

"You!" They pointed at me. "You!"

I had come up to speak to them. "You tried to get him shot!"
they cried, backing away from me. "Run, this minute, you are
trying to get Papa killed!"

The few travellers on the platform turned and stared at me.
What was all this? Was this a case for a gentleman to interfere?
Should someone call the police? I could see all these thoughts in
the faces under the dim lights. And I could see that the two girls
really did believe that I was trying to get their fat uncle shot.

"I'm sorry," I said. "Really, that's not true; you know I
wouldn't do things like that."

"You did, you did—you must have said something about him.
You hate him!"

"Maybe so—but, you must believe me, I did not do this, and
besides I am sure that Frumkin is all right. I know he will be all
right. Why, old Papa Frumkin could get out of *anything*, you
know that. Now, come now, don't cry, for God's sake. Here, let
me get you some tea. Now, Anna, look here, Anna—do you *think*
for a moment I could hurt old Papa Frumkin? Really, do you
think such silly things as all that! Nonsense, why you ought to be
ashamed of yourself. Here, use my handkerchief . . ."

With one more or less under each arm I led them along that
dreary platform and down to the station restaurant.

"But you're trying to get him killed right now!" Anna renewed. "You're going down to Sebastopol. That was what you were waiting for, to go to Sebastopol and do some more danger to him!"

"I'm not," I snapped. "I'm waiting to ride down as far as Kharkov with a girl I know. You come up when the train comes in and you'll see me go off with her."

"Well!" laughed Olga Ivanovna as the Kharkov train pulled out. "I must say I don't feel jealous—but you have broken their hearts, I can see. I never saw anybody weep so brazenly over a man. I won't do that when I say good-bye to you."

It was not love, I explained, it was a grisly death. But when I gave her the story of Frumkin she felt almost as concerned about it as the two nieces had been.

"You know—these things *do* happen," she said.

And Olga Ivanovna, as I discovered afterwards, knew what she was talking about!

One morning when I was in bed in Petrograd my door was flung open and in walked Death Valley Slim. He didn't knock, he just walked over and looked down at me:

"Boy!" he said, his bobbing Adam's apple showing that he was under great stress of emotion. "Boy! I just loped up here from Sebastopol to break some bad news to you . . . we've got a heap of trouble coming our way . . . I've seen Frumkin . . . hanging on in back of the bars like a big baboon. An' he's scared plumb out of his mind. He's got 125 charges against him, and"—Slim placed a sunburned finger on my stomach—"twenty-five of 'em is *you!*"

"Quit your kidding!"

"It's God's truth I'm telling you. Twenty-five of 'em is you!"

"I don't understand it."

"Neither do I. But listen . . . they don't all start with that Balaclava party with you and me getting pinched for that camera business. That's in what they call supporting evidence. That's what Korsakov told me it was. Anyway, weren't you and old

Frumkin up at Archangel, and didn't you and old Frumkin spend a lot of time talking and buying champagne for a couple of old colonels up there; and wasn't he trying to fix them two colonels, huh?"

"Something like that."

"Well—them two colonels ain't there any more; they're not there. No, they're out Siberia-way. Digging up salt, I guess. Anyway, 'fore they left they spilt enough to put you and Frumkin in the soup."

"What's the real answer?" I asked.

"I dunno. Frumkin pigged some graft money from some guys pretty high up, I guess. You know—holding out on 'em. How the hell he thought he could get away with *that*, I dunno. He's a pretty rich guy, old Frumkin—but he can't buy his way out of this. That's what's got him scared to death. This time some guy he's double-crossed is going to tack out his skin!"

Slim told me that the younger officers in the flying station had commissioned him to beg me not to come back to Sebastopol. It might make trouble for all of us. They had also suggested to him that it would be better if I did not try to leave Russia until this thing was cleared up. One never could tell what these sort of things could end up with.

Slim opened his mouth and his Adam's apple clucked. "He offered them half a million . . . *half a million!* That's what the station says. And they turned him down—cold! Ain't that enough to scare any man half to death? Somebody wants to croak you so badly he passes up half a million! Ain't that enough to make anybody feel a bit blue?"

It did sound impressive.

Chapter 24

JOHN REED

WITH Frumkin in prison, every one of us who had anything to do with him had to rebuild our Russian connections all over again. This did not matter much to most of the Americans in Petrograd, i.e., the Hotel Astoria assortment, because the "big" American millionaire who had tried to bulldoze me into getting his precious Frumkin freed, was rapidly and surely absorbing all their activities. If they themselves would not surrender the rights to let his company handle their business with the Russian Government, he would merely cable to his big New York banking group which would immediately get into touch with that particular company in the United States, whereupon its representative in Russia would get a wire saying that his services were no longer needed. The representation had been turned over to the big banking group.

In such fashion I saw one American after another broken, saying good-bye to us sadly, taking in all cases tearful farewells of the Russian women (whom they had found much more exhilarating and vital than the ones they were going back to) and leaving Petrograd with a feeling of secret disgrace.

The big millionaire got heavier, more arrogant, more predatory in his determination to gobble up all of us. He soon had an entire suite of rooms in the Hotel Astoria. He was like a big cannibal trout, lying in a deep pool, periodically raiding shoals of his little brothers. And, like the *ferox*, his jaw *did* change its shape. It got a nasty upward hook to it. I watched that man grow, I can tell you, because I was mortally afraid of him. His fat came from eating us! I was one of the little trout. To escape him I knew I had to go up into the shallow water, where he couldn't swim, or else make for some intricate undergrowth . . . where he would get tangled up.

That is why I went to the Grand Duke Serge Michaelovitch, then head of the Artillery Department, and at least put down on record, where I could refer to it, a straightforward bid on my stuff without any graft money included. That is why I spent a good many of my nights now travelling between Petrograd and Moscow, because, after my row with old Frumkin I had gone down there and opened up a connection with the Zemskie Soujouse with Howe of the Robert Dollar Co., an interesting, mystical creature who had represented that huge steamship and exporting company for some twenty years in China.

By the time midsummer of 1915 had come along the only Americans left in the Hotel Astoria were automobile mechanics and service managers, healthy, hearty one hundred per cent Americans—with American flags in their buttonholes—who had nothing to do but have a good time with the Russian girls—which they had!—see that their particular types of machines were assembled correctly, and obey the orders of the big millionaire. There was a charming Philadelphian from a big chemical company (who wasn't gobbled up by the millionaire simply because the millionaire did not know how to handle hospital supplies), and an extremely intelligent export manager of a big American motor-car and carriage works who managed to maintain his identity against the millionaire to the very end. He was the only intelligent American export manager I had met. The rest did not even know their geography, and thought it made no difference if they palmed off obsolete models after getting the order.

I did not, with one or two exceptions, find these people particularly exhilarating. They all considered themselves vastly superior to the Russians around them and made no attempt whatever to learn anything about the country they were in. They might as well have been in London or Paris or New York. Or else they "got sophistication" and began to argue with the head waiter about the vintage of every bottle of wine they bought, men who had never had a bottle of wine before they left the United States! I was bored with the "Good old U.S.A.!" stuff, and "These here Goddamned *moujiks*."

I kept darting about the pool with that human cannibal trout after me. I got cables from New York and London, showing that he was chasing me there. The reason that they were not effective at first was solely due to the fact that I had already got one big order, and to some masterpieces of letters I had written to both offices explaining the whole Russian set-up. Nevertheless, if I chanced to get in the same lift with that cheery, man-eating millionaire, and he began wishing me his usual hearty good morning and "How's things?" I would usually get out before the lift reached the ground floor.

"Say, when are you going home?" he asked me openly one night after dinner in front of a crowd of Americans in the smoky tea-room.

That question had now become an insult in Petrograd. And he had made it so more than anyone else.

"I don't know," I said. "When are you?"

"Oh, I'm here for the duration!" he laughed.

But his laugh was a growl. He was furious.

It is small wonder that when I looked down into the red and white dining-room of the Hotel Astoria one day and saw John Reed, I almost gave a cheer. I had met John in Greenwich Village when he was working for the *Metropolitan Magazine*, and I had been completely captivated by his Mexican stuff, when Pancho Villa had made him a general. Well, here he was in Russia, sitting with Boardman Robinson, an Englishman now a naturalised American.

Reed, as always, was shooting his hands upward through his rumpled waves of chestnut hair. Boardman was tugging at his red beard. Both were making jokes about the Russian officers and American business men around them and laughing uproariously. They were dressed in rough corduroy breeches, as if they had just come down from a fishing trip in the Maine woods.

They had, as a matter of fact, just come up from the Russian front—behind which lines they had been caught without the proper credentials—and when I sat down with them they told me that even then they were under "open arrest." Hence their raucous laughter at everybody.

An arrest of any sort, even an anaemic open-arrest that allowed one to eat *sterlet* and caviare with the courtesans of the Astoria,

was balm to John's Communist soul. A soul which later wrote
Ten Days that Shook the World!

"The Grand Duke Nicholas is threatening to shoot us!" exulted
John.

"Silly ass!" laughed the ex-Englishman, Boardman Robinson,
who, with masterful strokes, was drawing a caricature of a firing-
squad on the table-cloth. "It's perfectly gorgeous publicity!"

If they made that Russian summer a Nirvana for me, I was a
gold-mine for them. For about a week we did nothing but pick
each other's brains all night over the open-air dinner-table in the
courtyard of the Hotel Angleterre where they were living.

I gave them an inside view of the working of the vaunted
Russian steam-roller, about whose omnipotence all the fatuous
newspaper correspondents were sending out such unpardonably
optimistic newspaper accounts. It had no works inside it. With
John I went over every step of my career in Petrograd; my struggles with Frumkin, with the Dane and the *nine* men between us
and the War Department, with the venal Technical Department,
the futile interviews with the Grand Duke Serge Michaelovitch,
the picture of the great Russian regiments marching through the
snow to entrain—one with and one without rifles—and what ordinary talk was like among the American munition experts in the
Hotel Astoria.

I introduced them and we had several particularly interesting
meals with the little Englishman who was the secret representative in Russia of Sir Basil Zaharoff, the mystery man of Vickers
Co.—vast armaments net.

"When we were dickering with the Turks for a battleship,"
grinned Parnell, describing how they all sat on cushions in, he
tried to tell us, the Sultan's seraglio, "John Doe & Co. got on the
job and promised them a bigger ship. 'Righto!' said my boss,
'get out your pencils and design a bigger ship still with two more
twelve-inch guns than John Doe have offered.' So, of course, we
got the order."

Afterwards, when I was a journalist, I often searched to find
someone just like myself then; someone naïve and fresh and full
of rage and energy, who would just tear off the lid of a situation

and let one look inside. For I was one of the very earliest to come into Petrograd on war business with the Russian Government. And, as far as I can see, I experienced every shock and form of corruption and satisfaction that such an underhand enterprise could provide.

John went into ecstasies over having specific instances and names to quote. He gave me an education in what was and what was not news—and what material was necessary or sufficient to ensure that it could not be repudiated. By handing him over my dossier I gave him some most sensational stuff.

I also, it turned out, had given it to the Russian Secret Service Police. For of course all the days that John and Boardman Robinson and I spent talking together, they were being kept under close watch. When they were out of their rooms in the Angleterre their rooms were searched. Every document in them was read and re-read a number of times, my dossier among them. And that explained a sinister little notation I discovered written on one of the cables to me from London. I spotted it as I was going through my correspondence to write up a report. I came on a cable from the London office which had reached me during the time I was fighting to get my first war order—the days when both London and New York were being bombarded by the Danes to order me home, those ghastly days of uncertainty and delay when I had offered to remain in Russia at my own expense. The cable simply read:

WHEN ARE YOU RETURNING HOME?

But across it someone had now written:

JAMAIS!

Knowing full well the material John Reed and Boardman Robinson had collected behind the Russian Front and were collecting in Petrograd, and knowing only too well what use they were going to make of it, the Grand Duke Nicholas, Commander-in-Chief of the Russian Armies, finally gave them an ultimatum that they could leave Russia, *via Siberia*, within a stipulated time, or—face the consequences. The consequences left no alternative but imprisonment or a firing-squad. And this last was not at all far-fetched by any means. Men were being shot for less than John Reed had done.

Reed, it will be remembered, was already in trouble with the Allies through his foolish joke of firing a rifle up into the air from the German trenches. This was before the United States entered the war, of course. The French General Staff were screaming for his summary execution on the ground that he, a neutral, had probably murdered some French soldier. The French had too much power in Russia for either John Reed or Boardman to let themselves feel comfortable over that blot on John's escutcheon. But primarily they knew that everything was going to be done to prevent them getting their "story" on Russia into the American papers. The Russian "steam-roller" myth must be kept up. No one in France, England—or the United States—must be allowed to know the alarming weakness of the Russian allies. In the sake of such a cause an "accident" to two American newspaper correspondents was a mere nothing, and even an execution would be justified.

And Reed of course was already *persona non grata* with the American Government through his cynical disclosures of a big oil company's use of private policemen at Bayonne, New Jersey.

John and Boardman became more and more thoughtful as the days of the ultimatum expired.

It was not all politics, however, that we talked in those white nights in the little courtyard of the Angleterre.

I must have been rich for them! While John was baiting me like a picador in the bull-ring, Boardman would draw insulting cartoons of me on the table-cloth. (I wish I had kept them!) When John, relating the deeds of the Octobrists, held out such hopes for the Russian *Intelligentsia* in its efforts to throw off the Romanoff régime, I said that I would put him in touch with one of them.

This was Olga Ivanovna. I had met her that spring in a *cabinet privée* in the Villa Rodé at a midnight we were having with the gypsies out on the Islands. I had gone there with an Englishman, who had brought Olga along with him and another girl, and when we drove home that daybreak—facing the Admiralty golden steeple shining in the sun—we went back to Olga's place on the Letaney Prospeckt. She had a little apartment there overlooking a Mohammedan mosque. We called it the Mosque of the Seven Stars, because on its turquoise mosaicked dome we could see just seven stars from her bedroom window. We had sat up there all that morning, with two big sofas pulled so that they were facing each other, like the seats in a Russian railway train, and we played railway train—Olga insisted that we were Russian nobility being exiled to Siberia.

"Not," commented the Englishman, bored with such elephantine kittenishness, "that we should be travelling this way!"

Olga retorted that if the Englishman really wanted to know what the interior of a Siberian prison train was like, she could get hold of an ex-Siberian convict who had been in one, and whose brother had just been shot in Siberia.

The Englishman, very wisely as it turned out, said that he would just as lief not meet such an interesting fellow. But when John Reed and Boardman Robinson showed up on the scene, an ex-Siberian convict, it seemed to me, would be just the food for them.

By that time Olga Ivanovna and I had got to that point where we could sit up all night with the samovar, and she would tell me that her soul was sick, that Life held nothing for her but some ultimate great sacrifice; and she would listen while I told her what swine there were in the Russian purchasing departments, what a swine Frumkin was, what a swine the American millionaire was, etc., etc.—all of which, of course, was sheer bliss.

Supporting these conversations as chief listeners, and occasional contributors of sanguinary incident, were Rosa, Olga Ivanovna's steady girl companion who shared the flat with her, and a little hunchbacked Jew named Levitsky, by profession a wheat-broker, in secret life a hardworking enemy of the Tsar. It was his brother who had been shot in Siberia.

"He tried to protect a girl comrade from being ravished by a police officer. The policeman shot him. The Germans *must* win this war—Culture *must* triumph over barbarism!"

Levitsky, who was as brave as a lion, was also a brilliant conversationalist. He gave me a most *macabre* picture of the people who were "working under the floor" to overthrow the Romanoffs. He often came to us from meetings of his Comrades, and while he was discreet to the point of timidity about who they were or what they were planning, he did hint to me in advance of the two-day tram strike that nearly started the Revolution in Moscow in 1915. It was most dramatic. I was in Moscow and had just come out from being cooked alive in a Russian bath when I noticed that there was something "queer" with the street scene. I could not think what it was for some moments, then I saw that all the trams were stationary, some of them in the middle of a block—and that nobody was sitting in them. I thought the power had failed, but when I asked a bystander, an engineer, I could see from the green band on his cap, he smiled:

"No, something else is happening. I think this is IT!"

Levitsky groaned afterwards that if the Comrades had only had a little more guts, they could have had the Revolution in 1915. The Army was already ripe for rebellion over the way it was being massacred without proper ammunition to defend itself, the general populace, already queuing up for food and boots was growling that it was being starved to death, the newspapers were beginning to have to admit the inevitability of the German advance. There was not a factory in Petrograd, he claimed, whose workers would not have walked out at once.

"But we talk too much!" he said bitterly. "We do nothing but talk. And everybody wants to do it differently from everybody else. Russians must have a Master; they need a Brute—someone who can beat us into line."

"Like a Tsar?" I suggested.

"Well," he shrugged those hunchbacked, clever shoulders. "As a symbol, yes, he is the Brute. But have you ever noticed the statue of Alexander II before the Nicholas Station?"

This monstrous bronze horseman, done by Troubetskoy, was claimed to be one of the most superb works of Russian satire.

Alexander II, like the giant in a Fairy Tale, sits astride a Gargantuan horse. The great neck of the horse is bent, pulled in backwards by the bit, until its chin is almost against its terrific chest.

"But it's the reins! Look at its reins!" said Levitsky. "That is where the great jeer comes in! The horse you see is Russia—and its head is held by bits of string—if it just stretched out its head, it could snap them, if it sneezed!"

It was quite true. The reins were like toy ribbons with which a child ties a doll's hair. I looked at them, as I passed them at full speed, the day the Revolution broke out in 1917. I had been an unwilling witness of the first death of the Revolution—a conductor who tried to drive his tram through the mob a few blocks behind me on the Letaney Prospeckt. The machine guns were beginning their bop-bop-bop-bop. . . . And during the days of the Revolution, when I passed that Homeric figure in bronze, I looked for the little hunchback of Levitsky among the shouting Comrades that used it as a rallying place against the new surviving Tsar's police. But Levitsky was not there.

He had disappeared somewhere during the summer of 1915.

Seven Letaney Prospeckt amused John Reed for a night or so, but he immediately saw it for what it was.

"It's not the real thing," he laughed, with that absolute gusto for "seeing things happen" that made his eagerness for the Revolution, any Revolution, seem at times so childish. When this Revolution came, he said, it would be led by professional leaders of the proletariats, not the dilettante *revolutionaires*.

One day when I went in to pick them up for luncheon, I found both John and Boardman Robinson in an uproarious mood. They were amusing themselves by throwing pop bottles at a Russian Secret Service "plain" clothes man who was watching them from the street.

"You can always tell a Russian detective," said John, "because he wears a bowler hat like Charlie Chaplin, carries a little Charlie Chaplin cane, and wears patent leather shoes—like that!"

As he said this, he stepped back from the window and threw another pop bottle in a neat parabola into the street. Charlie Chaplin had moved to another lamp-post from which he was glaring at us.

"They replace them at regular intervals," said John. "We ruin the *morale*."

"We've had a gorgeous morning," said Boardman, with his deep-chested laugh. "They've been chasing us all day."

He then described one of their usual mornings of taking *droshkies* and giving them an address they never intended to go to —for the benefit of the lurking Charlie Chaplin's ears, then leaping out on either side as the *droshky* was galloping down the Nevsky. The frantic effort of Charlie Chaplin's pursuing *droshky* to turn and "dog" them again—how they would make a hurried rendezvous and then dart off in different directions, a frantic Charlie Chaplin not knowing which one to follow. Jumping on and off tram-cars and nearly breaking little Charlie Chaplin's neck. Going into the big Army and Navy Store, and, for the benefit of an eavesdropping Charlie Chaplin, asking the price of machine-guns, rifles, daggers and dynamite. Then going up and trying to speak to Charlie Chaplin. Little Charlie Chaplin becoming almost terrified at this distinctly unorthodox behaviour of the men he had been set to shadow, and no doubt quite reasonably terrified by big laughing John and Boardman, suddenly looking fierce and pulling his ferocious red beard—Charlie Chaplin on the run—just reversing the performance!—dodging like hell to get away from Boardman and John Reed!

No wonder the Grand Duke Nicholas wanted to have them shot! They deserved it.

"Bang!" The last bottle splintered at Charlie Chaplin's feet, which, when they reached the ground again took him hastily out of range. "Order some more soda, Boardman, the battery is running low."

"Today," said John, "we have had a great soul-stirring vision of what it means to be a citizen of those great United States. We have seen what the Stars and Stripes mean, how glorious it is to know that the Star-spangled Banner floats over the land of the

Free and the Home of the Brave. We know what this means to an American who sees that Flag of Freedom floating in Foreign Lands. We have been to our Embassy!"

John and Boardman had gone over to the American Embassy on the Fourstatskyia Oulitsa, that little two-storied building, to beg help from Ambassador Marye. Marye had been a Baltimore banker whose diplomatic post abroad had probably been obtained in the usual American manner of selecting its foreign Ambassadors, i.e., according to how much money they had contributed to the Republican Party's political campaign at election time. If, as Marye was coming down the lift in the Hotel Astoria, I happened to ask: "Well, Mr. Ambassador, what have the Germans been doing to us now?" the Ambassador to the Court of St. Petersburg would cock his top hat over the heel of his right thumb, in the manner of professional mourners at important funerals and declare:

"Mr. Farson, are you cognisant of the fact that the Teuton race . . ." etc., etc., *ad infinitissima* . . .

He could never use such simple words as "do you know"—it must be "are you cognisant"—and when John and Boardman came to him, he replied, according to John:

"Gentlemen, I regret exceedingly—the—ahem—shall we say, unfortunate predicament you find yourselves in, but—ahem—I would like to point out to your attention that you have wilfully, needlessly and may I say—ahem—quite unwarrantably created this—ahem—situation yourselves. Therefore,—ahem—I regret to inform you that the Embassy of the United States cannot take up your case. You have placed yourselves beyond the—ahem—outside my province—ahem—ahem, sorry."

"And this means," said John, "that you are not going to help us."

"You have—ahem—put the right—put the wrong complexion upon the situation, if I might say. It is no longer a question of my volition—I simply cannot do anything."

"Oh, yes, you can, Your Excellency," John is reported to have answered. "You can go to hell!"

It was afterwards that Boardman drew the cartoon of this

meeting which appeared in the *Metropolitan Magazine*. It showed Ambassador Marye, dressed in the comic semi-admiral's uniform that his Attaché Honoraire had just invented for the American Diplomatic Corps of Petrograd, his plumed hat almost burying his little head, his sword dangling between his legs, pointing to a sign above the American Embassy which, under a waving Stars and Stripes, announced:

NO AMERICANS NEED APPLY.

The British Embassy therefore took up the case. When somebody knocks an Englishman about, British foreign officials know by instinct what to do. If he is in the wrong, they will at least see that he gets a fair trial; if he is being maltreated, they will bring the whole force of Whitehall to bear on the unhappy foreign government, and if it is a little nation, it might even be paid a visit by a British gunboat. In either case, the British get him out. That's what the Union Jack means.

Boardman Robinson had been an Englishman before he became an American citizen. When he saw that the Grand Duke Nicholas meant to be nasty, and that the American Embassy was an utter wash-out, and that the days of the ultimatum were almost run, Boardman Robinson went over to the red British Embassy by the Troitsky Most, and had a talk with capable Benjie Bruce, now husband of the beautiful ballerina Karsavina, and then Counsellor. Bruce listened, saw the seriousness of the situation, and acted at once to prevent something tragic happening.

I was sitting in their bedroom in the Angleterre when Bruce brought over to John Reed and Boardman Robinson the telegram which the British Embassy in Petrograd had sent to the Grand Duke. It was over a page long, and it was to the effect that, in spite of their having violated Russian regulations by appearing behind the Russian Front without the proper credentials, and much as it was to be regretted that such a thing had happened, they were nevertheless two very eminent and respectable American newspaper men; that there could be no question of their having anything but the most impeccable attitude towards Russia, and that it would be an act of the greatest magnanimity if His

Imperial Highness, the Grand Duke Nicolai Nicolaievitch could see his way to permit them to leave forthwith via Sweden. With the highest respect, etc.

"I think," said the handsome Benjie Bruce, "that this will do the trick. I am sure that all he wants is to get you out of his mind as quickly as possible. So do we! But you must leave those poor wretched secret service men in peace!"

It worked. In a few days a wire came back from the Front, saying that John Reed and Boardman Robinson were quite free to leave Russia via Sweden, provided they did it forthwith. They did. I did not see John Reed again—not in Russia, that is—until the Revolution was in full swing.

Chapter 25

KNIGHT OF THE DOUBLE CROSS

IN THE summer of 1915 I don't think I ever went to bed before six o'clock in the morning. I know I saw every sunrise, because this was the time of the long "white nights," which are really green, when there was only about an hour of semi-darkness around midnight. Dawn is the most beautiful time to look at Petrograd when its great blocks of colour are softened in the pastel lights along the cool Neva, and the city is neither Europe nor Asia, but a fantasy of both. We were usually out on the Islands and drove home past the Admiralty, to be challenged by its great spire, shining like a golden spear in the early sunlight. The freshness of the green islands with the mists just clearing off them was at silent dawn a rebuke for the stuffy *cabinets privées* we had just spent the night in; full of cigarette smoke, the smell of young girls, red heads of dead crayfish and the echoes of crazy laughter and gypsy songs.

It was a summer of dejection, with deliberate dissipation as an antidote.

These Petrograd parties had a sinister efficiency, like the conduct of an established rake. In ordinary restaurants, like the "Bear," private dining-rooms were provided for serious love affairs. A brother officer's wife could be taken there. The waiters always knocked twice, and did not come in before the word, "*Moishna*," "it is permitted," was heard. In the road-houses out on the Islands, such as the famous Villa Rodé, it was just wild carouse. The *cabinets privées* there had windows that looked down over the tables in the main dining-room and were like box seats for the stage. On tables loaded with sweet champagne and piles of red crayfish, the wildest of our Russian girls put on shows that would have made the professional performers blush.

Then the waiters would begin to yawn, and we would see the tired attendants below sweeping and piling up the chairs. We would collect our girls and drive home.

Sometimes I felt like a scallywag as I came back to the hotel. I was going to bed just when everybody else was getting up. I would take a cold bath to wash off the night. Sometimes I could not sleep and would lie there through the melancholic morning, wondering where all this was leading me to.

But if we felt particularly gloomy we did not go home to bed. We carried on. We would take gypsies and girls to some other place. When Peter Serck, the Norwegian, got his war order from the Russian Government he gave a party that lasted three days. I entered it after the ballet, with the singer's sable stole around the neck of my dinner jacket. This was in the dead of winter, and I woke up the morning of the third day to find myself in an open Daimler car, far out on the foot of the Islands by the Royal Yacht Club. All the petrol had run out. I had no idea how I got there, and the Englishman who had been driving the car was still snoring over its wheel. Nothing but the alcohol in us, I suppose, saved us from being frozen to death.

It might have been wrong, although I don't think a more earnest soul would have found a better way; it was my way, at any rate, of trying to keep my sanity while struggling to do business with the exasperating Russian War Department. A week like this was usually washed out of my system by a long week-end out in the country at Murano, where I swam naked in the streams that ran through its birch woods, played golf, ate heaps of fresh cucumbers, and sprawled on a hundred-year-old croquet lawn at tea-time, to retail to my pretty hostess of the Millionayia Oulitsa all the scandal that I had been able to collect about our friends and notabilities.

As a tribute to our somewhat dormant sporting sense, Jack Hoth and I would occasionally go out on the William Island and shoot clay birds, thrown overhead from a tower, at the Krestoff-sky Pigeon Club—during the winter of course we shot only live pigeons out there—and I played a certain amount of tennis over at the *Midshipmanski Courts*.

But, no matter what I happened to be doing, nine-tenths of my thoughts were centred around the War Department, and what was happening to my orders. Whales, I believe, are still a riddle to science. No one seems to know exactly how long it takes to make a baby whale. All they know is that when it does arrive—it is a *whale*. It was very much the same with a Russian war contract; we never knew how long it would take to come through. But when it did we knew that it would be worth waiting for.

The golf course at Murano was an amazing affair. It was the only one in Russia, built by the English in a stubborn attempt to let nothing stand in their way of expressing themselves. But as it was all either sand-dunes or pine trees, one never knew when it was legal to ground one's club. Also the clumps of pine trees were full of Russian children who ran off with the ball the instant you hooked a drive, and then sold your ball back to you at lunchtime. We bought them back with a sigh of thanks, because golf balls were as valuable as awk's eggs in war-time Russia and just as hard to come by. The British Embassy had theirs sent out in the dispatch bags with the King's Messenger, but the rest of us had to hunt all over Petrograd for them. A broken club was a tragedy, which one had to repair oneself. Strange golfing costumes decorated the brave golf course at Murano. A veteran American war correspondent, for instance, used to play there in white duck trousers, a long-tailed morning coat and a straw "boater."

He had a *datcha*, summer bungalow, in the birch woods, where his wife, a professional pianist, had chicken and waffles—and everybody who could get invited there—for Sunday breakfasts.

Poor old Whiffen! One of the most fearless and hard-faced American newspaper men I ever knew; he had a hidden romantic streak.

When he died in Soviet Russia, we discovered it. He said, in his Will, he wanted to be buried in Russia, the country that he had damned day in and day out as a professional journalist. Not only that: he wanted to be cremated, taken up in an aeroplane and from there to have his ashes strewn over the Red Square in Moscow.

He died (murdered by a filthy hospital operation) in dead winter. No plane could be obtained for some weeks, so Walter was cremated and put in a jar, and his successor came to live in Walter Whiffen's apartment. His successor was a New York Jew, who noticed that the Russian servant always managed to get flowers, even in dead winter, and put them around a little jar that stood on his breakfast table. He asked her about it one morning, why she did it. For Mr. Whiffen, she replied; he had been such a kind man.

"But Mr. Whiffen is dead."

"Know it"—the girl pointed at the jar on the table by the marmalade—"*Gaspoden Whiffen tam!*"

"Jesus!"

Reinhart took one look at the urn holding all that was left of courageous, romantic old Walter and fled from the flat. He couldn't be made to come back to it.

"Jesus!" he said. "And me eating breakfast there every morning with *him* on the table!"

When an aeroplane finally was secured, flying up over the eagles of the Kremlin, and the pilot leaned over the side to let Walter sift down gently on to the heads of Russia's proletariat, he dropped the jar, which just missed a Red soldier walking harmlessly through the square. Walter, I believe, hit just this side of the Cathedral of St. Basil, whose architect had his eyes gouged out by Ivan the Terrible so that he could never build another.

Nor will there ever be another Walter Whiffen.

Letters from home that summer informed me that most of my friends were becoming millionaires out of war orders. New York had a fever like a diphtheria chart. This was all very disturbing to someone who saw himself on the verge of being broken in all senses of the word at any moment, and Olga Ivanovna and I used to have long talks about it. She wouldn't marry me (not that I ever asked her to) she said, but she was quite willing to go to America with me and be my wife without benefit of clergy. With my sort of family I tried to make her see the utter impossibility of such a thing. Then, she said, why go to America? Stay on and live one's life here in Russia. The roses of the Crimea were finer than those of any other country.

We used to have luncheon every day, after I had paid my ceremonial call on the Technical Department, on the Hôtel de l'Europe roof. There we could look out over the enamelled domes of Petrograd, and a little shaven-headed Tartar waiter would leave us alone with our wine in the latticed kiosk all the afternoon if we chose to stay there.

Olga Ivanovna, I learned there, had been in love. It was a Cossack officer she had nursed when she was with the Red Cross at the Front. I never knew his name; he was always "The Man from the War." She did not love him now, she said. That was what made her so sad—because he always kept writing to her. He was, he said, going to marry her as soon as he could get leave from the Front, but there were so many damned Austrians to kill yet!

One day when I came up on the Hôtel de l'Europe roof, Olga Ivanovna was not there. Instead, the girl friend, Rosa, was there. Rosa, never a pretty girl, had been weeping. Her nose was red and her eyes were swollen. "Negley!" she cried. "The Man from the War is back!"

"Well, what of it?"

"He—he is going to kill Olga Ivanovna!"

"Rot!"

"He tried to—*he tried to kill her this morning!*"

"For God's sake—why?"

"You—Olga Ivanovna told him about you!"

In a kiosk, full of tears Rosa then told how the bell had rung, how the Man from the War had been standing there, how he had pushed Rosa aside and rushed furiously around the flat looking for Olga Ivanovna. When he found her, still in bed, he had seized her by her beautiful white neck and said:

"If I don't have you, nobody shall have you!"

To me it sounded very much like the lines of David Warfield in *The Old Music Master*, and I couldn't repress a smile. Rosa went frenzied at that:

"He pointed a revolver at her head. 'Speak!' he told Olga Ivanovna. 'You will marry me now? I am here!' "

But Olga stuck it out. Apparently, without saying anything to me about it, she had written the Man from the War, telling that hot-headed Cossack that she loved another, and he was acting just as any good Cossack would upon receipt of such news.

"Does he know who I am?" I asked.

"Yes, of course. Olga Ivanovna showed him your photograph!"

"Well, that was tactless of her—what am I supposed to do now?"

Rosa then said that Olga and the officer had both got so excited that the officer had dropped his revolver on the sofa and got down on his knees on the floor, with his arms around her legs. Olga shoved him loose and got into another room.

"And I picked up the revolver," said Rosa.

"Sure?"

"Here it is."

She opened her bag and showed me a wicked little Colt. I *was* glad to see it!

"But are you sure," I asked, "he hasn't got another?"

"No," said Rosa, "only his silvered dagger." Which, I thought, remembering those double-edged fluted blades, was quite enough.

"Well," I said, taking a deep breath, "you go into the phone booth and call Olga Ivanovna, and ask her what she wants me to do. Tell her I will come up now if she wants me."

The phone booths were covered with green baize, like a billiard table, with a little elliptical glass peep-hole. I spent a bad two or three minutes looking through that. Russians are never altogether curt to each other over the telephone, and it seemed to me that Rosa and Olga would never finish with each other. And I wanted to know my fate as soon as possible.

"This," said Rosa when she emerged; "Olga Ivanovna wants you to do this. Stay in your room in the Astoria until she telephones you. She has told the Man from the War that she will marry him. She is going to take him out for a drive. She will drive him about all the afternoon, out to Sisteretz, I think, and then she is going to come back to the flat and tell him to leave her as she must have time to pack. That will be about six o'clock, she said, and she is going to tell him not to come back until 9. That will give you about three hours to get her out. She will go 'way with you."

Rosa had forgotten something: "You see, Olga Ivanovna has

told the Man from the War that she will go to Finland tonight, she will go with him to Terioki."

"Tell her I'll be waiting," I said, and put Rosa on a Nevsky tram.

Then I went back to the hotel. It was no joke to cross a love-sick Cossack, even if you did happen to have his automatic. And Olga Ivanovna's time-table did not look any too good for me. If I had been that Cossack, knowing Olga as I did, I would have spent from six to nine o'clock outside her apartment door. And unless he was an absolute fool that was exactly what he would be doing. Therefore—what about me?

I took a sheet of Astoria notepaper and carefully printed out Olga Ivanovna's address. Then I put it in an envelope and sealed it. Then I went downstairs to the room where lived the Third Secretary of the American Embassy.

"Ryan," I said to him, "I want to borrow your heaviest walking-stick—that cane you've got. (It was a hefty Irish blackthorn!) And I want you to do me one great favour."

"Okay, kiddo. What is it?"

"See this letter? No. I don't want you to open it. I want you to keep it. And if I don't come and get it back from you, say, before lunch-time tomorrow—or telephone you in the meantime— I want you to open it."

"And then what?"

Yes, what then? What could he do?

"Well, there is an address inside it. If you haven't got a luncheon date or anything like that, I wish you would go up to that address by yourself just as fast as you can get."

"Boy! What is this? Ain't you up to something nefarious?"

I grinned. He was a stout fellow, Ryan; he might smoke long thin stogies, so as to make himself look like the American Senator Uncle Joe Cannon; he might talk politics and send postcards home to all his constituents in preparation for his expected Congressional career; but I did not know anyone whom I would rather see turn up at 7 Letaney Prospeckt the next morning in case I did not show up to get that letter back.

"Promise?" I said.

"Abso-bloody-lutely!"

Then I went upstairs to my room and sat down and read Tolstoy's *Resurrection*.

At six o'clock prompt the phone jangled. It was Olga Ivanovna. "Come," she said. "Hurry!"

Then the phone clicked.

I picked up the blackthorn, crossed myself, and pressed the lift-button.

Seven Letaney Prospeckt was an apartment house built around a courtyard. There was nobody at the outside entrance except an old dozing *schwitsar*. Olga Ivanovna's entrance was diagonally across the court and I looked up at her windows. They were all closed. Then I began to climb the stairs.

"There are double-doors into her flat," I muttered to myself. "It will take some time to open them both. I will listen. If I hear that *pssing-pssing* of an officer's spurs, I won't look—no, I will just take one wild swing with this blackthorn inside the door."

That, I thought, ought to give me the advantage right from the very start. It was a crude bit of *tactique* but I could think of no better one.

> *Twice blest is he who knows his cause is just*
> *But thrice blest he who gets his knock in fust!*

But I thought of those lines afterward. Almost the instant I rang the door bell Olga stood before me. Her head was wrapped in a towel, her eye and face were swollen. She pulled me inside. She was a terrible sight.

"Well"—I began, looking around the room for the Man from the War—"where is he?"

If anybody had dropped a book then I would have jumped five feet in the air.

"He promised not to come back before nine," she sobbed. "But I do not believe him."

"Neither do I," I said. "For goodness' sake, get some clothes on you."

While she was dressing the bell rang. I picked up the black-thorn again. This time *I* would open the door, and once again I had the same resolve, if I heard that *pssing-pssing* of spurs—to take one wild swing. If I hit the wrong man I could apologise about it afterwards. But this was only little hunchbacked Levit-sky.

"What's the matter?" he asked, looking at me clasping the blackthorn. And I explained things.

"Well," he said, "when I saw Rosa just now she looked rather excited. She was running down the street as if the police were after her!"

Olga had sent Rosa off to get a spring dress back from the cleaners.

"Well," added Levitsky, with great wisdom, "we don't seem to have much time, do we?"

He was, as it happened, a cupid who had flown in on us just in time. I gave him a handful of roubles and sent him off post-haste to the railway station.

"There's an eight o'clock for Moscow," I said. "Get Olga Ivanovna and Rosa two sleepers on that. We'll meet you at the station."

Half-way to the station Rosa remembered that she had forgot-ten to get back their passports from the *schwitsar*, and I had to leap out of the *droshky* and rush back for them. He made an awful stew about handing them over to me, I at any minute expecting to see the love-maddened Cossack roll up, and when I did reach the station the Moscow train had gone, so had Olga and Rosa, and so had Levitsky.

Two days later I went down to Moscow by the same train to ride down as far as Kharkov with Olga Ivanovna. She was going on down to the Crimea, to Theodosia, that poplar-shaded para-dise by the Black Sea where her delightful ox-heart cherry eyes had first opened on this glorious world. I rode back to Petrograd with Rosa.

"I wonder," she mused. "Where is the Man from the War? I would like to know where he is."

"So would I," I told her.

And for weeks after that I could never pass a Cossack without a sudden desire to sprint. For one thing, I knew that at least he must want his revolver back.

I never heard from or saw Olga Ivanovna again—not until in the little Russian church in Welbeck Street, London, I was holding the golden crown over the head of the Russian Naval officer who was being married to Olga Ivanovna's sister. Looking over my shoulder from that tiresome position of being the "best man," I saw Olga Ivanovna looking down at me from a bench she stood on along the church wall. She had left by the time the ceremony was over. I did not try to look her up.

There is no point to this story. It's just Russia.

Chapter 26

SMASH UP

THE SUMMER of 1915, thank God, was coming to an end. The days were getting noticeably shorter and Petrograd was beginning to be cloaked in those evening mists that make it such a dreary place before the snows. It's the worst season of the year for that "eye into Europe" that Peter the Great built with a knout out of the swamps.

Frumkin was still in prison. We expected any day now to hear he had been shot. I had never been able to re-establish myself with the War Office after my break-up with Frumkin, and now with him in prison charged with being a German spy my former close association with him had put me under a cloud. My friendship with John Reed also helped to make officials somewhat gunshy of me. The Artillery Department was a dead letter as far as any chance there was concerned, and I was in a tight corner with the big American millionaire, that cannibal trout, waiting lazily outside it to gobble me up.

Also, owing to the attitude of London and New York, I was hard pressed for money. I was really very hard up, and it was no longer a case of all-night soirées out on the Islands of Petrograd or crayfish with the gypsies at Yar's or Strelna's in Moscow. I was beginning to get as economical with my funds as shipwrecked sailors with their last keg of fresh water on a raft. I doled it out to myself, drop by drop.

For this reason I made an arrangement with Howe of the Robert Dollar Co., the big American steamship and exporting concern, and we decided to pool our interests as far as the approach to the Zemskie Soujouse was concerned.

"But you must not think that there is no graft here!" he declared. "I know it is not in places higher up. Lvov, of course, would see that the man was shot whom he caught taking palm oil—but it's there! It's all through the small fry in the organisation. They have to be 'fixed' or they will stymie every approach we make. I'm already giving it."

He then introduced me to a man who would have made the perfect *gigolo* for some sex-starved American millionairess travelling abroad. Of him I can remember only three things clearly. That he was a Pole, that he had a dog that was continuously winning prizes at Cruft's Dog Show in London—or perhaps it was only the same prize he was always telling us about—and that his name was Baron Ripp.

"*Bonjour! Comment ça va?* Ah-ha! Ah-ha! Mr. Farson—and how are we today?"

I eyed him with gloomy distrust.

The trouble with Baron Ripp was that although we gave the required bribe-money to him, we could not find out who he was giving it to. We did have what might have been interpreted as one or two startlingly successful results, but I pointed out to Howe that it might have been through our own efforts.

"I think he keeps it," I said.

Howe was not much use in this. When things got too complicated he would go over and stand in one of the churches of the Kremlin and do a Yogi on himself. He had picked up that habit of temple contemplation in his twenty years of China. Then he would come back and read Elbert Hubbard and Omar Khayyám, after which combination he would have a sort of mental colic and become quite unable to think.

He *saw* things!

"I can *see* Ripp now," he said. "And I *know* that something is wrong!"

"What's he doing?" I asked.

"I don't know. That's just what I want to know."

And Howe would rub his brow with his finger-tips.

Howe frightened me. I took to going over to the Kremlin too. I had always been fascinated by those red walls beside the Moskva River, its unbelievable piles of onion-shaped domes, its rich feeling of the past. I would have liked nothing better than to have been care-free enough to wander about it for days and days. Life in Moscow could so easily have been sheer enchantment. I still think it is the most mentally exhilarating city in the world. But Howe and I were half sick with worry.

The summer had gone far enough for the ballet season to be opened. Or it might have been a special performance, I do not remember which, but it was a very distinguished night with some of the most important dancers on the stage; and I remember it quite distinctly for two specific things. The first was that I went there alone with one of the French military attachés who had been given one of the Imperial boxes, where we sat in solitary grandeur. The next was that that was one of the last nights that I was to walk about freely on my own two legs.

That morning had opened with a cold drizzle that marked the beginning of winter, and that was unfortunate, because on this day we were to have a test of our machines. In this case they were to be some motor-cycles, with machine-gun attachment on side-car platforms that we were to demonstrate out on the flying field. We had all our stuff out on the field except one machine which had been left at the hotel by the Russian motor-cycle "expert" we had engaged to drive for us in the tests.

"Drive?"—or should I have said ride? At any rate I knew nothing about motor-cycles; I had never been on one in my life. And we were aghast when the Russian "expert" did not show up. The "expert" was a Russian soldier, a big tall fellow, with three St. George's crosses. With his breast covered with black-and-orange ribbons he would easily have been noticed in any crowd, for one reason alone: everybody would be turning to look at him. He was a very fine fellow indeed; but he did not show it at the one time when it would have pleased us most.

We waited until the last minute, then Howe got a *droshky* and—as there was no hope of finding anyone else to do the job now—I got on the motor-cycle, and after a few kicks at the starter, the machine jumped off! My first attempt in twisting the handle grips almost snapped my hat off my head. It was a terrifying experience. I went half-way round the square before the Hotel Metropole, before I could stop. It was an American machine, fearfully heavy, and when I stood up and carelessly let it lean away from me it pulled me over flat on my face. Then I more or less got the hang of it, and we went sliding and jumping and lurching out to the flying-field.

I, of course, knew how to drive a car, and by this time I had more or less got the hang of things, at any rate, I was in for it now. I took the brute over the bumps that had been selected out on the flying-field, made it go down into a ditch and jazzed it up the other bank, and then the commission asked me to give them an exhibition of its acceleration and speed. After which we would couple it up—showing how quickly that could be done—and go through the machine-gun side-car test.

There is, or at least was, a long, winding cobbled road along the edge of the flying-field, which was shut off from the main highway by a board fence. I took this with the hand-grips fully twisted, my hat long since blown off my head. A driver of another machine that was to be tested rode along beside me, ahead of me in fact, till we came to some of the turns. Here I picked up a bit and on one turn I passed him, tried to straighten out, and felt the wheels failing to grip on the greasy cobbles, and sitting helpless like this I sailed, slightly sidewise, clean over a shallow ditch and completely through the board fence. . . .

"It's still running!" was the first remark I heard clearly, and found myself being pulled out from under the roaring machine and helped to my feet. And even then I wondered at the unkillability of that thing! I seemed to have nothing more than the breath knocked out of me, a ruined double-breasted blue suit, torn to shreds in places, and a few cuts. My legs, though, looked bad enough to bandage on the spot, which was done by some of the air force sanitars. The front forks of the machine had been smashed, however, and we were out of the test, a thing which as it turned out did not do us any harm. We eventually got the order. Everybody present had been much too impressed by how little damage it had really suffered after knocking such a big hole in that thick board fence. I was feeling the same congratulatory mood about myself.

It may have been the annoying woman we had supper with after the ballet. "It's too *muscular!*" she chattered at us as we ate cold sturgeon around the fountain in the Hotel Metropole. "Look at their *legs*—they're like cart-horses! It's so *vulgar* . . . leaping about like that. I much prefer the sinuous, sensuous dance of *Spain* . . . don't you, Captain—er?"—at any rate I felt ill.

Two nights later, in a private room at Pivato's in Petrograd, I fell across the table in a faint. I had a violent streptococci infection.

It was over a year before I was able to walk without crutches again.

In the meantime the whole roof caved in.

The big American millionaire, the cannibal trout, did not even bother to eat me now. He merely cabled New York what had happened, and I got a cable saying all business was now in his hands. My Power of Attorney was cancelled. But I did not get another draft for my expense account. . . . They couldn't, however, break the arrangements I had made with Howe for the Zemskie. He got the order, a small one, but he got it. And then he also got the sack. He came into my room one morning when I was tossing about with 104 degrees, trying to dream of ice-fields covered with oranges.

"I'm off to China," he said. "Christ—but I'll be glad to get out of Russia!"

"So would I!"

As did all my friends, to keep me company in that Astoria Hotel bedroom, he ordered his meal and sat down and ate it beside me. He gave me a sip of iced white wine.

"Well, so long," he said.

For the first time since I had left it I wired my home for some money. I got it in about a week from my guardian, with the cryptic question: "WHAT'S WRONG?" I had not told them of course, and when he saw me being carried off the boat at New York he got the shock of his life. Among other things I had dropped from thirteen stone to ten.

But that was months later. There were several Gethsemanes to be gone through with first. One of them was having some bone removed, where my bed was the operating-table, the chloroform mask was made from the back of my old writing-pad, and the surgeons . . . well, perhaps the less said about them the better. One of them to whom I telephoned one night, when I was half out of my mind, for some morphia, left his lady friend at the supper party in his room, painted a round disc with iodine on my thigh with a shaky hand, and *threw* the hypodermic needle at it—

"Bull's-eye!" he gasped.

My pretty English hostess of the Millionayia Oulitsa heard about such goings-on. How, for instance, to keep my mind off myself, my friends used to hold midnight poker parties in my room, games in which I usually took a hand. And she had a talk with those doctors!

I hear that one of them is running a garage in the United States now. If so, I must be careful to whom I take my car.

She discovered that they were not giving me morphia at all. They were doping me up with innocuous iodides. And, when it came to a show-down—she pressed them to that point—they did not know what to do. They then told her they didn't think it of much use to do anything. I would not last long.

In the meantime Jack Hoth had given me his valet—Alexander. Alexander used to sleep by my side on a couch, rolled up in comforters in pigeon-egg-blue silk underclothes. I should imagine he had picked up his fashions at Monte Carlo and Nice where Jack used to take him for the winter before the Great War. And the magnitude of Jack's sacrifice can be gauged by the fact that until Alexander took a tram back in the morning, all the way out to William Island, Jack Hoth could not get out of bed. Alexander served two masters, and he served them both well!

"Poor, poor Mr. Farson," he used to say—tears in his eyes. "Can't I do *anything* for you?"

"Turn me over," I said, "I'll try to see if I can't get to sleep on the other side."

One day when he had half-carried me into the bathroom he found that I had fainted on the toilet. I had grabbed at the wash-basin as I saw it coming, and my head was hanging in there over my arm.

"Poor, poor Mr. Farson . . . !"

I came to, to find Alexander patting my head.

"This simply can't go on!" said my pretty English hostess one morning, her cheeks pink from the cold snows. "This is simply horrible. They'll kill you! I can't stand it. I'm taking you over to my place."

"But I can't!" I protested, "I can't leave—I owe this hotel too much money. I haven't paid them for eight months!"

"Stuff and nonsense—call Louis."

I did, and that little Frenchman came up. Little Louis, the cynical manager of hotels in Nice, Paris and Petrograd. Louis Terrier, one of Europe's great *hôteliers*. Dapper little Frenchman in his immaculate morning suit. I explained things to him after my hostess had gone.

"Of course," I said, "I can pay you part of it."

"Mr. Farson—*please!*"

Louis had leapt up. With a most exquisite gesture he rejected my money. He was, he said, horrified that I should suggest such a thing.

"Nothing!" he said. "We can talk about that when you are better."

A Scotchwoman and a Frenchman—and a Finn. What fine friends they were!

For, of course, Jack Hoth insisted that Alexander must accompany me to the Millionayia Oulitsa. He wouldn't sleep there, of course—

"But there are certain little odd jobs about a sickroom that you'd rather have Alexander do."

I was now getting gaunt enough to be interesting, and I appeared at dinner parties with the lower part of me wrapped up in blankets in my rolling chair, and above-decks in a dinner-jacket that Alexander had got on to me in the most ingenious fashion. I thought it was cruelty at first. I thought it was callous the way my pretty hostess would bait me for being an American before all the other dinner guests. I knew her caustic wit and that the "snottier" I could be about the English, the better she would like it. What she was really doing in fact was to keep my

brains and my blood moving and to get me accustomed to being
"up" as much as possible, so that it would not be too much of
an effort when I made my stab at reaching New York. Their
kindness was marvellous. Her husband would even come into
my room in the evening and kneel down in his immaculate dinner-jacket, and put on my shoes for me.

She had, I might add, got me a Russian doctor, and a very
good doctor he was, too.

So at six o'clock one morning with Alexander quite tearful,
we drove through a snowstorm to the Finlandski station, and I
was carried into a compartment. There had been a last touch of
the Frumkin affair when the police at the frontier wanted to
take the bandages off my leg to see if I had anything concealed
underneath them. Only my Red Cross nurse succeeded in preventing them doing it. They did pinch my leg to see if they
could feel the crackle of paper beneath my dressings!

Three days later I was carried aboard at Gothenburg, the guns
in all the rocky grey fort fired a salute, and the *Stockholm* (late
the German *Potsdam*) started off on her maiden voyage for the
United States. Most of the directors of the steamship company
were travelling in their new liner and a bottle of champagne had
been placed in each cabin. I asked my Red Cross nurse if I could
have a lobster salad and she said yes.

"*Skol!*" I said to her, holding up my glass. "Your health, my
health, everybody in Sweden's health!"

Chapter 27

ROMANCE FOR REVENGE

WE HAD an amusing time on the *Stockholm*. This was her maiden trip, and the first thing she attempted was to run the British blockade. On the second day out we noticed that her engines had stopped. We rolled in the Atlantic swell. Then a feather of black smoke appeared over the horizon, a destroyer materialised at the nose of it, growing larger every minute, and a little British midshipman climbed up our side. He saluted our huge, red-faced Swedish skipper.

"Sorry, Captain—but you will have to put back to Kirkwall."

"The English!" damned Torsten. "By God!—what right have they to do such things to us Swedes!"

We lay in Kirkwall two days while the *Stockholm* got her hatch covers off and gave the British a good look inside. I saw several sacks, which I was told was contraband mail from Germany, taken off her. Then we were allowed to proceed to New York. The Swedes were furious! Aside from the indignity, the charter of a ship like the *Stockholm*, in those war-profiteering days, was worth about £3,000 a day. Torsten was angry because he was rushing to the United States on a mission from the Swedish Government to buy a huge quantity of food supplies (I always thought they were to liberate other Swedish foods to go into Germany); and I was none too happy about the delay myself, because it was a nip-and-tuck question with me whether I would have time to reach a New York operating-table alive.

That was no joke; and Torsten, with his baby blue eyes, was also furious with the British on my account.

There was a touch of comedy in Kirkwall. Beside us lay another steamer. The gold lettering on her bows read *Oscar II*. It was Henry Ford's ridiculous Peace Ship.

"It's a battleship!" screamed a man who had been thrown off it and on to the *Stockholm*. "All they do there every night is fight all dinner long! God, to think of a crowd of idiots like that going over to try and stop a war in Europe! Hell! they can't even keep the peace among themselves!"

This fellow was a newspaper correspondent, one of the worst sort; he knew everything. And to give him some more of this we made up an imaginary campaign on the Russian Front. We told him about the terrible battle of *Stakan Chai*, where General *Moroshnie* swam his regiment of Cossack *Oodkas* across the Lena to take the Austrians in the rear. How the Austrians killed every last *Oodka!* He snapped out his note-book and took it down. The Censor, we told him, would never let that story get out of Russia. He would be the first one to print it. He would have a world scoop.

That was as we neared the shores of America, when we particularly detested him. He had tried at the last moment to have an affair with my nice nurse. She and I were very much inclined to let that story of *Stakan Chai* go into print. But then, I reflected, it would absolutely wreck his career. The American papers at that time were quite capable of printing anything—and his managing editor would never forgive him for selling them this pup!

So I called him down to my cabin, told him that *stakan chai* meant glass of tea, that *moroshnie* was Russian for ice-cream, that *oodka* meant duck, that the Lena was a river a thousand miles from any Austrian Front, and more or less asked him to forgive such a silly joke.

But I had to become a newspaper correspondent myself to learn what they are capable of doing in the way of revenge! The next morning when the steward brought my breakfast-tray there was a card beside the grapefruit, and it read:

> Miss Anna Goertz & Mr. Negley Farson
> Beg to Announce
> Their Engagement.

S.S. *Stockholm.*

Anna came in completely shattered, and said that there was such a card on every table in the dining-saloon. We did not know then, until after the ship had docked, who had caused them to be printed; and just when we were about to send for the ship's printer to try and find out, a note came down from the *Stock-holm's* captain, saying the ship would like to give us a dinner that night—did I think I was well enough to be taken into the dining-saloon? After that, there was nothing to do, of course, but go through with it. I have never to this day been able to grasp why we did not both simply deny it, but I suppose she felt with anyone as ill as I was on her hands, that the line of least resistance would be easiest for me, and I had some mud-dled feeling of chivalry that a denial would be a slight to her.

"Bear up," I told Anna, "I might have been worse."

She was in tears, and only her professional concern about get-ting my 10 stone of misery into the dining-saloon made her face the ordeal at all. There was a heavy sea running. Our table had been banked with flowers which had evidently been in the ice-box since the ceremony of the send-off of the maiden trip; and the Swedish captain stood up on his gallant sea legs and made a very pretty speech. . . .

I replied. In normal health, I shudder at the mere thought of making a speech of any sort. But I wedged myself between the table and a pillar of our alcove and thanked the captain, praised the fine ship and, nodding at Torsten, remarked what a pity it was the descendants of the Vikings had become such puny men.

There was a bellow of laughter from all the gigantic Swedes, who all raised their glasses to six foot six Torsten, who there-upon rose, with his baby blue eyes, and calmly told the gather-ing that he was going to be my Best Man!

And as a matter of fact, he was, but that is quite another story. I heard Anna sobbing. . . .

"Smile!" I hissed. "Get up and say something! Quick!"

She stood up, opened her pretty mouth, and then quite un-consciously reached down for the napkin and began to wipe her tears. . . .

The effect was terrific! The whole dining-saloon stood up and cheered. Never had they seen such a radiant pair! They started *"Skoling!"* everybody . . . and I was carried back under one of Torsten's mighty arms.

"You devil!" I groaned at him from my bunk. "You and your Best Man business!"

That vengeful newspaper reporter kept it up. When the *Stockholm* moved on to her slip, saluted by the sirens of all ships in the harbour of New York, awaited by every ship reporter in the City, Anna and I found ourselves facing a battery of cameras. This, said the reporters, was great stuff!—Ocean Romance! First page stuff. . . .

So it was. The Directors of the *Stockholm's* line were merely snapped once, all lumped together in a bunch. And the next day when I was being given an enema for my operation, the hospital orderly (a Russian, by the way!) handed me a New York paper with our photos on the front page!

"Dot's lovely!" he said.

Anna did not think so. Her young man in Philadelphia saw our photographs in the *Bulletin*, announcing our ocean romance, and immediately broke off his engagement to Anna—thereby just about breaking her heart. There simply must have been fire, he insisted, where there was so much smoke! She rushed up to New York, and was, in fact, the very first person I was allowed to see after my operation.

"You've got to straighten things out!" she cried. "There's a man outside the door *now*, trying to interview you for the New York *American*—they have a Sunday story about us! It covers a whole page of the *American!*"

I begged my nurse to let me speak to the *American* man just for one minute (he and I afterwards became the best of friends):

"If you print that story," I growled, "I'll sue the paper. Every damn word of it is a lie!"

"Ah, go on!" he begged. "Let it go in. It's a whale of a good story! Why spoil it! Why don't you go ahead and marry the girl?"

He did not print it. But he did send me the proof—and I read it over in my darkest moments. It was a romance—such as only Dunham's fertile brain could have imagined. And I wrote Anna's young man a letter which put everything all right. Before I left hospital I received an announcement of their wedding.

Chapter 28

WAR ORDER MADNESS

I DID not see New York for months, because I lay securely strapped to a board on the top of a down-town hospital. By turning my head I could look over its roof tops, and below me was always the roar of the traffic in its streets, and at nights I could see the lights on the river. But for many months the three most important things in the day to me were breakfast, lunch and dinner—with of course the dread day when the surgeon would do my dressings.

It was a good time to improve one's mind, and almost the first day I was allowed to see anybody John Reed turned up with an armful of books.

"You're a born Communist," he said, "even if you don't know it. I think you could do anything in the world that you wanted, if you would only put your mind to it. Here's some brain fodder."

John was already earning the hate of United States officialdom that was to pursue and persecute him to the day of his death from typhus in Moscow. He did not seem to care, but it was making life very difficult for him. He was very hard up. He was feeling the weight of public opinion against anyone who tries to tell it an unpleasant truth. Some of the magnificent stuff he and Boardman Robinson had done on Russia had got into the *Metropolitan*, but not all of it. They had struck a submerged mine when they tried to blow up the great Russian "steam-roller" myth. And perhaps that dramatic issue of the *Metropolitan* has not yet been forgotten where, after having come off the press, it was sent back to have a new cover design stamped over its old one. The magazine was coming out with a sensational exposure of Rasputin and had an enormous figure of the Mad Monk on its jacket. Then the Russian Embassy at Washington got wind of it, as did the Allied diplomats, and the *Metropolitan* changed its cover design. A new design was stamped in heavy colours over the figure of Rasputin. But by holding it up to the light one could see through the cover, and there the sinister figure of Rasputin showed up like a figure coming towards one on a dark night. It was, as it turned out, somewhat symbolic.

The Americans did not want to be told anything about the myth of the Tsar's "steam-roller." They did not want to hear anything that was bad for business. And the skilful propagandists of the Allies at Washington were determined that the U. S. should not see such a weakness among the Allies. The American Embassy at Petrograd does not seem to have been any better than the Allied diplomats in their failure to realise how the corruption at Petrograd was rotting the heart out of the brave Russian Army.

John Reed lost his job trying to show up that situation in 1915.

New York had gone completely crazy, lost its bearings in the flood of Allied war orders. The horn of plenty had been turned upside down and from it was pouring a shower of simply unescapable riches. Profits were pyramiding so miraculously that their possessors grew dizzy at the sight of them. Factories and export companies were springing up like mushrooms all over America. The outskirts of our cities were ringed with new munition works.

"Export managers" were being appointed by every company with money enough to rent an office on Broadway. Most of them bought a book on the export business, which was a best seller at the moment; and from it they learned what "C.I.F." meant, and from its elementary pages on foreign exchange they got brain fever. The lobbies of the big New York hotels were full of them. All of them tried to get on a steamship for Europe.

"The ships are lousy with them!" laughed John.

J. P. Morgan & Co. immediately put a fast one over on the rest of the American fraternity by managing to secure all the purchasing for the British War Department. Caught napping in the scramble, the Guaranty Trust Co., and the National City Bank were fighting it out to corner what was left of the staggering Allied hand-out of riches. They did not have to persuade the Allied staffs to buy anything; their armies were blowing everything to bits much faster than the Americans could manufacture it, or else the Germans were only sending it to the bottom of the ocean; and the question was which companies in America were going to get this unbelievable business. And when the Allies did not have enough money to pay—we shipped the goods without it.

Half of the United States was being packed into ships and sent to Europe—where it stayed. For the interesting thing about American insanity at that period was that the Allies never had such a purchasing power. That is the answer to the riddle of the War Debts.

It was maddening to have to lie in hospital while all this excitement was going on and not be a part of it. I had become accustomed to having people treat me tolerantly when I tried to tell them some of the facts about the Russian War Department. My only wish now was to get out and get back to Europe as quickly as possible. My guardian, although he could not afford it, had had one of the best surgeons in America do my operation. He made a splendid job of it; so good that I was an exhibit for a few days after he became sure that it was successful, and he brought one or two prominent New York surgeons in to have a look at me. After several months I was removed from the board and placed in plaster of Paris. Then I was taken up to my guardian's house on the lake in New York State.

A trained nurse went with me. I found my old fishing rods, one of them bent like a bow, because someone had leaned it against the boat-house wall after he had been using it. But a couple of them were all right, and shortly after the ice melted I was daily carried down to the canoe where, with a paddle, I was just as good as a sound man; and I began to fish for bass again.

At nights I worked on my plans. For I was on my own now, employed by nobody; and I was going back to Russia again.

I did not see how I was going to make it at first, and I would have had a much harder time if it had not been for a bit of luck in Stockholm. When some clumsy train-porters, assisted by my Red Cross nurse, were half killing me as they tried to lift me into the train, a Swede appeared and took off his hat to us. He was about six feet seven, with eyes of baby blue.

"Please!" he said.

He then picked me up in his arms and walked with me into the train as easily as if I had been a basket of grapes.

He was now my partner. Torsten, his Christian name, he said, when translated literally meant "The Hammer of God"; and that seemed just the right name for him. He was being sent to the United States on a mission to buy foodstuffs for the Swedish Government. On the way over and when he came up to visit us at Lake Mahopac, we decided that we would build up an export business. So every night now, on the new portable typewriter I had bought, I wrote reams of letters to business friends of mine and to companies whom we wished to represent. And by the time I was able to get about we had our company fairly well launched.

Chapter 29

LANDBY AND FARSON INC.

THE BUSINESS that Torsten and I had in mind was to have one main characteristic; and that was, it was to be permanent. I was going back to Russia this time to live there, if I could. I liked that life in Petrograd. Business was not the sole thing for which one lived, and Russia was big enough to offer one all sorts of lives. At Imitra, in Finland, was some of the best trout fishing in the world, and as for shooting, of course, Russia had everything. And even business itself became an adventure in opening up new fields. It would be like starting out in the United States with the pioneers.

There were large parts of Russia that were still entirely unknown, and rivers running up into the north that had only been travelled by the natives who lived along their unmapped banks.

A meteor fell in Siberia some time during the war and blotted out an area as large as all of Belgium; yet it was 1923 before anybody heard about it. Heard about it, that is, in Moscow or Petrograd; for the natives around that region had already invented a thunder god to explain the catastrophe and had invented new totem poles to put up before their lodges.

There was something grand in starting a new life in a country as unspoilt as all that! Business itself, too, had so little affected the mode of Russian life that as the head of my own business there I could live a practically feudal existence.

So when I set out on my barnstorming trip in the United States to collect agencies, I went out for stuff that, I hoped, would not be for simply these flash-in-the-pan war orders. I had forgotten about all the civil engineering I had ever learned, but I wanted the base of the new business to be engineering supplies. To make money quickly, and I hoped easily, I wanted to get two distinct types of American motor-cars: one very good one, and one very cheap one. Then, as I had learned the technique by the blood of my soul in Petrograd, I got several firms to let me place their agencies for them in Scandinavia on a percentage basis. I was to get a small commission on the first two years' business. It was not such a badly planned scheme, and if the Revolution had not hit us I think that Torsten and I would have made a good thing out of it.

We had our cards and stationery printed, and they looked very imposing. Too imposing, I thought, when I got the bales of writing paper with the neat little black heading:

LANDBY & FARSON INC.

New York—Stockholm—Petrograd

We were lucky in the fact that the people who first sent me to England, opened up a branch for us in their New York office, and put a perfect genius of a young mechanical engineer in charge of it. Torsten had registered us in Stockholm. When I got to Petrograd, I registered the company under my own name in the Second Guild of Merchants of Russia.

As I hadn't a hope of competing with the big exporters, like the Cannibal Trout, the big American millionaire in Petrograd, I realised that my only virtue lay in my smallness, and that I must capitalise on that. I must handle very few things, and, whatever they were, they must be the best of their kind that I could secure. And these people themselves must see the virtue of the small company that Torsten and I had planned. In fact, that was our only chance of ever putting the idea across.

In that mania for sheer bigness in business this was almost an original idea, and it worked beautifully in Indianapolis. The first thing I was told in that big motor-car company's head office, was that they were practically ready to place their agency for Russia. They were ready to sign with the Cannibal Trout.

"But he's so big!" I said.

The president of the company looked at me in amazement. "Big?" he said. "I don't see what's the matter with being big. What's that got to do with it?"

"Only," I said, "that you'll be one of twenty."

Then I gave them a list of the motor-cars that I knew that big group was handling. I listed a few other things that had nothing whatever to do with motor-cars. I gave them in fact what I think was the reason for that big Cannibal Trout's collapse after the war, for the top-heavy business that he had built up during the hey-day of war-order madness was as variegated as a huge department store. He just wanted to sell everything.

"If you want to put your fine car in with that galaxy of business," I said, "all right, but don't be surprised, if he finds you hard to push, if he puts you on the shelf and sells somebody else's car."

The president whistled and then laughed at me.

"Well, Jack the giant killer," he said, "that sounds pretty sensible. I never looked at it in that way. I know damn well we wouldn't do business that way in America."

"Then why should you in Europe?" I asked.

They told me to give them some time to think it over, and I went back to my hotel where I could not eat my lunch from anxiety. If I got this contract, I knew that I was not only getting one of the finest cars built in the United States, but that it would help me to get other contracts. When a bell boy came in and said that I was wanted on the telephone I was almost afraid to go to it. It was the company's export manager.

"You've got it," he said. "I'm coming down to pick you up, and then we'll give you a turn around the Speedway."

Whistling around the curves of that famous racing track, I had to laugh with sheer gaiety, for at almost the first shot I had scored a bull's-eye against that Cannibal Trout in Petrograd. No matter what he did now, he couldn't get his paws on this motorcar for two years anyway.

I bought two of its famous Bulldog models. A dark, cherry-red one for Torsten, which I thought ought to go well with the Swedish snows, and a coal black one for myself.

During that barn-storming trip to close agencies, I had one or two startling examples of the hysteria of America's mushroom export trade. One company that I had decided to get, attracted by its advertisement in all the trade journals, turned out to be just a half-empty warehouse. It was waiting for war orders, with the intention, I suppose, of sub-letting them. The decrepit engineer in charge nearly wept when I left after just a look at the place; he thought I had come with an order for them. In one city I signed a contract with a company giving me their Scandinavian and Russian agencies, and I had hardly got back from New York before I got a wire from its vice-president in Cleveland, asking me not to do anything with my contract until he came east to see me. He was an extraordinarily decent person and laid his cards on the table. Their export manager, it seemed, had secretly gone so far with another company that they were threatening suit if they did not get the agency. He asked me to tear up my contract, and I did so.

The first motor-car agent I called on in Christiania handed me a letter he had just received from the United States offering him the Scandinavian agency for a motor-car I had been appointed to handle. I showed him my contract. He wrote a letter to the American company turning down their offer. He also told me that he would warn his friends in Scandinavia. As far as I know that company did not place an agency in Scandinavia that year. I know they did not in Russia. I took care of that. When I sent them back my contract, with a letter telling them what I thought of their idea of doing an export business, we were bombarded with cables and letters for some weeks afterwards asking us to change our minds.

Half the troubles that the Americans encountered in the mushroom war export business was that they did not pattern themselves on the old American export firms who had realised long since that the most essential thing in doing business abroad is to have an untarnished reputation for living up to your word or sample; and, without that, nothing else could take its place.

Swedes have both a flair and a weakness for inventions. And my partner was no exception. The result was that half my time in New York was fighting with some sleek patent lawyers and inventors over some inventions that Torsten had bought. They were good inventions, but our patent rights seemed literally fringed with infringements. To a layman like myself, it was a bewildering mess. The American patent law, I discovered, was even worse than the application of its criminal law, which is as full of loopholes as a fish net.

One of the inventions was a printing process. Its inventor was the same man whose original patents now form part of the printing-press processes used all over the world. The chief trouble with his new process was that it overlapped the old one. It was impossible, without a legal battle, to tell how much of our patent he really had the right to sell.

Another patent was for making boxes and such things out of wood pulp. Its inventor was a charming person, but, it seemed, he was taking all the money we gave him to perfect his process and putting it into his yacht. This was a big cabin cruiser and I took it up Long Island Sound with him one night, and he steered us into a slanting spar buoy and nearly sank us. He did cut off our superstructure as clean as if it had been done with a knife. But he got her repaired again, so that when I next tried to catch him (chasing him one night across New Jersey in a motor-car) to make him sign some release documents, he got his yacht down through the Raritan canal before I could locate him. And when last I heard of him he was off the coast of California, where both he and the yacht seemed to be doing very well.

In the end it developed that we could not sell the patent rights to Europe unless we wished to turn patent sharks ourselves.

During this time my guardian died, and we opened a Pandora's box of frightening discoveries. All of the catastrophes that he had been staving off in secret for a long time descended upon us at once. He died before I was well enough to leave the lake, in the room next to where I was lying in my plaster cast. As I sat out taking my sunbath the next morning, a New York paper called us and asked for an obituary, and I sat down to write it. As I did so I thought what a novel could have been written of his career. His two lives. One, the steel hard financier who would risk everything he owned, and much more unfortunately on some big deal. A man who could, and did, lose millions without ever turning a hair. And the other man, the old Yale athlete, who liked nothing better than to get off somewhere alone in the woods on horseback. The man who had actually cried when he saw them carrying me down the gang-plank of the *Stockholm*.

Then I looked down at his lawns that ran down into the lake, the paddock shining in the sun, and the sail-boat lying so quietly beside the boat-house. These had gone. Not a stick of furniture on that place belonged to us.

That chapter was closed.

I felt like a coward when I sailed from America this time, for I felt that I was running away from things I ought to stay and face. I left my old grandmother and her two daughters to face life alone. When I returned and saw them again after the war was over, I realised that they were the most heroic people I would ever know. My two aunts, totally unprepared to have to care for themselves, had gone into New York and both made careers. They had succeeded in a place where I had failed.

Chapter 30

GHOST IN A HAT SHOP

Before leaving New York, I had a sensational finale. I was down in Knox's Hat Shop in lower Broadway, buying a felt hat; and as I dented its crown and looked in a long mirror to admire the effect, I saw a face. It was a large, triangular face, growing wider as it reached its lowest extremity. It might have belonged to a bulldog, or a catfish—or a ghost! And as I started, and opened my mouth in astonishment, it opened its mouth. Its two round little eyes disappeared in rolls of flesh, its little round nose quivered. . . .

"Frumkin!"

"The same as ever!"

I held his fat hand:

"I thought they'd shot you?"

He rubbed his thumb and forefinger, one against the other, the Russian sign for bribe money. "My best friend got me away from getting shot," he grinned.

"When are you going back to Russia?" I asked.

A twitch of fear stiffened his coarse features. "When I ain't got no more brains."

He plucked at the lapel of my coat. "Do you know," he said, "I believe you're sorry they didn't shoot me."

"Yes," I said, "I am."

"Well"—Frumkin's huge face divided into a broad grin—"if *that's* the way you feel about me, come out and have a drink."

He had, he said sadly, been forced to give up every dollar he had in the world in order to buy his way out of prison and Holy Russia. He was settling down in America now, beginning all over again. He wanted me to meet "the wife."

"But of course, you know her!" he said.

It was Anna, his niece.

Chapter 31

SCANDINAVIAN TYCOONS

THE LITTLE *Danske Fly* was a travelling circus of the war tycoons of that time. Practically everyone on her had made, was making, or was expecting to make more money than he had ever hoped to possess in his wildest dreams. Topping them were three Scandinavian "shipping barons": Louis Hannivig, Brosgard, and Johannson. Little tow-headed Louis Hannivig, Norwegian and not yet forty, had, said the smoking-room, made over 40,000,000 dollars selling out his ship-building contracts to the British in New York. Brosgard owned the big line of Danish sailing ships. Johannson was Johannson of the Johannson Line. For not much more than a month's charter they were getting as much for the use of their ships as any one of their ships had cost them to build. They were in a typhoon of wealth. They simply could not get away from it. They were coasting before it on the glittering crest of life's wave. Similarly swept along by unescapable richness were assorted Scandinavian motor-car and business men. Men who, in a bleak, spartan little country like Norway, had never even imagined such ornate lives as they had been living every day in New York, and—if they could manage it—would live for ever after in stern Norway. There was a garrulous, over-friendly, poker-playing American ex-German Jew, who was just "taking a toot across the Pond," to smuggle back a cargo of unobtainable drugs on the *Deutschland*—one of the two super-submarines the Germans built to run under water across to New York. The *Bremen* actually did make the passage and came up in New York harbour.

They began drinking champagne in the *Danske Fly* almost before they had had their morning bath!

There was, however, in the second class a particularly beautiful and yet wistful Norwegian girl, who, out of all that assembly of happy tycoons, seemed to be the only person aboard returning to her own country much poorer and more distracted than when she had left. She was, she told me, a child's governess, whom her mistress had thought too young and pretty to be left alone with the child's father out on a Long Island estate.

"So," she smiled, her hair shining in the fresh morning air, "I was fired!"

She felt doubly out of things on the *Danske Fly* because the Captain of that wretched tub was so infernally smug and "proper" that he had ordered her off the boat-deck reserved for the first class. The officers of the *Danske Fly* were incredibly class-conscious.

I thereupon organised what we called the Corporation. We took only twelve members and would allow no one else in. That made a class barrier inside the first class which had precisely the effect I desired to create—it abolished boredom. Everyone outside the Corporation was trying to get in. We each paid in five dollars as an initial membership fee, and we agreed with the bartender that no member of the Corporation should ever pay for a drink at the bar. He would merely give him one of the Corporation's chits. The money to pay for this prodigious fund we collected by means of a kitty at our two, almost continuous, poker games. The Corporation had a set of laws and by-laws and the first of them read:

"The chief object of this Corporation is the total corruption of the ship."

As President of the Corporation I carried this out. I invited the pretty Norwegian girl into my cabin for dinner, ordered caviare and hot toasted rolls and two bottles of champagne, and signed the Corporation's chit. When I was hauled over the coals for it by two poker tables in full session, I merely produced the copy of by-laws, which I had typed out.

"I have," I said, "fulfilled the first one."

If they had known how very innocent that little party really was, they might have thought the president merely a sheep in wolf's clothing.

The Corporation then bought a baby—and we named it. I named it, Heaven preserve it! Atlanta Flyvia . . . and its mother wept in gratitude.

For, impossible as it seemed, the diminutive *Danske Fly* had a steerage class; and somewhere down in the bowels of that little ship as we were approaching the rocky shores of Norway, a baby was born.

"Please!" said the ship's doctor to me. "The family is very poor. Could—could not the Corporation give it a little present—to get a start in life?"

He was the best of the ship's officers, that doctor!

"May I," I asked, "*buy* the baby?"

He went white at the very idea of such a thing.

"Because," I said, "if you will let the Corporation buy it, to have a real live baby of its very own, we will each of us give it ten dollars as a birthday present. Ask the mother if she will let the Corporation be its godfather for the rest of the trip."

I thereupon assessed a levy on the Corporation and told them about it. We got the money from the steward in fresh bills and gave it to the doctor. He came back with tears in his eyes, he was so happy. He then said he thought it would be a good idea if we suggested a name for it.

I wonder what "Atlanta" is doing now? I hope she has grown up to be as pretty as that blue-eyed creature who drank the two bottles of champagne (I hate the stuff!) to help me corrupt the *Danske Fly*.

And, as an example of the hearts that sometime beat under those barren Norwegian exteriors, I will cite the case of the Herr Direktor. He was a wizened, aloof little man, a director of one of the state railways, who with his wife, carried their own trunk off the gangway to save the tip when the ship touched at Bergen. His exit was followed by furious glares from cabin, dining-saloon, bar and deck stewards, to whom he gave the most minute of tips, if any, but when he learned that a baby had been born on board, and that the Corporation had raised a fund for it, he came along to me the next day:

"Please!" he smiled—he was really very sophisticated—"I know I am not allowed to be a member of the Corporation. But may I give this?"

He placed a five dollar bill in my hand.

Christiania and Stockholm I found fantastic. The Scandinavians were living in a fairy-tale of wealth. Especially the Swedish capital. Among the sturdy timber, iron, and shipping magnates, slow-growing and substantial as their own pine forests, had sprung up a vegetable growth of war millionaires. It was quick-growing, lush undergrowth that perished ruinously in the cold blare of the depression that swept over Scandinavia in 1921, from which only the stronger of the big shipping and iron men emerged.

"I've still got my ships!" said one of them to me often that time, as we sailed out through Stockholm's beautiful islands and fleets of new Marconi-rig racing yachts. "We are all of us just about broke and perhaps that will do us good. We Swedes will return to our simple lives again—to crayfish and sailing!" But while it was lasting, this vegetable growth of war tycoons nearly wrecked Scandinavian morals. It had completely upset the proprieties of Swedish life. And, as always happens in such cases, this was immediately evinced in the night life. The Operakellern at midnight was like an UFA film of the *Rake's Progress*, the German version of the way the aristocratic man-about-town always goes to Hell in a dress suit and opera cloak, cynically flicking the ash off his gold-tipped cigarette. The blue eyes of Sweden were bloodshot in the mornings.

"Till's" was the *dernier cri* for Sweden's gay dogs. It was a sort of layer cake of organised high-class lechery, built up of tiers of balconies of *cabinets privées* all looking down on a stream-ered dancing-floor, whereon every midnight twinkled the toes of six lusty Lancashire dancing girls whom a far-sighted British Government propaganda department had shipped to Scandinavia to hold the Swedes from the arms of the Germans.

Some inquiring statistician, I was told, had just produced a graph, showing where immorality was most congested in this world; and, instead of being a circle around Paris, it ran straight through Stockholm. I never could understand what he based his definition of immorality upon. Stockholm, in the dawn, I had discovered a shockingly respectable place; cold, Calvinistic in its reproachful propriety. And even at fetid "Till's," if you went outside for a breath of air after midnight, you could not come back again. Its doors were hermetically sealed at twelve sharp. I found a little man outside like this one night. He was a swarthy, wildly excited little personage, with an enamelled order dangling down the immaculate white front of his evening dress. He was without hat or coat in dead winter time. A giant of a Swedish policeman was holding him at bay in the snow with an upraised palm.

"*Nay!*" said the policeman.

"But I am ze Blank Minister!"

"*Nay!*"

It was about ten below zero. I waited to see the little man freeze to death. He clapped his cold hands and jumped up in the air again.

"*Je suis le Ministre de Blank!*"

"*Nay!*"

The Minister from Blank blew on his frozen knuckles. He clenched his fists.

"I am the Minister from Blank!" (In Portuguese.)

"*Nay!*"

"I am the Minister from Blank!" (Spanish.)

"*Nay!*"

The policeman then advanced one step and gave the gesticulating gentleman an official shove. He was, said the policeman, obviously too drunk to understand that he could not get in again. He was calling the upholder of the Law by bad names. He must go home to bed, like other naughty gentlemen when they have too much drink taken. There were so many these days.

At that moment, a young British diplomat came out of the door of "Till's" to see what had happened to his friend; and the situation and the Minister from Blank were saved.

But when the Swedes got down to the office in the morning they were very much on the job, and I discovered an astonishing amount of their business was being conducted with the Germans —wherein the Allies were taking part!

A certain dye, for instance, for the French uniform could be obtained from nowhere else than Germany, and was coming through daily via Copenhagen or Stockholm. *Salicine alizarine black* was another dye that the Allies winked a blind eye about. If they didn't they would never get a sight of it. And I went down myself on a commission from Julius S. Bache, in New York, to see if I couldn't get some electrodes from the Siemens Schurgert works in Berlin. I met the negotiator in the Castle Hotel in Copenhagen. And sitting in a wicker chair before a cocktail in that exciting hotel I met my American ex-German Jew poker-playing friend of the *Danske Fly*. He was waiting for his cargo of precious drugs to be put aboard the *Deutschland*, the German super-submarine which was then intending to run a cargo through the British blockade to New York. With him was his German agent, who gave us a demonstration of how he had dodged conscription in Germany so far by feigning G.P.I. He nearly frightened a waiter out of his wits by suddenly going goggle-eyed, sticking out his tongue, and sliding limply out of his chair.

"Boy!" said my *Danske Fly* friend, "there ain't a room in this dump that hasn't got a story in it! I'm afraid to take off my pants at night for fear somebody will swipe 'em!"

"I do this two or three times a day," said the German trench-dodger, "because you never know who's watching. Sometimes —I feel as if I *was* getting that way. I catch myself thinking about going to a doctor—to see if he can't cure me!"

And they both looked over their shoulders before they talked.

Even the Danes, most level-headed of all people (you will never find a good Dane who does not live far below his income); even the Danes were drinking champagne at eleven a.m.!

In Sweden I made a few business trips, to places such as Upsala, where I got a warm vision of the richness of life in that little university town; and I made one or two trips to far-flung little towns whose whole life was built around the local iron or wood works, and where the head of the works had an almost feudal prestige and sense of obligation. One of these was Ljusne Woxna on the Baltic, to which I drove from an inland northern railway line through snow at forty below zero, with Count von Ecker-mann—to whom everyone immediately took off their hats. And in this isolated community among modern mills that were making the plates for their own steamships, I saw men before the flame of a little iron furnace that had been going for over a hundred years.

At Ljusne Woxna I was given the Russian rights for the new Swedish semi-Diesel motors that are now at last adopted, some twenty years later, to run the modern rail-cars.

When I started to go into Russia I discovered that the Russians were not at all anxious to have me back!

It might have been my association with old Frumkin, and the long list of espionage charges of which it had cost him his fortune to buy his way clear; or, as after events seemed to confirm, it was probably my friendship with John Reed.

I feel pretty sure it was Reed, because when I was afterwards put on the black list of the Lusk Committee, and my name was among those who were being considered eligible for deportation from the United States on the *Soviet Ark,* John Reed's name and that of Ginsberg, of the Stockholm Nyea Banken, were among the charges laid at my door. One accusation was that I had done business with the Germans, via the Nyea Banken in Stockholm —which I had; the other was that through the adroit Herr Ginsberg (who actually did bring a high Russian Minister and some German officials together) I had been in contact with Lenin— which I had not!

The whole charge against me on the Lusk Committee was a farrago of nonsense, like most of that Communist witch-hunting which is still going on in the United States; but it is to my ever-lasting regret that the charge of having been in contact with the great Lenin at that date was not really the truth.

I did, as a matter of fact, see Lenin later on in the company of John Reed.

At any rate, in 1916, when I tried to get a Russian visa for my passport in Stockholm it was refused. And it was refused very rudely. For me, it meant the crash of a future.

"Sorry," said the American Legation, "but the Russian Government has issued a new order that no passport can be visaed for Russia—*except in the country of origin.*"

"But that means I would have to go back to the United States!"

They said it did look like that. It was a pity, because the law had been passed a couple of days after I had sailed from New York and was still on the water. They were amazingly nice and friendly about it; and I would not have been at all hurt if they had let matters ride. After all, an American Legation cannot do more than make an official protest to the Russian Government, which it was then getting ready to do.

But there were three extremely able and friendly people in our Stockholm Legation: MacGruder, the First Secretary; Francis, private secretary to the Minister; and Ira Nelson Morris, the Minister.

Morris laughed when I chided him that an old Andover man was going to let another Andover man down. I had just happened to notice a photograph of Phillip's Academy behind his desk.

"The old school tie, eh?" he smiled, telling me to compose myself. "And you have bought your ticket to leave tomorrow?"

I told him that matters had finally come to that point. I had my sleeper, the Russians were refusing to visa my passport, and I was being told that I would have to go back to the United States to get a Russian visa in the country of origin.

"Country of origin, eh?—well, that's a cinch!"

Morris pressed a button and asked a secretary to come in. "Cancel Mr. Farson's passport," he said. "Wire Washington for permission to grant him a new one—a new one here in Stockholm. Make out a fresh passport for Mr. Farson—and give him a diplomatic pass. I am going to make him a messenger, carrying our bags to Petrograd."

"That's the stuff to give 'em!" he said to me. "Now you rush out and get six photographs taken just as fast as you can."

It was the only passport photo I have ever had taken that showed me with a smile. But there were not smiles around the Russian Consulate when I took my passport back there the next morning. They simply had to stamp the new one because I was complying with the rules—I was asking for a visa in the country of origin—and, also, I had a diplomatic pass from the American Government.

The little shaven-headed underling of the Russian Foreign Office held me up just as long as he could. He sat there scowling at me, and then at the clock, like an angry rat, until at the last minute he slowly took a rubber stamp and stamped it over some Russian stamps and writing on my passport. I snatched it from him. The Legation dragoman and I raced for the train going to Happaranda. It was just pulling out. Torsten was trying to hold it back! He was running beside it yelling at a pig-faced conductor, who was waving him off. My bags were already on. I sprinted after the train, jumped, caught the last handrail on the last car and, waving farewell to the "Hammer of God," I went on into Russia.

Chapter 32

RUMBLES OF REVOLUTION

Russia had changed terribly since I had been away.

"Nobody expects Russia to win the war now!" were the first words I heard from an Englishman. "No, not even the poor devils at the front, and from all accounts they feel pretty sick about it!"

A covering gloom hung over the streets of Petrograd like a fog. Defeat and disaster were both in the air. One heard it openly from crippled soldiers who stopped one and whined for money in the streets, and from healthy truculent soldiers who openly sneered that they were deserters. One heard it in the wails of the wounded in hospitals, who screamed out they had lost their legs or arms for nothing. And one heard it in the gloomy mutterings of the American war order hunters who were still lingering about the Hotel Astoria.

One heard it everywhere—except in the Allied Embassies.

Then—Rasputin had been killed. And even Englishmen, who would have laughed if you had told them they were superstitious, went about remarking half under their breath:

"Well, you know what he prophesied—if anything happened to him it would be the end of the Romanoffs!"

The average Russian went about in gloomy apprehension of the Nemesis he felt sure to come now that the Mad Monk had been murdered. Instead of being national heroes, Prince Yussopoff and the Grand Duke Dmitri Pavlovitch (who had been exiled to the Caucasus) were almost universally hated for their courageous deed. Rodzianko was openly called a fool for having supported them.

The slender young Grand Duke Dmitri told me years afterwards in Cairo, when he was a cavalry officer in the British Army, "Being exiled to the Caucasus, however, was the one thing that saved my life. If I had been in Petrograd, I would have been murdered. When the Revolution came on I managed to escape from the Caucasus into Persia, and—here I am!"

I pressed him to tell me whether it was he or Yussopoff who fired the first shot. He would not tell me. I believe that for a long time they had pledged each other that no one present on that night would reveal who struck the first blow to rid Russia of that amazing peasant.

Then the streets of Petrograd and Moscow presented not only pitiable but frightening signs of privation and starvation. There were queues around each provision shop that sometimes encircled the whole block in which it stood. In Moscow I actually saw a boot shop that had a queue which had been standing there for days that went twice around a large city block. White bread had vanished from the tables of the rich. I was living with an Englishman then, who had bribed government officials to get flour to make white bread, and every mouthful we ate we regarded as preciously as if it had been cake.

Tales drifted down of breakdowns on the Archangel line. The four sections of the single-track railway to Vladivostok were waging an internal war. This was chiefly over the right to rolling stock. This was going to pieces under the strain. In the old days, when a Russian locomotive driver slept, his locomotive "slept" with him, but now the engineers sleep inside their cabs while another engineer takes over, so that these over-worked engines are never allowed time for vital repairs or even a few seconds to let their tired metal rest. From Vladivostok came alarming stories of war supplies being landed and then sinking under the sands of the beach—at, it was claimed, the rate of seventeen inches a day, for lack of transport to carry them off to Petrograd, Moscow, and the front.

With its two mouths—Archangel and Vladivostok—choking with the food of war, Russia lay like a prostrate Mars, starving to death. It was a process of wastage that one could witness on every side. As plain as watching a man die from phthisis in a hospital ward. A man who was becoming rotten inside. The tales of high officials who had been caught and shot for corruption became more frequent every day.

We lived in an atmosphere equivalent to being in a city in the last days of siege.

The gypsy love songs of the violinist Gianescu had begun to cloy. The Roman Holiday atmosphere of the Hotel Astoria was gone. Fear had now taken its place.

When I looked over the ground again I found these things. The big American millionaire, the Cannibal Trout, was still swimming about the Astoria. His room, which had enlarged to a suite before I left, had now swollen to take up an entire floor. But whereas he had always tried to make his entrance into any gathering or conversation take on the nature of an event, he now seemed content to remain in the background. The reason for this was not hard to find: by utilising Russian corruption for all there was in it, he had managed to secure the exclusive right to the steel supplies for the Russian War Department—and then the Russian Government had demanded a huge loan. Caught between the promises they had made to secure a monopoly of these steel rights in the U.S.A., and the plain fact that the Russians could no longer pay for them, the big New York banking group that was backing the American millionaire in Petrograd had to make the huge loan. They made it—more than likely not knowing what the big man in Petrograd knew. He knew that it was extremely unlikely it would ever be repaid. Therefore he was somewhat less arrogant than in the care-free days when he was chasing us small fry about Petrograd in 1915.

His clerks and minor executives, however, did not see that far. A new class of Americans had come to inhabit the Astoria. Swift-risen, assured young clerks, who had not a worry in the world— let the Company do that! and who considered themselves the overlord of every Russian they met. They made me feel like a veteran, and I had almost an affectionate regret for the former naïve crowd with the Stars and Stripes in their buttonholes.

Most of the young Englishmen were gone. Two of the best had gone down with Kitchener as his A.D.C.s when the *Hampshire* struck a mine off the Norwegian coast. Others were in British khaki scattered about the Russian Empire trying to scrape up war supplies. A few were still working night and day to keep the Russian factories going. The life in the New English Club in the Moskayia had dwindled to nothing; and the beef-steak dinners had vanished for ever. There were no more beef-steaks, and soon there would be no New English Club.

English missions were pouring in in a frantic Allied effort to keep the Russian "steam-roller" going. They went to munition works, chemical and explosive plants throughout Russia. The Americans sent in the great engineer Stevens, famous for his work on the Panama Canal, to try and keep the Russian railways from collapsing. The British sent a mission through Petrograd to burn the oil wells in rotten Roumania, and the Hotel Astoria had a brief flash of glory in Locker-Lampson's British Armoured Car outfit. A gallant Scotchman of this body thrilled us later with his exploit of fighting a rear-guard action in the retreat from the Carpaths; against it seemed half the Austrian army, which he held off with a battered Ford and two machine-guns.

The husband of my hostess on the Millionayia had at last come into his own in the Russian scene. Realising the integrity of the historic old trading firm he represented, the Russian Government turned to him in its desperation after seeing the mess into which it had got itself by letting the corrupt Technical Department line its pockets in dealing with the American and British war profiteers. But it was much too late. There was a death-cell solemnity about every Petrograd office by the end of 1916.

There was a dramatic contrast in two Christmases I spent in that year. The first was in Stockholm and the second was the Orthodox Russian Christmas, which I had in Petrograd thirteen days later. The Stockholm Christmas was a Lucullian affair, all of us heavy with the food and mulled *glog* of a preposterous dinner we had managed to get through on Christmas Eve. Conversation had been almost entirely devoted to what a fine mess the Germans were making of the Russians. Germany was popular with the Swedish army; Swedish business men were insulted and infuriated by the arrogant methods of the British sea blockade, and it must be remembered, there were very few Swedes who believed in the rights of the Allied cause. Few of them do today.

In Petrograd the Russians, as only Russians can, had temporarily decided to forget any ugly realities of life for Christmas Day. But a cake with white flour in it was as rare as any gift—and there were indeed very few gifts. Except for expensive establishments, like Faberge's, and a few fantastically expensive sweet shops, like Eliesieff, the stores of Petrograd were almost as empty as Mother Hubbard's cupboard.

Conversation at that Christmas table was of a cousin who had just been killed at the front, of the sullen attitude of the wounded soldiers in a hospital run by the mill, of the menacing attitude of the mill-workers themselves, of the increasing difficulty of obtaining food or clothing, of the unpatriotic way the soldiers talked when they were on leave from the front; of executions, dismissals, and changes of faces in high official quarters; of when would America ever get ready to come into the war, of what would we all do when Russia lost the war?

That was it, this last thought—certain defeat. And that was what every intelligent person in Petrograd was talking about. Always, of course, excepting the Allied Diplomatic staffs. After listening to the American Ambassador Francis, discoursing about the armies of the Tsar, anyone who had been keeping an ear open to what was being said in Petrograd's streets, or who was then trying to do any business with the Russian War Department, felt that there was simply nothing left but to go out somewhere and shoot himself. If he did not, and things were allowed to go on like this, the Germans would soon be in Petrograd to do it for him.

The ostrich attitude of the Embassies in Petrograd in those days was too incredible to bear description.

Jack Hoth I found the same. He had the correct idea toward war: that it was futile to be killed in it. And he was having as good a time as he could on the Petrograd Front.

"I've got a new pair of Purdys," he said casually. "We'll try them on Sunday."

This was at the Kresstoffsky Pigeon Club, the "Society That Loves to Shoot," as it was officially called on the little golden

"Fish" that one used as counters for the purchase of live birds from the Club secretary.

There they were: Count Schuvaloff, and Sherimeitieff, and Jack Hoth, and Kazanskoff (winner of the Grand Prix at Monte Carlo); a dozen or so round a table groaning with vodka and the finest zakuska, betting their heads off—as if the sound of our shot-guns was the only firing that was going on in this world. The Grand Duke Nicholas was the patron of this club, but he was now demoted to commanding the Russian Army of the Caucasus.

I usually left that club on the snowy islands much poorer than when I had driven over to it. The betting was done in twenty-five rouble blocks. If you were the ordinary good shot you had to bet 3-1 against yourself, and as your name was called, the various men around the table held up their hands. You nodded to the men whose bets you wanted to take. Betting seventy-five roubles on yourself every time you went out to shoot made it an expensive affair if you hit a streak of bad luck. The rouble was still worth about 2s. (50 cents).

But the excitement was worth it. The entire front of the club-house was one huge plate-glass window, like the most expensive jeweller's. The men left their vodka and crowded to this window as you went out to take your shot. You shot from so many metres, seventeen, I think, up to twenty-eight, at pigeons which might be sprung from any one of a semicircle of five boxes before you.

You were allowed two shots on any or every bird, but you must not lower your gun until you had taken them both. Or, if you were satisfied with one shot and lowered your gun, then you had finished shooting at that particular bird. This was very important as a bird was sometimes knocked down by the first shot, and then, when the shooter confidently dropped his gun—and the dog was released to retrieve the bird—the bird suddenly came to life and flapped and fluttered until it reached the boundary wire of chicken-netting and climbed over it. That was counted as a missed bird, even if it did drop dead outside. Similarly, a bird shot in the air, killed stone dead, that chanced to drop outside that circular wire barrier was also counted as "missed."

People like Kazanskoff, a professional, who made their living by gambling on their shooting at the Kresstoffsky Club, always gave a bird the second shot. But when people like Kazanskoff shot, the bird usually crumpled up, hit by the full charge.

There were shoots where people like myself had a chance against even such shots as Kazanskoff. These were the Miss-and-Out shoots. You put fifteen shells in your pocket and stayed out there on the platform until you made your first miss. Theoretically perfect shooting would of course give you fifteen birds, which of course was hardly ever made. The best shot in the place might miss his first or second bird. In one such shoot I beat Kazanskoff, who missed his second bird, and then I went on to kill eleven straight and win the shoot.

It was about the only success I had in Petrograd that winter. Meanwhile the Revolution was brewing.

When I found that the ports of Archangel and Vladivostok were choked, and that even if I did place new orders it would be next to impossible to get my stuff shipped, I decided to make a quick *volte face* and devote myself almost entirely to trading inside Russia.

I did this with the most charming little Jew, named Pinkus Solomonivitch Citrine. He was a Russian Charlie Chaplin with large soulful eyes and an overcoat about five sizes too big for him. But if Mohammed could have utilised him, Pinkus Solomonivitch would have made the mountain go to Mohammed.

I never saw anything like him. He had a positive genius for unearthing hidden treasure troves of war material inside Russia. It was nothing to him suddenly to think of a cargo of wool, down in the Caucasus, for a distracted English mill manager who was vainly trying to get the same thing from Australia.

"But somehow," complained Pinkus to me, "I never got rich!" I know there can be nothing more honest than absolute honesty, but Pinkus seemed to have a quality about him that excelled even that. Therefore, when he asked me for some money almost the first day I met him, I handed it to him and refused to take his note.

It was in Moscow, and Pinkus saw me in the Hotel Metropole. He came trotting across to me with his ridiculous Charlie Chaplin earnestness:

"Please—may I have some money?"

I looked in my pocket and saw that I had about a hundred odd roubles, and my railway ticket that night to Petrograd. I offered him seventy-five roubles.

He blushed and looked very uncomfortable. "Perhaps—perhaps you don't want to loan me any money?"

"Of course," I said, a little nettled. "But that's all I've got."

"Well"—sadly—"I need two thousand roubles. I've got a chance to double it by ten o'clock tonight. What a pity!"

"Wait a minute," I said, when I saw his distress, and I wrote out a cheque for the two thousand and a note. "If you can't get this cashed at the bank," I said, "take it to the Englishman I've given you this note to. He will give you the money if you give him my cheque."

Pinkus sat down and started writing out an IOU. I told him I did not want it.

"But they always do! No one trusts me!" he said. "Mr. Farson, you do not know me!"

"I know the man who sent you to me," I said, "and I know what he told me about you. I do not need your note."

He blushed to the roots of his curly black hair, gave my hand a frantic shake, almost a hug, and rushed out of the Hotel Metropole. A week later in Petrograd he took a cab and drove twelve versts outside of the city to find me. He had two thousand roubles in an envelope, which he handed to me, with his little astrakhan hat clutched in his hand.

Until I left Russia, and even after I left it—for I left it with an open account for Pinkus Solomonivitch to draw upon—Pinkus and I never signed a document between us and every rouble he made out of the various deals we had together he split meticulously fifty-fifty with me. The only time Pinkus ever doubted *my* honesty was one time when I was a little bit too tender-hearted.

I had sold a ton of the famous *salicine alizarine black* dye to another Jew named Simon (an amazingly honest man himself) at a perfectly outrageous profit. The dye was almost as precious as diamonds, and, of all places, I had got hold of a ton of it by cable in New York! Simon paid me the usual 12½ per cent down, which in Russia is known as the *zadotik*. And almost immediately after he had paid it, the rouble broke. Instead of being two to the dollar it went to nearly eight.

Pinkus rushed out to me in a perfect sweat. "Simon's got you!" he said in alarm. "He's going to hold you to it!"

"You go back," I said, "and tell him to read that dye contract over again. It says two things. The first is that the remaining 87½ per cent of that money must be paid at the rate of exchange *quoted in New York on the day the dye is shipped*. That means that if the rouble drops to a 100 on the dollar, Simon's got to pay me a 100 on the dollar. The second thing says that the dye is to be shipped by the first 'available' steamer leaving New York. If a steamer is not 'available' for twenty years—I can keep Simon's *zadotik* for twenty years. Now, Pinkus Solomonivitch—go back and tell Simon that."

"*Oi!*" grinned Pinkus. "*Oi-Yoi!*"

Then, one day, I gave Gaspodin Simon his money back. He didn't want to take it at first.

"You're selling those dyes to somebody else!" he said.

"Not a bit," I said wearily. "I merely happen to have volunteered for the French Aviation Service, and I'm leaving in a couple of days for Paris. Here's your money."

He was sitting in his marble walled mansion that was a veritable palace in Petrograd. It made one think of the *Merchant of Venice*. We sat in the conservatory; and he walked out of it with his hand on my arm.

"He gave me my money *back* . . . !" he said to the palms.

When Ginsberg of the Stockholm Nyea Banken asked me to whom could he sell some German dyes in Petrograd I gave him Simon's name. He wired Simon using my name. Then Ginsberg telephoned me:

"Come over here—I've got something that will please you, Mr.

Farson—Mr. Simon says he wants to do this business through you!"

It gave me a warm feeling to have little Simon send such a wire. When I heard afterwards of a Simon who had risen to a position of prominence under the Soviets I always hoped it could be he. Yet, when I first told Pinkus Solomonivitch Citrine that I had given Simon back his *zadotik*, Pinkus looked shocked.

"I do not understand, Mr. Farson—what are you doing?"

The moment I did persuade him that there was not anything fishy about it, he merely changed his opinion to the conviction that I had gone crazy!

Pinkus and I did business together (at least he did it) long after I had left Russia. Our partnership ended abruptly when the Bolsheviks seized a cargo of lycopodium we were shipping to Sweden in November 1917.

The Swedes were using this precious dust, from a species of Russian moss, as a substitute for talc. It had suddenly become of tremendous value in the making of certain medical supplies. We had cornered the lycopodium market and would have had a nice little fortune in Swedish kroner if that shipment had not been seized when it was already half across the Finnish frontier.

Our claim against the Russian Government for that amount of lycopodium (not in roubles) is registered at Washington under the name of Landby & Farson Inc. to this day.

But Pinkus seems to have vanished. I searched all over Petrograd for him when I was back in Russia in 1928, but he was one of the ghosts of that tragic city—

"I don't know why it is, Mr. Farson, I make plenty money. But somehow—I never get rich!"

Chapter 33

END OF THE TSAR

One morning when I had gone up in the Singer Building to see North Winship, the American Consul, I saw crowds collecting below us in the snowy streets. We were accustomed to menacing crowds by this time, and the Nevsky in front of the Cathedral of the Virgin of Kazan was a conventional meeting place when trouble was afoot. We did not think that anything was amiss even when we stood watching a *sotnia* of Don Cossacks come jangling down the streets.

"But look there!" cried Winship. "Have you noticed it?—the Cossacks are *laughing!*"

That was disturbing. Generally the Cossacks, whose profession it was to kill, took a delight in riding rough-shod into crowds. But the short horses of the Janissaries from the Steppes were moving about peacefully among pushing people, and their riders were leaning down and talking and nodding, and waving to each other across the sea of upturned faces. They were waving their *naigaikas*, their wicked little whips, tipped with steel, that could cut a man's face open as swiftly as a knife.

"This is the Revolution!" I said. "This is It!"

It was. And that was the way we saw the Kerensky Revolution begin. We stood out on the granite balcony of Winship's Consulate and watched the crowd beginning to build up its own nerve. It did not know what it wanted at first; it was simply collecting. It had no movement or sense of direction. It was just people voicing their discontent. It was like watching some savage beast that has broken out of its cage and did not yet know where to go; it might head for anybody—it might make for you.

When the policeman on traffic point tried to make the crowd open up to allow a tram to pass the people merely laughed at him, and the policeman threw up his hand, stared wonderingly, and then stepped aside. Under the leadership of a few spirits that had materialised in its midst the black mob began to move slowly down the Nevsky towards the Letaney Prospeckt, and as it moved, the shopkeepers along the route ran out and hastily began to pull down the steel shutters over their windows.

"We had better get our business finished," said an Englishman who was with me. He was in the uniform of the Russian Army; but he was in fact Landby & Farson Inc.'s sole Petrograd staff. I had employed him about a month previously as secretary, typist, and interpreter; he had been born in Russia and had lived there all his life. "There will be trouble," he said.

We ate our lunch unheedingly in the Hôtel de France, where I collected five bottles of White Horse whiskey I had discovered in a *cache* in its cellar. Whiskey was almost unobtainable in Russia then, and I was giving four of these bottles to an Englishman who owned a big woollen mill up the Neva. I was living with him at that time, and we found his huge coachman, Arsenie, waiting for us in a sleigh outside the Hôtel de France.

"*Plokha, baren*," he said, shaking his bushy head. "It is bad."

There was, he said, trouble in the streets.

When we turned out into the Nevsky it presented a deserted prospect, for the steel blinds were now pulled down over all its windows. Yet the sidewalks were crowded. There was still no sense of any purpose that one could feel in this mass of mulling people. It was more like a holiday. Work had stopped and the people were walking about. That was all, except that some of the trams stood still and deserted in the middle of the long blocks.

Going along to the Letaney Prospeckt we saw the Cossacks clearing the sidewalks. They were riding along the sidewalks close to the barred windows, knocking people into doorways and out into the gutter with their horses' rumps. They were laughing, however, and joking about it, although I saw one or two women knocked off their feet. Women who had children with them were scuttering down side streets. When we got to where the broad Letaney crosses the Nevsky we saw a black mass of people that completely choked both streets. Here Arsenie suddenly reined up the horses. I ordered him to drive through the crowd.

"Hold up!" said the Englishman. "Don't do that. They might kill us. This *is* the Revolution. I was here in 1905—I know!"

We waited there. The Englishman remarked that he wished he were dressed in any other clothes than the uniform of an officer in the Tsar's army.

"It might," he said, "make us a target at any minute now."

As we were discussing this probability we saw a detachment of Russian "Uhlans" coming towards us down the Nevsky. They were at full gallop, snow flying under the hoofs, and their lances were pointed at us like a row of long bayonets.

We watched them in a dazed fashion as they piled up on top of us, expecting to be spitted at any moment. There was an avalanche of flesh, yells and steel, and the Uhlans swept past us into the crowd. Their momentum carried them clean through it, and their wake was a scatter of black shapes rolling about in the snows.

Whether anyone died as the result of this charge I do not know, nor did we stop to find out. At the last instant I had seen the Uhlans throw up their lances so that they passed us, lances upright, and then they seemed to be giving the butts of the lances to the mob. But the mere impact of a horse at that speed would be enough of itself to kill most people. As Arsenie lashed the horses through them I saw people rising to their feet screaming and shaking their fists at the Uhlans, who were re-forming to charge them again. And at that moment a tram conductor tried to drive his tram through the mob.

I believe he was the first person killed in the Kerensky Revolution; for in an instant that tram was buried under a mass of shrieking people, the tram conductor was dragged out and beaten to death with his own brake-bar.

"I think," said the Englishman coolly, "it's about time we shoved off."

Arsenie did not need any directions. He knew a Revolution, too, when he saw one; and he had probably already had an inkling of what was afoot from the mutinous workmen at the mill. He galloped to the end of the Nevsky, swept past that elephantine statue of Alexander II, sitting on his monster horse facing the Nicholas Station, with the little ribbon-like reins still holding back that Gargantuan horse's head, and then Arsenie gave the horses their heads up the Schlusselberg road. This was the mill district and its streets were thronged with people, many of whom made half-hearted efforts to stop our sleigh. Arsenie used his whip on them right and left.

When we drove over the road which had been made across the broken pack-ice of the Neva, we found the Englishman and his family at tea. They might have been sitting down in Kent somewhere. The Englishman's wife, a Russian herself, asked how many lumps did we want.

"Yes," said the Englishman casually, when we told him what we had seen, "the office telephoned me. All the shops are still closed, but I think it will blow over by tomorrow. Protopopoff, the Prime Minister, has the situation in hand. I hear he has posted hundreds of police, with machine guns, along the roofs of the Nevsky."

The whiskey from the Hôtel de France was the only thing the Englishman was excited about. He up-ended a bottle against his palm and rubbed it on his sleek black hair with a sensuous gesture!

"This is all that matters!" he laughed.

His wife was furious with him, for she was a Russian "Intellectual" herself, a secret friend of some of the most courageous Russian women revolutionists, and she smoked one cigarette after another at that tea, talking about Plekhanov and Kropotkin and the figures whom she erroneously believed would appear on the Russian stage. The Englishman's pretty daughter, to whom I was engaged to be married at that time, was too young it seemed to appreciate the seriousness of anything.

The next morning when I was dressing to go into Petrograd the telephone rang by my bed. It was the Englishman talking to me from the mill.

"Are you going into town today?"

I told him I was, and that Arsenie was already waiting for me at the door.

"Well, take a look out of your window first!" he said. "All hell's broken loose!"

I went to the window. It was a bright winter morning. Russia was blanketed with fresh, glittering snow. Looking down along the Neva to the accustomed blue line that marked the buildings of Petrograd I noticed nothing unusual at first—and then I saw a thick column of black smoke that stood up straight as a plume in the windless sky. It was from the flames of the Nicholas Station, which the revolutionaries had set on fire.

"Arsenie is *not* waiting for you," said the Englishman, when I went back to the telephone. "I ordered him not to take a sleigh out today. In a few hours I think we will all be in a state of siege here—like we were in 1905. Look after Vera and her mother, will you?"

As I was getting into an old suit of plus fours, Matilda, the maid, rushed into my room.

"*They're coming!*" she cried.

"Who?"

"*They!*"

My room faced out on to the private lawn that lay between the river and the great mill. When I put on my dressing-gown and went into the front room to look, I found Vera and her mother leaning against the window. Their eyes were fixed on what they saw going on over on the Schlusselberg road. Across the broken pack-ice I saw a long ribbon of black which was enough to show that the banks of the Neva were lined with people. But as I looked I saw figures above the crowd—horsemen—and I saw the flash of swords. Then I heard the faint *pop-pop* of shots and these figures began to topple down. I saw one last sword glittering and flashing like a windmill blade in the air.

Then the crowd broke. The black line disintegrated. It gathered in large blobs.

I remembered then that there was a loaded Browning down in the hat-rack, and I went down and put it in my pocket. I did not know what I would do with it. I had no precedent to guide me in revolutions. The only thing I could think of was to have that Browning ready when it was needed. I pictured some rather terrible possibilities; and I hoped I would be equal to them if they came. The person I was most afraid of on that bright sunny morning was, of course, myself.

So I went down and put the Browning away. It would be useless, I realised, to try and hold off that crowd that was now jumping across the pack-ice of the Neva towards us like a thousand black goats. I might get excited and shoot somebody, and precipitate the murder of all of us! Across the road built on ice swarmed a stream of people that must have been three or four thousand strong. We could see that they were the workers from the Aboukoff Ironworks and the other mills that lined the other side of the Neva. They were making for our mill.

The Russian mother and her daughter continued their dressing, and as I went in to stand beside Vera again, she said in a resigned voice:

"I suppose they will kill all the foreigners. We had a squadron of Cossacks to protect us in 1905."

I confessed I had no idea what they wanted. "I suppose what they really want is to get your work-people out and then march into Petrograd?"

This was what they did want, and the two English brothers who were running the mill stoutly faced a mob of some four thousand yelling Russians at its wooden gates.

"Put down that club!" the eldest brother ordered the Russian ring-leader, and something in the tone of his resolute voice made that Russian obey. "Now then—what do you want?"

These two Englishmen were of Lancashire stock, with an ancestry accustomed to dealing with mill-workers. Their supreme feeling at this moment was one of outrage that the workers should be trying to take matters into their own hands, and that this mob of Russians should be trying to push two Englishmen about!

"You come in here quietly!" the two Englishmen addressed the waiting mob. "And don't you break anything!"

I believe these two English brothers could actually have sent that mob back, had it not been for a Ford full of students which now rushed into the mill yard. I was standing with the Englishmen when the students rushed up. They had two machine guns sticking out of the back of the Ford, and, oh, climax of irony! I saw that they were the selfsame guns that Frumkin and I had been trying to sell to the Russian naval aviation corps on the

Black Sea. In their excited, trembling hands, they were brandishing some cocked revolvers. They pointed these at our stomachs as they talked.

"Put those *down!*" cursed the Englishmen in Russian. "Fools! Do you want to shoot somebody!"

The hot-faced students all began to shout at the same time. The gist of their babel was that they represented a Workers' Cell, that they were in command of this demonstration along the Schlusselberg road; and that if we did not let all our work-people come out at once they would destroy the mill.

"All right," said the Englishmen, "take 'em—and be damned to you!"

The work-people poured out in a yelling river. In a few minutes, with the Ford in their van, we watched them parading across the river. From the top of the Ford someone was waving a red flag.

When I went back to the house I saw that the Englishman's wife had tied a red band around the elbow of her primrose-coloured jumper.

We were a mixed gathering in that house. Staying with the Englishman was an Italian count and his Roumanian wife, their tall languid daughter, and a young professor who had been the daughter's tutor, but was now intent it seemed on becoming the countess's lover.

This family had managed to escape from its estate in Jassy, Roumania, and was now trying to make its way back to Rome. The count was a charming creature with a Nebuchadnezzar beard and immaculately polished brown riding boots. He had a high, hooked Roman nose; and although he looked as fierce as a vulture he was in reality a simple man who was still unable to get his bearings in the flood of misfortunes which had swept him off his pleasant farming land in Roumania.

"Call me Beppo," he insisted. "This is no time for formalities."

The second day of the Revolution, Beppo and I had gone across the pack-ice of the Neva to see if there were any signs of Tsarist life still left along that tragic Schlusselberg road, where we had seen them murdering all the mounted policemen. There had been no snow for two days, and the roadside around us was mottled with tell-tale red patches. Beppo, suddenly becoming philosophic, was dissertating on the needlessness of such ugly death, when a rattle of rifle shots rang out just behind us.

I do not know what Beppo saw under my feet. But I saw him, without bending his knees, leap a couple of feet straight up into the air. It was like levitation—for we both seemed suspended there for a second—and when our feet came down again we found that we could not run. We just stood there.

Then a motor lorry, packed like a market basket with red-bannered comrades, turned into the Schlusselberg road and jolted along towards Petrograd. As they went they sang the "Marseillaise" and fired their rifles in the air.

That night, after another outbreak of murder along the Schlusselberg road, we found three women and a boy in a palatial limousine that had been overturned in a ditch. We took them back across the Neva to give them food and shelter in the mill house.

The woman was the wife of the Court Chamberlain. She and her two daughters were dressed in the uniform of Red Cross nurses. She told us that they had received a telephone call at their Red Cross station asking for someone to come quickly to a barracks to attend to a wounded colonel.

They did. And when they got there they found the old shaven-headed colonel, a man whom they knew, lying on the floor of his barracks stark naked. His body was a mass of holes from bullets and bayonet stabs, and his head had been split open with a sabre cut. . . .

"It was their idea of a joke," said the Chamberlain's wife.

The next night I saw a little scene of the Revolution. I saw a police captain trying to escape with his life.

I happened to go into the library about ten o'clock, and while I was rummaging about there I noticed a figure in the corner. It did not move. The room of course was quite hot, because this was dead winter; but this figure had on an astrakhan hat and had

Its fur-coat collar turned up so that it covered Its face. It also wore dark glasses. It did not speak. It might have been a dummy as far as any sign of life was concerned, but I could actually feel Its eyes.

These eyes, I knew, were following every movement I made. They made me so uncomfortable that I gave up looking for the book I had come in for and left the room. As I did so, I passed the Englishman who was my host. He looked strained, and as he passed me he whispered:

"Don't come back!"

I saw that he had an armful of clothes.

About an hour later the Englishman came back into the room where we were sitting, and he looked as if he were sweating.

"He hasn't got a chance!" he said bitterly. "They'll catch him and kill him before he gets half-way across."

He then told me that the figure I had seen crouching in the corner of the darkened library was the captain of the police *pristaff*, the district opposite us on the Schlusselberg road. With that astrakhan hat and a civilian's overcoat over his uniform he had been in hiding for two days. He had managed to cross the pack-ice in the darkness that night, and now, in civilian clothes, he was trying to make his way across the fields behind the mill to a forest about half a mile off. We heard afterwards that a policeman had been caught in the snow out there and killed. Whether it was he or not I do not know. But I can still see that motionless figure in the library with the dark goggles over its eyes.

"I had to help him!" said the Englishman. "Damn it all—when a fellow's down like that!"

The Englishman, of course, was taking a chance with his own life by helping a detested police captain to escape.

The workers along the Schlusselberg road were hunting every policeman in that *pristaff* to the death. No quarter was given; it was to be murder on the spot. The workers said that when they had wrecked the police-station they had found two corpses immured in its walls.

These wretched Russian policemen were the chief victims of the Kerensky Revolution. Practically every one of them was caught and killed. It took seven days to do it. It was quite true that Protopopoff had posted hundreds of them along the roof tops of the Nevsky, armed with machine guns to fire down into the streets. Many of them were found frozen to death beside their machine guns, most of them unwounded. It was claimed that Protopopoff had deliberately brought the Revolution to a head, with the cynical belief that he could force it prematurely, lance it, and kill off its leading spirits. To accelerate this, he had purposely created a food shortage. This would make the population desperate. We ourselves had noticed the alarming length to which the wretched queues had suddenly grown, that stood all the twenty-four hours outside the bread shops in the working district. Before a quarter of these queues had filed past, the remainder were informed there wasn't any more bread until the next day, but they still hung on there desperately, afraid to lose their places. And there is this much to be said in support of that criminal charge against Protopopoff; at least half of the vast warehouses along the Schlusselberg road were afterwards discovered to be full of food—food that had been allowed to rot.

The first hysterical reaction to the sudden freedom from this terror of the Romanoffs was this eight-day frenzy of revengeful murder in Petrograd. The police, as symbols of Tsarist oppression, were naturally the first victims. Then, as each regiment mutinied, it usually killed its officers. If the officers were wise enough not to go back to their barracks, the men from other regiments either killed them or publicly humiliated them in the street. The sailors from a British submarine that was over in Hango told me that they saw an old colonel walking down the street, his hands pressed together before his face in the attitude of prayer, being followed by four sailors.

"He had a bald head," said the Britishers, "and walking behind him was a sailor with a cutlass. While we were looking, and before we could stop him, the sailor took a swing and cut the poor old blighter's skull wide open!"

It was a common occurrence for a sailor or a soldier to stop a superior officer in the street and ostentatiously demand a match. Some old general or admiral, expecting death any minute, would fumble about helplessly in his tunic, produce a box of matches and murmur, "*Pajalst!* Please!" Then the sailor would give him a shove and some of the worst of them would spit in the general's face.

One could not blame the officers for not retaliating. It was a case of *sauve qui peut*. They had no cohesion, no way of communicating with each other to form anything like a body of opposition. It was infinitely worse than the front, where at least one *knew* one's enemy. Here any man walking beside you in the street might suddenly turn nasty and make a scene. And a scene usually meant that the people would murder you. Some of the officers, anxious to get the suspense over, deliberately went back to their barracks, where they knew they would be shot. It was shattering to drive past some of these pink plaster barracks and know that only a day or so before all the officers of such and such a regiment had been butchered there by their men, and then see these same men joking and laughing in a disorderly crowd around the barracks' archway. Some of the officers, when the soldiers and sailors took to stripping them of their epaulets in the Nevsky, got out of uniform and into mufti as quickly as they could. I had a tragic example of this.

I had taken a ground-floor flat on the corner of St. Isaac's Square, and had got as far as having its floor polished and the first of my furniture moved in, when the Revolution broke out. I had no clothes there or any valuable belongings, but it had been badly shot up during the Revolution; several bullets had broken its windows, and, in particular, had scarified my new wallpaper. I was standing outside examining the damage, when an officer came up and asked me could I lend him some clothes.

It was a young captain I had often shot with out at the Kresstoffsky Pigeon Club. He was a minor princeling of a sort, and was in a crack cavalry regiment. It was a regiment that had killed its officers.

"I must get into mufti," he said. "I'm too conspicuous. They don't like Guards' officers, you know. I tried to get into my flat, but the *schwitsar* told me it was full of soldiers. I can't get any clothes."

It was a poignant moment. He was in grave danger, so I told him that of course he could have anything I had, but my clothes were at the Englishman's place up the Neva. I called a *droshky* and we both jumped into it.

"Bad, bad, bad!" he kept muttering to himself. "Everything is bad! I have nothing to do—no place I can go!"

Then suddenly he laughed, stopped the driver and jumped out. He pointed to his own slender body, and then to mine.

"Why, of course," he said, "it's ridiculous! You're twice my size. I'd look like a figure of fun in your suit. Good-bye."

I never saw him again.

This was in the first eight days when nobody knew exactly what was happening in chaotic Petrograd. It was possible for instance to drive in perfect safety down the Nevsky and imagine, if one wanted to convince oneself of that, that the Revolution was already over. Then such reflections would be broken by the sound of shooting going on round the corner. It would be another regiment just mutinying, or, and I will have more to say about these heroic youths, the Corps de Pages having a foray from their armoured car with the Revolutionists.

As the first frenzy of murder subsided another took its place. A new Republic was being born, and hundreds of new officials were being created overnight. The ones we first came into contact with were the self-appointed police. These were mostly university students who got themselves up in whatever uniforms they could collect. They tried to look as militaristic as they could. It was quite *à la mode* to wind strips of cloth round their trouser legs to look like puttees. As every one of them had a rifle, and hardly any one of them knew how to use it, they were a dangerous crowd. It was dismaying to have one of them suddenly leap out and challenge you. You never knew if it was a policeman or one of those bands of guerilla robbers that wandered through Petrograd for months after the Kerensky Revolution was officially over. A banker I knew, who had a palatial flat on the Neva quay, had his flat entered one night by a band of men posing as police. They forced him to show them where he kept whatever money he had in the house; then they demanded to be shown where he kept his wine and food; and for several days they kept him out of his own house. When he finally did get back into it the place had been wrecked.

Perhaps the thing that was most irritating was to have an eager young Russian dash up and say: "Now we are just like you. We are a Republic—like America!"

But the foreigners who had the most trying time of it during the aftermath of the first Revolution were the English mill owners and mill managers who were trying to keep their plants going through it all. The workers were like sheep who had been let out of their pen, and the English managers could not get them back. They had no idea what freedom meant, but most of them took it as an invitation not to work. There was a daily drama in every mill yard. In the one I was most acquainted with the 3,000 workers had immediately elected their own Soviet, which was insisting that it should now have a say as to how the mill should be run. It met and drew up a list of demands which, aside from the orthodox stipulation of an eight-hour day, demanded an impossible increase in wages forthwith. There was no question that under the Tsar the workers had been forced to live under almost unlivable labour conditions. Out along the Schlusselberg road district, it was the custom for entire families of workers to occupy one badly ventilated room, and the dark, dirt and wet inside the mill, where they slaved out their days, were no better. But this was the opposite swing of the pendulum; and they were demanding things which the mill managers simply could not give. The English mill managers had no force to use against these demands of the Workers' Soviets except ridicule and tact—and their policy soon turned from flat opposition or attempt at compromise to one of yielding as slowly and as gracefully as possible to each new demand.

The reason for this was that no one knew where this Revolution was going to lead the working class. The workers themselves had no knowledge of outside conditions and working hours; and the more cynical among their leaders thought that the only way to see how far they could get was by trying it on. As soon as the Englishmen thought they had come to some decent arrangement with a Workers' Soviet, therefore, the extremists among the workers' leaders were immediately demanding further concessions.

It was enough to drive a man mad.

I watched an Englishman go through this ordeal day after day, trying to reason with his workers in the mill yard. So that he could address them *en masse* he stood on a table and harangued the crowd. Using simple comparisons he tried to explain to them why they would have to be content with certain concessions he had just made. The price of labour, for instance, was just like the price of wool. He would begin by saying they were all running the mill together, and the mill wanted to make money so that they all could make a living from it. Now, they would not pay several thousand roubles a *pood* for their wool, would they? No, growled the workers, they certainly would not! Then, he demanded, why ask the mill to pay them such ridiculous prices for labour?

For a moment the mill crowd would look thoughtful, and some of the steadier hands among them would begin nodding their heads. Perhaps, for a moment, the Englishman would carry his point, and the Workers' Soviet would be satisfied because it had just managed to get some concessions which increased its prestige in the workers' eyes. But always, often before the Englishman had got down from the table, a wilder spirit would jump up.

"Fools!" he would yell at the crowd. "Why stand here and talk about it? The mill is ours. We will liquidate the situation and throw out these foreigners and run the mill ourselves. *Deloie boorjoie!*"

This last cry—"Down with the Bourgeois!"—was the prelude to the real Revolution of Lenin's. It was not heard much at first, but to a careful observer these local committees of soldiers and workers' deputies were the centres for the final explosion that was coming later on. It was the cry that the foreign mill owners and managers were most in dread of because they knew it was no longer aimed at the Tsar but at their class.

The Scottish and Lancashire mill foremen could afford to be more abrupt than the Englishmen higher up, who had responsibility for the mill. When a Russian department manager came to them and complained that a machine had broken down they would jeer at him.

"O-ho! So it's broke, is it? Now ain't that too bad! Tsit! Tsit! Well, Ivan Petrovitch—you're running the mill now. You fix the machine."

Then, to me, they would add:

"And they can bloody well run 'em to hell as far as any help they'll get from us is concerned."

Even in the beginning the appalling lack of a foreman class among Russians was making itself felt.

But bad as this situation was with the workers all over Russia, the political pandemonium was infinitely worse. Kerensky was head of the Provisional Government. But there were something like twenty-one different political parties bickering behind his back for the control of 180,000,000 people. And Kerensky, as I have said, was a political chameleon.

Kerensky's sole virtue (if indeed one wanted to call it that) was his power of oratory. His political prestige was based exclusively on his spirited defence in the Bayliss ritual case, when he had been a young lawyer. And against a cold implacable intellect like Lenin's he was as purposeless as a weathercock.

I heard him make a speech one night in the Marinsky theatre. One of his best speeches, in fact. On that stage which had seen the glories of so many gorgeous *ballerinas*, with the boxes of the absent Grand Dukes filled with the flower of Allied diplomacy, the leader of the Provisional Government excelled himself. Russia, undefeated, Russia unconquerable, would go on and on to win the war. Russia would never desert her allies, and Russia, re-born, would emerge victorious. The brave soldiers at the front, the brave sailors . . .

It was stirring. Even with my faulty Russian I could get enough to be thoroughly moved by it. The Englishman I had gone with told me it was a magnificent speech; Kerensky was telling 'em what for! Kerensky, with his flat-lidded eyes and black hair *en brosse*, shook his clenched fist: "Our soldiers—"

"*Svallitch!*"

It was the Russian equivalent for son-of-a-bitch, and someone had called Kerensky that from the first row of the orchestra, a distinguished position where, before the Revolution, no one below the rank of General could have sat. We turned our heads to see who it was and watch him being removed. But what we saw was a gigantic sailor standing up and shaking his fist at Kerensky.

"One of those sailors from Cronstadt!" came the half-frightened exclamation from the seats around us.

"Ho!" said the sailor. "So *this* is what we fought the Revolution for—*this!* To go back and get killed again! Well, listen to me —you fool!—we didn't fight on the barricades for the *boorjoie!* (Capitalists). We fought this Revolution for us—LAND—LAND AND FREEDOM! *Deloie boorjoie!* Down with the Capitalists!"

We held our breath. Nobody moved to touch the sailor. In fact, as the man from Cronstadt shouted "*Deloie boorjoie!*" a storm of cheers swept the galleries. Added to which were savage shouts—"Down with Kerensky and the Provisional Government!" and "All power to the Committees of Soldiers and Workers!"

"You're worse than the Tsar!" said the sailor.

And there stood Kerensky!

Even the least of his admirers, I should imagine, would not deny his physical courage. He was still standing there, with his clenched fist upraised; and, as the shouting died down, the fierce histrionic fervour on his face changed to an ingratiating, friendly smile.

"Comrades," he said. "Brothers."

With a startling alertness the head of the Provisional Government continued his interrupted speech. So quick was his political shift that he seemed to be taking the words out of the sailor's mouth, to be carrying on, in fact, from where the sailor left off. His oratory reached lyric heights. From a flat oration on the glory and necessity of Russia continuing to carry on her part in the World War, it now switched swiftly into a plea for all true Russians to unite—a Centre speech. A plea to save Russia from being plundered. And in this new Russia there would be a new life for everybody. Its people would be free—free—as the brave sailor from Cronstadt here had said they should be. He went on and on, in a masterpiece of placation and compromise. Land and wealth would be more equally distributed! From a militaristic beginning he brought his fiery eloquence to the task of making a straight labour speech. Words, words, words; it was in this way that Kerensky held the stage for seven months between two Revolutions.

In 1933 I had luncheon with Kerensky, together with Bruce Lockhart and Alexander Woollcott, in the Carlton Grill in London.

Kerensky, like all the White Russians, was thinking in terms of his eventual return to Russia and, even at this late date, of the downfall of the Bolshevik Government. He refused to listen when we tried to persuade him that the coming "young" Russians would never have any trace of the old régime in power again. He was furious with Woollcott over what he eventually told Lockhart and myself were the great New Yorker's "wisecracks" about Russia, which quite naturally to Kerensky was a most tragic subject.

We wondered where we were. People you met in the street now had a preoccupied look on their faces. In the old days you would have known that such an expression of intentness meant that this man was thinking of the pretty woman he was taking to Kontant's for luncheon, and debating whether it would be rushing things too fast to try to seduce her that very first time in a *cabinet privée* or wait until a more certain opportunity presented itself; that man would be thinking of a war contract he was after, wondering if the bribe money he had given had really reached the right person; that pretty Englishwoman would be pondering over the dinner party she would give that night, and how the people should be seated at the table.

But now . . . Now we knew that everyone was absorbed in the problem of self-preservation. For very few of us (particularly those who were trying to do business in Russia) thought that the Provisional Government was going to last. Kerensky was too ephemeral—and there was too much misery knocking about Petrograd. It seems amazing, how vastly much more informed were the business men in Petrograd at this juncture than were the Allied diplomats or staff officers. Whether it was the usual mumbo-jumbo that diplomats and statesmen feel that they must give off over any situation, even if they, by chance, have already seen its hopelessness; whether it was that so-called statesmanlike manner or just pure ignorance, I do not know; but I do know that people in certain Embassies strongly resented having the truths of this situation pointed out to them.

Most of us in making our plans during this epoch usually thought out what seemed the most obvious and logical turn for events to take, and then fortified ourselves against the direct opposite. Life in Petrograd had become a great gamble. But the only thing we were certain of was that it was not going to continue—at least, not so far as we were concerned.

One day, in that fashionable barber shop opposite the Hôtel de France, where aristocratic Russia had its head shaved and its moustaches curled, a complete stranger came over to me.

"This is not Russia!" he said to me earnestly. "I assure you, this is not Russia!"

The barber told me he was, or at least had been, a great landowner down in the Crimea; but his peasants had told him they would kill him if he ventured near his estates.

One day, after the weekly luncheon of the American Club at Kontant's, I was walking back to the Consulate with North Winship, the American Consul. At the luncheon we had had the American Ambassador, the Hon. David R. Francis, as a guest of honour. He had called for a toast to the twelve members of the Provisional Government, and, although it was drunk in sweet fruit juice, called *kvass*, we responded with enthusiasm. For upon the efforts of these twelve men and their continuity in office depended the bulk of what we had in this world. These men, we could see even then, were just hanging on to power because of their previous popularity, but the coming into power of the fast-forming committees of soldiers and workers was holding them up seriously in their efforts to re-establish a sane régime. We drank their health with the wish, first, that we had drunk it in good wine instead of fruit juice, finally, that we wished we could have put some real heart into it.

Winship's consulate was in the Singer Dom, an office building built upon a supposed likeness to the American plan. It stood opposite the Cathedral of the Virgin of Kazan, before whose buff-coloured colonnades Winship and I had watched the Revolution break out.

As we walked across the grass before the Virgin of Kazan we noticed that all the *droshky* drivers in the Nevsky were going in the same direction, and one and all were whipping their stallions furiously! These old philosophers were wonderful trouble barometers, and when you saw them all dashing in one direction you could be sure that there was something in the nature of a riot whence they were hastening.

Down by the Nicholas Station a sea of red seemed to be pouring into the Nevsky. The whole thoroughfare, about twice the width of Fifth Avenue or Piccadilly, became scarlet. The effect was staggering in its immensity. I remarked to Winship that this must be the father and mother of all demonstrations, and he replied that he did not know there was that much red bunting in all the Russias. We were used to these processions by now; thousands of chanting people, faces uplifted, marching behind red banners, demanding—LAND AND FREEDOM—but this one was sinister.

Shopkeepers, bored with so many threats of disaster, began to come out and wearily pull down the steel blinds over their windows. Much familiarity with street disturbances had bred a good technique in their long-suffering souls.

But as we walked toward the procession we noticed that a large number of soldiers were running away from it. They were yelling loudly and shaking their fists at it! And they were shout-

ing indignantly for their comrades to assemble. This was something entirely new in the way of demonstrations!

As we passed the *Balshoi Kanushnayia* or Big Stable Street,
where were the barracks of the *Praeobrajinsky Polk*, the *élite* of
the Guards Regiments, we saw a mob of them rush out and run
along the Nevsky to a spot opposite the Kazan Cathedral, where
a giant among these magnificent six-foot guardsmen was haranguing an excited group of them. Trouble in Russia always seems
to break out in certain spots, and the miraculous Virgin of Kazan
had looked down on some of the bloodiest scenes in Russian history. It was from beneath her benign gaze that Father Gapon led
the mass meeting of protest in 1905 to kneel before the Winter
Palace, from whose balconies hundreds of them were murdered
by rifle fire . . . the answer of a badly frightened Tsar.

By this time the main body of the procession had about reached
the Hôtel de l'Europe, a block away, and its forerunners were
already upon us. They consisted of children, anywhere from
twelve to fifteen years old, running sidewise, hand in hand, like a
May chain. These infants tried to prevent anyone from cutting
across the street ahead of the procession. That was their rôle;
and they were very important about it. They were all gaily
chanting some Red version of the "Marseillaise."

Then about half-way up the square advanced a soldier, a
workman, and a sailor, bearing aloft a huge red banner with the
words:

"WELCOME! LAND AND LIBERTY!"

About twenty paces in their rear came an assortment of some
forty of what seemed to us, at that time, the most potential black-
guards it had ever been our misfortune to see. They were, as a
matter of fact, these "irregulars" who had been making life such
a trial for us as we drove in and out through the barricades they
had established around Petrograd. These men all carried rifles, in
any sort of manner. Many of them looked a bit sheepish.

Following them came an inspiring sight, a bevy of factory girls
marching arm in arm; their shawl-enveloped heads tilted sky-
wards; their placid Slav faces lighted with a look of perfect
ecstasy, and they sang as if inspired the Hymn of the Revolution.

It was impossible not to be moved by such a profound, even if naïve faith in their new-found freedom. And then I saw IT!

I have seen a few gruesome sights in my life, but I have never seen anything that gave me such a shock.

It was a huge black banner, with a white skull and crossbones, which seemed to be grinning over the words:

"WELCOME, ANARCHY!"

Actually, the Jolly Roger! I had thought that such things had vanished with Captain Kidd. But here it was in real life! There was something loathsome about it, as if it were a flaunting invitation to indulge in all sorts of beastliness. Our genuine sympathy for the Revolution had then been for this! Turning to Winship, I caught a stare of absolute horror on his face. He said, "I'm getting out of this; that filthy thing makes me sick!"

I tried to persuade him to remain for a few minutes, as I thought there would be some excitement.

"No, thanks," he said sensibly. "I've been watching those soldiers, especially that big fellow; and I think there is going to be some shooting in a few seconds."

"Never!" I said—for I thought I knew my Russia.

Caught up by the emotion of the whole affair, I walked over to the group of soldiers now standing in the middle of the Nevsky. The big guardsman, his hat shoved on to the extreme back of his head, was roaring at the oncoming procession.

"Devil take you—swine! You want ten roubles a day for eight hours' work, do you? And our soldiers—eh? We are to work twenty-four hours a day in the trenches for seventy-five kopecks a month! *Boorjoie!* Capitalists! Go back to your factories!"

This was, as it turned out, the last protest of the soldiery against the Communist element in the Workers' programme. The *Praeobrajinsky* was one of the last regiments to go whole-heartedly Red.

"Back to your factories!" shouted the guardsmen, and spread themselves out as if determined to block the street—to hold back some thirty thousand people!

An answering snarl came from the hooligans with the rifles. The Jolly Roger Brigade was obviously at a loss as to how to proceed.

My faulty Russian had been just good enough to allow me to grasp what the guardsman had said. Here was a Man; but it was perhaps more the personal satisfaction of having understood and agreed with his words that made me suddenly feel so excited about things and slap him on the back.

"*Harasho!*" I yelled at him. "Good! Good!"

He turned, and seeing that it was a foreigner smiled delightedly, his broad face beaded with sweat from his emotions, and then he began cursing the procession again. His enthusiasm was contagious. I caught it, and turned to call Winship, only to see him at that instant diving into the Singer building. I still had my hand on the big guardsman's back. There were about twelve of us around one of the big bases of the tramway pillars. And as I turned to enthuse with my soldier friend again—I found myself looking straight into the muzzles of about forty rifles. . . .

My heart did not flutter, but I think it stopped altogether for a few moments.

It seemed ages, waiting for those rifle shots, and then they came:

"Cr-u-u-mp! Pop! Pop!"

A volley and a couple of stragglers.

The big soldier fell away from my hand. I was still holding it up—where his back had been—when I saw his arms go up, and then he lay sprawled at my feet. As I reached to turn him over I saw another soldier fall near the base of the tramway pillar and two others drag him over and fall on top of him. At the moment I wondered whether they had also been shot, or if it was a heroic effort to protect him with their own bodies. The Nevsky tram pillars are over a yard wide at the base. But I did not wait to investigate.

The big guardsman, for whom I now felt a strange sense of personal responsibility, was quite dead. A bruised hole under his hair was enough to show that, without having the evidence of those pinkish brains, like sweetbreads, oozing out of the back of his skull.

Suddenly I realised what had happened! My time reaction was a little late in coming; but when it did I lost no time getting out of that street. I looked up first, expecting to see a mob through which I would have to force my way, and found to my astonishment that the Nevsky was empty.

Half-way down to the corner of the Hôtel de l'Europe I could see the "gunmen" retreating in confusion, obviously appalled by what they had done. I could also see that the procession was fighting inside itself; I saw red banners waving about crazily, and then being snatched down; I saw the whole procession, some thirty thousand people backing up on itself, rising and falling like a sea-serpent's undulations or like the freight cars in a crumpled toy railway. The orderly demonstration had suddenly become a shambles.

I saw Winship waving to me from the balcony of the Singer building; whereupon I suddenly stood up and raced for it.

From the balcony we watched the procession re-forming itself. When a few hundred yards of it had again passed our door I decided to go down and walk along with it. A fellow from the American Red Cross had come up to Winship's office and said he had heard that the soldiers were collecting and were going to attack the procession when it reached the Marinsky Square.

We followed them into the square, where they came to a halt. They then began an orgy of speeches. Speeches, speeches, speeches; a scene we had long since grown tired of. Every student, with a green band around his hat, had collected a crowd round him. Some had obtained boxes; some seemed to have raided the Hotel Astoria for chairs; those who couldn't get anything better were haranguing the mob from the lamp-posts. It was infuriating, because the impression one got was that everybody was talking, and, as long as they could talk, they would never do anything. And no speech would have any relationship to the very next speaker's diatribe. One would be shouting—"Arrest Lenin!" —and the man next to him would be provoking cries of—"*Deloie Boorjoie!*" Down with the *Bourgeoisie!*

And just across the Neva, Lenin himself was speaking! I saw him, on a raised platform, before the home of Kschensinska, a former *première ballerina* and favourite of the Tsar. A short, dumpy figure, with an enormous dome of a head, high cheekbones giving a sinister contemptuousness to his Tartar eyes. The great Lenin! But he was not "great" to any but a very few people then. He was just this undersized new agitator in an old double-breasted blue suit, his hands in his pockets, speaking with an entire absence of that hysterical arm-waving that so characterised all his fellow countrymen.

"Yes," he was saying, "it is the Capitalists and our diplomats who make the wars. Not the people. They get rich, we get killed. You left the soil and the factories to go to war, and when war is over—what? You will go back to the soil and the factories to work under the Capitalist system again—those of you who are left alive. *What do you get from war?* Wounds, suffering, and death."

Town workers, *moujiks*, soldiers and sailors looked up and listened, and then they looked at each other:

"*Da*, yes, he is right! What do we get out of this war but wounds and death and starvation. Back to the factories!—take them! Take the land! *Deloie boorjoie!*"

Lenin's usual platform, before he had to flee temporarily to Finland, was this palace of the Tsar's favourite directly across the Troitsky bridge from the British Embassy. I always like to think of that picture of him standing there, absolutely sure of his purpose—an alchemist of human emotions—while in the square red building of the British Embassy across the bridge, the best diplomatic corps in Russia was guessing which way the cat was going to jump; and further on, on the Fourstadtskayia Oulitsa the Americans were doing likewise; and further on the Italians and the French; and further out the whole world; all guessing. And John Reed saying to me:

"The next time you hear the machine guns, old boy—you put on a red necktie. It's going to be the only safe colour in Petrograd. And this time it will be a *real* revolution."

He had just come back from seeing Lenin for the first time, and his eyes were still half-blinded, as if he had seen a vision, as if he had seen God!

For some reason the Allied diplomats were not sufficiently impressed by Lenin at that time. It was possibly because they would not go out and listen to the talk in the streets. One English business man said to me:

"I say! There's an amazing fellow over there on the other side of the Troitsky bridge; he's talking rank anarchy! Immediate peace, no annexations, the Dictatorship of the Proletariat, world revolution! Never heard anything like it in my life!"

"Well, there's nothing new in that," I told him.

"Isn't there! Well, this fellow is talking about it *now!* Advocates the soldiers coming back from the front and the overthrow of the Provisional Government . . . *now!* Doesn't he know there's a war on?"

"He'll get over that all right," I assured him. "Besides, the people will mob him or he will be arrested!"

"You go over and see for yourself!" he said significantly. "That's just what they aren't doing—they're listening!"

And so, chiefly owing to the failure of the authorities to appreciate his calibre, Lenin was allowed to stand there in full view of Petrograd, on the balcony of the Tsar's mistress, and carefully sow his seeds of discontent and sedition.

We watched this on the afternoon of the Nevsky shooting affair. The Red Cross man and I went back to my flat on the Gogol. While there, Korsakoff, an aviator from the Black Sea naval base, dropped in. The Revolutionists had killed Admiral Nevitsky, he said; and no planes had left the water on the Black Sea since the Revolution, as the officers were in deadly fear of their mechanics and expected a general massacre to be held on them any day, and, like the Guards' officer, could I let him have a suit of clothes as his uniform merely made him a mark for disturbance?

Commander Utgoff, he said, had held off the Revolutionists on the Black Sea for a time by a reckless act of courage. When the local Soviet had passed its order, commanding all the officers to give up their side-arms, Utgoff—the first man that I flew with in Russia—had leaped into the naval launch and rushed out to the flying base at Kiln Boutha. As he entered the officers' mess he passed his comrades who, with flushed and averted faces, told him of their disgrace. They had already given up their arms.

"Then I began to cry!" said Utgoff himself, as he told me this story afterwards.

He ran from the mess and out to a hangar, where he jumped on the wing of a seaplane and pulled out his little Webley-Scott automatic and unsheathed his little ceremonial dirk, with its black-and-orange St. George's knot.

"See!" he cried, weeping before his men—"these are my side-arms! Come and take them. I have fought side by side with you men for three years, and now you wish to drag me in the mud!"

Korsakoff said the men were ashamed to see their commander weeping.

"Come on!" cried Utgoff, levelling his revolver at them. "You come and take them—for I swear before Christ I shall never give them to you!"

The result of this, said Korsakoff, was that Utgoff's personal mechanic rushed across to the plane, put his arms around Utgoff's legs and lifted him high in the air. The sailors then cheered him, and the local Soviet passed a new order saying that the officers should be allowed to keep their side-arms.

Korsakoff some time later painted a terrible picture of what the Russian officers had to endure in the Crimea. Sebastopol was some 2,000 miles from Petrograd, and the Red of revolution was slow in seeping down there. At first the officers entertained the hope of being able to set up an independent Crimean Government. As late as June 10th, some of the loyal sailors from the fleet had sacked the Sebastopol office of the Bolshevik party. They were not yet ready for the Red slogan:

Immediate peace on all the outer fronts . . . and war at inner fronts!

But this sacking had reached the ears of Cronstadt, the naval fortress, fifteen miles outside of Petrograd, then the stronghold of the Reddest revolutionaries, and a delegation of propagandists was at once dispatched to Sebastopol. They said to the sailors of the Black Sea:

"*Pfoui!* You are cattle, sheep of the Revolution! Why are you afraid of your officers?"

The Black Sea sailors, amazed at first at this accusation, soon began to be convinced that they had been entirely too subservient to their Tsarist officers.

"Look at your comrades on the Baltic!" demanded the propagandists from Cronstadt. "*They* are not afraid of these damned, yellow-epauletted officers!—these fragments of the old régime. They exterminated them all in the glorious Revolution!"

And they reminded the Black Sea sailors of the slaughter of their comrades in the 1905 *Potemkin* massacre!

To prove to the Bolshevik emissaries their lack of fear towards their officers, the Black Sea sailors began to make it a point to practise open disobedience, to make demonstrations of open contempt. The officers then knew it was only a question of time before death came to every one of them, and Admiral Kolchak called them together:

"My officers," said this tragic "Rock of the Crimea," "we are like men in an open powder magazine. We must go carefully. Bend, but do not break. Let no man among you be provoked into striking the match that would blow us all into eternity."

For his exceptional bravery in the Russo-Japanese war, the Tsar had given Kolchak a golden sword. The second highest decoration or award that could be bestowed upon a Russian officer was the right to wear "golden cold arms."

"If they once start it will be a general massacre; we shall all be killed. That is not the way to save Russia. My officers"—Admiral Kolchak touched his golden sword—"we must *live* to use this for Russia!"

"And that's the way things are in Sebastopol," said Korsakoff, "that nice, warm, sunny Crimea, where you used to have such a good time with the pretty Russian girls!"

The story of Kolchak's golden sword symbolised both the tragedy and the comedy of Revolution.

On July 10, 1917, under the auspices of the Cronstadt propagandists, a monster mass meeting of sailors was held at Koulikovo

Field, on the outskirts of Sebastopol. The Bolsheviks wanted to persuade the Black Sea Fleet to provoke its officers into some action that would invite retaliation. After an all-day harangue, the Bolshevik emissaries convinced most of the meeting that immediate disarmament of their officers was an absolute necessity. As Russians never do things by halves, that meeting appointed a delegation with this all-embracing of all slogans. It was:

Immediate disarmament of all officers, and to hell with the Soldiers' and Workingmen's Committees if they do not concede!

As the Soldiers' and Workingmen's Committees were fighting for exactly the opposite of what the Tsarist officers were trying to retain, this resolution seemed to have included both sides of the controversy.

Special delegates were then sent to the palace of the former Commander-in-Chief of Sebastopol, where was now sitting the Committee of Soldiers and Workingmen which was to be sent to hell in case it did not concede. This committee, intimidated, and believing that the propagandist "flying meeting" on Koulikovo Field really did voice the will of the people, agreed. A deputation was then sent in its name to make Admiral Kolchak sign the *ukase* ordering the officers of his fleet to give up their arms.

The Admiral was on his flagship, *St. George the Vanquisher,* lying in the basin near the harbour entrance. He received the delegation on his quarter-deck.

Kolchak must have sensed the seriousness of their mission, for he received the delegation with his hand clasping the hilt of his golden sword.

"Never!" he said when the sailors told him what they had come for.

"It is the will of the people," said their spokesman.

For a few seconds Kolchak stood there and faced them; then his hand slipped limply from his sword, and his shoulders sank. He seemed to shrivel. "*Harasho!*" He spread out his hands to show his impotence. "So be it."

He entered his cabin and wrote out the humiliating order to his officers to surrender their side-arms. To a Russian officer, brought up in the tradition that his sword was his honour, he must have felt he was writing those words with his life's blood. But he did what he thought was right under the circumstances; he was almost Tolstoyan in his submissiveness.

When he emerged from his cabin the setting sun was colouring the waters of Sebastopol a rich red gold. He walked to the head of the delegation and handed him the order. Kolchak then turned to re-enter his cabin. But the delegates stopped him.

"Your sword, Admiral?" Their leader pointed to the token of honour.

Kolchak paused, and looked down at his weapon—the golden sword that the Emperor had given him with his own hands. Then he slowly unstrapped his treasure, and, with outstretched hands, held it before him. The sailor approached to take it from him—and reached out a grimy paw!

It was too much. The sword that he had won in honour could not be desecrated. Kolchak backed away from the reaching hand, and threw his sword over the heads of the delegates. A faint splash and a few concentric circles marked the spot where Father Neptune had taken it to his bosom. It was safe there, thought Kolchak.

"But Kolchak," said Korsakoff, "surrendered to an illusion. The day after he threw his sword away look what Utgoff did!"

After Utgoff had refused to surrender his side-arms, and defied his men to come and take them from him, the sailors sent a deputation to the Committee of Soldiers and Workingmen demanding that all the officers at the flying station should have their side-arms returned to them at once. The committee agreed.

Not only that, two days later all the officers in Sebastopol had their side-arms returned to them. *Divers were sent down to recover the golden sword of Kolchak!* After two weeks' search they discovered it, and it was solemnly forwarded to the Minister of the Navy at Petrograd, with instructions that it should be returned to Admiral Kolchak.

At the same time the Sebastopol Committee of Soldiers and Workingmen passed a resolution "to declare a dispraise (disapproval) of Kolchak for allowing such an insulting order (officer disarmament) to be issued. . . ."

With such things going on it was no wonder that people in Russia could not know what was going to happen to them from one minute to the next. And perhaps Korsakoff was right when he declared that had Kolchak obeyed his fighting instincts (like passionate Utgoff) and not surrendered to an illusion, he might have saved the Black Sea and been alive today.

But none of these experiences could equal the fantastic adventure that then befell Utgoff himself.

Chapter 34

A RUSSIAN ACE

COMMANDER VICTOR V. UTGOFF was the first man to fly from a ship during the World War. Nine hours after Germany had declared war on Russia he was flying about the Bosphorus. He was one of the original Russian "aces," that sporting lot who, when they weren't playing tennis at Monte Carlo, went in for flying for the love of the sport. He was the Viking type of Russian, a lean fair-headed fellow with amazing greenish eyes, and a willingness to do anything provided there was excitement in it. When I first met him, with Frumkin, in 1915, the first thing he showed me was his scrap-book which as far as I could make out was nothing but a ghastly record of the crashes he had made. There were photographs of every conceivable type of land or seaplane, all smashed to bits, with Utgoff either standing proudly on top or else being fished out of some floating wreckage. He must have cost the Russian Government a pretty penny to train him. But he had more than made up for it by the time I met him, for his trim white naval tunic was heavy with decorations, and as I said his little ceremonial dirk bore the coveted St. George's knot.

By the time the Revolution came along Utgoff was in command of the mobile seaplane forces of the Black Sea Fleet, and after that upheaval he carried on with his fighting, having to watch not only the enemy but his own men.

"It was as if I was always fighting two persons," he said to me. "One in front and another behind me who held my arm every time I tried to strike my natural foe!"

Utgoff's case was so typical of the thousands of those desperately gallant Tsarist officers who carried on in the face of difficulties that would have stopped a more practical race that his story is almost a saga of the White Russian officer. To begin with, he could never understand why his story bored the world.

"Even my nationality now appears to be a guilt!"

He was exactly my age, and he laid bare to me the heart of a

Russian officer throughout the Revolution and its aftermath. What they were thinking, what they said to each other, why they did what they did—and didn't do many of the things that they ought to have done—why none of them ever seemed able to find his feet again in a purely Western civilisation.

As a vivid analysis of White Russian psychology his talks to me while I lay in hospital gave me a clear look at what has been an almost unwritten page of Russian history.

"From the age of about nine," said Utgoff, "the Russians of my class were educated to be scientific destroyers. Our fathers were the same. When we were still children we were always packed off to the *kadet* schools, which were walled in from the world like monasteries, and we were taught the dead arts and how to kill. We knew nothing of the world or real life. We were like Carthusian monks. Then we were graduated to join a class, a caste. We neither worried nor thought about the realities of existence. There was a groove already shaped for every one of us. And along these grooves we ran like marbles to come out at the other end . . . with grey hairs, a safe pension, an atrophied brain, and, of course, a few decorations to pin on our tunics at village fêtes. We could tell you what Napoleon had for breakfast on the day of Waterloo, but we could not tell you how even the houses we lived in were paid for or built."

"Not even that charming little flat of yours hanging over the Black Sea at Sebastopol?"

"No. And I don't mind telling you I wouldn't mind changing places with Matvé in it right now!"

Matvé had been his batman, personal attendant, and butler-wetnurse-cook to Utgoff's family.

"Then came the Revolution. All the grooves were smashed, and for the first time in our lives we had to take care of ourselves —and to think. It was awful; many of us couldn't do it! We who had been taught nothing but how to destroy were now faced with the task of creating a new rule to lead an army of 12,000,000 people. An army which incidentally had revolted against our caste. I have read your Wild West stories; cowboys riding for their lives before a herd of stampeding cattle. Well—that's the way I felt when I looked up from the radio message giving us the details of the Petrograd Revolution. I saw a stampede of 180,000,000 people coming down on us. And we couldn't run— we had to stick it out there and lead."

Then he gave me his own gorgeous adventure.

"It was in June 1917; and we lay in the seaplane carrier *Imperator Nicolai Pervyi*, about twenty-five miles off Constanza in the Black Sea. Constanza was then held by the Germans and the Bulgars. My job was to fly over the city and try to pick out some suitable landing place for the troops. We were going to try and take Constanza from the sea.

"The crew of the seaplane carrier numbered about 600 men. They had already elected their local Soviet, their Committee of Soldiers and Workingmen, to which in those early days they were kind enough to include a few officers. *Ispolkom* was the wireless name for such committees. Twelve sailors and one officer was the form of our ship's local government. We had one in every ship. Every ship was a world of its own—and *Ispolkom* was its government. It took a bit of doing to have the patience to deal with that.

"In the *Imperator Nicolai Pervyi* we had only about twenty-five officers to try and control this trouble that was always boiling inside the steel sides of our ship. The seas overside were just as fresh and familiar as they had always been, but our lives on the sea were such as we could never have dreamed they would be.

"Our rule was one of following the path of least resistance, of wit, of chicanery, of strong personal example, and sometimes the force of utter desperation when we would have to chance everything and revert to the old iron fist.

"When my seaplane was about to be lowered overside the president of our local Soviet came along and asked old one-legged Captain Kovanko:

" 'Is this expedition to be *defensive* or *offensive*?'

"The sailors were then of the opinion that if we did not attack the enemy the kind-hearted Germans would reciprocate by not slaughtering us!

"Old Captain Kovanko replied without thinking: 'Oh, just

photographic. We're only flying over to pick out a landing place.'

" 'That's all right, then,' said the Soviet's president and let me go to my seaplane.

"The seaplane was a Shchetinin 9, Russian make, with a 150 horse-power Salmson motor. The first thing I noticed was that there were no bombs in the racks under the wings. My mechanic, Oskolkoff, who had been with me ever since 1912, when I first started flying, was standing by the engine. 'Where are the bombs?' I asked him.

" 'Oh!' he said, looking rather foolish. 'I did not think you wanted any. I did not know that this was an *offensive* expedition!'

"Well," grinned Utgoff, "you can imagine what I wanted the bombs for. I wasn't going to miss the chance of laying a few eggs on the dirty Bulgars! Besides, you know what an easy mark our seaplane carriers are—when they have to stop to take the planes aboard. Perfectly stationary target—the thing that submarine commanders just dream about!

" 'Put those bombs on!' I told Oskolkoff. And he did.

"The plane was lowered to the water and I took the air. It was a gorgeous fresh day, with the sea far below me. I didn't think much about the Revolution up there. I think I sang all the twenty-five miles to Constanza. Normal times I would have been listening with my heart to the engine! But now I did not care. The blue waste of the sea tumbling thousands of feet below me once meant an ugly death if my engine failed. Now—it seemed almost friendly. Only when I got near the coast did I begin to think about my objective, to do my job of photographing, and then race back for that little black spot that was lurching on the swells of the Black Sea. The Salmson hummed like a contented bee.

"Soon, down below, I saw the white line of surf breaking along the coast of Roumania, and looked down on that flat, lake-dotted, unhappy land. A haze forced me to come down to a 1,000 feet before I could get the proper visibility for aerial photos, and I dived down through the 'Archie' bursts and swept along the coast photographing all the spots that looked like likely landing places.

They were crazy to get me. A nice little burst of incendiary rockets missed me by inches. I did not take the time to drop any eggs on them, it was too hot! And I gave a yell of relief when I had shot my last plate and got clear of those 'Archie' bursts.

"But I did not sing on the return flight to the ship. The show, perhaps my last show, was over. And it would be no fun, being picked up and lifted on board again—not like the old days.

"We were instructed to fly around the ship several times in wide circles before taking the water. This was our precaution against submarines who knew that the ship would have to come to a full stop to take any returning plane aboard. I had done so hundreds of times. But this time when I did so, there, sliding through the soapy green sea towards the *Imperator Nicolai Pervyi*, I saw a long grey cigar. A sub.!

"For a moment," said Utgoff, "I just stared at it. I simply couldn't believe my luck! 'By God!' I said, 'I've got you!' I banked to come up into what I could see from the *Imperator's* smoke was the course of the wind; and at my signal, Oskolkoff, who had also become bloodthirsty at the sight of the enemy, sighted carefully and pulled the bomb clutch.

"There was a burst of white sea. I did a sharp turn to come back over the spot. But the sub. had vanished. She couldn't have submerged. She had gone down too quickly! I don't think I hit it; we seldom do, but I had probably opened her up. But, my God, the terror that must have been going on inside that submarine. I know the panic that follows those ghastly vibrations in the water, when all the lights go out and you're falling all over the machinery and the crew goes mad with fear. I shook for a moment with sublime satisfaction; those are the peaks of life's emotions.

"Then I came back to earth, or rather to the water, and taxied over to the *Imperator Nicolai Pervyi* to be picked up.

"When I was being swung inboard I saw the sailors talking in excited groups. But I pushed through them and made my report to old Captain Kovanko. Then I went over to my cabin, took off my things, and lay down. The reaction was setting in and I wanted to think. Our ship was ploughing along on her way back to Sebastopol. What a difference our homecoming would have been in the old days of the Tsar! And, among other things, I was thinking as I lay in my bunk, how lucky it was I had really spotted that submarine—the picture of some six hundred of us struggling in the water was not nice to contemplate.

"While I was thinking this a sailor knocked at my door and then came in, where he stood, scowling at me. 'Commander Utgoff,' he said, 'you will report immediately before our Executive Committee!'

" 'Can't it wait till tomorrow?' " I asked.

" 'No! You will report now!' And without saluting he left my cabin.

"I got up and put on my uniform and went over to the sailors' mess, where sat the men. In the big room they had pulled all the tables into line, and behind sat the members of the Executive Committee. In the yellow light I could see that all the sailors not then on duty were gathered in the room. About two hundred of them. The smoke from their cigarettes filled the room, and none of them were dressed properly. One lout, a member of the court, had his shirt open all the way down to his dirty navel. In that sulphurous light their shaven heads looked like a field of enormous eggs. I walked to the centre and stood underneath a swinging lamp opposite the middle table.

" 'Now, Commander,' began the presiding judge. 'Will you kindly explain to us why you dropped a bomb on a peaceful submarine which went out of the harbour to get some fresh air? Our Comrades at the front do not fight any more—so why are you here "provoking" an offensive spirit? Tell us that.'

"I lost my temper. I shook my fist at them:

" 'You damn fools!' I began. Then I called them every name I had learned since a child—and the Russian language is very expressive. Once started on that tack there was no use backing down. Besides, I was crying—crying from sheer outraged common sense! I was so wild with them that I walked across and pounded the table before the court's faces. That shook 'em a bit. And do you know, that awful language of mine recalled them to the old régime. It was like old times, and many of them, without thinking about it, began buttoning up their clothes and one or two got up to their feet. Then I knew that I had them, and my own feelings began to cool down. I knew that I had navigated the worst stretch of it—but I could not leave them in that frame of mind. Each one of them would think that he had shown himself a coward before the others—and a few minutes after I would leave them, they would all be down on us like a pack of wolves. I had to make them *friendly* before I left.

" 'Why,' I said, laughing—and I took off my hat—'you're like the Russian rabbit! You know, you know the story—how he ran like hell out of Russia and then sat down under a bush and went puff! puff! puff!

" 'A German rabbit came up to him and said: "Vot's de matter? Vy do you sit dere and go puff, puff, puff like dat—eh?"

" ' "Because," said the Russian rabbit, "I have just heard that all the elephants in Russia are going to have their noses cut off!"

" ' "But hell," said the German rabbit. "You ain't no elephant!"

" ' "Know it," said the Russian rabbit. "But first they will cut off my nose, and afterward I shall have to prove that I am not an elephant!"

" 'And so,' I said to them, 'after that "peaceful" submarine had torpedoed you, all you would have had to do was swim over to Constanza—only twenty-five miles—and tell them that it was all a mistake—we had only flown over Constanza to take harmless photographs. You would have to prove you were rabbits!'

"For a moment the men looked solemn, as if I had been insulting them; then somebody laughed—then they all laughed. They roared with laughter. Though the *Imperator Nicolai Pervyi* was lurching heavily, they took me on their shoulders and carried me along to my cabin!

"While I was sitting there in a perfect stew of mixed emotions old Captain Kovanko came along. He was smiling like a bridegroom. 'Utgoff,' he said, as he sat down beside me, 'in those good old days in Monte Carlo, those dear old days! I saw beautiful women win strong men with just a smile. But you are not a woman—and you are not beautiful, and yet, so, with a joke, you win back the control over six hundred men!'

"Old Kovanko shook his grey head. 'I shall go out now and throw my useless *Regulations* into the sea! In Sebastopol I shall buy a joke book. It is the New Era. A command that I thought irretrievably lost . . . you regain with a laugh!

" 'But, believe me, Utgoff—when someone tells me that joke again, which will be about the two-thousandth time I've heard it —I shall not be able to laugh!' "

Chapter 35

OFFICERS' HOSPITAL

ABOUT the time these things were happening to Utgoff and my friends, I was having a bad time of it myself. The wounds that I had received in 1915 in Moscow broke open again, and I was taken to a little log hospital on the William Island, where I was operated upon by Dumbroffsky, the Tsar's doctor.

It was a sad spot, full of badly wounded officers, with two soldiers' wards, which were full of the most wretched-looking cripples.

"There is no use talking about the glories of dying for one's country to them," said an Interne, speaking of the peasant soldiers. "They've seen through war. Do you know that some of these fellows are getting letters from their villages, saying that if they have lost an arm or a leg they had better not come home —they would only be a burden to everybody."

One of the officers was a horrible case. He had been speared by a German Uhlan; the lance had entered at the knee and come out of his hip. He had got necrosis of the bone from bad care at the front. He had to be dressed every morning. And, as the dressing consisted of scraping some twelve inches of exposed rotting bone, he screamed the house down. In England or France he was one of those cases to whom they would give a whiff of gas or ether before they dressed him. But there was not enough to spare in this half-starved hospital. I can still hear that officer's screams. We all had on paper bandages ourselves, and they used to clot.

I lay there for a long time during that summer. Most of the time I was convalescing, I lay out under the birch trees. The fellow with the necrosed bone eventually died, but he used to ask me every morning, as we were taking our sun-bath: "How do I look today?—better, don't you think?"

And I would have to go through the pretence of looking at

him closely, and then say that he did look better than he had yesterday.

One night some Bolsheviki got a machine gun up on the roof of the Stock Exchange and sprayed the Winter Palace. Then they shot up a mass meeting of women on a lower Neva bridge. Then they sent a few shots into our hospital. They did not kill anybody except a Chinaman, but the officers thought that this was to be a fight for it, and I heard them asking to be given back their swords and revolvers. Except for groans, their wards were usually pretty silent; but now I heard them laughing and shouting to each other from their beds.

The poor Chinaman was a coolie, one of the Chinese labour corps imported before the Revolution. But his suit of blue coolie cloth showed that he would never go back to China again. He had stopped too many machine-gun bullets. Dumbroffsky was very sympathetic about him.

"Poor fellow," said the old surgeon as he was doing my dressings. "He was so far from home!"

I was beginning to feel the same way. Most of my friends got out to see me at one time or another; and the one person I wanted most to see came every day. She rode all the way down from up the Neva in one of their carriages, or else she clung on outside a packed tram like any peasant girl. She was splendid about that. But she was too young to stand up against outside influences; and I could see that the Revolution had changed everything as far as we were concerned.

Suddenly I began to hate Russia.

Chapter 36

VOLUNTEER FOR FRANCE

When America entered the war, I did what most Americans did who happened to be abroad: I went to the Embassy and handed in my name.

"You stick around here," said old Bailey, that charming Southerner. "There'll be plenty of doings for us Americans in Russia —yet!"

I was half-offered a post in the American Secret Service, out in Siberia around Vladivostok, which I wish I had taken; and I was offered a post up at Archangel which I am glad I did not take; and then I resolved that as soon as I got well enough I would see the real thing.

I would join some flying corps, and I really didn't give a damn which.

I went out to Finland to recuperate and lay there by the sea, where the pine trees and the hills and the whole Gulf seemed asleep in the sunny haze. Out there I made one more attempt to prevent being parted from the only person I really cared about. But it was no use. One night, in a rage, I threw my stick into the Gulf, having the immediate humiliation of having to climb down the sea wall and retrieve it again; and the next day I went to Sweden.

Torsten, "The Hammer of God," met me there.

I explained to him the way things were in Russia, the whole thing was coming to pieces; and we had better get out with what we could save as quickly as we could.

This was at luncheon, and after lunch I left Torsten and looked up an address in the telephone book. When I got there I crossed a courtyard and pressed a bell.

The servant ushered me into a room.

"*Captain Thomas?*" I asked of the man in it. "*Le Capitaine Thomas?—est il ici?*"

"*Mais, mon Dieu! M'sieu!—Ceci, c'est la Legation Autri-chienne.*"

"My God!" I said in English.

"What do you want?" he asked, also in English.

I laughed.

"I've come to volunteer for the French army," I said.

"No! Oh, no!—it isn't possible!" He took my hand. "What a marvellous joke!"

We both roared with laughter, and he called some of his colleagues into the room and told them about it. They gave me a cigarette and asked me if I would not sit down and have a liqueur. They had been at their luncheon table themselves.

"Why don't you join *us?*" they said. "We're not such bad chaps!"

"No," I laughed. "You certainly aren't—but where *is* that French Legation?"

"Regrettable!" they said. "Very regrettable—you are certainly missing a lot by not fighting this war with us. However—*voilà!*"

They opened their door, bowed and waved their hands to the diagonal corner of the courtyard where I saw a shield bearing the Tricolour of France.

"Best of luck to you!" they said.

Captain Thomas, the French Military Attaché, gave me a cigarette and some papers to fill out.

"*Bonne chance!*" he smiled as I signed my name. "Lucky dog —you will soon be in Paris!

"But why . . . ?" he said, opening his cigarette-case.

"Oh, for a variety of reasons," I said.

The next night I was on the train back to Petrograd, and around my stomach was strapped a new grey suède money-belt; and it itched and was heavy because there were a hundred gold sovereigns in it.

"The Germans," said "The Hammer of God" confidently, "will probably take Petrograd or cut the line through Finland before you get back. Gold will be the only thing that will be of any use then. You can use it to get out Archangel way."

He, a level-headed Swede, was losing a fortune in Russia himself; but you could never tell it from his smile.

"All the best!" waved "The Hammer of God" as the Happaranda express headed toward the Arctic Circle again.

I was, I thought, entering Russia for the last time.

Chapter 37

JOHN REED IN TROUBLE

JOHN REED had come back to Russia.

He was out at Smolny every day. He had been refused a visa in the United States, and I think the Americans had tried to prevent him from getting away from New York—we were all for keeping down "these damn Radicals" now that we were in the glorious war—and I ran into him in Petrograd under rather dramatic circumstances on the first day of my return.

I was going into the Hôtel de l'Europe to get a cheque from a man who owed me some money when I bumped into a burly figure in a trench coat by its door. It was John, with Louise Bryant; and he had just had his pockets picked.

We did not know it at the time, and I did not find it out until long after the war, not, I think, until after John had died of typhus in Moscow. Perhaps he never knew it. But John Reed's pockets were picked by the Russian Secret Service Police in connivance with the American Embassy in Petrograd.

An account of this appears in Laurence Houghteling's book. Houghteling was attached to the American Embassy at that time; and, after I had read the story in his book, I gave him the other half of it in Chicago, in 1924. MacGruder, Chargé d'Affaires in Stockholm, also told me about Reed and the way he (Mac-Gruder) had managed to have Reed taken out of the coal-bunkers of the Finnish ship off Abo, when John was trying to get back to America from Russia to carry on propaganda for the Soviets in the United States. MacGruder and I had luncheon and a heated argument about it at the Legation in Sweden in 1927. I told MacGruder how the old New York *Sun* had asked me to do a page on John Reed after his Abo arrest, how I did it, and how I got it sent back—with a telephone call from the Sunday editor:

"Sorry, old boy. Agree with every word you've said. Know

Jack myself. Great chap. But—my God, we couldn't print stuff like that!"

The editor then said he had sent my story on to somebody else. When I asked who, he said, of all papers! one of the editors of Hearst's New York *American*. And from him I got the same reply:

"Sorry. Personally I agree with you—professionally I've got to say I think you're cock-eyed! Say, I'd like to see old John over there! How is the old scout?"

I told him of my last night in Petrograd with John Reed.

I must have been pretty stupid, but I did not realise at first how John Reed was being dogged this way by the American Government. I knew the trouble he had been having in the States, ever since he had tried to blow up the Russian "steam-roller" myth in 1915. But I did not realise how long was the arm of a very peevish Uncle Sam. I was a little hurt, for instance, by the way both the American Consulate and the American Embassy in Petrograd treated me when I appeared with a smiling, curly-headed John Reed in tow. John had not been particularly anxious to go to either of these places at first; but I persuaded him, I found erroneously, that I had such good friends there that they would help him out of this hole he was in after getting his pockets picked.

"Sorry," said Bailey at the Embassy. "The Embassy can't do anything. Why don't you go to the Russian police, Mr. Reed?"

Bailey's manner of asking that should have been enough to warn me that something was up. But I was hurt with him for the cavalier way I thought he was treating my friend. Then at the Consulate:

"Sorry—the Consulate cannot do anything. Why don't you go to the Russian police, Mr. Reed?"

The contents of John's pockets, including his wallet with his letter of credit, had all been very expertly "lifted off" him as he strolled down the Nevsky. So I gave him the cheque I had just collected from the man in the Hôtel de l'Europe. It was for two thousand roubles.

"That," I said, "ought to hold you for a time."

The next morning John came into my room before I was up and handed me back my cheque.

"Most amazing thing!" he said. "I went into the Consulate this morning, just on the half-chance—and the very first thing they did was hand me back my wallet! The letter of credit was there, and all that was missing was a few hundred roubles in cash! Now, how the devil . . . ?"

John could not understand how the thief would know enough to return his wallet to the Consulate, or why, after being cynical enough to pick it out of John's pocket, he should be tender enough about John's circumstances to return it to the Consulate. Neither could I. It seemed an *Alice in Wonderland* sort of pick-pocketing to me.

And so it was. His pocket had been picked by the U. S. Government and the Russian Secret Police in conjunction, to get copies of letters John had to some prominent Bolshies in Russia. When the Secret Police photostated them and pocketed the ready roubles inside, as is the way of secret police the world around, the wallet was returned to John, and—the people to whom he had letters were watched.

It is small wonder that when I got out on the Finlandski Station that midnight in Petrograd, thinking with what different thoughts I had landed there one snowy midnight three years before, and found no one to greet me, that I was terribly disappointed. For had I not wired Bailey at the Embassy:

"WILL EITHER YOU OR JOHN REED KINDLY TRY ENGAGE ROOM ME HOTEL ANGLETERRE ARRIVING FRIDAY NIGHT."

Nobody there. People being welcomed, hugged, and kissed. Nobody but half-starved porters and *isvostchiks* fighting to welcome me. In mournful meditation I drove down the wide old streets again.

"No," said the *concièrge* at the Angleterre, "there is no message for you. No, sir, there has been no telephone. No, sir—I am positive."

The first thing I did next morning was drive to the Embassy. Yes, smiled Bailey; he had received my wire. Then the "Old Judge," as they used to call him, oldest man from point of service in the American Diplomatic Corps, leaned back in his chair.

"Farson," he said in his charming Kentucky drawl, "the very next time that you link my name with John Reed—IN A CABLE TO THE AMERICAN EMBASSY, MY GOD!—the very next time you do that—you are going to be what they call *persona non grata* with Mr. Bailey. Boy!—where *have* you been all these years!"

Bailey then said, what he had been trying to tell me for months, that John Reed was just about as popular as a rattlesnake with the Department at Washington. He had, he insisted, been trying to make me stop going about with Reed for a long, long time.

"But you're one of those mule-headed fellows. Now you know. I'm downright sorry about your hotel. What you doing for lunch?"

"I think I'll call up John Reed," I smiled.

But it was an American Negro who provided one of the only things I felt I could heartily laugh at during the whole Revolution. Bailey also had a grievance with me about him!

Gordon—Willie Gordon, he called himself—"Champion Heavyweight of Roumania!"

He had opened the door of the Embassy for me that first snowy morning when I had returned from the United States.

"Jes-sus Christ!" he said. "Ain't it cold!"

From that he progressed to asking me to feel his arm. It was like a bull's thigh. He was about as broad as he was high, with a grin to match.

"Yes-suh! Ah sure used to knock 'em about down in li'l old Bucharest! 'Fore the Germans almost got me. Ah was going strong in that town!"

One day when he opened the door he was resplendent in a blue uniform with silver buttons, the regulation Service uniform for its liveried staff.

"I'se been promoted," he said. "Ah's a sec'tary now. Ah's done been made Secretary of the Door!"

Two doors down the Fourstadtskyia Oulitsa on which stood

the Embassy, was the Palace of Prince Levin, one-eyed patriot who had fought as a private in the Russian Army, and whose one delight in life was a Spalding Bros. punching-bag. I introduced Gordon, "Champion Heavyweight of Roumania," to Prince Levin.

In a week Gordon was all the rage with the young Russian bloods. He was giving lessons all over the place. In them, his diplomatic career stood him in good stead.

"Prince, dat's a mean li'l hook you got! Ah felt dat one! You got me right under de heart!"

Or:

"*Doucement*, Prince—'member dis yere nigger's got a livin' to make. Jes you pull yo punches a bit!"

Levin met me in the street one day and proudly showed me a split lip. "Gordon," he said. The Negro's success was phenomenal. Sporting young Russians used to bring their muscular young friends up to Levin's just to see Gordon give them a black eye.

But this morning I found that if my heart was low Gordon's was gone. The great smile was bent downward. My coat was taken away by a drooping figure which dragged its feet as if they were weighted with death. I heard a deep groan.

"Why, Gordon!—what's wrong?"

"Nuffin'!"

"Are you sick?"

"No, suh. Ah ain't—sick."

"Well, then—what's the matter? What's troubling you?"

"Oh—Ah'm in *bad!* . . . awful bad! You—you ask Mister Bailey."

So I asked Bailey now.

The gentleman from Kentucky picked up a card that lay before him on his desk, smiled at it, and slid it across to me. It was about the size of a postcard. On it was the photograph of a huge, naked Negro, arms folded, biceps bulging like black knobs of ebony—and the glowering, fighting face of:

WILLIE GORDON—CHAMPION LIGHT-HEAVYWEIGHT OF EUROPE

BOXING LESSONS

Address: THE AMERICAN EMBASSY, 14 Fourtstadtskyia Oulitsa.

"The Ambassador," said Bailey, "is just about wild over this!"

Bailey grinned at me. "You, and your John Reed, and your one-eyed Russian princes—and Willie Gordon. Boy!—your name is getting well known around this place!"

I told him that perhaps it would be better if after all I did lunch with John Reed. I then told him what my real plans were.

"Let me know," he said, "before you go. We'll make you a Messenger and let you carry the bags. That will give you a diplomatic pass to get you across the frontier."

And, sentimental oaf that I was, I took that pass.

Chapter 38

RUSSIAN WIND-UP

I say I was sentimental to take that diplomatic pass from the American Embassy, because it tied my hands from doing what I wanted to do. Now I could not smuggle anything out of crumbling Russia. Which, after all, was the one thing I had come back there from Sweden to do.

The point is that the diplomatic pass of a State Department messenger means that your baggage is never gone through at the frontiers. It and your person are supposed to be immune from search, and it was a particular point of honour in those days, before the U. S. Government took to using U. S. Marines as messengers, that those of us who were given such passes would not abuse them. Therefore, for the next couple of days, I regretted that I had said I would take it; but after two days I saw that it did not make any difference.

My first scheme for getting our money out of Russia was to buy jewellery; diamonds or any precious stones, any form of small objects which, in capsule form, would contain about 154,000 roubles. But I was not the only person who had that brilliant idea.

When I went in to price things at Faberge's on the Moskayia, I found that if the rouble was dropping, the prices were shooting up at treble the pace. Any price would have been worth paying as it turned out. But I did not see that far into the future then—although John Reed was begging me to. But it was little Pinkus Solomonivitch Citrine who put me on to the other scheme.

Waiting for me, like a "frozen" badger behind the potted aspidistras of the Hotel Angleterre, he dusted an incredibly soft powder in my hand. Then he told me to rub it. I did, and it seemed to vanish. "Well?" I said.

"Lycopodium!" said Pinkus Solomonivitch.

If he had bought an unripe persimmon and a dead cat in the Caucasus I knew that Pinkus would already have someone in mind who had need of such things, so I listened to him. He waved his arms, walked up and down, made gestures to indicate barrels, and how they would have to be painted with tar to keep the lycopodium from seeping through seams that even beer couldn't penetrate. He talked about the use of lycopodium in hospitals—how the Swedes were buying things for the Germans. Then he outlined a pilgrimage of his through the Russian marsh-lands where this moss grew.

I wired Sweden, and Torsten replied:

"ANY AMOUNT BUY ALL YOU CAN NO LIMIT DEMAND ALREADY ASSURED SUBSTANTIAL PROFITS."

And that's how Pinkus Solomonivitch Citrine and I "cornered" the Russian lycopodium market!

I took Pinkus Solomonivitch over to the American bank to which I had transferred my account. I shall never forget Stevens' face when he saw that grotesque, Chaplinesque figure trotting after me into that gilded former private ball-room on the Neva. Nor Stevens' face when I told him I was leaving Russia, and said:

"I trust this man absolutely. I leave the whole account for him to draw against. Pay out against his bills of lading until the whole 154,000 roubles are gone. Now how much Foreign Exchange am I allowed legally to take out of Russia for my own personal use?"

"Five hundred roubles," said Stevens.

I took that in Swedish kroner, because I had given some of my golden sovereigns to V.'s father, to help him and his family get out of Russia when the storm broke. And John Reed, as he promised he would, eventually got them safely across the frontier with Bolshevik visas. That was a matter which, after all, did not mean very much to me now, but it was perhaps why I was so infinitely touched by little Charlie Chaplin Pinkus Solomonivitch, who clasped my hand as we were driving away from the bank.

"What a pity!" he said. "Why do you go, Mr. Farson? You and I could do such things together."

He was weeping at the Finlandski railway station two morn-ings after; his soft doe-like brown eyes were the only ones that had come to see me off. I told him I would never forget him, and I never have.

After leaving the bank I picked up John Reed.

"The day after tomorrow," I said, "I leave Russia. Come out. I'm going to have an absolute blind tonight. We'll go out to the Islands and hear the gypsies sing."

I tied up or cut other knots during those last few days. I went to see Shura Alexandra Georgievna Tomachova. She, after all these years, was again in Petrograd and had been asking about town if anyone knew where *Gaspodin* Farson was. Jack Hoth was away. But finally she did find someone who told her and she immediately hired the most ornate *isvostchik* she could find and drove out to the Englishman's private home. They happened that week-end to be in from Finland, and they told her I was in Sweden. She insisted on leaving her address—in case I ever came back.

And they had sent it to me. . . .

There was no mistaking her now. She was, unfortunately, just as they had described her. And she had again fallen for a scarlet, Gainsborough hat. I must have winced when I saw her in that cheap hotel bedroom. So different from the Shura I had laughed and wept with at Archangel.

"Aren't you going to kiss me?" she said.

I told her I did not feel like kissing anybody. But she saw deeper than that.

"So . . . ?" she said.

"You shouldn't have gone out to those English people," I said.

She jumped up. For a second she was the young Cossack again. Her face flamed with colour:

"*Ranche*," she said, "*Vuie builie gentleman—Sechas nyett*." (Before, she said, you were a gentleman—now you're not!)

"Perhaps," I said.

"Very well then," she said. "I am being kept by a Russian. He's fat and old and ugly. I sleep with him every night. I have been sick. I wouldn't let you kiss me if you wanted to. Goodbye."

The last night I spent with John Reed. I put him and Louise Bryant in a *droshky* and stood on the pier as the barge towed it across the dark Neva.

"Good-bye," John waved back, and called—"Good luck to you."

That night he had tried until the last minute to persuade me to remain with him and see the real Revolution in Petrograd. I remembered this and I cupped my hands.

"Good-bye, John," I called, "you'll need good luck more than I will, I think!"

Those were the last words I said to him, and I could not see him even then. They were prophetic words.

When I came back to Moscow in 1928 the first place I made for was John Reed's grave under the walls of the Red Kremlin. It was just a rough slab of black granite beside Lenin's tomb. I stood there for about an hour and just stared at it.

Chapter 39

ROYAL FLYING CORPS

In London I went to our Embassy where I found a letter from Jo-Jo waiting for me. It was dated 1914. I had written him from Manchester, saying that if he still felt that way I would take a year off with him and go any place on earth. "I make only one stipulation," I wrote. "If we haven't made good at the end of that year; and by that I mean, if we haven't got hold of some life that leads somewhere—then I'm going back to work. Say the word. . . ."

Jo-Jo's answer was to invite me to join the French ambulance corps. He had already signed up with it by the time he received my letter. His invitation was now three years old.

Then I went around the Hotel Goring and volunteered for the American Air Force.

It was Colonel Colvin, the American Military Attaché in Stockholm, who had talked me into that. On my way down from Russia, with French papers in my pocket, Colvin had pointed out, "If you're going to fly, the chances are you will be smashed up. And the way you are now isn't too good a shape anyway. What you need is a good hospital always handy. And about the last place *I* ever want to be in again is a French hospital. Join the Americans, my lad—our hospitals are swell!"

In the Goring, spurs clinking, I found an American army captain. He did not have wings up, but he knew enough about flying to know that I did not know anything.

"Flown?" he said.

"Certainly."

"Ever land a ship?"

"Er . . . yes."

"Solo?"

"Er . . . no."

"Then you don't know a damned thing about flying. Landing is the only thing that counts. Any damn fool can fly as long as he stays up in the air. It's the ground that kills people—and don't you forget that!"

I wouldn't have minded that so much, if he had not followed it up with:

"You go back to New York."

He gave that like an order—as if he was already over me.

"Maybe I won't," I said. "Will you pay my passage back?"

My money was just about running out now. I had not been able to take enough out of Russia, and what I had taken in Sweden had got me just about as far as I was.

"Why should we?" he asked arrogantly. "Couple of fellows came in here all the way from South Africa the other day and they paid their own passages first class back to New York."

"Well," I said. "If my government wants me to go back and be a good little American and fight for it—it can damn well *send* me back first class. I'm not going to pay out any more hard-earned cash to get killed. I've come all the way out of Russia as it is."

"Where's your patriotism?"

"I don't know—I must have left it somewhere."

"You're a hell of an American!"

"And it's a hell of a government that won't pay my passage back home—the British would."

"The British!"

"Yes—the British!"

"The hell you say!"

"Yes—the British—and, what's more, I'm going to join the British army right now."

"The hell you will!"

"The hell I won't!"

After this sparkling dialogue I left him and took the train up to Manchester, where were the only Englishmen in England I knew. I was shocked when I reached the works to be told of the number of people I knew who had been killed.

"Brothers," I said. "I want to join the British Royal Flying Corps."

He had not changed a hair, although he had lost many of them in these last three years. Brilliant, facetious, Brothers was as dangerous as ever to be serious with.

"Another blow!" he muttered. "Just when I thought we British might win the war! Why do you Americans come over here and spoil things? Now Fritz will never give in."

But that night he took me down to the Midland Hotel where I found another Englishman I had known in 1914, now a captain in the R.F.C., and he gave me a letter, and I took the next train back to London, went to Bolo House, swore I was a Canadian—born in Montreal, father born in Calgary (how he swore when he heard that!)—and a few weeks later I walked into the Goring Hotel and saluted.

"Yes, sir?" said an officer, with spurs on, behind his desk, very politely this time; "what can I do for you?"

"Nothing," I said.

He looked up with a start, and then he recognised me. He laughed.

"Well, I'm damned!"

"That's all," I said. "Cheerio, Captain Fitzgibbon."

Then I walked past the gates of Buckingham Palace three times, just to see the sentries salute me. I felt transcendent in my new uniform. I had fifty quid from Bolo House in my pocket. Major Conran had given me the address of his tailor and told me to charge everything.

"You stick to that fifty pounds!" he said. "Blow it all in London on a good time."

It was ten years before I paid that tailor's bill. And when I did I found that it was the mistake of my life. I still use him, and, I hope, always will, but he has never had the same respect for me since; nothing like the interest he felt in my welfare when I owed him £110.

There had been a little contretemps at first. Because I had had a commission in the 2nd Regiment of Philadelphia the U. S. National Guard, which I could prove by my card to the Rifle Range—marked with the coveted "sharpshooter" grade—the people in Bolo House said I would not have to be a cadet. They were legally able to give me a commission forthwith. They knew I was not a Canadian, just as well as I did, and the whole thing amused them.

"You're a Canadian, aren't you?" said old Colonel Cameron.

"Er . . ." I looked him in the eye.

"Canadian! Aren't you?" he barked.

"Y-yes, sir!"

"Well, sign there!"

"You go down to Farnborough," said another officer. "We will send your Commission along."

Then they lost my Commission. . . .

At Aldershot I took a taxi all the way out to Blackdown Heath; and when I had got there, and tipped him, I found that I had exactly fourpence left in this wide, wide world. I entered the gates.

" 'Ere—you!" An N.C.O. slung a palliasse at me, an assortment of khaki, and directed me to the tailor's hut. Other N.C.O.s chased me about camp until when at last night fell I was lying down in a cold hut with a split-tail flying tunic by my side, a pair of heavy "K" boots, and a bed made of three boards that nipped chunks out of my behind even through the straw of that wretched palliasse.

Next to me was an Eton boy—I knew what that blue-striped black tie meant by then—and, it seemed to me, he was young enough to have just run away from Eton. He had not even got his uniform or palliasse yet. And for a pillow he was trying to use his bowler hat.

"Don't do that!" I said. "The way to do it is to take all your old shirts, stuff 'em in a clean one, and tie the arms of it around it like this." I showed him mine.

"Oh, I say!" he said, almost blushing. "You *are* kind!"

I would have given a lot to have been able to see into our two dramatically different minds that night. Mine was full of great, gold, onion-shaped church domes, piles of colour against a blue sky. . . . It was cold as the devil in that hut.

"F-o-o-orm Fours! As-you-were!"

The next day a Bateman Guards sergeant-major chased us about like barnyard chickens through the mud. . . . There was a battalion of the 5th Londons beside us—a "penal" battalion I was told. And I must say they looked like it; their defaulter's parade in the mornings seemed to include their entire strength. Ours was not much behind it, and when I looked at some of those haggard, white faces of "masquerading officers" that the M.P.s had picked up in the early hours in the Strand I began to see why shop-keepers were chary about taking a Flying Corps cheque.

One day, one of us laughed when the sergeant-major slipped into the mud.

"Y-a-a-a-a!" he came at us. "I've sent twenty . . . five . . . thousand . . . men . . . to . . . France . . . and if any of —— ——! F'm fours! As-you-were! F'm fours! As-you-were! F'm fours! *As*-you-were!" etc., etc., etc. . . .

He was monstrous! Terrifying! He made the blood drip out of our veins. . . .

I borrowed two quid from him the next day.

"Whatcher want it for?"

I told him I wanted to go up to London and see about my Commission; they must have lost it somewhere. There had been a boxing match the previous night, when the Flying Corps boxed the Army. I had not wanted to box because of my condition. We had no heavyweight; but at the last minute I felt excited and a Flight Sergeant Sugarbread and I put on a six-round bout. I got a draw with him. On the strength of this our Adjutant had given me a pass up to London, and a little chit about the bout to use where it might do me the most good in Bolo House. As our terrifying sergeant-major was the Mother Superior of our boxing team I felt that I could work him for a loan.

"You come back 'ere, mind yer!" he said. "If you don't you bloody well send them two quid!"

While I was up in London an epidemic of measles hit Blackdown Heath. Bolo House told me it had been quarantined and sent me off to a Cadet Corps at Hastings. I had borrowed another £5 in London, and the first thing I did was to give one of these to the sergeant-major at Hastings. I wanted a good billet, I said. The first thing he did the next day was tell me to take a detachment over to a "buzzing" class.

They were, most of them, ex-Princess Pat's who had been fighting in the trenches since 1915 and had been transferred to the Flying Corps as a form of rest cure. They eyed my whipcord breeches with particular disfavour. They also stood there, waiting for my commands. And I did not know one English command—except "Form fours" and "As-you-were!" So I stepped into the middle of their group and said to the biggest of them: "Go on, you take over."

"Don't ever do that again!" I said to the sergeant-major that night. "Just leave me alone!"

"Right you are, sir. You just watch the others and you'll soon twig how it's done."

But I had an awful time with those Canadians. The fellow I shared a basement with was from Montreal; and when I told him I was born there he was always wanting to talk about old times. I had, I told him, left Montreal as a small child. I did not remember anything about it all now, although I was always hoping that one day I would go back.

(I did, eventually, to be operated upon in the Royal Victoria Hospital in Montreal, 1921; and the man who cut me up and excavated the hole that the Clerget motor had made in my shin bone, was Doctor Keenan of—Princess Pat's!)

Then one day, when we were holding a sweepstake to see who could be quickest in picking a Vickers' lock, an Ack Emma appeared at the door of the machine-gun class.

"Is Mr. Farson in here?" he asked.

"*Mister* Farson!"—the lock-spring shot out of my hands. "Did I hear someone say *Mister* Farson?"

The N.C.O. Instructor grinned and handed me a slip of paper. It was as casual as toilet paper, but on it was written that if I presented myself at the Hotel Cecil, Strand, London, I would receive my Commission and £50.

I looked at the N.C.O. He nodded. Then I stuck on my little forage cap and blew him a kiss.

"Good-bye, Sergeant!" I said.

And, after several lobster salads at Scott's while I was waiting for my uniforms to be finished, I appeared at the Wantage Officers' School with five pounds left.

Chapter 40

DESPONDENCY IN EGYPT

A few months later Jack and I sailed for Egypt. We had both been put on scouts, little single-seated fighters, which pleased our vanity enormously. To fly scouts was the ideal of every young pilot in those air-salad days; and as we were both around six feet high, and built accordingly, it pleased us that they had found us delicate enough with our hands to handle these sensitive little machines. As a matter of fact, the arrangement of the little Camel did make it too small for my legs, and I flew S.E.5's.

Jack, I might say, was no lady. He had come over from Canada with the "Little Black Devils"; and a German, by sticking a bayonet through his foot, had persuaded Jack that the air was the best place to be when a world war was on. He was an American, of the "Black" Irish blend, who alternated between bursts of the most unregenerate gaiety and prolonged moods of the most abysmal gloom. He was typical of thousands of young officers. He felt utterly impersonal about the war. He neither knew nor cared who had started it, or what it was all about; he was only afraid that someone would stop it, and then he would lose that gift from God—Cox's Bank Account.

Being in it, he quite expected to get killed before it was over and that gave him complete absolution from whatever he did when he was on leave.

The war, he said often, would be the only real vacation he would ever have in his life. The army should worry, what happened to him! Back home, to which the prospect of eventually returning so depressed him at times, he had sold magazine subscriptions for a publishing company.

He was a veteran campaigner by the time I met him. Our course through the British army was followed from squadron to squadron by a despairing note from a little tailor in Rouen, asking why Lieutenant Jack would not please pay that small bill for the tunic he had made in 1915.

"Sure I'll pay that tailor!" blustered Jack, when Adjutant after Adjutant laid the accusing bill before him. "What do you think I am—a crook!"

Faced with such a brazen invitation to be candid very few adjutants could collect themselves quickly enough to take advantage of it; but one weary soul in Cairo seemed to have been waiting for Jack and told him in so many words he was a swindler.

"It is people like you," he said coldly, "who are ruining the reputation of the British officer in Egypt. Before the war, when an officer wanted anything in this country, all he had to do was walk into a shop and sign a chit for it, giving his name and his regiment's. Now they won't even take our cheques! It will take us years to live down what you people have done to Egypt!"

More than a grain of truth in that, too. For the breed ran low during the war, and the Egyptians saw a type of "officer and gentleman" that for ever destroyed their *sahib* complex. It was much the same with the Indian troops when they came to France, and most regular Indian Army officers bitterly regretted taking them there.

But in his heart Jack was mortally shocked by the way the Adjutant had talked to him. He covered it up, as was his way, by sneering about it.

"Maybe I will pay that tailor," he growled to me, as he was teasing his wretched pet monkey afterwards, "if I get through. If I don't—well, that's just too damn bad for that little tailor in Rouen—ain't it, Sultan Fuad? I should worry!"

Our last night in London saw us separated. When we met again at Victoria Station at six o'clock the next morning, there was no one—not one single person to see either of us off.

"Any money?" asked Jack.

"A bit."

"Well, let's drown it. I've got a mouth like the bottom of a birdcage!"

I had had the most amazing experience. Sitting in the Savoy, having tea with a Russian girl, I saw a little Flying Corps officer with a face like a gladiator.

"If this wasn't London," I said to my Russian friend; "and if that officer wasn't in the uniform of a British officer—I would say that that fellow sitting there is one of my best friends. I spent three years in college with him."

"Well, that's strange," she said. "He's been looking at our table ever since he came in! I thought it was *me!*"

I got up, and as I ascended the red-carpeted steps I got a blow between the shoulder blades that nearly floored me. It was Brint Hill, the third member of our Triumvirate.

"Well—of all the people in the world, Neg Farson! What are *you* doing in that uniform?"

"What are you?"

"Oh, the Americans couldn't make me dizzy with their damn fool medical tests—they put you in a basket and spin you, you know, so I went up to Canada and sold my soul to the British. I'm flying Bristol Fighters, and I'm off to France the day after tomorrow!"

We spent the night together, talking about Jo-Jo, the other member of our Triumvirate—neither of us knew where he was— and we ended it up in a large double bed in the Savoy Hotel, with a bottle of Johnny Walker for which we had given the night porter one pound.

When I forced myself into my uniform about five o'clock, I saw the wings of Brint's tunic over the adjacent chair. I had to laugh, when I thought of the days he and I used to cruise down the Chesapeake Bay together! This was funny, this scene. He told me to go to hell when I woke him up to say good-bye.

One of the first newspapers I read in Egypt was the *Egyptian Gazette*. I read: "Killed in Action—France—Robert Brinton Hill, R.F.C."

He must have got it on one of his first trips over the line. Some time later I got a letter from my father:

"I know it will interest you," he wrote, "to know that Jo was killed at Château-Thierry. He was killed as a Captain in the

American Army. His father told me Jo was mentioned in dispatches twice before he died and had been cited for another decoration. One of the men of his company wrote Jo's mother, saying he was walking beside Jo when it happened. Jo, he says, never knew what hit him. It must have been a direct hit with a heavy shell. He was walking beside Jo one minute—and the next minute he was gone. . . . Just disappeared off the face of the earth. . . ."

So that was the end of our Triumvirate, I was in a hospital myself, pretty well smashed up by a crash, when I got my father's letter about Jo-Jo. Years later I anchored one night, quite by accident, alongside his old yawl down the Chesapeake. The *Anna* had fallen into unholy hands. She was rotting in the sun, the canvas covering of her cabin was cracked and blistered like sunbaked mud after a heavy rain. No one loved her any more.

Before we reached Egypt Jack had already made a small reputation for himself.

We rode down through France on the top of our passenger train, and although we ruined our uniforms we saw an amazing amount of fair France. Why we weren't killed on the top of that train, hurtling through tunnels, I shall never know, except that God must have been industriously watching over us, for we were usually sitting up there on top with a bottle of red wine for each of us.

Even Jack was moved by the beauty of Provence. When we first saw Arles, its yellow, dusty, dozing streets under the sycamores were full of grinning African *spahis*, and every bloomered warrior of the sands had a nice, fat white French girl under each arm.

"The French must be a mixed race!" said Jack.

We saw Marseilles at its very best as a colourful sink of iniquity. Cox's were a bit obtuse in Marseilles (they hadn't got on to the curves of the Temporary Gentleman yet), and they allowed every officer to draw £5 a day as long as he was in a Transition camp. As a result we saw a glittering riot of life as it is lived over by the harbour where the Mediterranean shipping ties up alongside the sidewalks, and we were broke in Egypt for months afterwards.

We saw Marie's, the most famous brothel in the world, with its staggeringly obscene movie. In those days the star film was a French comedian, *à la* Charlie Chaplin, seducing a dairymaid in the barnyard. When I saw it again in 1930, on my way back from India, the style had changed. It was now strictly Lesbian and homosexual.

Jack and I both admitted that anything more calculated to take all the enthusiasm out of a man, than watching that movie in cold blood, could hardly have been devised.

In Marseilles I also saw Gaby Deslys dance with Harry Pilcer and I ate *bouillabaisse* twice a day before the transport hauled me away from it.

To eat *bouillabaisse* in Marseilles was one of the things I had marked down to do in my life—just like eating caviare at Astrakhan—and praise be to God I have done both of them, lots of times.

We went out on the old *Kaisr-I-Hind*, at that time one of the P. & O. Company's crack boats. We were missed by a submarine just outside Malta, the torpedo passing just under our stern and just ahead of another transport—I think it was the *Malwa's* bows—with the result that the convoy began to zigzag like a drunken sailor, and the destroyers raced about the horizon blowing it up with depth-charges. Nothing was hurt, except our feelings, for we lay in Malta for two days, as gossip said you could walk from Malta to Alex. on the top of German periscopes.

Lying dolefully in Valetta Harbour, gazing longingly at that little buff-coloured town where we were told by returning majors and colonels there were ices galore and fresh-looking English girls, we got up a boxing match.

The chief bout on the card was to have been a match to the death between two professional pugs we found among the enlisted men. But, being professionals, they got together and decided to split the purse. It was the only thing they did split. And for the honour of the officers, who had started this show, the Irish major who was managing it insisted that there should now be a strictly "Officers' Card."

It was pretty rough, because we felt that we must put some spirit into it before the caustic Tommies. But the *pièce de résist- ance* was the performance that Lieutenant Jack, Royal Flying Corps, provided.

Jack and a fellow named Bellamy, first man to fly up the Khyber Pass, were to box a captain and the adjutant of the Leicesters. It was to be a blindfold show. All four men were to have their eyes bandaged and be in the ring at the same time. This held out infinite possibilities, and before going into the ring Jack asked the captain of the Leicesters if that animal on his tunic lapel was really a pussycat, and Bellamy, as his gloves were being tied, informed the Leicester captain that he need not worry as no one could hurt anybody with such pillows on his fists. Add to this that Jack was an obvious American and that Bellamy was an obvious Canadian, and that the two Leicester men were both out-and-out English Charterhouse boys—and you see the ingredients of something that everybody was lusting to get started—particularly the Charterhouse boys.

There was blood in it!

Jack and Bellamy had arranged a secret signal, so that in that blind carnage they could call and come to each other's aid. The signal was "Here, Jake!"

For a minute after the tap of the gong it was a grand free-for-all, with wild swings and misses, and everyone hitting everyone else—including himself. Then the Charterhouse captain seemed to sense that it was Jack's hairy chest he was leaning up against (the Japs say they can smell an Englishman, so why shouldn't an Englishman be able to smell an American?) and he pushed Jack deliberately away and then sent in a bitter punch that almost went through Jack's stomach.

"Here, Jake! Here, Jake!" called Jack, faintly.

We watched with an awful fascination as we saw the brave Bellamy feeling his way blindly towards his partner. The heavy P. & O. boat had a slight, slow roll in that gentian sea. These fellows were all big men, mind you; and when they hit they hurt. Then the captain of the Leicesters seemed to smell Jack—and he hit him again. It was a horrible wallop. Jack steadied himself on his wiry, muscular legs and drew back; then he lammed back a punch that would have knocked out that Leicester captain if it had touched him even a glancing blow. It did not, however, for it landed flush on Bellamy's jaw, knocked out the Canadian and, as they toppled over with the roll of the ship, Jack sprained his ankle. We had to carry off the whole side.

The men, who were sobbing with laughter, said it was the best officers' show they had ever seen.

Then there appeared a pale yellow line along the horizon, the tufts of three solitary palms, and a strange burnt smell—Egypt!

Shades of everything I had ever read! Here was I, a British soldier, going into Egypt. I was astonished to find myself shivering with emotion. It was strange, but everyone on board seemed to feel sentimental about it. An Englishman, dressed in khaki, feels he is fulfilling something very definite when he disembarks in Egypt.

We hung out from boats and rails as we passed through that long line of sunken funnels and masts that the Austrian submarines had now made the prelude to Alexandria breakwater. Forced to straighten out, we put on a little extra spurt of speed to reach the safety behind those yellow rocks; then we were passing slowly through one of the most amazing masses of shipping in all this world. Great ocean liners, their sides zigzagged with colouring as if they had leprosy; Greek barques and Levantine trading ships; yellow, red-sailed Arab dhows with open hulls and naked, turbaned crews gaping up at us; slanting feluccas, sailing across the blue water below us like butterflies; stocky little British tramps and coalers, as dour as Yorkshire business men; two solemn British monitors, the grey sides not a foot above wateredge; a couple of Japanese destroyers, doing torpedo drill, their smart little sailors darting about before their macabre-looking flag of the Rising Sun—and thousands of bumboats whose Gippy occupants were already beseeching us.

"Meester Captain, Meester Captain—High Life shawl, real amber, Meester Captain! Real scarab from de tombs of de Pharaohs! Real rhinoceros-tail whip, Meester Captain; can use him as walking-stick . . . Meester Captain—gib it! gib it! . . . very nice, veree good, veree cheap . . . *Ya Allah!* . . . *Baksheesh!* . . . Meester Captain, I got private girl, harem girl—veree nice, very good, veree clean . . ."

"Why, God damn it!" said Jack, vastly disappointed. "They talk *English!*"

A pile of coloured blocks, buildings came down to the water-edge; the homes of Greeks, Italians, French, and ubiquitous Levantines. Behind them the fingers of minarets pointed wistfully into a cloudless sky, the sun shining on mosques of gold and turquoise—the sweet stink of sewage—and over all, flanking it, guarding it and guiding ships into Egypt from the sea, the great yellow column of Ras el Tin lighthouse, beneath whose dead beam I was soon to lie in hospital on the long, hot afternoons when the doves cooed in the frangipani outside. . . .

We were sent out to Aboukir, in whose pellucid bay Nelson fought the French. Flying over it we could still see the dark patch below water of a sunken frigate. There was a little Arab town there, with a mosque and a fetid bazaar where the flies crawled over sewage and piles of dates and the children's eyes. There was an oasis of tufted, friendly palms. And far away, on the edge of a sandy aerodrome rutted with tail skids, there was a long strip of white sandy beach. On two wretched donkeys, Jack and I raced for it, threw off our uniforms and dived into the sea. . . .

"Boy!"—Jack's black curly head appeared above the blue water —"Do you know this was Cleopatra's old bathing place? Wish to hell she was here now!"

Chapter 41

JACK

JACK and I, *faute de mieux*—both being Americans—were destined to bunk together from the day when we first faced each other in the ex-student's study we had been given to live in at the Wantage Officers' School. Looking each other over carefully, we saw that we were both of exactly the same height, weight, and, it appeared, temperament. We slid into a state of armed truce with each other that was always on the point of breaking down. In England we fought over who had pinched the last cigarette; in France it was who had taken the last of that bottle of red wine; out here it was over our daily allowance of water, and whose golf stockings were whose when the laundry came in.

He was, I should imagine, the most unpopular American in the British Army. He epitomised everything that the Englishman hates in Colonials, particularly their muscularity. His unthinking bombast laid him wide open for subtle ragging, or at least ragging that thought it was subtle. And Jack's only answer was an invitation to step outside and settle it that way.

"I dove on him!" declared Jack one day in the Mess, describing a dog-fight.

"You—*what?*"

It was about 110 degrees inside that sagging tent.

"Dove—you bastard—dove—D-O-V-E!"

"Oh, you mean you *dived* on him?"

Jack snatched up a plate. I grabbed his hand. "Forget it!" I said as always—"Don't let them get you so serious about things!"

Then in our tent afterwards, Jack would burst out: "Well, I'm not going to have *him* trying to tell me how to talk English—a bloody New Zealander! They think they *are* English! I tell you, I *dove* on him!"

We had made a golf course on the desert out of Three Castle tins. It was all right, if you did not mind picking your ball out of a tin full of lizards. One day we had a tournament. An ex-jockey from the Argentine turned in the best score.

"He's a liar!" yelled Jack, when the scores were read out after dinner. "He takes five strokes before he can hit a ball! Send somebody around to count with him!"

In this case we all thought Jack was correct in his judgment. The ex-jockey from the Argentine never forgave him for it. Jack, aside from the wretched monkey—"Sultan Fuad"—had a pet chameleon. When I came out to Aboukir again, after a spell in Ras el Tin Hospital, I found the whole station giving Jack a boycott. Nobody would speak to him. When I asked him what he had done now, he said that the ex-jockey's chameleon had bitten the tail off his chameleon.

"I told him," said Jack, describing how he had taken reparations from the Argentine jockey; "I said to him, 'You're too damn small to hit!' So I gave him a boot in the pants. Now they all call me a roughneck!"

He was nursing his poor livid chameleon with tears in both their eyes.

Jack had an adventure out by the Mamouidah Canal, where the slanting rigs of the feluccas add their arabesque to the date palms on cool starlit nights, and it was some time before we were tentmates again, in Cairo, where he turned up with some Grand Guignol reminiscences. It was out in the desert that I suddenly realised he was sick. I told him that if he did not report himself, I would report him.

"If you don't go over and see the M.O.," I said, "I'll do it for you. I've got an open wound—and I'm not going to take any chances. Not with you, swiping and wearing my things every time the laundry comes back!"

For just one instant I thought that *Der Tag* had arrived—the long-expected battle between Jack and myself was about to begin. He heaved himself off his camp cot and jumped across the marquee. In its darkness, which was almost like night after the blinding glare of the white desert, I could plainly see a frenzied desire to kill me in his eyes. Then he suddenly thought of himself, went a sickly green under his tan, and without a word walked out of the tent and across to the M.O.'s marquee. Half an hour later he swaggered back.

"Ya—funny! You can just stay here and rot! I hear a *kham-seen's* coming. You can eat sand for three days. I hope you choke. I'm off to Alex., I am!"

When Abdul the Damned began to pack his kit for him, Jack hit him a vicious whack across his broad, jibbah-clad bottom.

"*Mushquiece!* Meester Captain!" Abdul whined—and held up his monkey-like paws in supplication. It was sickening.

"One of these days," I told Jack sullenly, "one of these days, you'll hit one of those black sportsmen with the gashes on their cheeks—and then God help you, my lad. They're not Cairo Arabs —they're Sudanese. They hit back!"

Yet, the day I crashed in Cairo, Jack wept!

It took them seventeen minutes to cut me out of what was left of the little Nieuport. Jack heard of it in the Mess and left his breakfast to come running out to the Maccatam Hills, where I was tangled up, kissing a rotary motor, in a tangle of R.A.F. wires, castor oil and blood.

"If Farson dies!" Jack told an uninterested but occupied crowd of Ack Emmas and the M.O., "I'll never fly again!"

I did not know anything about this, of course, for I was unconscious; but when I came to, eighteen hours later, I found Jack looking down at me. He had told a tale to the adjutant to allow him to remain in Cairo that night; and at various intervals, I learned afterward, he had telephoned the hospital from places I could very well imagine. Near dawn he had come and sat outside on the cool balcony. Then I awoke. Said Jack:

"Hello, you big bum!"

A couple of weeks later, when I was allowed to sit upright, he came in, inquired about my health, gave me the gossip of the squadron, borrowed my remaining £5, and left that night for Alexandria to sail for England.

When I tottered back to my squadron, I found all my nice new Viyella shirts missing. So were all the decent knitted khaki neckties, so was my one pair of whipcord breeks. As I had crashed in the very best gaberdine uniform I had (I had been going into

Cairo to play tennis that day at the Gezireh Sporting Club) I discovered I now had no uniform to go about in, except the rather heavy khaki slacks I had on.

"Where's shirts?" I demanded of the frightened Abdul. "*Fen* clothes?" I shook my stick at him. "Hurry! *Eggerie!*"

"Me no know, Meester Captain—Captain Jack—he take 'em."

"*What!*"

I reached out for the batman, who, as I could barely walk, escaped me by jumping two paces off.

"Meester Captain, Meester Captain"—they always called you Meester Captain, whether you were a corporal or a colonel—"Meester Captain—Captain Jack—he take 'em!"

A protest which, knowing Jack as I did, I finally believed. With an overdraft at Cox's, a tragic loss of flying pay due to my long stretch of hospital, I would have been in a pathetic situation were it not for three Scotsmen, two of whom killed themselves shortly afterwards, but all of whom lived long enough to "keep" me in Egypt, buy me ices at Groppie's, buy me whiskey and sodas and Gold Flakes at the Mess, tea at the Gezireh Sporting Club, and give me a farewell beano by letting me eat all the prawns and mayonnaise at Shepheard's. Even more; at the "sun-down stand-up" at Shepheard's bar they used to fight their way in through the ranks of thirsty colonels and majors to get my drinks for me. And one of the saddest tasks I have ever had laid upon me was to send a note to the father of one of them. The son, Herron, until he looped an S.E.5 into a Bristol Fighter, thus ending his own and the lives of two Australians, was the finest pilot I have ever seen in my life—then or since. His father was a gardener near the Bridge of Allan.

Herron and I once had the fantastic notion of putting in for the Egyptian Air Force. There was talk of such a force being organised at that time. It would have been our solution of the post-war problem. And that is why, with Abdul the Damned in the hot afternoons of the desert I kept him sitting on his hunkers, teaching me Arabic.

"*The eunuch is in the garden of the Caliph* . . . Now, Abdul . . ."

"*Oh, sahib!*" Abdul would go into convulsions of laughter. Why I should begin learning Arabic with eunuchs was a thing which that Arab simply could not fathom. Neither could I. But I believe that is one of the very first sentences one is given to learn in "Hugo's Arabic." It was not, as it is in learning every other language from *amo, amas, amat* up—"I love, you love, he loves. . . ."

"*Ya vass lublu* . . . I love you!"

Damn those words.

Perhaps Dr. Hugo also had a love affair that went wrong? If so, how appropriate!—"*The eunuch is in the garden of the Caliph!*"

Chapter 42

THE DESERT

It was all part of the scheme of life that I should come to Egypt, just at this moment—the Land of the Dead! For, without being maudlin or dramatic about it I also was dead inside. One of the lowest mornings of my life was that six o'clock on the Victoria platform, waiting for the train to pull out.

Less than half a block away, was an hotel that I dared not drive past on my way to the railway station. In it, sleeping like the healthy young creature that she was, was the only person I cared about. Her people had got out of Bolshevik Russia, with the help of John Reed, who had helped them as he promised, and for a few days the whole of my Russian life seemed to be coming together again. Then it fell to pieces; I lost my head, I destroyed everything. When I was told that nothing could be decided now —"as you might get killed in the war, you know!"—I flung out of the hotel in such a rage that I even left my British "warm" behind me. It was sent down to me two days later, with its pips missing. They had been kept as souvenirs. And it was still pip-less when I stood with Jack on Victoria platform. I didn't have the courage to put them back!

When the train pulled out, I went through all the feelings which, I imagine, a young, lusty monk must feel when he enters a monastery and closes the doors of the world behind him. And it was in this mood that I saw Egypt.

I welcomed that early morning flying in the desert. It had a beauty that completely wiped out thoughts of anything else.

"Four o'clock, Meester Captain—me tellum you fly!"

Abdul the Damned would have his hand under my mosquito net. His favourite method of awaking me was by pulling my big toe. After a night of bridge and Johnny Walker even that hardly worked.

"Four o'clock, Meester Captain—four *o'clock!* Fly! *Sabe?* Fly!"

I would get up and climb into cold, greasy shorts. They would be sticky with castor oil from the rotary engines. Then into short flying boots. Then stumble across guy-ropes and tent-pegs to where the candles guttered on the tables of the mess marquee. Here we would eat a comfortless breakfast of unripe bananas, condensed milk, and luke-warm tea, the familiar roars from the hangars recalling us to our responsibilities.

"Suck in?"

"Suck in."

"Switch on?"

"Switch on."

"Contact."

In the chill air, the fur around my goggles was warm on my face. There would be bursts of roars from the rotary engines; and with our eyes still half closed from sleep we would taxi out on the 'drome, head into the listless wind, and tap-tap-tap along the desert until we felt that smooth rhythm that told us we were in the air. We would climb, until the sand-coloured marquees of the camp were barely a spot on the desert below us. Then we would look into the "office" and out at the ailerons. It all seemed so intimate in all this space; the steadiness of those struts and R.A.F. wires!

Then the sun would rise. Out in the Libyan desert it was like a strip of red fire along the horizon. We would be staring into a bowl of blazing colour. For a few minutes the world below us would be veiled in a flamingo mist—but only for a few minutes. Then the desert would lie under us everywhere, endless, everlasting, yellow and spotted as a leopard's back.

I was in the desert during the moon of Ramadan, when all true believers fast all day and feast all night. There was a tribe of fanatic Senussie in a wady near us. They made a cynical contrast, those two camps. When we were coming down from our last flight at sunset, the Arabs were on their knees, praying towards Mecca. We were having a sun-down whiskey and soda in the mess marquee. When we were playing bridge with more whiskey at midnight, we heard the plaintive ul-ul-ul chanting from the Arab fires, and the thud of their tom-toms. With his religion, and the life of the Koran, in his mind all his waking hours, I could sympathise with the Egyptian's resentment of the materialist civilisation the British were slowly forcing him to live. I agreed with the desert Arabs, but when it came to Cairo and Alexandria, I was glad the British had given Egypt a bath.

One morning when I flew over the Nile Delta, the sun rose below me. It was one of the most beautiful dawns I have ever seen. The whole floor of clouds below me turned a light rose pink. I started up the Nile—or, at least, where I thought the Nile ought to be. And when the sun began to tear holes in the clouds I spun, and dropped through them.

I came out directly on top of a fleet of fishing feluccas. They were coasting along the blue water like so many butterflies. Coming lower I saw their black crews looking up at me, men out of the Arabian Nights, naked except for loin-clout and turban. Then I straightened up and flew into the Nile Delta, past the green swamps, with more white butterflies standing out across them, until I reached the tufted palm trees and yellow sands . . . and heat!

That was the one side of Egypt which paid me for everything. The other side made me feel all the more regretful for what I had lost.

I envied those flowered homes along the Mediterranean out at Montazah and Stanley Bay, with the *bougainvillaea*, climbing over their yellow walls. I envied the Egyptian life there of the British Army officer; cool-jawed under his helmet, playing polo out at the Gezireh Sporting Club. These men had careers that were rich with action and romance. I even envied their correctitude, the way they carried themselves. And I felt sorry for myself and the other officers who haunted the Rue Ramleh at nights. We had a hunger that that street could not answer.

In Egypt I seemed to stand just on the edge of the perfect life I had dreamed of as a boy. America had no lives such as were held out by the British Empire. We had no India, no Egypt, no Africa—with their exciting, glamorous, yet complacently practical careers. Richard Harding Davis, with his *Soldiers of Fortune*, among the islands of the Caribbean, was the gaudiest adventure-area in which our younger sons had a chance. It must have been in a short story I had once read; but on Gezireh Island one day I had tea in an officer's garden, and there it was; every rose—just as I had imagined it would be!

So my years in Egypt will remain to me: a coloured strip of those yellow camps along the blue Mediterranean, those burning dawns and cool nights of the desert, the unsatisfying mockery of our own lives, and that perfect other life which I still see with all the unreality of a mirage.

Chapter 43

CRASH

WITH the spring came a flurry of rain that lashed us in the face and then vanished into the sands. Now we learned why that camp of Senussie had been waiting there, with their black tents, muffled women and bleating little fat-tailed sheep. In the wady which held their tents a faint green fuzz appeared that seemed to be nurtured from some river flowing under the sands; and they prepared to harvest their annual crop of barley before they and their camels moved off into the mysterious waste that stretches all the way across Africa to the Atlantic.

I was sent to Cairo, where I switched over on to S.E.5's. It was a marvellous little scout, whose long nose held a sweet and powerful Hispano-Suiza motor. But one morning after breakfast, to get out of the heat, I took up a Nieuport. The only thing I had ever noticed that was particularly difficult about Nieuports, was their habit of slewing right or left the instant their wheels touched the ground, when the torque counter-action came off. But this one must have been tricky, or perhaps it was that unbelievable heat and thin air. At any rate, at four hundred feet I found myself in a violent spin.

There was a Flying Corps commandment in Egypt that no one should turn a scout below five hundred feet in taking off. But on this frying morning, as I walked out to the bus, a group of bored people in the shade of a hangar, said: "Give us something to look at."

I took off in a climbing turn. It was at about four hundred that I felt that slew and wrench that told me I was spinning. It all happened so quickly that I did not have time to think over my past life, as people are supposed to do when facing death; I did not have time enough even to be frightened. I simply knew that this was IT! And it was happening to ME! I would end up with a crankshaft through my chest as many of my friends had done.

"Your engine has failed!" my brain roared to my heart. "Open her up wide and dive for it!"

So I opened the bus up full wide and tried to dive out of it. It was a futile attempt, because I couldn't have been a hundred feet up. But that was the thing that saved me. Just as the sands swirled into my face, I heard a crash like the sound of a peach-crate smashing before I passed into the darkness. I went clean through the bus, the crankshaft passing under my arm, to end up against the sharp fins of the rotary cylinders.

It was with a feeling of the utmost astonishment that I woke up. A face was leaning over me, a pretty face; and it was repeating—in that kittenish firmness those V.A.D.s had: "You—must—not—sit—up! Understand? You—must—not—sit—up! Now be a good boy!"

That was what my crash was like. I felt around carefully, and found that both legs and my head were bandaged, and it felt as if someone were sitting on my chest.

Nasrieh Hospital was not bad, except that it was full of septic cases, and it took that overworked staff two weeks to discover that, aside from concussion and a shattered left tibia, I also had the bones of my right foot broken; and it was nearly a year later that a bearded naval surgeon tried to set that right by taking some bits of bone out of it at the Royal Naval Hospital at Chatham. In fact, from that day on, somebody, somewhere, was always trying to take bits of bone away from me.

A flap of ear that was hanging down was sewn back by the doctor with a couple of quick stitches before they shoved me into the ambulance.

"Perhaps the dirt and castor oil did it," he said, when I thanked him for such a good job afterwards. "I never took the trouble to clean it—didn't think it was much use, you know."

All of them, including Jack, of course, thought that my number was up. And, as evidence of the way Nasrieh Hospital viewed my case, I have the episode of one, named Fergusson.

"Are you Farson?" he asked one morning—a gaunt Punjabi officer, with a head bandaged until it looked like a Mohammedan's turban. "If so—we ought to meet. The doctor says you and I are the only two men in Nasrieh with solid ivory skulls!"

Fergusson had been shot from the side through his forehead, the Turk's bullet going in one side of his skull and out the other, and apparently nothing had happened to Fergusson.

"I'm always a bit silly anyway," he grinned. "So I don't think anyone will notice any difference in me."

One episode in that hospital still embarrasses me when I think of it. My people had been notified of my crash by the War Office, when, at first, things had looked serious for me. And one morning, when I could see people, Hampson Gary, the "American Consul-General and Diplomatic Agent," as he was sonorously named, came in and sat beside me. He looked rather embarrassed, and then finally he laughed and handed me a letter.

"I should not do this," he said. "It is a breach of professional etiquette. But I am sure it will amuse you."

It was a letter to him from my Aunt Edith in New York. "My nephew is such a wild, reckless boy." Would Mr. Gary not try and get me transferred from the Flying Corps to some safer arm such as the Royal Service Corps?

I groaned. If Mr. Gary had not been such a good sort I should never have lived it down. Poor Edith—she had some weird ideas about safety and the gallant Royal Service Corps at that.

There was a deal of palaver at Nasrieh Hospital, as I started to navigate again on crutches, about sending me to a Rest Home down by Montazah on the Mediterranean. Which was the one thing I distinctly did not want. Once caught in the toils of a Medical Board I might as well have been in a prison camp. I wanted my freedom—and I also wanted my ten shillings a day flying pay.

So, the day I got out of Nasrieh I took a gharry out to Heliopolis and went straight to the doctor's hut. He was an amazing person, the Nth degree of British sportsman. We used to take him up as a passenger and let him take over when we were in the air. But one day he climbed into the back cockpit of an Avro, telling the mechanics he would warm it up, and after buzzing it for some time he told the Ack Emmas to pull the chocks away. They did not know what he was going to do. Perhaps he did not himself? At any rate, after a prolonged buzz, the Avro began to move across the sands—ruuumph-ruuumph-tap-tap-tap . . . our doctor was in the air! He flew all over Cairo in giddy freedom by himself, afraid, he told us afterwards, to come down. Then he saw that he would eventually run out of petrol, so he brought the bus back—and landed 20 feet up! He washed off an under-carriage and lost his job. But he had flown solo; a busted Avro proved that.

With a doctor like that one can talk openly, and I told him my fears.

"Yes," he said candidly, "if a Medical Board gets you, you're for it. Doesn't look to me as if that leg will ever heal in the state that it's in."

He made me take off my shoes and socks and close one eye. Then he made me touch a pencil with my big toe. "How's your nerve?" he asked. I told him frankly I did not know, and I wouldn't know until I had flown solo again.

"Well," he said, "to be perfectly realistic about this, I think you are just as fit as you were before the crash. Your legs might bother you on the ground. But in the air you should be just as good a man as you ever were. I'm going to pass you fit for service —to hell with red tape in this case!"

Our major signed a chit for the required seven hours dual after hospital and I gave it to a friend of mine, a regular Indian Army Officer, who took me up in an Avro forthwith. I threw her about in rolls and loops and spins until I had satisfied both him and myself that my nerves were all right. Then he pointed down at the 'drome and signalled me to land her.

As I taxied the bus up to the hangars he made a rotary motion with his hands to signify that I should keep buzzing the motor. I saw him unstrapping his belt. Then he climbed out and looked up at me:

"Take off!" he yelled quickly. "Get into the air! You're all right!"

With a few rump-ruumps I was tapping across the 'drome and

was in the air again. I soared over the Macattam Hills and looked down to see if I could spot the dent I must have made in Egypt when I crashed. Then I flew over and looked down into Cairo, and I circled about over the Waza, that naughty huddle of streets near the tombs of the Mamelukes which was out of bounds to troops. Then I flew over to the Nile and took a look at that. The Pyramids next occupied my attention, and I nearly crashed against the wireless wire that had been strung to the broken top of Cheops. Then I stared down at the hole in the head of the Sphinx. Then—then I began to think about my petrol. If I had had enough petrol of course I should have been flying yet. I had only left hospital that morning; and now I began to think that I had overdone things.

On the contrary, when I did put the bus down I made the most perfect three-point landing of my life.

"Wouldn't have broken an egg!" said Arthur, the Indian officer. "And now, my boy, you're free from medical boards—you've been solo. At any rate, they can't take your flying pay away from you without the hell of a lot of trouble for everybody."

The next day I was back on S.E.5's again.

All would have been well had not our doctor tried his solo business and faded away and a new doctor turned up. He saw me, walking around in shorts and our usual golf stockings, with a stick and a bandage on my left leg.

"Let's take a look at that," he said curtly. Then: "What are you doing, walking around Egypt with an open wound like that? Don't you know this country is simply lousy with infection!"

"Yes," I smiled, trying to placate him. "But that hole in the bone is simply chock full of iodoform—I dust it in there every morning."

"Huh!—you do, do you! Well you won't in my squadron. Now, don't get shirty about things; I know what is right. I'm sending you to hospital. I'll send you down to Alex., where it's nice and cool by the sea. They can try and do a skin graft on you."

That's how I entered Ras el Tin Hospital and became blood brother to a Scotsman of the Black Watch. He was operated upon just before I was; and when I came out of the chloroform I was told that a piece of him had been left over and put inside me.

"How am I?" he used to ask me in the mornings, when we lay in the old cow-shed overlooking the sea. "You know we're blood relations of sort—what?"

"You're dead," I told him one day. "The M.O. took you out this morning."

And, aside from the swimming and sailing native feluccas about the harbour in my pyjamas, the one bright spot of Ras el Tin was when I interviewed the Sultan of Egypt in bed. I was in bed.

Chapter 44

SULTAN OF EGYPT

IN THOSE days when Ahmed Fuad Pasha was not yet King of Egypt, but merely its Sultan, he received more pomp and ostentatious ceremony from the British than they would have dared to give their own King. The British know how to placate the "lesser breeds without the law"—after they have compromised them—and with Fuad they laid it on with a spade.

Fuad was much too sophisticated a gentleman not to realise quite clearly that it was all part of the great show. But it went well with the *fellaheen*, and even his own politicians; and that did not displease him in the least.

We used to see him most frequently at the horse-races of the Alexandria Sporting Club. His imposing entrance was preceded by a squadron of Lancers, red and green pennants fluttering in the sun, Fuad lolling in his barouche.

Then he would climb out, and the plump little Sultan in fez and Italian morning suit would mount to his private kiosk.

Meanwhile, all the British officers on the course stood at stiff salute . . . as if petrified. It was part of the game. But underneath our breath we swore at him for driving his sharp-tyred carriage down the centre of the turf.

Then this morning the Commandant of Ras el Tin Hospital stuck his nose in the ward and said, "Who talks French here?" As my bed was nearest to the door I said that I did. "Right," said the Commandant and disappeared. I thought it would mean a chance to do some interpreting, perhaps a meal down in Alex. at the Union Club; and they would not find out that I did not talk enough French to order a meal until I already had the job.

"What's it all about?" I asked the sister, when I saw them sweeping and polishing the brasses again.

That was an ominous sign. We were periodically inspected at Ras el Tin by "personages," one of whom was General "Bull"

Allenby, who roared at us so that some of us shivered and shook for days afterward. But this looked like a very, very special inspection. I knew something dreadful was going to happen when I saw all the walking patients being chased about the yard and put back to bed. They did not look sick enough standing up. And at the last minute one cavalry officer was caught at the gates, making for Alex., and put back to bed with his boots on—a flying splint strapped over his now perfectly good arm.

Then a sister came along and pinned a blue band on my pyjama sleeve.

"Say!" I called in alarm. "What's this for? I haven't got my clothes on yet!"

"You'll see," said the sister, with feminine spitefulness. "You just lie there and try to be good. Do you want me to comb your hair for you?"

All our clothes had been taken away from us and thrust into lockers, so there was nothing left but to lie there—and just wait. Could it be Allenby! But French . . . ?

"Bull's at Gaza," said a colonel, fresh down from the line. "Must be another brass hat—Boyle?"

"So—you talk French, do you?" said my neighbour. "You low, pushing American."

As it turned out afterward, he really did talk perfect French; as he proved to the ward.

The hot morning waned, the doves began to coo and make love in the frangipani outside our windows, a soft breeze from the Mediterranean gently stirred our gauze curtains. I dozed in delicious security, then . . .

Rrrr-whummph-whummph . . . five red motor-cycles slithered into the yellow walls of the old fort. A gorgeous red Rolls-Royce came silently to full stop. The Sultan of Egypt stepped out!

"Cripes!" An orderly still with his tunic off slid along the linoleum to some screens.

A shiver slid along the ward as the plump little man, dressed in the khaki and silver of a Colonel in the Egyptian army, came towards us. He paused, with his staff behind him, at its entrance, and then walked into the ward. He stood there—obviously searching for something.

"Ah—*voilà!*"

He saw the blue band on my arm, smiled, and came over to me.

I could have died. My tongue stuck to the roof of my mouth. What, I thought, my mind in a stutter, is the bed-salute to give a Sultan?

"*Vous êtes blessé, Monsieur?*"

"Ah"—in my French—"Yes, Your Altitude!"

I saw the officers of his staff stiffen.

"Where were you shot?"

"I am not shot, Your Altitude. I—I did beat myself against the ground . . . whoop-ziiip!" I made crashing sounds and imitated an aeroplane disaster. "Flying, Your Altitude."

By this time the face of Ras el Tin's C.O. had gone a fishy white. The Sultan smiled compassionately. "Ah—your legs are broken?"

"Yes, Your Altitude, she was."

By now something like panic was spreading behind the Sultan. The British officers of his staff eyed me in a way that thoroughly shook any composure I had left. The hospital C.O. had his hand half out, trying to lure the Sultan off to some other officer. But the Sultan of Egypt was enjoying himself. He, poor man, probably detested hospital inspections, and—he had never heard French like this!

He asked how long I had been in Egypt, and then where had I come from. I said from Russia.

"Ah—you were there during the Revolution?"

"Yes, Your Altitude."

"That must have been very exciting?"

"Yes, Your Altitude—she did."

"Ah . . ."

"Did you see Lenin?"

"Yes, Your Altitude."

"Ah. . . . He saw Lenin!" he said, turning to his staff. They all scowled obediently. I—who the devil was that madman lying there?—he had seen Lenin. "Ah . . . well," said the Sultan, and he put out a neat, gloved hand; "I wish you good health."

Then the Sultan went home. He turned on his heel and without another look at the long line of colonels, majors and captains waiting there like sardines on toast for his inspection, he left Ras el Tin Hospital.

The nurse came along and took the blue band off my arm.

"Nice boy," she said. "You can go out and play now." How we detested that patronising playfulness of the V.A.D.s.

The long line of colonels, majors, and captains just lay there and stared at me.

Across the courtyard a phonograph was playing, "What did you do in the Great War, Daddy?"

Then the man in the bed next to me translated our entire conversation.

I was given an extra whiskey and soda at luncheon on the strength of it. It was about the last thing I did in Egypt.

Some time later I was appointed one of the four flying instructors to the Denikine show in South Russia and left for London.

Chapter 45

GETTING MARRIED

LONDON again. I felt that I had my teeth into life again now. Colonel Maund, who was in charge of the Air Force attached to the Denikine Expedition, had vetted me and marked my chit, "An ideal type of officer. . . ." I was immensely flattered, and happy to be under him. I had seen him in Petrograd in 1915. I had a cubicle in the Royal Automobile Club, down by the shower baths; and nearly every day we officers sat in Bolo House before a map of South Russia, and held conferences about the supplies we should take out.

There were four of us who were to be pilot instructors, later command squadrons, and seven technical officers, with a complement of mechanics and R.E.8 planes. Winston Churchill was over in Paris off and on making contact and arrangements with the White Russian officer *émigrés* over there. We were told not to talk too much about the Denikine show in London; and one day I understood full well why. For walking out of one of our conferences in Bolo House I bought a copy of the evening *Star* in the Strand, and read Lloyd George's statement to the House:

"ALL BRITISH TROOPS BEING WITHDRAWN FROM RUSSIA."

One of my first contacts with that official mendacity that was to give me such an ironic relish in exposing when I was a foreign newspaper correspondent.

My life seemed to have zest in it these days; at any rate, it had purpose, and I particularly liked the crowd with which I was going out to Novorossisk. Then one day came a telephone call. The whole of my Russian affair with V. was reopened. We were to get married right away. And on the strength of that I went down to the Hotel Cecil and resigned from the Denikine show.

It was terribly humiliating.

"I suppose you know," said the major, looking at me with

330

thinly veiled scorn, "it will be almost impossible for us to get another officer to take your place?"

And he showed me the chit the Colonel had written, when they put me on the strength. It sickened me to look at it.

"Well . . . ?" said the major.

The chief complaint against me as a prospective husband—and not an unreasonable one, if you like—was the fact that, now my Russian business was lost, I had no visible means of support. I had to get started again in real life. I had to do it, even if it did cost me the respect of some of my recently-made friends in the R.A.F.

"I must resign," I said.

"Very well, then."

The major took up a pen, dipped it in red ink—and drew a line through my name!

"Good morning," he said coldly.

My engagement then broke down for the last time.

I think it was at Eastchurch, waiting to be repatriated, that I hit rock bottom. I had left New York in 1914—it was now 1919 —and I had lost every solitary thing I could think of.

Russia was gone—and I hardly knew anybody any more in the United States.

I asked to be operated upon out of boredom more than anything else, and had more bone removed from my right foot at the Royal Naval Hospital at Chatham. Then my left leg broke down, and I was sent to the R.A.F. Hospital at Eaton Square, London. Here I underwent the painful experience of having the skin of my leg pulled across my open shin-bone—and tacked down with gramophone needles. It was not a success.

And so passed the spring and summer.

Autumn saw me sailing up the Delaware, staring out moodily through the porthole at the serene stretches of the bay down which I used to sail as a boy. Not much had changed there. Off the old Farson place at Marcus Hook, now the Government Quarantine Station, the S.S. *Haverford* lay at anchor, while I had the dismal introspection of seeing the same lawns from which

I used to set my night-lines for eels and catfish. And at Phila-delphia my family met me. My brother, who was an officer in the U. S. Navy, had married by then. He was two years my junior, and that night his wife said to him:

"I thought you told me Negley was happy-go-lucky! Since he has been home he hasn't said one blessed word. Why, he is one of the bitterest persons I have ever tried to talk to!"

I stayed at home a few days and found that I was completely out of gear. Most of my friends had made so much money that I did not know how to talk to them. That did not bother me much, as I had so few friends—I had not really been home since 1910. I missed Jo-Jo terribly, but then he was dead, so there was no use mourning over that. And most of the neighbourhood thought I was a Communist because I insisted that Lenin was a great man, perhaps the greatest produced by the war, and not the conventional, bomb-throwing Revolutionist that our Govern-ment was trying to make him out to be. I wrote an article on Lenin, and one on the reasons why the United States Government should recognise Soviet Russia. When I showed the latter to my father, he exclaimed:

"Print that—and the Government will put you on the *Soviet Ark* and ship you back to Russia."

"I hope they do," I said, and he was furious when I told him that I hoped the Lusk Committee would go ahead with the case they claimed they had against me.

The article trying to get the U. S. to recognise the Soviets was given a half-page display in the *New York Sun and Herald*, March 14, 1920; on March 30 I actually managed to get a similar one printed in the leading paper of my father's home town! And on July 11 the *New York Sun and Herald* printed my Lenin article.

But during all of that time I was in hospital again, going through some unnecessarily awful operations this time!

I had returned to the United States on a British passport. When I joined the British Army I lost my American citizenship, and actually was an Englishman (as far as passports and uniform were concerned) for nearly three years. This gave me a considerable amount of pleasure when I went up for operation in New York. I was to be operated upon at the —— Hospital in New York, under the British-American reciprocity hospital scheme. A high British official said to me:

"You might let us know how you get on at the ——. You are the first British officer to be operated upon there. We have had nothing but complaints from the Tommies, and we are curious. Be very kind of you if you tell us how you get on."

He thought I was a Canadian! The British passport said I was.

I had heard something about the graft and corruption and the filthy bullyragging that went on in the American soldier hospitals, but I was not quite prepared for what I got. To begin with I asked if I could have a private room.

"Yeah? What for?" snapped a major, with spurs on, behind his desk. "Why should *you* have a room, I'd like to know?"

"Because," I said, "if I am going to have another bone operation I know that I shall be here a long time. I want to work. I am writing newspaper articles and magazine stories to make a living."

(I had just had two Russian articles accepted by the *New York Sun and Herald* and a short story on Egypt bought by Bob Davis, of *Munsey's Magazine*, and in my naïve manner I thought that I was launched!)

"You do, do you? Well, let me tell you—the war's over! And an officer isn't any better than anyone else—see? I don't care what they do in England, this is New York."

"All right," I said. "When shall I be X-rayed?"

He told me to go upstairs and have it done then. I did. A nasty little kike took off my bandage and laid it—bloody side down— on a dusty packing case. Then he X-rayed me and, after ordering me about like a criminal, tried to put the same bandage back again!

"Wait a moment!" I said, hardly able to speak. "What are you going to do?"

"Put this bandage back."

"The hell you are!"

I jumped off the X-ray table and rolled up my trouser leg. I grabbed the mess of dirty bandage. Then I walked down three floors of the —— Hospital followed by the X-ray man, a growing trail of protesting nurses, and the eyes of all the visitors then in the hospital. I was happy, happy, happy . . . ! I went into that major's office and dropped the bandage on his desk.

"Now," I said, "just listen to me for a few minutes. I'm not an Englishman—I'm an American. I was asked by the British to tell them how I was treated in this hospital—and I'm going to tell them plenty!"

It was marvellous! All the venom that I felt for that bully-ragging atmosphere of American officialdom had its chance. My resentment against all the cocksureness of the America that I loved had its day. Before I had finished the major was begging me to forget the episode, and he insisted on bandaging my leg himself. I felt humiliated about my exhibition of temper—but not mollified. When I stood up I said to him that I was going out to write that letter forthwith, and, I said:

"I shall do everything in my power to stop an Englishman, officer or just plain Tommy, from ever entering this hospital again."

I did. Prefacing my letter by the fact that I was sorry to have to say I was an American under such circumstances, I wrote out a report to the British Consul-General in New York on the —— Hospital. The British made no reply, other than to thank me for my letter, and direct me to secure suitable accommodation in a private hospital in New York and send the bill to them.

Then I fell into the hands of one of those surgeons whom they call "daring." I haven't the heart to picture those summer months in New York, when I lay under a Murphy "drip" of chlorine with my shin-bone sticking out through a mass of sluffing flesh from my knee to my anklebone. It was pretty grim. Just one little incident might illustrate it.

Sometimes, the surgeon dressed me. But it must have embarrassed him, for he usually let one of the nurses do that job. Three or four times, when the doctor did come in, I suggested that the bone graft he had done on me had failed. The new bone was dead.

"Sheer nonsense!" he laughed.

One day, when he was dressing me, I asked if I could have the probe for a minute, and as I asked I took it from his hand. Then I flicked a large slab of bone out of my leg on to the hospital sheets.

Neither of us made any remark. There was, of course, nothing to be said.

I kept my sanity going by writing all day and most of every night. The Sunday Editor of the *New York Sun and Herald* came up to see me and said, "You know I will get my ears clipped if I go on printing stuff like this about recognising Russia and all that—give us some Egyptian stuff." Major Wardwell, of the American Red Cross mission that was in Russia during the Lenin Revolution, came up to see me and gave me his diary.

"I read your story on Lenin," he said. "I liked it so much I wanted to meet you. Here is my diary. You will see that when I saw Lenin for the first time I went home and wrote almost the same description that you did—but if I tried to talk like that down in Wall Street they would say I was a Red!"

That was the time that the Americans (and the British) believed that the Soviets were nationalising Russian women to provide public concubines.

When I tried to get back to England again I found I could not get an American passport for months. Our Government had just realised what a gorgeous racket they had overlooked in the passport game, and now Washington was making more fuss about "documents" than old Tsarist Russia in the Nihilist days. Thousands of desperate Americans were queued up, waiting to pay their $10—plus $10 to every country they wanted a visa from—and, as is invariably the case with American officialdom, the clerks in Washington and all our Consulates abroad were being just as rude as they could be over the job. Give an American a government job and he can become more bureaucratic than any official on the globe! My mind had cleared by this time, and I saw my way ahead.

My reasons for going back to England could brook no delay.

I had never felt more determined about anything in all my life. There would be no delays or frustrations this time. So, putting my British passport with its little lion in my pocket, I collected my crutches and went down to the British Consul-General.

"Can I," I begged, "use this passport once more?"

"For the sake of services rendered," smiled that kindly official, "you can. But you must promise me to turn it in to our people the minute you reach London."

Eve met me on the dock. We took the night boat across to Dublin together, and then went down through Sinn-Fein-ravaged Ireland to Killarney, where we stayed at Flesk Castle with her friends. On the lakes of Killarney I knew I had found what I wanted. We went down to Dingle and swam off Inch Strand. We hauled nets at night with the Irish peasant fishermen. Eve was really Irish herself. We went up on horseback through the Gap of Dunloe—riding within three yards of a Sinn Fein ambush that an hour later bush-whacked some British officers. And we caught dozens of the little spotted trout where the Flesk River flows through its osiers into the soft blues of Killarney Lake.

My partner Torsten came down from Sweden to be my best man. He stood there, quaking and cracking his knuckles while old Padre Chapman married us in the Chapel Royal of the Savoy. Chapman, who was a great friend of Eve's family, excelled himself on the benediction with which he blessed what he called this Anglo-American alliance. Then Eve and I took the night train for Southampton—and America.

I had just £100 in the wide, but now very interesting, world. I had the promise of a job—in South America. When we were half way across the Atlantic a wireless message informed me that the South American market had fallen flat. So had my job.

We got that news with the Marconi the steward brought in with our morning tea.

"Well," I said ruefully. "It looks as if we start from here at zero again!"

"We do!" laughed Eve. "And as I've been seasick up to now we are going to start with a good breakfast."

It was in such a mood that I brought an English girl to face the skyscrapers of New York.

Chapter 46

AMERICAN JOB AGAIN

NEW YORK. Much as I hated the thought of having to work there, I knew I would rather make a new start there than in any other city. Its tempo was so exhilarating. But we did not begin in New York.

The XYO Oil Co. offered me a job in India. I was all for it. But Eve, whose father had been Chief Commissioner of the Northwest Provinces, had been born in India; and she knew enough of that country to save me from taking a job in Madras. Then the company which had offered me the job in South America made me another offer

"*Chicago?*" I gasped.

"Why not—what's the matter with Chicago?"

My God, I thought; here is a man who has the nerve to ask me what is the matter with Chicago!

I went back and talked it all over with Eve. She had married me with the full knowledge that I did not have one penny in the world. That did not worry her in the least. And it was an unbelievably strengthening feeling to know that you were married to someone who would take any and all sorts of chances with you. But Chicago. . . . Eve's knowledge of Chicago, of course, was based strictly upon the reports of British newspaper writers, and visiting novelists who came to the United States to lecture us about Life.

"It sounds pretty grim!" she said. "Why not go out and look?"

"That's just what Fulton said," I told her. Fulton was the President of the Mack International Motor Company; and when I had shown my dismay about working in Chicago, he had immediately retaliated by expressing his doubts whether the Chicago manager would like me enough to give me a job. "You've got to go out and see Bob Black first," he said. "If you're O.K. with him, you're all right with me."

So I went.

One of the blackest nights of my life was spent in the Blackstone Hotel, where my modest room faced a shaft, down which some dirty snow was falling dismally. So, I thought, life has brought me to this—to Chicago!

The next morning I met the man whom I like and respect perhaps more than any other I know. No one would have guessed, to look at Bob Black now, that he had been one of the fastest quarter-milers in America as a schoolboy. Certainly, he would never have mentioned it. Nor would anyone guess that inside that comfortable, well-cushioned business man, smoking that long black cigar, was the heart of a romantic. Nor would they have known that this poetic soul of Bob's was functioning all through his business hours. To see him waving a cigar at you, you would never have guessed that.

"Times are pretty tough," he said, as the opening gambit of our conversation. It immediately put me into the position of having to press for a job.

"They are for me," I said. "But I've noticed they get better."

"Yes? What have you been doing?"

I told him—part of it.

Bob was Vice-President of the company, put out into the Middle West to kill off the competition. A great war was being waged among the four biggest motor-truck companies for the control of the Middle West. Who was going to dominate that market? It was the Golden Age of that industry. Anything went —so long as you made good—and as I looked at the man before me I thought of the battles the Chicago packers had fought out on the Western plains, when they deliberately sent out gunmen to shoot the poor sheep "nestors." And as we talked, salesmen came in and had interviews with the efficient, too efficient salesmanager in the office next to us, and the service station roared with the exhausts of the tremendous Mack Bulldogs that were the standard motor-truck for the United States Army. Great dump trucks lumbered out, destined for the roads and buildings that were springing up around Chicago. I heard one of the salesmen showing off the fine points of a giant motor to a Swede—a Swede who could hardly speak a word of English—buying a $6,000 long-distance delivery van.

"Have lunch with me," said Bob. "It's not my say-so whether you work here or not. Jelke is the sales-manager. You've got to pass him."

Jelke just about epitomised the one thing that frightened me most in the United States—he was a hundred per cent Go-Getter, a live-wire; and he read Correspondence School Courses on Salesmanship Efficiency. Nevertheless—he sold motor-trucks. I put a muzzle on myself, answered the questionnaire he put me through as meekly as possible, and sweating like a pig afterward, went down to the Princeton Club to have lunch with Bob Black.

That day, although it was the last thing that I could have imagined, began a friendship that I value more than any other I have ever made. I could not have suspected it at that luncheon; because, knowing his own inner sensitiveness, Bob Black went through life always "on guard." And so depressed was I with the idea of starting life all over again in Chicago, that I stopped off in Pittsburgh to see the only rich relative I have. At a twitch of his eyebrow all life could be made smooth for me. And it was the first time in my life that I felt like appealing to him.

I went to the Fort Pitt Hotel, took a room, and asked the telephone girl to put me through to his home. I waited there in a cold sweat at the booths.

"Number Thr-e-e, please!"

I picked up the phone, heard a voice at the other end, and put the phone back on the hook again.

"When," I asked the clerk at the desk, "does the next train leave for New York?"

"Er—aren't you keeping your room, sir?"

"No, I've changed my mind. . . . I mean, I'm giving it up."

"It's Chicago," I told Eve, as we ate our modest dinner in a little New York restaurant. "But now for our honeymoon!"

My father, incorrigible old water dog, was then enjoying the last of his yachts. She was a forty-foot motor-cruiser, the *Kirawan*. She had two cabins, a huge one amidships, with a neat galley and toilet forward and a little one aft, which Eve and I pre-empted. Then we went down the Delaware River, through the

Chesapeake and Delaware Canal, and passed out of that moss-overhung, dozing old cut into the Elk River and the open waters of the Chesapeake.

There was not a point or a town we passed, even the sleepy old wharves up almost forgotten creeks, that I did not know by heart and have some vivid association with. There were the same drowsy old locks along the canal, where I had first come through in *Nimrod*, and then time and again in the *Anna*. The sleepy farms whose fields ran down to the quiet wind-ruffled waters of the Elk. That great fourteen-mile-wide stretch where the Susquehanna, Elk and North rivers pour into the Chesapeake. There were the Chesapeake Bay "flats," one of the best duck and goose grounds in the world, where Ned Cochrane and I nearly lost our lives trying to cross them at midnight during a gale. The trees of Pool's Island, rising up out of the heat-haze, looking as they always did, as if they were floating in mid-air. . . . And there were the same old "niggers," with their dug-out canoes, crabbing off the Severn River at Annapolis. There was the same unbelievable stink from the phosphate works, the night we lay in harbour at Baltimore.

At Annapolis, the Naval Academy, my brother did the honours. He had had a regular commission in the U. S. Navy, and Annapolis was the pride of his eye. As well it might be, for it is one of the finest institutions of its kind in the world. My brother, realising my wife was English, showed her the only Royal Standard that had ever been captured from the British. It was hanging, most treasured, in Bancroft Hall. He showed her other things we had done to her countrymen—to all of which Eve remarked— "Oh, yes. How interesting," in a manner which made poor Enoch think she was bored to sobs. Finally, to shake her composure, he led us to a crypt.

"This," he said, "is the tomb of John Paul Jones!"

"And who," said Eve, "was John Paul Jones?"

"*What?*" My brother swayed and leaned against the mausoleum. "John Paul Jones! John Paul . . . Say!—have you ever heard of *Nelson?* Well, he was your John Paul Jones! John Paul

Jones!—never heard of him! My God, my God . . ." He stag-gered along beside us. . . .

Then at luncheon Enoch put his foot in it for fair. He was lecturing me on life. He always did that. He was two years my junior, but he was growing a moustache when he was twelve.

"You knock about too much. The trouble with you, Neg, is—you don't stay put. First you leave the United States and go to England. Then, after a couple of months—you go to Russia! Then, instead of joining the American Army, you join the British! And now look at you."

"Yes," said Eve, who had been sitting quietly through all this. "Do look."

"Er—what? I don't see what you mean?" Enoch looked at her rather warily. "I was just telling Neg. . . ."

"I don't see that you've done so much," said Eve. "Why were you such an idiot as to leave the Navy?"

"I—er—I'm married, you know."

I loved Enoch—when he was baffled like this. He was like a puppy that was being smacked because it was trying to be friendly. He had been telling me about life, all for my own good of course.

In Eve, I could see quite plainly, he realised that a new element had entered into our family. An element that had to be reckoned with. And, of course, it was the one thing to make Enoch like her.

"That girl's got a head on her!" he told me afterward. "But, my God—do you think she had *really* never heard about John Paul Jones?"

English schoolchildren, I told him, were kept in a state of the blackest ignorance regarding the loss of the American colonies.

My father, who knew nothing about motors, could always make the *Kirawan* start. Enoch, who had a genius for all things mechanical, went down below, touched the motor, and we were laid up for three days trying to restart it at the Naval Academy.

Eve outraged my father's sense of seamanship by jumping off the *Kirawan* in mid-ocean, whenever she felt like taking a swim.

Then I left the America that I adored and went back to New York again.

"Are you a salesman?" demanded the personnel officer in charge of the huge motor company's training school.

"I suppose so," I said.

"Well, how much better than a salesman are you? Are you a good enough salesman to sell Mack Trucks?"

I laughed outright at that remark.

"Are they as hard to sell as all that?" I asked.

He eyed me. Then he laughed:

"Listen, mister," he said, pointing a mock schoolmaster's finger at me. "You pay attention. There's a lot more to this motor-game than perhaps you expect. Do you, for instance, know anything about the cost of transportation?"

I did not. And when James L. Horine put on his heavy glasses, took his slide-rule out of his pocket, and started talking about running motor-bus lines all the way across the United States, and freight-feeders that would run 300 miles to feed railways out of at present desolate districts, I began to see those Mack Trucks climbing mountains, trundling across deserts, working like shuttles through the maze of city streets. I began to see all this as a new, perfectly concrete problem of scientific mechanics. An exact science that could be mastered!

And at once my heart warmed to my work.

Horine, and those transport engineers of the Mack Company, showed American genius at its best. He was just as glad as I was to drop all the footling sales talk. There were *facts* buried under this dense mass of ignorance over handling this new arm of transportation, the motor-truck, facts that were just as finite as those which underlay the working of railroads. Some of them had been already discovered and pointed out. Some were suspected. But there was a great field ahead of us that was totally unexplored. And we could be the pioneers.

I, of course, had to begin life in Chicago as a motor-truck salesman—in which I distinguished myself by selling exactly one motor-truck.

That was to a Swede, who couldn't talk English, whom I kept in the office by leaning my back against the door—with Bob Black waiting upstairs and missing his dinner until I completed the job.

"Yust von leetle thing," began the Swede for the hundredth time.

"Now, for God's sake, Swanson," I said. "Don't try to re-design our whole truck! You know it's the best in the world. It costs the most, doesn't it?—and we sell the most. And the body will be painted all in bright red, with a place for you to sleep in it over the driver's seat—and your name will be in big gold letters —SWANSON—S-W-A-N-S-O-N! Now you sign!"

"Yust a leetle minute . . ."

"Sign!"

Swanson signed.

"Now," I said, "you've got the best motor-truck in the world —and don't you forget it. You treat that truck well, and it will make a good living for you."

"Sure," grinned Swanson. "I knew dot all de time! Dot's why I came in here. I vos going to buy von, anyway. Dere's yust von leetle thing . . ."

Chapter 47

MARRIED LIFE

Eve, like most English people, was appalled by life in the United States—at first.

When I was taking my gimpy leg up and down Chicago, trying to sell motor-trucks, she looked for flats. On the specifications one night, she seemed to have found a possibility; the rent was unbelievably cheap. Then I looked at the address and saw that she had found us a flat directly in the centre of the Negro quarter out on Prairie Avenue.

"I'll have to carry a shot-gun to take us home at nights," I said to her. "Still—if you like it—we'll take it."

We did.

But, after we had agreed to take it, on the verbal statement of the real-estate agent that it would be put thoroughly in order, we found that he had not kept his word. It was just as the last Negro occupants had left it. And they had not been clean Negroes. I called on the real-estate agent.

"I said, 'As is,'" he said. "And 'As is' means 'As is'!"

"Does it?" I said, blowing up. "You old mutt! Give me my ten dollar deposit back."

"Nope," he said confidently, wagging his billygoat beard. "That ain't right. Deposit's mine."

"You filthy old crook!" I called him. "Give me that ten dollars —or I won't leave this place."

"Nope! Ten dollar's mine!"

I was sitting there, talking to him and telling him and his clerks what I thought of him, when Eve came in. She gave him a taste of some British shot and shell.

"You're a swindler," she said.

Eve thought of things to say that I could never have imagined. The real-estate agent's girl typists began to titter. He began to look very uncomfortable. Finally he snapped:

"Tell the cashier give these people their money back. Don't

344

want nothing to do with people like them. Never want to see them again!"

"You won't!" we told him.

Then we went over to Everett Avenue and took an apartment overlooking the cool lake that cost us just ten dollars a month less than I was making. Eve cooked her first meal for me, or indeed for anybody.

I hate to say this, but it was less than six weeks before Eve had jaundice and I was in hospital with a gastric ulcer.

I thought it was peculiar that we should be having cold lamb for dinner—without ever having had any hot lamb. So I mentioned this fact.

"Oh," said Eve. "*That* part of it I bought in a delicatessen shop."

Then, not having yet sold a motor-truck, and with a monthly rental that was just two pounds a month less than my whole salary, I asked the company to give me a motor-car. They did. "You're an expensive proposition!" they sighed, as they gave me a Ford coupé.

And that is how we got "Henry"—in which that first Sunday we drove a hundred miles out of·Chicago trying to find a real hill. This was not an easy time for either of us. We knew no one in Chicago and were really very poor by American standards. It was often a question whether I would buy a packet of cigarettes or not. We loathed the climate of Chicago, both winter and summer, and my leg was going to bits again on these city streets.

We spent eight months in Chicago at that time, during which I tried frantically and vainly to sell motor-trucks. It was a period of depression in the States, the 1921 panic, and everybody was afraid. Some days I made thirty calls, and was almost kicked out of most offices. I talked to every nationality on the face of the earth, now metamorphosing into what it thought was a hundred per cent American, and I might just as well state frankly that I detested most of them.

I was again and again to learn that truth: that nothing could be more brutish than the suddenly-successful emigrant in the United

States—unless it was that emigrant's son. Chicago was a maelstrom of wills, every person in it trying to impose his will on some other person.

It is not always the flower of European manhood that emigrates to America. Nine times out of ten it is the scum!

But my colleagues faced up to this with a sportive exuberance.

The flat on Everett Avenue survived. We took a boarder. We charged him fifty dollars a month for his room and would not even give him a cup of tea in the morning. He was a charming person, studying law at nights; and he used to sneak into his own room when he came in and saw that we had company, but apparently he had never slept in linen sheets before and was enraptured with ours. That gave us sixty dollars a month to live on. On the strength of that we hired a maid. The first was a Swedish girl, whose dreams of life in America had quite obviously been shattered. One morning she announced, "Ay tank Ay bane quit!" The next one was a negress, Bessie, who stuck it out with us to the end. I don't know where she had worked before, but she could never get over her confusion at having to bring our breakfast in to us in bed, and she would call my wife "Honey."

"Honey—does you all want waffle dis mawnin?"

She was charming.

Eve, of course, born in India where a clap of the hand or call of "*Qui hai!*" would bring twenty servants running to command, and then Ireland and England, where servants had been almost as plentiful, must have faced a terrific feminine ordeal at the housework which the average American woman is prepared to do herself. And Eve had a good healthy distrust of all labour-saving devices. She put the polish on our boarder's floor herself in our pre-maid era. Then, we were always just beating cheques to the bank—which was a new experience for Eve to whom an overdraft was like an earthquake. But in some miraculous fashion we never seemed to feel the pinch of life; we had lobster salad occasionally and took cheap seats at movies; and then one day when I got home I found that Eve had been crying.

This was something entirely new, but I almost bellowed too when I found the reason for it all.

An express man had arrived with a box, sent by *express* rate from England—charge $79.79. We just happened to have exactly $80 in the house, and Eve gave it to him. Then, seizing a meat chopper she had hacked open the case; as it was from her mother it must obviously be full of valuable things—things for our flat.

She found that it was full of books, her old books that she had been only too glad to leave in safety behind her. Also, about half of them were completely ruined with sea water.

"Our eighty dollars!" gasped Eve. "What shall we do for this month's rent?"

All I could mutter was: "And she sent them EXPRESS across the Atlantic!"

That case of books nearly sank us.

During all of this time, of course, my dud leg had to be dressed every morning. This was usually done by an interne at the American Veterans' Hospital on Biddle Avenue, and I would have been operated upon at that hospital had it not been for a lucky chance.

One day an advertisement appeared in the paper from two wounded American privates in the hospital, saying that they were both going to have a serious operation and they had been told they ought to go off somewhere and build up their strength first. Would someone please loan them a car so that they could go off and spend a couple of months in the country.

We decided to give them "Henry."

It was a pang to give up Henry. He saved my life in the hot streets during the daytime; and he saved both of our lives on the hot nights when we used to drive far out from the roar and smells of the packing works and find a real tree and lie under it. So we went down to the Biddle Hospital with a strong feeling of martyrdom.

"Yeah?" said a be-goggled doctor in its office. "And what do *you* want—see that sign?—this ain't visiting hours."

"I know," I said, handing him the advertisement we had seen in the paper asking for an automobile. "I came to see those two men."

"Well, you gotta come at three o'clock—see?"

I told him I could not. I had to work in an entirely different part of Chicago.

"Well, that's nothing to do with my life!" he said. "Three o'clock is three o'clock."

"But what about these two men; am I to be allowed to give them my car, or am I not?"

"I told you once. Three o'clock is three o'clock. This is an Army hospital."

"Yes," I said, "it sounds like it."

That saved me. When the interne at the out-patients' ward of Biddle Hospital told me my leg was getting in such a state that the bone was dying again I wrote to London.

In three weeks a letter came back telling me that the Canadian medical authorities would forward me full first-class passages for myself and wife to Toronto. We went to Toronto where they treated us with the old familiar decency, and, when Eve told them that she had friends in Montreal, they gave us further tickets there instead.

In Montreal I was operated upon by Doctor Keenan, D.S.O., surgeon to "Strathcona Horse" in the South African war, doctor of "Princess Pat's" in the World War. I had a private room in the Royal Victoria Hospital that would have cost a private patient fifteen dollars a day. And I was told to stay there until I felt good and well.

And here I got a letter from the Mack Motor-truck Company in Chicago—*enclosing three months' advance salary!*

"Don't worry. Your job will be waiting," it said. "Hope this little cheque will see you through all right. . . ."

If I seem a little rough on the American post-war hospital treatment of soldiers it is not without reason, the treatment that most of the returned soldiers were forced to put up with was disgraceful and the graft of the Army hospital under the Harding administration shocked the country when it was brought to light. In Montreal, after I had been in hospital for two and a half months and asked them what I owed them, I was presented with a bill for four dollars for some newspapers. This is the kind of treatment that soldiers will not forget if it is ever a question of fighting for Canada again.

In the treatment of war cases I believe that international commissions found Canada to stand ace high in this regard, and the United States rock bottom.

In Canada began two of the most glamorous years of our lives —beachcombing in British Columbia.

Chapter 48

BEACHCOMBING IN B.C.

WE ARRIVED in B. C. with just $30 left in the wide world, but we had my shotgun, a couple of trout rods and a typewriter; and with a bit of luck we felt that we could get along pretty well in that part of the world on those. We had to, in fact. Now was the time, I said to Eve, when some of my useless virtues would have to make good.

I had always said that the only three things I was any good at were no use at all as far as making money was concerned. My passion for sailing, shooting and fishing had brought me nothing else but trouble up to date. On the other hand, I would rather fish than eat; and I had always felt that one day these three early fevers of mine would come in useful. This apparently was the day. It was a case where, if I didn't shoot or fish we just jolly well wouldn't eat! Such being the case, we felt utterly unconcerned. With Eve's passion for home-making we knew we could take care of ourselves in the woods.

We had scandalised both our families and our friends by this B. C. adventure.

"But people don't do such things!"

"Some do," said Eve.

It was all so unorthodox. People seemed to take it as a matter of course that life was business and business was life, and that a life in the city was therefore the ordained order of things. The woods they regarded as a place where a person went on a vacation or a hunting trip. But to live there . . .

"You aren't *serious?*"

"Serious as hell," I assured them.

To make our B. C. expedition seem less fantastic I explained that my doctor had ordered me to go out somewhere and live in the open sun. He had in fact admitted that it was a toss up whether another bone operation would do me any good or wreck my much-hacked-about leg entirely. He also said that hammer-

350

ing it about on hot city pavements would be fatal. Which was all the moral support we needed to turn our backs flatly on city life.

So from the Royal Victoria Hospital in Montreal we sent a telegram to Eve's "Uncle Dick."

Uncle Dick was one of four brilliant Irish brothers. One was Bram Stoker, red-bearded, eccentric, who wrote that horror *Dracula*, and who had been Henry Irving's manager; another was Sir Thornley Stoker, the Dublin surgeon, Surgeon to the King, and a great connoisseur; the third was Thomas Stoker, my father-in-law, who after twenty-five years in India had retired as Chief Commissioner of the Northwest Provinces. He was blind by the time I had become engaged to Eve; Bram and Thornley were dead; and he said of Uncle Dick:

"I've got a brother. He's mad. Lives in a hut like a Red Indian . . . somewhere on an island off the coast of British Columbia!"

Uncle Dick, I learned, was a retired Indian Army Colonel, who on his way home from India to settle in Tasmania had seen Vancouver Island and immediately given up all idea of living anywhere else. It was symbolical of Uncle Dick's hatred of show that, although he was a full colonel in the Indian Army, he was always called, and appeared to have no other personality, than Dr. Stoker. He had never even completed his homeward trip to Dublin. That was some forty years ago. None of his family had laid eyes on him for over fifty years; but once every year, around Christmas time, when the cockles of his heart thawed a little, the old Irishman wrote an annual letter saying that someone of the family really ought to come out and visit him. And this time we took him up on it.

Uncle Dick, I also learned, had spent some twenty years of his life in Tibet, and in the days of his youth, in Ladakh, had enjoyed the unusual sensation of being under bow-and-arrow fire.

He showed me these arrows out in British Columbia, dangling among his salmon rods. He was mad, I suppose, by conventional standards. But he was nothing to the recluses around him, all of whom in their own fashion—and for their own private reasons— were living lives that defied every convention in existence.

Perhaps the one thing that really clinched the B. C. adventure was Eve's passion for mountains. When we saw the Canadian Rockies at dawn from Calgary, Eve had been sitting up all night to catch the final glimpse of them; and we sat there all day in the tail of the observation car, completely enraptured with our own futures.

We had a bit of trouble in Vancouver city itself. The Canadian army medical authorities had "boarded" me there. Being surgeons, they immediately wanted to operate. I had feared this. Everything hung upon whether they would let me go, and give me back my small wound pension. I could see that it positively pained them to let such a marvellous chance for a bone-graft experiment slip through their hands. While they were fighting with their better natures we saw that our $30 was gone! A few days in its sumptuous hotel had already put us in pawn to the Canadian Pacific Railroad. Part of our reasons for being so broke, I might say, was that Eve's bag was snatched on a Montreal tramway, with $150 of our precious capital in it. Then the doctors' better nature won out.

Two nights later, with shotgun, rods and typewriter, we stood on the shore of a mountain lake in the heart of Vancouver Island. For the first time we faced that long, lovely, lonely stretch of water on which we were to live for two years.

It is essential to see the background of the B. C. tapestry. The woods out there have a feeling that is different from any other forest on earth. It is chiefly a feeling of freshness. The trees are old; there was a stand of giant fir at the head of the lake whose ten-foot thick trunks had been saplings when Columbus set out for America. They were like a great woodland cathedral, with massive pillars rising to a hundred or two hundred feet before the branches began to make its ceiling. Yet a herd of elk roamed through this with all the freshness, and curiosity, of the fifth day of Creation.

The rivers and the forests and the mountains are peopled with the legends and ghosts of the Siwash Indians who believe in the Salmon god, and that if a squaw eats salmon eggs she could be turned into stone; men who still dance with beaked, wooden masks on their faces to Tootich, the Thunder Bird, who used to carry whole whales up to the mountain tops to eat them. Eve and I had the luck to see the last *potlatch*, we think, where the Haida Indians danced to their heraldic totems of wolf, bear and eagle; and Old Louis, the Chief, gave all his wealth away in Hudson Bay "four-stripe" blankets and phonographs to acquire merit in the future world. The Canadian Government puts them in jail for doing that!

Yet all this was fresh. The legends and ghosts, and some very material Siwash Indians were still there. But they did not give the slightest feeling of time. Watching the dawn arise far up the Robinson River, I had the feeling that I was the first white man to see this scene. And, as far as that particular spot was concerned, I very likely was.

This freshness of B. C. gave life itself a quality that was like being reborn.

I can only say that when an Englishman and I later tried to find an unused trail to cross the main range of the Caucasus, everything we found down there seemed both old and *used*. We rode for four weeks without ever once seeing a road. Part of this time we rode with a tribe of Turco-Tartars who had hardly changed a utensil since the days of Jenghiz Khan. We rode with them through the passes, with their great herds of horses and cattle in search of grass; great, trackless forests bedded with unbelievable yellow azaleas—yet every tree and flower seemed old. The dust of Asia's centuries was heavy over everything. And among the strange tribes that we found in the pockets of isolated valleys were some sullen primitives who went about in chain armour, with round metal shields on their backs; men who carried swords and had seven Crosses on their kaftans—although they could not tell you why. Some wandering Crusaders could have told you a story! But these people would not have been interested in it. They were old and weary with their scene. Nothing fresh and new would come out of their life—except, perhaps, the Bolsheviki!

Another thing about this life in the woods of B. C. was that though a family could live comfortably on £ 10 a month it was almost impossible to make it there.

But these were the things that we discovered later on—just the way I discovered that Shaw Creek in the upper lake had rainbows that weighed six pounds lying thick as sardines off its bouldered mouth. Our first sight of that lake on which we were to spend the next two years of our lives was just the long plaque of gun-metal water at the foot of which was an unpainted, plank shack that was both the local general store and post office. Below it, lying along the high bank of the river pool, where the lake prepared to pour down thirty mountainous miles to the sea, was one of the strangest communities I have ever seen.

These were the "house-boaters," a colony that lived in pine shacks that had been built on rafts of huge cedar logs. This relatively urban community was, in fact, the real working population of the lake. On one raft, in a shack with lace curtains at its windows, lived the hatchery-man, English "gentleman" from Penshurst, married to the storekeeper's pretty sister; the next two rafts held Swedish loggers; on the next was another English gentleman, a "Remittance Man," this one; and in the handy little outfit dwelt Ken, local martin trapper, and most dangerous poker-player on the Island.

With the exception of the Remittance Man these people all had a vocation in the woods. And coming down among them on mail days, after a long run down the lonely lake, the sight of so many people talking together at one time always gave me the impression of coming up to town.

These houses built on rafts had all the amenities of a house on shore—plus mobility. They had wood-piles and chopping blocks out on their rafts; one or two had porches around them, with railings to prevent babies from falling into the swift water; and every one had its flower boxes. I saw sweet peas and nasturtiums in full bloom on those house-boats when I arrived in October.

This house-boat colony had a form of social life of its own, where, if one felt talkative, one could either cross a gang plank or walk along shore to the next house-boat. But above them social intercourse as such simply ceased to exist. The remaining twenty miles of that lake were inhabited by five of the most dramatically different families one could conceive of. And each one seemed to have settled as far from the other one as it could get. Each family had its own "story" and as a result its own hospitable, aloof or even hostile personality.

About four miles up, in a slash of dead-woods, was the *schloss* of Captain von Hauptmann, ex-officer in the Kaiser's army, whom the French wife of the English game warden insisted simply must have done something queer out in German East Africa. Hauptmann, who was bearded to his navel, went about in an abbreviated khaki costume which was open in front to his waist, belted, and pinned with a safety pin to resemble a kilt. There was nothing underneath. Below decks his hairy legs were encased in calf-high Siwash moccasins. On his shaven pate he wore a jaunty Basque beret. That was when he was dressed. Usually he went about his place naked, which was a great surprise to passing trout fishers; and he sent a photograph of himself this way to Chicago and won a beauty prize. Captain von Hauptmann was a man.

He was, in his sullen, unpopular, and disregarded way, the most powerful personality on the lake. As time makes the others grow dim he becomes ever more vivid in my mind.

Across the lake from him, and hating him like poison, lived the game warden and his French wife. The game warden had been postmaster general, or something like that out in British Nigeria. Blackwater fever bowled him out of Africa and his career. He and his French wife had been living for years in a nine by eighteen foot floating shack. They were the *literati* of the lake. But as Titheredge would never call a cormorant anything other than a *corvus marinus*, sea-crow, conversation with that family was difficult without a dictionary. When he got on the subject of trout flies I realised that conversation with him was impossible. Our relations were a state of armed truce that kept up until I left the lake.

I poached deer out of season just to ease my feelings about Titheredge.

"What's this!" said Titheredge, eating luncheon with old Dr. Stoker. "Why, this is *deer* liver!"

"Sure it is! What did you think it was?"

"But—"

"Isn't the season open?"

"Yes . . . but . . ."

Titheredge, to give him credit, was too fond of the old gentleman to embarrass him by asking how he came to have deer liver, when the season had only opened at daybreak that morning. But the Doctor was inwardly furious. I had given him the liver, and he had accepted it unthinkingly.

"You mustn't do things like that!" said the Doctor to me afterwards. "Damn it all, man—think of Titheredge's conscience!"

About four miles above Captain von Hauptmann lived an English "rancher," heir (except for three healthy elder brothers) to one of the oldest peerages in England, living as far away from his creditors at home as possible. The most peculiar thing about his *ménage* was that for some three months of the year, in the rainy season, it was nine feet under water. He did not discover this until after he had bought it—from an advertisement in an English sporting periodical. When he did realise it, he realised it every year, with the result that he soon built a house on stilts, like the South Sea Islanders. But on top of this, his wife, gallant daughter of a gallant British general, had made a little bit of old England itself. Open fireplace, chintz chair covers, Georgian silver, the *Sketch*, *Tatler*, and *Bystander* lying on the drawing-room table beside a tea that might have been laid out in any "county" home.

Algy Cunwall was one of those Englishmen whom the war and a changing sense of values was driving out of British life. He was a country gentleman of the purest type, a man simply bred to inherit and inhabit a country estate. His entire knowledge was limited to horses, hounds, and the shooting and rearing of pheasants. Before the war he had been an estate agent to a peer. In coming out to B. C. to "ranch" he had merely fulfilled the traditional exile of a British younger son. He was shocked by the swindle that had been perpetrated upon him in the sale of the submerged ranch, and made cynical thereby; for Algy, as soon as he saw his plight, inserted in all British sporting publications a duplicate of the advertisement that had inveigled him into buying this dubious stretch of sub-aqueous land.

Another Englishman rose like a trout and paid Algy's lawyers in England his life savings to purchase a half share in the British Columbia "ranch" . . . "splendid pheasant, grouse, deer and bear shooting, with two salmon rivers on the estate," etc.

He could have got salmon, he soon saw to his horror, from the drawing-room window.

He was Algy's unwilling, lugubrious partner when we came out to B. C.—tied by the leg to a ranch that was under water for three months of every year.

His useful life had been spent planting tea in Ceylon. Now all he did on the useless ranch was saw wood, wash dishes, walk about glowering at the scenery, and mend holes in his high white rubber boots. He was called "the Pessimist," as well he might be! An occasional day of trout fishing was his only divertissement. To make matters worse for him, he had to be pleasant at meals when Nancy Cunwall invited people up from Victoria during the summer months.

Above the Cunwalls' was the place of old Tread. Old Tread claimed:

"A man can keep alive, but not much more. I guess I've raised everything that can grow, crawl, fly or flap in Creation—and I've gone broke on all of them. Now, with my teeth gone, I'm right back here on the shore of the lake where I started from. And that's over forty years ago."

Tread came from Canterbury originally, where rumour had it he was related to the Archbishop; and when I asked him what had held him out in B. C., fighting the jungle all these years, Tread gazed off to where the mountains were just a haze in the golden sunset.

"Well . . . I don't exactly know . . . maybe it's been because I've always been my own boss."

Tread was the only *bona-fide* settler in the region. He was also the first white man to come to the lake. With an axe, saw, rifle, and his entire worldly wealth, he had walked up the Siwash trail some forty odd years before. On the exact spot where his greatly enlarged log cabin now stood he had tried to hack himself a plantation out of the woods. It was so thick, so impenetrable with its neck-high choking undergrowth of salal bushes, that for the first years he decided to live on a raft. All one summer he worked alone in the forest, felling huge cedar trees so that they pitched into the lake water; and on these logs he built the first house-boat. Then he went back down the trail.

He came back with a young bride, daughter of a retired naval captain; and on that raft, on a bed made of straw like a Greater before them, his two sons were born. Tread was himself the midwife; there were no doctors in that part of the world. They cooked on a square of dirt placed on the floor of their shack, the smoke going out through a hole in its roof, just like a Siwash fireplace. And, when Tread and his young wife grew bored with any particular view, they would simply pull up their house-boat's moorings and let it drift—just to see where they would wake up in the morning.

When we first saw them, their two sons were eighteen and twenty-one years old. The log cabins had now become several log cabins joined together to form a sort of rambling house. The smoothly polished log walls were poignant with the childhood of the two boys; there were the horns of the first deer that Peter and Tom had shot; there were treasured collections of birds' eggs (in a glass case now); there was a pathetic library of the literature that children read, early books of adventure and derring-do sent out by friends from far-off England; and—there were school books. The Tread boys had never been to school; old Tread and his wife had taught them by first carefully poring over the school books themselves. "That's the way I learned algebra all over again!" chuckled old Tread.

Peter had never been further afield than Victoria, to which vast metropolis he journeyed when the Treads once bought an old second-hand donkey-engine in a logging venture. Tom, who was so silent nowadays, had volunteered at seventeen to go to the Great War.

"Tom has never been the same since he came back," was the

curious mutter of old Tread. "Something must have happened to Tom in France."

Whatever it was Tom did not say. He had (and that certainly should have made him talkative) ended up the war as a sergeant-major in one of the toughest Canadian regiments. But whether he had received some nerve-shock in battle, or whether he was finding this lonely life in the woods almost unbearable after the dissolute life of a soldier in Europe, one never knew. We never shall know, because poor Tom was killed by a falling tree almost on the day we left the lake.

If, in their pathetic efforts to win the heart of the pretty young Cunwall daughter, both Peter and Tom tried to court her by showing what good rifle shots they were . . . well, to excel in such virtues was their idea of what made a man desirable in woman's eyes, much as a city gallant would drive by in his sporty motor-car.

That these courtships were both hopeless can be judged from the constant assertion of Aline Cunwall to her own pretty self— "I'm going to go back to England—and I am going to dance with the Prince of Wales."

She did.

The saga of the Treads could be told from their clearings back in the forest. In the days of Tread's prime he had hacked huge acres for himself out of the pressing jungle. Then as his strength began to wane, the jungle took its own back. As his two sons grew to strength they fought with the jungle to win their fields back again. One day, when I had been trout-fishing off their river and we had dropped in at the Treads' for tea, Peter came dashing out of the woods and rushed back with his rifle. Half an hour later he returned to announce that he had shot a bear in one of their clearings. The poor bear had been so absorbed eating black-berries that it had been waiting there when Peter got back.

Characteristic of Tread life was the fact that the three men immediately set off for the clearing to bring back the "meat." Some of it was kept fresh to be eaten after it had "hung" for a few days. The rest was carefully salted and stowed in a cellar-pit, made by a spring near the log house.

"Meat for the winter!" mumbled old Tread. "But not for me!"

He was toothless now, living on soft-boiled eggs, and rarely ventured back into the heart-breaking jungle which he had fought from sunrise to sunset all his life. He spent most of his days studying Eugene Christian's diet course—*Eat and Grow Thin.*

"Guess I'm skinny enough!" he said ruefully. "But I've got something wrong with my insides."

As I said, the lake was twenty miles long, which gave it a total shore-line of some fifty or sixty odd miles. On this left shore, within ten miles, lived this strange assortment of people. There was also a hermit, bobbing in one of the most ramshackle house-boats on the lake: "Old Louis," the French-Canadian trapper who could neither read nor write. It was one of the weirdest sensations of my life, having to spell out the letters—T-O-B-A-C-C-O to Old Louis, and then tell him what they meant. He knew the brand of tobacco only by the shape of the tin; tomatoes had a tomato on the front, so did corn, pears, and peaches, to which last Old Louis was very partial.

But Old Louis could glance at a patch of shore mud, and tell you a beaver had passed, how big the beaver was, and how many hours back he had gone by.

In the thirty forested, irregular miles of the right shore had once lived a remittance man, up the lonely North Arm. He had been paid two dollars a day by his relatives in Ireland never to come home. Four times a year he rowed down to the store to get this remittance and get drunk. But he had been found dead in his blankets two winters before we saw the lake.

"Been a heavy snow," said the trapper, Ken, who had led the search party over Bald Mountain to find the corpse. "But when the letter had been waiting there for him about two weeks we knew that something must be up! He was dead all right—never saw such a sight!"

They found hundreds of whiskey bottles stuck in the earth to line the path Mead had made through his apple orchard.

But, added Ken, one could tell that Mead had been "a gentleman once."

"Now how on earth could you tell that?"

"By his blankets—they were black. His whole cabin showed that Old Mead had never learned how to take care of himself! That man had been used to servants, walking around and picking things up after him, he had!"

Now the only person who lived on that lonely right bank was Uncle Dick.

The hut, which my father-in-law had so contemptuously spoken about in London before he died, turned out to be a solid bungalow, built in a weird mixture of Indian and backwoodsman style. It was constructed of huge, peeled logs; but it was all built around one high central room, in which, during the winter, water would freeze on the table within ten feet of the fire.

For forty years, after India, Uncle Dick had lived in this with Aunt Sue, going down in the winter to a real house he had built among the English retired Service officers in their colony thirty miles below.

Aunt Sue, once a blue-eyed Dublin girl, had left Ireland in her teens to go out to India to marry Uncle Dick. She had seen some twenty exciting years of Tibet, but she had never once in her life been inside a theatre or even seen an aeroplane. Aunt Sue cut out the advertisement for *lingerie* in the *Tatlers*, *Bystanders* and *Sketches* that Nancy Cunwall sent her before she passed them on to the next settler on the lake. She thought they were improper.

They were Irish, and therefore witty old Uncle Dick and Aunt Sue could never have been called mid-Victorian, as was their epoch. They were two of the most charming and exhilarating old people I have ever met. They lingered on a few days at the lake to initiate us into the mysteries of their estate. Then they left us with their cabin, a kitten that was just learning to walk, and a hundred tins of pea-powder soup to face our first winter in B. C.

"Put the milk on your finger," advised Aunt Sue in parting, instructing me how to mix the milk-powder she had left. "The kitten will have to take it that way first."

"And don't let the coons get it!" warned Uncle Dick. "The coons ate Titheredges' last cat. And Mrs. T. hasn't got over it yet." Brushing aside many thanks, they handed over to this unknown niece and alien nephew practically everything they had in the world.

Chapter 49

THE LONELY CABIN

WE WERE never lonely in our two years in B. C., although, aside from my weekly row down to the store for mail and supplies, there were weeks on end when we did not see a living soul. We got to a point when we did not want to see anybody. The tempo of our own lives had become so silently geared that it was a positive jar to have someone break in on us. It was a strain to have to make conversation, or listen to anyone else's. After a few months our life of splendid isolation made us so *farouche* that far from wanting company, we shunned it.

To get at us people would have to come across the lake, as we were the only people who lived on our side of the lake and there was no road to us. When we saw them coming we would often make off into the woods. The forest of pine and fir was so thick behind us that there were no trails through its choking undergrowth. The first winter we were there two timber cruisers lost their lives in it. They had tried to take a short cut down the lake from the ridge of Bald Mountain, but they were unable to get through the woods and finally fell exhausted in a snowstorm. They were not found until spring when the back of one of them appeared through the melting snow. The other man was found in the hollow of a rotted tree. They were less than three hundred yards from an old clearing.

I have shot a pine grouse from Uncle Dick's clearing, seen it fall and carefully marked the spot, and yet been unable to find it when I got there. The thing that made these B. C. woods so difficult to penetrate was the floor of fallen trees. They had been falling and piling up one across another and rotting there since history began, and through these was a dense growth of salal berries. Trappers, for instance, would never go over into the Nitinat country except in pairs, as a man would surely die in that jungle if he broke his leg. Up there in a hollow tree was found a skeleton with an old flintlock rifle and a broken leg. It must have been one of John Jacob Astor's fur-trading expedition, which was massacred by the Indians.

"But what did you do all the time out there?" was the inevitable question from our friends when we eventually did come back to Chicago. My answer was that I probably worked harder in B. C. and read more books at nights than I ever had in any city. Our friends sent us most of the new novels from London or New York, and we subscribed to the New York *Times* Literary Supplement and to the London weekly *Times;* and, of course, everybody on the lake passed their reading matter on to everyone else, so that we had quite a good little circulating library of our own.

Cutting firewood alone was a full-time job, because, of course, we had to use it for both cooking and keeping our cabin or house-boat warm. In the winter we had our little iron kitchen-range going all day long.

It was my task to cook the breakfasts. It was a bitter job in winter to have to get up in the cold and start that fire. But it was grand when the spring came along. After I had put on the coffee to boil, and a few strips of bacon, I would take a quick swim overside. We used no bathing suits in that part of the world. After breakfast I sat down at the typewriter and tried to earn our living, while Eve worked in the garden she was always making somewhere on shore. When we had our house-boat we even had a garden on the end of its cedar raft. We filled the interstices between the logs with brush on which we carted sacks of dirt. We grew lettuce and radishes there. Always being watered this way the lettuce shot up like the trees, and the radishes were hot as pepper.

After lunch I considered that I had earned my day and then, if I did not chop firewood, I went out in the skiff to fish or shoot. One of the great tragedies of living in this lake, so far from the sea, was that the salmon were already so far with spawning by the time that they got there, that we hardly ever caught one that was fit to eat. My first one, which weighed 12½ lbs., I caught in a squall at the mouth of the Robinson River. I took some forty minutes to land him, and by that time I was a physical wreck from sheer nerve-strain. But when I got him into the boat I saw that he was too far gone to eat. At least I thought so, but Captain von Hauptmann's wife took it and boiled it, and preserved it.

Twice a week, when we were not frozen in, or on some shooting or fishing expedition up the lake, I rowed five miles down to the store for our mail and supplies from the Hudson Bay Co. For about nine months of the year our main food was supplied by my shotgun and fishing rods. But there were always such groceries as coffee and tea, and sugar and salt. And in the winter we bought eggs by the gross and huge sides of bacon, which were sent up from Victoria.

The store was the general meeting place and gossip centre of the lake, and, according to the seasons, I always took a rod or my shotgun with me on the row down. Trolling the five miles down and back, I could nearly always count on a couple of rainbow or cut-throat trout for dinner. One day, waiting in the pool below the store for the auto to come up from the railroad with the mail, I got three salmon: 12½, 8½, and 7½ lbs.

When the duck season was on I would row down close along shore and put up the mallards from the patches of water lying back among the trees. They made beautiful shots as they came out over the trees. One day when Eve came down with me to the store, feeling that she wanted some social life for a change, I got a couple of golden-eye ducks and one widgeon, and Eve got the best trout we caught in B. C. It was a 6¼ lb. rainbow.

One sunset I had a grand surprise. It was snowing and I had been shooting golden-eye at the mouth of Bear Creek. This was a short stream of water between a little isolated lake and the big main lake. The ducks were lying in the lonely inner lake, and, as they always follow the water when they are put up, I was firing an occasional shot to put them up and then shooting at them as they came out. I had been overboard once, up to my armpits, trying to get a wounded mallard that got away from me in the flooded underbrush, and when the snow set in in earnest I was just preparing to row for home.

Then I saw something coming into Bear Lake through the

sunset. As it came at me, it cocked its wings and I knew that it was a big game-bird of some sort. I shot at it as it was whistling straight at me, but my little 16 ga. did not seem to phase it. Then, as it swept past, I lurched around and shot it in the trousers. It fell with an enormous splash. When I rowed up in the darkness to retrieve it the first thing I saw was that tell-tale white "V" on its neck.

"A Canada goose!" went my yell into the lonely pines of Bear Lake.

The five-mile row home was nothing now. I saw the square of light shining from the cabin, for we lived on shore that first winter. As I opened the door I called to Eve:

"Put plenty of wood on, make a good fire; for tonight we eat." Not only did we eat. We ate that whole goose.

One day when I got my mail at the store I found a little square envelope instead of the usual rejection slips I had been beginning to collect at an alarming rate. In it was a cheque for $150 for a short story I had written on Egypt. That $150 meant three months' good living at least. At a pinch we could have stretched it out for more. One Scotsman's bill at the store was only $85 for a whole year. That was the same day that I caught the three salmon. As I rowed back that sunset I felt that I was truly bringing something home to Eve. Our experiment of trying to live out in B. C. was working out all right. It was that night that we decided to take a house-boat of our own.

Chapter 50

SWANSON, THE BIG SWEDE

ONE WINDY sunset of that first autumn I was standing on the point of our place meditating whether I would try the sunset flight of ducks or see if I could get one last rainbow trout in the evening rise. Food of some sort was essential. As I stood there I heard the roar of a motor-boat coming down lake, then a shot, not a hundred yards around the point from me, and the sound of the motor stopped.

A few minutes later Swanson, the Swede, came around the bend in his skiff with the old Buick automobile motor in it. And across Swanson's bows dangled a nice fat buck.

"Yust picked him up!" grinned Swanson, who had seen the deer standing on a rise. "Damn fool yust stood there looking at me. Couldn't help it."

The apology, it might be said, was because Swanson had thus shot a fine deer two weeks before the deer season legitimately opened.

"Seen the game warden?" asked the huge Swede anxiously.

Titheredge, I told him, had been at my place not an hour back. He had gone off in his boat somewhere. I did not know where he was.

"Dot's bad. Catches me with this an' I'm for it, I am! Say, will you help me cut dis feller up?"

We slung the deer in our wood-shed and with our axe we soon turned that lovely, brown-eyed creature into chunks of red venison. Then we sank the hide and antlers in the lake. Then we washed our hands and the axe.

"Well, dot's done!" grinned Swanson. "Dot game warden gives me a pain in de ass."

When he roared off down lake again in his home-made motor-boat Swanson had given me the liver and chops.

I was a little annoyed at first. I had an idea that the haunch of venison was the best part of the beast. But, as I discovered the minute I tasted it, the liver—made pungent by eating salal berries —is the most prized part of a deer in B. C. And the chops are the tenderest. For being an accomplice to his crime Swanson had given me all the best parts of his kill.

We soon became bosom friends.

Swanson had a *saga*. He had come out to the West Coast eighteen years before—184 days around Cape Horn, in a windjammer from England's Hull. In the ice off the Horn—"Cape Stiff," Swanson called it—the Captain's wife died. "Chips" made a coffin, lined it with copper, and "we pickled her in whiskey!" But she leaked! Steering on dark nights, said Swanson, he never could get his mind off that floating corpse in its box, lashed just forward of the wheel. Off Cape Stiff, also, they had had a near mutiny. Ice and seas smashed open the forecastle, and in his wet blankets the oldest member of the crew began to die. The sailors in a body went aft and begged the officers to take the injured old seaman, Saul, into their cabin. But the bucko mate drove them forward with his revolver. "We just didn't have no guts!" explained Swanson sorrowfully. Old Saul died, and was slid into the icy seas. The battered barque crept up the West Coast of South America. But young Swanson brooded upon things. . . .

"Dot first mate!" said Swanson. "He knew I didn't like him anyway! He was always making life hell for me!"

At San Francisco the barque lay beside some old oil tanks, her bowsprit extending over the street.

"So I says, 'Here's for it!' When the mate comes along I lets him have it—right in the ribs!"

Swanson stuck a knife into the detested first mate, ran up the bowsprit, and dropped—into America.

For eighteen years since that day he had been wandering the West Coast from San Francisco up to Fort Yukon in Alaska. When I asked him what he had been doing all those years, the huge Swede grinned:

"Yennerally I was yust huntin' a yob!"

When I got to know him, Swanson was "push" (foreman) of a little Swedish logging outfit—five husky Swedes who had managed to get hold of an almost exhausted donkey-engine. And Swanson lived in one of the finest little house-boats on the lake. Its brightly painted shack was surrounded with flower boxes brilliant with sweet peas, nasturtiums and a much-treasured rose.

Beside it, stuck on the bank where its builders had left it, was another almost-completed house-boat, whose two Swedish owners had just gone off into the Peace River Country on a gold rush. I told Swanson I wanted it, when I found that he had been left in charge. How much?

"Well"—Swanson scratched his hairy chest over his first real-estate transaction—"do you tink $10 a month would be asking too much?"

It was, in fact. But I did not yet know the scale of values in B. C.; so I told Swanson I would take it.

"But," I exclaimed, pointing to the solid forty-foot raft of huge cedar logs so high and dry on the bank. "How can we ever get it into the water? I want to take it about six miles up lake."

There was a lonely bay I had had my eye on up there, an elbow in the mountain where nobody would be within five miles of us.

"Ho!—dot's nothin'!" exulted Swanson in his strength. "Me and a couple of oder fellers'll yust get a yack and yump her off in de morning!"

The next day I watched five Swedes, with their jack and peevies, slide our new home into the lake. The winter was just breaking; and that night, after an all day tow, we moored *Mole End* in her quiet bay.

Chapter 51

A CYCLE OF BRITISH COLUMBIA

THE NEXT day I started to work. With an axe, I entered the forest, picked a slim fir and drove the blade deep into the wood.

My first task was to fell three trees that I wanted for mooring booms to keep my house-boat fixed permanently off shore. Being single-handed I had to pitch the big trees so that they fell into the water. I dropped the first one so close to the house-boat that I raised a scream from Eve who was staining the floors inside, and who thought that this time she was done for. We fixed our floating home a little too permanently in one spot in fact, for when a sudden cold spell halted the melting of the snows, the lake fell swiftly one night, and we stuck.

It was about two o'clock in the morning when we first felt that sickening bump that told us we were aground. Feeling over the side with a push pole we saw that we had about four feet of water all around. We should have had at least a foot of clear water under us, but still we experienced those dull mysterious bumps. There was nothing for it but to strip and go overside for a look. It was one of the coldest jobs of my life when, stark naked, I dropped off into the ice-water and did a quick submarine crawl under our craft. I found that a submerged tree stump was jammed between the underside of our cedar logs. By standing in four feet of water and pushing the brute, I moved our house-boat along until she was clear. Then we took up some more of our outlying booms and rode in safe water again. If I had not freed her, we would soon have been left at an angle against the shore—for the rest of the year. When what was left of my frozen body managed to crawl back on to our raft, Eve, who was holding a lantern through all this, shrieked with laughter at my goose-fleshy hide.

"You look like a pickle!" she said.

That was one of the things that could happen to us on the house-boat. The other, strangely enough, was that she would nearly sink under the deep snows. When the Thirty-Year blizzard came the next year I spent several nights staying awake and every hour or so going out to scrape the snow off our roof and shovel it overside. And, as Eve is seasick if she even sees a steamer's sailing list, she had rather a bad time of it when a gale came down lake.

While I worked on the shore, Eve worked in our home. For $1.50—the same price I paid for my trousers, marked "Pride of the West"—she had bought oak stain and brushes at the store; and she coloured our doors, floor and window-sills a warm brown. This gave a sort of English half-timber effect to our home and killed the hard glare of fresh wood. She made little curtains of checked gingham for our windows and she filled boxes with earth, tacked slabs of bark over them, and planted sweet peas and nasturtiums.

The shack on the raft had two rooms, with, oddly enough for that part of the world, several large windows. One of these we made our bedroom, with a cougar-skin on the floor for its rug. The other was our kitchen-sitting-living-room, with a solid little iron range we had got from the Hudson Bay Co. and a library of books that gradually grew along the entire length of one wall. We had oil lamps, of course, which after all are the most comfortable light to read by on long winter nights. I think I read more out there in B. C. than I have anywhere else, except the three years I spent in hospital beds; but my reading was often made restless at nights by the tantalising sound of a salmon leaping somewhere in our quiet bay.

We made most of our furniture. It cost us hardly a penny. A most magnificent chest of drawers was made from old coal-oil crates. A sumptuous piece. I took my time over the job (there was no mass production in B. C.), and I planed and polished and rubbed so that when I had finished, and stained it a dark brown, the drawers slid in and out easily, the way the cheap factory-made furniture of our flat in Chicago seldom did. Furthermore—I had all the exquisite pleasure of craftsmanship. And it was pleasant, after a day of such satisfying work, to take a quick dip overside and then sit down to a dinner of fat rainbow trout.

Before the trout would take a fly that spring, I rigged a night-

line from our house-boat. Nearly every morning I found two
or three trout swinging about in the clear water. We often had
them for breakfast then. Our usual way was to boil them and eat
them the next day, cold. When we felt like having a beano, and
had enough trout, we would fillet the rainbow and serve them
with mayonnaise.

I'll never forget the effect of the first mayonnaise trout on
Swanson!

Sometimes we would stuff them full of rich parsley dressing
and bake them in butter. Sometimes we would grill them with
strips of bacon inside.

"You people know how to live!" said Swanson, the highest
compliment he could pay.

So the seasons rolled along. It is banal to say that we forgot
what day of the week it was. We did not do that because Wed-
nesday and Saturday were mail days, and therefore my row down
to the store. But we never knew what the date was and had only
the haziest idea of the time. The passing of time to us was borne
in by more tangible things than a calendar. The approach of the
rainy season, for instance, was heralded by a sullen, continuously
grey sky. Then we knew that for some six weeks or so the rain
would rattle day and night without ceasing on the cedar shakes
of our roof. The woods would become almost impassable. We
would go about soaking wet most of the time and our tiny room
was always full of steaming drying clothes. Life was very dis-
agreeable then. Better lay in as much fire-wood as we could cut
now, so that I wouldn't have to be drenched to the skin cutting
wood in the rain. When the leaves turned I got a deer one moonlit night. I shot it in a glade when the deer were feeding. It was
almost as clear as day and the leaping deer that sprang off after
my shot made the scene in the glade look like an heraldic tapestry.
When the mountains began to lose their shadows and take on
that hard, metallic blue, we knew that winter was coming on.
This was serious. And for days, as the last of the deer season
closed, I would pair off with someone—usually Captain von
Hauptmann—to swing a saw and chop wood all day long. When
the snows came down it would be almost impossible to keep us

in fire-wood without an immense amount of effort bordering on the edge of sheer physical pain.

The approach of winter, we knew, was also the time when we would begin the heaviest inroads on our capital; for while the lake was locked in ice and snow, we would have to buy all the food we ate. Our bills with the Hudson Bay Co. shot up alarmingly during those three or four months. Heavy mackinaws and rubber boots also had to be bought.

The feeling of this change of season was like the prelude to some great opera, listening to the orchestra tuning up. Winter: cold, heavy, with its shrill winds. When the snows were deep around our log-cabin we would wake up to see the tracks of animals: deer, cougar and the long, finger-like tracks of coons. I set traps, baited with dead ducks and one morning saw a domino-eyed creature staring at me from the base of the tree. It was an enormous coon. I caught two whose skins I tanned to make Eve a fur collar which she occasionally wears even in London today.

And then the pipes of spring!

The snow would drop from the trees. The sun would be hot and fresh in our faces as we walked outside our door in the mornings. The mountain across from us would be beginning to lose its hard, blue stare and take on its deep shadows. Instead of that melancholy black of the open water in dead winter, the lake would be almost a blinding blue, shimmering in the heat haze. The woods would begin to fill with trilliums and dogwoods and little wild pink lilies.

Then I would put my trout rods together again.

But the great pageant of B. C. was the death of the salmon. If you once see that tragedy you will never forget it. And I watched it for two years.

Rex Beach has called it the Silver Horde. But then he spoke of the salmon when they were still in salt water, live, eager things. When I watched them, high up in the mountains, they were red and weary and covered with white sores. Millions of them. A red host, fighting its way home, to spawn—and then die.

It was fearful to see them. I have sat in a skiff for hours on end and watched them passing silently underneath. They were so intent with their urge that they did not even notice me. Nor, at first, the spinning baits with which, until I got sick of it, I used to catch them, just to see how they fought. No scientist has yet been able to give a satisfactory explanation of why all the Pacific salmon should only spawn once and then die. Their life cycle is limited to either two or four years, depending upon their species. At the end of their appointed time the great silver hordes in the ocean turn with one accord and make for the very stream they were born in to end their lives, on perhaps the very same riffle where, with sac attached, they first emerged from the egg.

With the rains came the salmon. In from the vast Pacific, they would one day appear to lash the salt-water inlets into a froth of white-caps with their leaps. They would fight their way past the nets, weirs and salmon-wheels of the canners, up past the shallow runs where the Siwash stood on banks hurling spears at them; up, up into the roaring mountain streams. Here we would watch them resting in the deep pools, hundreds of them milling about sullenly before they attempted to clear the waterfall. Then a month or six weeks after they had started this pilgrimage of death we would see them far up in the mountains, wobbling feebly across some shallow reach, heedless of our hands if we reached down to touch them. Up here the fat bears scoop them out and flap them on the bank, to get a good glut of salmon meat. And up here, with their tails, they would wash out a pebbly nest; the female would deposit her eggs and the male would fertilise them with his melt. The bucks would fight on these spawning beds. Ugly fish, whose jaws were now hooked like a dog's snarl. But once the spawning process had been completed they began to die. Their lives had been lived—and fulfilled. The water would fall and the spent fish would rot on the banks, so that for weeks after the rainy season the woods of B. C. literally stink of death.

I went down and fished the run when it first entered the salt bays of the coast. And down there I speared salmon with the Siwash Indians. They used a strange, two-pointed spear, which they hurled in a parabola in the same way that the ancient Greeks threw the javelin. It was tremendously exciting to throw a spear into a big 15 lb. dog salmon as he passed up a shallow reach. The squaws sat behind us, gutting and smoking the salmon on the banks. They just threw the entrails anywhere beside them. The stink of a Siwash village in the salmon season is something that sticks in one's nostrils through life; it is almost as bad as a whaling station. And I have had both.

But then, I also helped in the birth of the salmon. Hardinge, the hatchery-man, enlisted me for that.

A *chinook* had been bowling in from the Pacific for three days. Great streams of storm had been whipping in over the mountains. The lake was filled with white mist and slanting rain. The giant firs swung before it, their heads bent in the gale. And each stream had become a yellow torrent, sweeping boulders, dead wood, even live trees along with it to roar into the great lake.

It was a time when most sensible persons remained indoors, but there was a thud against our house-boat and I came out to see dripping Hardinge and the hatchery launch.

"Going up the Robinson to strip salmon," he announced. "Need another man to help us haul up the skiff. Want to come along?"

Our progress up that mountain torrent was both slow and painful. While two men poled, Hardinge and I hauled us along by grabbing the next branches of the submerged undergrowth. It took us about an hour to get up the quarter mile to where Hardinge had his beloved salmon-trap.

Here, the quiet English "gentleman" became a rabid, cursing High Priest. A fanatic.

He stood there, in his sea boots, on the rim of the fish trap, his "public school" calm cast completely aside. He had a salmon clasped by the tail. With a quick flip he imprisoned its head under his right elbow; then, holding its fighting tail with his left hand he slid his right fingers along its stomach towards the vent—and a stream of carnelian globules shot into the pail. Beautiful things, these salmon eggs, about the size and colour of a currant.

"Ha!" grunted Hardinge. "A fine fish!"

He spoke as if he were milking a Holstein.

My designated job was to dip the net into the box formed by

the boards of the fish trap and chase around a salmon till I caught it. I passed it up.

"Buck," said Hardinge, after the merest glance.

His mitted left hand closed over the tail, the practised right fingers slid along towards the vent. A stream, fluid this time—quite milky—shot into the pail. Hardinge diverted its stream into another pool of those carnelian red eggs. Then he flung the buck back into the swirling stream.

Like some alchemist of old Hardinge now leaned over his buckets, and gently, ever so gently! he let a soft flow of water seep down over the brim and across the fertilising eggs.

"*Look!*"

I watched the miracle taking place in the bucket. A gossamer mist floated over the eggs, almost imperceptible, so fine was its texture. It was the changing of colour. Now each egg was distinct, wrapped in its own little robe of Creation. A white spot on each showed that Life was now there.

As we shot back down the Robinson a hooded merganser duck came up it, hurtling past us.

"Damn that bloody bird!" said Hardinge. "Every time he dives he comes up with a fish in his mouth!"

"But he's nothing to the canners," said Hardinge, as we were going back down lake in the dripping hatchery launch. "They're a godless lot of crooks—almost as bad as the American and Canadian politicians they've bribed not to stop them from putting every salmon in Creation into a tin can!"

Hardinge, with his beloved hatchery-tanks full of inch-long salmon babies, was one of the happiest mortals I have ever seen.

"Nature," he announced, "gives a salmon egg a 1,000-to-1 shot against reaching maturity. I am bettering the odds."

Chapter 52

TRAGEDY STRIKES THE LAKE

THERE were other tragedies on the lake. The big logging camp that had just brought up its logging engines to desecrate the mountainside above old Tread's place was, I was told, full of men who "had a story in them." The bulk of these loggers of course was provided by husky Finns and Swedes. But there were other men there, Englishmen and an occasional American, who, for reasons of their own, had preferred to drop out of the world for a time. In these camps they usually took a new name, and found sanctuary.

In No. 1 camp, for instance, a high-rigger fell out of a tree. High-riggers, the highest paid job in the woods, are usually Finns and ex-sailors. They are the men who, with ordinary linesman's spikes, climb to the top of giant 200-foot firs and cut off their tops, so that they can be used as derrick masts to swing out the logs. With their spikes dug into the swaying tree, and a rope around their waist, they lean out and swing their two-bladed axes with the unconcern of a domestic man chopping firewood on the ground. But, sometimes, the axe slips. . . . Pavel, of No. 1, had cut himself down. Fallen a hundred and fifty feet to crash through some underbrush and land in a pulpy heap.

When the loggers were trying to move him, the camp's little time-keeper rushed up.

"Leave him be!" he said. "For Christ's sake, don't touch him until I have had a look at him first."

Then while the loggers stood agape the little time-keeper examined Pavel. He then ordered the men to split some wooden splints in the fashion he directed and bandaged Pavel's legs and arms. He then directed how Pavel should be put on to a hurriedly constructed stretcher and placed in the logging camp's launch, where he was carefully taken down lake and transported in a motor-car thirty miles to the nearest hospital.

"He'll live," said the surgeons examining Pavel's broken body down there. "But it's a damn' good job you had a doctor up there to patch him up."

"Doctor?" said the astonished loggers who had brought Pavel down. "We ain't got no doctor—our time-keeper's the guy that fixed Pavel up."

And that was the way Dr. Y., ex-abortionist from Brooklyn, gave his show away.

Most important people in these rough camps were the cooks. They were paid $250 a month, the same as a high-rigger, and had assistants whom they called "flunkies" to help and wash the dishes for them. But the cookee seldom lasted more than a couple of months at a camp. Then the men got tired of him and chased him down the trail. The standard of food was amazing. The piles of hot scones, buckwheat cakes, hot and cold dishes, coffee, etc., that they expected at breakfast alone nearly made my eyes pop out one day when I shared it with them. And they saw that they got it.

Two cookees, however, were famous on the coast and a camp thought it was lucky if it was able to hang on to them. They were Champagne Shannon and Hoot Mon MacDonald.

"Champagne was very particular," said the foreman of No. 1 camp, when I stayed there one night. "He always wore a frock-coat when he cooked."

The trouble with Champagne and Hoot Mon, it seemed, was that as soon as they got a month's pay they quit any camp they were working at and went down to Vancouver where, with the ladies of Railway Street, they drank it all up.

But these camps were outside our existence. We seldom saw them; and we hated their proprietors for scarifying the lake. With corruption so prevalent in British Columbia politics at that time they never felt obliged to obey the reforesting laws. When their donkey-engines and Lidgerwood "Sky-Line Fliers" had finished snatching giant trees from a mountainside they left it such a barren waste that no tree would ever take root there again.

Captain von Hauptmann, that first winter, provided the tragedy that nearly broke our hearts.

Hauptmann had come to the lake in B. C. long before the war. He came from German East Africa, where he had—so he said—been growing seisel, and flogging Swahili, and things like that.

Out here, in the heart of the wilderness, he built himself a *Schloss*. It was an ornate affair of scroll-work and gables and queer curlicues. He had the boards portaged up trail from the saw mill by the sea, plasterers come up from Victoria, coal delivered by pack train. His walls were grinning with the heads of East African game. Stands of rifles stood in the corners, spears on the walls, assegais, arrows, short stabbing spears.

In a land where all doors swing open to the touch he introduced brass locks. He had a fence built around his ground, an impressive wire barrier, with a bell at its gate and a white enamelled shield bearing his name:

CAPTAIN VON HAUPTMANN

Settlers called him "The Count."

He had the grand air, and, it was rumoured, he was a natural son of King Ludwig of Bavaria.

Some things he told me. For instance, when he had left Germany to come to his mysterious exile in B. C., his mother had packed all of his clothing with scented violets. Then he had been told on the ship, that if he put a five dollar bill carelessly on the top of his trunk, the Customs officials at New York would not examine his baggage. But they apparently took the five dollars and ransacked the lot, violets and all. Then he told me how he had married Elsa, the red-headed housekeeper that his mother sent out to him.

One day, at the end of the second year she had been with him, he suddenly thought of it, and asked Elsa to marry him. I suppose he was reconciled to perpetual exile by then, for von Hauptmann was a high-caste German, and Elsa had worked as packer in an Odol Tooth-Paste factory.

They took the train down to Victoria; Elsa in her best finery, von Hauptmann in an old morning suit. They were married and ate a marvellous dinner.

"And," said Hauptmann, showing the only emotion I ever saw him display, "I made the orchestra play the whole score of 'Lohengrin'!"

Then they took the train back to the *Schloss* on the lake.

Elsa was a good wife—she fed the Herr Captain handsomely—and on the little tea-cosy she had stitched the motto: MAY THE HOUSEWIFE BE HAPPY AND FAITHFUL.

Then came the war. Von Hauptmann underwent a sort of open internment. The game warden and his French wife, particularly the latter, saw that Hauptmann did not budge. And one day, even, a Canadian soldier, in tin-helmet, called upon von Hauptmann and took away his firearms. When they demanded his shotgun as well as his rifles, the poor desperate German cried in dismay:

"Damn it all—you'll be taking my fishing-rods next!"

Then the war ended, Germany passed through its Gethsemane, the mark broke—and Captain von Hauptmann was destitute.

Then Elsa really stood by. She was keeping the von Hauptmann household going by sewing when we first saw them. But still, they still had their *Schloss*—nothing could rob them of that —their cameras, their tools, the ingredients of a dozen hobbies—and within those walls, hung with his African trophies and photographs of his regiments, the gallant captain was still an important personage.

Then, just about the darkest hour of dawn one winter morning, I heard someone shouting my name:

"Farson! . . . Farson . . . !"

My God! I thought, sitting bolt upright in bed—what was that!

"Farson! . . . Farson . . . !"

I cannot tell you how ghastly that sounded in the middle of the night, when the nearest person to me lived over five miles away.

We were still in the log bungalow then, and I leapt into my

slippers and rushed to its door. A cold wind shot through my pyjamas. Then came the cry again:

"Mr. Farson . . . !"

It was a woman, this time; and I recognised the voice of Elsa von Hauptmann. Then I saw her.

She was struggling in the underbush, stark naked it seemed, with a moaning, slobbering man—all that was left of von Hauptmann, ex-officer of the Kaiser's old army.

Together we lugged him into our bungalow. I threw some logs on the fire. Elsa, who really had been naked, had crawled into my bathrobe. Hauptmann, beard sunk on his breast, was wearing an old opera cloak with his feet thrust into sacks.

"All gone. . . . All gone. . . ."

They kept repeating this to each other. Their *Schloss*, their all-in-all in this world; everything they possessed had gone up in flames.

"Oh, but it can't be!" I protested, agonised by their grief.

Then von Hauptmann pulled himself together. He took the scalding hot coffee we gave him and drained it at a gulp. He carefully pulled his long beard into its conventional shape. Then he sat up.

"You must excuse me," he said. "We are not—not quite ourselves at this minute. We have had a shock, understand? A shock. It is terrible—but my house has burned down."

It was just about as bad as trying to console a mother after her child has died. I just sat there and made coffee for them until day. When it was daylight I rowed Elsa von Hauptmann across to the black pit of ruins.

She shoved about in the wreckage, gashing her hands on bits of twisted metal and broken glass. I tried to stop it.

"What are you looking for?" I asked.

"A timble."

"A what?"

"A timble. A timble. A timble!"

Elsa was already starting her fight with life; she was searching for a thimble.

In the pit of black ash I spotted one of those grotesque little

German bread plates of theirs. Its china rim showed me from whence Elsa had got her motto, for it said:

SEI DER HAUSGRAU HERRLICH UND TREU.

I stuffed it under my sweater to give it back to them when they felt better about things.

It was amazing the way that community chipped together to put the von Hauptmanns back on their feet again. The wives of the Swedish loggers suddenly discovered that they had a lot of sewing to do—and didn't have time to do it—so would Mrs. Hauptmann be kind enough to do it for them? They would pay her, of course. Swanson turned up off the burnt *Schloss* with an old house-boat in tow. An English colonel, thirty miles down trail, read of the fire in the local weekly newspaper, and sent up some sweaters to Hauptmann and a pair of almost new jodhpurs —of which Hauptmann promptly cut off the legs.

"The English," he said to me ungratefully. "They have no calves! Legs like pipe-stems. Yah?"

During this time we kept the Hauptmanns in our bungalow. But in a strange way Hauptmann soon had the neighbourhood all against him again. Swanson, for example, wanted an extension put on the roof of his house-boat and employed von Hauptmann to do it.

Now, if there was one thing that von Hauptmann was proud of, it was his ability to use carpenter's tools. He had had a perfect little workshop in his house, although, as near as I could see, he never made anything useful in it. Now here was a chance to do a real professional job. Swanson borrowed the tools for him and von Hauptmann set to work. When he had finished, poor Swanson's roof had a hump in it like the back of a fish!

"By God!" said Swanson. "Yust look what you've done!"

"Can't help it," said Hauptmann. "I know my measurements were correct."

"And I know my house-boat looks like hell! You come around my place again and I'll bust your face!"

Even with me, von Hauptmann managed to bring out all the

devil in a man. During that first frightful dawn I had left Eve to make the coffee for them and taken a row across lake to see if there was anything I could save of von Hauptmann's burning house. The house itself was a mass of flames, but the shed near it was only just beginning to catch fire. I found a bucket and managed to put this out. And in doing so I got fairly blistered in spots. When the Duncan's weekly newspaper wrote the account of Hauptmann's tragic loss they mentioned my effort to salvage something from the wreck. Hauptmann, reading the account, looked up and glared at me.

"You wrote this, I suppose," he said.

I could have killed him.

And so the two years passed away.

My conscience had lain dormant. What was life, anyway? Weren't we living a good life out here? Weren't we both making good at it? Wasn't I getting pretty sure now that I would sell a short story or an article when I wrote it? Well, then—why these occasional qualms?

To do Eve justice I will say that she never had one. She was making a great go of things, and, courageous little Briton that she was, had already established a firm place for herself in the community.

And we were saving money. In two years we had accumulated $1,800, more than I had ever saved at any one time in my life— except, of course, my lost funds in Petrograd.

There was really no logical reason why we should leave except that these fits of conscience began to get more and more frequent on my part. We had even planned to spend that summer sailing around Glacier Bay in Alaska, and had gone to the point of writing to a man up there to get us a sail-boat. Then I broke the news to Eve.

"We're going back," I said.

She wept.

I admitted that I was not at all sure I was right, but I felt that I owed it to both of us to go back and have a go at life in the cities again.

"We want to see the world," I pointed out.

So we left.

As we were sadly packing up the few belongings that we meant to take with us Swanson told me that the steelheads were running. I thought I would have one last chance at the fish, so I put my rod together and went down to the river at the foot of the lake. I waded down the wonderful waters under the friendly sun. Hundreds of steelheads were coming up. I nearly went crazy at the sight.

"But they won't take a thing!" called a voice from the opposite bank. It was from an American, a sportsman from Seattle, who had come up the island to fish the big steelhead run, and tried every fly in his book.

I cast over them all day and never rose a fish. One beauty, about 10 lbs., did turn and look at my fly. There was a split second when he looked as if he would take it. Perhaps it is just as well that he didn't; for my resolution to return to Chicago was running a bit low as I watched those miraculous fish.

If the steelhead had been taking that day, I would probably be in B. C. now.

Chapter 53

MACK TRUCKS—AND MANY OF THEM

Bob Black met us as we stepped out of the train at Chicago, and we all had breakfast together at the Blackstone Hotel.

"What are you going to do?" asked Bob.

"I don't know," I said. "One thing—I'm not going to sell motor-trucks."

"You never have," said Bob.

When we had finished laughing about my previous woeful efforts to sell motor-trucks, I asked him to let me make my own job. "Call me the Promotion Department," I said. And for several very interesting, but I must say unproductive, weeks after I got back to Chicago I sat at a desk and tried to figure out new uses and appliances for motor-truck transportation. Then the Milwaukee manager ran amok and someone had to be sent up to try and straighten out that branch. By an incredible bit of luck I was selected for the job.

It was exciting and yet rather frightening work. The salesmen were all at each other's throats. The cellar was full of old traded-in trucks, absolute junk, that were valued anywhere up to $2,000 on the New York books. And the battle for the dominance of the territory was in full, unregenerate swing between the five biggest motor companies in the States with no quarter either given or asked. It was so easy to make a colossal mess of things.

I called in the second-hand man and took him down the cellar.

"How much is this truck worth?" I asked.

He looked at its ticket. "$1,500," he said.

"Forget that," I said. "How much do you think you could get for it?"

Tony, who always carried a revolver about with him on his job—in case, he said, he should meet an old customer—took a long look at the truck and then said:

"Well, maybe I could get a coupla hundred bucks for it. But that's all."

"All right," I said. "Stick a sign, $200, on the nose of that truck."

"Say . . . Mr. Farson! . . . that truck was traded in for $1,500!"

But we did that with every truck. I took a half page in the Milwaukee *Journal* and advertised a sacrifice sale of second-hand trucks, no promises given, no arguments—one price—take it or leave it.

We cleaned out that basement—and took a staggering loss on the New York books. A howl to heaven went up from there on that! But the deed, horrible as they thought it, was done. Then I got a room in a hotel, where we had a dinner, and a practically all-night argument with the salesmen. When we left it each salesman knew where his territory began—and stopped!

Then, with that amazing fervour that it seems only Americans can throw into such work, we spent the next thirty days and nights selling motor-trucks. Those salesmen were a marvellous crowd. And at the end of that month they had brought the Milwaukee branch "out of the red." Even with the ghastly loss we had willingly taken on the trade-ins to begin with, the Milwaukee branch showed a small profit for that month.

Bob Black took me down to New York to report personally on Milwaukee to the President of the Company. He was out at Watch Hill, Rhode Island, on his yacht; and we had a cocktail picnic out there on an island, where, pressing my Milwaukee good luck, I asked Fulton if he would send me to Europe or China or anywhere to let me get back into the export business again.

"You stand in line," he said, with what seemed needless brutality. "Go back to Chicago and stand in line and take your turn."

That, I thought, was a tough way to treat a person. But I understood the next day. I was standing beside Bob Black in the Princeton Club in New York, while he took a shower bath. It was a ghastly hot day. Bob beat his chest under the spray.

"How'd you like to be Sales Manager for Chicago?" he said.

I laughed. "You're crazy," I said.

"Am I?" he said, stepping out from the shower. "You don't know it—but you've been Sales Manager for Chicago ever since yesterday afternoon."

When he told me what my salary would be I told Eve that our worries were finished, as far as financial matters were concerned.

"But," warned Bob, "this is a cruel world. You are up there now, where everybody will be shooting at you. Alibis aren't wanted by the head office in New York. If you don't make good —even if it isn't your own fault—you're out! Uneasy lies the head that wears the crown . . . the whiskey's on the window-sill."

Chapter 54

"B"

IT WAS a pretty tall jump from the house-boat in British Columbia to this job.

When I held my first meeting as Sales Manager, facing my old colleagues, every one of whom was a ten times better salesman than I was, I felt like Daniel in the lions' den. And as they did the job the story of that spectacular Chicago year had better be told by the life of one of them.

One day, when I was sitting in my imposing-looking glass box of an office with my gallant secretary, sweetie of a well-known gunman, a desperate-looking young man stood before my desk. In some way he had managed to get past the protecting barrier of employees I had established in front of me.

"I want a job," he said.

"Ever sold trucks?" I asked.

He laid a card on my desk. On it was the name of an inferior rival of ours.

"I can give you references," he said. "But it will be no use writing to them. They'll give me a black eye."

This was something different from the usual 100 per cent go-getters that besieged me all day for a job.

"I haven't sold much of anything," he said.

I thought it was merely a new line at first. A smug modesty meant to "sell" me. Then I saw that he was desperate. Desperation simply stared at you from every rigid line of him. It was shocking.

"Give me a try," he asked.

I asked him something about his record, and to my surprise he informed me that he was an Annapolis graduate and had been a regular officer in the United States Navy. He had been partially deafened by an explosion in a turret and had taken a bounty to leave the Service. Since that day things, for him, had gone from bad to worse. His grim jaw showed it. I don't believe in the strong jaw theory, and I have usually found that the strong silent man is just plain dumb. But B impressed me. And I liked him at once.

I went in to see Joe Donnelley, the Branch Manager, a cynical Irishman when it came to judging either horse- or man-flesh. But a big man.

"Joe," I said, "I've got a fellow in my office who looks like the last half of a wasted life. He looks like hell. He told me not to write to any of his old companies for references—so I won't. But I'm going to take him."

"O.K.," smiled Joe. "It's your loss."

For weeks that fellow never seemed to be even near selling a truck. He came in in the mornings looking even more haggard than usual. One morning, when I saw him sitting there so forlornly—and uselessly—on a bench among the standing motortrucks, I went out and sat down beside him.

"I'm not going to fire you," I began, "so don't feel worried by what I'm going to say. It's none of my business to begin with —but do you take dope?"

"God, no!"

"Do you drink, then?"

"Sometimes. But I know what you mean—drink has nothing to do with it."

I was flummoxed.

"It's something else," said B.

There, I knew, I had reached a point where any more questions must stop. Then, trying not to sound too Pollyanna, I said:

"Look here. I don't know what it is, and I don't want to know —but if you've got something on your chest like this, the only way to get rid of it is by just drowning yourself with hard work. And hard work doesn't do a damn bit of good unless you are getting somewhere. . . . Come on into the office and let's go over your list of prospects. There must be somebody out in your district you can land for a big order."

We spread out the reports he had made all across the glass top of my desk. There was one thing about them—they were pretty candid documents. They held out no false hopes. But that was refreshing. Then B picked out one showing a call he had made on one of the biggest mail-order companies in Chicago.

"I got on there pretty well with the Service Manager," he said. "I might sell that one."

Now my chief contribution to Chicago salesmanship, and the experiment that was either going to make me or break me, was a "STAR" system I had inaugurated. I put it in primarily to lure the salesmen away from going after the small one-truck orders and concentrate all their amazing energies on the big stuff.

It was no virtue on my part; it was a case of do or die. I had seen so many sales managers broken, who had tried to fulfil their quota by taking any kind of orders that they could get, that I resolved if I was going to hang on to the Chicago sales manager's job I had better go after nothing but big stuff. In each salesman's territory I had picked out twenty of the biggest accounts to whom we had been unable to sell anything up to date. We made a study of each account; and to make the salesmen go for them I put on a bonus that made them forget everything else.

That was just the trouble at first, for the Star System worked so well that nobody sold anything for a time. The salesmen were out all day trying to capture almost untakable strongholds of our enemy motor-truck companies. New York became alarmed, and even Bob Black got nervous about things. He used to come into my office, pumping his hand up and down in that way that he had and say:

"I don't want to press you," he would begin. "But that board looks pretty blank—doesn't it?"

This was the Star System score-card that hung behind my desk. It was a daily reproach, at first; because for over a month it stood there as naked as the day I had drawn it up.

This was the year of a presidential election, when business is always upset in the United States. Everybody was holding off buying until he saw how the elections would go. Even in booming times an election year will temporarily slow down business in the United States. In that year it brought it to almost a full stop.

As part of the system was that I should go out every day with the salesmen myself, taking them in rotation, I could see myself that they were getting somewhere with the STAR accounts. I could feel that we were approaching some big sales; but, until desperate B stood in my office that morning not one had matured—and the one B had selected as "likely" was one of the most hopeless of all. It was pure luck that I did not turn him off it and direct him to try something more likely first.

We looked up its list of directors to see if any of them interlocked with companies we had already sold; we analysed its present fleet of trucks, how old they were and what were their chronic weaknesses compared to ours; we tried to get the mail order company to let us appraise them for trade-in values; in fact, we gave that mail order company "the entire works." And B got the order.

It was probably the most dramatic day of my short business life when B and I drove out there to close the deal. The managers of our three biggest rivals were sitting in the outer office as we came in. They smiled at us as we went upstairs. Upstairs we found the president of the company sitting behind a big cigar.

"I'm going to close with somebody this morning," he told us as we sat down. "It might be with you or it might be with one of those fellows sitting below. You have the first shot, but, remember, if you go out that door I close with somebody else. Now, I want so many thousand dollars for my old trucks. I know they're not worth it—but that's what I'm going to get. And I won't take one red cent less."

He was a high-power person, this president; but he had named a price that I knew we could give. We had already appraised his trucks and even had likely customers in mind for them. I knew what it cost to make ours, how much sales cost I must add on; and how far I could go before our backs were against the wall. We argued there for about an hour. Finally, when we had both moved towards each other quite some distance, only a few hundred dollars stood in our way. I offered to split it, and at the same time I wrote the final figures at the foot of the order and slid it across the desk.

People who think there is no adventure in business should experience some of the anxiety that B and I went through then, as we watched that big man chewing his cigar and making up his mind. In a way it was a sensational order, for not only were we trading in his whole fleet, but we were breaking into a new type of company which had been almost monopolised by our biggest rival. For some days, "Who's going to get the So-and-So order?" had been the talk of Automobile Row.

Then the president signed, and feeling slightly dizzy, B and I stood up. It was hard to keep from yelling as we went down the stairs. The other three sales managers were sitting there. The one I had feared most gave me a smile as we passed out.

"No use," he said sarcastically, "of me going up?"

"No," I said, taking the folded order out of my pocket, "not a bit."

It was a great day. After we had driven a couple of blocks B and I got out of the car and shook hands with each other in the middle of a crowded street.

That was the kind of life that made Chicago so exciting, and, unfortunately, it is a side of American business that foreigners never see. It wasn't the money of the thing, it was the sheer excitement that kept most of those salesmen on their toes. We had to contend with every type of person in Chicago, many of whom could hardly talk English. Spike O'Donnell, the gunman rival of Al Capone, was a customer of ours. We got him through City Hall. I talked with Spike one day out at his beer-running garage and the two drivers we were talking trucks with were both murdered by Al Capone's gang the next week. When the Star System started to go over it was thrilling to watch the way the salesmen finished that year. Their vitality was exhilarating, and there wasn't a day that didn't see an exciting battle of some sort. B, having tasted first blood, decorated his name on the board with a perfect constellation of stars. The whole system had an accumulative and contagious effect. Eve got accustomed to having me get home for dinner at any hour of the night. The branch got on headway like a big ship and at the end of the year we sailed evenly across that dread line which divides profit from loss.

Chicago, key point of the Middle West, had gone over, and I decided to throw up my job.

It was on the crest of this high wave that Eve and I decided we would get out of business altogether. After I had made it quite clear to Bob Black that I was mad enough to throw up such a good job, he asked me who I thought my successor should be. I recommended B.

He was given my job.

Chapter 55

WE TAKE ANOTHER CHANCE

SUNDAYS drove us away from Chicago. And I can remember the particular Sunday that did it. It was after a steaming hot night when we had tossed about hour after hour in our little flat looking out on a melting asphalt street; and in the room across the alley, which was so narrow that our hands could touch it, a phonograph was playing a tune of the moment called "Swinging down the lane. . . ." A maddening hammering sort of tune.

We were still stunned by Chicago, after our two years in British Columbia. . . . We were haunted.

> *And always night and day*
> *I hear lake water lapping*
>   *With low sounds by the shore.*
> *When I am in the roadway or on*
> *The pavements grey,*
>   *I hear it in the deep heart's core. . . .*

That phonograph mocked us. Swinging down the lane! God, what bunk. This was worse than Sunday in London. It is possible to get away from Sunday in London. In less than an hour you can be in real country, grass, trees. But we knew we could never get away from Sundays in Chicago. Queues of motor-cars stretched for twenty, thirty, forty, fifty miles in every direction. And wherever we went the blistering, flat cornfields would surround us. They would be smothering in this furnace heat.

The best thing to do was to go and sit all day in a bathtub of cold water.

We were lucky in our friends. We had made plenty by this time, and a jollier crowd we could not want. They were intensely hospitable, but the point was that their country estates around Lake Forest and Lake Geneva in Wisconsin were not our places, and we would have to become millionaires to own one. That was the premium one had to pay for merely comfort in America. It

was impossible to live simply unless one was rich. Unless someone invited us out into the country for a week-end we were sunk.

Janet Fairbank saved our lives in Chicago. Her wooden house
out at Lake Geneva had defied all the raucous progress of time
and mass production. It was almost a museum piece. And her
exhilarating house-parties would compensate one for purgatory
itself. Janet, most sophisticated creature, who had seen more of
the world and been deeper into her own country's affairs than
most women, *loved* Chicago.

Watching Janet always made us think there must be something
wrong with us.

But there was no mistake about this day. No one had invited
us away for the week-end and it lay before us, utterly, completely blank. Nothing but the thick piles of huge Sunday newspapers stared at us, and looking at them I knew why they were so
large and thick; they were the American anaesthetic for Sundays.

"What the hell are we going to do with ourselves!" I moaned.

"This isn't good enough," said Eve. "No matter how high you
get or how much money you earn we shall never have more than
that miserable two to three weeks a year to do what we really
like in."

I was right in the middle of my successful career as a sales
manager. The company had just given me a brand new motor-car.
It lay in the garage around the corner. But instead of using it
that day we got out an atlas. In the semi-darkness in which we
had to keep our rooms to prevent us from stifling we took a long
voyage. It was in our own boat—and we began at Rotterdam, in
Holland.

That night we went down into the Loop and had a marvellous
cold lobster salad. And all through it we cruised in our own sail-
boat.

"We're only going to live once," I said most profoundly.

"Hear, hear!" said Eve. "What's the use of waiting until we
are seventy?"

"People will say we have gone crazy again."

"Let them. You're making more money here than you ever
thought you would make in your life—and look at us!"

"Yes . . ." I mused. "We could buy a boat, a cabin yawl or something like that. There would be no hotel bills to pay, and no railways. . . . How much have we got in the bank? Lord! is that all?"

So I set out to lay siege to old Victor Lawson, that great and fearless American newspaper proprietor, who published the *Chicago Daily News*. It was John Bass, the American war correspondent, who backed me up in my desires.

"The *Daily News* Foreign Service," he said, "is far and away the best in America. Get a foreign job under Victor Lawson and you will have the finest job an American newspaper man can get."

It was a letter from Janet Fairbank that opened the gates for me. Old Lawson, the hermit, had a great respect for her, and it was Walter Strong, afterwards publisher of the paper, who was my secret accomplice in my almost insane efforts to see that great publisher. He inhabited, I knew, almost an attic at the top of the ramshackle building in which the great *Chicago Daily News* was still published. He read every word of the paper every day—even the advertisements. And, I had been told, he had been reading the newspaper work I had done for the *New York Sun and Herald* and other publications. Still . . . no word came down. Then one day Lawson sent for me and I opened the door of his sanctuary to see a rather small man, with a sharp beard and brilliant brown eyes, examining me.

"Won't you sit down?" he said. He was so deferential in his courtesy that he seemed almost a timid man.

"I like what you have written," he said.

It was the accolade. But it was a long, long way from being accepted on the foreign staff of the *Chicago Daily News*. Lawson spoke of Paul Scott Mowrer and Edgar Ansel Mowrer with almost a resentment that I should think myself fit to be taken into such company. I knew their work; it was reading their lucid accounts of what was happening in Europe that had been my one way of keeping in touch with what was going on over there. In every big capital in Europe and the Far East Lawson had a man who was at the top of his rank as a journalist. Lawson's genius presided over everything, and Lawson was a frank, fear-less, resolutely independent man like C. P. Scott of the *Man-chester Guardian*, at that time probably the greatest newspaper in the world on the correct reporting of foreign affairs.

My bid to get on the foreign staff of the *Chicago Daily News* was that I would show another, and perhaps more realistic, face of Europe than could be seen in the capitals. Beginning at Rotter-dam, I intended to sail across Europe. I would buy my own boat; my wife would be the sole crew; we might take six, eight months, even a year over the job. I would end up where the yellow Danube poured into the Black Sea from Roumania. I would write what I saw.

"I'm going to do it anyway," I told Mr. Lawson. "But I would much rather do it for you than for anyone else."

The great editor sucked his thumb like a child while my des-tiny hung in the air. Then he nodded.

"It is a splendid idea!" he said. "Do it!"

To leave the Mack company was a terrific decision to make. I was tasting American business at its very best. I felt almost cer-tain that I would never again work for such a group of really big men. The men at the head in New York were "big shots"—great gamblers, if you wish; but the kind of men who inspired respect by their own personal example. You were all right with them, as long as you made good. And they were intensely human. You could spend money like water as long as you were producing results with it. There was no niggling in that broad-minded or-ganisation over the details of expense accounts. It did not attempt to make money by seeing how much money it could pare from its own employees. I felt that I would never find their like again. But I was wrong in that; for under both Victor Lawson and Walter Strong I found the same sense of independence and man-liness, the same generous treatment in working for the *Chicago Daily News*.

That was 1924. When Walter Strong died in 1931—and I was holding the coveted London post—I felt that it was my own as well as his obituary that I was sadly typing out for the English Press. A great American newspaper publisher had dropped dead, one of the last of the "independents"; he was gone—and I prepared myself to meet changing conditions.

I met them.

Chapter 56

GOOD-BYE TO A GRAND JOB

THE MACK company gave me what, to me at any rate, was an astonishingly large bonus when the season ended. Although my expenses had always managed to keep slightly ahead of my salary in Chicago, no matter how much I was making, this bonus, plus what was left of the money we had saved in British Columbia, allowed me to pay our fares to England and buy a twenty-six-foot Norfolk Broads, centreboard yawl.

Before I left, the Chicago branch gave me a farewell dinner at the Illinois Athletic Club. They had taken a private room and had one of our Italian customers, an ex-saloon keeper, bring down a section of his brass-railed bar and put it up in the private dining-room. Old Tony Giuseppe, for sentimental reasons, had kept that slab of mahogany he had so often leaned across. These were Prohibition days; and I was led into the room, up to the bar; and old Tony, like a fat ghost, said:

"What's yours, Mister?"

With a grand furore of speech-making and some genuine pangs of separation my generous old crowd gave me a Mannlicher rifle, a beautiful Graflex camera, suit-cases, a revolver, and various other things that would come in useful to "the Farson outfit."

It was princely.

I had carried the season through into the early spring. B had the reins in his hands. There was a farewell round of cocktail parties and dinner parties with our other friends, during which time Eve and I were undergoing daily inoculations for para-typhoid, cholera and being vaccinated against small-pox—so that our arms stuck when we tried to lift a cocktail glass to our pale lips. Then the train pulled us out through the stockyards and was soon hurtling through the night to New York. Down there I faced Fulton and "Red" Mike Masury, president and vice-president of the Mack company. Masury, also consulting engineer to the United States Navy, was lost later when the huge dirigible

Akron went down off the New Jersey coast. Both of these men typified all that was "big" in American business—and they were both fanatic yachtsmen.

"Well," grinned Fulton when I had tried for the final time to explain to him my reasons for leaving such a good job, "you never did have any money urge. I suppose you must get this off your chest. All the best to you. By the way—what kind of a boat are you going to use?"

They were like that, those men.

Chapter 57

DOUBLE DUTCH

SOUTH KENSINGTON again, with the ease and assurance of English life and a tremendous welcome back. But only for a little while. With Maurice Griffith, now Editor of *Yachting*, I drove 1,200 miles around England in search of a yacht. I found *Flame* in Kemp's shipyard at Southampton. I bought her at once. I took my pen-knife and tested her keel and garboard-strakes. She was sound as a bell.

A few weeks later I was bobbing up and down at the bows of a filthy old British tramp in the traffic-infested waters of Rotterdam.

"Mynheer Snook, you have failed me!"

"That is sorry," said Mynheer Snook.

Mynheer Snook was one of those amphibious Dutchmen who make their living on the water of Rotterdam. That curious life where the customs of land and water are inextricably mixed, where every calendar on shore shows the time of the tide, and every barge has its dog, its garden, and the washing hung out. I had engaged Snook to help tow me up to the Royal Den Maas Yacht Club, which fine group of sportsmen had made me a member while I was fitting out in preparation for my 3,000 miles' cruise across Europe.

Perhaps it was the solidity of his wooden shoes that misled me. For Mynheer Snook did not turn up.

"I will watch the little board by the fish market," he had promised me. "It says when a ship comes past the Hook. It is two hours from Hook of Holland to Rotterdam. When *Nyroca* comes—I'll be there."

I sat on a slip from seven o'clock until three, watching the family life in the Dutch barges. At three, the *Nyroca*, having been fog-bound off the Hook, warped in, got her lines out, and made fast.

" 'Ullo!" said her mate. "And 'ow does Rotterdam hit you?"

I told him. "Of course," I said, "it makes things difficult when you can't speak a word."

"I never go ashore," said the mate.

By this time the stevedores had the hatch covers off, the don-key-engines were clanking, and my heart was in my mouth to see the way they were man-handling *Flame!* It wasn't until she lay safely in the water, twenty feet below, beside a green, slippery wall that I felt the absence of Mynheer Snook.

"Have you seen my Dutchman?" I called up to the mate.

"No, what's he look like?"

"Short little man, blue cap, wooden shoes."

"Wot? They all look like that."

"Name's Snook."

"Snook! 'Ullo, Snook!" the mate bellowed along the length of the dock. His red face peered down at me from the *Nyroca*. "Sure that's his name?"

"Yes!" I screamed, clawing at the green wall with my finger nails. "For God's sake hurry up!"

I don't know any place more isolated than the fore-foot of a steamship. Try and picture this scene: the little 26-foot yawl, with her spars, masts and gear piled every way on her deck, bouncing about on a mud-coloured sea at the bow of that filthy old Liverpool tramp. See the row of curious, placid faces staring down from the dock. But I could not even hang on where I was. By the time the mate of the *Nyroca* came to her rail again I was clinging on to the bow of the *Jaribu*, fifty yards further down the stream.

"He ain't here," called the mate.

"Well, get someone else!" I shouted. "Someone to give me a tow."

"I've just been telling you," yelled back the mate, "I don't know any more about this town than you do."

"Well, get someone who does. What do you expect me to do?" The mate told me.

But a passing yachtsman saw my plight and towed me up to Den Maas where the sporty little *Flame* looked like a tramp

among the beautiful carved *schuits* and *boejers*. And here, at
sunset, Mynheer Snook found me.

"You are here," he said, regarding me stolidly.

I went on with my work.

"I didn't come here for money," he said, speaking slowly, apparently addressing the figurehead of the yacht next to us. "I
don't do things like that. I have a good name and I want to keep
it. I don't like to see other people robbing the English, I—"

"I'm not English," I burst out. "I'm American. Clear out!"

The yellow hairs of Mynheer Snook's eyebrows all pointed
upward, giving him the curious expression of having just been
surprised. I saw pain in his blue Friesland eyes—these foreigners!
Stepping out of his wooden shoes, he came into my boat. "Sir,"
he began, and in a manner tentative yet determined, he told the
tale of his absence. From the little board by the fish market he
had calculated the time of *Nyroca's* arrival to the minute—no
mistake about that—but, having two hours to spare, he had gone
off on another job in the meantime. "Because," he explained, "I
didn't want to charge you for the whole day." The other job
made him late.

"I'm disgusted," I said. "In England they told me I could de-
pend on the Dutch. The English seldom speak that way of anybody but themselves . . . they are careful whom they com-
mend . . . so that was a very fine compliment."

"*Ja!*" agreed Mynheer Snook. "The Dutch do fine work. I
am a captain."

This explanation over he was filling his pipe. Evading my glare,
his eyes saw the steering gear of Southampton. "That is not
right!" he said, using his pipe as a pointer. "It should have a
sleeve—so! That is dangerous."

In an instant he had suggested the much-needed changes. He
went over my boat like a doctor. I handed him tools. I saw
Flame under his skilled, battered hands becoming a crack little
craft. And he, looking up, saw my smile of contentment.

"Double Dutch—eh? That's what they say in America. Double
Dutch—but not dumb."

I re-engaged him at once.

Chapter 58

THROUGH HOLLAND

IT WAS fun fitting out in Holland. The men of the Royal Den Maas were just preparing for their own great race, where they sail for a week day and night. The basin was full of broad-bosomed *boejers* with their gold inlaid sideboards. They never tired of reminding me that I was a member of the Royal Den Maas—and immediately asked me to have a drink with them. Some of the *boejers* had their own little cocktail bars inside them. From breakfast to sunset, grimy as a pair of plumbers, Mynheer Snook and I worked in the *Flame*. Then I would have a cold shower, get into cool flannels, and eat long, talkative dinners on the Den Maas verandah overlooking the masts, funnels, and derricks of Rotterdam harbour.

The sky-line was never still for one moment.

Then one May afternoon I said good-bye to these sporting Dutchmen, left my card in the rack, and hurriedly ran back to *Flame* to get into dirty ducks again. I was off! The heart- and purse-aches of fitting out in England and Holland were over. Three thousand miles of Europe lay ahead of me.

"Cheerio!" called the mate of *Nyroca*, who was anchored in the stream. Then, leaning over her rail with cupped hands, he called after me with true British humour, "You're going to have your blinking hands full, me lad—good luck!"

I had my hands full already. The traffic of the Meuse off Rotterdam is worse than Fifth Avenue or Piccadilly in rush hours.

I would have appreciated some policemen or street signs at that moment—or even some distinctly numbered buoys. There were none. Just a welter of snorting, business-like tugs, tows half a mile long, of heaving mud-coloured waters and black hulls lurching past. Traders for the Rhine, for the Seven Seas. Barges for Dordrecht, for Haarlem and Delft, steamers for Batavia and the Plate. Belgians bringing coal from the Ruhr. And through it all, sailed the unconcerned, lumbering passage of the red-sailed, broad-bosomed Dutch *boejers* and *schuits*.

"*Den Lek!*" I called, laying myself alongside a passing tug and five barges.

"*Ja!*" Two men who were standing in the water that over-lapped a barge amidships, nodded, waved their arms, and pointed —each in a different direction.

The skipper of Sir Thomas Lipton's *Shamrock* had advised me to take the Lek, lower Rhine, up through Holland to get into Germany.

"It's a peaceful river," he said. "The real Holland."

Eve, who had come over from England, had gone up to Gouda where she wanted to see a stained-glass window. I had told her that morning that I would pick her up off Lekkerkerk about sun-down. But now it began to look as if we were parted for ever.

An American, sailing an English boat, in a Dutch river, with a German chart, is a confusing enough combination. Add to this that the scale of the chart was in kilometres, not miles, that none of the buoys were numbered, and that the shore-line was honey-combed with waterways, and you have some idea of my feelings. Realise also that while an island is an obvious thing on a chart— there it is, with the water all round it—it is a deceitful affair in real life. If it is big and lies close to shore you are not sure whether the open mouth of water you see at its foot is merely the mouth of another river or not—it might not be an island. You cannot fly over to look, nor is it always possible to rush up and see if there is water on the other end of it. You have to chance it, trust your luck, and spurn all enticing water mouths until your instinct tells you that you have reached the one you are bound for. Canals every few hundred yards do not tend to simplify matters. . . .

But then I got out of the thick traffic. The stone walls, docks and factory stacks of Rotterdam lay far behind, and I felt sure that the curving, rush-lined river ahead was the Lek. A brown-sailed barge went before me, wing-and-wing, her main sheets almost sweeping the bank. A woman, wrapped up against the cold, grey drizzle of rain, leaned her broad stern against its carved tiller.

"*Den Lek?*" I called, and she nodded, regarding me curiously. Then she waved a sunburned hand straight ahead.

Some ducks, alarmed by my voice on this quiet river, paddled out from the rushes, headed into the wind, and with a frantic splashing, took the air and shot past me. They circled, and I watched them come over, drop down close to the water and disappear up the winding river ahead. I saw flat green country, with the roads raised above, little tufts of green willows and beyond, around the curve of a bend, the red roofs of a village, its church steeple pointing finger-like into the sky—peaceful Holland.

Suddenly my whole soul filled with deep contentment. I lay back in the cockpit, my elbow against the wheel-spokes, delighted that it was raining and that I could feel the roughness of that old tweed collar against the weather. Our lives and nearly everything we owned in this world were in that snug cabin at my feet. Life, I felt, could hold no greater feeling of comfort and independence —and it never has.

At Lekkerkerk I put in for Eve. A man on the dyke waved an eel at me, in welcome. To a young Dutch boy on the bank, who was exploiting his English, I gave the command that he should meet the bus coming from Gouda.

"Girl?" he repeated, smiling.

I nodded.

"My girl?"

"No," I said, frowning. "My girl. Go and meet her."

He went away with a bevy of little Dutch girls.

They came back at the head of a cavalcade, most of whom were carrying parcels. Eve had been shopping.

We cast off. There was a friendly flutter of hands from the bank. At the bend we looked back. The man with the eel stood at the end of a long row of red roof-tops that were peeping over the dyke. He looked like a weather-vane as he waved the inde-cent carcass aloft in final farewell. We looked ahead. In the far distance, under a pastel of low-lying clouds, the arms of a wind-mill caught the air, waved once, and then twice as the night closed down.

Chapter 59

LIFE IN *FLAME*

Out in British Columbia, in our two-roomed little house-boat, we used to think we were very ingenious, the way we made use of space. Life in the *Flame* often made us wonder what we could have put in all that room. The cabin of *Flame* was six feet by eight. We had to stoop to get into it, and stay stooped until we sat down on our bunks. Then we had head-room.

Ahead of this cabin was a forepeak, like the toe of a boot, into which we used to crawl to get fresh changes of clothes, books, medicines, and our reserve of tinned provisions. That forepeak, occasionally, leaked; and when we arrived in Budapest, and were at once summoned to dine at the American Legation, I found that a spare American flag I had put in my suit-case had transferred its Stars and Stripes to the bosom of my only clean evening shirt.

"But you should have *worn* it!" exclaimed old Judge Brentano. "The Hungarians would have thought it so patriotic!"

It was not that *Flame's* forepeak leaked so much, but that our two suit-cases and two duffel bags—our only baggage for nearly a year—had to be stuffed up into the nose where some sixty fathoms of chain rested upon them.

To get into a dinner jacket in *Flame* I had to lie on my back in my bunk with my feet in the air, taking extraordinary care as I came upright not to put a crease in my shirt.

It was even more remarkable to see the way Eve could emerge in full rig for a party!

And yet that forepeak, in which every solitary inch of space was put to some use, simply reeked of Romance.

I have crawled there on a wet night, to get a pair of dry shoes, and have just sat there, fascinated, listening to the lashing of rain on our deck and feeling the thrum of the lower Rhine or Danube against our keel. There was a spare anchor in there, a great mud-hook, and when darkness caught us just above the rapids at Vilshoften one night it seemed to me that I would never get it out of that tight little forepeak quickly enough.

There was a bunk on each side of the cabin about eighteen inches wide, covered with green waterproof canvas cushions. By pulling these out at nights, we gained another three inches and thus made two beds. At the head of the bunk on the port side was a compact W.C. with a pump. Ahead of the starboard bunk was our galley; the single Primus stove on which we did all our cooking.

There was a centre-board well running down the middle of the cabin, with a flap on each side that when turned up gave us a fine, varnished teak table about four feet by three. The cushioned bunks were our seats.

Miracles were performed on this table every night. Breakfast, of course, was no trouble at all. We merely dropped the eggs in the coffee and let it come to a boil. But dinner, our only other hot meal, was more elaborate. Dinner was only too often the reward for a back-breaking day. Dinner meant rest.

We were a little rusty at first. The bacon would be cold before the eggs were half done; potatoes would appear a soft soggy mass. The coffee would be ready about the time we were yawning with sleep. No three things ever appeared simultaneously. Then Eve got her hand in. Three course dinners would materialise in the middle of a howling gale. We always started with a big bowl of soup—which, in fact, was the only way we could cook the wild ducks that were our staple food in the marshes of Roumania.

It is extraordinary how much one thinks about food as soon as it becomes scarce. We used to lie in our bunks in the wastes of Bulgaria thinking about duck and green peas and sausages and roast beef. Actually, of course, there was always *something* to be had, though often pretty nasty. But in Bessarabia for two days there was literally nothing. We had run short of provisions and we just boiled our tea leaves over and over again. But that was because of an unexpected scrape we had had with the Roumanian frontier guards, who had an order to arrest me.

It was a marvellous sight to watch Eve stalking a village market, determined to find at least something we could eat. On the Rhine we used to take on our supplies of bread, eggs and vegetables without ever going ashore—shop from the market boats that lay out in the stream. In Bavaria—land of *hock* and honey—shopping was sheer delight. Every little village had its market stalls in the square. One night in the Frankischer Jura mountains the nuns of a convent supplied us with a heaping sack of green beans.

There was a melon market in Bratislava that might have been in old Virginia. Water-melons, cantaloups, and little yellow melons, like oranges, in great, sweet-smelling pyramids. Milk, for some strange reason, was always a mystery—and usually goat's. In Hungary goose-liver paste—almost *foie gras*—was cheaper than butter. Partridges and venison cost less than ordinary meat. In the Balkans we lived on a sweet corn diet, they called it *kuckruts*, and usually gave it to us. When a Czecho-Slovak had me under arrest, I saw Eve in their cornfields being given armfuls of maize. White bread was unknown in the peasant villages. We bought slabs of the grey stuff, held it against our chests, and hacked off great hunks; but we could not eat the Balkans' buffalo butter. It both looked and tasted like lard. And, oddly enough, we had done 1,500 miles on the water before we bought our first fish.

We had a "frost box" made of porous clay, which, after we had soaked it in water, would keep our food cold on the blistering days. There was a tank under the after-deck holding ten gallons of fresh water. An African water-bag, worked on the process of evaporation, gave us three gallons of cool drinking water.

Each morning presented a new problem to be solved by our wake. To judge what distances we would attempt to make each day. To pick a safe anchorage at nights; some spot in the river where we could turn in and sleep without fear of being run down by some steamer or rolled out of our bunks. Anchors, riding and running lights, sails and motor—these had to be right. I would always test how our anchor was holding before turning in—and then sleep with one ear open.

With the lamp gently swinging in its gimbals we would lie in our comfortable cabin on raw, rainy nights and fall to sleep with the most soothing sound in the world in our ears—the croon of swift-running water.

Flame was our world.

Chapter 60

THE INVISIBLE LINE

THAT voyage of eight months gave us a shocking view of the worst side of Nationalism.

The trees were just the same across the German frontier, that invisible line, yet the streets of Emmerich were sullen with desperate men. It made us hate the fat dinner we had had at Arnhem in Holland, among the retired Dutch *nabobs* a few nights before. That invisible line. Austria was like entering a house of mourning, whose occupants were trying to murder each other; the "Hackenkreutzers" at the Communists' throats. Bavaria, that land of honey where every village was so beautiful we wanted to stop and live there for ever—Bavaria was full of *wandervogel* trying to walk away, to Hungary, to Roumania, to Turkey—trying to walk out of this world. Somewhere, they said to us hopefully, there must yet be a fine life? That invisible line. Wherever we touched it in Czecho-Slovakia we were arrested at once; everyone suspected everyone else—it was a new-born country, just given the lines of a frontier, and it was afraid to let anyone cross them. "The Czechs make trouble for everybody!" said some English officers in Vienna. Hungary, reduced to a third of its size, had a motto: "No! No! NEVER!"—that we heard at every turn. And in Budapest the feudal barons and officers were weeping openly at an opera where a hussar swore he would get back the shako he had lost in Transylvania. Inside the invisible lines that held the kingdom of the Serbs, Croats, and Slovenes we found them all plotting to assassinate each other, so that they could have separate frontier lines around themselves. Belgrade, that peasant capital, was still the spy-centre of Europe, with French, British, and Italian diplomats and commercial agents with government missions all trying to further their own political designs. One man in every seven in Belgrade was in a uniform of some sort; and at eleven o'clock every morning, when the *Politika* came out, everyone bought a copy of that disturbing newspaper and retired to a café to read and plot.

In Bulgaria, they shot at us, chiefly because they were drunk—and had we not tried to cross over from the Roumanian side of the river? Nevertheless, we carried away a great admiration for that stout little country.

The day we landed in Sofia a colonel in the army shot the Mayor, George Madjarov, and then blew out his own brains.

"There are two bodies lying over there in the Levsky," said the waiter as he put down our breakfast. "Colonel Tomov just shot the Mayor and then killed himself." He dusted the table-cloth to put down our eggs. "You can see them if you want to."

Sofia was so used to assassinations that it had its black flags out, merely furled, before all the public buildings, so that all they had to do was pull a cord to put the city in full mourning at once.

The Bulgarian Army had been reduced to 30,000; and fuming under its resentment every man in it was being trained to become a non-commissioned officer. The regiment of the Iskarskaya gave us a luncheon—and toasted the next war.

Along the new invisible lines to which the Roumanians had been allowed to move soldiers stood in a long line with needle-like bayonets; and when we penetrated into the forbidden land of Bessarabia we found them sticking these bayonets into the throats of ex-Russian peasants and shooting them as they tried to escape across the river at Kishenev. From one end of Roumania to the other—inside that invisible line—every official we met seemed to have his hand held out, not to greet us, but for a bribe of some sort.

That invisible line. Where the Treaty of Trianon had been imposed we found villages where the houses of the people were in Hungary and the railway station a few yards off was in Rou-mania. Hungarians had to go back country forty miles to find another railway station for their town. The power plant for the electric lights of a factory would be in Roumania, and the factory in Hungary—and therefore silent. Rivers which began in one country were having their courses diverted, so that they would not flow through to the enemy across that invisible line. A peasant's home would be in one country and his cattle's grazing-fields in another. He had to take his passport with him before he attempted to enter his own fields.

These lines had been drawn in all seriousness by a commission of supposedly intelligent Allied officers. Yet they were so patently absurd that even countries who hated each other were being forced to recognise ten-mile-wide neutral belts along such lines so that life could conduct itself.

We saw the Germans watching the French black troops strolling impudently along their boulevards in the Rhine and Ruhr; this, in 1924, when—if the French had permitted—the Allies could still have come to some peaceful arrangement with desperate Germany. We saw the Germans already preparing themselves for Nazi rule. In the Theatre Café, in Bamberg, I talked with a young German student and expressed my astonishment at the athletic activity I had seen all along the Rhine and Main; the swimming, sports, marching clubs and rowing-shells I had seen from one end of Germany to the other. They seemed a nation in training, I said. He smiled:

"Would you like to see our aeroplane factory?"

I was secretly conducted to what had been an Uhlan barracks before the war. Inside it was a class of German youth, both boys and girls. They were being shown the skeleton of a fuselage, mounted on small wooden horses. A blond young man clicked his heels as I was introduced.

"Herr Müller," said my student friend, then aside to me: "He brought down ten English during the war."

The plane they were building was a *Harth*—a famous glider. The workers were volunteers, students, enthusiasts who found the time after hours. Three of them were girls. For their work in helping to build the glider they received instruction in aeronautics and flying. They were burning with eagerness to take part in the big gliding tests in the Rhone valley. One was a dentist.

"They tried to tie our hands!" laughed Herr Müller, speaking of the victorious Allies. "They won't let us use bigger planes. So they make us learn how to fly like birds with these. We have found that we can do as much with a 20-h.p. motor as we used to do with a 120-h.p. during the war! Necessity is the mother of invention, you say—*ja?* And, of course," he added, "for the big work—we do that in Japan."

General Goering's material was being prepared for him in every village in Germany in 1924.

In the Ludwig's Canal my engine broke down, and a young man on the bank, with a scar on his forehead, came down to sit beside me and help me to repair it. As we talked I discovered he had been a pilot in Baron Richthofen's squadron—the dreaded Red Circus. He had been wounded three times, the last machine-gun bullet of an unknown Englishman creasing his forehead and ruining his eyesight. Otherwise, he asserted, he would now be flying in Morocco with the Riffs. Several of his friends had gone down to try and help Abdel Krim—and get a job.

He became so attached to us that he went along with us to Ratisbon in Bavaria, sleeping in a *gasthaus* or wherever he could on shore at nights. He sat in our cabin and drank *Schnapps* until midnight—talking about the next war without restraint. He began with the French, execrated them, said that all the German children were being taught as part of their regular lessons what the French were doing in the Ruhr. And why not? Wasn't that merely part of the school course in German history? Children could understand its meaning much better than dead dates in ancient history, he said. All sport carnivals, he declared, had one great purpose—to fit German manhood for war. He was intense in his hate—fanatical. German youth, he said, his voice shaking, had but one dream.

There would soon be another war—between Japan and America. Japan, of course, would win. England would make a vain, but half-hearted effort to help the United States. That would leave Germany free on the Continent. She would then subjugate France. Japan, flushed with victory, would overrun China and Siberia. Germany, master in Europe, would absorb European Russia.

Then the stage would be set. THE WAR! A Germanised Europe against a Japanese East. The only war of real importance.

That would be something to live for.

"Well, well!" we said, and put the cork back in the bottle of *Schnapps*.

I watched the French manufacture Hitler.

And it was what I saw among the peoples themselves, the boiler-house of resentment that the Versailles Treaty was making of each country, that stood me in such good stead in the next ten years reporting the fiasco of conference after conference where the French, skilfully evading any disarmament, were trying to inveigle the rest of the world into keeping Germany a third-rate Power.

There was nothing academic in this SAILING ACROSS EUROPE view of what was going on. There were plenty of real things to write about—mostly misery and hate.

That invisible line.

We set out from smug Holland in May. We ate our Christmas dinner in Angora, the capital of the new Turkish Republic. The Turks were fighting about a frontier line. They were on the verge of going to war with Great Britain over Mosul. British negotiators, knowing that Mosul had oil there, had skilfully managed to draw a line including Mosul inside British mandated territory at the optimistically-called Peace Conference of Versailles. Clemenceau had just apologised to his French public for giving it away, because, he pleaded, he hadn't known there was oil there. Mosul, as it happened, rightfully belonged to the Turks.

"The Turks," philosophised a distinguished British war correspondent, as we ate dinner on the train going up to Angora through Anatolia, "have nothing on their side in this case—except right. And precious little good that will do them!"

With Mustapha Kemal Pasha, his senses hurt, growling around his new palace in Tchankayia, and the Five Strong Men of Turkey assuring me that they might go to war with England at any minute, I talked with a Young Turk whom the British had imprisoned in Malta.

"But if you go to war with Great Britain, Chukri Bey!" I exclaimed, "it will mean the death of your Young Turkish Republic!"

Chukri Bey, who was bent like a bow from the articular-rheumatism he insisted he had acquired in the damp dungeons of Malta, drew himself up.

"If it comes to death," he said, "the Turks know how to die. Mosul belongs on our side of the line."

Chapter 61

SAILING ACROSS EUROPE

YACHTSMEN have sometimes expressed a wish to me that I had written a little more about the details and difficulties of navigating in my sailing across Europe from the north to the Black Sea. Buoys, shoals, rapids, customs regulations, etc., etc., I couldn't; I was too appalled by what I saw.

The hundred and twenty-five miles across Holland were the most peaceful of the eight months' trip. Time and again I thought regretfully of them; those gentle days on the Lek, where they swung their little pontoon bridges down-stream to let us pass, and little carved country carts waited at sandy roads that stopped at the water-edge for us to pass up. On hot, drowsy days, peaceful Holland always gave us the feeling of sailing along through a corner of some well-kept country estate. It was fascinating to cruise this country and win bend after bend, always with the pleasant expectation of seeing what lay beyond. On blue days, or grey days, when a sweater felt so comfortable, watching church steeple after church steeple come nearer across the Dutch sky. Or at nights, to lie off a little village like Schoonhoven, with its high green wall and red arch through the dyke, and hear—as we smoked our last cigarette—the tinkling church bells on shore playing little dance tunes, selections from opera and the music of the '80's. No wonder the Dutchmen were placid.

Above Emmerich we were caught in the maelstrom traffic of Rhine and Ruhr. For the next 265 miles, to Mainz, the Rhine is probably the most congested marine highway in the world. We moved among a never-ending concourse of steamers, and tugs with tows of barges at least half a mile long. Off the big Krupp works at Hochfeld we saw hundreds of 2,000- and 3,000-ton barges lying out in the stream. We got a tow up the Rhine, lashed alongside a tug, as our puny engine could not buck that current. The Rhine towns turn their best faces to the river. No advertisements mar the banks. The Germans know how to keep their Fatherland's beauty. Every town had its *schwimmbads*, and it seemed as if all Germany was lying naked in the sun. So we went—Dusseldorf, then for hours the twin spires of the peerless cathedral of Cologne loomed purple-grey through the rain. We lay in the basin of Cologne all one night, and Eve and I looked up the German officer-family in whose garrison town in the Black Forest she had been "finished" just at the outbreak of the World War. They were Guards officers, only one left alive; terribly wounded, he was acting as interpreter for the Allies in Cologne. "I get along well with the British," he said. "I like them. I am afraid to talk to the French. I am always afraid they will make me do something silly. I hate them so."

The bridge of Bonn, now undergoing repairs with its gargoyles painted red; by the Drachenfals; past Coblenz—black French troops strutting under the lime trees—and then the Rhine gorge, the legendary Rhine! Promenades, *bier-gartens*, vineyards like shelves; and the famous ruined castles, perched so neatly on their crags that they might have been a stage setting.

Above the rocks of the Lorelei our dinghy heard the call of the sirens. We caught the last inch of its painter as it whisked over the transom. In the Binger rapids we nearly lost *Flame*. Special pilots are taken aboard the tugs before ascending these rapids where the Rhine is less than fifty yards wide. The pilot of our tug forgot about *Flame*, being towed here by every inch I dared spare of our hemp warp to cushion any shocks. *Flame* was snatched through a permanent wave of white water and her bow-bitts were completely yanked out. Fortunately, I had taken the extra precaution of making the last of the tow rope fast around the mast. It just held. We passed the Mouse tower—now used as a signal station, with a white ball on its shaft to show when the rapids are clear—and entered smooth water.

Here we passed out of the gorge into a broad Rhine again, a tranquil Rhine, running through a rolling farm land, its hills soft, hazy blue in the pastel of distance. But it was only a temporary easement of effort, for at Mainz we crossed over and entered the Main to begin the 240-mile climb up to Bamberg.

For 190 miles of this trip we were hauled up by a continuous submerged chain into the mountains of Bavaria.

The Main is an enchanting river.

Its steep mountain slopes are dotted with villages like the old German illustrations for *Grimms' Fairy Tales*. Goose greens, high wedge-shaped little roofs, and storks' nests on the chimney tops.

Under our own power, and by much hauling and pushing, we got up as far as Obernau above Wurzburg, but there we had a rebuff. The Main swept us back; and at Aschaffenburg, below the palace of Mad Ludwig, we had to make fast to the *Kette-Boot*.

The *Kette-Boot*, the chain-boat, that pulls itself up on one continuous chain the 190 miles between Aschaffenburg and Bamberg, is one of the weirdest marine monsters afloat. Its grinding motors pull the chain in at the bow and disgorge it from the *Kette-Boot's* stern. And, with eight barges in tow, and *Flame* lashed to her side, we anchored off Dorfprezelten that first night. Grinding along, hauling ourselves up against the current of the Main, from six in the morning until eight at night, we had made exactly thirty-three miles. That was our pace.

That gave us plenty of time to see the countryside. The deep-forested mountains, the little villages with their ancient stone walls still intact (walls along which I used to run, trying to find a gateway to buy butter and eggs for our breakfast) and then the deep hills of vineyards which supplied the fine white wines we drank so freely all day.

Even ascending the Main to Aschaffenburg, we had climbed through twelve red-sandstone locks in fifty-four miles. Now, at Bamberg, we dropped the *Kette-Boot* and entered one of the most beautiful canals in the world—the old Ludwig's. It had been begun by Charlemagne and was now almost dying away. We were probably the first and last craft of our type to go through it. Four miles longer than Suez, twice as long as the Panama, it was then the only fresh-water link across Europe connecting the North and Black Seas. Probably the most unknown and least-used waterway in the world, the German Consulate had never heard of it when we tried to find out in London if it was still open for even small craft. It climbed over the fabulously beautiful Frankischer Jura mountains in a series of steps—101 locks in 107 miles.

So shallow and so overgrown with weeds was it, that we could not use our motor, and I hauled *Flame*, with a rope around my waist, over the Frankischer Jura range! As soon as breakfast was over, I would go out on the towpath and turn myself into a horse. *Flame* was 2½ tons dead weight, and it took me three weeks to pull her over the mountains that 107 miles. There were places where, straining on my rope, I could look down on the roofs of villages lying below me.

This was the Prince-Bishop country. A deep land of convents and monasteries and castles on towering crags. A legendary land to which we had brought the *Flame*. It was also a land of drowsy afternoons, when I would sprawl for hours, drinking my beer slowly (for even tow-horses drink), with the reminiscent keeper of some almost-forgotten lock. I was in no hurry to leave this gentle land. I shot deer up here with the *burgomeister* of Maiern. The great buck stood in a cleft in the forest, and above him I saw the turrets of a castle perched on its grey needle of rock. It was like an ancient tapestry.

Wandervogel came and sat on the banks beside us at nights, banks flowered with millions of glow-worms. They told us their troubles, their hopes, their fears. Sometimes they would look uneasily over their shoulders into the dark forest:

"Many men and women sleep in these woods at night!" they said nervously.

We knew what they meant. We had encountered them. Hungry, haggard people, who just came to the water-edge and there stared at us sullenly without ever saying a word. "Desperate characters," men and women, who would stagger on—sooner or later to provide a ghastly tragedy of some sort. Near Nuremberg one night the police surrounded the woods and arrested forty-one people. Five they hauled off to prison—they were criminals.

For three enchanted weeks we climbed over the Frankischer Jura mountains, then we locked out into the pleasant little Altmuhl, went down that tributary, and there—racing and grey—

was the upper Danube beginning its 1,600 mile journey to the Black Sea.

Three hundred miles below us lay Vienna. There was the old stone bridge below us at Ratisbon to shoot, rapids and rocks to wreck our craft. But we had crossed the Frankischer Jura, the backbone of Europe. We began the long descent to the Black Sea.

We missed disaster by inches shooting the A.D. 1300 bridge of Ratisbon. Once out in that swift current of the Danube pouring out from its gorge above Kelheim we were helpless. The steeples and roofs of Ratisbon simply raced at us as *Flame* hurled her 2½ tons dead weight at the one navigable arch of the bridge. We had taken our masts out to get under this arch. Not until the last minute did I see that the peasants at Kelheim had directed us to steer through the wrong arch. It was choked with rocks so that a white froth of rapids was sluicing through it. I had to swing *Flame* sharply to the right and try to hit a small open hole of arch by the town wall. We just made it, grazing it as we shot through. All I saw of it was a row of open mouths from the Ratisboners wondering what on earth was this craft doing up above the bridge, some yells as we shot down perilously at the bridge—and then the sun was shining on the back of my head again. The bridge was being snatched away into the distance behind us, Ratisboners wildly waving us a good-bye salute.

At Vilshofen we shot the rapids and hit a rock ledge just as we went into them. This broke our keel. We got her down the two hundred odd miles to Vienna, running below the great castles of the Wachau valley. We shot the Struden below Grein—a real whirlpool—and in a blinding white cloudburst ran on the rock ledge off the robber castle of Aggstein; passed the Benedictine Abbey of Melk, the Medelite of the Nibelungen, and anchored one windy night below the castle of Durnstein, where Richard the Lion-Hearted had lain prisoner.

Finally, we ran *Flame* right into the heart of Vienna and came to rest in the Schottenring.

The next day I took *Flame* over to a shipyard for repairs, and

Eve and I took a taxi to the old Meissl und Schaden, in which hotel for the old Viennese we lay for hours simply revelling in a hot bath.

It was a rapid descent in civilisation after leaving Budapest.

Hungary we adored. Admiral Horthy, Regent of Hungary, invited me to a partridge shoot out at Göddöllö, the old hunting lodge of the Hapsburgs, where I shot with five admirals—not one of whom now had a ship. And as His Serene Highness and I got covered with mud that day, trying to push the Royal motor-car out of a ditch, I had to sit in a bath-tub in the Palace while my shooting clothes were dried.

The Admiral, Regent of Hungary, came into the bathroom with a decanter of brandy and two glasses in his hand. He filled one for me and sat down on the edge of the tub.

"You shot very well today," he told me.

I almost drowned from sheer pride.

At Göddöllö, old Baron Pronay, "the last of the real Hungarians," drove off in his own coach and four. He still refused to ride in a motor-car. But before he left he commanded me to see the State stud farms at Mezohegyes and then to go up to the Puszta—and live with the Hungarian cowboys.

"There!" he said, with his blazing Magyar eyes, "on the Puszta you will see the Hungary of three hundred years ago."

Hungary since then, Baron Pronay seemed to think, was not up to much.

So I went down and shot partridges at Mezohegyes on the Roumanian frontier; and then we were the guests of the city of Debreczen out on the Hortobage, the great Hungarian plain of *Fata Morgana*. On a sky-line so bleak that a horseman could be seen for miles, we drank red wine and sang with the Magyar cowboys:

"For I am a csikos of the Puszta and not a gulyas,
I will wind my lasso on my shoulder,
I will saddle my white-footed horse,
And I will pull down the brilliant stars of heaven. . . ."

Mournfully they sang as our fires died down:

"The wild geese and the herons cry,
Good man, you will remain alone, alone on the Puszta,
For here no one has a winter refuge,
Every bird hastens to his quarter."

These cowboys of the Puszta have not changed much since the days of the Mongol invasion. Their faces, cast in the firelight, were Mongol themselves. The costumes they wear today have merely duplicates in the famous Esterhazy collection in Budapest. And they have the arrogance of their "own Attila."

"God in His Heaven," they say, "is certainly a great God; but neither am I a dog!"

In Yugoslavia a Serbian frontier guard loaned me the money to get to Belgrade, as I could not get my letter of credit cashed before there. "Don't worry," said Dragan, "send it back to me whenever you feel like it—from America, if you want." *Flame* lay in the Sava for a couple of weeks while Eve and I motored across Bosnia and Herzegovina, that stronghold of Allah, to the Adriatic coast. We saw the veiled women of Sarajevo and Mostar, and in the deep mountains far back we saw a Mohammedan fanaticism that was obviously growing more bitter each day as it watched the Westernisation of Egypt and Turkey. After a few days of sensuous loafing and swimming at Ragusa we went up Mount Lovcen into Montenegro. I accompanied the American Professor Shotwell—fulfilling his mission from the Carnegie Foundation—to see who had really started the World War.

Eve and I started one ourselves against the bed bugs we found.

In Bulgaria they shot at us one morning, because they thought we were smugglers, and gave us a regimental dinner the next day. We ate with the regiment out on an open cliff overhanging the Danube, with the widows of four wars around us. Eve danced the Horo with the *Iskarskayia* regiment's colonel that night, and I danced with its sergeant-major until he collapsed me on the floor.

The regiment carried me around the square on its shoulders

after they had made me get up and make a speech—which nobody understood—not even I.

In Roumania they began by offering up a prayer for us in church. That was Father Bufanu in the little village of Coronini, at the head of the rapids of Drinkovo and the Gorge of Kazan, where no ship ever stops or road passes. Father Bufanu insisted, when we turned up off their village, that he had a dream about me the previous night. "Distinctly—I saw a man with fair hair like you—and he came to us in a ship." After we had that awkward sensation of bowing down on our hands and knees on the church floor among the peasants while we heard him calling up to God in our names, Father Bufanu gave us a luncheon of turkey and caviare, and a little list of notes. "These are the things you must do!" he insisted. They were:

1. Get a small dog to give warning when the Bulgarians attack you.

2. You are on the edge of a very dangerous part of the Danube. No one is allowed to proceed below Drinkovo through the rapids, the Gorge of Kazan, and the Iron Gates, without taking a pilot. You must be sure to get a good pilot.

3. When in Bukarest you must see our Queen.

Unfortunately, or perhaps fortunately, we did none of these things. The Bulgars had already shot at us before we had time to think of a dog. We shot the rapids of Drinkovo, and obtained permission to shoot the Gorge of Kazan and the Iron Gates on our own. Sweeping down through that miraculous gorge we passed directly under Trajan's old legend, cut clearly in its grey walls of sheer rock:

IMP. CAESAR DIVI. NERVAE F. NERVA TRAIANUS AUG. GERM PONT MAXIMUS TRIBI.

His first Dacian campaign!

A line of seven black buoys marked the dreaded Iron Gates. These Iron Gates had been an obstacle to us even back in Chicago. The Germans used locomotives to tow steamers up through this race of water during the World War. It takes a special towing-steamer two hours to climb this downpour of the Danube. We shot down it in precisely six minutes.

All we lost were some cups and saucers that a lurch or sudden wind swept off the deck.

In one place we slept in three different countries in three consecutive nights. We blew in before a stiff gale to Turnu-Severin in Roumania; rolled the next night off Radujevac in Serbia; and on the third evening watched a crescent moon tip the minarets of Bulgarian Vidin.

Nothing could stop us from reaching the Black Sea now but winter—or the Roumanian police.

At Galatz in Roumania we had to beach *Flame* again to have her repaired. The keel I had broken up at Vilshofen, and repaired in Vienna, was broken again. Her stem had also been smashed against a rock. We nearly foundered before Turnu-Severin. Winter nearly got us while I fumed and fretted at Galatz. The ship workers tried to murder our boat. Galatz was not a lovely town. It was distinguished by two things. One was its eunuchs, a Russian religious sect, nearly all of whom were cab-drivers. And this seemed to me an ideal solution of the tough taxi-driver problem. The other was a sign in our hotel:

LADIES AND GENTLEMENS WILL PLEASE RETURN TO THEIR OWN ROOMS BY MIDNIGHT.

The winds of winter were howling now.

They were distressing winds that howled across the flat Roumanian marshes and went on shrieking down the high yellow bluffs of the Bulgarian shore.

This was late December.

With an army shirt, leather vest, two sweaters and coat of thick Harris tweed, I felt my flesh congealing inside me. Eve looked like Bibendum, wearing practically everything she had in layers under a thick rubber sea slicker. In a gale that would be blowing the tobacco out of my cigarette we would often sit there in the cockpit, struggling with *Flame*, wondering whether it was worth while to go on or just run in behind the lee of the first point we met. We would have on many an occasion if it had not been that we were now racing winter every foot of this last lap to the Black Sea.

There was no danger, of course, as far as ourselves were concerned. But it would be only too easy to lose the *Flame*. Following a raft of ducks one day, I grounded *Flame* in some sand bars near the Roumanian swamps, and wept with fatigue before I could get her afloat again. She weighed 2½ tons, dead weight; and that was almost an impossibility for one man to push off a bar up against a four-mile current. When I had done it (helped by a steamship's wash) I lay in the cockpit and sobbed.

In the lower Danube there are broad, shallow stretches where the wind can pick up a sea that almost exposes the river mud. We had to go through a day like this trying to make Corabia in Roumania. *Flame* rolled in these waves until I thought she was going to turn over. We had some aluminium plates washed out of our cockpit. And at one time, a sheltered point on the Bulgarian shore seemed the most tempting haven of my life. I felt that if I could reach it nothing else mattered.

But when we reached it, Eve and I looked at each other and nodded. It was not to anchor, but to go on. We took a few minutes' breathing space, watched by some Bulgarian shepherds on the high bank, and then we shoved out again to wallow across the yellow seas. And at nightfall we ran inside the sand bars off Corabia. We had made our objective.

But everything inside the *Flame* was soaking wet. We had no food except some cold unappetising boiled duck, and so we sat there and drank the whole of a bottle of Cointreau to cheer us up. It was the only thing to drink we had aboard, and we were too dead beat to go ashore.

With envy we thought about our friends who went across Europe in railway trains.

That was a sample of one of those last days. I can give you another—when we went down the wrong side of an island—couldn't get back against the wind and current, and *Flame* rolled in a rough sea until everything inside her was a shambles. A day when we contemplated spending that night—and more days—on an uninhabited swampy island, and poor little *Flame* looked so nearly done for that I actually took out her insurance policy, "Navigators and General," and buttoned it in my back pocket in case we had to make a quick swim for it at the last moment. We would very likely have got to shore all right, but *Flame* would have been finished.

That was the trouble of taking a boat like *Flame* across Europe, a boat whose yacht register was 5 tons, and whose dead weight was 2½ tons. It is so easy to lose her. If ever I make that trip again I will do it in a canoe. You have no responsibilities there.

There were days when the wild geese skimmed in black lines over the wave crests.

Fine days—to talk about afterward. There was a daybreak off Turski Cebar, in Bulgaria, when in a peach-coloured dawn I looked upon minarets drenched with rain and Mohammedans in ragged red turbans fishing for sturgeon in a yellow-green sea.

The night off Radujevac in Serbia was as black and ominous as a tiger's throat. Then for some reason the stars suddenly appeared in the sky, and from the black silhouette of trees on shore we heard the squirling music of flutes, and the drums going. There was a savage Eastern rhythm to those drum thuds—like a tom-tom.

Long, windy nights, when we slept to a long length of cable and *Flame* rolled in the waters.

In the Roumanian swamps we wandered around in a lost land where the water ran like the veins in an anatomical chart. This wilderness was the "bandit country," land of the celebrated Cocosh and Varlan, the last of whom was a merry brigand who had a theatrical wardrobe of disguises that ranged from a shoe salesman to an admiral in the Roumanian Navy. And a very good admiral he would have made, too. The whole Roumanian Army tried to catch him and couldn't. And here was the only time in our eight months' cruise that I wanted to use the revolver that I had so casually carried past the customs officials of a dozen countries—neatly tucked under the seat of our little W.C.

I woke up to find Eve's face almost touching mine.

"Someone is on the boat!"

We were in the heart of the swamps with not a village for miles. We had tied up behind the wreck of an old barge for that night. I thought Eve must be crazy; then following her hand my eyes saw a naked leg from about the ankle up, smack against the porthole over my very head.

In the lurch I gave to get that Luger, strapped under the W.C. seat, I forgot that I was sleeping in a "flea-bag." I landed with a crash on the *Flame's* cabin floor. At the same instant there was a great rocking of the boat, then a heave, to tell us that someone had jumped ashore.

When I got out into the cockpit, with the automatic, I found myself alone in the empty moonlight. I thought it must all have been a mistake—until I noticed that someone had pulled up our line attached to the barge, so that he could step down on to our boat from the barge's projecting stern. We cast loose and with a couple of duck loads in my shotgun we sat up that night to await our stranger's return.

Chapter 62

THE BLACK SEA AGAIN

ALL GREAT expectations as they near fulfilment frighten one just a bit. I had begun to rap wood three times every time I mentioned the Black Sea. When the Dutchmen laughed at us when I said I intended to take *Flame* across Europe, I told Eve to say we were only going as far as Vienna. That was talking softly . . . and within what seemed probability. But as country after country rolled in our wake—we began to say, "When we reach the Black Sea."

I used to console myself that if everything went wrong—we could float down. Then:

"Because of low water this year it is feared the Danube will freeze over early. The steamers loading at Galatz . . ."

The British Consul at Galatz read this out from his paper to us as we were having tea. The clay-stone in his cosy home was going full blast, yet I felt a chill race down my spine.

"Surely. . . . But the Danube simply can't freeze over—like that!"

He smiled, the somewhat sarcastic smile of the well-born Englishman: "The Danube," he said, "has been known to freeze in a night. It was in 1923, I think, that we had forty ships locked in the river."

He was a nice Consul, who had provided us with baths, and he added sympathetically: "But that was exceptional. Usually it is just jam ice, floating down from the tributaries, that clogs the river. Nevertheless, I should hurry."

I couldn't hurry. The dead-head I had hit above Novisad had not only broken our stem and keel—the engine of *Flame* was broken. A new propeller-shaft was being installed. She was high and dry on the beach. Each morning had found a new set of promises and delays.

"Oh, yes!" said a British skipper, when I asked him about the chances. "Why, we've had 'em frozen in as they were leaving Galatz. Right out in the middle of the river—stuck there all winter, too—couldn't get 'em to shore.

"I'm clearing out," he said.

I watched them go. Down through the marshes to the open sea. . . .

Padmore, Liverpool; *Wright*, Stockholm; *The City of Naxos*, Chios; *Taxiarchis*, *Gastein*, Trieste; *Naperadak*, Split; *Arta*, Bremen; the *Leonidas* from Antwerp. . . .

Grim, great, rusty with the salt of white seas; the tramps and grain ships of Europe were clearing out. They went down, one after another, waved . . . and their smoke died away.

Galatz, the big grain port from the Pruth, is ninety-two miles from the sea, and the Danube, capricious as ever, widens and deepens there, so that one feels it would be like trying to freeze over the ocean. Then, where the ruins of an old Greek church rise from the bushes, it suddenly begins to fray out. One leaves the broad river, enters a narrow little branch to the right, swings past the town of Tulcea in the Dobrudja, and enters what looks like a creek cloaked with willows. That is the Sulina Canal, the only open outlet of the Danube in thousands and thousands of miles of flat marsh. This is the famous—or infamous—Danube Delta and it looked like the grave of my hopes.

I had crossed Europe nearly 3,000 miles, and on the very last lap of it I might lose my race. *Almost* to reach the Black Sea would be worse than never having started at all. I had no philosophy against defeats like that.

I sat on the beach and watched the ice forming in pools. I put on more sweaters, I walked about nervously, came back—to seize a spanner myself; raved like a maniac when I caught them trying to *drive* the propeller-shaft through the stuffing box, instead of taking it down. I made myself so unpopular that the Roumanians were glad to get me out of Galatz. At 2.30 one afternoon *Flame* was slid into the water, given a quick try-out, and Eve and I slung our duffel aboard. Without waiting to stow things we pushed off down river.

That night, after butting along into an icy head sea, we ran on until late in the moonlight, and only when the moon slid down behind the black willows did we anchor above the island of Isaccea. I heard drums and flutes and saw lights through the tracery of trees. The peasants were dancing on shore. Their crops were all in, they had money to spend on wine, and the long winter when they would sleep on the top of their stoves was about to descend. We turned in with all our clothes on, dodged the dripping sweat from the cabin roof—congealed by our faithful little Primus cooker. But—

"When we reach the Black Sea," said Eve, "we simply must get some kind of stove."

She had said "when" and not "if"—because *Flame* was cruising again. We were racing the winter.

Dawn, a gold-clear cutting day, and I was glad that I had drained the water from my cylinder-jacket and intake pipes the previous night. Our drinking water had a surface of ice. It was a stupendous day, and we were off as quickly as we could get started after dawn.

As we bore down on our first objective, the old Greek church in the swamp, the S.S. *Albanian*, Italian Mail, came slowly past us. She was manoeuvring to hit the cut, and then we saw her charging into a clump of willows. "Good God!" I thought, "her steering gear has gone wrong!" But she was in the Sulina Canal. The Sulina Canal—a straight dash now to the Black Sea.

Come on, winter!

A man came out of the little white house on the bank that bore the red-white-and-blue flag of the European Danube Commission, rushed back for his binoculars, put them down to wipe his eyes, and stood there looking as if he could not believe what he saw. Then suddenly he took off his hat, waved it, and made us a deep bow. We waved our arms wildly in return. Turning to face what was ahead of me I saw just a flat yellow strip under a world of grey sky. The world was suddenly empty of everything except that long desolate low sky-line—the great delta of the Danube.

At sunset we came to a patch of hard ground along which some peasants were strolling in strange, beautiful hats. They were also celebrating the fact that their harvest was in and the cold winter could not harm them now. In this abundance of rushes their huts had a thatch that was two feet thick, and the sides of their houses were covered with another layer of rushes like cloaks; and in this wind-swept world each thatched little hut stood in a wind-proof fence of rushes which had been plaited like a mat.

"Please, Mister," said a Yugoslav employed by the Danube Commission, "you stop by here tonight?"

We told him we would, and we anchored just aft the E.D.C. sounding boat. He insisted that we come aboard and have some cognac and jam. We came out in the sunset to see a sky of flamingo over the marsh and heard some fishers singing as they swept past in their skiff; and looking over a rush-plaited fence we saw a bride and groom dancing under the apple trees, three fiddlers stamping time with their feet and a tom-tom player giving queer, little yelping shrieks as they thumped the drum-heads and the peasants clapped their hands.

What queer dreams that night—of the countries that lay in our wake.

The world was an infinity of sky over a featureless marsh, and here, suddenly, we felt the sea—a "lift" in our senses. There was nothing to mark it—just the "feel." We knew it was there. Then like a dream, some fanciful port in a reverie of adventure, appeared the gold-crossed, fantastic red Russian towers, the lighthouses, the slant sailing rigs and the black hulls of the ocean tramps in Sulina. We ran down past a medley of foreign shipping, saw the snow-swept English lawns of the Danube Commission, faced the red and green lighthouses at the Danube's mouth—and there, coffee-coloured, pounding and white, raced the everlasting waves of the barbaric Black Sea.

We had sailed across Europe.

Chapter 63

FORBIDDEN BESSARABIA

THE NIGHT we reached the Black Sea a snow-storm almost sank *Flame*. We woke up in the morning and found our cockpit one big drift. It was dangerously cold. A rain-storm came along and that froze, and our mooring ropes became long sticks of thick ice. We had to wait some time at Sulina, we did not know how many days, to get a steamer of some sort to take us away. All the big grain ships had finished for that season and we had to trust to luck. During this time we thought we would make a dash into forbidden Bessarabia, where I wanted to get off with the Russian sturgeon fishermen in the Black Sea.

Bessarabia was really a forbidden land, where a reign of terror was going on. A special visa was required before you could get into it. They had refused us visas in Galatz, so we walked aboard a little steamer called *Basil the Wolf* at 5 A.M. in Sulina one winter morning and were having tea beside the Governor of Bessarabia in Ismail that night. He obviously couldn't have known who we were because, as we learned afterwards, he must have had the order for my arrest from Bukarest in his pocket. Or maybe it only reached him after we had gone on.

Ismail, shivering, inexpressively lonely, with its patient bearded *isvostchiks* and Orthodox Greek church with its piles of Byzantine cupolas, was as Russian as any tale of Chekov. It is really impossible to beat the dullness, ugliness and loneliness of those provincial Danube-delta towns. I found my man there, Valparaiso Politikin, a Roumanian naturalised Argentine—if you can imagine such a combination—and after rouging his lips, rice-powdering his cheeks and getting into a perfumed shirt of crossed golden hunting horns, he showed me his commode—"Genuine Limoges— *n'ech pas?*" he said with a strong Spanish lisp—and then he took me out to mix with the *haut société* of Ismail. It would be a *thé dansant*, said Valparaiso, and would be *"très, très distingué!"* because the Roumanian officials and their wives would be there, together with some exiled Russian aristocracy. One of which last would be the Prince from whom he had bought the Limoges commode with the Cupids inside it.

The White Russian *émigrés* were a desperate and destitute lot, and it was quite patent to the eye that one or two of the prettier women among them were facing the fate of concubinage to keep some rouged Roumanian officer warm through the long, cold, otherwise weary Bessarabian winter nights.

Valparaiso asked me if I did not think Ismail charming?

The next day we went on to Wilkowo, the Roumanian sturgeon centre, where I left Eve to sleep on the top of a Lipovane peasant's stove and went down in a fishing *lodka* to the Black Sea. The *lodka* was sailed by five bearded, barbaric-looking Russians who looked like some men from the Golden Horde of Jenghiz Khan. They called themselves the Tshahinka Fishing Co., and that night I slept in their hut in the Danube marshes.

It was a clay hut, inside which was an enormous clay stove. After we had drunk the two bottles of vodka I had brought along, Feodor Tshahinka and I exchanged first names and then we all went to bed on the stove. The old grandmother and grandfather were given the place of honour, which was up on the heel of the stove over the burning rushes. Feodor placed himself thoughtfully between me and his pretty young peasant wife, and the other four men from the Tshahinka Fishing Co., stretched out beside me like sentinels. When one turned, we all turned. It was all very *gemutlich*—and stuffy.

"Sometimes," boasted Feodor, "we get a sturgeon as big as this skiff!"

They catch the sturgeon down there with nets made of bare hooks. Hung from buoys these deadly rakes hang a few inches above the sea floor. The great sturgeon, nosing their way along the Black Sea to enter the Danube to spawn, touch these hooks, give a frightened flick—and are impaled.

We were coated with ice. Feodor and Matve pulled in the glistening hooks while the two others held the boat steady in the heaving seas. They hauled in a black and white sturgeon as big as myself, and in a murderous tangle of flying hooks they beat it to death with wooden clubs. It had great, cold, moon-stone eyes. Another sturgeon, hammering the floor-boards with his steel-hard head, was small enough to keep themselves. They hacked him to bits as we neared shore and stuffed all of him down inside their black leather boots. "For our dinners!" laughed Feodor.

They did not laugh much. For they had to surrender the big sturgeon to the Roumanian Government for whatever the corrupt officials at Wilkowo chose to offer. These officials, claimed Feodor, were in the fish business as middlemen themselves. And on every point of hard land that we passed in the marsh there was a soldier, with a bayonet, who made us come in and show him our catch.

That night we ate rich sturgeon soup, all of us from the same wooden bowl (it was good manners, I learned, to lick your spoon clean before you put it back to dip again); and I dreamed of the great sturgeon, climbing up the Danube with their cold moon-stone eyes.

The ice cracked and boomed in the frozen marshes around us.

Back in Wilkowo the next afternoon Eve told me of a disquieting episode she had had with the Port-captain. Coming back to the Lipovane's hut after a walk she had caught him, red-handed, going through our baggage. His hand was in my suitcase, in fact.

"You should be more careful," he said blandly. "You should lock these when you go out."

Eve thought it half-funny and half-infuriating, until the peasant woman whispered to her that the police had been asking her about us that morning. I had half expected to be picked up in Bessarabia, but I wasn't going to let it happen if we could help it —too far from a white man's Consulate of any sort—so I ran back to the sturgeon wharf, found Feodor (we were blood brothers by now), and told him that we would go back with him.

We spent that night in the lonely marsh, and the next day, instead of going out for sturgeon, the Tshahinka Fishing Co., in great style, sailed Eve and me in their black *lodka* down the Black Sea. It was a cold clear day with a bright sun and Feodor sailed her beautifully across the sparkling waves. Having left it unannounced and unseen at 5 A.M. one morning, the next Sulina saw of us was when we came sailing in a Bessarabian fishing *lodka* from the Black Sea. We saw the British Vice-Consul's youngest son, just out from a public school in England! Waving to us from their office:

"Stay on board your boat!" he called.

Then he rowed across and told us that the Roumanian police were going to arrest me. They had been looking for us everywhere, they told his father, who, quite truthfully, had told them had not the faintest idea where we were!

It was a tiresome, irritating third degree that they put me through, as can be seen from the verbatim transcription of the letter which the Greek who interpreted for me (he was a clerk in the Consulate) gave me before I left. "In case you have trouble," he said:

"REPORT OF GREEK-ROUMANIAN INTERPRETER OF CONVERSATIONS BETWEEN NEGLEY FARSON AND THE RUMANIAN SECRET SERVICE POLICE

"On presentation of Mr. Farson's passport to the Secret Police, the rekown Siguranta for the obtaining of a visa for Bessarabia the individual charged by the Roumanian head quarters of the secret police for the granting of such visa informed me that he was unable to do so as he had every reason to doubt Mr. Farson's visit to Bessarabian territory, he added that he will ask for instructions and that he will let me know whether he is going to grant one or not. He requested me to inform Mr. Farson that he is ill and that he was not visible.

"On the next day about two P.M. he informed me that he is not going to grant the visa.

"As Mr. Farson proceeded to Tulcea he was very anxious to know whether he intends to land at Vilkov or not. As he was informed by me that I did not know where the gentleman proceeded he bombarded all the towns in Bessarabia with telegrams reporting the arrival of Mr. Farson. He did not finish with me before he was certain of obtaining no information whatever with regard to Mr. Farson's visit to the country in question.

"On Mr. Farson's return to Sulina, he asked me to find out on his behalf where he has been how he came back and what he states. Of course he was not successful.

"On the 9th of December he rang the office up and asked for Mr. Farson to present himself in the Secret Police offices for interrogation. On my presenting Mr. Farson he told me that he had instructions to arrest him but that he was not going to do so for some apparent reason. He said that he could not grant a visa to Mr. Farson to go to Bessarabia as the whether emanating from Russia was too cold. Mr. Farson asked him whether he could obtain a visa in summer when he smiled and states that he does not know. He then asked Mr. Farson to produce his papers and requested me to remain in his offices pending Mr. Farson's return with his papers in the course of my stay there he told me after opening a draw containing some Roumanian money that why I do not tell him what Mr. Farson is after and that he has every reason to believe that Mr. Farson is after spying on some mission entrusted him.

"Mr. Farson returned to the Secret Police offices and he was asked all sorts of questions which were put down on a form. This form I was asked to sign and Mr. Farson signed. On Mr. Farson asking him for a blank form he stated that he has to account for the forms that he uses and that they were expensive and he had better apply to Bucarest for one. He finished by saying that the sooner the Journalist goes the better, that he will take steps to find out why Mr. Bibescu at Washington granted Mr. Farson a diplomatic pass. He does not like the visit and murmured some thing which was of a nature, stating that he is not a damned fool.

"(Signed)

"NEMITAC"

The Consul and I went duck shooting out in the Delta, which was all the Roumanian King's game preserve. He had been given the right to shoot on it and, as he was a fanatic sportsman, that made Sulina's exile bearable, as far as he was concerned. For the women, it must have been a living death.

That Englishman and his family saved us from the worst of

Sulina. They let us have a bath in their warm home every day. And on the last night, when it was agony to sleep aboard frozen *Flame* any longer, they took Eve over to sleep with them. The next morning, when I found that I had to chip the ice off the companionway doors with a screw-driver to get out into my cockpit, I decided to put *Flame* ashore.

The Danube Commission beached her for me. She disappeared under the succeeding days' snow; and one night Eve and I went over and sorrowfully said good-bye to her.

The next day an Italian mail steamer was taking us down the Black Sea to Constantinople.

Chapter 64

TEN YEARS WANDERING

FOR THE next ten years I watched the world come to bits. For the first six years I was not in any one country for over six months. I talked with Dictators, I shot the great fin-whale with the dean of Norwegian gunners, I sat with Gandhi under his mango tree at Karadi, and I went up to Lossiemouth, to talk with Ramsay MacDonald, at "The Hillocks," after the fall of the British Labour Party government. I watched ten years of conferences fulsomely announce that they had "agreed on all major points," and then collapse. After an absence of seven years I made a trip back to my own country, to sit with the strikers, listen to the wails of my taxable friends, talk with the drought-stricken farmers and cowboys of the Dakotas, to see if America was really getting a new sense of values under Roosevelt. I talked with Roosevelt in the White House and had a private view of John Dillinger, naked on the slab, after he had been shot. I watched Stalin review the Red Army in the Red Square. I met some great men such as Roosevelt and Gandhi. And I met some *good* men, such as Lord Irwin, Viceroy of India, and George Lansbury. The strongest Englishman I met was Stanley Baldwin.

But for the rest of the world's public figures I am still waiting to see their retribution which is so long overdue.

Chapter 65

KEMAL DEFIES THE BRITISH

THE MINARETS of Stamboul rising up through the rain were all that Pierre Loti had led me to hope as our ship came down the Bosphorus. But they were there in defiance. The streets of Pera had succumbed to progress. Except that they were extraordinarily painful to climb they had been reduced to the monotonous level to which Western ideals would reduce all our sensations and scenes. They would have been exceedingly dull were it not for the fact that all Turkey was in turmoil at that moment.

Mustapha Kemal Pasha was in the throes of the Westernisation of the old Ottoman Empire. To break the grip of the Church over the State he had abolished the fez and driven the teaching away from the mosques. Death was the penalty for disobedience, and his Tribunals of Independence were hanging rebellious Turks wholesale—*pour encourager les autres*. That was an inside war, mostly against the entrenched *mullahs*. Against the foreigner the Ghazi had his motto "TURKEY FOR THE TURKS"—(especially the Anatolian Turks)—and the *Cercle d'Orient* in Pera was full of furious Englishmen who were railing against the new restrictions placed upon foreigners both in commerce and legal matters. In reality about all Mustapha Kemal Pasha had done was to abolish the amazing privileges that the foreign Powers had previously been able to bribe or threaten from the Sublime Porte. The Greeks had a more poignant point of view as they had been driven into the sea with the burning of Smyrna, and most of their properties in Turkey had been confiscated—with just a Turkish promise of compensation.

The Greek Ambassador, a superb type of Parisian *boulevardier*, sadly said to me, "There are three things, M'sieu, a man should not do: have a wife in Roumania, a ship in the Black Sea, or own land in Turkey—he will lose all three!"

The poor Greeks looked to the British to back them in their pathetic efforts to make the Turks pay for confiscated property, but the British had already burned their fingers in Lloyd George's rash policy of backing the Greeks against the Turks—and the British had a private row of their own just beginning with the Kemal Pasha. The British with their habitual innocence, had managed to see that the rich Mosul oil fields were included inside the line of their mandated Iraqui territory—and now the Turks were trying to get them back. The British had never quite reconciled themselves to the new Turkish Republic; if the Turks wanted to go to war over Mosul—well, that was just too bad for the Turks.

In the meantime the French, playing their usual game, were secretly supporting Turkish Nationalism and getting ready to sell out the British, as Franklin Bouillon eventually did.

The Americans had a Commissioner accredited to the new Turkish Republic, Admiral Bristol, who occasionally got in the way of British imperialistic aims.

It was a lively situation to step into, made all the more exciting by the very charm of the Turks themselves. At a dinner one night at what was the American Embassy, Hikmet Pasha, Admiral of the Turkish Navy, said to me:

"Why is it that all you foreign correspondents are so nice when you are here? You are so charming and you are such good company, and yet—when you go away—you write such unpleasant things!"

Hikmet Pasha, who had red hair and freckles, and might have been taken for any Englishman, was a most charming person himself. I told him that was the very reason.

"You are too pleasant yourselves," I remarked. "When we are here we like you too much. It is only after we go away that we think about the unpleasant things you do to—the Armenians?"

"Ha!" said Hikmet Pasha quite seriously. "That is *your* fault! You Americans and British, with your missionaries—you gave the Armenians a national consciousness—and so we have to kill them."

Then he asked me if I had ever seen the Turkish *Red Book*, which they brought out during the war, showing the atrocities the Armenians had perpetrated upon the women and old men in some Turkish villages, when their young Turk husbands and sons were at the front. I told him I had: Brewster, the American Military Attaché with Djemal Pasha, had shown me it in Cairo.

About the Armenian question—I saw enough to agree with the American Armenian Relief Officer in Constantinople, who is supposed to have said finally to a crowd of shrieking Armenians besieging his door:

"You must go away! If I am to save you—*I've simply not got to know you!*"

Night life in Constantinople at that time centred around three places: The Turquoise restaurant, where every waitress was said to be a Russian princess (available), and usually was; the Rose Noir, cabaret, where naughty Turks and hopeful-to-be-naughty Europeans collected; and Maxim's, an all-night cabaret run by an American Negro, Thomas, late of The Hermitage, Moscow, where a hungry man could get a marvellous beef-steak with horse-radish sauce.

Thomas was one of the three most interesting Negroes I have met in Europe. I have already mentioned one, Willie Gordon, Champion Light Heavyweight of Roumania, Secretary of the Door at the American Embassy in Petrograd. The other, whose dark, sad, intelligent face will appear later, was playing the trap drums in Saragossa, Spain.

Thomas was very sophisticated. He had married a Russian refugee, of noble family, and had two *café-au-lait* babies. When a big White Star liner came into Constantinople with a shipload of suddenly-wealthy American tourists on a round-the-world trip, all of Thomas's Russian girl waitresses jumped into Turkish bloomers, and Thomas put on a fez, got out his prayer rug and prayed towards Mecca. Maxim's was Mecca, to a Negro who had once lorded it over The Hermitage; but as soon as he really got his cabaret on a paying basis, the Turks, with their motto: TURKEY FOR THE TURKS!—took it away from him.

We had watched the American tourists being rushed around Constantinople all day in charabancs. They entered Maxim's like a chorus themselves, rushed to the tables around the dancing floor and stared at the bloomered dancing girls.

"Very Turkish!" explained their guide-interpreter. "Just like a harem—what?"

Half an hour later he stood up and looked at his watch.

"Ladies and Gentlemen—this concludes our trip to Turkey. Ship sails in twenty minutes. Transportation is waiting for you outside the door. All aboard! All aboard for Jerusalem and the Holy Land—we will now follow the footsteps of the Master!"

When more than two American families ever gather together abroad, the Europeans always treat them like that. We are such a trusting race.

Thomas salaamed them out, bowing with pressed hands—"Good-bye, Effendi. Good-bye, Effendi!"—then he took off his fez and became a nice Mississippi Negro again.

Not all Turkish women were pleased with Mustapha Kemal's attempts to emancipate them. One of them was the wife of a Turkish Naval Attaché who had seen several European capitals, including Berlin.

"I would much rather remain behind the veil," she told Eve. "I *had* my husband then."

The morning we got to Angora we could hardly see across the street for the corpses. The Tribunal of Independence had been at work again, and seventeen Turks who had voted the wrong political ticket were dangling from hastily erected little wooden tripods in the main street. They all looked as if they were listening, with their heads cocked over, and each one had a fez on his head. On a night-gown which had been pulled over their bodies and arms before execution was a placard on each, whereon was written the reason for his plight. Slippers dangled from their dead toes. Driving past them through the mud and Anatolian donkey caravans went the sleek motor-cars of the *Corps Diplomatique* at Turkey's new capital.

That evening the Turks were selling picture postcards of the corpses. And we understood now why the *muezzin* from the minaret opposite our window was calling the Faithful to prayer, in a bowler hat!

The Mosul affair was a nasty business. The Turks lost, of course; and since the Mosul pipe lines have been opened in 1935, an Armenian in Paris (who long ago got the original concession from the old Ottoman Turkish Government) gets 5 per cent of the oil; the French and the U. S. Standard Oil (which horned in on the job) got 22.5 per cent each—the French got enough oil to supply their entire navy. The British got 50 per cent, and the Turks do not get one drop.

It looked for a time as if the Turks might make a fight for it. Albert Sarraut, the French Ambassador, seemed to think that they might. He assured me of this one morning as he took me for a walk around the walls of Angora. Wonderful walls, on the hills where Tamerlane fought Byazid, and the Ottoman Turks first entered Europe as a band of horseman raiders; walls built of wrecked Persian lions and the statues and ruins of countless civilisations. And Albert Sarraut, sitting before the huge Gobelin tapestry he had brought from the magnificent French Embassy to his hutment in crude Angora, was a wonderful Ambassador!

The Russians gave the Turks an alliance in the middle of the Mosul affair to help them make up their minds—but it was a defensive, not an offensive alliance—and the Turks very wisely refrained from picking a fatal quarrel with mighty England at that time.

Most of us, writing about it, thought it was the worst case of Big Power gunmanism we had seen in our time.

Chapter 66

ST. GEORGE'S HOSPITAL

IN THE three months in Turkey I spent a couple of weeks around Brusa, that fascinating capital of ancient Turkey on the other side of the Sea of Marmora, where all of the primitive machinery is turned by water-mills, and in the great bazaar native craftsmen would make you a saddle, or a felt rug, or cut out a pair of wooden sandals while you watched them sitting cross-legged in their *suks.*

And over there I caught myself swaying in the streets. My leg was going bad again. It seemed the foot this time. One morning, when I found I could not put my left shoe on, I mournfully abandoned all the plans Eve and I had made for a motor trip across Kurdistan and Persia to enter India through Baluchistan— and rushed for the Orient Express just as fast as I could.

In London I was given a room by that kindly and most competent institution, the St. George's Hospital, where a friend of mine, Gideon Colquhoun, then its House Surgeon, operated upon me, and, as a recompense, sent me in a bowl of real turtle soup and lobster salad afterwards, from Scott's. I would like to pay my tribute to everybody in St. George's, where I lay for several weeks, listening to the London traffic, milling around Hyde Park corner.

They were splendid to me there.

But I came out of it with my left foot in a black, felt hospital boot. Something was definitely wrong, and Giddy warned me, "It will only be a question of time before you will want me again!" He was right.

But Janet Fairbank was in Paris. Eve and I flew over to join her, and it was like a pick-me-up to come within the range of that exhilarating personality again. In Paris we saw why the French hate us so much. The franc was crashing. American tourists and English were standing in the banks, hesitating to cash their letters of credit.

445

"Wait! Wait a few minutes and we'll get a hundred for a dollar!"

They were laughing about it. And Eve said she saw one American light a cigarette with a five-franc note. Watching this ghastly performance were the English clerks in some of the banks—who were being paid in francs.

But—it is useless to deny!—how much we enjoyed, for the first time in our lives, being able to eat at Foyots'.

In Paris I got a wire:

"BRITISH PREPARING GENERAL STRIKE. . . ."

I flew across that day. That night, outside the Houses of Parliament, I saw the buses with the red flags waving from their tops. I tried to talk to Jim Thomas and J. H. Cook as they rushed out of the House. Cook flung me off.

"We wanted peace! We wanted peace! Baldwin couldn't have it! Now it's a fight to the finish!"

Thomas was weeping and being helped along by two women.

I watched the police baton-charging the crowd down the shining asphalt of Whitehall. The crowd ran jocularly just ahead of them. When the police caught a Bloomsbury Communist with a red banner they seized him, broke the banner's standards across their stalwart knees and gave the agitator a half-friendly whack across the behind.

" 'Ere, you—hop it! Go home to bed."

In less than twenty minutes the sound nerves of the British public had re-established themselves, and people were joking and laughing about how they would get down to business in the morning, or even get home that night.

Over at Victoria the great trains all lay stationary, their steam dying down.

"But I've got to get to Brighton!" screamed an old lady.

"Sorry, madam, last train's gone."

"But I *must* get to Brighton, my son is waiting for me there. When *can* I get a train to Brighton?"

"God knows, madam; ask Mr. Baldwin."

The gateman shut and locked his gate and politely touched his hat.

The next day I saw the great British middle-class mobilising in Hyde Park. By magic, this class of Englishmen and Englishwomen appeared with their own motor-cars and a sound set of steady nerves to lay at their country's feet. They did not hate the strikers—most of them were sorry for the wretched coal-miners and their plight—but they simply were not going to have such a thing as a general strike interfere with personal rights.

No other country in the world can mobilise a class—an hereditary officer class—of good-natured people like that.

These were the days when the British crowd would joke with the special constables. They, and the raw nerves of The Depression, had not begun to make them the red flag to a bull that they are to any British crowd today. Such, for example, as when the hunger marchers reached London in 1932.

But down in Wales, *in the valleys of despair*, down there one saw things that made this London scene look like the most bitter caricature.

I went through the General Strike, riding on the back of a motor cycle, with Evan Davis, Leader of No. 2 Glamorganshire miners, sitting in the side-car, rushing about the silent collieries to speak from coal-tip after coal-tip. In Pontypridd, I saw thousands of Welshmen standing bareheaded in the pouring rain, singing "Land of My Fathers" and Evan Davis pleading with them: "For God's sake, keep cool. Keep your hands in your pockets! Keep your heads! For God's sake and for the sake of our women and children, don't any of you men let an *agent provocateur* tempt you into doing anything desperate. If you do that—we are lost!"

Yes, and the sensational Press in London, cabling to the world stories about the rioting Welsh miners.

"GIVE US MORE BLOOD" one American agency cabled to its London man who was trying to report the General Strike as he saw it. So he went out and bought a copy of Winston Churchill's *British Gazette*.

With even the London *Times* reduced to an edition of one

quarter-size sheet the truth was cut off during the great General Strike.

In the Admiralty a government propagandist held daily meetings for the Press. A splendid old gentleman from some Civil Service job, he was highly complacent in dealing with Fleet Street and the foreign correspondents. He thought, alas, he could be subtle. One morning, he said:

"There is no truth in the report that striking railway men have murdered a Scottish soldier in Perth."

"Where was that reported?" asked a tall, blond-haired Swede.

"I—er—I don't know. I merely tell you there is no truth in the report."

"Who ever said there was such a report? Do you know what you seem to be doing?—You are trying to get us to deny that a railway mob killed a British soldier who was trying to protect the railway lines! Do you know what that means?—That our readers will believe that railway mobs *are* killing soldiers in England. Denial of such rumours only confirm them—you know that. Gentlemen"—the Swedish journalist turned to the other pressmen in the room—"I vote we do not mention this denial."

That is where I first saw Eric Swenne of the *Svenska Tagerblatt*, afterwards, for seven years, President of the European Correspondents Association in London.

As my foot was in such a state that I could not drive myself, I hired a big Daimler limousine, at a shilling a mile, and drove down through the night all the way across England to Cardiff. I shall never forget the drama of those dead railroads—the red and green signal lights standing unmoved in the night. It was like being alive in Conan Doyle's *Poison Belt*. Dawn, and I passed through Cardiff and up the Rhondda Valley. At Glenellen, I saw a crowd of Welshmen standing around a galvanised iron chapel. They were the overflow from a meeting that was assembling inside. Evan Davis, leader of No. 2 Glamorganshire miners, was among the crowd at its door. I asked him if I could go in and hear what they were saying. "I'll have to ask the men," he said.

I heard him inside on the platform, asking them. Then I heard a wild Welsh voice:

"Let him in! Mates, if our Cause isn't good enough to be heard —then it's no cause to fight for! Let him in! Let him in!" came the shouts.

"Speak to them," said Davis, as he indicated a chair for me beside himself on the platform. "Some of them might still be suspicious. Explain who you are."

I stood up. I was frightened at first. Then I looked down into the pale faces of those eager, earnest men. They were all looking up at me with such seriousness in their faces. And most of the faces, I noticed, were pock-marked with little blue dots from explosions in the coal.

"I am an American," I said. "I have no sides to take in this strike. I don't even know what it's all about. Neither do the people in America. They want to know. That's why I'm here. My syndicate of papers has another man in London who is reporting that end of the strike. I want to try and show your side. I'll write what I see, and—after I have sent my dispatches—you are free to read them right here. Is that all right?"

A mumble, a looking and turning of faces at one another, and then a sober nodding of heads.

"That's right," shouted someone. "Show them our side!"

There was no cheer. Evan Davis was on his feet:

"Men . . ." he began.

It was one of the most moving scenes I have ever watched in my life. The Daimler was waiting outside, ticking up shillings even while it stood still! And the moment that meeting was over I raced back down to Cardiff to send my dispatch. I began it with the first words of the miners' leader:

"KEEP COOL STOP KEEP YOUR HANDS IN YOUR POCKETS STOP THESE ARE COMMANDS LEADERS GIVING STRIKING WELSH MINERS. . . ."

I raced the Daimler back to Pontypridd, discharged it, and for that week I rode beside Evan Davis from meeting to meeting in the Rhondda Valley. I saw Tonypandy, hot-spot of Communism, and Merthyr, which was called "Little Moscow" at that time. I saw them all again, in 1929 and 1934—dead—dejected—the men just standing with their collars turned up and hands sunk in their pockets, men who stood all day on the street kerb, men with no present or future life—men waiting ten, fifteen, twenty years for the Old Age Pension to come along.

As I approached one coal-tip near Tonypandy during the General Strike, the crowd listening to Evan Davis noticed the taxi I had left in the road and turned to see who was coming. As I came nearer they began to mumble, then growl, and several of the younger men came towards me. For some reason, they looked menacing. Then I heard Davis shouting over the crowd's head:

"Mr. Farson! Mr. Farson—you come up here beside me!"

Then the men who were approaching me smiled, some of them, I thought, in a sheepish sort of way, and the crowd made an aisle for me to pass through it.

"Indeed to goodness!" whispered Evan Davis, when I stood by his side. "You should be more careful—and announce yourself. Know what was the trouble? Why, you're the living spit and image of the owner's agent in these parts!"

Most of the Welsh mining leaders I talked with were furious that the railway men had come in to join them on this strike. They were powerless, because the railway men were going to fight out the General Strike until the last miner was left.

"It'll lose our Cause," the miners told me again and again. "It'll put the back of the country against us, this General Strike—stopping the plain people's trains and things like that! Our Cause will be lost!"

And they were right.

Thinking, or at least accepting him automatically without thinking about it, I had always pictured Ramsay MacDonald as the Great Labour Leader. And I was astonished during the General Strike how seldom I heard the miners mention his name—how little they expected from him.

But I came to see why quite clearly in 1931.

Chapter 67

FASCIST FRAME-UP

OUR MAN in Italy had got himself into a position where he was about to fight a duel with a Fascist.

That he was the victim of a Fascist frame-up we realised after it was all over. His courageous reporting of Mussolini's castor oil technique and the Matteoti affair was making it advisable to get him out of Rome. But at first it looked like a very unfortunate and possibly dangerous private affair. At a dance one night a Fascist ex-employee of the *Chicago Daily News* came up and slapped Hiram Moderwell's face. Moderwell was too amazed to do anything for a moment. Besides, he had the wife of a colleague on his arm, who shouldn't for any reason have been at a dance—she was just about to have a baby—so Hiram led her to a chair.

The next day a row broke out over Carol in Roumania and Hiram Moderwell flew to Bukarest. Rome rang with the tales of American cowardice; how Moderwell had been slapped in the face by a Fascist and immediately flew from Italy. When poor Hiram came back he was the centre of an unpleasant situation, where even some of his best friends felt that there was no way out of it but to fight a duel. One friend in Paris, who had done some amateur fencing as a sport, volunteered to fly to Rome to give Hiram lessons in the art. Newspaper men all over Europe were talking about nothing else.

Then Hiram took the Fascist bull by the horns and gave it a good punch. Walking over to the Press Club he confronted the Fascist and said:

"In my country we do not fight with swords. We do this!"—and he knocked him flat on the floor. "Now," he said, as the Italian got up, "I challenge you to a duel with swords or anything you like."

That was going too far.

The Italians got together and a sort of Grand Council was appointed which sat on the case. I have forgotten, but some

Italian nobleman was its chairman; and, finally decided the council, there could not be a duel. Why? *Because Mr. Moderwell was not a gentleman!*

It was a fantastic situation.

And poor Hiram Moderwell, furious now with everybody in the world, demanded that the paper give him another post. He had done his duty all round, he said. Rome would be impossible for him now. He met me at the railway station in Rome when I landed there to take over.

"Gosh!" he laughed. "You've got a job on your hands. I won't ask you to dinner, and I don't want you to ask me to anything. I'm going out into the country tonight, where I'm going to cool off. Then I shall shake the dust of classic Italy off my blooming feet."

Mussolini's jaw!

I saw that everywhere I went in Italy. My paper was distinctly not popular with the Fascists, and they kept me waiting an hour and a quarter in the Foreign Office, when a colleague took me over to Palazzo Chigi to present my credentials. The Party man, the man the Fascists had put in to break the Press, stamped up and down like a mad Mickey Mouse when he did consent to see me—all the time pounding a copy of the *Chicago Daily News* that lay on his impressive desk.

"Imperialism! Imperialism!" he kept shouting at me. "That's what you say about us! We mean to fight! We mean to make war! Imperialism! Imperialism!"

He resumed his Mickey Mouse parade again.

I looked over and saw the red-pencilled dispatch. It was one of Paul Scott Mower's of, I think, May 3rd.

"Why!" I said in surprise, almost without thinking. "I was sitting right beside Mr. Mower in Paris when he *wrote* that! Imperialism? Why—he hasn't said that! See this part here—what he said was that Mussolini evidently felt that Italy had come late to the banquet which was proportioning Africa among the Allies—and that Italy felt it had some just grievances. If it couldn't get what it wanted by peaceful means—then there was every likelihood that Italy would one day go to war."

Then I saw what had made the Fascist so wild:

"Mr. Mower says," I pointed out, "that as Italy has not got nearly enough coal and iron she probably won't be able to go to war for some time."

"Yah!" riled the Italian.

"You don't know!" he said, clenching his fist.

It was all very funny—and embarrassing. When I went to the American Minister and asked for some help from him to get Mussolini to consent to see me I got absolutely zero assistance from that staunch Republican.

But my opinion and reporting of what Mussolini was doing for Italy had to be based upon the creative work he was doing and the way he was invigorating that country with a new sense of self-respect. Perhaps my final conclusions could be summed up in a single scene. A little Contessa had invited me to a discreet tea, where I was to meet a gathering of prominent anti-Fascists. They were professors and men of intelligence in Italian affairs. They were charming. But the instant I broached the subject of what they would propose as an alternative to Mussolini they all fell to quarrelling with each other. Their voices rose, and the quiet tea became a madhouse.

The Contessa tried to restore order, then she shrugged her pretty shoulders and laughed to me:

"Well . . . you see . . . perhaps Mussolini serves us right!"

In Rome I saw the classic tragedy being enacted of rich American girls angling for Italian noble husbands. And I heard the sad stories of many American girls whose fathers had bought them for them. One even got so far as to escape in a steamer for New York with her child, when the husband pursued them in a seaplane and forcibly took the child back to Rome. Even so, I thought, with this beauty of Italy to help them endure it, their married lives must have contained more of Life itself than they would have got out of some stucco palace on Long Island Sound.

When I was in Italy, Mussolini passed his Syndicalism pro-gramme which forbade workers to strike. I went to Augustino Turati, General Secretary of the Fascists Party, and asked:

"The workers of the world have always considered the strike as their ultimate weapon. Now that they have been forbidden it won't they feel both helpless and hopeless?"

"You," said blue-eyed Piedmontese Turati, "you go on the principle that every government is dishonest!"

"I do!" I laughed.

"Well, let me prove to you why it would not pay our govern-ment to be dishonest—not with the workers. Fascism must find a solid base in the whole-hearted support of the working class . . ." etc., etc.

Which, perhaps, explained why 70 per cent of the disputes settled the next year before the Labour Courts were adjudged in favour of the workers.

When the Eucharistic Congress was being held in Chicago, which Rome said was "the greatest manifestation of the Divinity of Christ mankind has shown," I went to a Cardinal and asked him if he believed in the power of mass thought.

"Of course," placidly waving his jewelled hand. "Did not the Crusades start that way?—people all over Europe suddenly acting because they had all been thinking about the same thing."

Then I asked him if the Church of Rome would mention the subject of gunmen when its Cardinals were in Chicago. Call on the people of America to get rid of their corruption in politics, for instance. Our municipal politics, I suggested, were practically the private monopoly of Irishmen. They would listen to the voice of Rome?

The Cardinal frowned.

The most peaceful spot I found in Rome was in the aura of Sir Rabindranath Tagore. I found him gently waving a fan at himself beside a bowl of red roses.

"Do not ask me," he said, " 'What will happen after Mussolini dies?' Everyone asks me that!"

Chapter 68

PAIN

STOCKHOLM.

It was refreshing to be back among the Swedes again. The paper had asked me to write my own ticket after Rome, and I had suggested driving a motor-car up into the Arctic Circle through Lapland, crossing over into Norway, and shipping the car down on a whaler from Narvik to where the roads began again on the Norwegian coast. No one had done that (nor has anyone yet), and I saw the chance for a vivid series of sketches from the Scandinavians.

Waiting in Stockholm for the Ford I had bought to have special tanks, etc., put on, I flew across to Helsingfors to cover the World Y.M.C.A. Conference erroneously called "The Voice of Youth." To get a cross-section of the population of the world some eighteen youths from different countries were placed in each class; and there they were asked such questions as: "Do you believe sexual intercourse is necessary to good health?"

In the days of my youth I had been taught that it was positively injurious. I wondered what the American boy in that class would now think—of the picking-up of girls, for instance— when he got back to God's country again.

"I don't know," answered the Polish boy delegate, "because we have no prostitutes in Poland."

"No prostitutes!" said the Hungarian lad. "Well, you'd better go back home and get some—to protect your sisters."

I asked one of the heads of the Y.M.C.A.'s, the general soothsayer of the Conference, what he thought about the advisability of all this.

"When I was a boy," I said, "I was always warned that immoral intercourse with women would give me a headache and make my hands clammy, and things like that. It didn't—but perhaps it was just as well that for a long time I was afraid that it would."

He made some sort of reply that I did not pay to send to the *Chicago Daily News.*

In these classes they asked such questions as: Do you believe in the omnipotence of God?—or why not? And at the end of the day a professor from the Calvary Theological College in America added up the score of each class on a blackboard. He wore tortoiseshell-rimmed spectacles, and was the picture of collegiate efficiency as he analysed God this way—with a piece of chalk and a slide-rule.

CLASS A. Belief in Omnipotence of God.
Aye—15. No—4.

"Now, gentlemen . . ."

A German delegate jumped up. He was a baron, ex-officer, horribly disfigured and maimed in the war.

"STOP!" he shouted. Then he banged his one fist against the rail of the seat before him as he tried to control his voice. "This is hideous! You must not talk of God like this! This is blasphemy! The way to Christ is not through gymnasiums and shower-baths. No, no. No, I TELL YOU! You must read the Bible—the words of Christ Himself! Oh, God . . . !" He sank his face in his hands and shook there before us, ashamed of the scene he had made.

Several of us afterwards, cynical correspondents—drinking whiskey out of tea-cups in Prohibition Finland—confessed that we had all had the same feelings as we watched that scene: we wanted to cry. And each one of us had the same desire: to walk over and put an arm around that lonely man.

That Conference was not a success, thank God.

Instead, it was the most profane exhibition I have ever seen. In the figure of that wounded German was a mad hunger for real faith.

With a Ford that had extra petrol tanks along both of its running-boards, tents and duffel bags resting between its bonnet and front wings, and four extra tyres sticking out of the stern like Mrs. Katzenjammer's hair, we took the golden, high roads that are raised above the floors of the green forests as you go upwards through Sweden. Our hearts sang with the joy of being alive in that lovely land. Eve was about to have a baby, and we felt that this prelude to Dan would always make itself felt in future years in that forming mind.

We hoped he wouldn't be born on an ice-floe or introduced to this world among whales; and every night Eve and I used to argue this point in the little white Swedish inns, with the red geraniums before their clean windows.

"You must go back," I said.

"Never! He's got to take his chance."

We always spoke of a boy. I don't know what would have happened if a girl had come forth; we should have been so surprised. Even down in Venice, when Eve said she felt that things were about to happen, we always spoke of Dan.

Daniel Negley Farson.

Well, he wasn't born on an ice-cake. His father saved him from that by going into hospital himself. And there I stayed, in Sweden and then London, for eight months.

We had reached Dalecarlia. Dalecarlia with its bronze pines and blue lakes, where Zorn painted the Swedish peasant girls standing naked in the sun. In that open air I felt strong; even if I was still carting a left foot along in a medical boot, I felt strong as a bull from the waist up. I drove bare-headed with my chest open to the sun and my muscles felt firm and hard when I climbed out of the blue water from a swim. I was fit. . . . In the water I was fine.

But the night we reached Lake Siljan we got lost in the woods. It was the old type of Ford that you work with your feet. Something snapped in my left foot up in the woods. We saw the lights of the hotel shining through the pines. We reached it, took a couple of small bags up to our room, and went down to dinner. I fainted across the dinner table, spilling the coffee.

A special stop was made of an express train to take me aboard at a crossing in the forest trail the next morning. I was operated upon in Stockholm the next day. . . . Phew! how my fever soared: 103, 104, 105. . . . Another operation in two days: 101, 104, 105. . . .

"But this is madness!" said desperate Eve.

The surgeon who had operated upon me had gone away, leaving instructions that I was not to be touched. In the big bone of my left foot he had cut a hole, and in that hole he had stuffed a hard packing of gauze plugging. Corked up, the infection was eating its way through the bone. I felt like a boiler whose head is about to blow off. But nobody, not one single doctor, dared touch me.

Where was the other doctor? They did not know; he was off shooting somewhere, they thought.

Eve went berserk.

"He's dying!" she said.

The Swedish sisters just stared at her blankly. The House Surgeons tried to keep out of her way. Just at this moment a wire came from London. Giddy Colquhoun had heard that I was down again. His wire asked if I would like him to come over to Sweden to operate on me.

This was one of the kindest things that had happened to me. I shall never forget it.

But I did not know it had come. I was passing through patches of delirium. It was too urgent to wait for Giddy, welcome as that Scotsman would have been. Then Eve broke through all medical etiquette.

There was a brilliant surgeon in Stockholm, a Communist, named Silversjold—may his gallant soul for ever rest in peace— and he flung all the mumbo-jumbo of his high profession aside the instant he saw my leg.

"I must operate upon him at once!" he said. "This is very serious."

But it was P. C. Wren who probably saved my life.

I had been operated upon that evening. Silversjold had bored a hole completely through my foot. I was lying there, feet in the air, and the left one full of drainage tubes, still extremely dicky around midnight. *Beau Geste* was lying on the night-table beside my bed, and I reached for it.

Soon shrieks were heard from my room. A frightened Swedish sister came running in. She saw me, in that grotesque position, laughing and crying in turns. She dashed out: "The American has gone mad!" A house surgeon came in, at the double, and slowed up.

"What's the matter?" he asked.

I showed him the book; the part where the two unregenerate Legionnaires have that miraculous fight with the cook on the ship going across to Africa.

"I haven't," I sobbed to the doctor, "read anything that has made me laugh so much in years!"

That broke my fever. Some time during the night my hands began to feel as if they belonged to me again. The next morning I begged for a soft-boiled egg for breakfast, made such a row that I finally got it.

I was out of the danger line now. I had been asking them to cut off my leg the day before. Now I wanted to keep it again. But I was just entering on what was to be the third of my three years in bed from the day I crashed that Nieuport in Egypt's sands.

Cairo, Alexandria, Chatham, London, New York, Montreal, Vancouver—now Stockholm was added to the list.

I have had a great deal of fun in hospitals. They always improve my mind, such as it is; I do not think I even had one before I was smashed up. I lived for brawn and not brain.

From the day when I was fourteen and a strapping big Canadian nurse undressed me, and then whisked the sheets off me to give me a good bath from top to bottom, I have had many adventures in bed. In Russia, as I have written, I came within an ace of witnessing a second battle of the Alamo, when the officers' hospital I was lying in was being machine-gunned by the Bolshies. And, in hospital, I have even engineered an elopement from my bed. This was the Royal Air Force hospital in Eaton Square, where I helped a South African to marry the night nurse.

At first, I opposed the marriage. He had been shot through the leg and could not walk; he would probably be a cripple for life. Also, he wasn't quite sure that he loved the gal.

"But she's a nice one," he insisted, "and, hang it all, I've been in bed for two years!"

"Is it a change you're after," I asked him, "or a wife?"

She didn't have any doubts about it; she wanted this poor broken bit of humanity. But she was afraid of the matron.

"Well, all you've got to do," I said, "is to get him an outpass, so that he can go out on his crutches and get a licence. Then the next thing for you two to do is to go to a registrar's office somewhere and get it over with. Then you can tell the matron to take a long run and jump in the Thames."

I had forgotten all about it. Sunk in our usual bridge games I had not even noticed that the South African had been out all day. And then, just at ten o'clock, closing time, he came sliding down the slippery ward on his crutches and plunked himself on my bed.

"I've done it!" he said, red as a beet.

"Done what?"

"Married—you fool. Whoop! We got married this afternoon!"

His wife, the night sister (who had a ten o'clock pass) turned up very primly to put him to bed. She came over to give me my sleeping-draught.

"How's the best man?" she whispered.

"Waiting to kiss the bride," I said. "Turn the lights out."

"Go hon!" she said. "You're delirious."

The Sophiahammet in Stockholm was a gorgeous place to lie up in. The old Dowager Empress had given it to the people. She was very religious, and a law had it that no doctor could attend a woman patient unless he was a married man himself. There was a religious motto over every door—graded to the scale of charges. Over the sumptuous thirty-five-kroner private rooms it said: GOD WILL HELP YOU. DO NOT FEAR. But as the rooms became lower in the scale this assurance grew less firm. In the four-bed room where I spent my first awful night it merely said: GOD HELP YOU.

The nurses all dropped a curtsey as I was wheeled into the operating theatre—every one of the three times.

"*Goddag!*" they said. "*Goddag!*" said I. The surgeon getting ready to cut me up, came across and bowed: "*Goddag!*" said he. "*Goddag,*" said I. The sister who was to give me the chloroform leaned over me with the mask in her hand: *"Goddag!"* said she. *"Goddag!"* said I. Then I was off.

I have, once or twice, been cut before I was under. I take an unconscionably long time to go out. So—to let them know I'm still there—I always wiggle the first finger of my right hand.

But would those little Swedish sisters let me do that? Not they! They seized that finger—they belayed it—they tried to push my hand under a fold of my hospital shirt. I fought, with the mask over my face, summoning all the Swedish I knew.

"Det er min finger!" I gasped. *"Det er min finger! Leggo!"*

And, as I said, it does improve my mind. In bed that eight months I wrote two novels which were published—unfortunately—and was part-author in a play.

My share of it was one of the worst plays ever written. I won't have that distinction taken away from me.

Daniel Negley Farson was born January 8, 1927, at 4 A.M. in London. At that moment his father was sitting upright in bed in a room two floors below writing the last chapter of a novel he had determined to finish in thirty-one days flat, and which had already started running as a serial. One of the last things poor Eve had done had been to bring me down on a stretcher from Stockholm, and in the library of my mother-in-law's house in South Kensington I was to lie for another six months. With my leg transfixed in an iron surgical boot I could not get up to see Eve. And in the worst hours of that momentous night, she heard me typing that abysmal love story, for which, she declared, she would never forgive me.

Having thrown in his lot with us Dan was to see the world. He first entered salt water in France; he had his first love affair in Berlin with a little Siamese princess he met in the Tiergarten; he was taught to swim by Janet Fairbank, junior, in Lake Geneva, Wisconsin; and he has just caught his first trout in a mountain lake of Yugoslavia.

He is a practical child.

When we were telling him about the wonderful new Zoo at

Whipsnade, where all the lions and tigers and elephants ran freely all over the place, his only comment was:

"But what about *us?*"

And, sure enough, a camel did bite him.

In Berlin we all got the dachshund craze, and immediately we got back to London we bought one for Dan. Anyone who has ever had one of these enchanting little beasts will know just how we feel about our Liesel. She is the fourth member of our family.

Chapter 69

KILLING A WHALE

MY BOSS on the *Chicago Daily News*, who was also my friend, used to allow me a great deal of liberty as to where I should go to get a good series of articles. With a heavy plaster cast on my leg the field seemed pretty limited. But one of the books I had been reading while I was laid up was *Whaling, North and South*. My friend, Frank Morley, had written the Northern part of that exciting treatise on whale-killing; and Frank arranged that I should go off with the same whaling outfit that he had.

If I had known what I was in for, I don't think I would have taken my leg up there; I cannot imagine anything more monkey-like than climbing up the steel ladder of a whaler's bridge, with one leg in a plaster cast and a camera in one hand and the whaler bucking like a horse in the seas. The daring young man on the flying trapeze was not in it.

I got to Olna Firth about midnight, felt my way gingerly along the stringpiece of a deserted wharf and dropped down on the steel deck of the *Skeena*. I was colliding with iron bitts and the unforgiving bulks of machinery, in the most unlooked-for places on a ship, when a hand in the darkness seized mine. It was a hand like the flipper of a turtle, hard and crusty. Its owner did not speak, but pulled me along and up the steel rungs of a ladder to the charthouse; and there I faced him—Olsen, dean of Norwegian gunners—killer of 2,600 whales.

"Dere iss no hvales," said Olsen. "I haf said so."

"Where are they?" I asked.

"I don't know. Dey came up here, making deir eastward passage in de spring—but now I don't know. Maybe dey go down between de Faroes and Iceland. Maybe dey're in dose waters up nord of Alaska. I dunno. No von knows about de hvale."

These Norwegian whalers, I was soon to see, had a grand, careless manner of speaking about this world. They spoke of the sounds off Chili as if they were in their own back yard. It had been a long speech for Olsen; and the reason for it was that I had come aboard the *Skeena* at a most dramatic moment—a strike of the Norwegian whaling gunners was afoot. Olsen, king of them all, did not want to kill any more whales that season. He wanted to go home.

But Olsen had his chink in that turtle-like figure of his, and I found it; he was preposterously vain.

"Well, damn my eyes!" I said dolefully. "This is bad luck—they told me in Scotland that you were the best gunner afloat; they said: 'You ought to see Olsen kill a whale!'"

"Well—maybe we get one," said that king of the sea.

The *Skeena* was the last word in whale-chasers. One hundred and five feet long, she had no keel from amidships aft; she could turn quick as a polo pony to follow the antics of the whale. She carried a harpoon-gun in her bows, with 2½ lbs. of smokeless powder in its barbed tip. And attached to the lanyard of this bomb-tipped harpoon was a third of a mile of six-inch whale-line. This line ran up through two huge shock-absorbers along the steel mast—"accumulators," they called them—fastened aloft and on deck to giant steel springs. A steam windlass aft the mast was the *Skeena's* monster fishing-reel.

Yet the first big fin-whale we shot, it was eighty feet long, fought the ship for two hours, and at one time had the little *Skeena* pulled down by the head.

Eleven Norwegians manned the *Skeena*. When I asked Olsen if there were any whale gunners in the world who were not Norwegians, he scratched his skull and said:

"Well, dere's a Yap, off de coast of Formosa—but he ain't up to much!"

I differentiated the crew and officers of the *Skeena* by their tattoo marks. One had a dancing girl, naked, done on his chest. To amuse us at nights we used to make him strip—and then wiggle his skin with our hands. "Hoochy-koochy dance!" One had a snake tattooed over his wrist. "See dat," he scowled, "dat used to spell 'ANNA'—my best girl's name. She trew me down—so I put a snake over dat girl." A rose, on his right forearm, marked the frailty of another wench. But on his chest were two naked women, standing on either side of a heart; above this were crossed the Norwegian and American flags; underneath was the slogan ALL FOR LOVE.

"Had dat done in Brooklyn. Guy who did it had a bald head —and when he took off his hat and bowed dere was another face, grinning at you from de top of his head!"

"A two-faced guy," I said.

"Yeah—dat's right—a two-faced guy. Say, have you ever been to the island of Juan de Fernandez? Dat's a swell place—nobody on dat. Dat's de place I'd like to take my girl!"

It was fascinating, leaning in the bridge canvas beside Olsen as he took the *Skeena* out through Olna Firth. A pitch black night, with just the shape of the land slipping past us and the soft hiss of steam and clicking of valves from the engine-room. Gunnarson, the cook, had told me he had seen the aurora borealis going at 2 A.M. and had heard the "merry dancers."

"I heard dem 'merry dancers' crackling. It's going to blow."

And blow it did. When we hit the open sea I could have washed my face in the waves from the plunging bridge I was on. Another whaler, which was just coming in without a whale, passed us at dawn, rising high above us, and then sinking entirely from view in some amazing ocean trough.

Our hunting-ground was an ever-changing patch of the Atlantic about 200 miles long by 50 miles wide. As Olsen declared: "No von knows about der hvale," but a certain knowledge of their habits has it that in the months of early spring they come eastward past the Shetland Islands following the currents, full of shrimp, along the 100-fathom bank about 50 miles off land. In August and September they are supposed to come west.

But this time the whales had upset the dope. There were no shrimps. And we couldn't find the Gulf Stream. And so there we were, on this lonely night, scouring the empty seas for that white puff of vapour that tokens Leviathan.

"Dom dat Gulf Stream!" growled Olsen from the bridge canvas. "Yust like a voman! Never know where de devil she is when you want her."

We lay, not at anchor, but merely riding the long swells, with the seagulls that had been following us resting on the water around us like chickens in a barnyard. The sun was sinking in bars of black and gold. I was gloomy. Despite all this beauty, I was missing an epoch. Tomorrow the little 105-ft. whale-catcher was destined never to return to the land. I would never see the killing of the great fin-whale.

The day dawned crisp and clear. I lay in the stern sheets and tried to philosophise. Olsen, navigating by dead reckoning, was about to run home.

"*Blast!*"

The look-out man was leaning out of the barrel on the mast-head and pointing to windward; swinging wildly against the windy sky, he howled again:

"*Blast!*"

If an ordinary cargo-steamer had happened to be traversing that patch of the Atlantic, this is what she would have seen for the next two hours: a little grey steamer, with smoke belching from her red funnel, apparently gone crazy. A grey little ship that turned and twisted and raced back on itself like a game little polo pony. They would have seen the little steamer suddenly race madly over the sky-line. Then, for no apparent reason, it would turn and race back. Madness—except that they might have noticed ahead or astern, to port or starboard, of that mad little steamer—a faint puff.

A mere nothing. Like a puff of smoke from a man's pipe. But beneath it, racing through the immensity of the seas, was a great black and white shape, *and there he breaks again!* . . .

They came out of the green seas just ahead of us. Two great glistening backs like overturned ships—or Zeppelins—and they curved there unconcernedly. They broke again, forty yards on our right, so close that their sharp, pneumatic sighs sounded like valves in the engine-room. I suppose it was the shock of their sheer size, for I could not believe them. Mythological shapes from a mysterious sea. Olsen barked a command and the mate spun the wheel, sending the *Skeena* hard after them. Olsen, out-guessing the whale, hung on the plunging harpoon-gun on the bow, waiting until he got within forty yards to destroy the biggest thing in Creation.

At less than forty yards one of the huge fin-whales rose just ahead of us, rising, rising, rising out of its own waves until I thought my heart would burst with the tension. Then Olsen shot. There was a billow of smoke, a snatch-vision of hurtling lanyard, a dull explosion—and the seas were empty again. The seas were just as empty as if there had never been any whale.

But Olsen was down on his knees peering over the bow. Men raced about the steel decks to their stations. Then something peculiar about the mast-tackle caught my eye. It was the big metal block of the "accumulator," the shock-absorber on the whale-line. It was pulled half-way down the mast and was jumping up and down its steel springs. The six-inch whale-line was whizzing through it like a fire-jet. We were into him, and, just like any trout or salmon, the startled fin-whale was making his first run!

He came out of the green seas several hundred yards off. Grey like a ship, coursing along in a smother of white seas, the waves by his tail bright red with blood. At the sight of this, a cloud of seagulls shrieked and swept down on him. The great whale was silent. He lay there—and then charged again. He had taken out two lengths, nearly a quarter-mile of six-inch Manila rope, and we played him on the end of it.

He charged along the surface and left a bright crimson wake. He rolled. He jumped. He "sounded," boring down towards the sea floor, straining against the reversed engines of the ship. He broke again—thrashed the waves. He had been shot just aft the back fin, and although the 2½ lb. smokeless powder bomb had exploded inside him, none of his vital organs had been touched. He was still fresh and fighting.

The mate and Olsen were hurriedly reloading the harpoon-gun. They stuffed in a bag of black powder, rammed it and tamped it home with reckless thuds of the steel harpoon. I expected any moment to see them both sail off into space clinging on to the harpoon barbs. Sailors were coiling and splicing on a new whale-line, with infinite dexterity splicing it to the harpoon just aft these expanding barbs.

"And now," said the mate, taking the wheel from me, "dis time he's going to get it—an' he's going to get it good!"

The best place to shoot a whale, he told me, was in the lungs, because then it pumps blood and quickly bleeds to death. But this whale was not having any. At the first jerk of that renewed torture when the *Skeena's* deck-winches were reversed, he went straight down towards the bottom. He kept on going down, until Anderson said he must be a good fifth of a mile straight underneath. When I suggested that that would be impossible, as the pressure of the seas would crush him, the mate gave a great guffaw.

"Ha-ha! *Crush a whale*—dat's good!"

It was decided to kedge him up. The windlass ground, but all that happened was that the little *Skeena* began to stand on her nose. We lay there, slightly down by the head, in mortal tug-of-war against that invisible adversary. Then the "accumulators" suddenly shot upward and the windlass clattered around as if it were coming to pieces. The *Skeena* rocked idly on the waves.

Our harpoon had pulled out. And when it came in over the bow, I saw ganglions of tendons in its barbs as big as a man's arms.

Just at sunset we shot it again. The second chase had been infinitely more exasperating than the first. The whale now knew what we meant. His antics had a purpose. Instead of going in long straight runs under water he kept switching directions, coming up after each dive to blow erratically, lying on the surface when we were not nearing and submerging just as we were almost within gunshot. He was obviously trying for a breathing spell; and that seemed to be our only hope—chase him so persistently that he would become desperate. He would have to come up within range.

There was something like two hours of this. At times he rose so close to the ship that I could have jumped from the bridge on to his back. I saw the gaping wound in his side with the white tendons dangling from it. Once he passed directly under the keel of the ship and Anderson remarked that if he came up at that moment—we would go down.

Then we shot him.

"Hi!" yelled the mate. "Dat's got 'im! Blood! Look at dat blood!"

I did. I was horrified to see those thick, heavy jets. The whale was labouring ahead, pumping out its life in gasping blobs. But even then he fought bitterly. The line suddenly whizzed through the "accumulator" and the seas thrashed again.

"Dey go crazy when dey die," barked Anderson, and yelled into the speaking tube to reverse the ship. "Dey go round in circles. You watch."

The whale shot off on his death rush, failed, and stopped to blow a low, laboured jet. He was dying. That great bulk rolled on its side, grey as a battleship (and, it seemed, quite as large), and then the whale stiffened. A strange head emerged from the waves, as if for a last look at the sky, and, across other waves a delicate tail curled out, massive, yet beautiful as a butterfly's wing.

They stayed there, the strange head and that beautiful tail and then they slowly slipped back into the water and sank beneath the waves.

We had killed our whale.

We hauled it up. When its white pleated stomach appeared beneath the bows a sailor leapt down and pushed a steel pneumatic air pipe into its side. The whale was blown up. Its beautiful tail was cut off. Lashed to the little whale catcher we towed it back to the land. The seas caressed it, outlining its body in green fire under the stars.

"You know," muttered the mate to me in the bridge canvas, "dat was a lady whale. She was going to have a baby. Dat's why she fought so hard."

Chapter 70

THE SPELL OF THE SHETLANDS

In the Shetlands, on the Island of Unst, I slept in a "great" house, with Georgian silver on its mahogany dining-table, a painting of Wellington—given to that family by the Iron Duke himself—and a fine library of old books. And the gateway of that house was the jaw bone of a whale.

Now the sailing ships that used to belong to that great house are just stranded hulks on the beach, and only a few mad sea-trout fishers (like myself, and Sir Robert Hamilton, M.P. for the Shetlands) keep the great house going.

I lived up at the head of a lonely voe with an ex-officer of the Black Watch, who was the last laird of his line. He was keeping his crofters alive by teaching them to knit, and selling their knitting for them in London.

And where the Atlantic thunders up against the cliffs of Eshaness, Eve and I lived a week in a croft where our bed was a hole in the wall. There is not a tree in the Shetlands, and with no place for lovers to wander, they used to do their courting in bed— "bundling," they called it—and for precaution a mother would tie her daughter's legs together. With the curtain pulled over the wall-bed they did their love-making while the rest of the family sat around the hearth. In this croft we cooked on a little iron triangle that stood about two inches above the peat embers and for once had our glut of mushrooms which grew in thousands round the croft door, but which no native Shetlander would touch. By the peat fire at nights they told us (half believing them themselves), stories of the seal-families of the Shetlands, where people could turn at will into seals.

I found people who had never seen a railway, or a streetcar—or even a street. Over on the island of Foula I found some who had never seen a tree. I actually talked with one old crofter whose knowledge of the world was so vague that he asked me which type of motor-car was used by the nobility of America.

See the Shetlands once, and they will haunt you for ever.

They are mad little islands, like a mountain range sunk below its timber line, forming a teeth of rocks between the Atlantic and the North Sea. There is not a spot in the whole hundred of them that is more than half a mile from salt water.

Their coast line is crazy. It is a sort of geologic debauch where the rocks have gone mad indeed. They shoot out of the sea in sheer cliffs—Foula's Atlantic side is one sheer cliff 1,300 feet high. They used to pitch their dead "over the Sneug." They called it a burial, as they had not enough earth to inter a corpse. The people of Foula used to live on just fish and guillemot's eggs (which bird to oblige them lays a lop-sided egg that won't roll off a rocky ledge); and if you go off to Foula in the mail boat, you may not be able to get back for weeks. The islands along the Atlantic coast are often just spear-points of red rock. There are rock arches through which one could sail a full-rigged sailing ship. The Atlantic rushes up to them, flings itself high up their sides and falls back in a lacery of white, broken seas. Spotted seals bask and call on the fantastic red shelves. The great whale blows off shore. Gannets, guillemots, fulmar petrels, shags and puffins scream from the serrated ledges of the cliffs, shoot past in staring flotillas on the tide and whirl in a feathered spray over the endless waves. For six hours each day the Atlantic sets through the Shetlands, sweeping in great swirling eddies to bring the flood tide. Then it ebbs, and the North Sea races after it, leaping and thrumming through the rips of Yell and Blue Mull Sound, so that even the connecting motor-boat has to fight to win the other side.

But inland all is monotony. Black peat, bogs and long lonely moors. A sheep is visible on any sky-line for miles. There are no real streams, only gurgling burns, which run almost unseen through the black channels they have dug among the peat, to empty into shallow windswept lochs, where the water lies black as coffee; and the lonely cry of the curlew is the only sound as you moodily cast your flies for the speckled Shetland trout.

I had an 8 lb. sea trout, on a frayed 3X cast, in Laxo burn for two hours and forty minutes!

They are lonely and dreary little islands; they are wind-swept and battered; and yet, if you have stood on their wine-red moors at sunset and seen the great swells of the Atlantic pounding in, you will never forget them.

Chapter 71

A CRUEL JOB

THAT age old argument that gives so much pleasure to literary log rollers in London pubs—"Do sailors love the sea?"—was put casually to Olsen and answered in the affirmative.

"I guess I must," he said. "I've been on it for fifty years."

Also when the whalers were yarning in the forecastle at night they would often make some remark about the things they had seen, such as the colour of the Antarctic ice, which showed they had been touched by the beauty of the scene. And that miraculous night when we lay rocking off the Gulf Stream and the sun went down in bars of black and gold, the splendour of that night moved even Olsen to exclaim:

"Dat's *fine*, ain't it?"

It was a natural expression of admiration that had more appreciation and understanding in it than a chapter of the most polished literary style. This was important. It was vastly encouraging to believe that the "men who followed the sea" did so, at least partly, for the beauties of the scenes their lives led them through.

But, with the exception of the two callow young giants in the forecastle, the whalers were mostly moody and meditative men; and the mate's face was a study in dissipation and remorse.

"I don't care if I never see the shore again," he told me one night, when I was standing beside him on the bridge. "I got no friends dere—now."

The most dejected sailors I have run up against were the men of the Shetland herring fleet. But this was chiefly because their profession had fallen on bad times; the islands of Unst and Yell were haunted by the ghosts of rotting wharves and barren granite mansions from which the great sailing "drifters" would never again set out. Lerwick, the herring port, was choked with ships, none of whose crews were making more than enough money barely to keep alive.

To an outsider, of course, Lerwick was a scene of almost alarming activity, its harbour packed with British, Dutch, Scandinavian herring boats. They lay along the stone walls of the little town packed tighter than fish in a tin. They jostled and bumped each other coming in and going out; and the lower air was a forest of masts, funnels, fishing floats and the stink of herring blood. The whole fleet put to sea at three o'clock in the afternoon and came racing back in the dawn, running to market with steam and sail, every ship straining to be the first to reach the sea wall, where in an octagon shed sat the fish buyers attending this daily auction of the catch.

Hundreds of Scotch herring girls in rubber boots and with bandages around their fingers—"their clooties"—were gutting the fish and packing them into pyramids of barrels. They worked on piece-work in teams of three girls each, gutting the herrings as fast as an ordinary man could pick up a fish. They waded in a welter of guts and salt blood, and their sturdy bare forearms were covered with scales.

It was only when one went off in a drifter that one got any idea of the sullen desperation underlying the whole active scene.

I went off in the *Kitchener*. We fished off the Skerries. And just as those cliffs were being painted rose by the sunset a black Swedish fisherman came out and shot his nets between us and the shore. Then the night came down and the *Kitchener* drifted there in the North Sea, riding to her two miles of nets.

It was an enchanting scene. The moon shone down on us through racks of cloud. It made pools of quicksilver on the heaving black seas. Around these pools, like the jewels of a necklace, rose and fell the riding lights of the herring fleet.

"It's better up here," said Constantinople, one of the crew as we sat on deck. "De stink in dat cabin will turn the silver in a man's pocket!"

It was true, the cabin beneath the wheel-house had an unbelievable smell. The ghosts of millions of herring spoke up from the bilge. We ate some boiled herring for tea, the men simply scraping the scales off them with their thumbs; and the tea was made by simply boiling it in the fire which made the steam for the windlass.

They had bought a knife and a fork and spoon for me, those friendly men.

"Get a land job?" grunted Constantinople, who had earned that nickname from serving in the British Mediterranean Fleet during the World War. "Yes, this minute, tonight, today. I'd leave the sea in a minute if I could get a land job."

The sea, he said, had only one virtue for him; a man who had a part share in his own ship was his own boss.

"That's the only ting dat keeps us at it. As long as we can keep out of debt—out of de big man's hands. Dey're always trying to gobble us up."

With her mizzen set and tiller lashed, the drifter rode to her two miles of net. Slap—slap—went the sea—whissh . . . roll . . . and plunge . . . and dive-whissh. The wind called coldly through the rigging and the gulls made complaining cries overhead.

Suddenly, as we talked, a monstrous shape rose beside us. It was round and smooth, and the moon glistened on its back. Pstsss! It gave a sudden sigh—like a puncture—and the night smelled as if someone had suddenly opened a dank cellar door—with something dead in it.

"Whale," said Constantinople, " 'e's got an awful bad breath."

The herring-whale played about us in the moonlight. Like a black rubber balloon. And then there was no whale.

" 'E's gone off to another boat. Hanging around here to see if there's anything doing for breakfast. Nothing doing—gone off to another boat."

But the whale came back when we started to haul in the nets, knocking the herring out of the gill-mesh with his tail.

I was aghast at the emptiness of that net. It came in black and glistening, phosphorescent. A few herring fluttered in its meshes and were snapped into the well or on the deck where they glowed like chips of iridescent metal. . . . I had expected to see a silver horde come in over the side. The fringes of the net were outlined in blue flame and twenty feet below the surface, swimming in a pale blue moonlight of their own cold fire, I saw the herring struggle to escape—to wrench their gills free—before it was too late. A gelatinous jelly-fish rolled helplessly along the mesh, ebbed clear, and shone in that eerie submarine world like a planet of the first magnitude. The captain grunted dolefully at the miserable result of the catch.

"Four crans," he said to me, indicating the herring baskets. "We've been working for nothing!"

There was one sailor in the *Kitchener* who was so tall that his nickname was "Hand-me-down-the-Moon." As a strong young man, he had gone to sea in the six-oared herring boats with which these hardy Shetlanders used to reap the sea. But, except for these perilous long rows off his own fantastic coast, Hand-me-down-the-Moon had never been outside the Shetlands. Hearing Constantinople and some of the rest of the crew talking of the world they had seen as sailors in the British Navy, the old fisherman turned to the captain:

"James Goodlad, you and me ain't seen nothing of this world. We was just as if we was brought up in a barrel."

At dawn we hauled the net again in a scream of gulls and diving sulphur-necked Solon geese. These gannets would drop from the dark sky like a plummet to spear a fish deep under water. And the Skua gulls, the real sea-hawk, were pursuing the other gulls to make them vomit their catch—which spewed-up fish the Skuas would often catch before it hit the water.

Orient, Venus Star, Children's Trust, River Nile, Camperdown and *Kitchener* raced back to port. Sailing drifters were racing ahead of us, red sails outlined against a grey coast. We went past the Bard of Bressay with the sheep like maggots on its high head. Past rain-spattered crofts, lonely in the green uplands, with the white smoke of the peat breakfast fire torn down wind. Bumping other boats about like cocoanut shells we joined the jam that was fighting to be the first boat along the market wall.

Hand-me-down-the-Moon and Constantinople took our four baskets of fish up to the auction ring. We heard the clanging of the auction bell.

"What am I bid? The *River Nile*—forty crans large fulls, gen-

tlemen. Twenty shillings? And two, and another—do I hear someone say twenty-five? Going, going—clang!"

A fish buyer had nodded calmly and made a note in his book.
Gutted and packed, these large herrings would probably be sold
in Germany. All the riff-raff among herrings were being bought
for the Russian market.

"Them Rooshins would even eat a mackerel!" said Constantinople, which fish, he declared, feeds on dead bodies. That's why
mackerel are so fat! Constantinople jangled some silver in his
hand and looked at the captain.

"Expectations," chuckled Hand-me-down-the-Moon. "Dey're
de only tings what keeps us alive."

But Captain Goodlad, kicking out his oilskins, spoke the verdict
of his life.

"Well—dere's annuder night dat won't have to be done again."

Chapter 72

COLOUR OF SPAIN

WITH the freedom that is given a foreign correspondent to roam the countries of Europe, I have always reserved Spain for my emotional adventures. The first time I saw it I was shocked. Anything less like "Spain" than San Sebastian on a wet winter's night could hardly have been imagined. I was the only guest in its main hotel; they charged me a pound for a dish of bacon and eggs; and a dog had forgotten himself on the red carpet under my table. I went to bed in sheer disgust.

Then I thought: "This is no way to enter Spain. Get up and bestir yourself!" So I dressed after midnight and went down to the sleepy concierge. "Tell me," I asked; "where do the Spaniards go in the winter time."

"Señor," he croaked, "haf you heard of the Bar Basque?"

"Certainly," I said. "It's in Biarritz. I was in it this afternoon."

"No, Señor—*le vrai* Bar Basque—*il est ici.*"

He summoned a moribund coachman, and in a few minutes I was in an underground café where the girls were dancing with each other before the bored dons, and where I met a young man who was wrapped in bandages from head to foot.

"I," he said, "am the best motor-car racer in Spain. Perhaps in the whole world. I don't know. Today I turn over in the race from Monte Carlo to Biarritz. Señor," he asked, having invited me to sit down, "what is Life?"

I snapped my fingers. "Nothing," I said.

"Precisely—you must let me drive you to Madrid."

I escaped that. But he gave me a letter to his amigo, the President of the Pamplona Bull Fighters' Club; and the next sundown saw me sitting before that Club, drinking white sherry and watching the "Promenade of the Pears," the nightly walk around of the pretty girls under the arcades.

Here I found Jesus Christi Basiano.

I got him out of a bottle. It was a bottle of Rioja Alta, that sour red wine of Aragon; and as we drained it I became Sinbad the Sailor and he became the Old Man of the Sea. But our metamorphosis was unknown to us, and we actually ordered another bottle and shook hands.

"*Amigo?*" he asked, with that strange, anxious stare—"Friend?"

"*Si, si,*" I said. "*Amigo*—friend."

Then he smiled and took my last cigarette.

Jesus Christi Basiano was a Basque. He was also a Spaniard. But first of all Jesus Basiano was for Jesus Basiano.

That, at least, was the way I first thought of him. I was five hundred miles and two months away from Jesus Basiano before I fully realised his excellence. I knew then the meaning of that strange look in his eyes, that fixed stare—as if something had just terrified him.

Jesus was an artist. In the days of his youth he had shown such promise that his government had sent him to study in Rome. But the promise had not panned out. He was back now, in Pamplona, with that strange look in his eyes.

The worst day I had with him was when he showed me his canvases. He had them stored away in an "art" store, where they sold gilt picture frames and brass lamps. He brought out his paintings, unwrapped them, and stood them against the wall. Then he stepped back and watched my face. I did not know what to say. They all bore the stamp of Something, but it looked like the mark of madness to me. Finally, I said, they seemed very good. But the trouble was, he explained, there were not enough other people who thought so. People who could pay for them. So when he had finished a painting of some lovely peak in the Pyrenees, Jesus would tack paper over it and put it away.

He lived down a side street, over a market where the peasants stood in the mornings with their lambs crucified on little wooden crosses. And up the narrow slit of his house Jesus had painted a floral design around its four windows to lend it distinction. He never asked me to come up. But he ate with me every day, or else sat silently beside me in the café. I thought at first that he was my guest—until I discovered that the two brothers who ran the hotel were not charging me for him. They loved him, he was their amigo—and that was enough.

I got this from one of the brothers who was president of the Bull Fighters' Club.

The café was always full. A haze of blue smoke, an everlasting rattle of dominoes against the marble-topped tables; waiters shuffling about with metal pots of coffee and goat's milk—and rows of Basque faces looking like acorns under their berets. It was the same every day. I wondered how Jesus could endure such a life.

Jesus just sat there. We did not know enough words to make a sentence in each other's language, and our efforts to converse via one of the brothers always went wrong. Then Jesus would revert to what had become a *leitmotif* in our conversation.

"Mista!—Ujue?"

Even then I didn't know what "ook-way" meant, but I had grasped that it was a place of some sort, and that Jesus was determined we should go there.

One night, worn out by a Spanish dinner, I nodded.

We drove all day. Even in winter the plateau of Pamplona was a painted scene. Under foot the soil was clay red, but the nearest bare hill was already a deep bronze, and then they rolled on and on in fading blues until we could not tell them from the sky.

It was an empty road, travelled by mules. Mules, eight in line, head to tail, tail to head, pulling hooded carts on high wheels. Mules in line, leading bullocks with pads of sheepskin lashed to their horns for yokes, hauling great loads of logs. Mules with wicker baskets and black-haired girls sitting on their rumps; mules with bundles of faggots, with high wooden saddles, with bulging saddlebags of purple and yellow and red; mules with wooden hooks and steps sticking out from their sides. Little trembling burros staggering along under great loads of brush with an old gnome of a goat-skin-clad Basque grinning at us from the swaying top. A man driving a pink pig with a little branch of green olive. All going at a slow walk—the pace of Spain.

It was sunset when we reached Ujue, a remote pueblo in

Navarre. To get into it we had to go out on a long spur of mountain and wind up around a circular road that led into the little labyrinth of stone buildings on its tip. Perched on the very top was an old yellow church, with its battlemented fighting top. And up here Jesus hauled me. He almost dropped me through its ancient beams, so eager was Jesus to get me to that ancient tower top. He scrambled ahead of me, as if he had some precious secret to show, until we stood on the old fighting tower looking half-way down into Spain. Below us lay the kingdom of Navarre, its bare mountains like waves against the low sun. The east was a deep sapphire, and along it was a high line of white, like the crest of a wave breaking in the sky. It was the snows of the Pyrenees.

We stood there in the cold wind until the mountains below us faded out and the tiny constellations of pueblo lights began to appear on their crests. Neither Jesus nor I had spoken a word. We did not need to. We understood each other now.

It was still night. The monks started to sing about five, chanting in Latin to greet the new day. They were kneeling, I knew, before Our Lady of Ujue, that beautiful little lady in the mountain church above. She sat in robes of silver, with a golden crown on her head, her hand raised, behind a rose-painted curtain which had little silver bells that would tinkle and give the alarm if some vandal tried to take Our Lady of Ujue away. Above her were the swords, crests, and golden crowns of the Kings of Navarre. Knights in armour slept with hands crossed on their tombs beside her. And at her feet—in a crystal casket guarded by four silver knights—was the black heart of Carlos el Malo, Charles the Bad.

The pueblo still slept. Its faded red roofs were like slabs of cork bark scaling the mountain crest. I got up and leaned over my balcony, watching the dawn strike through the Sierras. Their black crests made wavy lines in the steaming mist; and the mist made silver circles, widening, around the white sun. It was like peering down a burnished gun barrel. The low-lying clouds exploded in flames of yellow and rose. They burned fiercely. And then it was day.

Navarre lay below me. That cold, bare, glittering kingdom, keen as a sword.

Cats, dogs, pots, Spaniards, were all bunched together, as closely as they could be packed around the small fire. It was a fire of acacia wood, its tiny logs burnt in half, the pots bubbling in the embers. It was built on a hearth raised about a foot from the floor, and on a stool before this sat the señora, her knees under her chin, roasting a rabbit. The rabbit looked like a skinned baby, laying there on the low grid. Its glazed eyes seemed to appeal to me as she rolled it over from time to time and rubbed it with garlic.

Little Pepita who had been tottering about the tiled floor hugging a great loaf of bread, got up from sitting on it and handed it to her father. Jose took the knife with which he had just been slaughtering a sheep and hacked off a generous slab, which he handed to me. Then he smacked the cat. And we began our breakfast.

As we ate I could hear the morning exodus—the cattle being led out of the rooms below us and down the mountainside to graze in the terraced fields.

The pueblo is a city without numbers, or signs, or writing on its walls. This does not strike you at first, but then you realise that wherever you wander there will be nothing to guide you on your way back—nothing but instinct or memory. The streets are slopes of smooth rocks, like the beds of rivers in a drought, with here and there a little stream of sweet, milky sewerage trickling down through the stones. The walls of the overhanging houses hem you in like ravines. The streets are of stone and the houses are of stone, old, faded, yellow, so fused together in blocks that you cannot tell them from one another, and you pass, climbing, a succession of studded doors. And you begin to wonder if there is not something secretive about this labyrinth of mute stone.

But there is a stone crest over an arched door—and its lettering reads: "Anno Domini 1572." A plumed helmet surmounts the crest.

If you lie below the pueblo and look up you will see that noth-thing moves. It is like watching a painting. The fighting-top of its old church stands silently against the hills of Spain; and as you look you see its green bells turn completely over before their sound floats down to your ears.

Chapter 73

LOVE IN THE MOUNTAINS

"Love?" said Augusto. "There is no love in these mountains."

"But there must be love," I insisted, "in a place as beautiful as this."

I was spending the Christmas with Augusto in his casa up against the French frontier. There was no pass in his valley, leading over into contaminating France, and the Basques up at its head still went about in jerkins of hairy goat-skin, and wore sandals and breeches that were slashed and laced over white bloomers at their knees. It was a patriarchal civilisation in which Augusto's father (now absent in Spain with some sheep) was the Grand Old Man. Our village was at the head of the valley, where the loggers began to ride their rafts down through the dangerous rapids of the Pyrenees.

Augusto laughed. "The mountains—what do you think they mean to a peasant? Do they mean beauty? They do not. To the peasant the mountains are ugly. They mean danger—storms and hard work—and suffering."

"But what has that to do with love?"

"They haven't got time to love," said Augusto. "They work too hard. They are too tired."

"Now, that is nonsense," I replied. "Love is a thing without time. You do not put hours aside for it."

"Ho, yes, you do—that shows all you know!"

We were sitting under the black cone of his chimney. It made the entire ceiling of the room. A pot dangled over the fire from an iron hook on its chain. And his wolfhound dozed with his head on Augusto's knees. I had just ridden back through the rains and the snows of the upper Pyrenees from Aragon, and my two mules rested beside their sleeping mozo in the room below ours. The storm swept down the valley as we talked.

"Consider," said Augusto, "the day of a peasant. He gets out of bed before dawn. He eats his simple breakfast of *migas*—of bread-shavings and garlic and sheep-fat—and then he faces the mountain. He starts to climb it. Do you think he likes that—every day? He works there all day long. And at sunset he starts to climb back down the mountain. The mountain has taken it out of him. He is tired."

"And after sunset?"

"You have seen them—all the men go to the café. And where are the women?"

"Washing-up, I suppose."

"Why aren't the men with them?"

"I don't know."

"Because they would much rather be with the other men in the café. I am speaking in generalities now. My point is that if there had been a great love here between man and woman this custom would never have begun. No—when two peasants marry it is because their circumstances are suitable—their land and household possessions."

"Perhaps," admitted Augusto, "the peasants might know a few moments of love in the summer. In the summer they bring their flocks up to graze in the Alpine valleys. Up here, when the moon hangs over the beech forests—yes, the girls hunt for love there. Even the daughters of the poorer peasants who have been forced to work in the winter months in the sandal factories over in Manelon in France—they also come back to hunt their loves then. But it is a pagan affair. The night after a peasant is married, directly after dinner, you will see him coming back to the café."

Augusto, who spent his winters usually in Paris, was annoyed with what he termed the London-pub school of Pyrenean Romantics who wrote such fanciful tales of the high Pyrenees. He was also tartly realistic about life in his village.

"There," he said, "but for the grace of progress, go the dictators."

It was Sunday afternoon and we were watching the sunset promenade. The girls walked in twos and threes, followed at some distance by parallel sets of gawky youths. The women of the village were nowhere in evidence and the men were just leaning idly against its walls. Through this came five men, walking abreast, their coats flung over their shoulders like cloaks; and with a majestic aloofness they strolled down the village street and took the lonely mountain road. They were portly and elegant and each one stared sternly at Augusto as he passed. They were, said Augusto, the Chief of the Secret Police, the Priest, the Doctor, the Veterinary, and the Chemist. Attached to them was another man—the Richest Peasant in the Village. The Russians would have called him a *kulak*.

"They are the 'professionals,'" said Augusto. "The *gente de carrero*."

"But why dictators?"

He laughed. "You do not understand what the *gente de carrero* mean to a village! They form a club, a secret society of their own. They are banded together against the rest of the village. They are the intelligentsia.

"Charming people!" said Augusto. "They spend their lives eating, drinking, smoking—and criticising the village. 'Ah!' they say, 'what savages, these peasants!' And yet they are the very people who are trying to hold the village back."

For the doctor, the chemist, and the veterinary, said Augusto, the peasants of his village had to raise about £800 in taxes every year. For that the doctor was supposed to treat any cases free. But, said Augusto, a doctor who could not get anything better than a panel job in a village was no doctor to go to when one was really ill. If a peasant could afford it he always sent for a real doctor from Pamplona or Saragossa.

"And the grace of progress?" I asked. "How will it affect the dictatorship of these men?"

"Progress means roads," said Augusto, "and roads mean motor buses—and motor buses mean that our young men will go out. They go down to Pamplona, San Sebastian, and Saragossa. They see sophisticated people. And when they come back here, and the priest and the doctor and the others start at them again with their fairy-tales . . ."

"Yes?"

"Well—then the young men tell the dictators to go chase themselves."

That, said Augusto, was what progress meant to Spain. And that was why the priests in the valley of Roncal had fought the introduction of a motor bus line to the very last mile.

"The church was trying to hold the village back."

Even when I was with him in 1928, I could see that the "powers that be" in his village did not like Augusto Labyru. When I asked him to take me to Christmas Mass the priest almost stopped his service when he saw us, kneeling with the women, among the reversed chairs. The priest said to the Chief of the Secret Police afterwards:

"I know that Augusto Labyru is not a holy man. That foreigner he had with him did not look like one either! What do you suppose they could have been doing in church?"

We learned this through Augusto's own underground channels of information in the village; for he was even then working patiently for what he considered to be the freedom of Spain. In 1934, when I went back in the summer to spend some days with him in his village he led me proudly to three bullet holes in a door. This was where, in the first flurry of Revolution, the Gardia Civile had tried to execute him without trial. They killed his best friend—but they missed Augusto.

"They just stood us up against this door in the dark," said Augusto. "They fired at the whiteness of my face."

He placed his head so that the bullet holes made a sinister halo around it. When he discovered that he had not been hit, Augusto simply dashed off into the darkness and up into the mountains.

"I stayed there," he said calmly, "until word reached me that our side had won."

Chapter 74

MULES IN ANDALUSIA

Much as I liked Augusto I was dead against nearly everything that he wanted for Spain. The glory of his country seemed to be that serene, behind the Pyrenees she could remain a great farm, and Spain was too much out of Europe to be of any use as an ally in its political discords. She was lucky. There is a cathedral beside the yellow Ebro in Saragossa in which hang the flags of all of Spain's lost colonies. They seem to have covered over half the known world. It is a shocking sight. But it doesn't seem to have affected the Spaniards one little bit; their soldiers still know how to die—even if they don't know how to win wars. And the War Department is still the biggest building in Madrid.

If only the peasants had enough to eat! "I'm not hungry today —I've just eaten my cat." It shocked me to encounter the human scarecrows I saw walking about everywhere in Castile. One expects a peasant, at least, to be able to find food enough, even if a factory worker cannot—but it was not so in Spain.

My other shock, and it became almost chronic, was the abysmal propriety of the night-life of Spain. In search of fun in Bilbao one rainy night I encountered an American sailor off a mule-transport, from Texas. He was standing there in the square positively appalled by the evening promenade, that continuous walk-around of the young men and women under the arcades that takes place in every city in Spain as the sun goes down. His complaint was that all they did was walk. "They don't *do* anything!" he said. "They don't *get* anywhere!"

The propriety of the Spanish prostitute, I discovered, was deliberately put on to arouse the appetite of the Spanish don—who always wants to feel that he has made a conquest.

In Burgos I danced with the peasants on New Year's Eve. We danced with flutes, we danced to lutes, we danced to the tingle of tambourines. Two peasants who had got themselves entwined in a grape-vine decoration they had pulled down invited me to come inside. A Castilian in our van with sandals made from old American motor-car tyres had a bleeding bladder of goat stretched over a tin can. He was pushing a stick in and out of it to produce a series of grunts. Another peasant had a huge clock face strapped on his stomach; and to keep him up to date we moved the minute hand along as the hour of midnight drew near. In Burgos it is the custom to put a raisin in your mouth for each stroke of the clock that brings in the New Year. That brings you good luck. And as the bells of that superb cathedral struck the notes all dancing stopped and we put in our grapes.

I saw that two blonde girls, about a head taller than the Spaniards who had their arms around them, were standing and scowling at this scene.

"English!" squeaked a little Castilian, pointing them out to me.

As I put in my last grape I spoke to the girls: "Good luck," I said. "Happy New Year!"

"Don't be funny!" snapped one.

They were members of a chorus, they told me, which had broken down in Madrid. And going broke in Spain, they said bitterly, was worse than Buenos Aires.

"I'd like to slosh 'em!" said one of the girls in a good Lancashire accent as she looked at the Spaniards. "They don't know how to treat a lady."

They were in a bad way.

I bought a kilometre book and rode 1,000 miles third class to absorb the Spanish scene. I sat up all one night with a nun—talking about Galsworthy. There was a Guardia Civile and a travelling salesman with banana-coloured shoes in our compartment. He had a sausage wrapped up in his dirty undershirt which he insisted that we share.

After Augusto and I had drunk the "drink of departure," passing the leather wine-bottle back and forth in a pass in the high Pyrenees, I took my mules over into Aragon, where the Aragon itself was just a white froth of rapids hurling down the mountains, its water flecked with the red leaves of last year's beech. I crossed it on a terrifying bridge made of just three peeled logs, and El Caracole, "The Snail," my mule, signalled his dismay by semaphore with his upright ears. Then I went down to dirty, attractive little Perpignan in France, from which Eve and I and the Frank Morleys rode up on the top of charging motor buses into the little mountain republic of Andorra. Andorra was in a terrible stew of excitement because for the first time in years they actually had a man in jail. They were so ashamed of him!

And here I had a most poignant interview with Don Roc Palleras, the President. He was a peasant. And when he saw me coming across his fields he raced into his house and put on his frock-coat. But he had forgotten to take off his sandals. He had terrific dignity and a bad case of scrofula and his salary, he told me, was 18s. a year. When I asked him what were his principal duties he said: "Relations with foreign powers."

Then Eve and I bought a couple of mules and set off on a slow, lazy ride all the way across Andalusia. We slept in the little fondas frequented by the muleteers wherever night caught us, except when the smell of some town drove us to seek another one further on. Caught like this, debating whether to try and ride up to the lights of a town we saw shining above us in the mountains or just fall asleep in our saddles, a Spanish don materialised out of the darkness. He took us to his hacienda. It was an amazing place; its long white walls rose up like a fort in the night. And in the morning he had his bulls casually paraded before us while we were eating our breakfast. They would all die gallantly, he assured us, in the bull rings of Spain.

We almost wept when we had to part from Ferdinand and Isabella, our two mules, although Ferdinand did have one particularly nasty trick. When he was tired and wanted to get rid of me he would suddenly heave himself over on his side. Andalusian mule saddles are almost as square as table tops, and the first time Ferdinand did this without warning, he rolled on me and almost cut me in half. And he hated being cleaned at nights.

Hacienda and hovel, pueblo and castle. Water drawn from the well, clothes washed in the stream, food cooked on the hearth, the silver tinkle of the mule bells of Spain—would factory chimneys better this?

Once, in Andalusia, I felt almost sure. It was a hot day. The almond-trees, in full bloom, were clouds of pink against the grey limestone hills. The sky was pale blue. The bees were humming, and I drowsed in my saddle with the hot sun on my head through the sweet smell of almonds and warm earth. No, I thought; let this be. But then I came out from the almonds to face an interminable, blazing plain. It was a sweep of young wheat, dazzling under the sun. And just below me on a slope were forty men. They were working across the field, toiling in line—like prisoners—with an overseer at their back. They were bent over, turfing with little heart-shaped hoes, the baked earth between the young wheat. They were going to traverse that whole plain! And as I watched they called out wearily to a little boy who passed from one to another of them with a stone jug:

"*Agua! Agua!*"—"Water! Water!"

Without machinery they would always be the prisoners of the land.

Chapter 75

THE FAITHFUL HEART

THERE is a classic short story about the girl whose sweetheart fell into the crevasse of a glacier and who—so that she might recover his body—waited forty years at that spot for the glacier to pass. I met a living example of that in Saragossa.

He was playing the trap drums in a dingy Spanish cabaret.

"Yes, sir," he told me. "I've been all over the world—and to-morrow I'm going to be a young man."

"What do you mean?"

"I'm going to be sixty years old."

He took out his passport and I read—Albert E. Holeman, citizen of the United States, born in New York, 1868. He left me then to go to his drums and rattle out a jazz tune to the empty café. It had sawdust on its floor, with a square of it rubbed clean where the people could dance. He was a spare, dignified Negro, whose hair was just beginning to turn grey. He wore a dinner-jacket.

"Yes, sir," he continued when he came back to my table. "I've been in every country in the world—'cept one."

He had missed South Africa, he said, because on the way round from China, he had decided to come via Port Said.

"Yes, sir," his face twitched. "We decided we would work that winter in Alexandria and Cairo."

"Who was with you?"

"My wife."

I glanced quickly around the stale cabaret. The girls were all Spanish, sitting in postures of rectitude calculated to entice the Spanish dons. The propriety of the Spanish prostitute, I realised again, is without doubt the most lascivious thing in Spain.

"Yes, sir," Holeman was saying, with that faint quiver in his idol-like eyes that showed he was hurting himself—"my wife is dead. She died three years ago—in Madrid."

"She was from New York, too?"

492

"Yes, sir, she was coloured like myself."

"I see."

It was uncomfortable to confront the utter aloofness of his dark face. It was as if he were a spectator—looking at the world and me and this dingy café—from a distance where nothing could touch him any more.

"Tell me," I asked. "How long have you been doing this— going round and round the world?"

"Forty years."

"Good grief!—haven't you ever been home?"

He gave me a mirthless smile. "No, sir," he said. "My wife and I—we started out from New York with the *New York Star and Dramatic Company* in 1887—and we ain't been back there since. It was a coloured quartet. My wife and I was doing a singing and tap-dance act. We played Aspinwall first."

"*Aspinwall?*"

"Yes, sir—they calls it Panama now.

"Yes, sir—there were four of us and the manager. We disbanded at Aspinwall. I wouldn't say we exactly disbanded, though —we just bust. The manager, he just skipped out with the company's funds. He took a boat. This is where it's funny. We thought we might catch him. But no, no, when we all come running down to the dock the ship was just pulling out. There he stood waving good-bye to us over the rail. Yes, sir. And the cornetists of the ship's band was playing, 'Should Auld Acquaintance be Forgot. . . .' That's right funny, ain't it?"

"Awfully," I said. "How did you get out?"

"Well, that's another funny part of it. We got a boat to Havana. The captain said he would take us there if we worked our way, singing and dancing. Yes, that was right funny. We got seasick. We couldn't do nothing. Then the captain came along: 'Look here,' he said. 'What the hell!—if you ain't going to sing and dance you ain't going to get to Havana!' So we had to dance."

They had worked that season, said Holeman, in the islands of the Caribbean. Then his tale took me all over the world; up and down, around and around. "Moscow?" he said. "Yes, we worked there."

"Did you meet a coloured man, named Thomas."

"Thomas! Oh, yes, indeed. Thomas was head waiter in the Aquarium. Then he organised the Russian Waiters' Co-operatives, then he went off with a Russian count to the Russian and Japanese War, and—"

"I know," I said. "I just saw Thomas—down in Constantinople. He's running a cabaret down there now, a place called Maxim's. He's doing very well."

"Yes, I know. Thomas always was a great man. He didn't mean to run cabarets—he come abroad first to study the violin in Budapest. *His* wife died."

"Well, he's married again," I said. "Russian girl. They have three children."

"Me and my wife," said Holeman. "We always stuck together."

He frowned. "Coloured people ought to stick to their own folk. When I was in Paris the other coloured people used to say to me: 'You're scared; that's why you don't want a white girl. You's a timid nigger!' I told them to leave me alone."

Yes, he did look like an idol, with that black mask of his staring so contemptuously at those girls of Spain.

I asked him what country of all those he had seen would he prefer to live in and settle down.

"Germany!" he said, without an instant's hesitation. "The Germans are the most broad-minded people in the world."

"But what are you doing here in Spain?"

"I'm waiting for my wife."

"Your *wife?* But she's—"

"She's dead."

Holeman reached in the pocket of his dinner-jacket. "You see, sir, it's like this. When we come from Gibraltar my wife took sick. I got four doctors, and then I got a big specialist. I told my wife, 'You go to bed, and you stay there, you don't have to work no more.' We were singing and dancing, you see—partners. So when I was to work by myself I went out and bought these here trap drums. Primo, he liked jazz; and he used to give great big tips if he kept us for a whole night. My wife was sick four months and I was playing in the orchestras of Madrid—playing these here drums. And then she died."

Holeman carefully opened the long envelope he had been fingering and handed it to me. It was an American Consulate certificate attesting to the burial of Mary Elizabeth Holeman, aged fifty-five.

"It's these here regulations," said Holeman. "See what the laws says: Local law for disinterring remains . . . five years."

"Yes," I said, "I see."

"Well, that's why I got to wait. I got to wait around Spain here for two more years, and then I takes her home."

Chapter 76

WILD IRISH

I HAVE never written a word about Ireland without my paper receiving a deluge of letters asking who pays my salary: the paper, or the British Government? By the same mail comes another batch of letters calling me a dirty Sinn Feiner. One Irish-American outdid himself when he suggested that I was "just the usual bloody propagandist covered with a thin veneer of truth." So I don't expect anything I write about Ireland to please anybody, not even the British who are supposed to be paying me.

Anything funnier than the British Press before an Irish election, or a rumour of an Irish election, is hard to imagine. The British caricature the wild Irishman in their literature and they make an idiot of him on the stage; but they forget entirely about him at election time; and the funny part of it is, there are any amount of these Irishmen. That's why de Valera stays in.

The first time I talked with de Valera was in 1928, when he was out of office, sitting in the Fianna Fail headquarters over a shop in Lower Abbey Street. As I went in a girl clerk in his office handed me a ticket announcing I could get "A Beautiful Enlargement of Eamon de Valera" for sixpence. Along with most of the rest of the world I had come to the conclusion that de Valera was crazy even before I saw the man. And when I first talked to him he sounded to me as mad as a hatter. He said, for instance, that the Irish were exporting their best brains to America, and that the 25,000 young Irish men and women who left their country for the United States every year should stay home. When I asked him how they would live if they did so, he replied that the Free State ought to make jobs for them on Irish soil; the Irish ought to develop their own industries as a complement to Irish farming. As I said, the man sounded mad to me; and as I looked at those pinched lines beside his nose and faced the fire of his eyes, I thought I had better humour him a bit.

"Tell me," I asked; "there are only six votes in the Dail between you and President Cosgrave. If you are returned to office, will you try to make Ireland a Republic?"

"I will!" snapped de Valera. "I will do everything in my power, everything within reason."

Whether de Valera had exceeded the bounds of reason or not is not for me to say. I only know that the last time I talked with him he had gone a long and unmistakable way towards making the Free State free from England; call it a Republic, or what you like. I saw him in the Dail, the night that assembly passed the Bill abolishing the oath of allegiance to King George. I waited for him in his private office; and when he came in he was sparkling with ecstasy. That night I asked him the same old questions and he answered them the same old way; nothing had changed since that first conversation in Lower Abbey Street. But this time he was not so peevish; he was getting somewhere. I saw him that night in London, in the Piccadilly Hotel, when the negotiations with J. H. Thomas had broken down to end the Anglo-Irish economic war. This 40 per cent mutual tariff wall that had been erected between the two countries was ruining the most important enterprise in the Free State: the export cattle trade. Prices for cattle at the Free State fairs had dropped to less than half the normal price. J. H. Thomas was promising new restrictions against this most important Free State export if de Valera did not hurry up and pay Britain something like five million pounds overdue land annuities. But was de Valera blue? Not he. His calm on that night was so unusual that it was obvious there was something significant about it. What it was de Valera told me the last time I saw him, which was in Dublin, in the President's office, just before the last Free State elections when he administered such a crushing defeat to the combined forces of Cosgrave, Frank McDermot and the fighting General O'Duffy.

"The world slump and the British," he said to me, "are playing my game. With import restrictions springing up everywhere the world is closing its doors against us. The British are building a wall against our goods. The 25,000 young Irish people who used to emigrate yearly to America cannot go there any more. In fact, they're coming back. More Irish people came back to Ireland last year (1932) than went out of Ireland. We can't find jobs for them on the land—so we have to develop the industrial side of our country. That's what I have been trying to tell you all along."

He did not sound like the mad hatter then; not when one looked around at the autarchy sweeping over all the other countries. He seemed to be talking just plain common sense; although he had not changed a word from what he was saying in 1928. The only change I saw in him was in the man himself. When I first saw him in those shabby little Fianna Fail headquarters in Lower Abbey Street, he looked fretful and frustrated, a schoolmaster in an empty classroom. On this eve of the elections in 1933 he had just come in from standing in the rain to review the Irish Free State Army. He was dressed in plain black, with an old black felt hat; gaunt, not only physically, but with the burdens of responsibility. He made me think of Lincoln that day.

When I asked fighting General O'Duffy how he could account for the crushing defeat of his United Ireland Party, that famous Blueshirt (his enemies call him a stuffed shirt) replied:

"Ah, all the dead in Ireland voted before nine o'clock. The inmates of all the insane asylums voted before ten o'clock."

But it was not false registrations that returned President Eamon de Valera to office. It was the "wild" Irishmen that the British (and the Dublin politicians) had forgotten about. And they are not so wild. Part of their preference for de Valera was explained to me by a Senator who is one of the big men in the Irish Labour movement.

"You see," he said, "Cosgrave is an honest man, but he has the mind of a small shopkeeper. While Dev., mind you, he's a dreamer. Dev. sees things. Whether he can put them into action or not is another question; but we'd like to give him a try."

For the rest you must go to the west of Ireland where Cromwell and the cities of the United States are much nearer to the Irish than any living British statesman or even Dublin itself. Places in the Gaelticht, like Galway, Connemara and Mayo, where in many of the districts you won't hear a word of English spoken unless you speak it yourself.

Chapter 77

CONNEMARA

I FOUND him sitting on his stone fence in Connemara. He was watching three rows of unearthed potatoes that were drying in the sun. In the distance the Twelve Pins were a hazy blue silhouette across the waste of bogs, rocks, and torn lakes. Below him a red-sailed peat-boat was just setting out from a blue arm of salt water, and the rocks of the estuary glistened with yellow kelp at low tide. He had no shoes.

"There's enough spuds there," he announced, "to last me through the winter—but there's no money in it, mind you.

"I have a brother and sister still with me," he went on. When I asked him where, looking at his small one-roomed house with the cow gazing out at us from its wet dirty floor, he answered: "In Boston."

He said, "There's no place in the wide world today, excepting heaven, that's as fine as America."

"Then why did you leave it?" I asked.

"Ah!" He slowly rubbed his leg. "The Irish would leave heaven to get back to Ireland again."

He walked with me in his white bawneen coat as far as the local cross-roads store. There was no sign at the cross-roads except a whitewashed slogan, half obscured by some lolling youths, along a stone wall. It read: "BOYCOTT BRITISH GOODS." Inside the store a travelling salesman was trying to induce the shopkeeper to buy some of his wares while a political argument was going on. Said the salesman:

"Now, there's a pair of pants that'll come and go like india-rubber. They'll see you to your grave. Two-and-six a pair—know why I can sell 'em so cheap?—because they're Russian."

"Rooshin, are they! Well, so long as you keep 'em on I don't mind."

Said one of the politicians: "The Oirish don't know what the hell they want—but, by God, they're determined to have it! I'm as good a Republican as anyone—ask anyone in Ireland, they'll tell you that. Isn't that so, Jerry?"

"Jerry—hey!"

Jerry, who had fallen asleep on a packing-case, tried to look out through his muddled eyes; and then getting to his feet he staggered across and leaned himself against me.

"Mister, I want you to drink with me. Oim the happiest man in Oireland, in the whole world, in fac'—a son was born to me this day."

There was only one question on which the entire pub was united:

"We must have our Dev. He's the only man who knows how to handle the British!"

I was trying to sound out a political situation, and to do it I had gone straight across Ireland to the west coast to hear what was being said down on the Dingle peninsula, in Limerick, in the rock-walled country of Galway and Connemara, up in the bogs of Mayo, and in the cattle fairs of Donegal and the Golden Vein. Then I would drive back to Dublin to listen to Cosgrave and de Valera. I did this, covering Ireland, for seven years. And it always stood me in good stead, particularly where trying to make headway against the statements of belligerent General O'Duffy was concerned.

Leaving this pub in the rocks of Connemara I drove back to the heraldic dark glory of Galway, picked up a great Irish writer who was sleeping it off in his pub, and with an Irishman I had known in Rome and two bottles of whiskey, we drove out to Tilara Castle to watch the dawn rise from its slates. Then we all of us drove down into County Clare.

If a man is made by his environment, then to understand certain Irishmen and what is going on, you must know County Clare. I don't mean Ennis, the stronghold of de Valera, where you can get Irish Republicanism as neat as your whiskey on its pleasant golf course of rolling green. I mean the country out around the Atlantic, where the sun rolls off the nose of Black Head Mountain into the sea.

Padraic was the Irish writer's first name, and you can guess what his other was. It does not matter—he is dead now—but there is not an Irish writer who won't be glad to snatch off his hat at the mention of that name. You have probably never read a book of his, because he wouldn't allow them to be translated from Irish into English.

He might have been forty, he might have been fifty, it was impossible to say. His face was worn as the weathered rocks, creased with hard thinking—and a little bit of hard drinking. He stood in the wind with his hair flying off his round skull, his clothes flapping and his trousers curled around his bowed legs.

"I'd build a wall around Ireland! A wall thirty cubits high, the same as Tibet . . . a wall of brass around it. I wouldn't let in an idea. Not an idea, mind you—from the outside world."

He paused and stretched out his arm, palm down:

"Then I'd open it. Open Ireland after fifty years—and the stream of humanity would find that it had new life to put in its veins. Veins that had been sterilised by the standardists."

This talk had begun by my asking him why the Government was wasting every Free State official's time by insisting he must learn Irish. The Irish language, declared Padraic, was Ireland's only sure and safe frontier. It was their barrier against being denationalised. The previous day I had asked the same question of a nun in a convent. This was Sister Malachai at Spiddal; and she had smiled with an impressive confidence as she showed me the maps in the schoolroom—all done in Erse. And they did make Ireland look different. She pointed to the three Gaelticht districts of Ireland: Donegal, Galway, and Mayo. She spoke with a quiet air of satisfaction when she told me how Cromwell had told the Irish they could "go to hell or Connaught," throwing in Clare. Then she pointed out of the convent window over some kelp-covered rocks and a blue sea. She showed me the very spot where St. Enda had landed when he rowed across from Aran in a stone boat to found the ospedial from which Spiddal gets its name. She did not want the children to get the story of this land in any other language but Irish.

"Leave us alone!" said Padriac. "Let us run our own mad little island in the Atlantic . . . we want something with an instinct that is beyond reason."

I asked him what it was.

He looked at me and smiled without parting his lips. I did not talk Irish, he said; and there were thoughts in Irish that could never be translated into English. He knew that, because he had read the attempt of a man to translate one of his novels into English—and it was not the same thing. We could debate all we wanted about the perils of standardisation, the desire of most people to make the whole world alike; and, as he said, the fact that the Americans would one day level off the Rocky Mountains. We could talk about that—but he could not give me his side. How could a man explain an instinct that was so much stronger than mere reason?

Clare is Irish. It is like no other spot on earth. It is one of those grotesque landscapes of Ireland which, when you come on them suddenly, seem vistas from another world.

The world where we stood was so bare that the streams had no earth in their beds. They poured down, like fountains, over worn steps of rock. The yellow sedge grew in the limestone like patches of hair. At night, as a monstrous moon rolled down the nose of Black Head Mountain and into the sea, the white walls of the solitary cottages glistened like dead bones. This was the country of ogres—of one-eyed giants—and that eye in the middle of their chest. You don't wonder that this should have been the lair of the Long Black Hand. That fearsome Black Hand that used to reach down at nights and pull travellers off this road.

The land is so windswept and forlorn that its few trees are all twisted, leaning away from the sea, with their matted branches trailing out to leeward like a woman's hair.

Wild hair—like the hair of the girl who appeared from behind a rock when our car hit a sheep. She stood there, with her black hair flying and her lips parted. She was frightened, her white teeth were clicking and she pointed up to a man in an upper field. He stood there, staring down at us, half-turned, in his white bawneen coat. Then Padraic spoke to the girl in Irish and they fell to examining the sheep, and they found that its little legs were not broken, and so we drove on. But when I looked back the girl was still standing there, her hair flying in the wind, and there was a little lamb jumping up against her, kissing her hand.

Down off the Dingle peninsula, when I went off in a curragh to the Blasket Islands, nearest point in Ireland to America, the day was so rough that only the gannets were out, diving into the mountainous black seas. Papa, the Pope, faced forward in the frail skiff of canvas and slats, holding the mainsheet as he watched the mast, and a wild Irish fisher steered with two oars that he trailed behind in our hissing salt wake. The King of the Blasket Islands was a king in body as well as name. A giant Celt with a broad pale face dotted with red spots. And as we talked a boy played "Father O'Flynn" on a violin placed against his stomach, and Seamus danced in a daze on one spot of the sanded floor—his eyes fixed at some spot in the open sea.

The bard of the island was sitting with a board across his knees, writing a paean in Erse to a man who had just caught a record size fish. He was over ninety, and as I entered his home he took off his black islander's hat and said in Erse: "Welcome to this house!"

On the Blaskets there were only three or four persons who understood a word of English. The young girls had all emigrated to cities in America. The names of New York, Hartford and Springfield, Mass., were much nearer to the people of the Blaskets and the lives lived there more understood than was anything connected with Dublin. Aside from these place-names the only other English I heard on the Blaskets were the names "de Valera" and "Republic."

It was scenes such as these which were the sanctuary for the Irish thoughts of Padraic. I could well understand why he could not explain them. He did not need to. The country explained him.

Chapter 78

CATTLE FAIR

ONE SPRING morning in County Tyrone I drove in with the farmers taking their beasts to the Irvingstown fair. The roads were still fresh and cool from the night. The leafy beeches formed an arch over them. Smoke was coming from the whitewashed cottages on the green hills, and the farmers and their boys were walking slowly, with little sticks in their hands, whacking the rumps of heifers and bullocks and bulls. Carts full of pink pigs were trotting to market.

The pig carts were up-ended all along one side of the town's square. Their owners stood between the empty shafts.

"Look at the lovely lard on him!" said a farmer, when I looked into the cart. "Look at the grand skull on him!"

He stuck his broad finger into one of the little pale-eyed pigs to show me his excellence. He pulled him out from his warm bed in the straw, took hold of him by the tail and hauled him out from his nine brothers and sisters, and hefted him.

"Aye, there's nine weeks fine fattening in him!"

The pig shrieked with dismay.

"Glory be!" said a pig-seller, when he heard the price his neighbour had accepted for a pig. "Is he *bestowing* them?"

At the bend of the square the red cattle were being marshalled. There were no barriers; they just stood on the sidewalks, which were slippery with manure, with their owners whacking them into clumps and the buyers walking around them.

"I'll give you nine pounds."

"I'll not take it."

Two men are arguing before a stalled motor-car that is trying to get through this mêlée. They spit on their hands and whack them together. A third man speaks up, for it always takes more than two to make a bargain at an Irish fair.

"Divide the pound," he says.

"Will ye break his word, now?" demands the buyer. "Will ye split the pound?"

"I'll not."

"Will ye give him to me then?"

"I told you ten pound."

The buyer walks off.

"You'll be back now," cries the seller.

The buyer walks off and the men around the seller start berating him for his obstinacy. One of them runs after the buyer and seizes his hand, pulls him back, and smacks the buyer's listless hand against the seller's.

"Will ye break my word now; will ye split the pound?"

"I'll not!" says the buyer, and walks off again.

The buyer is called back, the sale is made and the buyer takes out his scissors and clips his mark on the yearling's rump. Then the three of them, seller, buyer and the Third Man, go off to have a drink at one of the steaming crowded pubs.

It's a grand scene. I've watched it when yearlings were being sold for ten pounds, and I've watched it during the Anglo-Irish economic war when British restrictions against Irish cattle had brought the price for a prime two-year-old down from thirteen pounds to six pounds, and the great fairs were almost dead. The Irish, they say, will always tell you what they think you'd like to hear. But it is watching these fairs that one gets the real *tempo* of Ireland—not listening to the politicians in Dublin. When Irish news gets "hot" and London newspapers start to write that a new election is impending at which the Irish will throw off de Valera, I cross over to Ireland and drive up the west coast. I watched a fair at Portumna before the 1933 elections where I saw hardly one beast sold all day. It was a terrible sight. But even then, with de Valera's tariff war with the British almost bankrupting them, these Irish farmers said:

"We will have our Dev! He's the only man who knows how to handle the British."

I love the little Irish farms, and I think that the forty-acre farm, with its livestock, is one of the best cushions against depression in the world. Two-thirds of any family on a farm are potentially unemployed anyway. And when bad times come the family can pull in its head, and with its own shock-absorbers of pigs, chickens, and ducks, ride safely through a slump that would ruin a big farm with hired hands. That is why the Anglo-Irish economic war has not made the Irishmen as desperate as certain British Cabinet Ministers had hoped they would be.

But forty acres is a fat farm; and a large part of the west coast of Ireland is so desperate that it could not be made any worse. This is the Gaelticht. The "blazer" country of Galway where the fields are so small that if you stand in the road and look across them nothing but ridge after ridge of stone walls meet your eye, and you can hardly jump a horse into one field and out of it without breaking his back. The torn bog of Connemara, where it is almost impossible to scratch a living from among the grey rocks. The deep, purple bogs of County Mayo.

They call the country around Belmullet in Mayo the "apathetic" area. People are so desperate they won't even try to work or find food. I drove down there with the medical officer when he was doing his rounds. Women, he told me, in that part of Ireland went through extra pains at childbirth, they were so badly formed from under-nourishment. And when they got them into hospital they had to bathe both the men and women by force. One of the first cases we visited down on the tip of the peninsula of Belmullet was a man with a badly battered head. He was sitting in his house with an impressive blackthorn club within easy reach. When I asked him how he had got his injuries he explained that he had been taking home his cow and he happened to cross a neighbour's field, and while they were in it the cow happened to stand there for a little while and graze. The neighbour happened to see it. He threw a stone which made a direct hit on this man's face. It knocked him down. More stones followed. But none of them accounted for that long gash on the back of his skull from which I watched the doctor take out several stitches.

"Ah," he said. "That one. Ah, when I was holding the man, so as he wouldn't ruin me altogether, the lady with him hit me on the head with a rock."

That, apparently, had knocked him out.

Solid land is so scarce in the wet bogs of Mayo that the peasants burn the bog to make land. They cut the bog and turn it over to dry in the sun. Then they set fire to it. It takes them years sometimes to make one of those wretched little plots of land which they till entirely by hand, the women carrying seaweed up from the sea in panniers on their backs to fertilise their little field.

The peasants were burning the bog this day. A great column of yellow smoke arose in the sky like a sacrificial fire. And on their knees on the point of the peninsula were a handful of Irish around a grave. A child was being buried that day. And as we came near them the note of a horrible keen went up into the sky.

In a black curragh the doctor and I went off to the Inishkea Islands which are about an hour's hard row off the coast of Mayo. The islands had just been the scene of a tragedy that had practically stopped their island life. Their whole fishing fleet of these frail curraghs had been caught by a storm and smashed against the rocky teeth of the mainland's coast. The frail curraghs, built of canvas and slats, were helpless before the gale. They had been fishing in the darkness for mackerel, and to try and save themselves some of the men in the curraghs had refused to cut their nets and run for it. They hoped they could use them as sea anchors.

"And I found them," said the father of two sons—making a horrid fumbling gesture with his hands—"like that!" He had found his two sons dead in their nets.

And at that moment the woman of the house threw her apron over her head and began to wail.

When we neared the islands we could see that all life had stopped. The men were just standing idly on the beach. One man was making a show at repairing some lobster pots, but when I asked him where he would use them, he shook his head.

"I'll not be using these again," he said. "There hasn't been a fish fished since that night."

The islanders had petitioned the Free State to take them off the islands. They did not want to live on Inishkea any more.

The most gruesome thing about the whole tale was that until late in the next day the islanders did not know how many of their men had been drowned. The storm cut them off from the mainland. There had been twenty-five of these frail canvas curraghs out mackerel fishing, with two men in each. Then one of the more daring among the islanders volunteered to ride before the storm in a remaining curragh to the mainland.

"If I get there," he told the islanders, "and our men are drowned, I'll build a fire in the top of the castle."

There was the fighting top of an old castle protruding over the backbone of the peninsula, and they pointed it out to me now.

"Aye, and we saw it burning," said the father of the two brothers who had been found among the rocks of the mainland tangled up in their nets. Nineteen curraghs had been lost and ten men were drowned along the rocks that fringed the wild coast.

When we were rowed back to the mainland that night in one of the frail curraghs the father came along with us. As we passed the old graveyard by Failmore he went up among the tombs on the sand-dunes and knelt down on a long patch of rocks. There were nine men buried in this one grave.

"We buried them together," said the old man, "because we thought they'd be happier that way."

I left him, praying open-eyed, facing the purple bog mountains of Mayo that swept up without a break to the lonely sky.

Chapter 79

BACK TO RUSSIA

Now THE great day had come—I was to return to Russia. I had had three years of it under the Tsars and saw the end of the Romanoffs; now I was to have a year under the Soviets. But Russia had left so many knots in my life that I was almost afraid to go back. My life had turned out to be so different from the one I had contemplated when I first crossed the frontier of Holy Russia in 1914 that I was almost tempted to let sleeping dogs lie. On the other hand I felt that if I went back and faced it again I might untie some of these knots that had a habit of suddenly making me so silent at the mention of certain names, scenes that were suddenly reminiscent, or when I heard certain songs. I thought this over carefully before I did what I had always known I would do: wire the paper thanking them for sending me there—and then rush out to get a Soviet visa.

But the Soviets refused it. And they refused it three times. Having once been branded almost as a Red in my own country, chiefly because I insisted Lenin was a great man, and the Bolshies were not fools, I was dumbfounded to find that the Bolshies considered me almost a White. I rushed across from Ireland to have lunch in Paris with the Counsellor and first secretary of the Soviet Embassy, and the first result of this meeting with those kindly, highly intelligent and cynical Communist diplomats was to make me more eager than ever to see Russia again. The next result was that we ran down the trouble, why Moscow had given orders not to give me a visa. One of my own colleagues had told the Soviets that I was not a suitable person to admit. He almost succeeded in keeping me out; and if he had known that I was one of the four Royal Air Force pilots attached as instructors to the Denekine expedition he most certainly would have. Even so, I re-entered Russia under a dark cloud.

This was the end of September and the greys of approaching winter were already making the fields deserted and forlorn.

I was so anxious to see everything that I sat there with my nose glued to the window from the moment we crossed the Polish frontier. At first I was astonished at how little things had changed. The heavy-booted soldiers in the Customs House, the smell, the hopeless confusion and crush at every railway station we passed, with the same furry peasants sleeping in their sheep-skins all over the floor; there had been very little change there—except in the uniform of the soldiers and the absence of epaulets. Outside, in the dreary waste of mud around Minsk the thatched huts of the peasants had not changed a straw. This was 1928, and the collectivisation of the land had not started yet. In the train, it is true, the waiters in the restaurant car refused a tip; but the *provodnik* gladly pocketed his when he brought me my glass of tea, and the train was neither cleaner or dirtier, faster or slower than it had been under the Tsars. This automatically put me on the side of the Bolshies, when a European traveller in the restaurant of a dingy station snorted to me:

"Look at them! *Look at those wretched peasants*. Just see what the Bolsheviks have done to these people."

"Madam," I said, "you ain't seen nothing yet. The peasants were always like that."

It was a fortunate note to strike at the very outset because it made me realise how all European tourists, and even journalists, who went to Russia in an inimical frame of mind triumphantly reported such scenes as these as being evidence of the failure of the Soviets. Yet they were seeing nothing else than they would have seen under the Tsars.

Leningrad, to me of course, was a city of ghosts. There wasn't a street in it that did not hurt. Restaurants where we had had long midnight parties in the first flush of being in the early 'twenties with Russia for my oyster: Eliesieff Frères, where I used to get candied apricots from Grasse for Vera (when the bread lines were two blocks long); even my old apartment—it still had the same wall-paper on its walls!—and I stood down in the street looking up into it, staring at the two familiar scars that some bullets had made during the Revolution, remembering the days when I bought my Peter the Great table and shopped at that

huge Army & Navy store to furnish my new Russian home with
Vera. It was like visiting a dead world to stand on the same spot
before the cathedral of the Virgin of Kazan, and try and recap-
ture my thoughts, when I first noticed that the Cossacks were
laughing with the people—not shooting them—and I knew that
the real Revolution had begun. My worst ordeal was when I
entered one of those tragic Soviet shops where they were selling
off the treasures of the lost age: faded finery, silver plate, gold
dinner services, remnants of uniforms, jewellery, walking-sticks,
meerschaum pipes, smoking jackets . . . the playthings of the
past. To show me how it worked an attendant wound up a little
jewelled music box and then set it down to watch it work. It
tinkled out a faded little tune of the '80's.

For a moment I hated the Bolshies for all I was worth. Then a
smug English tourist in the Hôtel de l'Europe made me a rabid
Red in five minutes.

Leningrad was full of memories for Eve too. She had gone out
there at eighteen as a V.A.D. with the Anglo-Russian hospital,
and goodness knows how many times we may have passed each
other on the Nevsky all unknowing.

But if Leningrad was now nothing but a shell from which the
life had been taken out, Moscow was that raw, red life itself. Just
as newborn babies are red, so was Moscow. Red—and squawling.
Moscow was simply palpitating with its newborn forming life. It
was impossible not to be exhilarated by its lustiness. Europe was
like an old *roué* compared to this awkward young boy. We got
there the day the Five-Year Plan was announced.

The commonest mistake that all foreigners make about Russia
both inside and out is their own fixed conviction that the Soviets
are trying to make all people alike. In New York and London it
was Public Charge No. 1 against the Communist ideology; and it
would have been a very sensible one if it were true. But a few
days in Moscow should have been enough to convince anyone
that the Soviet proletarians were competing with each other with
just as much, if not more, eagerness than any other community
on earth. The outstanding difference was that the Soviets awarded

different prizes, and had narrowed the gaps between the top and lower layers of life—hoping to make them both enjoyable.

It was an odd coincidence, but on almost our very first day in Moscow Eve and I picked up a young Russian girl as we hung on to the outside of one of those dangerously crowded trams— and, on the day before I left Russia a year later, I met this same girl again. She sat down and told me all that had happened in that year to her and her dreams—some of which had come true—some not.

She was a bright bit of colour in the sombre Moscow mosaic, so full of life that she couldn't stop talking about it—especially her own. We went out to Lenin Hills, and from there looked down on Moscow, which, from that distance, looked almost the same. The same old piles of painted church domes blazing in the sun. Nothing on that sky-line had changed except for the enormous towering haystack of the Third International's wireless mast. I repeated the old Russian proverb: "There's nothing above Moscow except the Kremlin, and nothing above the Kremlin except heaven!" Then I pointed out the wireless mast which now lorded it over everything.

The girl had been a textile worker in the Urals. But she had studied. She had won one of the seven scholarships to Moscow. And how I envied her excitement about that.

The scholarship, the "stipend," she called it, gave her some £3 10s. a month, and to keep alive in Moscow she did odd jobs of accounting or whatever she could find.

It was obvious even to my layman's eye that she was in the last stages of consumption. There was an exotic flush in her pale cheeks. And she had, she said, just returned to Moscow from a month's free rest in one of the rest homes in the Crimea. She told how heavy-workers, people who toiled with their hands, got a month's vacation every year and only worked eight hours a day; how brain workers got only two weeks and often had to work more than eight hours; how the Communists worked ten, twelve, fourteen hours a day. She seized my hands and gave a crow of a laugh.

"You'd only get two weeks!" she said.

She looked down merrily at her own work-worn hands. "I am a student!" she said. "Soon I shall be a textile engineer! If it had not been for the Revolution I would always have been a worker!"

There, I thought, was a nice little problem in class distinctions which pro- and anti-Sovieters could argue over until they were blind.

Then there was Peter. It doesn't make any difference where we met Peter, but, once we had, like the poor, he was always with us. He was a young Communist who was going into the Red Army on the 17th of the month. Meanwhile he wandered with us around Moscow. If what we saw were "set-ups," then it was propaganda on a scale that embraced most of the population of Moscow! Over in the Culture Park beside the Moskva River we saw something like 25,000 of the proletariat playing football, pushball, hockey, *gorodki*, giving amateur theatricals with amateur, and fairly frightful, orchestras, rowing (the most perfect eight I saw was made of girls), running, jumping, throwing the javelin, arguing—and discussing Soviet ideology, the Communist's philosophy. On another night we went to the Central Park, the summer club of the Soviet employees, where around an athletic field as large as possessed by any university in the United States, there were movies, theatres, libraries, cheap restaurants, and where Peter and I practised shooting in the target gallery, the targets being Austen Chamberlain and Chiang Kai Shek. To score a bull's-eye on Austen you had to knock the monocle out of his eye. Peter cheered when he hit it. And with a strange realism the shooting gallery made me pay for all the clay pipes that I broke!

"All this is ours!" said Peter, as we walked among the hundreds of pretty *komsomolkas* strolling around the dark running track. "We are young—and all this is ours!"

He could hardly get over that. Neither could I. One of my first and last reactions to Soviet Russia was the vitality and eagerness of the young people, and if I was going to be born again in this world, I would want to be born in Russia—provided that my father had not been a *kulak*. Peter presented the same problem in class relations. After he had been telling me how the Red army would not tolerate even the son of a *nepman* or a *kulak*, or the son of any other man who had once exploited the workers, I asked:

"But what are you going to do when you leave the Red army?"

"Why!" said Peter. "I'm going to learn a profession in there—Radio. *I'm* not going to be a worker!"

When I asked Peter if he did not mind the fear—always present in any Soviet Russian's mind—of living under the constant eyes of the G.P.U., Peter frowned and was silent. Then he said thoughtfully:

"*Da!* I do. But you must understand that it is *our* Russia they are watching over."

When, afterwards, I had luncheon in London with Kerensky, and I tried to explain this eagerness of Soviet Russian youth (some 2,500,000 more of whom come of age every year), that tragic figure of the Revolution simply could not see my point. Yet it is just this addition of fanatic youth to the mass of the Soviets that in my opinion makes the Bolshevik experiments certain to go on.

As an accredited foreign newspaper correspondent I was "conducted" very little around Moscow. When I tried to make contact with some of the workers in a textile factory I found it very difficult, but this was chiefly because the workers themselves were afraid of me, that being seen with me would draw attention on themselves. The manager of one mill chaperoned me on a tour of the new communal living quarters for the workers, where everybody seemed to be happy and holding meetings of some sort or another. But the next day I walked around behind the new barracks and into a badly lighted tenement where I was literally seized by the desperate occupants and drawn into a stuffy room. There I found ten people, men and women, comprising about five unrelated families, sleeping in beds along the wall.

"Look at us!" they all cried. "We are not Communists."

And one old codger seized his cup of tea and stuck his finger in it. It was so dark in the room, he declared, that that was the only way he could tell when his cup was full.

"Well, why aren't you Communists?" I asked.

There was a silence for a moment. Someone said that he had been waiting, and ten years of the Revolution had not brought much result. But the oldest and most dogged among them probably gave the chief complaint they all had against the new order of things—the inability to leave a job and move on. He mimicked a scene:

"In the old days, when we didn't like a job, we went to the boss and we took off our hats and we said, '*Baren*, I am going to leave.' And we were free to go somewhere else and find another job that we liked better. Here!—here!—well, if you leave one factory in the textile trust—you have left all of them! Understand? —you can't get a job."

But eventually, and over a considerable period of time, I spent weeks with one young textile worker. I talked to him at work on his machine, ate in the factory restaurant, went with him to his clubs, tried to buy a ticket and was refused when his mill had the entire Moscow Theatre for *The Armoured Train*, and spent nights with him in his home, which was but one room of a former Moscow merchant's apartment. His two children slept silently in their little beds by the wall. Lev and his young wife and I talked Communism, while they tried to convert me. In the next room lived an actor in the Vachtangoff Theatre and an engineer; we could hear them, as they always seemed to sit with their chairs tilted back against the closed double-doors, always talking about Culture. In the room on the other side lived a man and his wife who had been divorced, but were still forced to live together until the man found "living space." Lev belonged to an aeroplane club in his factory which had made its own glider. I expected to see him get killed in that, in the spring, but he got his arm torn off in the mill machinery before that, and I lost sight of him in a Crimean rest home.

But from Lev, whom the G.P.U. was watching of course, I got a fairly broad prospect on a Soviet worker's life. I felt quite certain that he was reporting every word that I said: but these were not so momentous, and I felt that as the Soviets were beginning to see I was trying to be objective in my job they encouraged

Lev to talk more and more openly with me. Not being a textile engineer, I could not tell, of course, whether the mill was being run well or not. Only the candid Soviet statistics showed the awful percentage of unfit goods which was being turned out. I could not even tell whether the people were happy or not, because half of them did not know that themselves, and the rest were too young to know anything of what life in a mill had been like in Tsarist days. The advantage of association with Lev was that it gave one a pretty clear insight into how the Bolsheviks were trying to build a house at the same time they were living in it; that they could not do what they had hoped to do in Nihilist days—rip down everything and build from the ground again—and that the structure of Communist life was a compromise at almost every point. It had to be, just as Lenin's resort to the *nepman* régime was merely a temporary retreat to enable him to jump further along the zigzag socialist road. While theoretical Communists outside Russia argue with definite intellectual preciseness as to just what Russian Communism is and is not, a Russian Communist will probably admit to you that he hasn't the slightest conception of what the future design of life should be. He's trying to find that out.

Just one thing stood out. The workers thought that the workers owned the factories, the tools, and the money to make them work. And as long as the workers felt that, whether it was correct or not, they weren't going to have any return to the system of private ownership.

In a place like Baku, for instance, which we saw in the very throes of its amazing prosperity from the comparatively easily exploited oil reserves, the Communist system seemed to be working so amazingly well to the workers down there that it was almost impossible to talk to them. They expected the world revolution to come along any minute.

Irritating as some of its exponents might be, such as the arrogant oil workers of Baku, I found a spirituality in Russian Communism that it is almost impossible to describe to someone who has not seen it. Compared to American and English youth, the Russians were planning with vigour. We seemed jaded and hopeless by comparison. And one could not help but envy their opportunity to forget their own personal worries in serving one great cause. But that, of course, is also the outstanding attraction of Fascism or National Socialism, or any State-cause. The point is, however, that America and England have neither of them yet produced a "cause" that has aroused any universal enthusiasm in the young generation.

Soviet Russia, in my opinion, is the only country in the world where the vast majority of the population does not grow up with envy in its heart.

Chapter 80

THE NIGHT VISITOR

Eve and I kept out of Moscow as much as possible. For the greater part of the year I was there, I was travelling consistently and freely, and usually third class, in some parts of Russia. Only once did I get into what might have been called "difficulties." And then I had got there on purpose.

Not so, our two friends from New York, those highly inquisitive Hooker girls, Helen and Adelaide—who walked straight into the arms of the G.P.U. at once. But then, Adelaide and Helen had gone out to Suzdal, knowing that there was a famous old monastery out there, and not knowing that the romantic monastery was now that taboo of all Russian taboos—a political prison. When the G.P.U. came upon them, they found Helen sitting out in the snows, doing an extremely good painting of its walls and Adelaide making photographic studies of its various gateways. The Hooker girls were brought back to Moscow under G.P.U. escort. But, apparently, they played "patty-cake-clap-hands" with the G.P.U. officers in the train: and Adelaide's only comment after they were released with much smiling and handshaking in Moscow was that "the G.P.U. had such lovely eyelashes!"

My small adventure was to get ourselves arrested on the Bessarabian frontier. We were placed under the guard of a resolute Young Communist with a loaded gun. While he tried hard to look terrifying I could see that the wretched Communist who had arrested us was being given very hell for it from the Odessa Soviet to whom he had telephoned to announce our capture and for orders as to what he should do with us. After listening with a paling face to that telephone he suddenly put it down and rushed across to Eve and me as if he feared he couldn't release us quickly enough.

The reason for Odessa's rage was that there was one of the usual "famine" scares going on in the outside world—and the Moscow diplomatic corps—about hundreds, thousands of peasants behind Odessa starving to death. I had been nosing around in a car behind Odessa without the benefit of a Soviet chaperon, simply because I had made a break for it the first day. But, while I had seen horrible hunger and seen the cattle dying on the plains, I had not been able to find any trace of actual starvation—although lots of villagers tried to make me believe there was. I found one peasant woman, for instance, who had driven eighty versts across the steppe to try and reach Odessa to sell a cart-load of chickens, geese, and ducks. They were all nearly half dead from exposure in her cart, and when I asked her why she was driving eighty versts to sell them, she said: "BREAD!—I have nothing to eat!" Bread, it was obvious, was life, the king of life to her; and like all Russian peasants she felt that without it she would starve to death. It had never occurred to her to eat her own ducks.

After a few days of this, I had driven back into Odessa and filed a dispatch to my newspaper describing exactly what I had seen—hunger, but not famine. And the Bolshies were grateful to have such an eye-witness report get out to the outside world. At least one Ambassador, they told me afterwards in Moscow, was telling his government that a serious famine was raging behind Odessa at that time. Therefore they had dropped any attempts to chaperon me, and were furious with the local Communist minor official who had picked me up on the Roumanian frontier, inside a closed zone where special permits to travel were required.

He was the most worried individual in that affair.

Almost as soon as we landed in Russia, Eve and I left Moscow for Nijni Novgorod, where we went by various steamers down the 1,500 miles of Volga to the Caspian Sea. We took our time about it and it was dead winter when we went down the Caspian from Astrakhan to Daghestan and the Caucasus.

The Volga steamers were a study in Soviet psychology, and what the hard-working Communists were up against. It was a sight to take one's breath away. The big *Turgeniev*, taking on an amazing mixed cargo of painted machinery up at Nijni, had seven hundred people from all the races of Russia waiting like sheep to pour into her hold, the ship's officers fighting like madmen to prevent these stubborn peasants from killing each other as they struggled to be the first up the gangway. Each one of them was carrying his entire worldly possessions on his back in three-ply wooden boxes and bags; and Tartar and Lett, Big Russian and Little Russian, Kalmuk and Kirgez—they fought for sleeping space between decks. The first ones up the gang-plank got some flat board shelves for bunks; the rest battled it out for a place to lie down on the deck, along the gangways, on the bales of the cargo, and I saw a baby put to sleep, wrapped up like a papoose, against one of the steam pipes leading to the donkey-engine. Mothers ripped open their blouses and stuffed their breasts into the babies' mouths the instant they found a spot where they could sit down to the job. A group of Communists among them had a Red Corner going almost before the *Turgeniev* had dropped Nijni behind, and next morning they brought out their own newspaper, one copy, which they pasted on a bulkhead.

It was an interesting demonstration of "culture," for hardly anyone among the rest of that human cargo could read or write. They were jolly and sang and danced and fed their babies as the great *Turgeniev* cut slowly down the sullen Volga; but once a landing stage was reached they began to battle again like frightened animals.

It was a babel, and it appalled one to think of the task that lay ahead of the Bolshies in trying to pacify it, to say nothing of trying to marshal it into line on the road to an entirely different life.

The Russian peasants were stupid as beasts—and they acted like beasts.

But to perpetuate this confusion the Bolsheviks were encouraging every form of racial autonomy. When that grotesquely lovely sky-line of Kazan appeared along the yellow flood—a long white fortress wall topped by cone-tipped Tartar towers—we went ashore to find ourselves in the Tartar Republic, with Tartar theatres, Tartar schools, and Tartar hotels, from which last may God for ever again save us. In the German Republic, lower down the Volga, we walked about a mile across dry river bed to find President Schwartz dictating a letter. He was dictating in Russian, but as he saw two obvious foreigners at his door he immediately switched into German.

Above decks in the *Turgeniev*, in airy clean cabins, and riding first-class, was a colourful assortment of engineers, doctors, school teachers, technicians and Soviet officials setting off to their out-post posts in the U.S.S.R. Four school teachers with whom Eve and I watched the human cargo piling into the *Turgeniev* at Nijni, told us that they were all going to different parts of Siberia. They spoke of it quite frankly as exile, but, they said, with what seemed genuine enthusiasm, they would be fighting the continu-ous battle of the Revolution along the intellectual front. In Tsarist days the chances were they would have been sent to the Siberian salt mines.

There was one priest aboard, also travelling first class. He was an amazing figure, dressed in a robe of russet silk with a silver cross dangling behind a beard that was as thick and as black as the back of a cat. He had the eyes of a fanatic, and looked strangely evil, I thought. Yet he was utterly fearless, and sat there on the deck of the *Turgeniev* as we steamed past some of the dead monasteries and convents along the Volga, pointing them out to us and telling us in a voice that he made no attempt to lower about the persecution of the Church in Russia. Whether he really wanted to get killed or not we could not tell; but we did feel certain that if he and priests like him won through this trial by fire that they were now undergoing in Russia, the new Russian Church would be a vastly different thing from the old decadent one.

We found three priests like him in the old Gregorgieff Mon-astery for the Black Monks outside of Old Novgorod. It was an amazing sight. The church domes of that monastery are all of gold and they sat like a cluster of tangerines on the top of the pine forest. It was so cold that I froze an ear even inside my fur collar, and I found the priests reduced to doing menial tasks, one of them carrying a yoke of water that he had obtained from a hole cut in the lake ice. One was repairing a broken window. They were black and greasy haired, but they were not in the least bit frightened of the local Soviet official who ordered them to show me the monastery.

Old Novgorod itself, that incredible place with its pink Kremlin rising off the waste of snows, was a perfect demonstration of the Bolsheviks' treatment of the Church. For in Novgorod I spent two days watching Davidov restoring some of the most precious ikons of the Novgorod school. It was alarming to watch him. He would take an already priceless ikon and pour some liquid over it. Then he set that alight and as the paint softened he would scrape off the upper layer of ikon with a palette knife.

"Watch!" said Davidov, with the fanaticism of the true expert. "You will now see that we are coming to a decadent age. The robe will have jewels on it."

Then a few beads of colour would appear showing a period when the old religious fire of the Novgorod school had been overlaid by these decorations. I watched Davidov dig down through hundreds of years until there slowly stared up at us the fervour of the face that only the Novgorod school seemed able to show. In the place of jewels on the robe was the round black circle and white cross that distinguished that school. All through that winter Davidov had been working under the Soviets to restore these religious paintings to their early purity.

In the same way I saw with my own eyes the Soviet Commissioners rebuilding the churches that had been blown to bits in the battles between the Reds and the Whites for the possession of Yaroslavl. In the church of "Nicholas the Wet" I climbed through the dark corridors still full of the sandbags of the Whites. I looked up and saw the hole through its shattered fish-scaled cupola, where a shell had probably hurled to their death a handful of Tsarist officers. It was dramatic to think of them falling down from those cupolas which they had used as machine-gun towers, to fall and die before the great altars with their staring ikons. The Holy Ghost, a wooden dove, lay on its back beside a dead crow. Yet, when I went outside again and looked up, I saw where the Bolshies with artistic care had already started rebuilding the shattered cupolas.

On the other hand, in Vladimir, a Communist took me into a church, put his foot up against the iconostasis, and, before I even knew what he was about, he ripped out a valuable brass ikon and handed it to me. "Keep it," he said. It now hangs beside our dining-table in London in a most treasured place.

In old Rostoff occurred a scene that nearly broke our hearts. A man tapped quietly on my door around midnight. He was the third timorous creature who had crept into my room that winter night. He peered behind him, down the black hotel corridor, before he closed the door. Then he stood there and fingered his hat. He was not an old man, although he had a stubble of grey hair on his thin cheeks, and his pale hands had no more flesh on them than a bird's claws.

"I have heard," he said, unwrapping a worthless bronze ikon, "that you are buying old things?"

My first visitor had been an old lady who first tried to sell me a bit of old lace, and then the wretched stole from around her own neck. The next hunted creature had been an old man, probably an ex-officer of some sort, who tried to sell me the illustrations he had ripped out of some books. "But these are all I have left!" he said frantically, when I started to shake my head. "This is the last."

It broke my heart to send them away. Yet I could not shoulder all their sorrows. It was impossible. When I had bought their old trinkets they had immediately gone out and found this man; and here he stood—quivering. In a bundle under his arm I was aware that there were other last possessions, bits of old belongings treasured against this evil day. And I knew, that treasured so tenaciously, they had acquired a fantastic value in his mind. It would be inhuman to disillusion him; and yet it was even more cruel to encourage him to go on. I shook my head.

"No," I said abruptly, "I do not want anything."

He smiled, to put me in a good humour, and then he began

again. With a terrible earnestness, watching my face, he slowly drew something from beneath his coat. "This?" he said.

If things had been different I should have laughed. For if ever I saw an imitation ikon, this was it. In the first place, it was painted on canvas and stuck on some unusually heavy wood. Then it had two fat, rubicund saints, pointing with shepherd's crooks at a full harvest moon. Its inventor had climaxed this caricature by stepping into its centre a solitary, shining bronze cross. It was so preposterous that I felt justified in telling this poor creature I would not have it at any price.

His lips twitched around again into that glassy grin and he began to sweat. He sighed as if he had suddenly become exhausted and sat down in the vacant chair. When he spoke again his voice was normal and strong—and desperate.

"It may not be old," he said, challengingly, "but my father bought it from the monastery here when I was but a boy. He always told us that it was very valuable. But—if it pleases you— you can give me what you like."

This was a direct appeal, and for a moment, in his desperation, he had made it quite plain that I ought to buy this ikon whether I wanted it or not. Gentlemen, he intimated, did such things when they found other gentlemen in distress. He was almost insulting in his quiet way.

"Have you always lived here?" I asked.

"I was born here. Our—our estate was here. Of course, as a young man, I was in the university at St. Petersburg. Then . . ."

St. Petersburg—what ghosts that raised! He had changed it to Leningrad almost as he spoke, as if he were afraid he might be suspected of anti-Bolshevik propaganda. But even then, as he stared at me, I could see he was wondering if he really had found a gentleman, in his sense of the word, or whether it was possible I could be so callow as to refuse his obvious appeal.

"It is hard to live," he said suddenly.

Then, as he saw my eyes return to the ghastly ikon, he boldly named a price. "Twenty-five roubles?" he said.

I shook my head. I was not looking at him, but I was aware that his moment of bravery and defiance had passed. His voice showed it when he asked, "Well, give me twenty roubles then?"

He had stood up and was again fingering his faded hat. "Fifteen?"

"Stop!" I said, "I like it—and I think twenty-five roubles is the right price."

He sucked in his breath.

I wanted to get rid of him as quickly as I could. I did not want him near me. In the space of a few minutes he had re-created a legion of things I had been trying to forget. His voice, his manner, the very gallantry of his despair. I wanted to put him and everything he stood for away from me for all time. While he was shoving my money into his pocket I almost shoved him out the door. I wanted, if possible, that he should leave me in a defiant mood, so that I should not feel so utterly miserable and tortured after he had gone. And because of this I forgot what had been my original resolve ever since he had begun our conversation, which was to give him the few hundred roubles I had in my pocket and say:

"Here is life—so many more weeks, so many months; whatever it is—take it!"

Instead I choked off his speech of thanks as he hesitated at the door. It was only after I was back in Moscow that I remembered that lost resolve. I was showing the ikon to Anisimoff, perhaps the most famous ikon expert in the world. He too laughed when he saw it. Then his brows came down and he hurriedly pried out the bronze cross.

"Where did you get this?" he asked. "This cross is sixteenth century! This gold-bronze of that period is now a lost art."

"How much is it worth?" I asked.

"It is impossible to say. The ikon itself is worthless. But this cross is a museum piece."

I was helpless. The man had come into my room at Rostoff, and I did not even know his name. It had been months since I had bought it, carting it with me around Soviet Russia; and, with the twenty-five roubles that I had given him, I wondered if my night visitor was still alive.

The cross hangs behind my back, in the dining-room of my London home. I often answer questions about it. But this is the first time that I have bored anybody with the whole tale.

Chapter 81

UNDER THE SOVIETS

In that year of travelling about Russia we saw some amazing scenes. In Kiev No. 1 Prison I saw 600 prisoners, 450 of whom were murderers. As ten years was the maximum sentence under the Soviets for anything except a political crime, and one-third of that is remitted for good behaviour, their average sentence was six years. When I asked a group of them engaged in making brass beds why they had committed murder, they laughed, slapped each other on the back, and said, "Love!"

That, it seemed, was the truth, for most of them were in there for killings in connection with a woman of some sort.

I watched the trial of a policeman who was facing a sentence for stabbing his wife. The judge was a woman. There were two assistant judges who were simply mechanics, seconded from a printing works. There was no jury, but there was almost a poignant effort on the part of all three judges to brush aside any legal red tape and phraseology and get at the plain truth. It was so much the antithesis of a Western court, particularly an American, that I could hardly believe what I was watching. Justice was being sought in its purest form. The policeman's wife testified against him.

"When he sat down to dinner," she said, "he had a knife. I did not know whether it was for the dinner, or for me."

The policeman, still in his uniform, sat there scowling while the woman judge forced his wife to give all the details of how he had been made a cuckold. Finally, the girl wife began to falter in her testimony, and the judge got her "on the run." Instantly the judge became prosecuting attorney as well.

"*What?*" she said, leaning forward, and opening the fur-collared coat she had been wearing in that cold court room. "Do you mean to tell me you don't remember when it was that you say he first tried to stab you!"

The girl wife sank in the witness-box. I saw her knees go out from under her. The whole audience in the court leaned forward. It was a simple sight; everyone knew that the judge had caught the witness in a lie. That was all. The girl wife became desperate.

"He loved me!" she cried, throwing her arms toward her scowling husband. "You ask him! After he had stabbed me he took me in his arms and he said, 'Thank God the knife did not find your heart!'"

The woman judge rose, and her lip curled with scorn.

"Love you . . . ?" she said. "*You?*"

Then she gave the court a recess with a look at the girl wife, which said as plain as looks could say, "You have no heart."

The policeman, I learned later, got a year in jail. But a bandit who had been sitting behind him, awaiting his trial, was sentenced to death. His case was shifted over on to the list of "political" crimes. He had been disturbing the peace of several villages in the district. Therefore his depredations and the eventual murder were construed as a crime against the State. He was shot.

Similarly, I saw a Soviet official serving ten years in Kiev No. 1 prison for absconding with the funds of a village Soviet. He had been given the limit, without remission, and was going to be deported to Siberia after that. Of four men who raped a girl in Leningrad, two who were Communists were shot; the other two, who did not belong to the Party, were only given ten years.

In Moscow I sat for two days watching the trial of Paul the Gypsy, the Pirate of the Volga. He had murdered fifteen people himself, and kept the details of how he had done it in a loose-leaf notebook in his pocket. His story was like a page out of the *Lower Depths.*

"One night in Nijni Novgorod," he said, "there were fourteen of us. Seven bandits and seven prostitutes—in other words, the entire religious congregation of the village."

This brought a laugh from that proletarian and atheist court, and it looked for a time as if Paul the Gypsy was going to get away with it. The court was thrilled when he described how he and his bandit companions had captured a Volga steamer from a rowboat. He was so pleased with himself and his exploits that he refused counsel and insisted on giving his testimony without aid.

His was one of the most evil faces I have ever seen, as I sat for two days watching him pour out this terrible record of murder. When he looked tired the judge invited him to sit down.

"Be seated, Comrade," he said. "You are tiring yourself."

Paul the Gypsy's plea before this proletarian court was that he had been forced into a life of crime because his uncle, who employed him, would not pay him a living wage. So he had killed his uncle.

"Tell me, Comrade," said the judge, apologising for interrupting Paul the Gypsy's account of a subsequent murder, "on the night of November 14th, in Nijni Novgorod, when you killed your uncle—did you also kill your aunt?"

"Just a minute," said Paul, hastily diving into his pocket. He got out the notebook and thumbed through its pages while we all sat in silence hardly able to believe this scene. Then he nodded his head. "Yes, Comrade—I did."

But Paul had gone too far. He had killed a Red soldier.

"It was a pity," he said, trying to explain himself to the court, "to kill one so young."

It was amazing to watch the chill descend over the court as Paul said that, and without waiting for the sentence I knew that Paul would be shot. He was.

The outstanding thing about the Soviet courts—always excepting any political or propaganda trial—was their simple effort to get at the truth, without having to wade through the undergrowth of legal qualifications and obstructions that have grown up in Western courts.

It was too soon to judge the effects of the short sentence and abolition of the death penalty in reducing and preventing crime. But in the Rubiaskevskayia Penal Colony outside of Kiev they assured me that their experiment of letting the prisoners, mostly murderers, go home to their villages to harvest the crops was working out all right. They always returned. They had another experiment. A prisoner on the farm could give the chief warder a list of his girl friends in Kiev. The warder would let one of the girls come out. All backs would be turned when the girl and the prisoner took a stroll into the woods on the farm.

"That," said the prison authorities, "does away with the worst evil of the English and American systems."

I should think that it did.

In Leningrad I watched my friend, Dr. Gant, operating in the laboratory of Pavlov; and I saw the respect with which the Bolsheviks treat that great scientist who is always tartly criticising them. And in Moscow, one snowy night, I passed up a "concessionaire's" feast (for Moscow) to sit for hours with Professor Andreev—the man who cut off a dog's head and then made it eat. Studying heart reactions, by putting a long knife down the jugular vein and cutting the heart's valve of dogs, he discovered he could bring people back to life that we ordinarily accept as dead, i.e., when the heart stops beating. He injects a serum counter to the blood stream and starts the heart beating again. He had "killed" dogs that way since 1912, and he showed me the graph of the heart action showing how it slowed down and then became a straight line.

"The heart has stopped. Now"—pointing to a faint stutter in the straight line—"I am injecting. You see the heart begins to pick up. Now the dog is active again."

He showed me the chart of a dog named "Sasha" that he had "killed" several times by chloroform, and then revived. "Sasha" finally died a natural death. He also showed me the dossier of a man he had revived who had died from spotted typhus.

"I kept him alive for twelve minutes—and then I let him go. His organs were too impaired to permit him to live."

Professor Andreev was very incensed over the newspaper stories that said he could bring dead men back to life.

"That is absurd," protested the hunched-up little man. "Those men were not dead. But if I can get to him before his blood begins to coagulate, I can restore many a man who has died from asphyxiation."

Nevertheless, that evening I spent with Andreev was one of the most macabre of my life. The brain, he said, is the part of a human body which is the first to die.

Chapter 82

JAPAN SHOWS HER HAND

FOR A foreign newspaper correspondent Moscow was probably the most exhilarating capital on earth. In other respects it was dull. Social life as such simply did not exist. The foreign colony was so small that the foreign correspondents were usually included in the life of the Diplomatic Corps. That Haroun-al-Raschid of Moscow, brilliant Walter Duranty, was always playing bridge with the Greek Ambassador. The Italians and the Germans had two splendid tennis courts. Madame Ceruti, the beautiful Hungarian wife of the Italian Ambassador, gave the best parties. Usually the correspondents lunched and dined each other and fought over every point in the Russian situation that anyone cared to bring up.

It was illuminating, these conversations, with men like Walter Duranty and Paul Scheffer of the *Berliner Tageblatt*, and William Henry Chamberlain, men who had been keenly reporting Russia for anywhere from five to eight years, always finding themselves in violent disagreement on their interpreting of the major events whenever they got together. It was such a contrast to conversations "outside," where everyone was so certain that everything he said about Soviet Russia was right.

These conversations also demonstrated the folly of attempting to prove anything about Soviet Russia—or any country—with statistics. The same old figures will prove anything, for or against.

Scheffer and I, for instance, went down into the Don Steppes and spent a fortnight wandering about getting material for what I think were the first two big dispatches on the collective farms. We rode together in the same autos across the dusty steppes, interviewed the same desperate old peasants who did not want to "come in," listened to the same boasting from the managers of farms that had already got under way, witnessed the tremendous enthusiasm of the youth on these farms—and the woeful lack of tractors and efficient *agronoms* (agricultural experts)—and we pooled our notes in nine pages of single-space typewriting which I did on my lap in the train on the way home.

Then, at seven o'clock in the morning in Moscow, Scheffer and I sat down to write our dispatches. It was a sensational story we had to report. When we showed each other our dispatches at noon the facts were identical—but the conclusions differed on almost every point.

Reading Scheffer's amazing dispatch years later in London, reprinted in his book, *Seven Years in Soviet Russia*, I was startled to see how clearly on that morning in Moscow he had foreseen the difficulties that made Stalin call a temporary halt in his policy of collectivising the land, the speech where Stalin told the "collectivisers" they were "dizzy with success!"

Yet, on the other hand, I think Paul Scheffer and I were the only two correspondents who, from the very first day, cabled our papers flatly that the Russians would not go to war with Chang Hsueh Liang over the Chinese Eastern Railway dispute. It was only when the American Secretary of State, Stimson, sent his asinine note to the Six Powers, accompanied by an alleged secret note suggesting that the Six Powers form a consortium to settle the question of that Manchurian railway, that Scheffer and I began to lose our nerve. For Stimson, by that incredibly stupid suggestion of foreign interference in Manchuria, very nearly did provoke a war between Russia and Manchuria. And Russia, in this case, would have been egged on by Japan.

This is a bit of secret history that Paul Scheffer and I wrote at length, getting it past the Soviet censors, to our newspapers, where, for some reason or other, what we thought were our amazing revelations seemed to fall on deaf ears. Yet, Scheffer and I, knowing its full significance, knew that we were getting a peep at Japan's long-distance policy of occupying Manchuria, the move that so startled the world in 1931, which move Scheffer and I, then working together in London, cabled day after day to our papers Japan would not stop.

To begin with, let me say simply this. Japan has mistrusted American policy in Manchuria ever since 1910, when Philander Knox, as Secretary of State, tried to neutralise Japanese and Russian concessions in Manchuria, and he and the famous Williard Straight suggested a foreign consortium for Manchuria to operate their railways there. When, in 1929, the Japanese watched the Chinese appealing to foreign Powers to come in and settle their dispute with the Russians over the Chinese Eastern Railway, the Japanese informed Chang Hsueh Liang (whose father they had killed in a railway "accident") that if he did not soon get busy and accept some reasonable Russian offer they, the Japs, would inform the Russians that they could cross the frontier into Manchuria up to certain distances—*without any protest from Japan!*

This scared Chang Hsueh Liang, who was nothing like the man that his father was, into suing for peace with the Russians. A Chang Hsueh Liang emissary was already on the way to Manchuli to meet the Russian emissary who was coming out from Moscow—when Stimson sent his ridiculous note. And what happened? Instantly Chang, seeing help held out from the foreign Powers, or at least, thinking he saw it, withdrew his emissary. The negotiations for a peaceful settlement broke down. Russia was almost on the verge of going to war. This happened about the end of July 1929. It wasn't until some time in December that the Russians had managed to bring Chang Hsueh Liang to a point where he would listen to reason again. Peaceful negotiations were again renewed. *And then Stimson sent another note . . . !*

The same performance began all over again and it was months and months before the Chinese Eastern Railway even got started running again. At that time I went to General Dawes, the American Ambassador in London, and did all I could to convince him of how plainly Japan had shown her hand in Manchuria over Stimson's unbelievable notes. Dawes, as a diplomat under Stimson, could, of course, do nothing other than listen politely to what I said. What that tart little realist was really thinking I do not know.

But if there is one thing I am proud of in my journalistic life it has been my reporting on Japan through all the humbug and hypocrisy of the 1929-30 Naval Conference and subsequent naval fiascos, and her definite aim to keep any foreign Power from getting a foothold in Manchuria. My Moscow insight into the Chinese Eastern Railway dispute was afterwards invaluable to me in reporting the attitude of the British, who very wisely refrained from following Stimson out on the end of the limb in his Japanese policy—a policy of empty threats that he could not back up for the simple reason that at that time Japan had a far better navy than ours. Moscow, as it seems to have worked out, gave me such a clear vision on the Japanese question that it cost me my job. For I was accused by the present publisher of my paper of having "so thoroughly absorbed the English point of view that you no longer report the passing scene as a detached American observer."

I was playing tennis in Moscow on the day that Stimson sent his note to the Six Powers. I was partnered with Von Dirksen, the German Ambassador. Our opponents were Cerruti, the Italian Ambassador, and Von Heidenstom, the Swedish Ambassador.

"We moost win!" said Von Dirksen, who was an ardent tennis player.

We did. And sitting around a table having tea under the trees in that pleasant garden of the German Embassy, I asked Cerruti if his government had got that note.

He nodded. "I am sorry to say we did."

Von Dirksen slapped the table.

"Now," he said, "we don't know what will happen. Up to this morning I would have said that you and Paul Scheffer were right —the Russians would not go to war. Now . . . I don't know."

In Moscow my leg had healed to a point where I could play tennis again for the first time in ten years. It was marvellous to get a good "sweat-up" again. But, I saw sadly, I was a flop. My tennis days were over. "The old waggon," as one of my colleagues kindly put it, had broken down.

Chapter 83

THEATRES OF MOSCOW

The theatres of Moscow that winter gave us a glut of emotions. We saw Kachalov's *Hamlet*; too mad, we thought; Moskvin in *The Brothers Karamazov*; Knipper Tchekova in her famous husband's own play, *The Cherry Orchard*; and through Danchenko and Stanislavsky we met many of the famous players themselves. We saw that amazing anniversary of the Art Theatre, with Stanislavsky playing his old part in *The Three Sisters*, and, for one night only, the Bolsheviks permitted many of the old Tsarist plays to be played for one scene. That night we saw people sitting in the Art Theatre with the tears pouring down their faces. They were tears of reminiscence. Nothing that I saw in Russia so brought back the old world as these old plays. And although Eve and I could hardly understand one word of Moskvin's in *The Brothers Karamazov*, his acting made us cry too. It was an emotional debauch that night. In the Art Theatre we saw the plays of the Revolution, *The Armoured Train* and *The Days of the Turbins*. The last was stopped temporarily, as it gave, in Communist eyes, too favourable a picture of the White Russians. And before we left we saw Stanislavsky and Danchenko forced to submit the marvellous little Art Theatre to that ghastly bit of propaganda—*Blockade*.

The amazing thing about the theatres of Moscow was that you could see a play being played at several theatres at the same time, and in several different ways. The realism of the Art Theatre, where reality was so much in demand that Stanislavsky himself always wanted to make the sounds of the birds in *The Cherry Orchard*. One could see a play being burlesqued in that marvellous Vachtangoff Theatre, and then being played in almost the fourth-dimension that Meyerhold could give his plays. We saw *Boris Gudonoff* as the conventional opera, with a bass of twenty-four who was believed to be a second Chaliapin—and then we saw Stanislavsky's production of *Boris*, where he had even gone

534

to the limit of ransacking the museums of Moscow to get the actual costumes that were worn at the date of the play. With anyone less great than Stanislavsky such an action would have been an irritating affectation. He made *Boris* so alive that I trembled when I saw him stride down the steps of St. Basil.

To hear that most tragic of all tunes, "God Save the Tsar," being sung by the White officers in *The Days of the Turbins* was unforgettable. It seemed to fill that theatre with ghosts. And when the three White officers, who have seen Germans, and Petlura, and Whites and Reds fighting to hold Kiev—when these three men lean by their window, listening to the roar of the Red artillery wheels entering Kiev—that I think is one of the most poignant moments I have seen in any play.

"Well!" cries one brother, flinging up his arm. "I'm going with them!"

He is going to join the Reds.

The two other gallant brothers face each other.

"What a prologue!" gasps one.

"Yes," says the other, "and what an epilogue."

No wonder the Bolsheviks stopped that play.

Eisenstein dined with us several times in our rooms in the Grand Hotel, telling us about his new picture, *The General Line*. The night we went to its uncensored version for a private showing, I took the daughter of one of the ambassadors with me. She was a girl with a rare sense of humour; but when we saw ourselves watching Eisenstein's unblushing reproduction of the love story of a bull—from where he first saw an attractive cow, all the way to baby bull—we did not know where to look. It was as hot as some of the movies I had seen down in Marie's brothel in Marseilles.

But, my God, what a film!

Chapter 84

IN THE HIGH CAUCASUS

DURING that winter, Alexander Wicksteed, the English hermit whose lair is Moscow, and only true love is the Caucasus, and I planned to try and cross the main range of the Caucasus by a forgotten trail. And, for three of the weeks we were riding on horseback over the Caucasus, *we never saw a road!*

We planned it all the winter. One of the men, whose Russian map-reading helped us select our route, is now a prisoner in Solovietsky monastery up on the White Sea. He was an engineer who for some reason fell foul of the G.P.U. During the winter, Alexander Wicksteed, delightful old, shaven-headed, grey-bearded philosopher, who would not wear a collar and tie, plotted how we would get food supplies. Usually we plotted in his room, for which Wicker had made all the furniture, in chairs that had a tendency to collapse and shut up on us as we sat down. Wicker's room in a Moscow tenement was like the White Knight's in *Alice in Wonderland* . . . things on things, under things, over things; things hanging on strings from the ceiling . . . and people sitting on everything.

Wicker solved his tea problem for the Caucasus by trading his once-used tea-leaves (in a proportion of 4 to 1) to the other families, each inhabiting a single room in the ex-apartment that his room was in, for their allotment of fresh tea-leaves. He collected almost a pound of tea that way. I think he mentioned this in his book, *Life Under the Soviets*.

My food problem was immediately solved by a cable from London, which announced that Sir Alfred Butt had bought the play that Dorothy Brandon and I had written called *The Black Ace*. The play, in spite of the fact that it was put on by Basil Dean, with that exciting star Raymond Massey playing the lead, only kept another good play out of the Globe for thirteen nights. But my paper was good enough to let me come out of Russia, for what was probably my first and last First Night, and on the

536

second night, in the middle of the second act, I reached under the seat for my hat, packed my bags (including sugar, tea, salt, rice, medicine and bandage for my dud leg), and went back the next day to Moscow and Alexander Wicksteed.

We sailed from Moscow. We went 156 miles down the Moscow River in an enchanting little steamer, across the fields, and got into the Oka at Ryazan. We went 400 miles down the Oka to where one sunset we saw the lights of Nijni Novgorod. Then we got aboard a Volga steamer and went 1,200 miles down that sullen flood, now swollen with the torrents of spring, to Stalingrad. At Stalingrad, Wicker and I then piled into a train and rode third class all the way across the Cossack country to Rostoff-on-Don, where we went down to Kislovadsk in the Caucasus. Here we got a mountain cart and rode up and over the first range in the Caucasus to fall down in the moonlight to where a silver cord of river flowed by the minarets of Khassaut. Here, as I couldn't walk far with my dud leg, we got horses—one for me to ride, one for our packs and the tarpaulins we used for a tent—and then our ride into the Caucasus really began.

No morning in my memory is as sweet as when I rode out, with the sun on my head, up that first river pushing down from the snows of the Caucasus. I found Wicker, who, because he had to walk, had started out about an hour ahead of me, sitting stark naked in an icy stream, with the sun glistening on him.

"Bully! Bully!" he was saying to himself.

Wicker, in my opinion, is one of the few men I have met who, I think, has really solved the problem of life. Most of his friends don't think so. They say he is like an old goat, sitting out there, with no shirt, in Moscow—defying every convention in the Universe. But I think he is a hero, and I hope that he lives long to teach thousands of Russian university students the English language by his own lazy method of simply refusing to learn Russian from them. And in the Caucasus, where he doggedly kept up the same slow stroll, either straight up a mountain or straight down it, or merely walking on the level (wherever there was such a thing), I saw him walk the very legs off those wiry Turco-

Tartars—some of the toughest little mountaineers on earth. There is no place in the world that will test out two men's ability to put up with each other like a long cruise alone in a sailboat or a lonely mountain camp—and Wicker and I clicked admirably. (Wicksteed died in Moscow while I was writing this book.)

From Moscow, to the night I had to sit until dawn at 9,400 feet, slowly freezing to death in the snows of the Khlukhor Pass (there was nothing to do when night caught me, but just stick where I was and try not to fall over a cliff), from Moscow down, our adventure was an odyssey of sheer beauty.

I sat up all one night to watch the sun rise over the Oka. I thought I was alone. But just before dawn I saw a girl sitting up in the bows of the boat down below me. Her head was resting on her folded hands.

"I love it! I love it! I love it!" she said, as we went down through Russia. She wanted to see every bit of Russia that she could. She had saved up some money; and she was travelling third class, walking, any way at all, so long as it was cheap, to cover as many miles as she could before her money ran out. She didn't know where that would be . . . she didn't know how she would live when she did get there . . . she was just going in a straight line across Russia as far as she could get. Just the sort of miraculous person with whom to watch the dawn rise on the Oka.

As soon as the sun topped the steppe the air became alive with birds. They seemed to spring up from the steppe and sing for joy in the sky. They swooped ahead of us down the shining green river, darted out of holes in its clay banks, soared upward and hung motionless above a forest of deep cool pines. Swallows played like dolphins before our bows. And looking over the side I looked straight down into a primitive dug-out with two fishers waving up paddles at us, like the spear-tipped blades the African Negroes use. It was an astonishing sight—but nothing like the sight I saw in their skiff. Lying on its adzed bottom was a fish as big as a man.

"I love it, too," I told the girl, as we were sitting up in the top of the Tartar tower, looking down on the bends of the Oka from above. "If I could, I would roam around Russia all my life." And so I would.

We had lots of time on the Oka to go ashore. Along that almost forgotten river our ship was trading cases of vodka for little crates of pigs. The cases of vodka went ashore over a gang-plank, along each side of which were posters illustrating the evils of drink. The lowest evil, it seemed, on the Soviet scale, was beating one's wife; the ultimate degradation showed the drunkard finally setting fire to a Soviet factory.

Wicker was a messy man on a boat. "Do you like salt?" he asked me. "I do. I find it adds another day to the life of your meat." I couldn't prevent him cooling our butter by simply dipping his dirty handkerchief in water and then wrapping the butter in it. But one day I struck. Opening the butter tin I found a half-eaten ham sandwich lying on top of the butter pat. "How the hell did that get there?" I asked. "I don't know. I must have forgotten to finish it." And down in the Caucasus one night I would have killed Wicker if I thought I would not have been unjustly punished for it.

I was cooking dinner and I asked Wicker to hand me the leg of sheep that we had bought and cut up two days before. We had already eaten the rest of it, and this leg of meat had been hanging under a flap of my saddle-bag as we rode through the hot valley that day. I saw Wicker examine it, dust something off it. Then as he brought it over to the camp fire for a look, I also took a look. And when I did I seized the leg of sheep from him and hurled it far down the stream beside our fire.

"Good God!" he cried. *"You've thrown it away!"*

"Do you mean to say you were going to *eat* that?" I said.

"Why, of course."

That leg of meat was simply crawling with white maggots.

Our programme in the Caucasus was to awake, which we did automatically, about sunrise, cook our breakfast of tea and rice cakes, and then ride on into the mountains until sunset. Usually, around that hour, we found a *kosh*. These are the huts made of piled rocks in which live the ragged roving shepherd tribes of the Caucasus. Sometimes there were tribes in the *koshes*, very often there were not. All along one valley we slept in *koshes* that couldn't have been inhabited for around a hundred years. This valley, incidentally, was the missing link which gave us the forgotten road over the Caucasus that the engineer had found with us in Moscow. There are no chimneys in these *igloos* made of stone. The smoke from the dung or log fires simply oozes out through the chinks in the stones. In one *kosh* I remember sticking my knife into the glistening tar that perhaps hundreds of years of little fires had deposited on the rock wall it was built against. My knife went in for one-quarter of an inch!

As we were often climbing all day through either rain or snow, one side of us would be half frozen as we tried to dry ourselves inside these primitive huts. The other would be blistered by our fire. We slept on straw, when a *kosh* was inhabited, on the plain dirt floor when it was deserted.

And what amazing people we met!

The migrations of history have left, it seems, almost every nation on earth in the valleys which form the pockets of the Caucasus. One night we would be sleeping with delicate, hawk-nosed, lean Persian types—the next we would be high up on a mountain shelf where the men were as big as Swedes and the girls had fair hair. And, as I have written before, when Eve and I went down through the Caucasus on the Georgian road to Tiflis, we came on the Khevsuries, descendants of the Crusaders, who wear chain armour, carry a little round, studded shield on their backs, long swords, and have seven crosses embroidered on their tunics; they are the worst drunks in the Caucasus.

But up here in these untravelled mountains the tribesmen could be truthfully called half-wild. They were so gentle. When towards nightfall we would hear that curious bee-like humming which, from a distance, was the bleating of some tribe's sheep, we knew that in a little while we would find some sort of people, whose like we had never seen before, nor they ours, who would make us a place to sleep, lying beside them and their women on the piles of straw, and that they would give us anything they had.

But once we started to *buy* anything from them—then a form of cupidity, a sort of arrogant pride, was aroused. They would not be bested in a bargain. At the very outset Wicker and I decided on the price we would pay for a sheep, a sheep that would usually last us three days. Seven roubles was our price. I don't know whether it was correct or not, but we fought about it over every sheep; and we never paid more nor less.

It was a gory performance. Once the price had been agreed upon, the sheep was brought in alive and held up for our inspection, much as a waiter will bring you a live trout in a London or Paris restaurant. Then the Old Man of the tribe—for, above 5,000 feet, Communism had not penetrated into the patriarchal civilisation of the tribes down there then—would take out his silvered, fluted dagger and cut its throat. This, incidentally, was all done inside the hut of stones, the whole bizarre scene of strange, staring faces, silvered saddles and Wicker and I lighted only by the log fire. The women would drain the sheep's blood into a bladder and hang it up. Inside each hut was an upright tree trunk, with one branch remaining that had been sharpened into a hook. The Old Man would throw the sheep against this hook, and with a few deft knife strokes, sever its head and pull off its skin like a shirt. The head would be handed to the children who would stick a stick up its nostrils and toast it over the fire. Then, while the girls were stripping the entrails and tying them in knots, the Old Man with an axe would split the sheep. He would wipe the blade of the axe, when it got too bloody, on his boot.

Then we cooked that delicious sheep. The head we always gave to the people who had owned it. They ripped its lower jaw off, split the skull with an axe, and made it into soup.

With a prong of green branch we toasted the sheep over the fire. Mountain sheep are sweet as nuts. And the Caucasian sheep we ate were as succulent as those Augusto and I used to gorge on in the high Pyrenees. But down in the Caucasus they had an added delight—as our bits of sheep were toasting and the fat nicely crackling over the rose embers, we took them aside for a moment and poured sour cream over them, and then we held them back again to toast. Sometimes we made *shashlik*, cutting the bits of meat into chunks and then spearing them on a green wand between chunks of fat.

Not that we always fed as well as that. Sometimes poor Wicker had to put up with my miserable rice cakes, which I could never make stick together without any eggs. They shook milk in a bladder to make butter; and down in the very heart of the Caucasus I had corn-pones, dripping with butter, as good as any I have had in Virginia.

Then—then came the Caucasian trout!

We had been riding for weeks with my trout rod strapped in an unbreakable case to my saddle. Time and again it had caught in things and very nearly shoved me over the side of a mountain; but now I was to use it in the headwaters of the great Kuban.

As we topped the bronze gorge in whose bottom lay Utch Khalan, I saw the ribbons of two rivers running through its bottom. One, coming down from the glaciers of Mt. Elbruz (3,000 feet higher than Mont Blanc) was an opaque rocky grey. The other, coming from lesser snows, was a vivid emerald green. Where they joined they ran together side by side like a two-coloured ribbon—then they crashed together in a rapids and shot down the purple shadows of a rocky gorge.

I fished down the gorge that first night, clambering to reach pools among its sharp rocks, and got seven fine trout.

They were marvellous fellows, snow trout, the colour of a skinned green grape, dappled with hundreds of vivid little scarlet spots. The Cossack girl who was looking after us in the school house on whose floor we had been permitted to cast our beds, put them in its porcelain heating stove over some rushes and forgot them. But it worked out just right; when I suddenly remembered them and took them out, they were crisp and brown, done to a turn in butter and garlic.

The next day I got thirty-five trout in the upper emerald stream. I do not think a fly had ever been put over those amazingly swift reaches of water before. Two Circassian horsemen who came down to the rocks couldn't believe it when they saw me snatching fish out of the stream with those tiny feathered things—not until I let them prick their fingers on the hooks. Then they appointed themselves my ghillies, and they and their horses went along with me until we reached a gorge down which even their cat-like little horses could not get.

An instructor in Communism, a Don Cossack, whom Moscow had sent down to Utch Khalan to teach the backward Turco-Tartars the values of Communism, had laughed at me before I started fishing the previous day. Flies! He smiled, sneering at what he thought were my trinkets—no!—anyone who knew anything about fishing knew that one used worms. He was a conceited ass. I could not argue with him then—but I could now.

Just as the entire slope of Mt. Elbruz—whose two breasts of snow are a mile apart—was turning a light flamingo pink against the sky, I started back for Utch Khalan. I had ten miles to make through the woods. It was long after dark when I got there. But I looked up the Instructor in Communism and invited him to dinner. I bought two bottles of Naperouli, that dark purple wine of the Caucasus, to celebrate the occasion. Then Wicker and I took a swim, holding on to a rock and letting the icy stream wave over us, to get ourselves in shape for the dinner of our lives.

"I'm a poor man," said Wicker. "I've never in my life had enough trout. But tonight—"

He stopped. He made a horrible look at his plate. He spit out his trout. I tasted my trout—and choked.

That horrible Cossack girl had cooked them all in sunflower seed oil.

"I told her to do it," said that conceited Instructor in Communism. "Don't you know that that is the only way to cook trout?"

He had the last of the argument—and the rest of the thirty-five trout.

We rode for two days with a tribe of Tartars who were taking their flocks over the passes in search of grass. Neither their manners nor their wooden bowls had changed a whit since the days of Jenghiz Khan. The old, decrepit men rode and their babies were tied with thongs to their saddles. They screamed all the time, with their heads jerking from side to side as the horse tried to find his steps. We went up through forests that were carpeted with yellow azaleas, and then where the trails were so worn that the gnarled tree roots had been rubbed bare and shining as dead bones. I rode ahead our last sunset as I wanted to be alone. When I got up above the timber line I saw a lip of the Caucasus where hundreds of sheep, cattle and horses were feeding in a surprising green bowl. Far out from me in darkening shadows of blue and bronze, I looked down for fifty miles along the ranges of the Caucasus. Below me, from the depths of the forest, came the hollow note of a cuckoo's call.

We pitched our tarpaulins, Wicker and I, that night so that when we woke up we could see that glory of the Caucasus in the early dawn. We sat by our breakfast fire and just soaked ourselves in the unbelievable beauty of it all, until the rivers in the valleys below us glistened in the sun.

That night the Tartars had built wolf-fires around their flocks. And the boys of the tribe sat up all night guarding the precious sheep. The next night in the mountains I knew that the Tartars would be somewhere, milking their flocks. The sounds of splashing from a thousand udders would come with the sunset's haze.

I now have to report failure . . . whether it was of courage or not, I don't know. It probably was.

We had seen Mt. Elbruz first from thirty miles off in the Don Cossack steppe. But once we were in the mountains of the Caucasus we did not see it again for weeks. We did not even see the main range. Then one night, when Wicker and I were in the valley of the deserted *koshes*, I went outside about midnight to attend a call of nature. I was standing there, in the moonlight, enjoying the fresh air, for we had been riding through a miserable day of storm and sleet. I was looking at what I thought was an extraordinary cloud stretching along the sky. Suddenly I realised I was looking at the snows of the Caucasus.

"Christ!" I gasped.

"Aha!" came the triumphal voice of Wicker from behind my

back. "Now you *know!*—now you know why I will never leave Russia!"

Well, from Teberda, I set out on June 27th to try and cross the Main Range by the old Khlukhor Pass. The Khlukhor had been cut in the face of the cliffs by the Russians of old Tsarist days, so that they could get across the Caucasus and down in the Black Sea littoral to exterminate the Circassians. But time and frost have cracked large parts of it off the cliffs. There is a small, very steep trail that is free from snow around the middle of July. And Wicker was right when he warned me in the valley of Teberda that he would soon see me back. He sat there, in fact, in Teberda, and waited for me.

With two Mohammedans, I got my horses up the face to 9,000 feet. Part of the way we went up over ice-age scrap, over snow-fields, where the horses often fell through to their bellies, and it was an awful job to get them on their feet again. Then for 2,000 feet straight up. At 9,000 we came on the glacial lake that is just 400 feet below the true pass. There was some green water on it in pools, and it did not look safe to cross. I fell through it the next day. We had to cross it, however, as one side of it was dead against a straight wall of precipice, and the other end was pouring in a waterfall over the cliff. I had to have the horses taken back.

This was just at sunset, and I watched the two Mohammedans doing that unbelievable task of taking the two horses down that steep face. Then I began to think about myself.

I walk in my sleep sometimes, and I did not want to walk over that ledge.

But there was to be no sleep for me that night. The moment the sun went down I began to freeze. I was sitting on some rocks in the snow, and that's where I had to stay. I had some "Solid Heat" tablets to heat the water to sterilise the dressings for my dud leg; and in a fit of desperation I used all of these to boil myself a single cup of tea. Then I sat there and watched the moon rise over the spear of Chachka. It was a beautiful peak, a great spear of rock rising against the bowl of stars.

The silence was terrific as I sat there and waited for dawn. Just before it those two incredible Mohammedan mountaineers appeared over the edge of the cliff and lay down in the snow in their goat-skin *burkas*. At 4 A.M. we tried to cross the pass.

As a matter of fact, we did get around what is usually considered the worst part of it—that shoulder of rock overhanging the glacial lake. I slipped there on the snow, as I was wearing nothing but brogues, and thought that my number was up. But the sapling I had cut down below to use as an alpenstock saved me by holding in the snow. Then we climbed up over the last wall of snow, and looked twenty-five miles down into the Black Sea.

It was a staggering scene. It was sub-tropic down by the Black Sea, but from where I was standing I was looking down into a bowl of white snow that was as unbroken as a tea-cup. And its sides were just as steep.

Below us was a precipice with a drop of a thousand feet or so. If we could cross about fifty feet of snow wall, and not fall, we might get to a slope where, even if we did fall, we would not go over the sheer precipice. If the worst came to the worst we would merely have a bad slide down into the bowl of valley. We tried to cross, and got about twenty feet out on the face. Then we hit a patch of soft snow that was over what seemed a slide of ice, and the whole thing began to move. That was a little too much for us.

We worked our way back and tested the chances with two boulders we managed to pry from a face of rock. One rolled away from us, took the far slope, and plunged for what seemed an interminable time down the snow face to the bottom of the valley. The other boulder, started in precisely the same spot, rolled from our hands—and shot over the precipice. We did not see it after that. We never heard it hit.

"No!" said one of the Mohammedans, shaking his head. "It is better to live."

And so we came back.

Chapter 85

FLIGHT TO INDIA

When I was in London, covering that shabby swindle, the 1930 so-called Naval Disarmament Conference, I got a wire from my paper: "WILL YOU RUSH INDIA?" I wired back "RUSHING," and twenty-four hours later I was in an Imperial Airways plane, flying to Karachi.

I was delighted to get away from all the humbug and hypocrisy of the statesmen in St. James's Palace. The American delegation, broadcasting across the Atlantic of the hypothetical savings they were effecting, were counting the ships they were boasting they had scrapped, at least one ship that had not turned a propeller since the Spanish-American war. The Americans at that conference increased their fleet by 146,000 tons, and their building appropriation from $50,000,000 to $200,000,000 a year, for the next five years. The French doubled their navy by the *Statute Navale*. The Italians would have to quadruple theirs if they wanted to get the equality they were demanding with France. The Japs did not have to do any extra building as they had been steadily building against the next Conference from the minute they had left the Washington Naval Conference of 1922. The London conference instead of abolishing submarines, legalised a new super-class, such as the French had built in the *Surcorf*, a submergible cruiser that carried a six-inch gun, a hydroplane, and could go all the way out to Hawaii on one charge of fuel. The British were the only people who did any disarmament at that London conference; they decreased their fleet by 98,000 tons. And the implacable Japs got the seventy per cent cruiser strength with the United States in the eight-inch gun class that they had come there to get.

"And yet," said Signor Grandi to me in Claridge's, "they have the audacity to call this a *disarmament* conference!"

I was equally furious, because my dispatch categorically accusing the American delegation of increasing our building appropria-

547

tion from $50,000,000 to $200,000,000 a year, giving the size, number and cost of the new ships we were demanding, did not get into the paper. The American delegation had complained that our dispatches on their actions showed an un-American attitude. Washington complained that we were more French than the French. Yet when Constantine Brown, my colleague, who did such a brilliant job reporting the conference from his intimate connections on the British side, took our combined dispatches to Mr. Stimson and asked him to point out where we had made any mis-statements, or where we had made any charges that could be construed as un-American, Mr. Stimson had nothing to say.

In the twenty-four hours I had left in London I knew it was quite hopeless to get any kit for India; and none of my own belongings were fit for the heat I knew I was in for. In my cupboard hung one suit that had always been Eve's *bête noire*. Eve pounced upon it.

"Ah-ha!" she said. "This ginger-coloured tweed is just the thing for you to wear out to India, and don't you dare bring it back!"

So on Boat Race morning at 5.30, I was going through the rain to Croydon. On the way we passed a policeman who seemed to symbolise all the might of the British Empire. His hand was upraised and the whole world stood still. As I sat there looking at that calm British jaw under its chin-strap I saw on his breast the coloured ribbons of all the wars within our time. When his hand dropped the world began to move again. Then I thought of that little 104 lb. naked figure that I was going to see, sitting under his mango tree, defying all the might of this great Empire.

We dropped in at Brussels for a cup of cocoa, and that night young Brancker, the only other passenger, and I were drinking cocktails called "Russian Petrol," with the *mädchens* of Nürnberg. As it was Lent they would not dance.

"Wake up!" At 4.30 in the morning the pilot of the plane was slapping my face with his flying helmet. "Do you want to sleep all day; we're flying to India!"

So as dawn rose I looked down from my seat in the cockpit where he let me sit beside him, into the forests, the red-roofed villages and the winding ribbon of the old Ludwig's canal, through which pleasant land of Bavaria Eve and I had hauled our little *Flame* one hundred and seven miles over the Frankischer Jura mountains six years before. Then we went down the Danube to Vienna; a thrilling sight to see those castles in the Wachau valley from the sky.

Lunch at Budapest. Then we flew over the steaming Alfold and came down that night at Zemun opposite Belgrade. Every foot of the world I had seen sliding beneath me had memories of *Flame*. And was it not lying at anchor opposite Zemun that Eve had mutinied!

In the Dragoman Pass, trying to get through the mountains of Serbia into Greece the next morning, we hit a nasty head wind. Grinding there, almost stationary in the black clouds, we looked nervously at our indicators, whose needles announced that our oil supply was beginning to give out. A pipe had split. We had taken off from Belgrade under a full golden moon. It was broad daylight now, but dark as pitch in the Dragoman Pass (which has now been abandoned on this flight); and as the pilot afterwards described his battle with wind, rain, and clouds:

"Two hours of it—all over the bloody sky!"

"There they are!" grinned the mechanic, as he did a swift repair by the minarets of Uskub, and he pointed to the black mountains behind. "There they are—sticking up—waiting for you when your engine conks out!"

Our pilot did a marvellous landing at Salonika, whose narrow little 'drome along the sea was probably the worst landing ground on the trip. He side-slipped the 105-foot wing-spread of the three-engined Heracles and did a swish-tail landing that brought us to rest almost on the tarmac. Whereupon the Greek customs officials swarmed into us like a cloud of bees.

They made so much bother with their tiresome regulations that it took us almost as long to get to our hotel as it had taken us to fly down from Belgrade—three hours.

This seven-day flight to India has been made as comfortable and as casual as a *wagon-lit* now. But this was the first trial trip through the Dragoman Pass; and, as we had had to go out of our way to take in Brussels the first day, we were trying to make up time to get the mails to Karachi. Also, as I wanted to see places like Cairo again, I stayed up most of the nights when we were down on the land. Counting it up I saw that I had thirteen and a half hours sleep in the whole flight to India.

We took off under a silver moon in the hydroplane from Salonika and landed at Alexandria in Egypt that sunset. On the way we dropped in at Athens and Crete. There was something grand about that. Flying down through the islands of the Aegean was a beautiful experience. Historic names, they rose up before us from the cobalt sea; rocky, grey, cloaked with pines, little white cities lying in their harbours, with the Aegean waves like white lace along their sides. The Greek coast emerged in cliffs of red 1,000 feet high. And a snow-tipped mountain moved by us with a tiny cloud resting on its tip. A fantastic coast with deep ravines of blues and mauves and pumice greys among the broken cliffs of red. In one deep cleft we saw the walls of a monastery. We flew over the Acropolis to drop down into Athens' harbour, and the roar of the engines stopped.

"We've got to go straight out to Crete," said the pilot. "I'll get you there on time. If this tail wind holds, Hopkins will get you across to Alex. tonight."

On the long grind out to Crete, where the thrumming of the engines weaved in and out like a tune in their synchronisation, a symphony of the sky, I fell asleep watching the ships trailing their white wakes far below us. Crete rose up like the humps of a camel from the turquoise sea: we cut into Mirabelle Bay, over the little fort of the leper colony, where people without any noses, etc., stared up at our fortunate plane—and then pilot and every-body snatched off their clothes (there were no women around) and dived into the cool sea. We had lunch on the Imperial Air-ways yacht; but as they had just fired their cook and the bacon was cooked by the engineer who cut it in slabs an inch thick—it was not a meal that we would rank with some of the others on the trip. For instance, in Fort Rutba, a little *Beau Geste* of an out-post, lying behind its barbed wire in Irak, they gave us cool lettuce salad.

Just as another ten minutes of sunset might have made it quite impossible, the able pilot Hopkins dropped into that amazing shipping behind Alexandria breakwater. I saw old Ras el Tin again, where I had lain for so many months during the war.

"Good hop!" said the Imperial Airways manager announcing that we had made the first flip from Salonika across the Mediter-ranean to Alex. in one day. "You've got about half an hour here before the train takes you up to Cairo. I've got a car here—like to see the town?"

"Prawns," I said.

"Don't you want to see Alex.?"

"Prawns," I said.

"Look here," I said, explaining things. "I've got a complex. I've been thinking of just one thing all the way from Crete. There's a café in Alex. called the Cap d'Or—and there's a gippy standing outside it selling *prawns that are six inches long*. At least he did stand there during the war. But I never had enough money then to get enough. I was always broke. Now I'm not, and I want prawns, prawns, prawns. . . ."

"And prawns you shall have," said he. "Don't say that the Im-perial Airways doesn't give every passenger what he wants."

But could we find prawns? Not a prawn. The gippy had died who once stood outside the Cap d'Or. And in the hotel a white-clad *suffragie* held up his hands:

"No prawns, Effendi—no find 'em."

"You damn well find 'em!" said the Imperial Airways manager, "or you'll know the reason why."

The barefooted *suffragie* hopped off and—just as we were rush-ing into the motor-car to race to the railway station—back he came—bearing a silver salver rimmed with pink prawns, in the centre of which rode a boat of beautiful mayonnaise!

"Oh, my God!" I said. "He's too late."

"Not a bit." The airways fellow seized the salver as we ran for his car. "Eat 'em," he commanded. "I'll drive like hell—we won't miss the train." "Won't you have some?" I asked. "Sure." So I dipped a prawn in mayonnaise and, as I put them into his mouth, I occasionally missed and put mayonnaise on his nose. We finished the prawns and ran for the train, removing our own mayonnaise dressing as we ran.

"Thank God," I said, as we shook hands good-bye. "That prawn complex of mine is now dead."

The next morning I stood on the 'drome out at Heliopolis and looked out at the spot under the Macattam Hills where I had spun my baby Nieuport into Egypt's sands, that crash, that at one time or another was to give me three years in bed.

Eighteen hours later, when I became conscious again, I had not been so sure on that morning that I was glad to be alive. But on this rose red dawn, flying out to India, I was sure of it. Another complex had died.

We took off at 5.15 and headed for the canal—"The Ribbon," the pilot called it. There was the same old brown desert again, streaked with its yellow waddies. The same old sun, white hot. The dull sheen of the Red Sea. The Canal was literally a ribbon of green between Port Said and Suez. I looked down on them both at the same time—with the big P. & O. boats going slowly through the Canal between them. Camels were strolling superciliously along the banks. Little oases of palms lay like pools in the sand-dunes. The blazing Gulf of Suez lay like white metal.

Then we faced those terrible mountains of burning sand that are the Sinai desert. How the old Pharaohs ever crossed it on campaigns that reached as far as Nineveh is incredible. Looking down into its trackless oven, one could well understand the agony of that exodus of the Israelites. Most of the sand-dunes were like high ridged cliffs. We flew on and on over this awful solitude, with an extra water tank strapped on the plane's floor.

There are some really unbelievable sights on that aerial route out to India. Perhaps one of the most incredible of them is the Imperial Airways station at Gaza. The British always know how to take care of themselves in out of the way places; but that flowered mess at Gaza seemed to me a very model of what such things should be. As a matter of fact, the accommodations provided by the Imperial Airways all along that picturesque route are excellent—even to the miraculous sauce that Mr. Jeans will give you with the dressed crab at Jask where he has spent twenty-seven years watching one end of a cable line on the Persian Gulf. He was, he told me—after I had played tennis with him and two Arabs on a cement court—going to retire on that sauce.

The Judean scenery was a garden of Allah compared to the terror of the Sinai sands. A pleasant land, with the black tents of the Bedouins splattered across it, and Jerusalem staring up at us from its yellow walls. Then we were flying over that septic sore on the earth's surface, the Dead Sea. Of all the gruesome spots to fly over I feel sure that this must be the worst. It is dead. Not a wave moved in that sullen mass of water that lies 1,300 feet below the level of the Mediterranean. It looks like the bottom of the world. It lies in a nightmare of scored and twisted uplands that seem to huddle together into a shuddering crowd before they fall headlong into that dead, green scum. Ten miles across the waveless sea the edge of the festering sore met our eyes in a rim of granulated ochre and red.

Beyond the Dead Sea you see unbelievable things like the queer pentagonal walls and circles of stone and the well-connected pattern that marks the fortresses of palaeolithic Man. At Kasr Azrak you see—without a stone changed!—the furthest outpost of Rome, the fort held by the 20th Legion, which later did such admirable work pacifying the savages of Britain. There are eighty miles of nothing but basalt out here, and below you when you reach the yellow sands again you will notice what seems a mere scratch. This is the famous "Plough Track," which actually is the track made by a plough, drawn six hundred miles across the desert by the Royal Air Force to provide a guide for the first motor-cars to traverse the Syrian desert. It took seven months to draw that one single furrow.

Drowsing, trying to peer down into the purple haze over unknown Arabia—where there still stand cities that no white man has ever seen—I find the plane suddenly circling to land—and we drop down outside little Fort Rutba, held by the Iraqui Camel Corps, very much occupied with camel bandits at the moment, as their convoy, bringing food out from Baghdad had been waylaid among the sandhills and cut up within ten miles of the Fort only two days before we landed. The Iraqui soldiery, silver-daggered and in burnouses, with their long black hair in plaits, were standing guard with bayonets fixed outside the barbed wire that encircled that crenellated little fort. Inside, in the welcome darkness after the burning sun we ate a meal of soup, fish-balls, chops, oranges and bananas, cheese and Turkish coffee. The Airways officer stationed at Rutba Fort told us that he amused himself shooting partridges and gazelle, with his nearest towns Gaza. 365 miles behind, and Baghdad, 250 miles ahead.

After we left Rutba, the desert was one everlasting and unbroken pink for two hundred miles. Two black spots revealed themselves as the bitumen pools, which show where crude oil has soaked up and come through the surface. Then one sights the fringes of ancient civilisation. A faint blush of green grass, and a herd of antelope scatter like buckshot across the plain. The shadows of clouds floated in pools of blue across the pink sands. Then a wandering ribbon of water curled through the flat meadows. In a few minutes we were over the Euphrates and making for the golden domes of the mosques of Baghdad. A jumble of mud-coloured blocks flanked by billows of date gardens beside the yellow Tigris.

Baghdad today is a horrible example of what the white man's civilisation can do to an ambitious East. Its cement streets were garish with sheiks in burnouses and American motor-cars, blubbering camel caravans, dirty babies, sore-eyed children, stinks and flies. Battleground through the ages for Turk, Persian and Kurd, its only remaining glories are the great mosques of the Shiah Moslems, whose shrines are still as rich with treasure as they were in the days of Haroun-al-Raschid.

The proprietor of our hotel was a Chaldean; our fellow guests were Englishmen in dinner jackets, and local women with shields over their eyes and stockings pulled over the outside of huge silver anklets. It was only in the last minutes of sunset, standing far out on its pontoon bridge, that the silhouette of Baghdad took on the eastern majesty that I had confidently expected to see.

Baghdad has a street which is probably the most evil in the world. Beyond a sign marked *"Out of Bounds to Troops"* is a narrow alley of brothels as open as the sidewalk cafés of Paris. Arabs from the desert stagger out of this street with dazed, dope-laden eyes. Prices descend in scale until at its far end only a piastre is required. When I got out of this street I clapped my hands for a servant in the hotel to pull off my shoes and dust my suit. I felt infected from just walking through it.

We flew out of Baghdad under a full midnight moon. The Tigris twisted below us like a silver snake. It is sixty feet lower than the Euphrates and in floods has been known to rise twenty feet in a day. The ruins of Babylon were black and gaunt below us. The huge arch of Ctesiphon was like a tent on the silvery desert. Between three and four we began to fly over the marshes. Scattered plaques of water under the moon, fringed with little dots from the fires of the untamable "swamp" Arabs. They have a penchant for shooting at aeroplanes and did manage to hit and kill the mechanic of a two-seater.

At Basra our unexpected arrival at that ungodly hour found the whole camp asleep and we had to circle it again and again before the sentries woke up the mechanics who put out some landing flares. The Air Force at Basra lies inside barbed wire and there is an order that any aeroplane on the ground must always be taxied inside this wire. After the roar of our 1,000 horse-power had finished we went into a lighted mess where, at about five in the morning, an immaculate, turbaned steward asked:

"What will the Sahibs have for breakfast?"

"Bacon and eggs," we replied in chorus.

"No bacon, Sahib."

"Anything else?"

"No, Sahib—eggs. Only have eggs."

"Well, then—eggs."

Basra was a city of mud stalagmites by the steaming Persian Gulf. This was the most dismal mass of mud and water on the earth. The flats of the upper Gulf have waterways that sprawl across their fetid ooze like the veins of an anatomical chart. This is a veritable no-man's-land, for no human foot would or could cross it. But where the Tigris runs into the Persian Gulf is a paradise of waving date palms.

We flew across the head of the Gulf to Bushire, which is nothing more than an island of solid ground in this mud, and there we found a wretched Englishman with the sweat dripping so much from his eyes that he appeared to be perpetually in tears.

"Ah!" he grinned, trying to be cheerful about it. "This is cold now. Come here next month and it's a regular bloody conservatory!"

Coming into Jask we flew over a salt desert where the damp clouds could barely lift themselves off the camel track. "Don't swim on the west side of the point," said Jeans, "an Arab fisherman had his leg torn off there yesterday by sharks." Swimming out there, Mallard (the pilot) and I suddenly saw an Arab fishing dhow coming at us across the opal sea. A red-turbaned steersman was standing in its stern shouting beats for the rowers. We were, we suddenly saw to our terror, swimming off the very spot where the shark had eaten the Arab's leg. Mallard and I broke all records getting back to that beach.

At Lingeh, the fat melted in the ham in our sandwiches as we took them out of the ice-box. There was a plague going on at Lingeh. There were no white men in Lingeh; and to keep us from venturing out where we might catch the plague the Arabs drew a circle with a stick round our plane. We had to sit under its wings.

Flying over the black mountains of the Arabian coast our pilot suddenly began to climb for altitude. Looking down, I saw among the scorched cliffs a little patch of level ground that from our height looked no bigger than a tennis court. That, said the grinning pilot when we landed at Lingeh, was at the moment an Arab battleground.

"And if you don't fly high they stop shooting at each other and shoot at you."

From Jask to Karachi the cockpit of the plane lurches along a lost world. This is a startling formation of plateaux along the Indian Ocean. They rise for hundreds of miles, unscalable, with little mounds of the earth's original dust on top of them. Behind, the mountains of Persia roll off in hundreds of miles of blue, steaming ridges. Off the coast of Muscat lie the giant rays and man-eating sharks. In some stretches we flew for hours over these rays, lying in long lines in the green sea, twenty feet between wing tips, working their obscene head flaps. The sharks made streaks of greenish-grey in the water.

Muscat is the cheapest place in the world to live—probably because no one, unless exiled, could be forced to live there. There is a Sultan exiled there now. Muscat has no customs, no passports, no port doctor; English whiskey costs only four shillings a bottle, and the best cigarettes are about seven and sixpence a thousand.

After Muscat the plane takes its last long jump across the Indian Ocean. Roar, roar, roar, the grotesque coast of Persia drops into the sea behind you, the yellow deserts of Baluchistan run along your left flank for a time, and then suddenly vanish in the heat haze. Then a faint pinkness begins to appear on the far horizon. The pilot gives a grateful smile, scans his gauges, opens her up a bit, and the Indian air mail roars over the native mosques, the Towers of Silence, where the vultures below can be seen picking the Parsee dead, the tennis courts of the Gymkhana Club, European streets, tumbled bazaars and the maze of shipping that lies off the coral strand of Karachi in India.

At Karachi I stepped right into it, that complacency of the British which gives all the rest of us such an inferiority complex. They are marvellous. A few British officials in topees and shorts were there to take over as we landed the plane. There had been a riot in Karachi the day before—ten Indians had been killed by the volleys of British soldiers—one of the Englishmen mentioned it casually to me. The Indians stood about in attitudes of obeisance. That night I dined at the Gymkhana Club. The next day I went to the horse-races and was given six winners by an Englishman who was riding his own horse in one of the races. I lost money on the day as I bet him twice what I won that he could not pick six firsts out of seven races. But between times I had been down in Karachi bazaar, seen the naked fakirs throwing ashes over themselves as the sacred cows ate all the vegetables at one stall in its coloured streets, the Indian women in their orange saris of sacrifice carrying brass bowls of salt water on their heads from the sea, to refine it to a few grains of salt to defy the British salt tax, and stood on the verandah of one of those incredible Karachi brothels where the girls were all Japanese, and the Madam, thinking I was there for the reasons that most men went, said to me, "Just a minute, Sahib, she will be through with that Indian in quite a minute!"

Before dinner in the Gymkhana Club I watched the tennis, and the British colonels and their ladies playing Badminton across a hemp net. Yes, they were a marvellously imperturbable race.

Then I went across the Sind Desert in a dust-filled railway train, saw the great yellow forts rocking in the heat haze, went down through Rajputana, with its red Jain temples and the grey monkeys scampering over the hills, down through the mud flats of the Gujerat to find Ashmead-Bartlett, with my Mannlicher rifle, waiting for me in Bombay. There Petersen, that brilliant London *Times* newspaper correspondent, gave me an amazingly clear outline of the Gandhi situation and Ashmead introduced me to the Bombay Yacht Club, which put me up and gave me a room as big as a squash court in its cool chambers. Ashmead died afterwards in Lisbon; Petersen, in a moment of despair, shot himself in the room next to the one he and I had occupied in Maiden's Hotel in Delhi; but we had many exciting Indian adventures before all of that.

The day after I reached Bombay I went up to Surat and drove across an arm of Baroda State with a Parsee. And there, at Karadi, sitting under a mango-tree, I faced Mahatma Gandhi. He was clad in nothing but a loincloth, a pair of ancient silver-rimmed spectacles, and two hats. Anyone else would have looked ridiculous.

But not the Mahatma. I realised, as I sat cross-legged on the ground before the little man, that I was in the presence of a Presence.

"Tell me," I asked, "why do you hate the British so much?"

"Because," said Gandhi, "they are sucking the life blood out of India. They do not give us schools, they do not give us roads. That village behind us pays a tax of 1,700 rupees a year."

"But 1,700 rupees," I said, "would not build a mile of road!"

Gandhi broke the cotton he was spinning into a string on his *takli*. It may have been an accident; I think not, for every time I seemed to get to the point of a convincing condemning state-ment against the hated British, he broke that thread. Then, with his little monkey-like tongue, he would spend a long time licking the broken ends and splicing the fibres of cotton together again— after which he would resume our conversation, talking about something else.

The students of his *ashram* sat around us.

"But to go back to the loom age," I asked Gandhi, "to take all India back to a village life—against the British—isn't that a good deal like sending naked men up against steel?"

Gandhi gave me a toothless grin. "Well, they aren't doing too badly," he said. "As long as we do not hit back, the British do not know what to do. After a while they will become ashamed of themselves."

What the Mahatma really had his eyes on that day in Karadi, as the grey monkeys swung through his mango-tree, was not the bazaars of India, swarming with young men in Gandhi caps shouting "*Gandhi Ki Jai!*" Nor did he care an iota what the *sahibs* in the Bombay Yacht Club or up at Simla were thinking about him. Gandhi had his eye on the British House of Commons, and on the face of American public opinion; both of which he was trying to horrify. That was where he thought he might win his fight. He longed to hold the British up as wife-beaters before a shocked world. The spirituality of his civil disobedience move-ment rested upon a masochistic base.

"Beat me, you brute!" Gandhi was encouraging Mother India to taunt the British. "Beat me, beat me, beat me. I won't hit back, and while you are doing it I am going to set up such an outcry that the whole street will know about it; even your own family will be horrified at you. And after you have stood this sort of scandal for a time you will be so ashamed of yourself that you will come to me and say, 'Look here, why can't we agree upon something?' And then you will have to give me my liberty of Dominion Status that I want.

"Otherwise you will have to go on beating me until you go crazy."

Facing the little man that sweltering day on the plain of Karadi this aspect of the Civil Disobedience movement did not present itself to me. I felt abashed in the presence of such apparent simplicity. It was only as I watched him at work that I began to see with what diabolical cunning such simplicity could be used. I saw the British driven almost frantic by it. Gandhi himself may not have started his Civil Disobedience movement with this masochistic intention; but when he failed to get full Civil Disobedience from the Indians (which would have paralysed the British Services within three days), he seems to have exploited this horror side of it. Even a Holy Man it appeared must employ guile to triumph. When I asked Lord Irwin, Viceroy of India, what he thought of Gandhi, he replied:

"The first time I saw Gandhi I was tremendously impressed by his holiness. The second time I was tremendously impressed by his legal astuteness. The third time I was sure of it."

"Of which, Your Excellency?"

Lord Irwin merely smiled and looked down into the Himalayas. "That is for you to decide," he said.

I saw quite a lot of Gandhi in the next few years, and even sat by his side at a vegetarian luncheon I had ordered for him and Mira Bey in London; and I still cannot be sure about him in my mind.

All that I know is that I have never for one moment doubted his absolute sincerity.

Chapter 86

SHOLAPUR

"Abdul, when did you buy this melon?"

"Tomorrow, Sahib."

"Very well, then. When you buy one yesterday, see that it has no spots on it."

Abdul was my servant—my life, my joy, my curse, my sole protection against the importunate hordes of India. I often wondered what I thought of Abdul; I am still wondering what Abdul thought of me. The last was very important. Upon Abdul's estimate of my importance, and character, depended entirely his attitude toward all the rest of India. For a real Sahib, Abdul would fight the whole world. And this means something amid the indescribable hubbub of Indian railway platforms. But he did not know Americans; we were a strange race; he did not know whether we were friendly or not with the British, and at first I think Abdul took me on probation. He never could make out what my business was.

"Sahib . . . wherever we go there is trouble."

"Yes, Abdul."

"Big trouble."

"Looks that way, doesn't it?"

"Why, Sahib?"

"The Indians make it."

A moment. Then Abdul would smile. A terrible performance, for his heavily-bearded face would slowly open to display a mouth blood-red with betel-nut, in the gap of which two solitary teeth stood like wounded warriors. Then he would nod and get on with his business.

We had a conversation like this on the Sholapur railway platform. Poor Abdul, he did not know what had sent me rushing up there from Bombay, but when we got there Sholapur was in a state of siege. At least, the railway station was, for it was being held by a handful of Europeans with machine-guns and a bazaar

561

of 70,000 Indians had sent down word that they were only waiting for darkness to attack us. A dozen or so Indians had been shot
that morning by British soldiers for trying to kill the English
police captain among the toddy palms. All the white women had
been evacuated from Sholapur and the surrounding bungalows
and sent down to Bombay—all but one, the husky Irish wife of a
mill foreman, who, with a black eye and a rook rifle across her
lap, was sitting patiently on the Sholapur railway platform waiting for the Indians to come on. "I'll let them have it!" she said.
The rest of the Europeans were sitting about armed with shot-
guns, sporting rifles, or what have you. A hundred Dogras of
the Bombay Grenadiers were posted around the railway station
and out along the road leading to the bazaar, with machine-guns
to absorb the first shock and try and shatter the expected attack.

It was a bad time, thought Abdul, to arrive at Sholapur. Eight
miles outside Sholapur our train had stopped to pick up an Englishman, who, with a bulldog and an ice-box, had been waiting
there all afternoon to get into Sholapur. He had been driving
towards there in his motor-car; but at this place some friendly
natives had warned him that if he went any further along the
Sholapur road he would be stopped and murdered.

I, too, thought it was a bad time to reach Sholapur, and that
night as a train stopped for a few moments on its rush to Bombay
I heartily wished I was on it. But a story is a story, and I had a
big one, all to myself. Beneath the jocular calm with which the
English were awaiting the attack was a tense seriousness, in a situation which the resident magistrate and the wounded English
police captain were handling with unruffled precision. It was one
of those situations for which the English have a long line of traditions; and they know automatically exactly how to behave. I'll
confess that I turned green when a major, giving me the lay-out
of the situation, mentioned the odds.

The Indians had attacked the little police-station inside the
bazaar and set it on fire. They had also killed three native policemen; and, it was reported, they had poured petrol over one of
them and set fire to him while he was still alive.

And it was just opposite this gutted police-station the next day, looking down at the pile of ashes where they had burned the body of the policeman, that I spent what were probably the worst ten minutes of my life. I have never been so frightened— before or since. Trying not to show it, by casually lighting cigarettes, I knew that while my hands looked steady my tongue was sticking to the roof of my mouth.

We had sat there on the railway platform all night waiting for the attack. Two amazingly brave native policemen had remained in the town in disguise to give the alarm when the attack began. They were hidden in the burned-out police *chowki*, and they would blow a siren of some sort. About two in the morning we got a false alarm and a bearded Dogra came running along under the stars to awake the police captain, who was trying to snatch a few moments' sleep in one of the railway carriages on the siding. I shall never forget the sight of that gallant Captain Knight—who afterwards died in a London hospital, chiefly because of the wounds he had received from the natives of Sholapur. He had not closed his eyes for two days. He was so dead-beat that when the Dogra woke him and he staggered to his feet, he fell flat on his face as he reached to pick up his revolver. Then he went past me, strapping on his Sam Browne, saying, "Oh, God! Oh, God!" —from sheer weariness. I was offered a shotgun, and I told poor unarmed Abdul to stick by my side. I was supposed to be a non-combatant—but there would be very little chance of trying to explain that if the Hindus once got past those station gates.

The attack did not come off. But next morning armed patrols in two motor buses were sent out from the railway station at regular intervals, periodically to parade through the bazaar. I went in one of them.

There were fourteen armed Dogras in each bus. Riding on the seat beside the driver of one bus was a native Hindu magistrate. There was a Mohammedan magistrate in the other bus. They were put there to give the legal order to the troops in case it became necessary to fire. I was the only white man.

The reason why the magistrates were put there, as well as for the buses' armed patrol of the bazaar, was to see that the order was not disobeyed—that *not more than four people in Sholapur should gather together in the street.* It was by that drastic order (frequently invoked in India during the Gandhi trouble) that the British hoped to prevent a crowd collecting. It is amazing to see a town with that order in force.

The bazaar lay about a mile from the railway station. As we approached the town a dust-storm came up, and through it I saw the natives rushing out to look at us, and then running back among their warren of wooden buildings with the little painted Hindu temples sticking up.

It was uncanny to *feel* that mass of Indians retreating before us as the two buses slowly went in second-gear through the streets of the bazaar. We knew that eyes were watching us from the latticed windows that almost touched in some places over our heads. But they did not come out in the streets until we reached the police *chowki.* Here, the street up above us suddenly filled with a mob. They stood there about a hundred yards from us and from them came a man. He was weeping and holding out his hands. Seeing me, the solitary white man, he came up to the other side of our bus and began to plead with me and cry. I could not understand a word he was saying, but the Mohammedan magistrate of our bus turned around and said:

"His child was killed yesterday. It was standing on that balcony and was shot. Poor man."

The rights and wrongs of such situations are confusing. The wretched father was standing with his feet almost in the ashes of the fire whereon it was said a live policeman had been burned to death, with the crowd holding the policeman's son where he had to witness the scene. On that morning I did not know whether that story was true or not—nor do I know now.

But then something happened which took our minds off everything but ourselves. Our bus broke down.

I had noticed that its radiator had been steaming even as we set out to drive to the bazaar. Everything was to tense that morning that perhaps its native driver had forgotten to fill it up. Anyway, it blew the radiator cap off now, just as we slowly turned into the worst, narrowest street in the bazaar. Then its driver poured a tin can of water into it and the engine cracked. And at once we lost our only safety—mobility.

When the crowd spotted that it began to advance. It came to within about ten feet of the first bus, and just stood there. Thousands of them began running around the streets behind us and adding to that crowd from behind. Sholapur was the home of a peculiar school of Hindus—professional bullies. Big Hindus were selected and trained there to attain a degree of physical strength so that they could lead the usually effeminate Hindus against the Mohammedans. We saw several of these professional thugs in the crowd now, sinister-looking men, who seemed not quite able to make up their minds what to do. It was very touchy.

Meanwhile the two native magistrates stood there arguing. They did not know what to do, either. The order that not more than four people should collect in any one spot was being jeeringly broken by a mob which was now several thousand, completely filling all the streets of the bazaar around us. The order to fire was what was puzzling the two native magistrates. Should they give it? And what would happen to us if they did?

Meanwhile the fourteen Dogras in each bus sat there, clutching their rifles. The two magistrates argued. And the two native *jemadars* of the Dogras, N.C.O.s, stood waiting for orders. I suggested that we get a piece of rope and tow our bus.

We tried to get one from the crowd and they jeered at us. We did find a piece of clothes-line under the seat of the leading bus. But when we tied it to our front axle, our driver forgot to take off the brakes of our bus, and the other driver jumped his bus off so quickly that the rope snapped like string. A jeer went up from the crowd and it began to come closer to us.

At this juncture the two magistrates got into the first bus and gave the order for it to move off. There was a large open square about two blocks up above us where there was more air—and less of these wooden balconies hanging overhead. I was left there, with a piece of clothes-line in my hand, facing the *jemadar* of our fourteen Dogras.

He did not know who I was, but as I was a white man, and he

had seen me about with the English officers at the railway station, he looked at me to see what I would suggest.

Then I had my brainstorm.

"Call that other bus back," I said.

He obeyed. He took his whistle and blew it; and the other bus backed towards us slowly through the wondering mob.

"Tell that other *jemadar*," I said, "to fall out his men and fix bayonets and line up on both sides of us. Fall out your men and line them up on each side of this bus."

He did it. Then, with the crowd standing there wondering what on earth was going to happen, I said something to my *jemadar* that brought a large grin to that fine fighting face.

"Now—push!" I said.

And with the Dogras, ready as cats for a fight, slowly walking along each side of us, the first bus slowly lumbered ahead, and our fourteen Dogras pushed our bus up to the large open square. We stopped pushing when we had the bus out in the middle of it.

It was during all this time that, as I was saying, my tongue was simply sticking to the roof of my mouth. I was scared stiff. I wanted a drink so badly I could hardly see, but the *jemadar* was all smiles to me now, and it had to be kept up.

"You stay here, with your men," I said, "and we'll rush round in that other bus and find a rope."

The Hindu and the Mohammedan magistrate both thought it advisable to come with me and two armed Dogras in the other bus. It seemed that they were dying for a drink, too. For the instant we found a garage and I rushed in and seized a big coil of rope without asking for it. I found them outside almost fighting with each other to see who would have the first drink from a brass jug of water. As they did not offer me any I just took the jug from them and drank about half of it myself. Then I felt better about things.

Then we rushed back to the stranded bus in the square where all the Dogras received us with delighted grins; and in a few minutes the Dogras were marching alongside as our bus was towed back to the station of Sholapur. On the way we passed a Hindu funeral. They were carrying a corpse to the burning ghats.

They were carrying it on a board on their heads, and everything except the face sticking up towards the sky was covered with a mound of white flowers of jessamine.

As we got back to Sholapur station and the magistrates told their British superior what had happened, two more buses were immediately equipped with machine-guns on their roofs and rushed into the bazaar. This was as a demonstration—to show that the British were still commanding that place.

Four Afghan money-lenders were standing at the gates of the railway station, collecting debts from a string of the fleeing Hindus who were trying to get away from the place. When the train came in, half a battalion of Bombay Grenadiers piled out to "relieve" Sholapur. We were certainly glad to see them. I was standing there, watching a captain falling in his men, when my *jemadar* came up and saluted him. The Englishman talked to him for a few sentences in his own tongue, then he laughed, said "Good," and turned to me.

"Know what he said? He said, 'We were in a very tight place —but the sahib found the solution!' What was it?"

"I told them to push the bus," I said.

He grinned. "Good idea," he said. The *jemadar* was immensely pleased when I took his photograph.

The most interesting spot I saw that day was the native garage from which I "lifted" the rope. To prevent their motor-cars from being stolen in the rioting at Sholapur—or to prevent them from being useful to the British—the Indians were taking off the wheels from all the cars.

Chapter 87

GUEST OF PATIALA

"IF YOU want anything just ring for it."

That was my introduction to the State of Patiala. The remark was made in my suite of rooms in the Guest Palace. The person who made it was the Minister of Finance, a charming thirty-year-old Oxford graduate. Press the button, he intimated, and the world or a Rolls-Royce was mine. In the face of such hospitality one's demands shrank to nothing, and I asked for a whiskey and soda.

Patiala had made me his guest when I came up to his State to ask him about the attitude of the Indian Princes, of whose Chamber he was the head. I was to lunch with him in his modest bungalow overhanging the forests of Simla, but for a few days I was first to be his guest in his State. The sporting Sikhs took me to their polo club, where, with their beards tied to their ears and turquoise and cerise turbans on their heads, they discussed sport of all kinds, drinking their whiskey just like any similar collection of sporting Englishmen. A Major Bulwan Singh had been told off to bear-lead me. He took me to the Sikh theatre—which was not allowed to start its play until we had finished our long and most excellent dinner—and when we did enter we found ourselves seated behind a table in the stalls, on which was a bowl of ice beside a siphon and a bottle of Johnny Walker. It was the most luxurious theatre seat I have ever occupied. I particularly wanted to see some nautch girls in action; and, as I could not very well press the button for them in the Guest Palace, I had expressed my wish to Major Bulwan Singh at dinner. Hence the theatre. Hence my fixed stare at the chorus. Finally, I said to Bulwan Singh:

"They're not girls—they're boys!"

"That's right," he said.

I pointed to some straw bumps on the figure of one that had

shifted. It was not my idea of what the figure of a nautch girl should be.

We sat up most of that night, talking about life in a Sikh State, after we had walked home in the moonlight past the red sandstone palace which, as a matter of fact, was all that I hoped the palace of some Eastern fairy tale would be. The Sikhs have strong heads, and I was feeling much the worse for wear when Bulwan Singh turned up at six o'clock in the morning already dressed for our shooting expedition. I had given my own Mannlicher rifle to Ashmead-Bartlett, who was off somewhere else in India shooting with it. The Sikhs gave me one of the Maharajah's double-barrelled Westly-Richards. It was the most beautiful sporting gun I have ever held in my hands, and in letters of gold down its web was H.R.H. Maharajah Patiala.

"I only hope I don't disgrace this!" I said.

In a car with a tub of beer bottles and ice at our feet we drove out across the yellow desert. The desert was pink, in fact, covered here and there with a scrub of acacia trees, through which were flying some flashing peacocks. Bulwan told me to shoot when we sighted a herd of black buck from the car. My hand was still a bit unsteady from the night, my sight made a little waving circle around the biggest of the bucks; when it was at the bottom of the circle I shot.

I missed—but the bullet hit the buck's horns. We saw the flick in the dust where I had shot some distance on this side directly below it, and at the same instant we heard the click of the ricochetted bullet against the horns. It was a beautiful beast and it gave a wild throw of its head as it bounded off with the herd.

For the next buck I got out of the car and stalked through the acacia trees, with the wild peacocks screaming about my ears. There was a magnificent buck, standing up in the middle of his females, out on the pink plain. Had I not had a bad hang-over I know that I should have missed. He was two or three hundred yards away, at least I judged that was the distance as I flicked up the leaf of the sight. I had a bad case of buck fever when I first saw him, so superb against that morning sky, but I was over that by the time I had crawled through the acacias to as near as I thought it would be safe to get without putting them up. I fired— and the herd bounded off. But the beautiful buck lay dying on the sands.

I must confess, I did not like it. It was the same way out in British Columbia when I had to face a wounded deer's eyes, and I felt like a murderer as we finished him off. But as soon as we had given him his *coup de grâce*, Bulwan Singh made a shandy out of beer and ginger beer; and we drank to the kill. I told him I did not want to shoot any more buck that day. When a huge blue buck stood within twenty-five yards of the car, presenting a broadside target almost as big as a cow, Bulwan, with Sikh hospitality, said: "Shoot! Shoot!" I picked up the rifle, and then shook my head. "I don't want to," I said. "I don't want to kill it."

I thought that I must have lost caste with the sporting Sikhs by doing that, and I was delighted when at dinner that night I heard Bulwan telling about this to the other Sikhs.

"Usually," said that old warrior, leaning out down the table to address me, "when we have foreign guests—they try to kill everything on the place!"

He then told the story how a Balkan prince, who is now a king, came to stay as the guest of Patiala, with his three Aides. The Aides had been taken shooting the same way that I was. As they passed a herd and Bulwan said, "Shoot," one of the Aides picked up a shot-gun, *loaded with 6's*, and blazed into the herd.

" 'No, no, no!' I told them," said Bulwan Singh, explaining that as he talked no French and the Roumanians talked no English he had had to give the rest of his warning in sign language. He, therefore, for our benefit, made a hole with his fingers about the size of a twelve-bore and then flapped like a bird.

" 'Little bird—big gun,' I told them."

He then pranced like a deer.

" 'Little hole,' I told them."

The Roumanians apparently understood that.

Then bearded Bulwan Singh went through the most fearful

antics. He roared, pawed his moustache and made as if to creep stealthily along the plain.

" 'Tiger! Don't shoot,' I told them."

Later that day the Sikhs lost the Roumanians, only to come upon them crawling flat on their bellies across an obviously game-less plain. They were stalking one of Patiala's pet camels!

Chapter 88

ARREST OF GANDHI

I HAD all the luck in India. Lord Irwin, the Viceroy, invited me the day after I reached Simla to lunch in Vice-Regal Lodge. After lunch, on the basis of an understanding that I would report nothing of what was said, he led me off for a long talk on the whole Gandhi business. Irwin, now Lord Halifax, has been criticised (and was being violently attacked both in England and in India at that moment by diehards) for what was claimed too soft a hand in handling Indian affairs. All I can say is that out in India I had one big Indian after another assure me that if it had not been for Irwin's character there would have been bloodshed all around. The Indians, particularly the Hindus, can understand and appreciate a saintly character. And if Gandhi was a holy man, Lord Irwin certainly was a saint. I think he is the finest Englishman I have ever met—with perhaps the exception of honest George Lansbury.

It was the fact that lots of the Indians believed in Lord Irwin's sincerity that kept them quiet.

"They are saying down in the Plains," said that tall figure, looking down into the Himalayas, "that 'you cannot govern India from the Hills!' Well, perhaps the Plains are too far from the Hills for the people to understand what is being done up here. Here are two more Ordinances that I am, very reluctantly, going to have to invoke tomorrow. You can have the first news of them to send them to your paper, if you like."

I think it was the Seditious Meeting Act—not more than four people being allowed to meet in one place, that was later invoked at Sholapur—and the Ordinance which made it legal to arrest a plotter even if he was in another part of India from the place where he was planning some disturbance.

It was watching these Ordinances being invoked, one after the other, that gave me the realisation of how the jaws of the British Raj were closing down to arrest Gandhi again. Ashmead-Bartlett and I were so sure of it that we even suspected the day. That's why he and I alone, of all the correspondents then out in India, got the scoop on Gandhi's arrest, and were standing there at six o'clock in the morning on the outskirts of Borivli, when the great Bombay and Baroda express roared around a cut, jammed on all her brakes for a full stop, and before the staring eyes of 400 startled Hindu and Mohammedan passengers, the little Mahatma was taken out of a supposedly empty restaurant car, calmly ushered into a motor that had been concealed in the bushes, and whisked off to Poona prison.

That *was* a morning.

The previous day, Sunday, I had been asked to go sailing by the Governor's A.D.C. He had a big yawl in which we used to sail nearly every sunset, and on Sundays, out to a little island where several yachts would anchor and we would all go in for a swim. A macabre island, for in the daylight its trees were full of "flying foxes," huge bats, hanging from the branches by their feet as thickly as grapes. On this Sunday both Ashmead and I were so nervous we could hardly sit down. We had such a strong hunch that the British were going to arrest Gandhi that we were afraid some of our own colleagues must smell the same wind. It was a story that, for a short time, was going to rock the world.

"I don't think I'll go sailing," I said. "I think I'll stick around Bombay today."

The A.D.C. did not know my reasons. Much as I sailed with him on those gorgeous sunsets, he never gave me one "inside" fact on politics. We were usually gabbing about sailing, in fact, on which subject we were both mad.

"Oh," he said innocently, "I'll get you back by eight o'clock."
That was it.

I went over to the Chambers, allegedly to get into a pair of shorts, and went straight to where Ashmead was trying to get some sleep under a whirling wooden fan.

"It's tonight," I said.

Ashmead was a genius for making people say what they didn't mean to say. We knew the official in Bombay who would know all about the Gandhi situation—because without his saying so, there just wouldn't be any arrest, and I sicked Ashmead on to him. While the A.D.C. and I and several pretty girls were eating our luncheon from ice-boxes over near Elephanta Island, fiery Ashmead was lunching with that official. At eight o'clock, the A.D.C., who could sail a boat beautifully, brought his yawl about among the yachts off the Yacht Club and we dropped anchor. Ashmead was waiting in the bar for me, leaning up against it.

"Borivli," he whispered.

He had the name of the place!

We ate a good dinner that night, because we knew that we weren't going to get any sleep in it, and more than likely no breakfast. It was great fun, sitting there in those deep chairs in the Bombay Yacht Club's cool bar, chatting with the Englishmen, and one or two of our unsuspecting colleagues, and knowing what we were going to do about midnight, with our motor-car already parked outside the Yacht Club. It had a great thrill of adventure, one of the things that makes the life of a foreign news-paper correspondent harder to give up than to leave off drinking.

Gandhi, we knew, was being arrested in his sleep in Surat, as we talked. He was to be secretly smuggled on board the Bombay and Baroda express and taken off at Borivli.

The express did not reach Borivli until six o'clock the next morning. But, even so, by waiting until almost the last minute on the railway platform at Borivli, we almost missed it all. The thought suddenly struck both of us at the same time, as we talked to the station-master, who was performing his ablutions in a bucket of water.

"What time does the Bombay and Baroda stop here?" we asked.

"No stop, Sahib. Express—she go right through to Bombay. Whussh!" he said, with a motion of his hands to show us at what speed she went through. "No stop!"

Then I said to Ashmead: "The British would never take him off the train, right here in the centre of Borivli—there's about forty thousand Hindus here—there'd be a riot."

Then we raced for our motor-car. Our only dilemma was whether they would take him off above the town or below it; and thank goodness we took the upper road. When we came to a crossing and saw that the gates were down, and two Englishmen in civilian shorts carelessly leaning over the gate on their side, we knew we were right.

"What are you two doing here?" they asked surlily.

"You're police, aren't you?" asked Ashmead.

"Yes, what of it?"

"We've come to watch you pinch Gandhi," smiled Ashmead.

If looks could have killed, as the saying goes, we would have been dead in a minute. Instead, the police had to stand for some of Ashmead's caustic wit. He found the Buick, hidden in the bushes, with a pink bridal veil around it.

"Talk about 'Buy British!'" came Ashmead's sarcastic laugh. "Why, you even have to arrest Gandhi in an American motorcar!"

We cheered them up and established a decent relationship by giving them a half share of our two thermos flasks of hot coffee. We did not take any whiskey with us on that mad drive up from Bombay during the night. We wanted cool heads to write the Gandhi story.

When that express came piling around the bend, I found myself shaking like a horse. It was indescribably dramatic as we heard the scream of the brakes. All the people inside it, of course, except Gandhi and his escort, thought they had hit something. Heads were sticking out of every window—great bunches of heads. And that expression about seeing the whites of their eyes! —when Policeman Condon ducked under the gate and put up his hand to help Gandhi alight, I saw a white circle widen around every one of those Hindu and Mohammedan eyes.

"Good morning, Mr. Gandhi," said Policeman Condon, taking off his sun topee to the Mahatma he had arrested once eight years before.

"Good morning," said Gandhi.

Clutching his white sheet around him in the cold morning air, the little man bowed to both Ashmead and me—he had talked with us both several times, and recognised us.

"Any word, Mr. Gandhi?" I heard Ashmead asking.

"Shall I say them now—or shall I wait?"

"You'd better say them now," snorted Ashmead. "In a few minutes you'll be on the way to Poona prison."

"Tell the people of England and America," said Gandhi, "to realise what is being done on this morning. Is this liberty? . . ."

Gandhi was marvellous, the only absolutely unruffled person on that scene. The English also were admirable. It was nip and tuck whether those staring heads wouldn't be pulled in from the windows and half a thousand Hindus and Mohammedans would come piling out to rescue their Mahatma. There were just the two cool policemen, armed with nothing but short little swagger sticks and a policeman and a doctor who had been with Gandhi in the train. Yet the English did not hurry Gandhi, and they apologised when they told him they had to cut short the story he was giving Ashmead and myself. The Buick, with its little pink silk bridal purdah, had been backed up for him.

"Are you ready, Mr. Gandhi," said the English doctor, dressed in civilian duck, but a Colonel in the Army Medical Corps.

"Ready," said Gandhi, and drew his white robe about him.

The instant he sat down in that motor-car it shot off down the road. At the same instant the great Bombay and Baroda express seemed to jump down the rails. I have never seen a train make such an astonishing start; and it was too late now, if any of them had made up their minds, for the Indians to rush out and try to rescue their Mahatma, or avenge him.

Ashmead, one of the two policemen, and I stood there alone on the railway crossing.

"Well," said the policeman, giving a quiet sigh that showed the strain he had been under. "I feel like a spot of breakfast."

"Know what we've been looking at?" asked Ashmead. "We've been watching the British Centurions arresting the Indian Christ—and old Dash (a high official of Bombay Province) is Pontius Pilate."

It was a joke that everyone in the Yacht Club appreciated that night—except Mr. Dash, who was slightly peeved with us over the whole affair.

Racing back to Bombay, knowing that nobody knew the story, we roared through villages and past palm groves, where we saw the "untouchables" around their miserable little breakfast fires. The story we knew would not be announced until some time that afternoon, when Gandhi would be safely behind the walls of Poona prison. So, when we got to the Yacht Club we woke up a bar attendant and ordered a bottle of Veuve Cliquot, two pewter tankards and some ice. We poured the cool champagne fizzing over the blocks of ice—then we toasted each other, and as the sun rose higher and higher, scorching Bombay harbour, we wrote page after page of the Gandhi story.

Owing to the curve of the world my story would hit all the afternoon papers in the United States. Poor Ashmead's couldn't appear until next morning's *Daily Telegraph*—and what a splendid story he wrote! But back in Chicago, out in San Francisco, on the cable desk of the *New York Sun* men "on the desk" were reading my first "take"—GANDHI ARRESTED AT BORIVLI SIX O'CLOCK THIS MORNING. . . .

Abdul kept our motor-car to rush back and forth between the Yacht Club and the Post Office; and then I began to jump into the car, riding down to see how the news of Gandhi's arrest would hit the Bombay bazaar. At first the excitement looked as if someone had thrown a bomb with its pin pulled out among the jam of natives down there. I wrote all day long, regardless of words, going-to-press time, and expense.

And when I was eating my dinner late that night I got the first cable back. It was from my own paper, asking me had I gone crazy "over-filing" like that—but then the papers of our syndicate began to wire my own—and after midnight I was awakened to be handed two or three cables that made me feel too pleased about things to even want to go to sleep again.

That was a day in a newspaper man's life.

But it wasn't always so pleasant as that. My dispatch on the fearful Maidan beating, where about four hundred Indians were taken to hospital and a jatha of twenty-five Sikhs were beaten almost insensible—because they had come there to sacrifice themselves and not hit back—that dispatch was held up by the Bombay censorship for eight hours. I did not find this out until seven hours after I thought that my first "takes" had gone. This was another tremendously hot story in which Karl Ketchum of the London *Daily Express* and I were the only two newspaper correspondents down there on that Maidan watching for the beating to begin. We stood within ten feet of the Sikh jatha when it was being beaten. We saw its brave leader fall again and again with the blood streaming down his face, and we saw the British sergeant of police, who, sweating so that the perspiration was coming through his white tunic, finally refuse to hit him. He dropped down his lathi.

"You can't hit a b—— again—not when he stands up to you like that!"

My dispatch, describing how I saw Indian women dressed in their orange robes of sacrifice, fling themselves on the bridles of the charging mounted police—how a Sikh mother held up her own baby for the police to hit—how I saw Hindu stretcher-bearers rush out to place a stretcher beside a group of men who refused to move, and were taking the rain of blows on their hands over their heads—that gory cable was held up.

For an hour I rushed about frantically in the post office, trying to find someone who would let my dispatch go through. I met one Englishman of the complacent type which hates Colonials and Americans, and when he got rude I told him that I was going to send an open cable to the Viceroy and give a copy of it to the editor of the *Indian Daily Mail*—saying that my dispatch, trying to tell the truth of what had happened, was not being allowed to get out to the outside world. I wired to London, to a naval commander friend of mine, who was a Member of Parliament, asking him to ask a question in the House. Because a lot of silly English officials at that time were trying to prove that there was no censorship on Indian news.

I had started filing about ten in the morning. It was now eight o'clock—and not one word of mine had been allowed through. Then I found Cliff, of the Secretariat. Cliff was in bed with a violent fever. But he came down to his drawing-room in his bungalow on the Yacht Club's front. I told him what had happened, and he asked to read my dispatch.

"Phew!" he said. "This is full of *blood!*"

"So was the Maidan," I said. "I deliberately sat still for half an hour before I wrote one word—I wanted to cool off."

"Do you give me your word," he asked, "that everything you say here really happened?"

"I do," I said. "I've underpainted the picture."

"All right."

He tottered to his feet, told his servant to bring his car round, and put on a heavy raincoat. The monsoon had broken just that afternoon (it saved Bombay from a riot the next day); and in that unbelievable downpour of rain, Cliff went to the post office.

My dispatch—*without one single word changed or deleted*—went through the air to America at once.

In that dispatch, I tried to show some of the inevitability of the whole affair. Motilal Nehru had insisted on holding a review of the Congress "army" on Maidan Field. The British had prohibited it. If the news had gone through India—where the "underground" wireless is quicker than the European's Marconi—that a couple of hundred thousand Congress wallahs had paraded before Nehru on Bombay's biggest playing ground, India would have been a riot the next minute. Motilal Nehru knew that. He also knew that hundreds of Hindus were going to be badly beaten, and some, perhaps, would be killed. But he wanted it:

"Beat me!" Mother India was yelling at the face of the British. "Beat me, beat me, and then I'll scream so that the whole street will hear it! I'll make you ashamed of yourselves!"

That was the whole strength of Gandhi's civil disobedience movement. A nation like the British held up their hands in horror at the idea of hitting people who refuse to hit back. It would have been different with the French. And all the world was watching how the English would handle such passive resistance. I was furious when I read the editorials that some of the American weeklies printed on my dispatch—what quotations they had made from it—*but particularly those they left out.*

The American daily newspapers, on the other hand, gave a

realistic and unbiased play to all our stuff. It was only the "easy oozy" sentimentalists of some of the magazines who refused to see both sides of this unbelievable affair.

The first two detachments of Hindus marching past Karl Ketchum and myself at six o'clock that morning were their stretcher-bearers and Red Cross Corps. There were several hundred of them. Watching them were several hundred Mahratti police, naked legged, with little round yellow turbans on their heads and bamboo lathis in their hands. I saw their Red Cross calmly laying out these stretchers beside the crowds of massed Hindus who were forming in round groups, standing there waiting to be beaten senseless. Thousands and thousands of them, with two battalions of the Yorkshire Light Infantry waiting down back streets, and a British General, with his staff on the field.

One of the most British sights I saw that day was an Englishman, in shorts, walk out for his morning round of golf from the Gymkhana Club. As all that slaughter was being staged he calmly teed up a ball and drove off.

Chapter 89

A RELIABLE COMMUNIST AGENT

ABDUL and I, and the ice-chest, travelled up and down India. Stationary, in an up country dak bungalow, he would draw back my mosquito net in the morning, bring me my tea and iced mangoes, fill my hip bath full of cool water, lay out my clothes, dress me, stand by to run messages, squat on guard over my possessions when I was out, and cheat me at every turn of the road.

But he would let no one else do it. In his own mind he had decided upon the commission he felt entitled to withhold from the money I gave him to pay for railway tickets, food and laundry, and to tip the safari of porters who accompanied our progress in and out of railway stations. What this commission was I never knew; but I always felt that honest Abdul would never take an anna more than that; that would have been stealing. And as far as leaving money and valuables about, they were safer with Abdul than in the Bank of England.

A Mohammedan himself, he was careful about mulcting tip-money in the Mohammedan districts—in Peshawar I don't think he held back a cent—but with the Hindus, he would just pocket half the tips and give them an arrogant snap of the finger on the head.

My importance with him took firm ground when he saw me spend two hours with Mohammed Ali, sipping pink sherbet, in the Khalifat headquarters in Love Lane. Evidently, whatever it was that I was doing, it was all right with the Mohammedans. And I was definitely accepted as his Sahib when I was the guest of the Brigadier commanding Ferozepore, and the bearer of that illustrious Indian Army name—Battye—came out to welcome me to Flagstaff House. Abdul had served a brother officer of Battye's when Battye had been a subaltern in his family's famous regiment, The Guides. Abdul recognised him at once, and after General Battye had shaken hands with him and asked him a few flattering

581

questions about old times, I could have done nothing that would have lowered me in Abdul's eyes.

Which was all very nice, because I liked Abdul very much; and I was immensely flattered, when a year later, in England, I got a letter from him.

"If you cannot come yourself, Sahib, please send me another Sahib, because I have no one but God and Your Honour for support. . . ."

Wily old Mohammedan!

Abdul and I stood by the water tank on the top of that huge mosque in Delhi, between two days of rioting, most of which took place between the mosque and the little police station across the street. We went out into the Punjab, on the rounds, with an English police captain who was visiting his village stations. He was trying to corner a notorious assassin, and one day as we rode across the pink desert we saw some camel police. The murderer, they announced, was dead. An outraged husband had killed him that morning in the next village we were coming to. Sitting beside the Englishman outside the police stations, with the peacocks screaming at us from the trees, I read some of the most extraordinary crime records one could think of. One village was highly agitated by a *fakir* who had just passed.

Thinking that he was a holy man, a village farmer had invited him to share his simple meal. The *fakir* dropped the seeds of some plant into the food, which he refused to eat himself; he lived on nothing, he said. And when the farmer's family came to they found they had practically nothing to live on as well. The deadly seeds had sent the family into laughing fits, during which the holy man had walked off with their money and clothes.

This police captain showed me how the village reforms, by taking the responsibility away from the head men of a village, had made it so hard to control crime. He was all for going back to the old days, making the four or five head men of a village directly responsible for its good behaviour.

In Delhi, I sat most of an afternoon in the garden of Shah

Jehan, where the crested "hoopoe" birds walked in stately pattern across the lawn, spreading their head-dress out like painted combs, and where the Arabic inscription around the marble pavilion reads:

IF THERE BE PEACE, THIS IS IT, THIS IS IT, THIS IS IT.

But there was little peace for Abdul and me on the day that we reached Peshawar. We got there on the morning when a Mohammedan woman had been shot by accident at the Kabuli gate. The bazaar had declared a hartel against the British; and two big lashkars of Afridis were coming down on either side of the Khyber Pass to attack Peshawar. These were the days when the "perimeter" wire around Peshawar cantonment was charged with live current; and the white women were evacuated from Dean's Hotel.

Petersen, the London *Times* correspondent, met me at the train; and Lowther, the political agent, took us for a cautious drive through the bazaar. I have never witnessed such a demonstration of quiet, implacable hate. The killing of the woman had been such an unbelievable accident that it was almost impossible to explain it had not been intentional. In the back room of the sentry-box by the Kabuli gate a white British soldier had been cleaning his rifle. It went off. From where he was sitting there was only a slit between the doors that showed the open street. The bullet took it, and went straight through the breasts of a mother and her baby who were driving at that moment in a *tonga* through the Kabuli gate. The bazaar, which had just finished that fierce rioting during which they built a fire under a British armoured car, was ready to start another one all over again.

As we drove slowly through the streets we saw that all the shops had their board fronts up. What few Mohammedans there were still sitting before the closed suks merely stared at Lowther, whom they knew, without a glance of recognition or a nod. At one corner, where our young native driver tried to push past a British cavalry patrol, Lowther gently tapped him on the shoulder with the little fly swatter he was carrying (instead of a revolver) and told him to go slow.

"One thing I would not like to do," said that hard-tried political agent with a smile, "is run over a child today in Peshawar bazaar."

The Peshawar rioting had already broken several of the best men in the Indian Services. The officers were playing tennis at the Club; and Peshawar, with its great shade trees and cool lawns, was the most "English" place I saw in all India; but the scene was as charged with potential trouble as the electrically-charged "perimeter" wire.

For six out of the seven nights I was in Peshawar I dined at Flagstaff House with General Godwin, C.-in-C. Troops of the Northwest Frontier. He was a splendid figure of British cavalry officer, in his white mess kit; and he discussed the fighting without the sense of its being anything out of the ordinary in the course of the day's duties. Neither was it. Sitting on the floor after dinner, with his long legs on either side of a map of the Northwest Frontier, he would discuss the next day's operations.

"They're trying to get Bura Fort. They cut the bridge going out there last night. What I'm going to do is take them on in this nullah. They'll be almost certain to try and get up to the gardens around Peshawar along that. I've got some cavalry now, out on the Bura road. . . . Some machine-guns will shake 'em up here. . . . What I'm doing, you see, is a converging movement. If I get them in there I can squeeze them. . . ." Then he would take a sip of his whiskey and soda and say: "You know, damn fine fellows, these Afridis. . . ."

He admired his enemy tremendously; just as the Pathans admired the British.

When the Pathans finally did succeed in killing a resolute Political Agent, who had brought many of their ringleaders to death, they sent down a request into Peshawar, asking if a deputation of eight or so of their big men could have "safety" to attend his funeral. It was done. They turned over their rifles at the gates, stood by the grave of their gallant enemy; then went back into the hills to resume sniping the British again.

The officers in, I think it was Landhi Khana Fort in the middle of the Pass, complained to me when I arrived there that they had been sniped all during the previous night, and several Afridi bullets had scored their new tennis court.

Although the Pass was closed, General Godwin got me up it, after I had threatened to weep if I was going to be refused the one thing I wanted to do most in all India.

It was a tremendous sight, to see Jamrud Fort, lying like a great yellow battleship at the mouth of those red rocks that form the Northwest Frontier. I went up it with a Sapper Major, who was more concerned about his precious pumps than whether we were going to be sniped or not from the hills above us. An Afridi lashkar, with banners up, was coming down along the mountains flanking the Pass as we went up. The rock ridges were full of British soldiers on guard. Most of them were Indian regiments, and we saw their turbans peering down at us from the little block-houses along our route. Where the Pass widened and we came on the little mud villages and cultivation, each village was a little mud-walled fort of itself, with men in its watch tower watching everything that went up the two roads. We passed two of these arrogant little forts facing each other at a distance of less than a hundred yards across our road.

"There are men in that village," said the Sapper, "who haven't dared step outside it for twenty years—blood feud, you know; and men in that other village across the road have been sitting there twenty years waiting for them to come out."

We saw a camel caravan, coming through on the slow-traffic road from Afghanistan. And by us passed a motor-bus—*en route* for Kabul. In all those forts by the main road, those British officers who were not on duty, had just finished their early morning game of tennis before the sun got too hot. Soldiers, both British and Indian, were kicking footballs about. Business-like British colonels were supervising the daily routine of life in the little worlds which they each controlled. Indian cavalry, in the picturesque coloured turbans of undress, were strolling about the cavalry lines. In the Mess, by the lowered pole across the road that marks the end of the Pass, I looked up into the snows of Afghanistan, as I drank the best iced beer I had tasted in India.

You can be sniped any minute, on a day that might seem as

peaceful as Sunday in England; but the daily games of tennis and football are worthy of note in the Khyber Pass.

"They're bitches!" complained the driver of the armoured car as we drove out to Matta Fort. He did not mean the Afridis (whom I was going out there to see shot up); he meant the locusts that came in through the eye-slit in the steel shield before us and squashed themselves against our eyes.

Badshah Gul had been raising forces to attack the British from the Mohmand country—a nightmare of rocky red, just across the Durand Line—and the village on this side, around little Matta Fort, was believed to be co-operating with that notorious renegade. The previous night a convoy had been ambushed at the village just outside the fort walls. The motor lorry had been overturned and set on fire. Its driver had been burned to death in the flames. Another man, wounded, had escaped death by crawling off into the green fields. He was a Mohammedan, and he had called to the mud walls of the village from where he lay. "Come nearer," the villagers called back from its mud walls, "and we will kill you."

We came on the wreck, the car still smouldering, and the cartridge-cases of some two hundred Martini-Henris and Pass rifles scattered all over the road. The villagers were grinning down from their mud walls as we stood there and examined them.

"I call this damned impudence!" said the General who was going out to take command over the bombardment of Badshah Gul from Matta Fort; and he discussed how it would be a good thing to take all that village's cattle away. To ambush a convoy right under the nose of the fort was simply going too far.

In the fort we leaned over the sand-bags around its little *Beau Geste* walls, while a Sikh mountain battery on the ground below us serenaded Badshah Gul. For it was hardly more than a serenade. The Afridis were in the caves of the mountains on the other side of the line. When the shooting got too hot they simply went inside. When they thought it had stopped for a moment they came outside and stared at us. I saw only one man killed that day.

It was a direct hit. Through the glasses, I was watching the mouth of a particular cave. In a lull in the firing I saw a little Afridi rush out. There he stood, and I could see his Pathan shirt-tail sticking out from below his vest. Then a mountain howitzer barked below us and a shell soared across the green delta, so peaceful, with its silver streams shining in the sun. Before the Afridi heard the sound of that shot the shell hit him. The mouth of the cave before my glasses rose up in a column of brown dust. When the dust settled no Afridi was there. While we were watching, a bomber from the Royal Air Force soared over the red hills and began laying eggs. We heard the thundering explosions and watched the great columns of earth and rocks rise up into the sky and slowly settle down. But I don't think the fellows up in that plane hit anybody. They might have had a lucky shot and blocked up the mouth of some cave. But when they had banked and headed back to Peshawar, we saw the Afridis come out, staring at us and taking some careful shots at us from the mouths of their caves. For a moment, one had the ridiculous desire of wanting to wave to them.

"They call me a bow-and-arrow soldier," said one of the Generals, leaning over the parapet by my side. He was a Gallipoli General, with a breast of decorations like a flower-bed. "They call me that, just because I keep telling them it's absolutely useless to try and use tanks and aeroplanes up in those hills. To get at the Afridis you've got to go up there on your hands and knees. It's a terrible country. I know. Why, I fought up in the Mohmand country when I was a boy, just come out to India. It's some of the most expensive country to fight a war in on earth."

Badshah Gul, as far as I know, is alive and fighting the British today.

As an example of how tricky all the fighting is around those parts, take the case of Petersen and myself getting back to Peshawar. As we were in a hurry to get our stories off to our papers we decided not to wait for the generals or the armoured car escort but to make a quick dash for it back across the delta to get into Peshawar. The delta of the Kabul River was a salubrious spot, its fresh water and cool green were startlingly beautiful under the frown of those sun-baked red hills. At one pontoon bridge crossing a swift stream, we did come on a bunch of about thirty Afridis apparently just lounging there in the rushes by its side. They watched us sullenly as we passed, and we speeded up to get away from their uncertain attitude as quickly as we could. But that was all. We were writing our descriptions of the Matta Fort story when the 'phone rang. It was from G.H.Q.

"Are you all right?" a voice asked.

"Of course—why?"

"Oh, nothing—they'd just telephoned from the fort that you two had cut back across country alone. Cheerio."

As I said, for six out of the seven nights I was in Peshawar, the general in charge was good enough to have me to dinner. I was to have dined with him on the sixth night—but at the last minute a bearer brought a note to Dean's Hotel, saying that the General was very sorry, but he would be unable to have me tonight. I could quite understand that. The Afridis were almost up to Peshawar's perimeter wire, in a dust-storm some of them had actually got into the gardens around Peshawar, and the only white woman in Dean's Hotel had been taken over by the Padre to sleep for the night in the Y.M.C.A. I had, in fact, refused an invitation myself to come over and spend the night at Flagstaff House. So I ate a lonely dinner and told Abdul that we were neither of us to go to sleep that night. I had been promised by the General that I could ride out with him the next morning to see the fight.

But the General did not show up. . . .

There is a bridle-path flanking all the main streets of Peshawar for the cavalry to use. I watched the slower units going out first. The field-batteries, the infantry, then the cavalry came jangling along. They were a grand sight. Then, a little while after they had cleared off, I saw the General's car turn into the street. I went out to meet it—and it drove past and left me standing there.

Now I did feel hurt!

Had I said something in my dispatches that had upset them? No—the General was not the kind of man to act like that; he would have tackled me about it, first. Then what was it? I sat there in a surly temper as I heard the shots of the story I had so much wanted to write. Then, just at sunset, the troops came back. I watched the same identical procession—foot-slogging, grinning infantry; haughty, jangling cavalry—then the General's car. This time, not to be snubbed again, I went back inside my room in Dean's. Then I heard a voice:

"Yes, General Sahib."

It was Abdul speaking; then another voice: "Farson, may I come in?"

The General stood at my door. I leapt to my feet and told Abdul to give the General a cool whiskey-and-soda, and then I waited upon what the General would say.

"It's been a damned hot day," he said.

"Hasn't it?"

"What are you doing for dinner tonight?"

"Oh, I've bothered you too much as it is."

"Not a bit of it—ah—that whiskey tastes good. See you tonight —same time."

Then, just at the door, he stopped and looked back. "Sorry about last night and this morning," he said. "I was fairly busy, you know."

"Yes, sir," I said. "I went over about midnight to give you this wire, and they said you were still at G.H.Q."

I handed him a wire which had been given to me at midnight the previous night. It was from my colleague in London, Constantine Brown, and it read:

"NEGLEY FARSON, DEANS HOTEL, PESHAWAR.

"RELIABLE COMMUNIST AGENT INFORMS RUSSIANS MASSING TROOPS BORDERS KASHMIR FRONTIER."

"I wouldn't have bothered you," I said, "but the fellow who sent this, Constantine Brown, has amazingly good contacts in London. I thought it might interest you."

"Hmph!—oh, these Russians again . . ." The General gave me a smile and went out. He left me more puzzled than ever. And that night at dinner I was more than puzzled, for the General had invited two other generals to dinner in Flagstaff House; and, as it was to be my last night in Peshawar, they insisted there was no hurry to go home, and they seemed to be going out of their way to be friendly with me. It was astonishing from such reserved men.

Lowther, the Political Agent, was smiling and very friendly, too, as he came down to the station to say good-bye to Petersen and me the next morning.

"See you again, Farson," he said. "Good luck."

I couldn't make it out.

But the moment we got into the train, with everything sealed up and its blue glass windows up to keep out the burning sun, Petersen opened his ice-chest and handed me a whiskey-and-soda. Then he broke down and simply roared with laughter.

"What on earth are you laughing at!" I demanded.

"I suppose," he said, "you have been wondering why you were treated like the white-haired boy in Peshawar—just after the General broke his dinner date?"

I had, I told him, been thinking about nothing else.

"Because," he said, "the cable that was forwarded to Godwin from Rawalpindi read: 'Negley Farson, reliable Communist agent, informs Russians massing troops on Kashmir frontier'!

"Just about that time," said Petersen, "you were wondering why the General had broken his dinner date; he was walking up and down G.H.Q. saying: 'My God—*and I've been talking freely to that fellow for days!*' "

The Political Agent down at Rawalpindi, it seemed, had got my wire on its relay from there to Peshawar, and had wired up to tell my hospitable hosts that they had a red-hot Communist in their midst.

"When they asked me about you," said Petersen, "how long I had known you, and had you been in Russia, and how did you talk about the Bolsheviks, I said you had been in Russia for years, and that you positively adored the Bolshies—then, damn it all, they looked so serious *I almost began to believe it myself!*"

"You're a nice one!" I said.

"It's all right," he said. "I told them that even if you were a

Communist agent—I could assure them you weren't a reliable one."

Still, that did not explain why the General had so suddenly changed his mind, and had felt easy about me again. I got that end of it at dinner in London one night, when there, in a drawing-room of South Kensington—stood General Godwin!

"Nearly arrested your husband once!" he said to Eve. "Thought he was a spy!"

I listened, fascinated, while the General told her how he had cleared all wires to London to investigate me after he had received that shattering wire from Rawalpindi. It was while he was out taking on the Afridis that the answer had come back from London that I was not a Communist agent.

"But dash it all," said the General, laughing. "I'm not so sure yet! When I was told first you were a reliable Communist agent, I thought, oh, no—he looks like a pretty decent chap. Then, blast it all, I suddenly realised—a *reliable* Communist agent would look like that!"

Chapter 90

EGYPT TO POLAND

"Tomorrow," said the bank clerk as I cashed my letter of credit, "you're going to see the finest sight in all India: Bombay—from the stern of a steamer going home!"

I was glad to be leaving. The monsoon was on in full swing. For days I had been living in air like hot steam. It had been dramatic, at first, to see those yellow rains hit Bombay—lashing horizontally down the streets, to watch the queer Indian rigs fighting up against the pumping tides of the bay, and the palm-trees over on Elephanta Island rise up like drowned men's heads through the stifling morning mists. But even under the wooden fan I could not get cool on my bed, my pillow was wet, cigarettes wouldn't light; and even an unbroken succession of whiskies-and-sodas and "gimlets" couldn't bring me the relief that white men seek that way. Even the Indians were too despondent to riot, and the few who were out wandered through the rain in that dopy fashion that they have when the monsoon soaks the muddy Gujerat.

At 4 o'clock on my last morning—with the great P. & O. boat waiting in her dock—I sat in the chambers of the Bombay Yacht Club to write my last dispatch. Sweat dripped from my arms to blot the carbon. For nearly five months I had watched the Gandhi movements in various parts of India. I had seen that little 7 stone, almost naked man bring the power of the British Raj nearly to a dead stop. And he had done it all with an Idea. I think that if the rest of the Indians had co-operated with Gandhi in the passive resistance he implored of them, "Civil Disobedience" campaign might have won the day. It was an unanswerable weapon to use against such people as the British. I watched Lord Irwin's answer to it, the Ordinances he invoked one after another from Simla, slowly pushing the Gandhi movement underground. I felt, as I left India, that it would break out again. But I had seen too much of the Indian politicians fighting amongst each other; and

I left India with the feeling that if I were an Indian, I would prefer to remain under British rule for quite a long time.

Abdul came in with tears in his eyes (I hope they were genuine) to pack my kit. He and his whole Mohammedan family were lined up on the deck to say good-bye. As I shook hands with him in farewell, he hung a wreath of overwhelmingly powerful jasmine blossom around my neck; and with this smell in my nostrils I went up the gang-plank. The smoking-room of the big P. & O. boat was full of people saying good-bye, people seeing friends going home on their first leave, red-faced old fellows saying good-bye to India for the last time; people from China, Japan, and people who had been washed down all the rivers of the Orient were watching this scene, which, with its hysterical gaiety and hidden heart-ache, they had become used to by now. Some Englishmen at a farewell party had practically wrecked my other leg, so that I could not walk. I got a deck chair, sat down —and began the long ride home.

The night we were reaching Marseilles, the steward handed me a Marconigram—"WILL YOU RETURN COVER EGYPTIAN RIOTS FORTHWITH." I wired back—"PROCEEDING EGYPT TONIGHT." I was so tired and hot, I felt like cancelling that wire; but instead, I wired poor Eve, who was waiting for me in Paris, to go on by herself to the French seaside resort. Ashmead-Bartlett and I hung over the rail as the great big P. & O. liner pulled into Marseilles and came to rest directly beside the little obsolete boat on which I had booked a cabin by wireless to take me to Port Said. Ashmead and I painted Marseilles a bright vermilion that night. It was indeed bitter to have to turn back with cool winds and seas almost within my grasp, and return to the heat and dirt I had just left. I was decanted into my bunk in the little boat, to wake up far out in the Mediterranean again. Egyptian troubles?—what were they? Ah, yes, the WAFD Egyptian Nationalism . . . Nahas Pasha, the man who had put on the mantle of Zaghlul. . . .

There was a riot in Arabtown in Port Said the night we were to get in at dawn. The Captain did not know whether we would be able to stop there and coal; the ship's doctor insisted that I take his revolver, in spite of my protests that this was the most dangerous thing he could give me to play with. On the shore at Port Said I engaged another servant, told him to wake me before the train reached Zagazig (which was the place where the doctor declared I would find his revolver very useful) and fell asleep.

The next day in Cairo, I sat before Nahas Pasha in the Saadi Club. Nakroshy Bey was our interpreter, finally taking over the whole conversation himself. I saw Sidky Pasha's troops preventing the WAFD, which held some 95 per cent of the seats, from getting into Parliament to vote his government out of office. Answering a midnight telephone call from Nakroshy Bey I penetrated the cordon of bayoneted Gippy troops drawn up around the Saadi Club and all around the streets leading to the Egyptian Parliament. I had talked to Sidky Pasha, the Premier, that afternoon—so it was no surprise to me to find them there.

But Nakroshy Bey did think he had a surprise for me. "I told you I would have a big story for you!" he said, pale and unshaved as he stood beside squinting Nahas Pasha under the granite bust of Zaghlul. "We have just held a meeting of Parliament right here in the Saadi Club. Enough of our members are also Members of Parliament to form a quorum. We have voted the Government Sidky Pasha out!"

It was a dramatic bit of Oriental statesmanship.

"But," I said, "while you have the votes—Sidky Pasha has the guns. I think he will tell you that your vote does not count—and the King will back him up."

And so he did.

Next time when a wire from my paper came, after a couple of stifling Egyptian weeks with the Nile in flood, I respectfully asked my paper to allow me to refuse to obey their order to remain on in Egypt and write a long series on Egyptian Nationalism. And this time I picked Eve up in France on the run and we headed for the Shetland Islands just as fast as we could make it. They seemed about as far—spiritually and geographically—from Bombay as I could get. It was up there on those cool, lonely

lochs, when I was beginning to feel like a human being again—
and catching some splendid sea trout—that I got a wire: "WILL
YOU RUSH BERLIN."

Hitler was expected to make a *Putsch* before the 1930 autumn
elections. We spent that winter in Berlin and Poland, where I got
into trouble with the polite Poles over having stuck my nose too
far into their alleged massacres in the Ukrainian revolt.

The Ukrainian peasants around Lwow were burning the wheat-
lands and the farms of the Polish landlords. Two Polish regiments
had been sent down into that district to quell the disturbance.
Their alleged method of quelling it had shocked the world. The
Polish Ambassador in Washington had thereupon made a speech
inviting American correspondents to come to Poland and see for
themselves. Reading this invitation of his, in Berlin, I decided to
take him up on it.

The Poles were kind, too kind, to me; and it was all I could do
to prevent some friendly Poles from accompanying me or meeting me at Lwow. In Warsaw, they asked me: "You will be sure
to call on the Voivode at Lwow as soon as you get there?" I said
I would and I did; but as the train I took happened to arrive at
eight o'clock on a cold winter morning, the Voivode was still in
bed, which was where I had hoped he would be, and I left my
card at the Voivodstow door with the message that I would be
coming back later on. I did not see him that day, because I was
arrested out in Gaje, the village I specially wanted to get into
without any Polish help.

To get out to Gaje, which was about twenty miles outside
Lwow, I took a taxi—and told him to drive me to a village which
was about twenty miles in the opposite direction. And in this I
was unusually lucky. The taxi-driver said he had to get some
petrol, as I knew he would, and in the garage I knew he was tele-
phoning the Polish "Defensive"—secret police—that the foreigner
was going to the village of X. The Poles, in handling people who
came down to investigate the revolt, never interfered with one's
person—you could go anywhere you liked—but a Polish official or
police officer insisted upon acting as a guide. Once the peasants
saw the Pole with you they shut up. Or else they did worse—they

talked volubly to convince you that nothing untoward had happened in *their* village. This is what must have happened to a big London newspaper's correspondent, who, in Warsaw, had told me he had visited two hundred villages—and never seen one authentic case of the alleged beatings or killings. Voight, of the *Manchester Guardian*, and I stood in Lwow itself on the day after my arrest, and in the sanctuary of the Uniate Church, Archbishop Shyptitski had the nuns remove the bandages from ten peasants of whose wounds both Voight and I now had photographs. There was no mistaking their character—some of the great, raw gangrened patches would probably never heal again, even with skin grafts. When the taxi-driver had taken me about a mile on the road towards the opposite village (also the scene of some horrible beatings), I ordered him to turn and take me out to Gaje *first*. He was a stupid person, and he did it.

Two miles this side of Gaje we got stuck in Polish mud, and I abandoned the car to walk over the hills. This, also, I had wanted to do: to be able to approach the village on foot; and walking through a light snowstorm I came on a peasant putting some winter reeds like a belt around his house. I asked him: Had the Polish cavalry been in that village. He said yes. Did they kill anybody?

"Yes," he said, "you know what soldiers are."

"What was his name?"

"Tiutku."

"Who was Tiutku?"

"Tiutku was a peasant boy."

"What had he done?"

"Nothing."

"Soldiers don't kill people for nothing—Tiutku must have done something?"

"Well, when the soldiers came—the boys ran off and tried to hide in those woods. The soldiers caught them. Tiutku told the soldiers he knew where some rifles were hidden in the thatch of the cottage in the next village. When the soldiers took him there Tiutku said there were no rifles."

" 'Why did you lie to us?' asked the officer. 'Because I hate you,' said Tiutku. And then the soldiers beat him to death."

This was verified when, after my arrest, and they knew I had the first authentic case of a killing without trial, the authorities in Lwow actually handed me Tiutku's dossier. But, they said, Tiutku died of heart failure—as well he might!

"They beat him," said a young man from Tiutku's village, who at the risk of his life sneaked into Lwow and up the back stairs of the hotel to my bedroom in Lwow, "until Tiutku was as black as *that!*"

He picked up my small black pocket comb from my bedside table.

Trying to get further details from the peasant woman who kept the little store in Gaje, a peasant heard me and rushed out to call a policeman. The policeman, spotless in all that sea of mud that had practically ruined my clothes, and with the courtesy of a good London Bobby, asked for my papers—did I have a revolver? what was I doing in Lwow? what had I been writing in that little book?—and then with the greatest politeness he told me I was under arrest. With the peasant leader of the village in a cart filled with straw we drove over the hills to find my stranded taxi. It had gone. So we drove several miles in the cart to a small town. On the way we stopped at a country pub and I bought some cold meat and vodka, as I had had no breakfast or lunch, and it was now sunset. The peasant leader drank with me. But the polite policeman refused. "I am on duty," he said; "but if you get out I would like you to have dinner with me tomorrow." He is absolutely true, that policeman; one couldn't have invented him.

In Lwow I spent the rest of the evening in the headquarters of the Secret Police, in a room full of photographs of gory corpses, bloodstained walls and bomb-wrecked buildings, which, I was informed, were specimens of the work of the U.W.O., the Ukrainian terrorist organisation. When they tried to get me to tell them what I had written in my notebook I refused. Then they said they would take it from me. I buttoned my coat.

"Take it," I said. "There are too many police here—I can't stop you—but you will have to take it by force—and I shall report this both to the Polish Foreign Office in Warsaw and to my

Minister. The whole world will know about it the next morning
—how you treat people who try to see the truth here."

"Now be a good fellow," they said. "Come on, now, just give
us a look. . . ."

At eleven o'clock, after about a half-hour's talk over the telephone with Warsaw, they released me. As I went into the hotel
I saw newsboys running about with placards, and I read:

NEW PROVOCATION
American Journalist—Negley Farson

etc., etc., etc., etc.

It occupied the whole first page of the evening's newspaper.
When I ate my dinner that night, as the orchestra in that sumptuous hotel in Lwow, run for the Polish land-owning aristocracy,
was playing "Victoria and Her Hussar," my table was directly
below a dais whereon were eating the smart officers of the crack
14th cavalry regiment—whom the peasants said had murdered
Tiutku.

At that moment the Socialist Press, in Vienna, had got wind
of my arrest, and it was being flashed all over the world—where
most people made too much of it.

The next day Freddy Voight of the *Manchester Guardian* came
down to Lwow, and together we saw the eleven half-murdered
peasants lying on their faces in the Uniate Church, with the nuns
caring for them. Rogovsky, the Pole who was handling the
Lwow business, had dinner with us; and he gave us the Polish
side of things that had happened. For there were two sides. The
next day I crossed over into Germany, hired a telephone wire to
my office in Berlin and dictated the whole story of Tiutku's
murder and the Lwow atrocities; and what Freddy Voight and
I had seen that morning where the Polish police and soldiers were
"supervising" the elections in Silesia.

Then I took everything out of my pockets, except money and
passports, and mailed the large packet of documents, etc., to myself in Berlin. Then Freddy Voight and I went back into Poland
to "cover" the elections.

For what they were like I recommend people to read the *Man-*

chester Guardian files. Freddy Voight's account was so frank and fearless that the Polish Government had a "case" against the *Manchester Guardian*. I think Voight's cables on those elections are some of the finest journalism I have read. Freddy Voight would be burned at the stake, rather than be frightened off a story. He was a most inspiring person to be with.

Only I would not advise anybody to go out with him in his outboard canoe!

But I saw other things in Poland. Their marvellous activity at Gydnia, their new seaport. The troubles that they were facing with their warring internal political parties, and their clamouring minorities, who were blocking Pilsudski's forceful methods of consolidating the country. Living in it, I realised for the first time what a very difficult position it is for Poland to lie between Germany and Russia. And I saw a national spirit that was just as indomitable as the Nazis in Germany. While I had to write some nasty things about them, I found plenty to say on the other side. While not its birth, I knew that I was watching the reconstruction of one of the greatest countries in Europe—and Poland would be permanent.

Watching the growth of Poland's influence in international affairs was one of the most interesting things I had to do during the next four years in London.

Chapter 91

TOO BRITISH

When I was given the coveted London post for my paper, I felt that at last my ship had come home. Eve and I bought the lease of two little workmen's cottages in Chelsea and knocked them into one. We ourselves painted the walls of our first permanent home and filled it with the loot we had collected in the wanderings of eleven years. The ikon that the Communist had ripped out of the altar at Vladimir hangs behind our refectory dining-table. And while Eve refused to let me bring back any "horns" from India, the cougar from British Columbia lies on my study floor. While the street may be a bit noisy in the mornings, our garden is quiet. The two pigeons who nest in the trees overhanging it were back there as usual this spring, and when I shoot with Fred Hardy down in Somerset, Eve always brings back some primrose and foxglove roots to plant.

But this spring I got a letter from my new boss, which said:

"You have so thoroughly absorbed the English point of view that you no longer report the passing show from the viewpoint of a detached American observer."

It was a pity, because for four years I had thought that reporting the English point of view had been my job. So I resigned. Under these conditions I could hardly obey the peremptory order to come back to Chicago and work on the local staff to be re-Americanised. So there I was; or, at least, where was I?

Over twenty years before I had deliberately left the United States to make my life abroad; I had reversed the process and was an American, emigrating to Europe. And what had I found? When I had written my letter resigning from the paper on which I had had so many happy years, I sat down and took stock. What were my assets now? I had no money, I had no job, and I had no expectations from anyone. For the third time in my life I found myself "out in the street again." I had lost everything I had in the Russian Revolution. In Chicago I gave up the best salary and most certain job I would ever have in my life, when Eve and I put our last dollars into *Flame* to sail across Europe. I was about to start from zero again. Materially, I was back at the point where I started from.

Perhaps I was richer in other things? But I was appalled how little assurance I had gained in these twenty years. Sophistication had brought with it merely increasing humility; experience, only a growing uncertainty. Perhaps what I had really been doing during all these years was searching for a good sense of values; and, in England, I felt that I had found them. For something like twenty years London, to me, had been like an island to which I would swim back after a period of years—only to be washed off again. London had become reward, just as that officer in the Cape Police had told me in the Libyan desert.

I love London and I was appointed to my post there at a most dramatic time; for it was only a few weeks before Brüning came to England and whispered in MacDonald's ear, "Germany cannot pay"—words so soon to be changed to "Germany will not pay!" —and I watched the financial blizzard strike Europe with all its force. In my conning-tower in London as a foreign newspaper correspondent, I watched country after country steering for the rocks. And, in London, I watched England ride the storm. If I had come to love England it was not without reason. And in the dark days of 1931 I wrote that if character counted, the English would be the first people to emerge from the world slump.

In London I had the luck to meet most of the important people of the day. The American Association of Correspondents made me its president; and, in making my usual ghastly introductory speech, I was in the chair for such a mixed bag as Amelia Earhart, when she had flown the Atlantic, Andrew Mellon, Ramsay MacDonald, Stanley Baldwin, Elizabeth Bergner, and Lord Irwin, when he came back from being Viceroy of India. For four years I was in contact with the British Foreign Office, or some section of the British Government, nearly every day. And many a time have I sat and talked with that good man, George Lansbury, in his home among his own poor people in Bow Road. As I said, it was not without reason that I have come to have respect.

If I have had to disagree with some of the statements of the ambassadors that my own country sent abroad, that is not my fault. No one, for instance, could agree with Mr. Norman Davis that the British were going to align themselves with the United States to force a 5-5-3 naval ratio upon Japan. One could only hope that such statesmen did not believe the things they said. And it was being realistic about such things that made me leave the great newspaper I had loved and served for so many years.

But that is the crevasse that lies across every newspaperman's path. I fell into it, that is all. What I wrote was not un-American; I was merely reporting what the British thought. I was an Englishman for two years during the War, when I joined the British Royal Flying Corps; but at the end of it I took back my American citizenship again. I did it automatically, without a thought, with the memory of my people's own careers as my background.

But it is no good at my age, and with my past, to return to the United States to try to pick up the threads of life again. Twenty years ago I left the States, and it looks as if the road does not turn back. I have given too many hostages to fortune to life outside. But there is a thing that troubles me.

In Dalmatia, where I am writing this, Eve and I entered the Bocche de Cattaro after an absence of eleven years. We first saw it when we were sailing across Europe in *Flame*, and it seemed we had found a paradise on earth. I could hardly wait to sit down and write about it. This time we looked upon a bare, dry, uninteresting land, and I did not want to write a word. We could not understand.

"I know," said Eve. "We are different. What we saw eleven years ago was within ourselves."